MCAD/MCSD: Visual Basic .NET XM

OBJECTIVE	CHAPTER

NOTE   Exam objectives are subject to change at any time without prior notice and at Microsoft's sole discretion. Please visit Microsoft's Web site (www.microsoft.com/traincert) for the most current listing of exam objectives.

SYBEX

MCAD/MCSD:

Visual Basic .NET XML Web Services and Server Components

Study Guide

MCAD/MCSD:
Visual Basic® .NET XML Web Services and Server Components
Study Guide

Pamela Fanstill

with Brian Reisman

and Mitch Ruebush

San Francisco • London

SYBEX®

Associate Publisher: Neil Edde
Acquisitions and Developmental Editor: Jeff Kellum
Production Editor: Liz Burke
Technical Editor: Helen O'Boyle, Gord Maric, Mike Stover
Copyeditor: Sharon Wilkey
Compositor: Interactive Composition Corporation
Graphic Illustrator: Interactive Composition Corporation
CD Coordinator: Dan Mummert
CD Technician: Kevin Ly
Proofreaders: Nancy Riddiough, Sarah Tannehill, Emily Hsuan
Indexer: Ted Laux
Book Designer: Bill Gibson
Cover Designer: Archer Design
Cover Illustrator/Photographer: Georgette Douwma, FPG International

SYBEX

To Our Valued Readers:

Thank you for looking to Sybex for your Microsoft certification exam prep needs. We at Sybex are proud of the reputation we've established for providing certification candidates with the practical knowledge and skills needed to succeed in the highly competitive IT marketplace.

We believe that the MCSD program, recently updated for Visual Studio .NET, better reflects the skill set demanded of developers in today's marketplace and offers candidates a clearer structure for acquiring the skills necessary to advance their careers. And with their recent creation of the MCAD program, Microsoft programmers can now choose to pursue the certification that best suits their career goals.

Just as Microsoft is committed to establishing measurable standards for certifying developers, Sybex is committed to providing those professionals with the means of acquiring the skills and knowledge they need to meet those standards.

The Sybex team of authors, editors, and technical reviewers have worked hard to ensure that this Study Guide is comprehensive, in-depth, and pedagogically sound. We're confident that this book, along with the collection of cutting-edge software study tools included on the CD, will meet and exceed the demanding standards of the certification marketplace and help you, the Microsoft certification exam candidate, succeed in your endeavors.

Good luck in pursuit of your MCAD or MCSD certification!

Neil Edde
Associate Publisher—Certification
Sybex, Inc.

This book is dedicated to Bill Carn, who taught me to have faith in my own abilities.
Thank you for all your support over the years.
—Pamela Fanstill

Acknowledgments

I would like to thank the editorial team at Sybex for all their help and guidance and for giving me the opportunity to write my first book. Jeff Kellum, the acquisitions and developmental editor, has been with this project from start to finish. Jeff did a great job of teaching me about the authoring process and how to create logical flow and structure for each chapter and the book as a whole. Liz Burke, the production editor, and Sharon Wilkey, the copyeditor, also made excellent contributions to the accuracy and consistency of this material. Many thanks to all of you.

I also send sincere thanks to my hardworking technical editors, Helen O'Boyle, Mike Stover, and Kyle Burns. They were responsible for testing all of the exercises and code found in the book, and making sure that my facts and explanations were on target. Special thanks to Helen for her security expertise and for making a major contribution by outlining and drafting Chapter 9.

My coauthors, Brian Reisman and Mitch Ruebush, also have my deepest gratitude, for stepping in late in the process (after just completing work on their own book) to take over Chapters 10 and 11 and to keep our schedule on track.

I would also like to thank some friends who provided the encouragement to undertake this project in the first place. My discussions with Joe Karam over the years have spurred my interest in the newest technologies and encouraged me to focus my work in the .NET direction. Joe also helped me to clarify my approach to the material in this book and provided feedback on my first drafts. Tcat Houser is my friend and coach, who kept me laughing and helped me with the many challenges I faced in completing this work.

I would also like to thank my family—my mother, Marion Fanstill, and my son, Tobias Ritter, for their support and understanding during this project.

Contents at a Glance

Contents

Table of Exercises

Introduction

Microsoft Certified Application Developer (MCAD) and Microsoft Certified Solution Developer (MCSD) tracks for Visual Studio .NET are the premier certifications for programming professionals. Covering the core technologies around which Microsoft's future will be built, these programs are powerful credentials for career advancement.

This book has been developed to give you the critical skills and knowledge you need to prepare for Developing XML Web Services and Server Components with Microsoft Visual Basic .NET and the Microsoft .NET Framework (exam 70-310).

The Microsoft Certified Professional Program

Since the inception of its certification program, Microsoft has certified almost 1.5 million people. As the computer network industry grows in both size and complexity, this number is sure to grow—and the need for *proven* ability will also increase. Companies rely on certifications to verify the skills of prospective employees and contractors.

Microsoft has developed its Microsoft Certified Professional (MCP) program to give you credentials that verify your ability to work with Microsoft products effectively and professionally. Obtaining your MCP certification requires that you pass any one Microsoft certification exam. Several levels of certification are available based on specific suites of exams. Depending on your areas of interest or experience, you can obtain any of the following MCP credentials:

Microsoft Certified Application Developer (MCAD)　This track is designed for application developers and technical consultants who primarily use Microsoft development tools. Currently, you can take exams on Visual Basic .NET or Visual C# .NET. You must take and pass three exams to obtain your MCAD certification.

Microsoft Certified Solution Developer (MCSD)　This track is designed for software engineers, developers, and technical consultants who primarily use Microsoft development tools. Currently, you can take exams on Visual Basic .NET and Visual C# .NET. You must take and pass five exams to obtain your MCSD certification.

Microsoft Certified Database Administrator (MCDBA)　This track is designed for database administrators, developers, and analysts who work with Microsoft SQL Server. As of this printing, you can take exams on either SQL Server 7 or SQL Server 2000. You must take and pass four exams to achieve MCDBA status.

 Both the Developing Web Applications and Developing Windows Applications exams can count as an elective for your MCDBA.

Microsoft Certified System Administrator (MCSA)   The MCSA certification is the latest certification track from Microsoft. This certification targets system and network administrators with roughly 6 to 12 months of desktop and network administration experience. The MCSA can be considered the entry-level certification. You must take and pass four exams to obtain your MCSA.

Microsoft Certified System Engineer (MCSE) on Windows 2000   This certification track is designed for network and system administrators, network and system analysts, and technical consultants who work with Microsoft Windows 2000 Professional and Server and/or Windows XP Professional. You must take and pass seven exams to obtain your MCSE.

    Microsoft will soon be releasing new exams on Windows Server 2003.

Microsoft Certified Trainer (MCT)   The MCT track is designed for any IT professional who develops and teaches Microsoft-approved courses. To become an MCT, you must first obtain your MCSE, MCSD, or MCDBA; then you must take a class at one of the Certified Technical Training Centers. You will also be required to prove your instructional ability. You can do this in various ways: by taking a skills-building or train-the-trainer class, by achieving certification as a trainer from any of several vendors, or by becoming a Certified Technical Trainer through CompTIA. Last of all, you will need to complete an MCT application.

How Do You Become an MCAD or MCSD?

Attaining any MCP certification has always been a challenge. In the past, students have been able to acquire detailed exam information—even most of the exam questions—from online "brain dumps" and third-party "cram" books or software products. For the new Microsoft exams, this is simply not the case.

Microsoft has taken strong steps to protect the security and integrity of their certification tracks. Now, prospective students must complete a course of study that develops detailed knowledge about a wide range of topics. It supplies them with the true skills needed, derived from working with Visual Studio .NET and related software products.

The Visual Studio .NET MCAD and MCSD programs are heavily weighted toward hands-on skills and experience. Fortunately, if you are willing to dedicate the time and effort to learn Visual Studio and Visual Basic .NET, you can prepare yourself well for the exams by using the proper tools. By working through this book, you can successfully meet the exam requirements to pass the Developing XML Web Services and Server Components with Microsoft Visual Basic .NET and the Microsoft .NET Framework exam.

MCAD Exam Requirements

Candidates for MCAD certification must pass three exams, including one Developing Web or Windows Applications exam, one Developing XML Web Services and Server Components exam, and one elective. You can get your certification in either Visual Basic .NET or Visual C# .NET, or both (you can mix and match languages). For details on the exam requirements, visit http://www.microsoft.com/traincert/mcp/mcad/requirements.asp.

MCSD Exam Requirements

Candidates for MCSD certification must pass five exams, including one Developing Web Applications exam, one Developing Windows Applications exam, one Developing XML Web Services and Server Components exam, one Solution Architecture exam, and one elective. As with the MCAD program, you can get your certification in either Visual Basic .NET or Visual C# .NET, or both (you can mix and match languages). For details on the exam requirements, visit `http://www.microsoft.com/traincert/mcp/mcsd/requirementsdotnet.asp`.

The Developing XML Web Services and Server Components with Microsoft Visual Basic .NET and the Microsoft .NET Framework Exam

The Developing XML Web Services and Server Components exam covers concepts and skills related to developing and implementing web and Windows applications with Visual Basic .NET. It emphasizes the following:

- Creating and managing Windows services, serviced components, .NET Remoting applications, and XML Web services

- Consuming and manipulating data

- Testing and debugging

- Understanding .NET Framework security concepts

- Deploying Windows services, serviced components, .NET Remoting applications, and XML Web services

- Maintaining and supporting Windows services, serviced components, .NET Remoting applications, and XML Web services

- Configuring and securing Windows services, serviced components, .NET Remoting applications, and XML Web services

Microsoft provides exam objectives to give you a general overview of possible areas of coverage on the Microsoft exams. Keep in mind, however, that exam objectives are subject to change at any time without prior notice and at Microsoft's sole discretion. Please visit Microsoft's Training and Certification website (www.microsoft.com/traincert) for the most current listing of exam objectives.

Types of Exam Questions

In an effort to both refine the testing process and protect the quality of its certifications, Microsoft has focused its exams on real experience and hands-on proficiency. There is a greater emphasis on your past working environments and responsibilities, and less emphasis on how well you can memorize.

Microsoft will accomplish its goal of protecting the exams' integrity by regularly adding and removing exam questions, limiting the number of questions that any individual sees in a beta exam, limiting the number of questions delivered to an individual by using adaptive testing, and adding new exam elements.

Exam questions can be in a variety of formats. Depending on which exam you take or which certification you are looking to achieve—whether it be MCSE, MCSD, or MCDBA—you might see multiple-choice questions as well as select-and-place and prioritize-a-list questions. Simulations and case study–based formats are included as well. Let's take a look at the types of exam questions you might see so you'll be prepared for all of the possibilities.

With the release of Windows 2000, Microsoft has stopped providing a detailed score breakdown. This is mostly because of the various and complex question formats. Previously, each question focused on one objective. The exams, however, contain questions that might be tied to one or more objectives from one or more objective sets. Therefore, grading by objective is almost impossible. Additionally, Microsoft no longer offers a score. Now you will be told only whether you pass or fail.

For more information on the various exam question types, go to www.microsoft .com/traincert/mcpexams/policies/innovations.asp.

MULTIPLE-CHOICE QUESTIONS

Multiple-choice questions come in two main forms. One is a straightforward question followed by several possible answers, of which one or more is correct. The other type of multiple-choice question is more complex and based on a specific scenario. The scenario might focus on several areas or objectives. These are the majority of questions you will find on exam 70-310.

SELECT-AND-PLACE QUESTIONS

Select-and-place exam questions use graphical elements that you must manipulate to successfully answer the question. For example, you might see a diagram of a computer network, taken from the select-and-place demo downloaded from Microsoft's website.

You are not likely to see this question type for Exam 70-310.

A typical diagram will show computers and other components next to boxes that contain the text "Place here." The labels for the boxes represent various computer roles on a network, such as a print server and a file server. Based on information given for each computer, you are asked to select each label and place it in the correct box. You need to place *all* of the labels correctly. No credit is given for the question if you correctly label only some of the boxes.

In another select-and-place problem, you might be asked to put a series of steps in order by dragging items from boxes on the left to boxes on the right and placing them in the correct order. One other type requires that you drag an item from the left and place it under an item in a column on the right.

SIMULATIONS

Simulations are the kinds of questions that most closely represent actual situations and test the skills you use while working with Microsoft software interfaces. These exam questions include a mock interface on which you are asked to perform certain actions according to a given scenario. The simulated interfaces look nearly identical to what you see in the actual product.

 You are not likely to see this question type for Exam 70-310.

Because of the number of possible errors that can be made on simulations, be sure to consider the following recommendations from Microsoft:

- Do not change any simulation settings that don't pertain to the solution directly.
- When specific information has not been provided, assume that the default is used.
- Make sure that your entries are spelled correctly.
- Close all of the simulation application windows after completing the set of tasks in the simulation.

The best way to prepare for simulation questions is to spend time working with the graphical interface of the product on which you will be tested.

 Microsoft will regularly add and remove questions from the exams. This is called *item seeding*. It is part of the effort to make it more difficult for individuals to merely memorize exam questions that were passed along by previous test-takers.

Tips for Taking the XML Web Services and Server Components Exam

Here are some general tips for achieving success on your certification exam:

- Arrive early at the exam center so that you can relax and review your study materials. During this final review, you can look over tables and lists of exam-related information.
- Read the questions carefully. Don't be tempted to jump to an early conclusion. Make sure you know *exactly* what the question is asking.
- Answer all questions.
- For questions you're not sure about, use a process of elimination to get rid of the obviously incorrect answers first. This improves your odds of selecting the correct answer when you need to make an educated guess.

Exam Registration

You can take the Microsoft exams at any of more than 1000 Authorized Prometric Testing Centers (APTCs) and VUE Testing Centers around the world. For the location of a testing center near you, call Prometric at 800-755-EXAM (755-3926), or call VUE at 888-837-8616. Outside the United States and Canada, contact your local Prometric or VUE registration center.

Find out the number of the exam you want to take, and then register with the Prometric or VUE registration center nearest to you. At this point, you will be asked for advance payment for the exam. The exams are $125 (U.S.) each, and you must take them within one year of payment. You can schedule exams up to six weeks in advance or as late as one working day prior to the date of the exam. You can cancel or reschedule your exam if you contact the center at least two working days prior to the exam. Same-day registration is available in some locations, subject to space availability. Where same-day registration is available, you must register a minimum of two hours before test time.

    You can also register for your exams online at www.prometric.com or www.vue.com.

When you schedule the exam, you will be provided with instructions regarding appointment and cancellation procedures, ID requirements, and information about the testing center location. In addition, you will receive a registration and payment confirmation letter from Prometric or VUE.

Microsoft requires certification candidates to accept the terms of a nondisclosure agreement before taking certification exams.

Is This Book for You?

If you want to acquire a solid foundation in developing and implementing XML Web services and server components with Visual Basic .NET, and your goal is to prepare for the exam by learning how to use and manage the new software language, this book is for you. You'll find clear explanations of the fundamental concepts you need to grasp, and plenty of help to achieve the high level of professional competency you need to succeed in your chosen field.

If you want to become certified as an MCAD or MCSD, this book is definitely for you. However, if you just want to attempt to pass the exam without really understanding how to achieve the skills necessary to use them in the real world, this Study Guide is *not* for you. It is written for people who want to acquire hands-on skills and in-depth knowledge of this topic.

How to Use This Book

We took into account not only what you need to know to pass the exam, but what you need to know to take what you've learned and apply it in the real world. Each book contains the following:

Objective-by-objective coverage of the topics you need to know   Each chapter lists the objectives covered in that chapter, followed by detailed discussion of each objective.

Assessment Test   Directly following this introduction is an Assessment Test that you should take. It is designed to help you determine how much you already know about the .NET Framework and Visual Studio .NET. Each question is tied to a topic discussed in the book. Using the results of the Assessment Test, you can figure out the areas where you need to focus your study. Of course, we do recommend that you read the entire book.

Exam Essentials   To highlight what you learn, you'll find a list of Exam Essentials at the end of each chapter. The Exam Essentials section briefly highlights the topics that need your particular attention as you prepare for the exam.

Key Terms and Glossary   Throughout each chapter, you will be introduced to important terms and concepts that you will need to know for the exam. These terms appear in italic within the chapters, and a list of the Key Terms appears just after the Exam Essentials. At the end of the book, a detailed Glossary gives definitions for these terms, as well as other general terms you should know.

Review Questions, complete with detailed explanations   Each chapter is followed by a set of Review Questions that test what you learned in the chapter. The questions are written with the exam in mind, meaning that they are designed to have the same look and feel as what you'll see on the exam. Question types are just like the ones you'll find on the exam.

Hands-on exercises   In each chapter, you'll find exercises designed to give you the important hands-on experience that is critical for your exam preparation. The exercises support the topics of the chapter, and they walk you through the steps necessary to perform a particular function.

Real-World Scenarios   Because reading a book isn't enough for you to learn how to apply these topics in your everyday duties, we have provided Real-World Scenarios in special sidebars. These explain when and why a particular solution would make sense, in a working environment you'd actually encounter.

Because the objectives for this exam cover a wide range of application types, some of the topics and details are exactly the same whether you are working with Windows services, serviced components, .NET Remoting applications, or XML Web services. The first four chapters cover creating and managing these four types of applications. Each chapter covers one type of application in detail. Chapters 5–7 focus on working with data. Chapters 8–11 cover testing and debugging your applications, understanding security concepts, and application deployment and configuration.

To help you prepare for certification exams, Microsoft provides a list of exam objectives for each test. Each chapter begins with a list of the objectives covered within it.

The specific exam objectives can be found at `http://www.microsoft.com/ traincert/exams/70-310.asp`.

Although we have tried to be as comprehensive as possible, writing a book that covers every aspect of distributed application development is almost impossible. Because this is a study guide, we focus on certification. Every effort has been made to cover the exam objectives in plenty of detail. In addition, we provide a little extra information that will make you a more productive developer but we don't burden you with unnecessary detail.

As you work through this book, you might want to follow these general procedures:

1.   Review the exam objectives as you work through each chapter. (You might want to check the Microsoft Training and Certification website at `http://www.microsoft.com/ traincert` to make sure the objectives haven't changed.)

2.   Study each chapter carefully, making sure you fully understand the information.

3.   Complete all hands-on exercises in each chapter, referring to the appropriate text so that you understand every step you take.

4. Answer the practice questions at the end of the chapter.

5. Note which questions you did not understand, and study those sections of the book again.

To learn all of the material covered in this book, you will need to study regularly and with discipline. Try to set aside the same time every day to study, and select a comfortable and quiet place in which to do it. Good luck!

Hardware and Software Requirements

In order to complete all of the exercises in this book, you will need to have certain software and hardware.

Required Software

You will need the following software to complete the exercises in this book:

- Microsoft Visual Basic .NET or Microsoft Visual Studio .NET
- Internet Information Services (IIS), which is required for all XML Web service applications

 IIS is included with Windows 2000, Windows XP Professional, and Windows Server 2003.

- Microsoft Desktop Engine (MSDE), Microsoft SQL Server 2000, or Microsoft SQL Server 7, one of which is required for all Microsoft SQL Server ADO.NET applications

Requirements for Microsoft Visual Studio .NET

The minimum and recommended requirements for Visual Studio .NET are listed here:

Processor

Minimum	Recommended
450MHz Pentium II–class processor	Pentium 4 1.6GHz processor

Operating System

Minimum	Recommended
Microsoft Windows XP, Home Edition*	Microsoft Windows 2000 Professional or Microsoft Windows XP Professional
Microsoft Windows NT 4 Workstation	Microsoft Windows 2000 Server
Microsoft Windows NT 4 Server	

* Limited functionality. Visual Studio .NET does not support creating ASP.NET Web applications or ASP.NET XML Web services when using Windows XP, Home Edition.

Memory

Operating System	Minimum RAM
Windows XP Home	160MB
Windows XP Professional	160MB
Windows 2000 Professional	96MB
Windows 2000 Server	192MB
Windows NT 4 Workstation	64MB
Windows NT 4 Server	160MB

Hard Disk Space

.NET Development Environment	Minimum Disk Requirements
Visual Studio .NET Standard Edition	2.5 gigabytes (GB) on installation drive, which includes 500MB on system drive
Visual Studio .NET Professional and Enterprise Editions	3.5GB on installation drive, which includes 500MB on system drive
Visual Basic .NET	2GB on installation drive, which includes 500MB on system drive.

Display

Minimum Monitor	Minimum Video Card
Super VGA (800 × 600) monitor	256-color

Other

You must also have a CD-ROM or DVD-ROM drive to install Visual Studio .NET.

Requirements for Microsoft SQL Server or MSDE

In order to complete the exercises that include Microsoft SQL Server access, you must have installed, at minimum, the Microsoft Desktop Engine, a scaled down version of Microsoft SQL Server 2000. It is included with some editions of Visual Studio .NET and Microsoft Office. The code in the book will work on all editions of Microsoft SQL Server 7 and 2000.

Listed here are the minimum requirements for Microsoft SQL Server 2000:

Edition	Operating System
SQL Server 2000 Standard and Enterprise	Windows NT 4 Server SP5 Windows 2000 Windows 2003

Edition	Operating System
SQL Server 2000 Trial and Developer	All of the above Windows XP Professional Windows XP Home Windows 2000 Professional Windows NT Workstation SP5
SQL Server 2000 Personal and Desktop Engine (MSDE)	All of the above Windows 98 Windows ME
SQL Server 7 Enterprise Edition	Windows NT Server 4 Enterprise Edition Windows 2000 Advanced Server Windows 2000 Datacenter Server
SQL Server 7 Standard Edition	All of the above Windows NT Server Windows 2000 Server
SQL Server 7 Desktop Edition	All of the above Windows XP Windows 2000 Professional Windows NT Workstation Windows ME Windows 95/98

In addition to these specifications, you will need at least 250MB of free hard disk space for the typical installation.

 We include all the exercises' code on the book's CD, so you don't have to rekey everything in. All of the exercises in the book assume that products have been installed according to the defaults. No consideration is given for additional customizations that you have made on the installation.

What's on the CD?

With this new member of our best-selling Study Guide series, we are including quite an array of training resources. The CD offers bonus exams and flashcards to help you study for the exam. We have also included the complete contents of the Study Guide in electronic form. The CD's resources are described here:

The Sybex E-Book for Developing XML Web Services and Server Components   Many people like the convenience of being able to carry their whole Study Guide on a CD. They also like being able to search the text via computer to find specific information quickly and easily. For these reasons, the entire contents of this Study Guide are supplied on the CD, in PDF. We've also included Adobe Acrobat Reader, which provides the interface for the PDF contents as well as the search capabilities.

The Sybex Test Engine   This is a collection of multiple-choice questions that will help you prepare for your exam. There are two sets of questions:

- Two bonus exams for 70-310—designed to simulate the actual live exam
- All the questions from the Study Guide, presented in a test engine for your review
- The Assessment Test

Here is a sample screen from the Sybex MCAD/MCSD Test Engine:

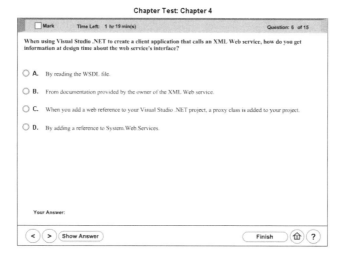

Sybex MCAD/MCSD Flashcards for PCs and Handheld Devices   The "flashcard" style of question offers an effective way to quickly and efficiently test your understanding of the fundamental concepts covered in the exam. The Sybex MCAD/MCSD Flashcards set consists of more than 100 questions presented in a special engine developed specifically for this Study Guide series. Here's what the Sybex MCAD/MCSD Flashcards interface looks like:

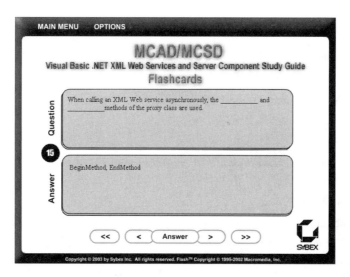

Because of the high demand for a product that will run on handheld devices, we have also developed, in conjunction with Land-J Technologies, a version of the flashcard questions that you can take with you on your Palm OS PDA (including the PalmPilot and Handspring's Visor).

Additional Files   The CD that is included with the book includes all of the sample code that is used for the exercises and any special files that you will need to complete the exercises. The code in this book was written using the 2002 version of Visual Studio .NET and will work correctly in Visual Studio .NET 2003, with a few minor changes. Please see the readme.txt file that is included with the code on the CD for the Visual Studio .NET 2003 changes and other notes for using the files to complete the exercises.

Contacts and Resources

To find out more about Microsoft education and certification materials and programs, to register with Prometric or VUE, or to obtain other useful certification information and additional study resources, check the following resources:

Microsoft Training and Certification Home Page

www.microsoft.com/traincert

This website provides information about the MCP program and exams.

Microsoft TechNet Technical Information Network

www.microsoft.com/technet

800-344-2121

Use this website or phone number to contact support professionals and system administrators. Outside the United States and Canada, contact your local Microsoft subsidiary for information.

Prometric

www.prometric.com

800-755-3926

Contact Prometric to register to take an MCP exam at one of the Prometric Testing Centers.

Virtual University Enterprises (VUE)

www.vue.com

888-837-8616

Contact the VUE registration center to register to take an MCP exam at one of the VUE Testing Centers.

MCP Magazine Online

www.mcpmag.com

Microsoft Certified Professional Magazine is a well-respected publication that focuses on Microsoft certification. This site hosts chats and discussion forums, and tracks news related to the MCAD and MCSD programs. Some of the services cost a fee, but they are well worth it.

MSDN Online

http://msdn.microsoft.com/

Here, you can get information on the latest developer trends and tools.

Cramsession on Brainbuzz.com

cramsession.brainbuzz.com

Cramsession is an online community focusing on all IT certification programs. In addition to finding discussion boards and job locators, you can download one of several free cram sessions, which are nice supplements to any study approach you take.

About the Authors and Contact Information

Pamela Fanstill, MCSD, CTT+, MCT, and MCSD for Microsoft .NET has over 20 years of experience working with information systems as a developer, instructor, and writer. Pam holds a B.S. in Information Systems Management from the University of San Francisco. She has been focusing on Microsoft development tools since VB 3 and earned her first MCSD certification in 1996. For the past few years she has been teaching Visual Basic and related development technologies as a Microsoft Certified Trainer for training centers nationwide. Pam has been enthusiastic about .NET since beta 1 and is one of the charter MCADs for .NET. Pam lives in northern California and can be contacted at pamf@austinsp.com.

Brian Reisman, MCAD, MCDBA, MCSD, MCSE NT/2K, MCT, OCA, CNA, and NET+, has more than two years of experience with the .NET Framework and more than five years of experience developing data-driven, client/server, and web-based applications. He was among the few Microsoft instructors nationally approved to present the Microsoft .NET Developer Training Tour. Brian is a coauthor of *MCAD/MCSD: Visual Basic .NET Windows and Web Applications Study Guide* (Sybex, 2003) and is also a freelance writer for *MCP Magazine*, CertCities.com, and ASPToday.com. Brian spends most of his time working with Visual Basic .NET, C#, and ASP.NET, targeting Microsoft SQL Server and Oracle databases. He is a consultant and instructor for Online Consulting Inc. (www.onlc.com), a Microsoft Certified Technical Education Center and Partner with offices in Wilmington, Delaware and Philadelphia, Pennsylvania. Brian is currently building a .NET developer community site at http://www.joltcoder.com.

Mitchell Ruebush, MCAD, MCSD, MCDBA, MCSE+I, MCSE for Windows 2000, and MCT, began programming in 1982 with Apple BASIC on an Apple II+ that he happened upon and decided was cool and something he must learn. Since then, he has expanded his abilities and still thinks programming is fantastic. Mitch has over 10 years of experience building client/server, data marts/warehousing, and web-based applications on Microsoft Windows and Unix with C/C++, Java, C#, Perl, VB Script, VB .NET, VB around Oracle, Microsoft SQL Server, Microsoft Exchange Server, and mainframes. Mitch also coauthored the *MCAD/MCSD: Visual Basic .NET Windows and Web Applications Study Guide.* He currently works for Online Consulting, Inc., a Microsoft Certified Technical Education Center and Partner headquartered in Wilmington, Delaware. He can be contacted at Mitch4161@joltcoder.com.

Sybex's e-mail and website are as follows:

Technical Support: support@sybex.com

Website: www.sybex.com

Assessment Test

1. You are creating a Visual Studio .NET application and you would like to use some existing COM components in your new application. Can you do this?

   A. No. .NET Framework applications cannot use COM components.

   B. Yes. Visual Studio .NET will take care of creating an interop assembly so that managed code in your Visual Studio .NET project can access the methods of a COM component.

   C. Yes, but only after converting the COM component to a Visual Studio .NET module.

   D. Yes, but only if the COM component has a dual interface.

2. What classes must be used to successfully deploy a Windows service when using an installer such as `InstallUtil.exe` or Windows Installer? (Choose two.)

   A. `ServiceInstaller`

   B. `ServiceSetup`

   C. `ServiceProcessInstaller`

   D. `ServiceProcessSetup`

3. You are creating a distributed application. You would like the client applications to use .NET Remoting to make method calls on server components. Which of the following describes an environment that is suited for implementing .NET Remoting?

   A. You are implementing an application that will support clients running various platforms; calls to the server are made over the Internet.

   B. All clients that will use the server components are located on the same network and are running the .NET Framework; however, the program that you wish to call from the remote host runs on a different operating system.

   C. All clients that will use the server components are located on the same network and are running the .NET Framework.

   D. All clients that will use the server components are located on the same network, but some clients are running older operating systems that cannot support the .NET Framework.

4. What type of application would be best implemented by running as a Windows service?

   A. An application that monitors server CPU usage. If usage goes over 75 percent, it should be logged in an event log.

   B. A data entry application for a busy call center.

   C. A spreadsheet application for financial calculations.

   D. An XML web service application to exchange B2B e-commerce orders.

5. You are creating a distributed application. You have decided to implement .NET Remoting to make method calls on server components. You have decided to use a TCP channel and the binary formatter. What advantage will that provide for your application?

    A. A TCP channel and the binary formatter will provide the fastest communication between components.

    B. A TCP channel and the binary formatter will provide the strongest security for your application.

    C. A TCP channel and the binary formatter automatically encrypt all data.

    D. A TCP channel and the binary formatter are supported by all platforms.

6. XML Web services are most useful when creating applications that meet which requirements?

    A. Your application must be able to provide the fastest possible performance in executing requests.

    B. Your organization has information that it would like to provide to a wide range of customers, without having to create a custom interface for each one.

    C. Your organization's departmental status reports must be delivered over the company intranet.

    D. Your application must support online transaction processing and provide up-to-the-minute information for call center operators.

7. You are creating a Visual Studio .NET application and you would like to take advantage of the distributed transaction management features that Windows Component Services provides. What should you do?

    A. You can't access Windows Component Services from a Visual Studio .NET application.

    B. Use classes from the .NET Framework `System.EnterpriseServices` namespace to support this functionality.

    C. Use classes from the .NET Framework `System.Runtime.Interop` namespace to support this functionality.

    D. You can create a Visual Studio .NET application that uses components that are registered with Windows Component Services, but the components themselves must have been created with Visual Studio 6.

8. Which set of underlying technologies provides the foundation for XML Web services?

    A. TCP and proprietary binary data formats

    B. XSD and UDDI

    C. HTTP, XML, and SOAP

    D. DCOM, XML, and SOAP

9. To implement Windows authentication and authorization in the web.config file, you must add the _____ element to grant access and the _____ element to prevent access to your Web service. (Choose two.)

    A. <allow>

    B. <deny>

    C. <prevent>

    D. <permit>

10. In a typical web-based application, most data returned by database queries is used to display data to the user. Which ADO.NET object can quickly and efficiently provide read-only data to your application?

    A. A DataSet

    B. An XMLDataReader

    C. A SqlDataReader or an OleDbDataReader

    D. A disconnected recordset

11. Your application needs to connect to a Microsoft SQL Server 6.5 database. Which .NET data provider should you use?

    A. The SqlClient data provider.

    B. The OleDb data provider.

    C. The ODBC data provider.

    D. You cannot connect to an SQL Server 6.5 database from ADO.NET.

12. What is one advantage of using a strongly typed DataSet in your application?

    A. Automatically generated SQL statements.

    B. Compile time type checking.

    C. No need to call the DataAdapter Fill or Update methods.

    D. Only strongly typed DataSets can be bound to controls.

13. For auditing purposes, you would like your Windows service application to write an entry to an event log every time it is started and stopped. How can you most easily accomplish this?

    A. Write code in the OnCustomCommand method of the ServiceBase class to create the log entry.

    B. Write code in the OnStart and OnStop methods of the ServiceBase class to create the log entry.

    C. Leave the AutoLog property of your service set to True. Windows Application event log entries will be automatically created.

    D. Leave the AutoLog property of your service set to Automatic. Windows Application event log entries will be automatically created.

14. What is the main benefit of adding XML-aware components to your application?

A. Applications can easily be converted to web pages.

B. It makes it easier to exchange data with other applications.

C. Applications can easily be converted to web services.

D. It makes it easier to share program logic with other applications.

15. Your application requires that you are able to support XML data files as input from your e-commerce trading partners, as well as supply results back to them in many formats of XML data files. What namespaces in the .NET Framework class library contain classes that can help you in your application design?

A. Only System.Data.

B. Only System.Xml.

C. The .NET Framework class library does not support XML.

D. There are many namespaces that contain classes that support working with XML data.

16. How do you easily change the setting of the Level property of a TraceSwitch?

A. Change the value of the switch in the application configuration file.

B. Use the category of each trace message to determine the level.

C. Set the level as a global variable in your application.

D. Set the level as a constant in your application.

17. Authentication is best described as the process of determining:

A. The permission set available to a user

B. Whether the .NET code is safe

C. Your identity to the system

D. All of the above

18. If you have set the Level property of a TraceSwitch to TraceInfo, which levels of messages will you receive?

A. Only those that test for Trace.Info

B. Those that test for Trace.Info and Trace.Verbose

C. Those that test for Trace.Info and Trace.Warning

D. Those that test for Trace.Info, Trace.Warning, and Trace.Error

19. When you use Visual Studio .NET to generate a strongly typed DataSet, what files are added to the project?

A. An XSD Schema and a class module

B. An XSD Schema and a config file

C. An XML document and a class module

D. An XML and a config file

20. ASP.NET supports only Windows authentication.

   A. True

   B. False

21. The CLR role-based security uses Identity and Principal objects to determine role membership.

   A. True

   B. False

22. Which method of deploying a serviced component should you use to deploy the component into a production environment?

   A. Use dynamic registration.

   B. Use `regsvcs.exe`.

   C. Generate an MSI file from the Component Services tool.

   D. Write your own script by using the `RegistrationHelper` class.

23. To authenticate a Web service request, you must use Integrated Windows authentication.

   A. True

   B. False

24. To enable static discovery, you must create a .disco file and place it in the web application's virtual root folder.

   A. True

   B. False

25. How can you best describe a Windows service application?

   A. It impersonates the identity of the user who is logged in.

   B. It runs in its own process with its own security account.

   C. It runs in the same process space as the web server with the identity of `IUSR_Machine`.

   D. It runs in the same process space as the operating system and must have Administrator privileges.

26. To create a .NET component that will be hosted by COM+, what should you do?

   A. Reference the `System.EnterpriseServices` namespace.

   B. Reference the `System.ComponentServices` namespace.

   C. Import the `System.COMServices` namespace.

   D. Import the `System.EnterpriseComponents` namespace.

27. When an object's lifetime lease expires, what happens?

    A. The client receives an exception.

    B. The object is marked as available for garbage collection.

    C. The client receives an event notification to extend the lease.

    D. The object is immediately removed from memory.

28. When creating an XML Web service application in the .NET Framework, what filename extension is used for your main source code pages?

    A. `.aspx`

    B. `.wsdl`

    C. `.asmx`

    D. `.disco`

29. In order to read all the rows from a DataReader, which method should you call?

    A. `myReader.NextResult()`

    B. `myReader.MoveNext()`

    C. `myReader.Read()`

    D. `myReader.GetValues()`

30. Which statement best describes the structure of a DataSet?

    A. A DataSet contains a set of records returned from the database.

    B. A DataSet has a collection of DataTable objects. In turn, each DataTable has a collection of DataViews and DataRows.

    C. A DataSet has a collection of DataTable objects. In turn, each DataTable has a collection of DataColumns and DataRows.

    D. A DataSet contains collections of DataTables, DataColumns, and DataRows. Relationships between these objects are defined by DataRelations.

31. Which statement best describes the way that an `XmlTextReader` works?

    A. The `XmlTextReader` enables you to load an XML data file in memory and have complete programmatic access to the data.

    B. The `XmlTextReader` enables to you to process each node in an XML file sequentially.

    C. The `XmlTextReader` enables you to work with your XML data as either a relational table or a hierarchical tree of nodes.

    D. The `XmlTextReader` enables you to convert text files into XML data.

32. What happens when you set the `Level` property of a `TraceSwitch` to `TraceError`?

    A. Output will be written only if there is a runtime error in the application.

    B. Output will be written only if the `Trace.Write` statement is in an error handler.

    C. All output messages will be written as message boxes that force the application to end.

    D. Output messages will only be written if you set the trace level to 1.

33. Which of the following best describes .NET Enterprise Services role-based security?

    A. It is no longer used, because it has been superceded by the CLR's role-based security mechanism.

    B. It requires that users be assigned to Windows groups, to specify the roles to which they belong.

    C. It can be used only when you are using other Enterprise Services such as transactions.

    D. It requires that classes using it inherit from the `ServicedComponent` class.

34. In order to allow an XML Web service consumer to specify the network credentials to pass into a Web service call, what property of the proxy object would you set to a `NetworkCredential` instance?

    A. `Credentials`

    B. `AuthInfo`

    C. `Identity`

    D. `Principal`

Answers to Assessment Test

1. B.   Yes, it is possible to use legacy COM components from Visual Studio .NET projects. Visual Studio .NET will automatically create an interop assembly that exposes the type library from the COM component in a form that is understandable to the Common Language Runtime (CLR). For more information, see Chapter 2.

2. A, C.   The `ServiceInstaller` and `ServiceProcessInstaller` classes contain the code necessary for the installer (`InstallUtil.exe` or Windows Installer) to write to the Registry and register the service in the service controller applet in Windows. These classes contain the code necessary for the installer to install, commit, roll back, and uninstall a Windows service. See Chapter 10 for more information.

3. C.   .NET Remoting is best implemented when all computers are on a closed network and all computers are running the .NET Framework. XML Web services are useful when you must support different platforms. For more information, see Chapter 3.

4. A.   Windows Services are best suited to applications that run without direct user interaction and that report their operations and errors to an event log. For more information, see Chapter 1.

5. A.   The TCP channel does provide faster transmission of data over the network; however, this channel is less secure than HTTP, which can use SSL and other web security features. All components involved in the distributed application must run the .NET Framework in order to use the binary formatter. For more information, see Chapter 3.

6. B.   XML Web services are most suited to creating applications that expose a simple, easy-to-access interface that is nonproprietary and cross-platform. Each of your customers can write application code to call your service and request information from any type of programming language and platform that they might be using. Although XML Web services can provide reasonable performance, because you are often accessing web services over the public Internet, fast performance is not guaranteed. For internal applications, such as intranets and online transaction processing, web services might not provide the best performance and security. For more information, see Chapter 4.

7. B.   You can register Visual Studio .NET components with Windows Component Services to take advantage of distributed transaction management and other features. Visual Studio .NET components that are to be registered with Windows Component Services must reference the .NET Framework `System.EnterpriseServices` namespace and inherit from the `ServicedComponent` base class. For more information, see Chapter 2.

8. C.   XML Web services use Internet standards such as HTTP, XML, and SOAP to maintain the greatest possible cross-platform accessibility. TCP implies the use of a lower-level protocol that might be blocked by a firewall. DCOM and binary data formats are generally proprietary and will run only on a single platform. XSD and UDDI are supporting technologies of XML Web services; however, they provide additional services and are not required for a simple XML Web service. For more information, see Chapter 4.

9. A, B.   The `<allow>` element is used to permit users to consume the service, and the `<deny>` element is used to prohibit access. For more information, see Chapter 11.

10. C.   A DataSet object is designed to store data in memory while users can update it and write changes back to the database. This capability uses system resources and is slower. An XML-DataReader creates an XMLDocument, which also requires system resources to hold data in memory. The SqlDataReader and OleDbDataReader are fast and efficient objects that provide forward-only, read-only access to data. The disconnected recordset is part of the older ADO object model and is not a part of ADO.NET. For more information, see Chapter 5.

11. B.   The OleDb data provider supports many databases, including older versions of Microsoft SQL Server and Access. The SqlClient data provider is customized for use with Microsoft SQL Server versions 7 and 2000 only. The ODBC data provider is for legacy databases that must use ODBC drivers. For more information, see Chapter 5.

12. B.   Strongly typed DataSets provide compile time type checking of your data columns. Object names are also available in Intellisense. No SQL is automatically generated for the typed DataSet; it is built based on a SELECT query that you define. You do still need to call the Data-Adapter Fill and Update methods when working with a typed DataSet. Any type of DataSet can be bound to controls. See Chapter 6 for more information.

13. C.   The default behavior of a Visual Studio .NET Windows service application is to automatically log Start, Stop, Pause, and Continue operations in the Windows Application event log. For more information, see Chapter 1.

14. B.   One of the main benefits of working with XML data is that it is a standard, nonproprietary, cross-platform format for data. It is easy to produce XML output that can be sent to other applications and easy to use XML input that is sent to you from outside sources. Although XML is often thought of as a web technology, the use of XML alone will not convert your application to a web page or web service. XML is mainly a means of moving data, not a component framework for sharing application logic. For more information, see Chapter 7.

15. D.   The .NET Framework class library has broad-based support for working with XML data. Although classes in System.Xml support core XML technologies such as XML Document Object Model programming and XSLT, ADO.NET (System.Data) and many other namespaces also contain XML-aware components. For more information, see Chapter 7.

16. A.   Using a configuration file to set the switch level enables you to change the setting as often as required without having to recompile source code. See Chapter 8 for more information.

17. C.   Authentication is the process of demonstrating to the system your identity. For more information, see Chapter 9.

18. D.   When you set a specific trace level, you automatically include all messages that are at a more critical level. So if you test for Trace.Info, you will also include Trace.Warning and Trace.Error as well. Trace.Verbose is the least critical level, so it will not be included. See Chapter 8 for more information.

19. A.   A strongly typed DataSet is described by an XSD Schema. A class module is added to the project that contains DataSet properties, methods, and events that are customized for the particular data definition. See Chapter 6 for more information.

20. B.   ASP.NET supports Windows, Passport, Forms, and custom authentication. For more information, see Chapter 9.

21. A.   The CLR role-based security uses Identity and Principal objects to determine role membership. For more information, see Chapter 9.

22. C.   Using an MSI file and the Windows Installer is the recommend approach to installing an application into a production environment. See Chapter 10 for more information.

23. B.   You can also use custom authentication. Passport and Forms authentication, provided by ASP.NET, are not recommended for XML Web service authentication. For more information, see Chapter 11.

24. A.   The presence of a .disco file in the virtual root of a web application will enable static discovery. For more information, see Chapter 11.

25. B.   A Windows service runs in its own memory process space and has its own security account, most commonly LocalSystem. A Windows service does not interfere with other users or programs running on the computer. For more information, see Chapter 1.

26. A.   To enable your components to be hosted by .NET Enterprise Services, you must set a reference to the `System.EnterpriseServices.dll`. For more information, see Chapter 2.

27. B.   When the object's lifetime lease expires, it is marked as available for garbage collection by the CLR. For more information, see Chapter 3.

28. C.   When working with ASP.NET-based XML Web services, `.asmx` is the filename extension used for your source code pages. The extension `.aspx` is used for standard ASP.NET pages. The `.wsdl` and `.disco` files contain XML documents that provide discovery and Web Services Description Language information. For more information, see Chapter 4.

29. C.   The `Read` method is used to advance the DataReader to the next row of data. The `NextResult` method is used when several SQL queries were run as a batch and there are multiple resultsets in a single DataReader. The `MoveNext` method was used with older versions of the ADO recordset and is not used in ADO.NET. The `GetValues` method is for retrieving column data. For more information, see Chapter 5.

30. C.   A DataSet contains a collection of DataTables. The DataTable in turn contains the DataColumns and DataRows collections. The DataSet, not the DataTable, also contains the collection of DataViews, available through the DataViewManager. The first option describes a RecordSet object from the older ADO object model. For more information, see Chapter 6.

31. B.   The `XmlTextReader` provides forward-only, read-only access to XML data. The XML DOM `XmlDocument` provides complete programmatic access to XML data. The `XmlDataDocument` enables you to treat your data as either a relational table or a hierarchical tree of nodes. There is no class that automatically converts text files to XML. For more information, see Chapter 7.

32. D.   You can test for the `Level` property of a `TraceSwitch` and use that information to determine which messages should be output. `Trace` statements can be placed in an error handler or anywhere else in code. `Trace` statements are output during the normal course of application execution, not only if a runtime error occurs. Message boxes that force the application to break are the typical behavior of `Trace.Assert` statements. For more information, see Chapter 8.

33. D. .NET Enterprise Services role-based security requires that classes using it inherit from the `ServicedComponent` class, as with any class taking advantage of Enterprise Services such as transactions and message queuing. It does not require that the programmer access any other .NET Enterprise Services in their code. It peacefully coexists with the newer CLR role-based security model; each has advantages and disadvantages that make one or the other the best choice in a specific circumstance. Unlike the CLR role-based security model, .NET Enterprise Services role-based security enables users to be assigned to roles that do not correspond to Windows groups. For more information, see Chapter 9.

34. A. The `Credentials` property of the proxy object is what should be valued and passed to the service. There isn't an `AuthInfo`, `Identity`, or `Principal` property for all proxy instances. For more information, see Chapter 11.

Chapter

1

Creating and Managing Windows Services

MICROSOFT EXAM OBJECTIVES COVERED IN THIS CHAPTER:

✓ **Create and manipulate a Windows service.**

   ▪ Write code that is executed when a Windows service is started or stopped.

✓ **Implement security for a Windows service.**

✓ **Instrument and debug a Windows service.**

   ▪ Configure the debugging environment.

✓ **Configure client computers and servers to use a Windows service.**

Windows services provide a means for application logic to run continuously on your computer, usually providing device driver or other operating system services. Windows services are useful for server applications that should always be available for clients' requests. If you are familiar with Microsoft SQL Server 2000, you will notice that it runs as a Windows service. An easy-to-understand example of a Windows service application is the Windows time service, which updates the clock you see on your computer's taskbar. Until now, it was very difficult to develop this type of application by using Visual Basic. The .NET Framework contains a set of classes that provide the basic functionality for Windows service applications. Now it is easy to make use of these Framework classes and use Visual Basic .NET to implement customized Windows service applications.

In this chapter, you will learn how to use Visual Studio .NET to create a simple Windows service application using the `System.ServiceProcess.ServiceBase` class. Then you will look at another .NET Framework class, the `System.ServiceProcess.ServiceController` class, to learn how to create Visual Basic .NET applications that can programmatically control and send custom commands to a Windows service. You will also review some considerations for setting security options and debugging that are specific to Windows services.

Introduction to Windows Services

A *Windows service* is an application that runs on a server or workstation computer and provides ongoing functionality without direct user interaction. Windows services are often used to perform system monitoring.

A Windows service will run in its own process, independently of users or other programs running on the same computer. Windows services are frequently configured to start automatically when the computer boots up. Unlike most applications, Windows services run under their own security identity, rather than under the identity of the currently logged-in user. They can start running, even if there is no user logged onto the computer. This behavior is exactly what is needed for applications that run unattended on a server or that need to be available all the time on a desktop computer.

The Visual Studio project templates and associated functionality that enable you to create Windows service applications are not available in the Visual Basic .NET Standard Edition. Neither is the Server Explorer feature. These features are included with Visual Studio .NET Professional, Enterprise Developer, and Enterprise Architect Editions.

When you create an application that will run as a Windows service, you must be careful not to include any user interface elements such as message boxes or other dialog boxes. A Windows service is not meant to provide a visual interface for users.

A Windows service will typically report its results and error messages to an event log.

 Real World Scenario

Using Windows Services to Monitor a Directory

You are a software developer for a medium-sized organization. You are hoping that some new features of the .NET Framework will help solve a problem that your department has been facing for some time. Your department is in charge of managing documents that are submitted for posting on your company's website. Documents are submitted by many departments throughout the company. End users simply copy the files to a designated network-shared directory.

Your department needs to know when new files are added to the directory. A consultant who left long ago wrote a system to periodically check the directory, but no one currently on the staff knows how to make changes or maintain the program.

A Windows service application is the perfect solution for this type of requirement. The service will always be running on the server, so administrators do not have to remember to check the directory or manually run a program. The .NET Framework even provides other useful classes, such as the FileSystemWatcher, which handles the actual task of firing events when files are added, deleted, or changed in the target directory. The Windows service can write to an event log, so there is an audit history.

By using the security features in the .NET Framework, your application can check the user's identity and permissions to make sure they are authorized to make changes. Other Framework classes provide the means to send an e-mail message, if necessary to notify administrators when new documents have been added.

It's clear that the .NET Framework provides a wealth of features to quickly and easily design solutions for this kind of common business requirement.

An administrator can interactively manage Windows service applications by using the Service Control Manager (see Figure 1.1). You can find this tool under different menus, depending on the operating system you are using:

- Start ➤ Programs ➤ Administrative Tools ➤ Services in Windows 2000 Server
- Start Settings ➤ Control Panel ➤ Administrative Tools ➤ Services in Windows 2000 Professional
- Start ➤ Control Panel ➤ Administrative Tools ➤ Services in Windows XP Professional

FIGURE 1.1   The Service Control Manager console

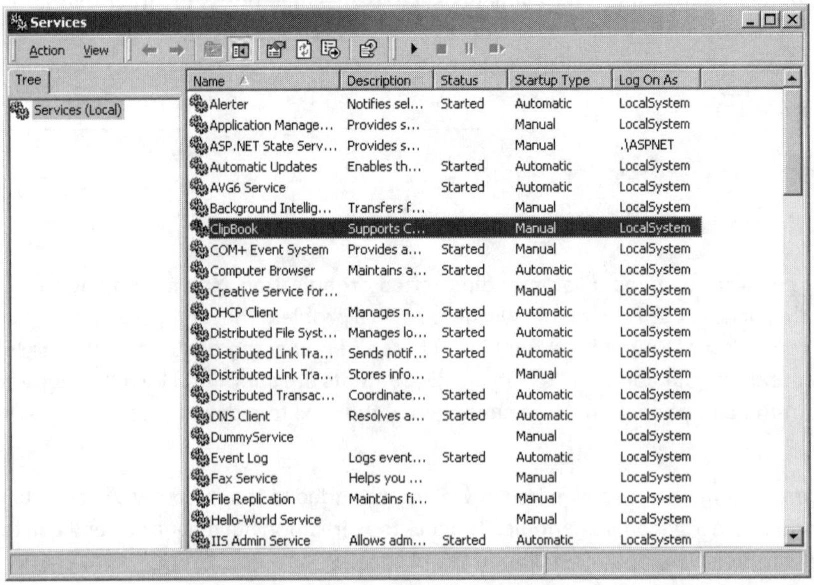

The *Service Control Manager* shows you a list of all services that are installed on the computer. For each service, you can see the name, description, current status (Started, Paused, or Stopped), startup type (Automatic—starts automatically on boot, or Manual) and the identity that the service logs on as. By using the menus and toolbar buttons, you can issue commands to start, stop, pause, continue, or restart the selected service. You can also view a Properties dialog box that enables you to change configuration options for a service.

Alternatively, you can view the Windows services running on your computer directly from within Visual Studio .NET by using the *Server Explorer*. To open the Server Explorer, choose View ≻ Server Explorer. Expand the node Servers, expand the node with your computer name, and then expand the Services node. You will see all the services that are running. When you right-click on a service, the pop-up menu provides options to start or stop the service and view the properties. You see a bit less detail here than in the Service Control Manager, but it is convenient to be able to start and stop the service from within Visual Studio .NET.

In Exercise 1.1, you will use the Windows Service Control Manager utility to view the existing Windows services that are currently running on your computer.

EXERCISE 1.1

Using the Service Control Manager

1. Start the Service Control Manager. For Windows 2000 Server, choose Start ≻ Programs ≻ Administrative Tools ≻ Services. (If you are using a different operating system, see the instructions provided earlier, immediately before Figure 1.1.).

2. Review the list of services that are running on your computer. For instance, select the Clipbook entry.

3. Right-click on the service and choose Start or Stop from the pop-up menu.

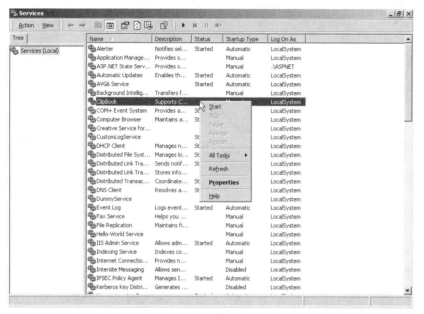

4. The status of the service changes in the Service Control Manager window. It is important to note that you should right-click the service name again and return the service to its original state. You don't want to inadvertently cause another application that depends on this service to fail or, conversely, to leave an unnecessary service running.

5. Right-click one more time and choose Properties. Review the choices that are available in the Properties dialog box.

Creating a Windows Service by Using Visual Studio .NET

The .NET Framework classes include a set of base classes, in the *System.ServiceProcess namespace*, that provide the underlying functionality of a Windows service application. Visual Studio .NET offers a project template that automatically sets a reference to `System.ServiceProcess` and also provides you some boilerplate code. This section describes the default setup in detail. When you create a project by using the template, you need to concentrate only on the unique features that your application will implement.

When you create a new project in Visual Studio .NET and choose Windows Service as your project template, the project will initially look like Figure 1.2. The default project contains one component class module (with the default name `Service1.vb`). If you view the code inside `Service1.vb` (see Listing 1.1), you will notice that a class has been created (also using the default class name `Service1`). This class inherits from the `System.ServiceProcess` `.ServiceBase` namespace. The template also adds an `Imports` statement for the `System.ServiceProcess` namespace.

FIGURE 1.2 Visual Studio .NET's default project setup for a Windows Service application

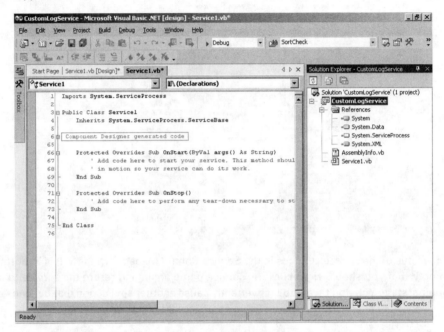

Listing 1.1: Default Code for a Windows Service Application

```
Imports System.ServiceProcess

Public Class Service1
    Inherits System.ServiceProcess.ServiceBase


'Component Designer generated code appears here


Protected Overrides Sub OnStart(ByVal args() As String)
        ' Add code here to start your service. This method
        ' should set things in motion so your service can
        ' do its work.
    End Sub
```

```
Protected Overrides Sub OnStop()
    ' Add code here to perform any teardown necessary
    ' to stop your service.
End Sub
```

```
End Class
```

If you expand the References node in the Solution Explorer window, you can see that a reference has been added for System.ServiceProcess.dll. Note that the .dll suffix is not present.

The default code also contains two procedure definitions for important methods of the *ServiceBase class*, *OnStart* and *OnStop*. You will add your custom code to these, and other methods, to implement the specific behavior of your Windows service application.

If you expand the region titled Component Designer Generated Code, you will see implementations for the New and Dispose methods, with code specific to how these standard Framework methods should be coded for a Windows service. There is also a Sub Main() procedure with some code needed for a Windows service to be started correctly (see Listing 1.2). The code in this procedure calls the Run method of the ServiceBase class and passes a reference to a new instance of your service. This is the code that enables your service to start when the operating system or a user invokes it.

Listing 1.2: Component Designer Generated Code

```
' The main entry point for the process
    <MTAThread()> _
    Shared Sub Main()
      Dim ServicesToRun() As _
          System.ServiceProcess.ServiceBase


      ' More than one NT Service may run in the same
      ' process. To add another service to this process,
      ' change the following line to create a second
      ' service object. For example,
      '
      ' ServicesToRun = New _
      '    System.ServiceProcess.ServiceBase() _
      '      {New Service1, New MySecondUserService}
      '

  ServicesToRun = New System.ServiceProcess.ServiceBase() _
          {New Service1}


    System.ServiceProcess.ServiceBase.Run(ServicesToRun)
    End Sub
```

Methods and Properties of the *ServiceBase* Class

Now that you have seen the basics required to create a Windows service application, you can concentrate on creating a service with custom functionality. To do this, you will provide custom implementations for methods of the parent ServiceBase class (see Table 1.1). The ServiceBase class also defines properties that you can set to affect the behavior of your service (see Table 1.2).

TABLE 1.1   Methods of the *ServiceBase* Class

Method Name	Description
OnContinue	Implement this method to run custom code when a service is resumed after being paused.
OnCustomCommand	Implement this method when you need custom actions that can be called programmatically by a ServiceController object.
OnPause	Implement this method to run custom code when a service is paused.
OnPowerEvent	Implement this method to run custom code when the computer's power status has changed—for example, a laptop computer going into suspended mode.
OnShutdown	Implement this method to run custom code before the computer shuts down.
OnStart	Implement this method to run custom code when a service starts. It is preferred to put initialization code in this procedure rather than in the constructor (Sub New method).
OnStop	Implement this method to run custom code when a service is stopped.

You will see how to implement the OnCustomCommand method later in this chapter, in the section titled "Executing Custom Commands for a Service."

It is preferred to use the OnStart method for any code that must run when your service is started. Code in the constructor method, Sub New, runs when the service is instantiated, before it is completely started and running in the context of the Service Control Manager. Also, the Visual Studio .NET documentation states that "there is no guarantee the objects will be reinitialized when you restart a service after it has been stopped."

TABLE 1.2 Properties of the *ServiceBase* Class

Property Name	Description
AutoLog	If this property is set to True, every time the service is started, stopped, paused, or continued, an entry will be written to the Windows Application event log. Set this property to False if you want to code custom log messages.
CanHandlePowerEvent	Set this to True if you have written custom code for the OnPowerEvent method. This will enable you to take special action if the computer that your service is running on experiences a change in power status— for example, a laptop computer going into suspended mode.
CanPauseAndContinue	Set this value to True if you want to allow your service to be paused.
CanShutdown	Set this to True if you have written custom code for the OnShutdown method. This will enable you to take special action before the computer shuts down.
CanStop	This value is usually set to True. It is set to False for some important operating system services, which should not be stopped by a user.
EventLog	If the AutoLog property is set to True, messages will be written to the Windows Application event log. If you set AutoLog to False, then you can specify a different event log for messages.
ServiceName	Gets or sets the service name.

Project Installer Classes

The Project Installers are "helper" classes that you add to your Windows service project. They provide important information that is used during the installation of your service application, such as the name that will be displayed in the Service Control Manager console, whether the service is started automatically or manually, and the security account. The *security account* is a Windows user login or system account that provides the identity and permissions that the Windows service will run with. Each Windows service project will have one instance of the *ServiceInstaller class* and one instance of the *ServiceProcessInstaller class* for each service that is included in the project.

When you are working in the Visual Studio .NET Integrated Development Environment (IDE), you can add ServiceInstaller components directly to your project from the Toolbox.

 If you prefer, you can also create these objects in code. You will see an example of that in Chapter 10, "Deploying, Securing, and Configuring Windows-Based Applications."

Setting Security Account Context for Windows Services

A Windows service runs independently of any user who might be logged onto the computer; therefore, the service must have a security identity of its own. When you create a Windows service application, you can select from one of four options for the security identity:

User   You create a specific username and password (using the standard Windows tools for doing so) for your application. Provide this username and password during installation. You must also provide this user with the appropriate permissions to complete the work of the Windows service application.

LocalSystem   *LocalSystem* is a built-in Windows account. It is the most commonly used setting for Windows services. It is a highly privileged account and is seen by other servers as an anonymous account.

LocalService   This is a built-in Windows account. It provides limited privileges on the local computer and is seen by other computers on the network as an anonymous user, so it is unlikely that code running under this identity will be allowed access to resources on other computers on the network. This account is available only on Windows XP and later operating systems.

NetworkService   This is a built-in Windows account. It runs with limited privileges on the local computer and can communicate with other servers as an authenticated domain account. This account is available only on Windows XP and later operating systems.

Again, the most commonly used security identity is LocalSystem. This built-in Windows account has a high level of privileges on the computer system. However, it is considered good security practice for applications to run with the least privileges required to perform their work. For example, do not allow the privilege to write to the system Registry if that is not needed to perform the core function of the service. To provide stronger security options, Windows XP and later operating systems have two new built-in accounts: LocalService and NetworkService. These two accounts have fewer privileges assigned to them by default. When installing a Windows service application, you should determine the level of privilege required and choose the best account.

These security accounts and other security considerations are discussed more thoroughly in Chapter 10.

Running a Windows Service

Unlike most .NET projects, you cannot run a Windows service application directly from the Visual Studio .NET IDE by choosing Debug ➢ Start from the main menu (or its equivalent toolbar or keystroke shortcuts). If you try to do this, you will see a message box that reads:

"Cannot start service from the command line or a debugger. A Windows service must first be installed (using `Installutil.exe`) and then started with the Server Explorer, Windows Services Administrative tool or the NET START command."

What this means is that you cannot interactively run your application for testing from within the Visual Studio .NET IDE. That is the way most Visual Basic .NET developers are used to working, and it's very convenient. Working with Windows service applications is a bit more structured.

You must first build and install your Windows service before you can test and debug it to see whether it is working correctly. Although this seems like a big drawback to developing this type of application, keep in mind that a Windows service application runs in a different context than regular user applications. It runs in the context of the Service Control Manager and under a different security context than the user identity that you are logged in as during development. To debug a Windows service application, you must complete the application, install it, and then attach a debugger to the running process.

We cover the steps to attaching a debugger to the process later in this chapter, in the section "Debugging a Windows Service." In Exercise 1.2, you will create a simple Windows service application. The steps for creating a *setup project* that will perform the installation of the service are included in the exercise. For a full explanation of creating setup and deployment projects, see Chapter 10.

For practical purposes, in real-world Windows service applications, you will probably want to create a Console or Windows Forms application to interactively test specific program logic before you add the code to your Windows service. After you are satisfied that your test code is working correctly, you can add it to the methods of your Windows service project.

For your first Windows service, you are going to design a simple service that uses a custom event log to record information about when the service is started and stopped.

You will create a new Windows service application project called CustomLogService. Next you will change some properties of the component. You will also add EventLog and Installer components from the Toolbox to the project. Finally, you are going to add code to the OnStart and OnStop events and also to the constructor method, Sub New.

EXERCISE 1.2

Creating a Windows Service by Using Visual Studio .NET

Setting Up the Project:

1. Start Visual Studio .NET and create a new project by using the Windows Service project template. Name the project **CustomLogService** and select an appropriate directory on your computer.

2. Using the Solution Explorer, rename the component Service1.vb to **CustomLogService.vb**.

3. Click on the design surface of CustomLogService.vb and display the Properties window. Change both the Name property and the Service name property to **CustomLogService**. Change the AutoLog property to **False**. Verify that the CanStop property is set to **True**.

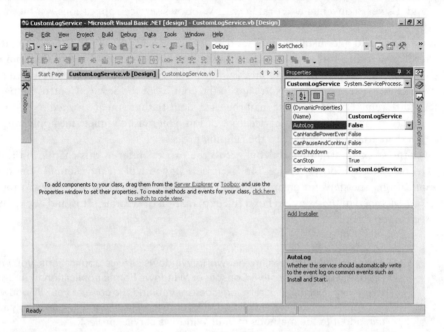

4. Display the Visual Studio .NET Toolbox and click the Components tab. Drag an EventLog component onto the design surface.

5. Click the EventLog component and display the Properties window. Change the name to **CustomEventLog**.

Adding Code:

6. Open the code editor for CustomLogService.vb. Verify that the class is named CustomLogService and that it inherits from System.ServiceProcess.ServiceBase:

```
Public Class CustomLogService
    Inherits System.ServiceProcess.ServiceBase
```

7. Expand the region titled Component Designer Generated Code. Add code to the New procedure. Code to initialize the custom event log is placed in the New procedure, instead of OnStart, because you want this code to run only when the Windows service is first installed, rather than each time it is restarted. Your completed code should look like this:

```
Public Sub New()
    MyBase.New()
    ' This call is required by the Component Designer.
    InitializeComponent()
    ' Add any initialization after InitializeComponent()

    If Not EventLog.SourceExists("CustomSource") Then
```

```
        EventLog.CreateEventSource("CustomSource", "CustomLog")
    End If
    CustomEventLog.Source = "CustomSource"
    CustomEventLog.Log = "CustomLog"
End Sub
```

8. Add code to the OnStart and OnStop event procedures. Here you will write an entry to the custom event log to keep track of when the service is stopped and started. Your code should look like this:

```
Protected Overrides Sub OnStart(ByVal args() As String)
    CustomEventLog.WriteEntry("The service has been started.")
End Sub

Protected Overrides Sub OnStop()
    CustomEventLog.WriteEntry("The service has been stopped.")
End Sub
```

Adding Installer Components:

9. Click the design surface of CustomLogService.vb and display the Properties window. Near the bottom of the Properties window is a link titled Add Installer. Click this link, and a new *component class module* called ProjectInstaller.vb will be added to your project. You will see that the design surface for this component has two other component icons on it: ServiceProcessInstaller1 and ServiceInstaller1.

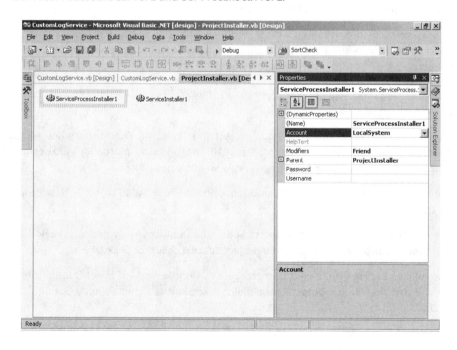

10. Click `ServiceProcessInstaller1` and display the Properties window. Select the Account property. Choose LocalSystem from the drop-down list. (If you decide to have your service running under a user account, you would also fill in the necessary information in the Password and Username properties here.)

11. Click `ServiceInstaller1` and display the Properties window. Select the `StartType` property. Choose Automatic from the drop-down list.

Building the Service:

Before you can build the service, you need to clean up some details.

12. Display the Task List window by choosing View ➢ Other Windows ➢ Task List from the menu. You will most likely see two errors; the first one says "Type Service1 is not defined." There is a remaining reference to the default name `Service1`.

13. Double-click the first entry in the Task List window, the code editor window will display the section of code where the error is located and the line of code that is in error will be highlighted. Change `Service1` to **CustomLogService**.

14. The next item in the Task List says "'Sub Main' was not found in 'CustomLogService .Service1'". This refers to the project Startup Object. Double-click this entry in the Task List window, and a dialog box pops up showing the new correct reference to `CustomLogService` . `CustomLogService`. Select this item and click OK.

15. Now you can build the `CustomLogService`. Right-click the project name in the Solution Explorer and choose Build, or choose Build ➢ Build CustomLogService from the menu.

16. Save the `CustomLogService` project. You will be using it for future exercises.

Creating a Setup Project to Install the Service:

Many details are involved in creating a setup project and deploying Windows service applications. This topic is covered in more detail in Chapter 10. The following instructions are designed to get your new application up and running quickly so you can test it.

17. In the Solution Explorer, click on the solution. Choose File ➢ Add Project ➢ New Project from the Visual Studio menu.

18. In the Add New Project dialog box, select Setup and Deployment Projects and select the Setup Project template. Name the new project **CustomLogSetup**. Click OK.

19. In the Solution Explorer, right-click `CustomLogSetup`. Choose Add ➢ Project Output from the menu. The Add Project Output Group dialog box displays. Select Primary Output and click OK.

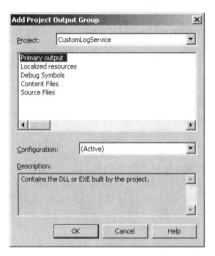

20. In the Solution Explorer, right-click `CustomLogSetup` again. Choose View ➢ Custom Actions from the menu.

21. In the upper-left corner of the work area, right-click Custom Actions. Choose Add Custom Action. The Select Item in Project dialog box displays. Double-click Application Folder, select Primary Output from CustomLogService (Active), and click OK. Your screen should look like the following one.

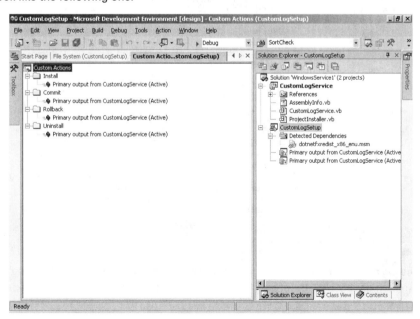

22. Build the setup project. Right-click the CustomLogSetup project name in the Solution Explorer and choose Build, or choose the menu command Build ➢ Build CustomLogSetup.

23. Save the CustomLogSetup project, because you will be using it again later in this chapter.

Installing and Testing the Service:

24. In the Debug subdirectory of the CustomLogSetup project directory, you will find a Windows Installer file named CustomLogSetup.msi. Double-click this file to start the installation.

25. This will start a Setup Wizard. Accept all the defaults and complete the installation.

26. Run the Service Control Manager to verify that your service is installed. To do this, click Start ➢ Programs ➢ Administrative Tools ➢ Services (or the appropriate sequence for your operating system version). You should see CustomLogService in the list.

27. Right-click on your service and choose Properties. Start your service.

28. Click Start ➢ Programs ➢ Administrative Tools ➢ Event Viewer (or the appropriate sequence for your operating system version) to view your custom event log in the Event Viewer.

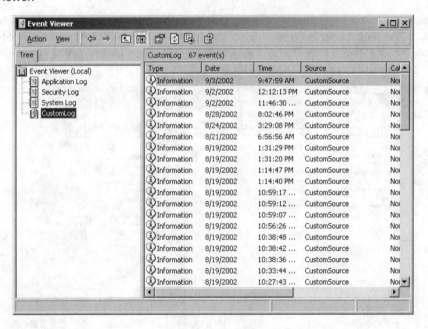

29. Click the log named CustomLog. Then right-click any one of the log entries and choose Properties (or just double-click the entry). You will see your custom message in the Properties dialog box.

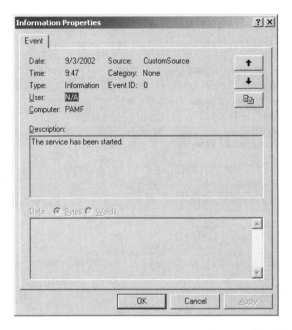

Debugging a Windows Service

Now that your service is installed and running, you can use the Visual Studio .NET debugger to attach to the service and use the standard debugging tools, such as breakpoints, stepping through code and others, to make sure your service is running correctly.

In Exercise 1.3, you will be attaching the debugger to a Windows service. You will be using a special capability of the Visual Studio .NET debugger that enables you to attach the debugger to an external process running on the computer. Because you have access to the source code for your service, you can set breakpoints. While the service is running, when a breakpoint is hit, you will go into break mode and can step through the code to examine variable values and perform other debugging actions.

EXERCISE 1.3

Debugging a Windows Service

1. In Visual Studio .NET, open the `CustomLogService` project. Right-click `CustomLogService.vb` in the Solution Explorer and choose View Code.

2. Set a breakpoint on the line of code in the OnStop procedure that writes the log entry:

   CustomEventLog.WriteEntry("The service has been stopped.")

3. From the Visual Studio .NET menus, choose Debug ➢ Processes. You will see a list of running processes on your computer. Make sure that the check boxes labeled Show System Processes and Show Processes in all Sessions are both selected.

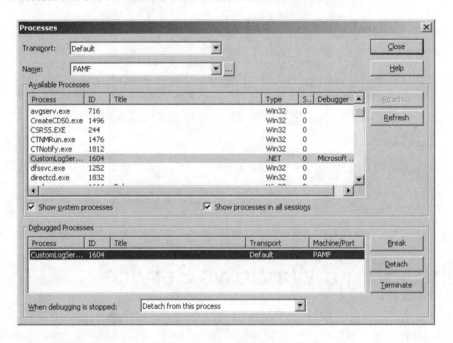

4. Select CustomLogService and click the Attach button.

5. The Attach to Process dialog box displays. Make sure that the Common Language Runtime option is checked and click OK. Close the Processes dialog box.

6. Back in Control Panel, start the Service Control Manager. Select CustomLogService and stop the service. A yellow highlight in Visual Studio .NET indicates that the breakpoint has been hit. The Service Control Manager will not be able to finish stopping the service until you release the debugger. Choose Debug ➢ Stop Debugging from the menu to do so.

WARNING   Be careful when using the debugger to attach to a process. Use this technique only when you are working with processes that you can control. Attaching a debugger to one of the operating system processes, for example, could cause your computer to hang up.

Configuring Client Computers and Servers to Use a Windows Service

Until now, you have been using the built-in Windows tools to view and manage Windows services. The .NET Framework also provides a set of classes that enable you to work with Windows services directly from your Visual Basic .NET application code. This can be very useful if you have created a Windows service that monitors and logs some system performance data, but you want it to run only while your application is running. You can start the service when your application starts up and stop it when your application closes. You can even add custom commands to your service and call them from application code.

In this section, you are going to learn how to use the *ServiceController class*. This is a .NET Framework class that has methods to programmatically control a Windows service. You will create a Windows Forms application that can start and stop services. A sample application called `ServiceControllerProject` is included on the book's CD and incorporates all the features covered in this section (see Figure 1.3). You might want to load the application code so that you can review it while you are reading this section.

FIGURE 1.3   The `ServiceControllerProject` demo

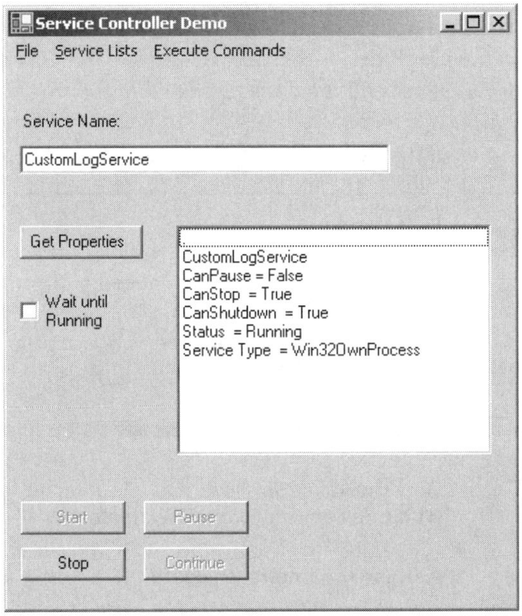

Exercise 1.4 at the end of the chapter is designed to take you step-by-step through the features of the `ServiceControllerProject` demo application. Exercise 1.5 provides some examples that modify the `CustomLogService` that you created earlier in the chapter to support custom commands and for building a service controller application of your own to test them.

Instantiating the *ServiceController* Object

When you instantiate a ServiceController object, you must supply two important pieces of information:

- The service name that you want to control
- The machine name that the service is running on

If you do not specify a machine name, the default is to look for the service on the local machine. Your project must include a reference to System.ServiceProcess.dll, and you should add an Imports statement for System.ServiceProcess as well. The ServiceController object can be instantiated as follows:

```
Dim servController = New _
    ServiceController("CustomLogService")
```

In the preceding example, the service name is passed to the overloaded constructor method as a single string parameter. The ServiceName property can also be set independently, as shown here:

```
Dim servController as New ServiceController()
ServController.ServiceName = "CustomLogService"
```

Properties and Methods of the *ServiceController* Class

There are several important properties of the service that you might be interested in testing. Table 1.3 shows some of the properties of the ServiceController class. The listed properties map to the properties of the ServiceBase class discussed in the first part of this chapter.

TABLE 1.3   Properties of the *ServiceController* Class

Property Name	Description
CanPauseAndContinue	True if the service can be paused and continued. (Read-only.)
CanShutdown	True if the service should be notified when the system is shutting down. (Read-only.)
CanStop	True if the service can be stopped after it has started. (Read-only.)
DependentServices	Gets the set of services that depends on the service associated with this ServiceController instance.
DisplayName	A friendly name for the service.
MachineName	The name of the computer on which the service is running.
ServiceName	Identifies the service that this instance of the ServiceController references.
ServicesDependedOn	The set of services that this service depends on.

TABLE 1.3   Properties of the *ServiceController* Class *(continued)*

Property Name	Description
ServiceType	One of the following: Win32OwnProcess, Win32ShareProcess (these are the types that can be created in Visual Studio .NET). Other system services might show a service type of Adapter, FileSystemDriver, InteractiveProcess, KernelDriver, or RecognizerDriver.
Status	One of the following: StartPending, Running, StopPending, Stopped, PausePending, Paused, ContinuePending.

Remember, you use the properties of the ServiceBase class when you are creating a Windows service. The CanStop, CanPauseAndContinue, and CanShutdown properties of the ServiceBase class enable you to set the behavior for your service. In the ServiceController class, these properties are read-only. The ServiceController instance can only test the property to see what was set when the service was created.

When you are working programmatically with a service, it is good practice to always test the service's state before you try an operation. For example, before you try to issue a Pause command to a service, test the CanPauseAndContinue property to see whether Pause is a valid action for that particular service:

```
If servController.CanPauseAndContinue = True Then
    servController.Pause()
End If
```

You also might want to test the current value of the Status property before issuing a command to change the status:

```
If servController.Status = _
      ServiceControllerStatus.Paused Then
          servController.Continue()
End If
```

The only valid settings for the Status property are defined by the *ServiceControllerStatus enumeration*, as Intellisense in Visual Studio .NET will show you (see Figure 1.4).

FIGURE 1.4   The ServiceControllerStatus enumeration

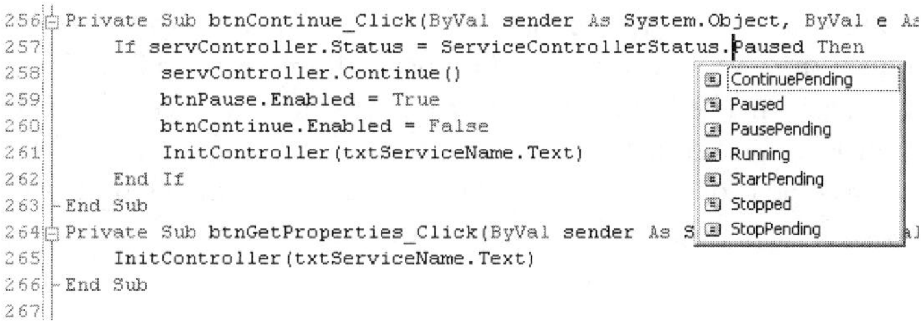

Table 1.4 lists the methods of the `ServiceController` class. These methods enable you to write code in a Visual Basic .NET application that can cause a Windows service application to start, stop, pause, or continue. Your code can also call custom commands and get other information about the service.

TABLE 1.4 Methods of the *ServiceController* Class

Method Name	Description
Close	Disconnects the ServiceController object from the service and releases any resources that were in use.
Continue	Resumes a service after a paused command.
ExecuteCommand	Executes a custom command on the service.
GetDevices	Gets a list of device driver services on a computer.
GetServices	Gets a list of services on a computer.
Pause	Pauses the service.
Refresh	Gets current property values.
Start	Starts the service.
Stop	Stops this service and any services that are dependent on this service.
WaitForStatus	Waits for the service to reach the specified status or for the request to time out.

The `Start`, `Stop`, `Pause`, and `Continue` methods are easy to understand. They work the same way in code that they work when you are issuing these commands through the Service Control Manager interface.

The `Refresh` method gets the current settings for the properties of the service that you are monitoring, without affecting the state of the service.

The `GetServices` and `GetDevices` methods populate an array of `ServiceController` objects, which in turn can access information about all the services installed on a computer (as shown in Listing 1.3). The `GetDevices` method gets those services that are of type `KernelDriver` or `FileSystemDriver`.

Listing 1.3 shows the procedure from the `ServiceControllerProject` demo that loads a ListBox control with the names of all services on the computer.

Listing 1.3: A Procedure to List All Services Running on the Local Computer

```
Private Sub btnGetServices_Click(ByVal sender _
    As_System.Object, ByVal e As System.EventArgs) _
    Handles btnGetServices.Click
        Dim servArray() As ServiceController
        Dim i As Integer

        servArray = ServiceController.GetServices()

        lstDisplay.Items.Clear()
        For i = 0 To servArray.Length - 1
            lstDisplay.Items.Add(servArray(i).ServiceName)
        Next
        servArray = Nothing
    End Sub
```

The WaitForStatus method takes into consideration that sometimes a particular service might take a long time to start or not start at all. Also, StartPending, StopPending, PausePending, and ContinuePending will appear as the service's status briefly, before they have completely reached a final state. You can test this with the ServiceControllerProject demo. After a service is stopped, click the Start button.

The display in the list box will show the status as StartPending. If you click the Get Properties button again a moment later, the display updates to show that the service now has a status of Running. If you select the check box labeled Wait Until Running, the code in the ServiceControllerProject demo will call the ServiceController object's WaitForStatus method and the code will block until the target service achieves the specified status. The display does not update until the service's status is Running. This is shown in the following code snippet:

```
If chkWait.Checked Then
    servController.WaitForStatus( _
        ServiceControllerStatus.Running)
End If
```

You can also call the WaitForStatus method by specifying two parameters: the status to wait for and a TimeSpan value, which indicates how long your code should wait before it times out and reports an error condition.

Executing Custom Commands for a Service

The ServiceController class offers a method that enables you to define truly customized functionality for your Windows service application. You have seen how to add code to standard methods that will fire in the normal cycle of events, as a Windows service application is started and stopped. The ServiceController class provides a means to call custom methods that you have designed for your Windows service application.

Let's return to the source code for your Windows service application named CustomLogService. You will add another event procedure to the service and then recompile and reinstall it.

When you create custom functionality for a Windows service, calls to any of your procedures are handled inside the single Windows service event procedure named OnCustomCommand. Inside this procedure, you can use a conditional test or Case statement to break out one or more groups of code that will be executed as part of a given command. The OnCustomCommand method accepts an integer parameter that indicates which section of code should be executed for any specific call to the method. The integer parameter must be within the range of 128 and 256. Values below 128 are reserved for system commands. If the *AutoLog* property of the service is True, calls to OnCustomCommand will be noted in the Windows Application *event log*.

The procedure inside your Windows Service application will look like Listing 1.4.

Listing 1.4: The OnCustomCommand Procedure

```
Protected Overrides Sub OnCustomCommand( _
   ByVal command As Integer)
    Select Case command
      Case 130
        CustomEventLog.WriteEntry( _
          "Command 130 successfully completed.")
      Case 140
        CustomEventLog.WriteEntry( _
          "Command 140 successfully completed.")
      Case 150
        CustomEventLog.WriteEntry( _
          "Command 150 successfully completed.")
      Case Else
        CustomEventLog.WriteEntry( _
          "ERROR: Unrecognized command parameter!")
    End Select
End Sub
```

For simplicity, your custom command does nothing more than write a log entry to verify that the command successfully completed. But that's enough to test your code in the ServiceControllerProject demo.

After you have the code in the Windows service application, you can write a method in your ServiceController application that calls the ServiceController.ExecuteCommand method. The ServiceControllerProject demo has a simple user interface that calls the method and passes a user-selected integer parameter (see Figure 1.5). As you can see from Listing 1.4, the OnCustomCommand method will recognize three valid parameter values: 130, 140, and 150. If any other value is passed, an error message will be written to the custom event log.

Listing 1.5 shows the code from the ServiceControllerProject demo that calls the Execute command method.

FIGURE 1.5   Executing a custom command from the `ServiceControllerProject` demo

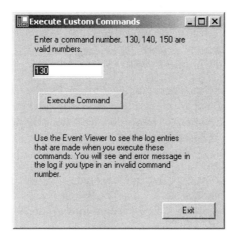

Listing 1.5: Executing a Custom Command

```
Private Sub btnCommand_Click(ByVal sender As _
   System.Object, ByVal e As System.EventArgs) _
   Handles btnCommand.Click

      Dim commandNumber As Integer
      servController = New _
         ServiceController("CustomLogService")
      Try
         commandNumber = CType(txtCommand.Text, Integer)
         servController.ExecuteCommand(commandNumber)
         MessageBox.Show("Command completed. " & _
            "Check the Custom event log.")
      Catch ex As Exception
         MessageBox.Show("Invalid command number.")
      End Try
   End Sub
```

One important thing to remember about calling a custom command on a Windows service is that all error handling must be done within the Windows service application itself. In this simple example, our "error handling" consisted of writing an error message to the event log. In a real-world application, you will need to consider your error handling carefully. The error handling implemented in the `ServiceController` client application guards only against sending a nonnumeric value as a parameter to the call to `ExecuteCommand`.

In Exercise 1.4, you will load the `ServiceControllerProject` demo and try some of its features that were discussed in this section.

EXERCISE 1.4

Trying the *ServiceController* Demo Project

On the CD included with this book, you will find a Visual Basic .NET project titled Service-ControllerProject. Open this project in Visual Studio .NET.

1. If you have already created the CustomLogService (see Exercise 1.2), the ServiceController-Project will immediately display information about the service when you first run it. If you do not have a service named CustomLogService installed, you will get an error message. If you get this message, type in the name of a valid service, such as **ClipBook**. Then click the Get Properties button.

2. Experiment with the Stop and Start buttons. You might also want to open the Service Control Manager and watch the service status changing there as well. You will need to refresh the display in the Service Control Manager each time you change the status by using the Visual Basic .NET application.

Because the CanPauseAndContinue property of CustomLogService is set to False, the Pause and Continue buttons are disabled.

3. Notice that when you stop and then start the CustomLogService, the status that is displayed is StartPending. If you click the Get Properties button again a few seconds later, you will see the status is now Running.

4. Select the Wait Until Running check box; then stop and start the service again. This time the ListBox display will not be updated until the service has been fully started and the status has reached Running.

5. Type in the name of a different service, such as **EventLog**, and view its properties. Remember, do not stop the system services or services you didn't create (especially if you're not sure what the service does); doing so can cause problems with your computer.

6. The Service Lists menu displays another form, where you can see a list of all the services installed on your computer. The GetDevices method shows all installed services that are device drivers.

7. Finally, the Execute Commands menu displays one more form. This form contains code to execute custom commands against CustomLogService. You can't test this feature yet. In the next exercise, Exercise 1.5, you will modify CustomLogService to accept custom commands.

In Exercise 1.5, you will uninstall and modify the CustomLogService you created in Exercise 1.2. To uninstall the CustomLogService, you will be using the Windows Control Panel application Add/Remove Programs. While looking at the list of installed applications on your computer, you will see only the entry for the setup program that installs the service. You will not see an entry for the service itself.

EXERCISE 1.5

Uninstalling and Modifying *CustomLogService*

1. Start the Windows Control Panel application Add/Remove programs. Remove CustomLogSetup.

2. Verify that CustomLogService is no longer installed by checking the Service Control Manager. Use Control Panel to open the Service Control Manager.

3. Open the CustomLogService solution in Visual Studio .NET (it should contain both the service and setup projects).

4. Add the following method to CustomLogService.vb. Add this code directly after the OnStart and OnStop methods (refer to the following screen capture):

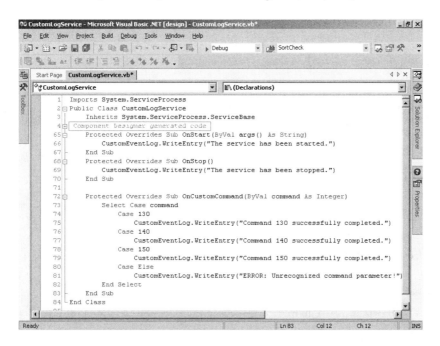

```
Protected Overrides Sub OnCustomCommand(ByVal command As Integer)
    Select Case command
        Case 130
            CustomEventLog.WriteEntry( _
                "Command 130 successfully completed.")
        Case 140
            CustomEventLog.WriteEntry( _
                "Command 140 successfully completed.")
        Case 150
            CustomEventLog.WriteEntry( _
                "Command 150 successfully completed.")
        Case Else
```

```
        CustomEventLog.WriteEntry( _
            "ERROR: Unrecognized command parameter!")
    End Select
End Sub
```

5. Save the solution. Right-click the `CustomLogService` project in the Solution Explorer and chose Build. Then right-click the `CustomLogSetup` project and choose Build.

6. Go to the `Debug` subdirectory under the `CustomLogSetup` project directory. Double-click the `CustomLogSetup.msi` file to install the revised version of the service.

7. Use the `ServiceControllerProject` demo that you used in Exercise 1.4 to verify that the `CustomLogService` is once again installed on your computer.

8. Start the `CustomLogService`.

9. Go to the Execute Commands form in the `ServiceControllerProject` demo and test execution of the custom commands. Try the valid parameter numbers 130, 140, and 150 and then try an invalid number, such as 155.

10. Open the Windows Event Viewer and look at the entries. Double-click an entry to display the Properties dialog box and view the message.

Summary

In this chapter, you learned about creating and managing Windows service applications. We covered the following topics:

- An introduction to how Windows services work

- How to view existing Windows services by using system tools such as the Service Control Manager and the Event Viewer

- How Visual Studio .NET helps you to create the foundations of a Windows service application

- The properties and methods of the .NET Framework `ServiceBase` class

- How to use Visual Studio .NET to add .NET Framework components, such as the Project Installers and an `EventLog`, to your project directly from the Toolbox

- How to add custom code to the `OnStart` and `OnStop` methods of a Windows service

- How to attach the Visual Studio .NET debugger to a running Windows service

- How to use the .NET Framework `ServiceController` class to control a Windows service from application code

- How to code custom commands for a Windows service and how to call them from a `ServiceController` object

Exam Essentials

Know how to create a Windows service.   Visual Studio .NET offers you a built-in template that makes setting up a Windows service easy. Windows service applications inherit from the `System.ServiceProcess.ServiceBase` namespace.

Be familiar with the properties and methods of the `System.ServiceProcess.ServiceBase` class.   Know how the code in the `Sub Main` method of a Windows service calls the `Run` method to instantiate the service.

Understand the security accounts that can be used with Windows services.   LocalSystem is currently the most commonly used security setting but it is a highly privileged account, which could lead to security breaches. Windows XP (and later) offers the opportunity to use accounts with lesser privileges: LocalService and NetworkService.

Understand that you cannot directly run a Windows service from Visual Studio .NET.   You must attach the debugger to the running process.

Know how to manipulate a Windows service application.   Know how to use the Windows utility Service Control Manager to manipulate a Windows service. Be familiar with the properties and methods of the `System.ServiceProcess.ServiceController` class. Know how to use the `ServiceController` to stop and start Windows services programmatically.

Key Terms

Before you take the exam, be certain you are familiar with the following terms:

`AutoLog`	`ServiceBase` class
event log	`ServiceController` class
LocalSystem	`ServiceControllerStatus` enumeration
`OnStart`	`ServiceInstaller` class
`OnStop`	`ServiceProcessInstaller` class
security account	setup project
Server Explorer	`System.ServiceProcess` namespace
Service Control Manager	Windows service

Review Questions

1. How can you best describe a Windows service application?

   A. It impersonates the identity of the user who is logged in.

   B. It runs in its own process with its own security account.

   C. It runs in the same process space as the web server with the identity of `IUSR_Machine`.

   D. It runs in the same process space as the operating system and must have Administrator privileges.

2. Windows services begin running:

   A. When the computer is booted, if the Startup type is set to Automatic

   B. When a user logs in

   C. Only when an Administrator starts them

   D. Only when called by a `ServiceController` object

3. How can you view information about the services running on a specific computer?

   A. By using the Server Explorer in Visual Studio .NET

   B. By using a method of the `ServiceController` class

   C. By using the Windows Service Control Manager console

   D. All of the above

4. Your Windows service needs to read some default values from a disk file every time it is started. How can you accomplish this?

   A. Write code in the `OnStart` method of your service application.

   B. Write code in the `OnCustomCommand` method of your service application.

   C. Write code in the `Sub Main` method of your service application.

   D. Write code in the `Sub New` method of your service application.

5. All Windows service applications support the same basic interface, because:

   A. The operating system will not load them if they do not implement all standard methods.

   B. They will not compile if they do not implement all standard methods.

   C. They all inherit from the `System.ServiceProcess.ServiceInstaller` class.

   D. They all inherit from the `System.ServiceProcess.ServiceBase` class.

6. If you leave the AutoLog property set to the default value of True in your Windows service, what behavior will you see when the service is running?

   A. Stop, Start, Pause, and Continue events will be written to a custom event log with the same name as your service.

   B. Stop, Start, Pause, and Continue events will be written to the Windows Application event log.

   C. No logging will take place unless you set the EventLog property to the name of a custom event log.

   D. No logging will take place unless you write code in the OnStart method to write entries to a custom event log.

7. You create a Windows service project that includes two Windows services. When you add installer components to your project, how many objects will be added?

   A. One ServiceInstaller object

   B. One ServiceInstaller object and one ServiceProcessInstaller object

   C. One ServiceInstaller object and two ServiceProcessInstaller objects

   D. Two ServiceInstaller objects and two ServiceProcessInstaller objects

8. You need to specify the security account that your Windows service will run under. How can you specify this while creating the project in Visual Studio .NET?

   A. Set the Account property of the ServiceBase class.

   B. Set the Account property of the ServiceProcessInstaller object.

   C. Set the Account property of the ServiceInstaller object.

   D. Change the Account setting in the Project Properties dialog box.

9. What is the most commonly used security account for running Windows services?

   A. Interactive User

   B. LocalSystem

   C. Administrator

   D. NetworkService

10. You have created a Windows service application and you would like to use the debugging tools in Visual Studio .NET to troubleshoot a problem with the application. You load the application in Visual Studio .NET. What should you do next?

   A. Select Debug ➢ Start from the Visual Studio .NET menu.

   B. Select Debug ➢ Step Into from the Visual Studio .NET menu.

   C. Select Debug ➢ Processes from the Visual Studio .NET menu.

   D. Select Debug ➢ Exceptions from the Visual Studio .NET menu.

11. You need to create an application that is able programmatically to start and stop a Windows service. Which .NET Framework class should you use?

    A. System.ServiceProcess.ServiceBase

    B. System.ServiceProcess.ServiceController

    C. System.ServiceProcess.ServiceInstaller

    D. System.ServiceProcess.Status

12. You are creating an application that controls a Windows service programmatically. You would like to be able to call the Pause method to temporarily disable the service while your application is running, but this does not seem to be working. What can you do to overcome this problem?

    A. You must set the CanPauseAndContinue property of the ServiceController to True before you can call the Pause method.

    B. You must set the CanStop property of the ServiceController to True before you can call the Pause method.

    C. Nothing. You cannot use the Pause method if the original designer of the Windows service did not set the CanShutdown property to True.

    D. Nothing. You cannot use the Pause method if the original designer of the Windows service did not set the CanPauseAndContinue property of the ServiceBase class to True.

13. You have created an application that is able to programmatically start and stop a Windows service. However, after using the Start method, your application always reports back that the service's status is StartPending rather than the Running status that you are looking for. How can you be sure that the service has successfully been started and is running, before your application takes any further action?

    A. Use the GetService method and see whether your service is included in the array of services that is returned.

    B. Set a Timer control to call the Refresh method until a status of Running is returned.

    C. Use the WaitforStatus method with ServiceControllerStatus.Running as the parameter.

    D. Use the ExecuteCommand method to run custom code when the service starts.

14. You need to create an application that is able to programmatically execute custom commands of a Windows service. How do you call custom commands from your application?

    A. Use the ServiceBase class OnCustomCommand method and pass an integer parameter.

    B. Use the ServiceController class OnCustomCommand method and pass a string parameter.

    C. Use the ServiceBase class ExecuteCommand method and pass a string parameter.

    D. Use the ServiceController class ExecuteCommand method and pass an integer parameter.

15. What does the OnPowerEvent method of the ServiceBase class do?

A. Enables the designer of the Windows service to write code that will run in the event of a power outage

B. Enables the designer of the Windows service to write code that will run when the computer shuts down

C. Enables the designer of the Windows service to write code that will run when a laptop computer goes into suspended mode

D. Enables the designer of the Windows service to write code that will run when a custom command is executed

Answers to Review Questions

1. B.   A Windows service runs in its own memory process space and has its own security account, most commonly LocalSystem. A Windows service does not interfere with other users or programs running on the computer.

2. A.   If the service's `StartUpType` property is set to Automatic, the service will be started when the computer is started or rebooted. If the `StartUpType` property is set to Manual, then the service must be started by using either the Service Control Manager console or by application code that uses a `ServiceController` object.

3. D.   You can view information about Windows services by using either the Windows Service Control Manager console or the Visual Studio .NET Server Explorer. The `GetServices` and `GetDevices` methods of the `ServiceController` class also provide information about the services that are running on a specific computer.

4. A.   The `OnStart` method is the recommended place to put code that should run when a service is started. Code in the constructor, `Sub New`, might not run when a service is stopped and restarted.

5. D.   To create an application that will run as a Windows service in Visual Studio .NET, you must inherit base class functionality from the `System.ServiceProcess.ServiceBase` class.

6. B.   If the `AutoLog` property of a Windows service application is set to True, `Stop`, `Start`, `Pause`, and `Continue` events will be written to the Windows Application event log without any further coding necessary.

7. C.   A Windows service project in Visual Studio .NET can contain more than one Windows service component class module. When you add installers to the project, one `ServiceInstaller` object will be added, and one `ServiceProcessInstaller` object will be added for each Windows service module contained in the project.

8. B.   Use the `Account` property of the `ServiceProcessInstaller` object to specify which security account the service should run under.

9. B.   LocalSystem is currently the most commonly used security account for running Windows service applications. It is a highly privileged account, which can pose a security risk. The new Windows XP accounts, NetworkService and LocalService, might be better choices from a security standpoint.

10. C.   To debug a Windows service application, you must install and run it. After it is running, you can attach the Visual Studio .NET debugger to this external process. Use the Debug ➤ Processes menu choice to display the Processes dialog box to choose from all running processes on the computer.

11. B.   The `System.ServiceProcess.ServiceController` .NET Framework class has properties and methods that enable you to get information about a Windows service and to control the service through application code.

12. D.   The original creator of the Windows service application sets the CanStop and CanPause-AndContinue properties of the service. The original designer might not want the service to be stopped or paused by a user, as is often the case with operating system services.

13. C.   The WaitforStatus method of the ServiceController class will cause application code to block until the desired status is reached.

14. D.   To call a custom command from an application that can control Windows services programmatically, use the ServiceController.ExecuteCommand method. This method takes a single integer parameter, which indicates the command that the user would like to run. Valid parameter values are defined by the designer of the Windows service application (within the range of 128 to 256).

15. C.   The OnPowerEvent method is intended to be used if your service must run on laptop computers. You might want to save data, for example, before the computer goes into suspended mode.

Chapter

2

Creating and Managing Serviced Components

MICROSOFT EXAM OBJECTIVES COVERED IN THIS CHAPTER:

✓ **Create and consume a serviced component.**

- Implement a serviced component.
- Create interfaces that are visible to COM.
- Manage the component by using the Component Services tool.
- Create a strongly named assembly.
- Register the component in the global assembly cache.

✓ **Access unmanaged code from a Windows service and a serviced component.**

The .NET platform offers many advantages for developing new applications. However, most organizations will not be able to give up their existing applications that were developed on and are running on the Windows 32/COM/COM+ platform, the standard for almost 10 years.

All code written by using the .NET Framework tools and designed to run under the Common Language Runtime (CLR) is known as *managed code*. Other applications that run on the Windows/COM platform, such as COM components and Visual Basic 6 applications, are known as *unmanaged code*. COM, or the Component Object Model, is the standard for *component interoperability* for all unmanaged code. COM defines a set of standard interfaces that enable components to discover the capabilities of other components and call their methods.

In this chapter, you are going to learn about using Windows/COM+ Component Services to host components created with the .NET Framework. By hosting the components in Component Services, you can take advantage of the infrastructure services provided by this environment; these are detailed in the next section. You will also learn how to call legacy COM components from a .NET application, how to call a .NET component from a legacy COM application, and how to call Windows Application Programming Interface (API) functions from a .NET application. Understanding when and how to use these different techniques will be useful to you as you start to integrate .NET technology with existing applications.

In any discussion of component technologies, you will find the terms *component*, *class*, *object*, and *instance*. It's important to work from a common set of definitions because sometimes these terms are used incorrectly. A *component* is a compiled unit of executable code. A *class* is the source code that defines an object. An *object* is an in-memory construction of code and data that can be created from a class. *Instance* refers to a single runtime instance of the object, which has its own unique set of properties and data.

Advantages of Serviced Components

Windows Component Services provide a hosting environment for *middle-tier components*. In a 3-tier application design, code is separated into a user interface tier, a business logic tier and a data access tier. The middle-tier components provide the business logic of your application. This hosting environment provides the basic infrastructure to support middle-tier components and help to optimize them for performance and availability to a large number of users. Some of the features of Windows Component Services help you to manage *distributed transactions*, enforce *role-based security*, and increase performance by using *object pooling*. Other features such as *message queuing* and event notification provide additional options for application design. These features will be covered in more detail later in this chapter. As a developer, you can take advantage of these features very easily and concentrate on writing code to solve your specific business problems, without worrying about the complexities of transaction management or security authentication schemes. By taking advantage of these services, you enable your applications to achieve better performance, reliability, and scalability with a minimum of coding on your part.

The History of Component Services

The idea for a standard component infrastructure was first introduced with the Windows NT 4.0 Option Pack. Microsoft Transaction Server (MTS) and Microsoft Message Queue Server (MSMQ) were included in the Windows NT option pack. MTS, due to its name, was mostly seen as a means to support distributed transactions (transactions involving more than one component, perhaps even running on different servers), but it also provided security and performance features. MSMQ works in conjunction with MTS, providing for asynchronous message-based communication within transactions.

Windows 2000 improved on MTS and MSMQ by adding new features and integrating more tightly with the operating system. At this point, the name was also changed to Component Services to reflect that this infrastructure did far more than just manage transactions. COM technology also received an update and is now known as *COM+*. When we create .NET distributed applications that use Component Services, there is another name that we can use: *.NET Enterprise Services*.

Another important concept to understand about Component Services is that of the declarative model of specifying attributes, rather than a procedural, code-based approach. The Component Services management console (which you will try out later in the chapter) provides many options to be set by an administrator. For example, if your application's security requirements change after the application is in production, the server administrator can make these changes in the management console. The component does not have to be updated at the source-code level.

When developing components with the .NET Framework, you can also apply attributes in your source code at the assembly, class, or method level to control the component's behavior when it is running under Component Services. All .NET components that will run under Windows Component Services must inherit from the System.EnterpriseServices.ServicedComponent base class.

Features of Component Services

Let's look at the features of Component Services in a little more detail:

Automatic transaction processing   This feature enables your components to participate in transactions that require coordination of code from multiple components. If an error occurs in any of the code that is enlisted in a given transaction, all the intermediate work that had been done up until that point will be rolled back. If all the code completes successfully, the changes (such as writing database updates) will be committed, or made permanent.

Just-in-time activation The feature improves performance and scalability by automatically deactivating an object—and releasing its resources—as soon as a method call is complete, even if the calling application does not release the reference immediately. The object's context is still maintained on the server, so the calling application still has a valid reference if it wishes to make another method call. If the calling application does make another method call, the server will activate a new instance of the object.

Object pooling This feature improves performance and scalability by maintaining a defined number of objects in memory at all times, ready to be activated when a calling application makes a request. You can tune application performance by adjusting the minimum and maximum number of objects to be maintained by the pool.

Object construction Object construction enables you to enter a construction string into the Component Services management console for a class in your component. This string is then passed as a parameter to the constructor method each time an object is instantiated for that class. This is useful when you need to provide information that might change after your component was installed, such as a database connection string. It enables the string to be changed by an administrator and doesn't require that the source code be updated.

Role-based security This feature enables you to define which groups of users (roles) are allowed to make calls on a component, class, or method. You can apply role-based security in source code through properties and methods of the `System.EnterpriseServices.ServicedComponent` base class, you can apply a `SecurityRoleAttribute` to your class, or you can assign roles administratively through the Component Services management console. This topic is discussed further in Chapter 10, "Deploying, Securing, and Configuring Windows-Based Applications."

Synchronization Synchronization manages multiple clients who want to use your component at the same time. This feature enables a developer to concentrate on business logic and not worry about complex threading issues.

Compensating Resource Managers (CRMs) CRMs provide transactional support for simple resources, such as disk files or the system Registry, so that changes to these resources can be committed or rolled back as a normal part of automatic transaction processing.

BYOT (Bring Your Own Transaction) This feature can be used in special circumstances when your component must participate in a transaction that was started by an external transaction manager, not Component Services.

COM Transaction Integrator (COMTI) This feature enables your components to interact with applications running in certain legacy mainframe environments.

Loosely Coupled Events (LCE) Unlike traditional event notification, LCE does not require that the event "subscriber" components stay running in memory waiting for notification. Component Services can start components when an event that they are subscribed to is fired by another component.

Private components   A component marked as Private can be called only from other components in the same application (in-process calls). It cannot be called from outside applications.

Queued components   This feature enables applications to make asynchronous calls on components. The information about the call is placed into a message queue (persistent storage) on the server, and the component processes each message when it is available. This is useful for making calls on an application on a remote server that might not always be online or for balancing peak workloads. Messages wait in the queue until the server component is connected and is able to process them.

Simple Object Access Protocol (SOAP) services   These services enable you to create an XML web service interface for existing components.

XA interoperability   XA interoperability supports the X/Open transaction-processing model. X/Open is part of the Open Software Foundation's Distributed Computing Environment, which is a set of standard middle-tier components that enable multi-vendor, multi-platform system integration.

Now that you understand the range of functionality that is offered by Windows Component Services, this chapter will concentrate on those that are most commonly used:

- Automatic transaction processing
- Just-in-time activation
- Object pooling
- Object construction

Chapter 10 covers role-based security.

Real World Scenario

Using Queued Components and Transactions

You are a software developer for a large organization. One of the tasks that you frequently face is transferring data from one application to another. The application that you are currently designing has a business requirement to generate summary information about transactions that have been entered each day. The application will run on a local server in each of your organization's 50 branch offices. Each of these branch offices must then send the information to an application at headquarters that consolidates all the branch office information.

You have looked at various models for transmitting the application and you have a few concerns. The first concern is that all 50 branches will be trying to connect to headquarters at about the same time each day; this might cause serious delays, and some connection attempts might fail. Your second concern is how to guarantee delivery if an error occurs at any point during either processing or data transmission. You have decided that .NET Enterprise Services and Queued Components can address these two design goals. You will create a message queue on the headquarters server that will accept the branch office data. This enables the branches to quickly connect to headquarters and submit their data without waiting for earlier requests to be processed. The application that consolidates all the data can process messages from the queue one at a time.

Support for distributed transactions within Enterprise Services makes sure that all the steps in processing, up to final delivery to the message queue, are a part of a single transaction. If an error occurs at any point, the entire operation is rolled back. You will not have to worry about sending partial results or a failure during message delivery.

Creating a Serviced Component

Now that you understand the advantages of using the features provided by Windows Component Services, you can create a .NET component that can take advantage of them. Here are the actions that are required when you want to use a .NET component in Windows Component Services:

1. Add the appropriate code and attributes to your .NET component.
2. Sign the component assembly with a strong name. Register the assembly in the Windows Registry.
3. Configure the component in the Windows Component Services management console.

You will look at each of these steps in more detail in this section. This section will also include a discussion of how to design components for better performance and greater scalability. Finally, you will learn about transactions and how to control them by using attributes and code.

Adding Code and Attributes to Your Component

To create a new component that will be hosted by Component Services, you will typically create a new project in Visual Studio .NET by using the Class Library project template. Then you must use the Solution Explorer to set a reference and include an `Imports` statement in your code module for the *System.EnterpriseServices namespace*. This namespace includes two important classes: `ServicedComponent` and `ContextUtil`.

Each class in your component should be marked as `Inherits ServicedComponent`. You can also add a set of attributes to your class that determine how your class will use features of the *ServicedComponent base class*.

Listing 2.1 shows an example of the code as well as some of these *assembly attributes*. Table 2.1 lists some of the important attributes that are available. For a complete list, see the Microsoft Developer Network (MSDN) .NET Framework documentation.

Listing 2.1: Creating a Class for Use as a Serviced Component

```
Imports System.EnterpriseServices
<Assembly: ApplicationName("TransactionApp")>
<Assembly: ApplicationActivation(ActivationOption.Server)>
```

```
Public Class Account
    Inherits ServicedComponent

    Public Function Credit(ByVal accountNum as String, _
        ByVal amount as Decimal) As Boolean
        'working code goes here
    End Function

    Public Function Debit(ByVal accountNum as String, _
        ByVal amount as Decimal) As Boolean
        'working code goes here
    End Function
End Class
```

TABLE 2.1 *ServicedComponent* Attributes

Attribute Name	Scope	Description
General Attributes—Assembly Level		
ApplicationActivation	Assembly	Library or Server. A library application runs in the same process with the code that calls it. A server application runs in its own process.
ApplicationID	Assembly	Enables you to identify your component by generating a Globally Unique Identifier (GUID) value.
ApplicationName	Assembly	Enables you to identify your component by a text name.
General Attributes—Class Level		
ConstructionEnabled	Class	Enables you to pass a construction string that is supplied at runtime via the Component Services console.
JustInTimeActivation	Class	Enables your class to take advantage of COM+ just-in-time activation.
ObjectPooling	Class	Enables your class to take advantage of object pooling.
PrivateComponent	Class	Can be called only from code in the same application, not by external clients.
Synchronization	Class	Determines how COM+ manages concurrent access to your class. The valid settings are SynchronizationOption .Required (default), Disabled, NotSupported, RequiresNew, and Supported.

TABLE 2.1   *ServicedComponent* Attributes *(continued)*

Attribute Name	Scope	Description
Security Attributes		
`ComponentAccessControl`	Class	Enables security checks to be performed before calling code in this class.
`SecurityRole`	Assembly, Class	Can be applied at assembly, class or interface scope. Use this attribute to name the role or roles that are allowed to call code in this component.
Transaction Attributes		
`Transaction`	Class	Determines how your class participates in COM+ transactions. The valid settings are `TransactionOption` `.Required` (default), `Disabled`, `NotSupported`, `RequiresNew`, and `Supported`. The transaction attribute also has a `TransactionIsolationLevel` property (values: `Any`, `ReadCommitted`, `ReadUncommitted`, `RepeatableRead`, `Serializable` [default, the highest level], and a `Timeout` property that can be set in seconds—but if not specified, is infinite by default).
`AutoComplete`	Method	This attribute is applied at the individual method level. When code in this method completes successfully, the object automatically votes to commit the transaction. If an unhandled exception occurs in the method, the object automatically votes to abort the transaction.

The next code snippets show examples of using these attributes in your code to do the following:

- Enable a construction string for the `DataComponent` class to be specified from the Windows Component Services console
- Reduce overhead through use of object pooling for the `BusyComponent` class
- Enable just-in-time activation to balance object activation time and overhead

```
<ConstructionEnabled(True)> Public Class DataComponent
    Inherits ServicedComponent
    'add methods of the class here
End Class

<ObjectPooling(Enabled:=True, MinPoolSize:=10, MaxPoolSize:=20)> _
    Public Class BusyComponent
    Inherits ServicedComponent
    'add methods of the class here
    End Class
```

```
<JustInTimeActivation(True)> _
<Synchronization(SynchronizationOption.Required)> _
   Public Class ActiveComponent
    Inherits ServicedComponent
    'add methods of the class here
   End Class
```

In addition to using attributes to make your class and its members, some methods of the ServicedComponent base class are commonly overridden to provide custom functionality for your component. These methods are described in Table 2.2.

TABLE 2.2 Methods of the *ServicedComponent* Class

Method	Description
Activate	This method is automatically called when the object is created or allocated from a pool. Used for custom initialization code.
CanBePooled	This method indicates whether the object is put back into the pool after being released by a caller Override this method to return true or false, as appropriate for your component.
Construct	This method can use the construction string value.
Deactivate	This method is automatically called when the object is about to be deactivated. Used for custom finalization code.
Dispose	This method releases the resources used by the serviced component.
Finalize	This method frees resources and perform cleanup before garbage collection.

Signing and Registering the Component Assembly

After you have finished developing your component, you need to prepare it for Component Services. The first step is to sign the assembly with a strong name. A *strong name* uniquely identifies an assembly by using a combination of the name, version number, and culture information, along with a public key and a digital signature.

The first step in strong-naming is to acquire a public key/private key pair. In a production environment, these keys, which are tied to your organization's identity, will be protected. The responsibility for strong-naming code before deploying it to customers or users will fall to a few trusted individuals. During development and for learning purposes, however, you can use a tool that is provided with the .NET Framework to create key pairs. This tool is *sn.exe*.

To use sn.exe, you will need to go to the Visual Studio .NET command prompt by using the Windows menus. Go to Start ➤ Programs ➤ Microsoft Visual Studio .NET ➤ Visual Studio .NET Tools ➤ Visual Studio .NET Command Prompt. At the command prompt, navigate to the directory where your application resides. Give this command:

```
sn -k myKey.snk
```

This will create a file called myKey.snk that contains the key pair.

You will also have to add a new attribute to your assembly:

```
<Assembly: AssemblyKeyFile("myKey.snk")>
```

The AssemblyKeyFile attribute was not included in Table 2.1 because it is a global .NET Framework attribute defined in the System.Reflection namespace. Any .NET assembly that requires strong-naming can use this attribute; it is not specific to only serviced components.

After you have created the key file, you can build your component and the resulting DLL will be strong-named.

The next step is to register the component. .NET Framework assemblies are designed to work without using the Windows system Registry, but because you want your component to interact with COM+, you must make a Registry entry for them. There are two ways to do this.

The first way is called lazy registration or dynamic registration; the component will register itself the first time it is called. The attributes that you included in your code provide enough information for proper registration. This technique is fine if you are still in development or if you expect only a single client application to use your component. The limitation of this technique is that any component that will be used by several different client applications and any component that is marked with an ApplicationActivation type of Server should be installed in the global assembly cache (GAC), which is a central directory on the computer that holds all shared components. For components that must be installed in the GAC, you must manually register the component and also manually install the component in the GAC.

Visual Studio .NET provides two more command-line tools to accomplish these tasks: *gacutil.exe* to install the component in the GAC and *regsvcs.exe* to register the component.

After you have completed these steps, you can use the Windows Component Services management console to view information about your component. Your will get an opportunity to practice these steps in Exercise 2.1.

 You will learn more about strong-naming, key pairs, the GAC, and other deployment topics in Chapter 10.

Configuring the Component in Component Services

The final step is actually configuring the component in the Windows Component Services management console. You can access the Windows Component Services management console in Windows 2000 Server by choosing Start ➤ Programs ➤ Administrative Tools ➤ Component Services. In Windows 2000 Professional and Windows XP, choose Start ➤ Control Panel ➤ Administrative Tools ➤ Component Services. Figure 2.1 shows what the management console looks like.

FIGURE 2.1 The Windows Component Services management console

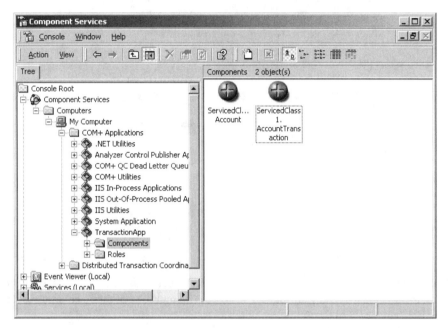

After you drill down through the Treeview control to locate your application, as shown in Figure 2.1, you can right-click it to access the Properties dialog box. The properties will reflect the attribute settings that you made while you were coding the component.

In Exercise 2.1, you will use Visual Studio .NET to create a component and add references and attributes. Then you will create a public key/private key pair that will enable you to create a strong-named assembly when you compile the component. You will install the application into the GAC and register it for use with Windows Component Services. In Exercise 2.2, you will create a client application that uses the component.

EXERCISE 2.1

Creating a Serviced Component

1. Create a new Visual Studio .NET project by using the Class Library project template. Name this project **AccountComponent**.

2. In the Solution Explorer, right-click the project name and choose Add Reference. In the Add Reference dialog box, select System.EnterpriseServices.

EXERCISE 2.1 *(continued)*

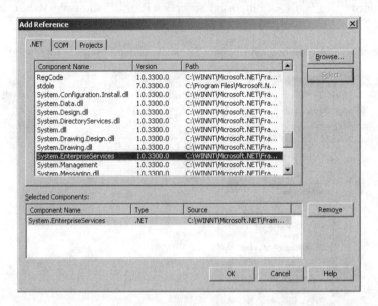

3. Add an Imports statement to the top of the module: **Imports System.EnterpriseServices**.

4. Create a class that inherits from the ServicedComponent base class, as shown in the following code. Include the assembly attributes as shown. The methods of the Account class do a simple calculation and return the result to the caller.

```
Imports System.EnterpriseServices
<Assembly: ApplicationName("TransactionApp")>
<Assembly: ApplicationActivation(ActivationOption.Server)>

Public Class Account : Inherits ServicedComponent
    Private acctBalance As Decimal = 1000

    Public Function Credit(ByVal accountNum As String, _
        ByVal amount As Decimal) As Decimal
            Return acctBalance + amount
    End Function

    Public Function Debit(ByVal accountNum As String, _
        ByVal amount As Decimal) As Decimal
            Return acctBalance - amount
    End Function
End Class
```

5. Open a Visual Studio .NET command prompt and navigate to your project's \bin directory. Use the strong name utility to generate a key pair. (The .snk file must be located in the same directory as the resulting DLL, or you will receive the error Error reading key when you build in step 7.)

```
c:\path> sn.exe -k myKey.snk
```

6. Add an additional `Imports` statement and assembly attribute to your code to support strong-naming. Replace `c:\`*path* in the code below with the correct path to the project directory on your computer:

```
Imports System.Reflection
<Assembly: AssemblyKeyFile("c:\path\myKey.snk")>
```

7. Build your component. Note: If you make changes to your component and need to build for a second time, make sure that you use the Rebuild Solution option on the Visual Studio .NET Build menu, or you might get an error when trying to use the component.

8. Back at the Visual Studio .NET command prompt, you will need to install your component into the GAC and then register it for Component Services. Make sure you are in the directory containing `AccountComponent.dll` and then use `gacutil.exe` to install it into the GAC:

```
c:\path> gacutil /i AccountComponent.dll
```

9. Use `regsvcs.exe` to register your component:

```
c:\path> regsvcs AccountComponent.dll
```

10. You can now start the Component Services utility by choosing Start ➢ Programs ➢ Administrative Tools ➢ Component Services (or the appropriate menu selections for your operating system version). In the treeview list on the left side of the window, click Computers to expand it, then click your computer name, then click COM+ Applications, until you can see your component listed under the `ApplicationName` (`TransactionApp`) you specified in the assembly directive. Right-click the component icon and choose Properties from the pop-up menu.

11. Save your project in Visual Studio .NET. You will be using it in future exercises.

Creating a Client That Calls Methods of the Serviced Component

1. Start a new Visual Basic .NET Windows Application project. Name the project **AccountTester**.

2. Set a reference to `System.EnterpriseServices`. You will also need to set a reference to the `AccountComponent.dll`, which you will need to browse to because your component will not appear in the list, under the .NET tab of the Add Reference dialog box. Be sure to select the component in the .NET tab, not the `AccountComponent` listed under the COM tab.

3. Your project should look something like the form shown here. You will need a text box to input the amount to be credited or debited and someplace to display the account number and new balance. You will also need command buttons to execute the `Credit` and `Debit` operations.

4. Add the statement **Imports AccountComponent** at the top of your code module.

5. Add the following code to execute the Credit and Debit methods from the Account component:

```
Private Sub btnCredit_Click(ByVal sender As System.Object, _
    ByVal e As System.EventArgs) Handles btnCredit.Click
        Dim objAccount As Account = New Account()
        Dim newBalance As Decimal
        Dim amount As Decimal

        amount = CType(txtAmount.Text, Decimal)
        newBalance = objAccount.Credit(txtAccountNumber.Text, amount)
        txtNewBalance.Text = CType(newBalance, String)

End Sub

Private Sub btnDebit_Click(ByVal sender As System.Object, _
    ByVal e As System.EventArgs) Handles btnDebit.Click
        Dim objAccount As Account = New Account()
        Dim newBalance As Decimal
        Dim amount As Decimal

        amount = CType(txtAmount.Text, Decimal)
        newBalance = objAccount.Debit(txtAccountNumber.Text, amount)
        txtNewBalance.Text = CType(newBalance, String)
End Sub
```

Now that you understand the basics of Serviced Components, in the following sections you will look at some additional topics, including designing components for performance and scalability, and using and managing transactions.

Designing Components for Performance and Scalability

When designing a component, you need to take a couple of considerations into account: performance and scalability. This is the primary reason for installing your components in Windows/COM+ Component Services. Just-in-time activation, which was introduced in Table 1.1, directly addresses these considerations.

Just-in-time-activation (JTA) is a feature that enables COM+ to activate an object instance very quickly when a client application makes a call on an object. When that method call is complete, COM+ can also quickly deactivate the object instance and release any memory or other resources that the object is holding. Other resources might be database connections, database locks, or open disk files. By releasing these resources quickly, they can be made available to other users.

JTA means that middle-tier components are not waiting for a client application to release resources in a timely fashion. There are many reasons why the client application might fail to do so—because the developer of the client application forgot to explicitly release the resource, because the end user of the application has not hit the Exit button, because the network connection was dropped, or any one of a dozen other reasons. Waiting for a client application to make decisions before releasing resources kills scalability.

JTA takes responsibility for managing this. As soon as each method call is completed, the object is deactivated. The memory and other resources that were being held by the object are released so that other user requests can be serviced. COM+ retains a certain amount of information about the object, so that if the client code makes another method call, the client will not get an error. COM+ will simply activate a new instance of the object so the method call will work.

There are two important things for the developer to remember here. First, because each method call is working with a newly activated instance of the object, any data from previous method calls is no longer available. This is referred to as a stateless model. There is no state, or persistent data values maintained from one method call to the next. Each method call to an object must be designed to pass all the data that is required for the object to complete its work. You cannot rely on the object "remembering" any data from previous method calls. Second, when you create components that will be used with Windows Component Services, you should remember that any code that must run when an object is activated or deactivated should be placed in the `Activate` and `Deactivate` methods as defined by the `ServicedComponent` base class. This is different from the .NET Framework standards of putting code into an object's constructor (`Sub New` in Visual Basic .NET) and destructor (either `Finalize` or `Dispose`) methods.

Using and Managing Transactions

A *transaction* is a set of operations that all must successfully complete together. If any one of the steps fails, then the results of all steps must be rolled back, or cancelled. A classic example of a transaction is a procedure that transfers funds from one account to another. You would not want to debit the first account until you were certain that you could successfully credit the second account. .NET Enterprise Services offers the Distributed Transaction Coordinator (DTC) to manage transactions.

The DTC can manage transactions that involve multiple objects and even multiple components. The DTC uses two-phase commit to poll each object involved in the transaction to see whether it has completed its work successfully; this is phase 1. If any of the objects involved in the transaction encounter an error, their "vote" to commit the transaction is negative. After receiving "votes" from all the objects involved in the transaction, the DTC sends an instruction to all the objects to either commit or roll back their work; this is phase 2. If any one of the objects involved in the transaction voted to roll back, then all the objects must roll back their work.

ACID

Whenever transactions are discussed, you often hear the acronym ACID. The *ACID properties* describe important features of how transactions work.

Atomicity   All the work of the transaction is completed, or none of it is. This is the commit or roll back behavior discussed above.

Consistency   The data used by the transaction must be in a state that meets all defined data integrity rules for the system when the transaction commits or rolls back.

Isolation   The data being used by the transaction cannot be seen by others until the transaction completes or rolls back.

Durability   The work of the transaction must be saved permanently once completed.

In order for your component to participate in transactions that are managed by .NET Enterprise Services you must use the attributes provided by the `ServicedComponent` base class. As you can see in the next code snippet, each class is marked with a `Transaction` attribute. You must also set the `TransactionOption` value of this attribute to one of the allowable settings:

Required   This is the default. This method must run in a transaction. If the code that called this method is already running in an existing transaction, then this method call will run as part of that transaction. If there is no existing transaction, then a new one will be started.

RequiresNew   This method will always cause a new transaction to be started. This object will be considered the "root" object of the transaction.

Supported   This method will run in a transaction if one already exists; otherwise, it will not require a transaction.

NotSupported   This method will not run in a transaction.

Disabled   The `Transaction` attribute is ignored.

Individual methods that will be used in automatic transactions can be marked with the *AutoComplete attribute*. When a method's `AutoComplete` attribute is set to True, the method's "vote" to commit or roll back the transaction will be set to Commit if the method completes successfully and set to Abort if an unhandled error occurs. This behavior will occur automatically, there is no need to add commit or rollback statements to your code.

The following code snippets show examples of using the `Transaction` and `AutoComplete` attributes in your code:

```
<Transaction(TransactionOption.Required)> Public Class Account
    Inherits ServicedComponent
```

```
<AutoComplete(True)>Public Function Credit(ByVal accountNum as String, _
    ByVal amount as Decimal) As Boolean
    'working code goes here
End Function

<AutoComplete(True)>Public Function Debit(ByVal accountNum as String, _
    ByVal amount as Decimal) As Boolean
    'working code goes here
End Function
End Class
```

The System.EnterpriseServices.ContextUtil class has properties that give you information about the status of the current transaction and has methods that you can use to affect transaction outcome. Every time a new transaction is started by .NET Enterprise Services, a new "context" for that transaction is also created and unique information about that transaction is available through the ContextUtil object.

Table 2.3 shows some of these properties, such as the ContextID, TransactionID, IsSecurityEnabled, and others. The *ContextUtil class* is a shared class, which means that you can call methods of the object without first explicitly instantiating it (this is similar to GlobalMultiUse classes in Visual Basic 6).

TABLE 2.3 Properties and Methods of the *ContextUtil* Class

Property or Method	Description
Public Properties	
ActivityId	Gets a GUID representing the current activity
ApplicationId	Gets a GUID for the current application
ApplicationInstanceId	Gets a GUID for the current application instance
ContextId	Gets a GUID for the current transaction context
DeactivateOnReturn	Gets or sets the done bit
IsInTransaction	Indicates whether the object is running within a transaction
IsSecurityEnabled	Indicates whether the object has the Security attributes enabled
MyTransactionVote	Gets or sets the consistent bit
PartitionId	Gets a GUID for the current partition
Transaction	Returns an object that represents the DTC transaction
TransactionId	Gets the GUID of the DTC transaction

TABLE 2.3   Properties and Methods of the *ContextUtil* Class *(continued)*

Property or Method	Description
Public Methods	
DisableCommit	Sets both the consistent bit and the done bit to False
EnableCommit	Sets the consistent bit to True and the done bit to False
GetNamedProperty	Returns a named property from the current context
IsCallerInRole	Indicates whether the identity of the user who called the method belongs to a specified security role
SetAbort	Sets the consistent bit to False and the done bit to True
SetComplete	Sets the consistent bit and the done bit to True

Earlier, you looked at how to use attributes to enable your objects to automatically vote on transaction outcome, simply based on whether a runtime error occurred during execution of the method. If you want an additional level of control over how your objects vote on transaction outcome, you can use methods of the ContextUtil class. These methods are *SetComplete*, *SetAbort*, DisableCommit, and EnableCommit. If you did any programming with MTS or COM+ components in earlier versions of Visual Basic, you will have seen these methods before. These four methods change the settings of important properties that determine what the final transaction outcome, either commit or abort, will be.

Each object participating in the transaction has two properties that show its status in regard to transaction outcome. These are frequently referred to as the *done bit* and the *consistent bit*. These are the terms that you will find in the Visual Studio .NET documentation, although the formal names of the properties of the ContextUtil class (as shown in Table 2.3) are DeactivateOnReturn and MyTransacationVote.

The *DeactivateOnReturn property* shows the current value for the done bit. If you call either the SetComplete or SetAbort method, it will have the effect of setting the done bit to True. You are indicating that, whether successful or not, your object has finished its work.

The *MyTransactionVote property* shows the current value for the consistent bit (this is sometimes also called the *happy bit*), which indicates whether your code has completed successfully. If you call the SetComplete method, the MyTransactionVote property will be set to True, and the SetAbort method will set the property to False. The SetComplete and SetAbort methods are straightforward and easy to understand.

There are two additional methods, EnableCommit and DisableCommit, which are a bit more complicated. As shown in Table 2.4, these two methods set the done bit to False. The objects are not deactivated at the end of the method call. These methods are typically used when the application design uses a root object, which in turn creates other objects that carry out the work of the transaction. When a secondary object returns from a method call with a status of

DisableCommit, it is communicating to the root object that the original method call did not succeed, but control is returned to the root object to decide whether the transaction as a whole must be aborted or whether other actions can be taken to resolve the error situation. A status of EnableCommit indicates that the current method call was successful, but the object should remain activated so that the root object can make additional method calls.

TABLE 2.4   Methods Used to Control Transaction Outcome

Method	Done Bit	Consistent Bit
SetComplete	True	True
SetAbort	True	False
EnableCommit	False	True
DisableCommit	False	False

Listing 2.2 shows how to use SetComplete and SetAbort in code.

Listing 2.2: Calling the ContextUtil Methods

```
<Transaction(TransactionOption.Required)> _
    Public Function TransferToChecking(ByVal _
    amount As Decimal) As Decimal

    Try
        'code here to debit savings account
        'code here to credit checking account
        'if successful
        ContextUtil.SetComplete()
    Catch
        'if an error occurs
        ContextUtil.SetAbort()
    End Try

End Function
```

Making a .NET Component Visible to COM

Some organizations might wish to start taking advantage of the .NET platform by developing (or redeveloping) certain key middle-tier components in managed code. However, they might still be using Visual Basic 6 or Active Server Pages for the user-interface tier. In this situation, you would want to develop new .NET components, which are visible to both COM-based client applications and managed .NET applications.

There are a few considerations for doing this. The first one is providing an interface that the COM components can understand. All classes and class members that should be exposed to COM should be marked as Public; they will be available by default. If there are certain classes in your components or members of a class that should not be used by COM clients, you can restrict which are available by applying the *ComVisibleAttribute*, as shown in the following code. Another important requirement is that you must provide a constructor method that does not require parameters (a default constructor), which is the only type of constructor that COM can use.

```
Imports System.Runtime.InteropServices


<ComVisible(False)> Public Class Account
        ' Insert class members here.

End Class
```

It is possible to mark your assembly or classes with the *ClassInterfaceAttribute*, with the `ClassInterfaceType` option set to `AutoDual`, and have an interface generated automatically for you by the runtime, as shown in the following code.

```
Imports System.Runtime.InteropServices


<ClassInterface(ClassInterfaceType.AutoDual)> _
    Public Class Account
        ' Insert class members here.
End Class
```

COM components communicate through interfaces and they expect these interfaces to always be the same (*immutable* is term you will find in the documentation). .NET Framework components do not require that the members of other components stay consistent, because the CLR enables components to discover available methods at runtime.

To keep a consistent interface for COM callers, you should create an explicit interface for your managed class (this can be done with the *Type Library Exporter utility, tlbexp.exe*), rather than relying on the automatically generated class interface. The automatically generated interface will reflect any changes that have been made to the managed component/class and will most likely cause an error for the COM component. The explicit interface will always look consistent to the COM component. You should also set the `ClassInterfaceType` option to None when providing an explicit interface. The other option for `ClassInterfaceType` is `AutoDispatch`. Use this option if you are creating components that will be used only by scripting clients, which communicate through the standard COM `IDispatch` interface.

Here is an example of how to use the Type Library Exporter from the command line:

```
C:\>tlbexp  myComponent.dll  /out:myComponent.tlb
```

The runtime creates a COM Callable Wrapper (CCW) class. This runtime always creates one instance of the CCW object, even if there is more than one caller accessing the underlying .NET-managed object. The managed object itself is subject to CLR garbage collection; the CCW is not. The CCW, like any standard COM object, maintains a count of all the references held on it by callers, and when the reference count reaches zero, the CCW releases the reference it holds on the managed object. The managed object can then be garbage collected. The runtime provides implementation for IUnknown and IDispatch, the standard interfaces that all COM components must implement.

In Exercise 2.3, you will create a component in Visual Studio .NET and then call methods from that component by using a Visual Basic 6 client application.

EXERCISE 2.3

Creating a COM Component by Using Visual Studio .NET

1. Create a new Visual Studio .NET project by using the Class Library project template. Name this project **InteropComponent**. Change the name of class file to InteropAccount.vb and the class name in the code editor to InteropAccount.

2. Add an Imports statement for System.Runtime.InteropServices. All the methods of your class that are marked as Public will be available to COM clients. Make sure your component has a Public Sub New constructor that does not expect any parameters. This default constructor is required for use with COM.

    Your code should look like this:

    ```
    Imports System.Runtime.InteropServices
    Public Class InteropAccount

        Public Sub New()
            'default constructor
        End Sub

        Public Function AddTwoNumbers(ByVal firstNumber As Double,_
           ByVal secondNumber As Double) As Double
            Return firstNumber + secondNumber
        End Function
    End Class
    ```

3. Compile your component. This will create InteropComponent.dll in the project's \bin directory.

4. Create a Visual Basic 6 client application to test your component. Name this project **InteropTester**.

5. Copy InteropComponent.dll file to the project directory of the Visual Basic 6 test client.

6. Open a Visual Studio .NET command prompt and navigate to the Visual Basic 6 project directory.

7. Use the command-line utility tlbexp.exe to export type library which will be called InteropComponent.tlb, from your .NET component:

    ```
    c:\path> tlbexp InteropComponent.dll
    ```

8. Use the regasm.exe command-line utility to register the component for use by COM:

    ```
    c:\path> regasm InteropComponent.dll
    ```

9. Use the Project ➢ References menu item in Visual Basic 6 to set a reference in the test client project. Use the Browse button to locate the `InteropComponent.tlb` file which was created in step 7, and is located in the Visual Basic 6 project directory.

10. Add the following Visual Basic 6 code to execute the `AddTwoNumbers` method from the `InteropComponent`:

```
Private Sub btnTest_Click()
     Dim objInterop As InteropComponent.InteropAccount
     Set objInterop = New InteropComponent.InteropAccount

     Msgbox CStr(objInterop.AddTwoNumbers(2, 2)), vbOKOnly, "Interop Test"
End Sub
```

11. Use the File ➢ Make InteropTester.exe menu item in Visual Basic 6 to compile the project.

12. This application will not run inside the Visual Basic 6 IDE; you must run `InteropTester.exe` from the Windows Explorer to test the `InteropComponent`.

Making a COM Component Visible to the CLR

Most organizations will not have the time or budget to rewrite their existing applications in .NET, no matter how desirable the features of the new platform are. Fortunately, it is easy to use existing COM DLLs with .NET applications. Working with COM DLLs requires that the information about the classes contained in the DLL be described in a way that that is consistent with the .NET Framework.

In the COM world, the file that contains information describing the classes in a component is called a *type library*. This type library information is embedded inside the DLL file or can exist in a separate file with a `.tlb` extension. To use the COM component from your .NET application, you must take this COM type library information and create a .NET interop assembly. There are several ways to do this—by using Visual Studio .NET, by using a command-line utility (the *Type Library Importer utility*, *tlbimp.exe*, that is supplied with the .NET Framework), by using .NET Framework classes from the *System.Runtime.InteropServices* namespace, or by creating custom wrapper classes. These last two options are outside the scope of this book and the exam objectives.

Remember that all COM DLLs that you want to reference from a .NET application must be registered on the computer that the application will run on (unlike .NET DLLs, which do not require registration). Use the command-line utility regsvr32.exe, or a Windows setup program to register the DLL. Figure 2.2 shows what this looks like.

FIGURE 2.2   The Regsvr32 utility

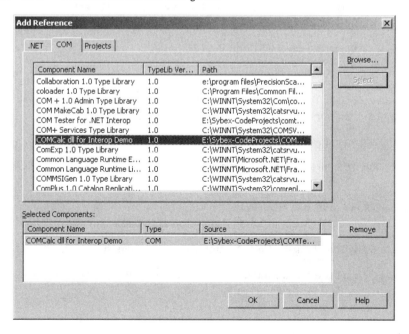

If you are using Visual Studio .NET, you simply set a reference to the type library file or the DLL; Visual Studio .NET does all the work. Figure 2.3 shows the Add Reference dialog box. After compiling your application, you will see a file in the \bin subdirectory for your project called Interop.*COMDLLname*.dll. This file contains all the information that the CLR needs to work with the COM component.

FIGURE 2.3   The Add Reference dialog box

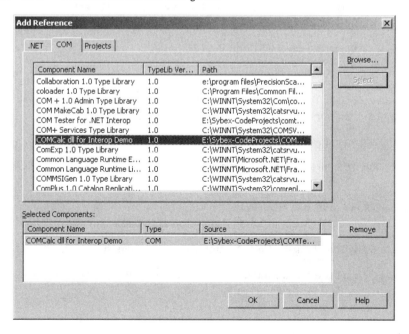

NOTE
Type library files (*.tlb files) can be generated from Visual Basic 6 by selecting the Remote Server Files check box on the Component tab of the Project Properties dialog box.

After you have referenced the DLL, you can instantiate objects from the class and use their methods, just as you would with any other component, as shown in Listing 2.3. This listing shows how to use a class called CMath, which has a method called Add.

Listing 2.3: Instantiating an Object from a COM Class

```
Dim Result As Short
Dim objAdd As CMath = New CMath()

Result = objAdd.Add(CType(txtNum1.Text, Short), CType(txtNum2.Text, Short))
```

In Exercise 2.4, you are going to add a COM DLL to a Visual Studio .NET project. You can use the COM DLL, named COMCalc.dll, that is provided on the CD included with this book.

EXERCISE 2.4

Referencing a COM Component in Visual Studio .NET

1. Create a new Visual Studio .NET project. Use the Windows Application template and name your project **COMTester**.

2. Copy the file \path\COMCalc.dll from the CD into your project directory.

3. To open a command window, choose Start ➢ Programs ➢ Visual Studio .NET ➢ Visual Studio .NET Tools ➢ Visual Studio .NET Command Prompt.

4. Navigate to your project directory.

5. Type **regsvr32 COMCalc.dll** at the command prompt. You should see a message box indicating that the component was registered successfully.

6. Close the command window and return to your Visual Studio .NET project.

7. In the Solution Explorer, right-click the project name and choose Add Reference from the pop-up menu.

8. Click the COM tab and then scroll down the list until you see the entry COMCalc for Interop Demo. Verify that this DLL is located in your project directory.

9. Click this entry. Then click the Select button and the OK button.

10. Open the Object Browser (from the Visual Studio .NET menu, View ➢ Other Windows ➢ Object Browser. This is shown in the following graphic.) You can expand the node titled

Interop.ComCalc. You will see that the component contains one class, called CMath. This class offers four methods. Notice the parameters that each method accepts.

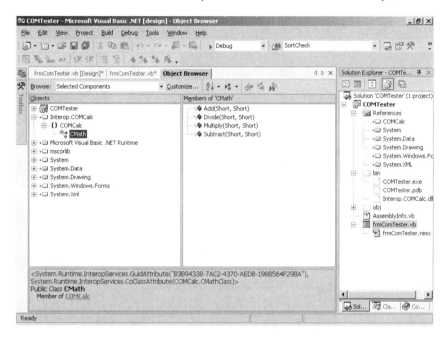

11. Create a simple user interface to test these methods. Your form will need three text boxes and two buttons, named as follows:

- txtNum1
- txtNum2
- txtResult
- btnAdd
- btnSubtract

12. In the Click event of btnAdd, add the following code:

```
Dim Result As Short
Dim objAdd As CMath = New CMath()

    Result = objAdd.Add(CType(txtNum1.Text, Short), _
      CType(txtNum2.Text, Short))
    txtResult.Text = CType(result, String)
```

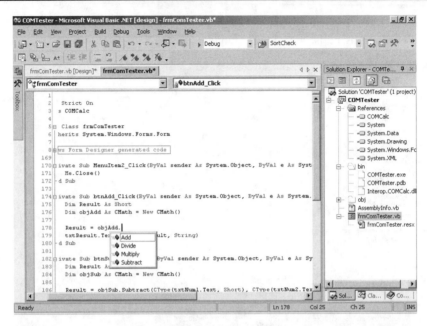

13. In the Click event of btnSubtract, add the following code:

```
Dim Result As Short
Dim objSub As CMath = New CMath()

    Result = objSub.Subtract(CType(txtNum1.Text, Short), _
        CType(txtNum2.Text, Short))
    txtResult.Text = CType(Result, String)
```

14. Run the project, enter some values into the two text boxes, and test each method. You should see results similar to those shown here. If you like, you can implement buttons for the Multiply and Divide methods as well.

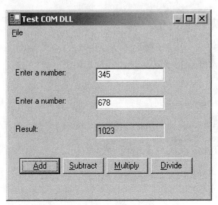

Command-Line Tools

If you are not working in Visual Studio .NET, there is also a command-line utility, `tlbimp.exe`, called the Type Library Importer, that can create an interop assembly from a COM type library or DLL. From the Windows command prompt, navigate to the directory that contains your Visual Basic .NET source code files. The next code snippet shows an example of using this utility to create a .NET interop assembly, called `myInterop.dll`, from a COM type library called `myComponent.tlb`. Use the `/out:` parameter to specify the name of the output file.

```
C:\path>tlbimp  myComponent.tlb  /out:myInterop.dll
```

Or, if you have only the COM DLL, the Type Library Importer can use that file instead.

```
C:\path>tlbimp myComponent.dll /out:myInterop.dll
```

You can use the .NET Framework's Intermediate Language (IL) Disassembler tool, *ildasm.exe*, to view details about the interop assembly that you just created. You can see the GUID identifiers for the original COM component. You can also see the classes that are contained in the component. You will also see the methods that those classes expose and the data types of all arguments and return values. Notice that the COM classes will also have a default (non-parameterized) constructor method.

You can start ILDASM from the command prompt, as shown in the following code. Figure 2.4 shows what the interop assembly that you worked with in Exercise 2.2 looks like in ILDASM.

```
C:\path>ildasm myInterop.dll
```

FIGURE 2.4   ILDASM

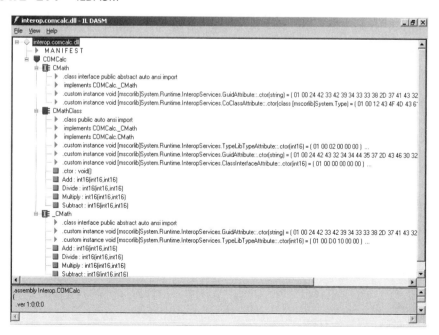

You can use the .NET Framework command-line compiler to compile your Visual Basic .NET application. Use the /r: parameter to specify that your application references the interop assembly. Use the /o: parameter to specify the name of the output file.

```
C:\path>vbc mySource.vb /r:myInterop.dll /o:myApp.exe
```

Calling Unmanaged DLL Functions

The .NET Framework class library has classes that provide access to most of the Windows system functions that your applications will need. In previous versions of Visual Basic, the only way to get to some of that functionality was to make calls, known as API calls, directly to the Windows system DLLs. If you find a function that isn't handled by the Framework classes or if you would like to continue calling a Win32 API function the same way that you did in Visual Basic 6, you can use the CLR's *Platform Invoke* (often shorted to PInvoke) capability to do so. Listing 2.4 shows an example of calling the PlaySound function in the Windows Multimedia DLL, winmm.dll.

In order to call functions in an unmanaged DLL, first add an Imports statement to your module that references the System.Runtime.InteropServices namespace. Rather than putting the declaration for the API function in the general declarations section of a module (the way you probably did in Visual Basic 6), in Visual Basic .NET you should create a separate class, which will wrap the function call. Each class can contain one or more function declarations. If you are using several related functions, it would make sense to make them members of the same class. All the functions declared inside the class are considered methods of the class. To call the functions from your application, create a new instance of the class and then use the familiar *object.method* syntax, passing any required arguments to the function. Look at the code in the btnPlaySound.Click event procedure in Listing 2.4 for an example.

Listing 2.4: Calling a Function in an Unmanaged DLL

```
Imports System.Runtime.InteropServices
Public Class Form1
    Inherits System.Windows.Forms.Form

Private Sub btnPlaySound_Click(ByVal sender _
    As System.Object, ByVal e As System.EventArgs) _
    Handles btnPlaySound.Click

    Dim myWin32Object As New Win32PlaySound()
    myWin32Object.PlaySound( _
        "C:\WINNT\Media\The Microsoft Sound.wav", 0)

    End Sub
End Class
```

```
Public Class Win32PlaySound
    Public Declare Function PlaySound Lib "winmm.dll" _
        Alias "sndPlaySoundA" (ByVal lpszSoundName As _
        String, ByVal uFlags As Long) As Long
End Class
```

Summary

In this chapter, you learned about creating and managing .NET components that make use of .NET Enterprise Services. We covered the following topics:

- An introduction to Serviced Components

- How to use Enterprise Services features such as transaction processing, object construction, object pooling, role-based sSecurity, and other features to improve performance, reliability, and scalability in your .NET applications

- How to add attributes to your .NET code to declaratively configure your serviced components

- How to use transactions to coordinate operations that involve multiple objects

- How to use the properties and methods of the `ServicedComponent` class from the .NET Framework to control transaction outcome

- How to make a .NET component available to COM clients

- How to make a COM component available to managed code

- How to call functions in unmanaged DLLs

- How to call functions from the Win32 API

Exam Essentials

Know how to create a serviced component.   Serviced components inherit from the `System.EnterpriseServices` namespace, `ServicedComponent` class. Know how to consume a serviced component from a .NET client application.

Be familiar with the properties and methods of the `ServicedComponent` class.   Understand when to add code to the `Activate` and `Deactive` events.

Be familiar with the properties and methods of the `ContextUtil` class.   Understand when to mark a class as `<AutoComplete(True)>` and when to use `.SetComplete` in your code.

Understand the ACID properties.   Atomicity, Consistency, Isolation, and Durability. These properties ensure that all of the work of a transaction is completed or everything is rolled back. They also mean that other users will not see the results until a transaction is complete and the resulting data will be stored permanently.

Understand the command-line utilities provided with Visual Studio .NET. The `tlbimp.exe` utility imports the type library from a COM component so that it is usable by .NET assemblies. The `tlbexp.exe` utility exports a type library from a .NET component so that it is usable by COM. The `regscvs.exe` utility registers a .NET component for .NET Enterprise Services. The `regasm.exe` utility registers a .NET component for COM interoperability. The `ildasm.exe` utility enables you to view the Intermediate Language generated by the .NET Framework compilers. The `sn.exe` utility creates a public key/private key pair that can be used for strong-naming assemblies.

Understand how to make a .NET component visible to COM clients. Know what attributes to apply to your code. Know how to expose an interface to COM clients. Know how to register an assembly for use by COM clients.

Understand how to call functions from unmanaged DLLs. In .NET you create a class, which will contain methods that wrap the unmanaged function call.

Key Terms

Before you take the exam, be certain you are familiar with the following terms:

ACID properties	instance
assembly attributes	Just-in-Time-Activation (JTA)
`AutoComplete` attribute	managed code
class	message queuing
`ClassInterfaceAttribute`	middle-tier components
COM+	`MyTransactionVote` property
component	.NET Enterprise Services
component interoperability	object
`ComVisibleAttribute`	object pooling
`ContextUtil` class	Platform Invoke
`DeactivateOnReturn` property	`regsvcs.exe`
distributed transactions	role-based security
`gacutil.exe`	serviced components
`ildasm.exe`	`ServicedComponent` base class

SetAbort	transaction
SetComplete	Type Library Exporter utility (`tlbexp.exe`)
`sn.exe`	Type Library Importer utility (`tlbimp.exe`)
strong name	unmanaged code
`System.EnterpriseServices` namespace	Windows Component Services
`System.Runtime.InteropServices`	

Review Questions

1. .NET Enterprise Services offers which of the following services?

    A. Manual transaction processing

    B. Tightly Coupled Events

    C. Windows security

    D. Role-based security

2. Your application design uses queued components. Which design goal indicates that queued components are the best choice for this application?

    A. Real-time updates from the database.

    B. User interface that is adaptable to many different devices.

    C. Reliable message delivery, but no immediate response required.

    D. Disk read/write performance is optimized.

3. To create a .NET component that will be hosted by COM+, what should you do?

    A. Reference the `System.EnterpriseServices` namespace.

    B. Reference the `System.ComponentServices` namespace.

    C. Import the `System.COMServices` namespace.

    D. Import the `System.EnterpriseComponents` namespace.

4. How can you indicate characteristics of your component to .NET Enterprise Services?

    A. Use the `Component` property of your class to set these values.

    B. Use the `/prop` switch when registering your component.

    C. Add methods to your class.

    D. Add attributes to your class.

5. You apply the `<ApplicationActivation(ActivationOption.Server)>` attribute to your class. What does this mean?

    A. Your component will run in the same process with the calling application.

    B. Your component will run in a different process than the calling application.

    C. Your component will run on the same computer as the calling application.

    D. Your component will run on a different computer than the calling application.

6. You apply the `<ConstructionEnabled(True)>` attribute to your class. What does this mean?

   A. Your component can be instantiated only by COM clients.

   B. Your component can be instantiated only by .NET clients.

   C. Your component can be instantiated with parameters supplied at runtime.

   D. Your component can be instantiated with parameters from the Component Services management dialog box.

7. Given this attribute setting:

`<ObjectPooling(Enabled:=True, MinPoolSize:=10, MaxPoolSize:=20)>`

What can you say about the object's behavior?

   A. If there are more than 10 concurrent requests for an object, object pooling will activate.

   B. If there are fewer than 20 concurrent requests for an object, object pooling will not activate.

   C. If there are fewer than 10 concurrent requests for an object, object pooling will not activate.

   D. There will always be at least 10 objects in the pool waiting for activation, but no more than 20.

8. The definition of a transaction states that there are four important properties of transactions. Which of these is one of those properties?

   A. Absolute

   B. Consistent

   C. Individual

   D. Distributed

9. You have created a component with attributes that state that a transaction is required. Which scenario best describes how your component works?

   A. Each time an object from this class is instantiated, the object will start a new transaction.

   B. Each time an object from this class is instantiated, the object will join an existing transaction or start a new transaction if none exists.

   C. If there is no existing transaction when this class is instantiated, a runtime error will occur.

   D. If another transaction is running when this class is instantiated, a runtime error will occur.

10. You create a .NET component that will be used by Component Services. What effect will the `<AutoComplete(True)>` attribute have on your component's behavior?

   A. This attribute affects the way synchronization is handled.

   B. This attribute affects the way object construction is handled.

   C. This attribute affects the way object pooling is handled.

   D. This attribute affects the way transaction outcome is handled.

11. You have created a .NET component that will be used by COM clients. What step should you take to make the component accessible to COM?

    A. Import your component's custom interface.

    B. Export your component's custom interface.

    C. Import the `IDispatch` and `IUnknown` interfaces for your component.

    D. Export the `IDispatch` and `IUnknown` interfaces for your component.

12. Before your .NET component can be used by Component Services, what step must you take?

    A. Register the component by using the `regsvcs.exe` utility.

    B. Register the component by using the `regsvr32.exe` utility.

    C. No special steps are required as long as your component has a reference to `System.EnterpriseSerivces.dll`.

    D. No special steps are required as long as your component imports the `System.EnterpriseSerivces` namespace.

13. You have created a .NET component that will be used by COM clients. Which .NET Framework namespace must you import in your code to support this capability?

    A. `System.Runtime.Serialization`

    B. `System.Runtime.InteropServices`

    C. `System.Reflection`

    D. `System.EnterpriseServices`

14. You would like to use an existing COM component in your Visual Studio .NET project. When you add a reference to the COM DLL, what action does Visual Studio .NET take?

    A. Visual Studio .NET creates a .NET interop assembly in your project's `\bin` directory.

    B. Visual Studio .NET creates a .NET interop assembly in your project's `\obj` directory.

    C. Visual Studio .NET creates a COM type library in your project directory.

    D. Visual Studio .NET creates a new class module in your project directory.

15. You would like to call functions from one of the Windows system DLLs from your Visual Studio .NET application. How do you accomplish this?

    A. Create a class in your project that contains the Win32 API declaration. When you want to call the function, instantiate an object from that class and make a method call on the object.

    B. Create a class in your project that contains the Win32 API declaration. When you want to call the function, instantiate an object called `Win32Interop` and make a method call on the object.

    C. Put the Win32 API declaration at the top of the main module in your project. When you want to call the function, use the code `PInvoke.`*`functionname`*.

    D. Create a class in your project that contains the Win32 API declaration. When you want to call the function, instantiate an object called `PInvoke` and make a method call on the object.

Answers to Review Questions

1. D. .NET Enterprise Services offers automatic transaction processing, Loosely Coupled Events, and role-based security to determine which Windows group a user belongs to.

2. C. Queued components enable you to deliver messages asynchronously to other applications.

3. A. To enable your components to be hosted by .NET Enterprise Services, you must set a reference to the `System.EnterpriseServices.dll`.

4. D. The `ServicedComponent` class from the .NET Framework class library defines many attributes that can be added to your assemblies, classes, and methods to set their behavioral characteristics. These attributes, including construction strings and security settings, are referenced by .NET Enterprise Services when the component runs.

5. B. Server components run in their own process. The `ActivationOption.Library` option directs the component to run in the caller's process.

6. D. The `ConstructionEnabled` attribute indicates that certain runtime parameters will be entered into the Component Services dialog box.

7. D. Object pooling enables you to specify the number of objects that can be "ready and waiting" when a client asks to instantiate an object.

8. B. The ACID properties state that a transaction must be consistent, which means that data integrity must be maintained when a transaction is completed. The other ACID properties are Atomicity, Isolation, and Durability.

9. B. `TransactionOption.Required` means that an object must run in the context of a transaction. If there is an existing transaction, the object will join that transaction. Otherwise, a new transaction will be started. If you always want to start a new transaction, use the `RequiresNew` option instead of `Required`.

10. D. The `AutoComplete` attribute states that if a given method completes successfully, the transaction vote for that object will be automatically set to commit the transaction. If any exception occurs, then the vote will be set to abort (or roll back) the transaction.

11. B. In order for COM clients to use your component, you must export your component's custom interface by using the Type Library Export tool (`tlbexp.exe`). The .NET runtime handles creation of `IDispatch` and `IUnknown` interfaces for your component, for use by COM clients. You would import a COM component's type library in order to access that COM component from a .NET project.

12. A. In order for Component Services to use a .NET component, the component must have an entry in the Windows system Registry; this does not happen automatically. The `regsvcs.exe` utility that is provided with the .NET Framework does this. The `regsvr32.exe` utility can be used to register only a COM DLL.

13. B.   The `System.Runtime.InteropServices` supports interoperability with COM components and clients. The `System.Runtime.Serialization` namespace includes functions to serialize and deserialize objects for storage and transport. `System.Reflection` allows access to underlying types. `System.EnterpriseServices` makes available Component Services, such as queued components, transactions, and so on.

14. A.   Visual Studio .NET creates a .NET interop assembly called `Interop.Projectname.dll`, in your project's \`bin` directory.

15. A.   When calling Win32 API functions (or calling any functions in an unmanaged DLL), you should create a class in your Visual Studio .NET project, which contains the Win32 function declaration. You can then instantiate objects from that class, and any functions declared in that class are seen as methods of your object.

Chapter 3

Creating and Managing .NET Remoting Objects

MICROSOFT EXAM OBJECTIVES COVERED IN THIS CHAPTER:

✓ **Create and consume a .NET Remoting object.**

- Implement server-activated components.
- Implement client-activated components.
- Select a channel protocol and a formatter. Channel protocols include TCP and HTTP. Formatters include SOAP and binary.
- Create client configuration files and server configuration files.
- Implement an asynchronous method.
- Create the listener service.
- Instantiate and invoke a .NET Remoting object.

The .NET Remoting architecture helps you create distributed applications by enabling your applications to communicate with other applications running separately on the same computer or with applications on a different computer. The Common Language Runtime also provides *application domains*, a new way of isolating managed code applications that are running on the same computer. Rather than requiring each application to run in a separate memory process on the computer, as in COM applications, you can run several application domains in a single process. Because managed code is verified to be "type-safe," it cannot cause memory faults that would crash the application. Therefore, running code in two different application domains provides the same level of isolation that would exist in separate processes. However, the additional overhead of making cross-process calls or switching between processes is not required. Running multiple applications within a single process increases server performance and scalability.

This chapter discusses some of the important features of the .NET Remoting architecture, such as selecting an appropriate channel protocol and format, selecting client-activated or server-activated components, creating configuration files, calling remote objects asynchronously, and more. It also covers the classes in the `System.Runtime.Remoting` namespace that provide support for Remoting object invocation.

Introduction to .NET Remoting Objects

.NET Remoting enables application developers to use a familiar object reference approach even when making interprocess communication between two applications. The client application can create an instance of the object running on the remote server and call its methods. To pass the call to the remote server, .NET Remoting uses a *channel* (you'll learn more about channels in the next section, "Channel Protocols and Formatters"). When you register your client and server channels, you specify important information, such as the protocol to use, the format of the data to be sent, the server name, and the port number that the channel will connect to. A proxy object is created on the client side to enable the client to make the remote calls and handle the responses as though the client were accessing local objects. The server logic can be hosted by any managed process, including any .NET executable or a .NET Windows service. To take advantage of enhanced security and other features, you might wish to host your server objects in Internet Information Server (IIS).

IIS hosting is covered in Chapter 10, "Deploying, Securing, and Configuring Windows-Based Applications" (Windows services, serviced components, .NET Remoting objects).

As you read through this chapter, keep in mind that .NET Remoting and XML Web services (which is the topic of the next chapter, Chapter 4, "Creating and Managing XML Web Services") can both accomplish the same end result of enabling different applications running on physically separate servers to call each other's methods. The technology that you choose for a specific system will depend on the requirements for a specific application.

In general, .NET Remoting is more appropriate for systems in which all components are running managed code on a closed network. This enables you to make use of the faster protocols and formats, perhaps even creating customized implementations, and to maintain more direct control over object activation and lifetimes. XML Web services, on the other hand, are useful when you need to connect to other systems that might be outside your organization or running on a different platform, accessible over the Internet.

Using Channel Protocols and Formatters

Channels are a .NET Framework class from the *System.Runtime.Remoting* namespace. These are the objects that transport messages and data across process or machine boundaries. A channel registered by the remote server application can listen on a specific endpoint, wait for an incoming message, and then send a response back to the calling client application. The channel registered by the client can also send and receive data and messages. Obviously, channel protocols and port numbers must match for the communication between client and server to be successful.

The .NET Framework provides two commonly used formatter classes. The formatter is responsible for writing the object's description and data so that this information can be sent across the network connection. This is called *serialization*. Serialization is the process of creating a representation of an object and its state that can be transferred across the network from one component to the other. The SOAP formatter uses a format of XML to write the information in a standardized way that can be understood by other applications. The binary formatter creates a binary data stream that is understood by other .NET applications.

In this section, you will learn the capabilities of these two classes and see some code examples.

Selecting a Channel Protocol and Formatter

.NET Remoting channels support two basic communication protocols; these are represented by the *HTTPChannel* class and the *TCPChannel* class.

The HTTP channel uses the familiar Hypertext Transport Protocol (HTTP), a widely used standard on the Internet, to pass data. By default, the HTTP channel uses the *Simple Object Access Protocol (SOAP) formatter* to send the message call as an XML document. The standard SOAP message format is also used by XML Web services and is explained in detail in Chapter 4.

The Transmission Control Protocol (TCP) channel uses a lower-level network transmission protocol and by default formats messages by using the *binary formatter* class, which creates a binary data stream. This results in a smaller and faster transmission, but requires that clients on both ends of the transmission are using the .NET Framework and can understand this format. The TCP channel also does not support some security mechanisms that are provided when using the HTTP protocol and hosting your remote server in IIS, such as Secure Sockets Layer (SSL) or Windows integrated security to authenticate users.

For the greatest interoperability and to take advantage of the enhanced security features, Microsoft recommends using the HTTP channel with the SOAP formatter. If you are working within a closed network, and all the applications participating are running managed code, you might choose the TCP channel for its faster performance.

You can also choose to use the binary formatter with an HTTP channel or the SOAP formatter with a TCP channel if your application design is better served by these options. This can be accomplished by supplying the type of formatter to use—either as a parameter to one of the overloaded constructor methods of the channel object or in a configuration file (configuration files are covered later in this chapter, in the section titled "Using a Configuration File"). It is also possible to extend the .NET Framework classes to create customized channels and formatters to add functionality to your applications—for example, to implement custom security features. However, this is outside the scope of the exam and this book.

Registering a Channel

The server application must register a channel before any clients can contact it. When you register a TCP channel or an HTTP channel, you must assign a *port number* so that communications can be directed to the application. Port numbers 0 through 1023 are reserved for common applications (for example, web browsers use port 80 by convention), so you should not specify these port numbers for your .NET Remoting channels. You can specify any other port number (up to 65,535) when you register a channel. Be careful that you are not trying to use a port that is already in use by another application running on the same computer. Microsoft SQL Server, for example, uses ports 1443 and 1434.

The sample code in Listings 3.1 and 3.2 shows how to register a channel and assign a port. Listing 3.1 assigns a port number of 8085 to the TCPChannel object. Listing 3.2 assigns a port number of 8086 to the HTTPChannel object. In order to use these objects in your code you will have to add a reference to your project to the System.Runtime.Remoting namespace.

Later in this chapter you will see how to register a channel and assign a port by using a configuration file instead of placing the instructions in your source code.

Listing 3.1: Registering a TCPChannel

```
Imports System.Runtime.Remoting
Imports System.Runtime.Remoting.Channels
Imports System.Runtime.Remoting.Channels.Tcp

Public Class Server

    Public Shared Sub Main()
        Dim myTCPChan As New TcpChannel(8085)
        ChannelServices.RegisterChannel(myTCPChan)
    End Sub
End Class
```

Listing 3.2: Registering an HTTPChannel

```
Imports System.Runtime.Remoting
Imports System.Runtime.Remoting.Channels
Imports System.Runtime.Remoting.Channels.Http

Public Class Server

    Public Shared Sub Main()
        Dim myHTTPChan As New HttpChannel(8086)
        ChannelServices.RegisterChannel(myHTTPChan)
    End Sub
End Class
```

Understanding Remotable Objects

Just as we make the distinction between value types and reference types in managed code, we refer to the objects that are exposed by remote servers as either marshal-by-value or marshal-by-reference objects. This specifies how object state and instance data is passed over the Remoting channel. In this section, you will learn about both types of remotable objects.

Marshal-by-Value Object

When a *marshal-by-value object* is passed between components, a complete copy of the object is serialized and passed through the Remoting channel to the caller. The object can then be transparently re-created in the caller's process by the Remoting infrastructure so the caller can use the object. All subsequent calls on the object or accesses of the object's properties are done within the caller's process. Marshal-by-value objects are created by marking the class with the `<Serializable>` attribute or by implementing the `ISerializable` interface in the source class and creating a custom serialization method.

When objects are passed as parameters, they are often passed as marshal-by-value. The ADO.NET `DataSet` class is an example of a common .NET Framework object that is *serialized* and copied whenever it is passed from one component to another. Although copying and re-creating the entire description of an object might take some time, slowing down the first call to the object, it can sometimes be more efficient than making several round-trips between client and server when you expect to be making multiple calls to the object.

The following code snippet shows a class declaration that uses attributes. The `<Serializable>` attribute marks the class as a whole as able to be written out to an XML stream and transmitted to another component. The `<NonSerialized>` attribute can be applied to individual members that will not be included when the object's state is passed to the caller.

Here is an example:

```
' An object that can be serialized
<Serializable()> Public Class myByValueObject

    Public variable1 As Integer
    Public variable2 As String

    ' A member that is not passed to the caller
    <NonSerialized()> Public variable3 As String
```

Marshal-by-Reference Object

When a *marshal-by-reference object* is passed between components, a *proxy object* is created in the caller's process. This object is a stand-in for the remote object, it shows the client the same interface as the remote object and allows the client code to make method calls as though it were calling a local object. When the caller makes method calls on the proxy object, the .NET Remoting infrastructure passes those calls to the remote server, and the call is carried out in the server's process. Marshal-by-reference objects are created by inheriting *System .MarshalByRefObject* in the source class. You should use marshal-by-reference objects when the object is dependent on using resources that can be accessed only from the object's original application domain (such as files located on a specific computer).

As we have mentioned, there is a trade-off between the time required to serialize an object and pass it in its entirety to the caller, and the total number of calls made to the object. If your server objects are very large and the caller is likely to be making only one call on the object, it is more efficient to use marshal-by-reference.

The following code snippet shows a class declaration that inherits `MarshalByRefObject`:

```
Public Class ServiceClass
    Inherits MarshalByRefObject
```

Activating Objects and Controlling Object Lifetime

Depending on how .NET Remoting objects are instantiated, they are said to be either server-activated or client-activated objects. This section describes the differences. It also discusses how to control object lifetime.

Server Activation

The lifetime of a *server-activated object* is controlled by the server. Although the object is instantiated by client-side code, this client call creates only the proxy object in the caller's process. The server-side object, which is ultimately responsible for executing code to complete a method call, is not created on the server until the client makes a method call on the object. This avoids a round-trip to the server when the client instantiates the object and also avoids tying up server resources until they're needed. A drawback to server activation is that only the default constructor (the constructor method that takes no arguments) is available for the object using basic .NET Remoting. Server-activated objects must be registered with the .NET Remoting infrastructure. When you do this, specify one of two `WellKnownObjectMode` values: either `SingleCall` or `Singleton`.

A *SingleCall object* exists only long enough to service a single method call from the client. A new object instance will be created for each subsequent method call or for additional callers. Any instance data that is passed to the object to complete the method call is destroyed along with the object. SingleCall objects are considered stateless.

An instance of a *Singleton object* can remain active on the server for many method calls and can service calls for many callers. Only one instance of a `Singleton` object is present at any time. When values are assigned to a Singleton object's properties, then those same property values are available to all callers. This type of object is useful for maintaining application-wide state information when all callers should access the same data. Later in the chapter, Exercise 3.4 demonstrates this. The lifetime of a Singleton object can last as long as the host application is running, or you can use `lifetime lease` settings to control when an instance is destroyed and a new instance will be started to serve new requests. Lifetime leases are discussed in a later section of this chapter, "Controlling Object Lifetimes."

The following code snippet shows how to register a server-activated object in the host application:

```
RemotingConfiguration.RegisterWellKnownServiceType( _
    GetType(RemoteObjectClass), "MyUri", _
    WellKnownObjectMode.SingleCall)
```

Notice the arguments that are passed to the `RegisterWellKnownServiceType` method. First we use `GetType` to expose information (the metatdata or class definition) about the remote class. Then we specify a unique string to identify our object to the .NET Remoting infrastructure. (This is called a Uniform Resource Identifier, or URI. In this example, we are simply using the string `MyUri`.) Finally we specify whether the object should be a SingleCall or Singleton. The preceding code shows registration of a SingleCall type of object.

Client Activation

The client directly controls the lifetime of a *client-activated object*. This can be useful when the client may want to keep an object activated and maintain its state information over multiple method calls. When the client code instantiates the object, a round-trip to the server occurs, the object is created on the server, and a *proxy object* is created on the client. The object will remain available on the server for calls from the same caller. If the calling client creates two instances of the remote object, two objects will be created on the server.

Your client code will use the following code to instantiate the object:

```
Dim MyRemoteClass As RemoteObjectClass = _
    CType( _
        Activator.GetObject(_
            GetType(RemoteObjectClass), _
            "http://localhost:8088/MyUri"), _
            RemoteObjectClass)
```

Notice that we are using the `System.Activator` class. The `GetObject` method creates a proxy for the remote object. We are passing three parameters to the `GetObject` method: a reference to the type information for the object that we want to create; the URL, which is a string that indicates where the remote server can be located on the network; and the class name. Later in this chapter, you will see some alternative ways to instantiate objects by using configuration files.

Controlling Object Lifetimes

The amount of time that a marshal-by-reference object remains in memory is determined by properties of its *lifetime lease*. After an object's lease time has expired, the *lease manager*, running in the server application domain, marks the object as available for garbage collection. (The lease manager is part of the .NET Remoting infrastructure.) A lease object associated with the marshal-by-reference object is created when the object is activated by a client. Lease object properties can be set at the time of initialization. Some lease properties are shown in Table 3.1. A client can also request to renew an object's lease time if they wish to continue using it.

TABLE 3.1 Important Properties of the Lease Object

Property	Description
InitialLeaseTime	This property can be set only at initialization. The default setting is 5 minutes. A setting of zero indicates that the object should have an infinite lifetime and will remain active in memory until the host process is shut down.
CurrentLeaseTime	This property shows the amount of time left until the lease will expire. This property can be changed by a call to renew the lease.
RenewOnCallTime	This property sets the amount of time that the initial lease time is extended after each client call on the object. The default setting is 2 minutes.

Remember that server objects that are marshaled by reference must always inherit from the .NET Framework class `MarshalByRefObject`. To set the lease properties, you must override the `InitializeLifetimeService` method of `MarshalByRefObject`. The code in Listing 3.3 shows an example of this. Notice that the code calls the constructor in the parent class and then checks the `CurrentState` property to make sure that the calls to change the other property settings will be allowed.

Listing 3.3: Overriding MarshalByRefObject.InitializeLifetimeService
```
Public Class MyLifetimeControlObject
    Inherits MarshalByRefObject

    Public Overrides Function InitializeLifetimeService() As Object
        Dim lease As ILease = CType(MyBase.InitializeLifetimeService(), ILease)
        If lease.CurrentState = LeaseState.Initial Then
```

```
        lease.InitialLeaseTime = TimeSpan.FromMinutes(1)
        lease.RenewOnCallTime = TimeSpan.FromSeconds(2)
      End If
      Return lease
   End Function
End Class
```

As you can see, the `RenewOnCallTime` property shows that each client call to an object extends its lifetime. Sometimes, however, you might want to explicitly extend an object's lease time. The following code snippet shows how to get a reference to the object's lease by calling `RemotingServices.GetLifetimeService` and then calling the lease's `Renew` method:

```
Dim obj As New RemoteType()
Dim lease As ILease = CType( _
    RemotingServices.GetLifetimeService(obj), ILease)
Dim expireTime As TimeSpan = lease.Renew( _
    TimeSpan.FromSeconds(20))
```

 The `TimeSpan` object is a class in the `System` namespace that can be used to specify a period of time. The preceding examples use the `TimeSpan.FromSeconds` and `TimeSpan.FromMinutes` methods as a standardized way to pass a value representing a time period to the `lease.Renew` method and to set the lease properties.

Creating and Consuming a .NET Remoting Object

So far we have discussed some of the important concepts and terms associated with .NET Remoting. Now, you are going to complete a set of exercises to create the various components that make up a .NET Remoting application. You are going to create four Visual Studio .NET projects:

- A class library project for the interface that defines your remote server

- A second class library project to implement this interface and provide the application logic

- A Windows console application, which will be your host server and will call the application logic

- A client application to make calls on the server

There is one more consideration for creating the client-side code that we haven't discussed yet. You need to provide a local reference for the client application. Although you could provide a copy of the server DLL to all your clients to reference and develop against, that would defeat your purpose of deploying to a single remote server. Your clients do not need the complete implementation DLL; all they need is an interface. This interface exposes any public properties and methods of your class, as well as the calling conventions for those methods. The interface shows what arguments are required for various methods and what data types will be returned.

Let's start with Exercise 3.1, in which you will create an interface that defines your server class and a server DLL that holds the implementation logic for your server.

EXERCISE 3.1

Creating the Server and Interface DLLs

Creating the Interface:

1. Create a new Visual Studio .NET Class Library project. Name the project **TimeInterface**.

2. Change the default code `Public Class Class1` to **Public Interface ITime** and change the name of the class file to **ITime.vb** by using the Solution Explorer.

3. Define the functions that will be included in the server. Your code should look like this:

```
Public Interface ITime
    Function GetServerTime() As DateTime
    Function GetServerTimeAsString() As DateTime
End Interface
```

4. Save and build your project by using the Visual Studio .NET menus.

Creating the TimeServer Class:

5. Create a new Visual Studio .NET Class Library project. Name the project **TimeServer**.

6. Change the default name `Class1` to **TimeClass** and change the name of the class file to **TimeClass.vb**.

7. Set a reference to `System.Runtime.Remoting.dll`.

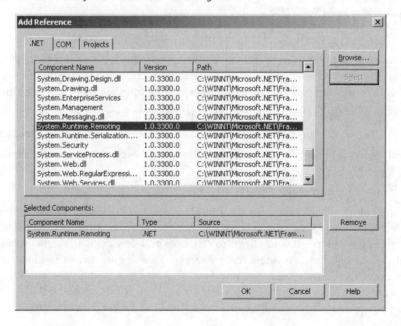

8. Copy the `TimeInterface.dll` from the `\bin` directory of the `TimeInterface` project to the project directory of the current `TimeServer` project. Set a reference to this copy of `TimeInterface.dll`.

9. From the Add Reference dialog box, select the Projects tab. Click the Browse button and then locate `TimeInterface.dll` in your project directory.

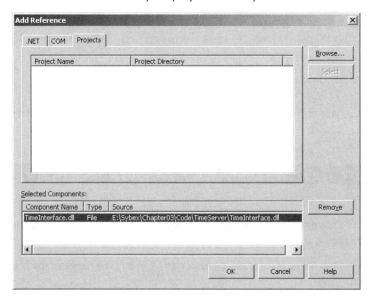

10. At the top of your class definition, specify that `TimeClass` inherits from `MarshalByRefObject` and implements `TimeInterface.ITime`. The class will have two simple methods: `GetServerTime` and `GetServerTimeAsString`. Each method will implement one of the methods defined in your interface. The code in each method will write a line to the system console (remember that the host for your `TimeServer` DLL will be a Windows console application) and then return the time from the server. Your code should look like the following:

```
Public Class TimeClass
    Inherits MarshalByRefObject
    Implements TimeInterface.ITime

    Public Sub New()
        Console.WriteLine("TimeClass has been instantiated.")
    End Sub

    Public Function GetServerTime() As DateTime _
        Implements TimeInterface.ITime.GetServerTime
        Console.WriteLine("Time requested by a client.")
        Return DateTime.Now
    End Function
```

```
    Public Function GetServerTimeAsString() As DateTime _
       Implements TimeInterface.ITime.GetServerTimeAsString
        Console.WriteLine("Time String requested by a client.")
        Return DateTime.Now.ToLongDateString
    End Function
End Class
```

11. Display the Project Properties dialog box by right-clicking on the project name in the Solution Explorer window. Verify that the Assembly name is TimeServer, the Root namespace is TimeServer, and that the Startup object is (None).

12. Save your project. Build the TimeServer project by using the Build menu.

In Exercise 3.2, you will create a Windows console application that will reference your TimeServer DLL and be responsible for accepting client calls to the TimeClass.

Creating the Host

1. Create a new Visual Studio .NET Console Application project. Name the project **TimeHostProject**.

2. Change the default name Module1 to **TimeHost** and change the name of the module file to **TimeHost.vb**.

3. Set a reference to System.Runtime.Remoting.dll.

4. Copy the TimeServer.dll and TimeInterface.dll files from their respective \bin directories to the project directory for the TimeHostProject.

5. Set a reference to the file TimeServer.dll. From the Add Reference dialog box, select the Projects tab. Then click the Browse button and select the file that you just copied to the host project directory. You must also add a reference to the TimeInterface.dll, because TimeServer depends on this interface.

6. Above your module definition, add the following Imports statements:

```
Imports System.Runtime.Remoting
Imports System.Runtime.Remoting.Channels
Imports System.Runtime.Remoting.Channels.Http
```

7. In the Sub Main procedure, add code to declare a variable for the TimeClass object, register a channel, and register the TimeClass. Also add a console message so you can verify that your host application is running.

8. Your code should look like the following:

```
Sub Main()
    Dim timeObject As TimeServer.TimeClass()

    'register the channel
    Dim timeChan As New HttpChannel(8080)
    ChannelServices.RegisterChannel(timeChan)

    'Register TimeClass as a SingleCall object
    RemotingConfiguration.RegisterWellKnownServiceType( _
      GetType(TimeServer.TimeClass), _
      "timeUri", WellKnownObjectMode.SingleCall)

        Console.WriteLine( _
            "Running. Press Enter to stop the host application.")
        Console.ReadLine()
End Sub
```

9. The following code shows another method of the ChannelServices .NET Framework class. You can add this code at the end of the Sub Main procedure to explicitly "un-register" the channel before your host application shuts down.

```
ChannelServices.UnregisterChannel(timeChan)
Console.WriteLine("Unregistered the channel.")

Console.WriteLine("Press Enter to stop the host application.")
Console.ReadLine()
```

10. Display the Project Properties dialog box by right-clicking the project name in the Solution Explorer window. Verify that the Assembly name is TimeHost, the Root namespace is TimeHost, and that the Startup object is Sub Main.

11. Build the TimeHost project by using the Build menu.

The complete code for Exercise 3.2 is located in Listing 3.4.

Listing 3.4: The Complete Code for the TimeHost Module in Exercise 3.2

```
Imports System.Runtime.Remoting
Imports System.Runtime.Remoting.Channels
Imports System.Runtime.Remoting.Channels.Http

Module TimeHost
    Sub Main()
        Dim timeObject As TimeServer.TimeClass()

        'register the channel
        Dim timeChan As New HttpChannel(8080)
```

```
        ChannelServices.RegisterChannel(timeChan)

        'Register TimeClass as a SingleCall object
        RemotingConfiguration.RegisterWellKnownServiceType( _
          GetType(TimeServer.TimeClass), _
          "timeUri", WellKnownObjectMode.SingleCall)

        Console.WriteLine( _
          "Running. Press Enter to stop the host application.")
        Console.ReadLine()

        ChannelServices.UnregisterChannel(timeChan)
        Console.WriteLine("Unregistered the channel.")
        Console.WriteLine( _
          "Press Enter to stop the host application.")
        Console.ReadLine()
    End Sub
End Module
```

Now that you have created your server DLL, the code library containing the business logic that your clients want to access, and you have created the host application for the remote machine, you can turn your attention to creating a client application. This will be done in Exercise 3.3, which is a simple Windows Forms project. Please note that when you register the channel in the client code, you can leave it set to port 0; the .NET Remoting infrastructure will select an available port for the client.

EXERCISE 3.3

Creating the Client

1. Create a new Visual Studio .NET Windows project. Name the project **TimeClient**.

2. Change the default class name Form1 to **frmTimeClient** and change the name of the form file to **frmTimeClient.vb**.

3. Set a reference to System.Runtime.Remoting.dll.

4. Copy the TimeInterface.dll from the \bin directory of the TimeInterface project to the project directory of the new TimeClient project. Set a reference to this copy of TimeInterface.dll. From the Add Reference dialog box, select the Projects tab. Then click the Browse button and locate TimeInterface.dll in your project directory.

5. Create a user interface that looks like the next graphic. Add the following controls:

    ▪ Text box named **txtDisplayTime**

    ▪ Command button named **btnTime**

    ▪ Text box named **txtDisplayDate**

    ▪ Command button named **btnDate**

EXERCISE 3.3 *(continued)*

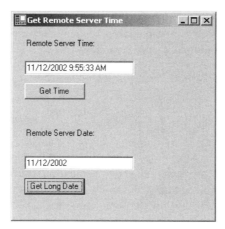

6. At the top of your form module, add the following `Imports` statements:

    ```
    Imports System.Runtime.Remoting
    Imports System.Runtime.Remoting.Channels
    Imports System.Runtime.Remoting.Channels.Http
    ```

7. Create a Form Load event procedure and add code to this procedure to register the channel. Your code should look like the following:

    ```
    Private Sub frmTimeClient_Load( _
      ByVal sender As System.Object, _
      ByVal e As System.EventArgs) Handles MyBase.Load

        Dim channel As New HttpChannel(0)
        ChannelServices.RegisterChannel(channel)
    End Sub
    ```

Instantiating and Invoking a Remote Method:

8. In the Click event procedure for the `btnTime` command button, use the `Activator.GetObject` method to activate the object. Use **localhost** as the machine name in the string that is passed to this method. This indicates that you are running the server on the same machine on which the client code is executing. Note that in production applications, this should show the name of a remote computer. You are also specifying port number 8080 and a URI string of `timeUri`; these must exactly match the values that were used when the channel and object were registered in the host application. Finally, call the `GetServerTime` method of the `TimeClass` object.

    To do all this, your code should look like the following:

    ```
    Dim timeObject As TimeInterface.ITime = _
        CType(Activator.GetObject(GetType(TimeInterface.ITime), _
        "http://localhost:8080/timeUri"), _
        TimeInterface.ITime)

    txtDisplayTime.Text = timeObject.GetServerTime()
    ```

9. Create another Click event procedure for the btnDate command button. The code should be substantially the same as for the preceding step. Remember to change the line of code that calls the method on the remote object to the following:

    ```
    txtDisplayDate.Text = timeObject.GetServerTimeAsString()
    ```

10. Make sure the startup object specified in the Project Properties dialog box is set to frmTimeClient. Save and build your client application. The complete code for the client application is shown in Listing 3.5.

11. Test your .NET Remoting application by opening a Visual Studio .NET command prompt and navigating to the directory where the compiled executable of your host application is located. Start the host application. You should see a command prompt window with a message that the application is running.

12. Start the client application and test the buttons. You should see messages display in the host command prompt window and you should see the results displayed in the text boxes on your Windows client application.

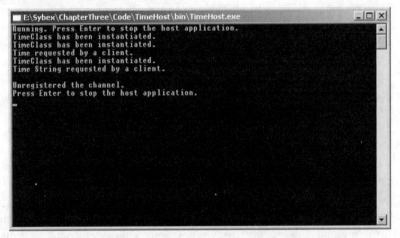

13. If you have another computer accessible over a network, you can move the host executable, the TimeServer.dll, and TimeInterface.dll to the other computer. In the URL in your client application code, change the machine name from localhost to the name of your remote computer.

14. When finished, go back to the command prompt window in which you started the host application and press Enter twice to stop the application.

Listing 3.5: The Client Application

```
Imports System.Runtime.Remoting
Imports System.Runtime.Remoting.Channels
```

```
Imports System.Runtime.Remoting.Channels.Http

Public Class frmTimeClient
    Inherits System.Windows.Forms.Form

'Windows Form Designer generated code

Private Sub frmTimeClient_Load(ByVal sender As System.Object, _
  ByVal e As System.EventArgs) Handles MyBase.Load

  Dim channel As New HttpChannel(0)
  ChannelServices.RegisterChannel(channel)
End Sub

Private Sub btnTime_Click(ByVal sender As System.Object, _
  ByVal e As System.EventArgs) Handles btnTime.Click

  Dim timeObject As TimeInterface.ITime = _
    CType(Activator.GetObject( _
    GetType(TimeInterface.ITime), _
    "http://localhost:8080/timeUri") , _
    TimeInterface.ITime)

  txtDisplayTime.Text = timeObject.GetServerTime()
End Sub

Private Sub btnDate_Click(ByVal sender As System.Object, _
  ByVal e As System.EventArgs) Handles btnDate.Click

  Dim timeObject As TimeInterface.ITime = _
    CType(Activator.GetObject( _
    GetType(TimeInterface.ITime), _
    "http://localhost:8080/timeUri"), _
    TimeInterface.ITime)

  txtDisplayDate.Text = timeObject.GetServerTimeAsString()
End Sub
End Class
```

In Exercise 3.4, you are going to make a few changes to the server and host project to illustrate the difference between SingleCall and Singleton remote objects.

EXERCISE 3.4

Using a Singleton Remote Object

1. In the TimeServer project, make the following modifications to the code:

   - Declare a class-level integer variable named counter.

     ```
     Dim counter As Int32
     ```

   - In each of the two button Click event procedures, increment the counter variable and modify the console message to display the variable:

     ```
     counter += 1
     Console.WriteLine("Time requested by a client. Request#" & counter)
     ```

2. Save and build the project.

3. Copy the new version of the TimeServer.dll to the TimeHost project directory.

4. Open the TimeHost project. In the Solution Explorer window, expand the References section, right-click on the TimeServer reference, and choose Remove from the pop-up menu.

5. Right-click on the References section. Locate the new version of TimeServer.dll and select it.

6. In the code in the Sub Main procedure of the host application, change the WellKnownObjectMode parameter from SingleCall to **Singleton**.

   ```
   RemotingConfiguration.RegisterWellKnownServiceType( _
     GetType(TimeServer.TimeClass), _
     "timeUri", WellKnownObjectMode.Singleton)
   ```

7. Save and build the TimeHost project.

8. Now you can test this in the same way as in Exercise 3.3. You will see results similar to the following graphic.

Creating More Manageable Applications

Now that you understand the basics of .NET Remoting, you are ready to look at some additional topics that will help you create more efficient and manageable applications. First, you will learn about using application configuration files for making common .NET Remoting settings. In the preceding examples you made these settings in source code. Changing a configuration file is much easier than changing source code when you need flexibility at deployment time. Finally, you will look at a technique for using .NET Framework callback delegate objects to make asynchronous calls on remote applications.

Using a Configuration File

.NET Remoting settings are one of the many features that you can specify by using *XML configuration files* for your application. XML configuration files are used to hold application specific settings. The advantage of making these settings in configuration files rather than directly in your source code is that an administrator can make changes without having to change and recompile the original source code. For example, if a conflict in port numbers becomes a problem after your application is deployed, this setting can easily be changed in the configuration file without a need to change the compiled DLL.

Configuration files can be provided on both the client side and server side. The .NET Framework defines a common set of tags that can be used inside the configuration file. Refer to the Visual Studio .NET documentation for a complete set of all available application configuration tags. Configuration files are typically placed in the same directory as your application's executable file and follow this naming convention:

ApplicationName.exe.config

Remember that XML parsing tools expect all XML tag names and attribute names to exactly match uppercase and lowercase characters as defined. Make sure your configuration files follow the examples or you will get an error when you run your application.

The next two code listings give examples of some common settings that can be made in the configuration files. Listing 3.6 shows XML configuration settings that specify a server-activated object. These XML configuration settings are the equivalent of the code shown earlier in this chapter in Listing 3.4 when using the RemotingConfiguration.RegisterWellKnown-ServiceType method.

Listing 3.6: A Server-Side Configuration File
```
<configuration>
    <system.runtime.remoting>
        <application>
            <service>
```

```
        <wellknown
           mode = "SingleCall"
           type = "RemoteObjectClass, RemoteAssembly"
           objectUri = "myUri"
         />
       </service>
     </application>
   </system.runtime.remoting>
</configuration>
```

Listing 3.7 shows an example of settings that you would place in a client-side configuration file. These settings provide the same information that was used with the `Activator.GetObject` method in our earlier examples (see Listing 3.5). When you use a configuration file to specify these settings, you do not need to call `Activator.GetObject` to instantiate the remote class. Instead, your client code will call a method to access the data in the configuration file and then simply use the New operator to instantiate the object. This is shown in Listing 3.8.

Listing 3.7 Client-Side Configuration Options

```
<configuration>
   <system.runtime.remoting>
      <application>
          <wellknown
             type = "RemoteObjectClass, RemoteAssembly"
             url = "http://localhost:8080/MyUri"
          />
       </client>
     </application>
   </system.runtime.remoting>
</configuration>
```

Listing 3.8 Instantiating a Remote Object That Uses a Configuration File

```
Public Shared Sub Main()

   RemotingConfiguration.Configure( _
      "MyApplication.exe.config")
   Dim objRemote As RemoteObjectClass = New _
      RemoteObjectClass()

End Sub
```

Making Asynchronous Calls

When implementing a production application that uses remote calls over a network, the time required to complete a method call can take considerably longer than what you have seen so far in your practice code. In cases when a user might have to wait a few seconds for a call to complete, it is preferable to make the remote calls asynchronously—that is, the client code does not block (or wait) while the call is connecting to the remote server and executing. The client application's user interface will be active, and you can give the user an indication, by using status messages or a progress indicator, that the application is working. Without asynchronous calls, a user might think that their computer has locked up and try to reboot if a call to a remote server takes too long.

Asynchronous method calls can be implemented simply by using .NET Framework Delegate objects and an *asynchronous callback function.* (If you are unfamiliar with using Delegate objects, you should refer to the Visual Studio .NET documentation for more background information.)

Listing 3.9 shows two procedures that use the `System.Delegate.BeginInvoke` and `System.Delegate.EndInvoke` methods to make the remote call asynchronously. The first procedure, called `asyncExample`, starts by using `Activator.GetObject` to declare and instantiate the remote object, just as you did in the earlier examples (see Listing 3.5). Then we declare and instantiate two Delegate objects. The first delegate represents the method that we are going to call on the remote server, and the second delegate represents the method that will accept a "call back" from the remote server when the original method call completes. Notice that we have a delegate declaration at the top of the module. The method signature of this declaration must match the method signature of the remote method we want to call. In this example, our remote method takes no arguments and returns a value of type `DateTime`. The second Delegate object is of type `System.AssemblyLoadEventArgs.AsyncCallBack`. Both delegates use the Visual Basic .NET `AddressOf` operator to specify the functions that they represent. Now we can call the remote method by using `Delegate.BeginInvoke`.

When calling `BeginInvoke`, you can pass any arguments required by the remote function (in this example, there are none), the name of the callback delegate, and a third parameter that is an object reference that might contain some state information (in this example, there is none, so we use the Visual Basic .NET keyword `Nothing`).

When the remote method call is complete. the .NET Framework event mechanism will notify the client application by calling back to the designated function, in this example `MyCallBack`. The `MyCallBack` function declares some local variables, one to hold the result data, one `AsyncResult` object to read the results, and a new delegate, declared as the same type as the delegate in the first procedure that called `BeginInvoke`. Then we can call the `Delegate.EndInvoke` method and retrieve the results.

Listing 3.9: Asynchronous Calls

```
Imports System.Runtime.Remoting.Messaging
Public Delegate Function MyDelegate() As DateTime

Private Sub asyncExample()

   'this code is the same as previous examples
   Dim timeObject As TimeInterface.ITime = _
     CType(Activator.GetObject( _
     GetType(TimeInterface.ITime), _
```

```
        "http://localhost:8080/timeUri"), _
         TimeInterface.ITime)

    'now declare the delegates
    Dim timeDelegate As MyDelegate = New MyDelegate( _
      AddressOf timeObject.GetServerTime)
    Dim timeCallBack As New AsyncCallback( _
      AddressOf MyCallBack)

    'invoke the method
    timeDelegate.BeginInvoke(timeCallBack, Nothing)
End Sub

Public Sub MyCallBack(ByVal ar As System.IAsyncResult)
    Dim result As DateTime
    Dim aResult As AsyncResult = CType(ar, AsyncResult)
    Dim tempDelegate As MyDelegate = CType( _
      aResult.AsyncDelegate, MyDelegate)

    result = tempDelegate.EndInvoke(ar)
    txtDisplayTime.Text = result
End Sub
```

 Real World Scenario

Distributed Applications

You are a software developer for a large organization. When developing Visual Studio 6 applications in the past, you were used to creating distributed applications that took advantage of the *n*-tier architecture model to centralize business logic on middle-tier servers. You would like to use this same design in your new .NET applications. Several other members of your team have been to some .NET presentations and they are very excited about using XML Web services. You think that XML Web services are a great idea for offering external clients access to selected functions on your servers, but are not sure whether they are the right choice for your internal applications.

Your primary goal is to simplify ongoing maintenance and support of your business logic components, by having a single installation of the components on a central server. You are not overly concerned about security features because all the users of your application are already logged on and authenticated by the corporate network. You do not have to worry about cross-platform support because all client computers will be upgraded to run the .NET Framework.

You have looked at .NET Remoting and like its simple model, which is similar to the distributed computing model that you've used in the past. You like the flexibility of choosing different types of channels and protocols, and expect that this will enable you to optimize performance. You also like the idea of setting options in configuration files, so you will not have to make source code changes and redeploy a component if a simple change, such as a port number or server name, is needed.

It's clear that the .NET Framework provides many options; it's up to you to make the best choices for each application.

Summary

In this chapter, you learned about creating and managing .NET Remoting applications. We covered the following topics:

- An introduction to how .NET Remoting works
- How to select either an HTTP channel or a TCP channel
- How to select either a binary formatter or the SOAP formatter
- How to register a channel
- The differences between client-activated and server-activated remote objects
- The differences between SingleCall and Singleton remote objects
- How to control object lifetime by using the lease object
- How to extend an object's lifetime lease
- How to create a .NET Remoting object by creating a .NET DLL that contains server logic and a host application to accept calls on the server
- How to consume a .NET Remoting object by instantiating an object and invoking methods on a remote server from a client application
- How to create an interface DLL to distribute to clients who want to make calls on the remote server
- How to use configuration files to register channels, activate both client-activated and server-activated objects, and specify lifetime lease properties
- How to call a .NET Remoting object asynchronously

Exam Essentials

Know how to create .NET Remoting objects.   Create a host application that listens on a channel and registers the classes from the server DLL with the .NET Remoting infrastructure. Create a client application that instantiates remote objects and invokes their methods. Remember, .NET Remoting applications reference the `System.Runtime.Remoting` component.

Be familiar with the choices for channels and formatters.   The TCP channel uses the binary formatter by default. The HTTP channel uses the SOAP formatter by default. Know how to register a channel in both client and server code.

Understand the object serialization versus proxy objects.   Marshal-by-value objects are marked with a `<Serializable>` attribute or implement the `ISerializable` interface. When a remote call is made on a marshal-by-value object, the entire state of the object (and its data) is serialized and sent to the caller, where is it re-created in the caller's process. Method calls execute in the caller's process. marshal-by-reference objects inherit from `MarshalByRefObject`. When a remote call is made on a marshal-by-reference object, a proxy object is created on the caller. Method calls execute in the host process.

Understand the difference between client-activated and server-activated objects.   The client directly controls the lifetime of a client-activated object. When the client instantiates the client-activated object, it is created on the server. When a client instantiates a server-activated object, a proxy is created on the client. An object is not created on the server until the client calls a method.

A server-activated object can be SingleCall—a new instance of the object is created and destroyed with each method call for each client. A server-activated object can be a Singleton—a single instance of the object can exist for an extended period of time, and service multiple calls and multiple clients, and the Singleton exposes the same data to call clients.

Understand how lifetime leases affect an object's lifetime.   Certain properties of the object's lease can be set only at initialization time. The caller can extend the object's lifetime. When the object's lifetime lease expires, the object is marked as available for garbage collection.

Understand how to use configuration files.   Many properties can be set in XML configuration files. When using configuration files, you can instantiate an object simply by using the New keyword.

Understand how to use an asynchronous callback with remote method calls.   Asynchronous calls keep your client's user interface responsive. Use the .NET Delegate object's `BeginInvoke` and `EndInvoke` methods to make asynchronous calls.

Key Terms

Before you take the exam, be certain you are familiar with the following terms:

application domains	client-activated object
asynchronous callback function	HTTP channel
binary formatter	lease manager
channel	lifetime lease

marshal-by-reference

marshal-by-value

port number

proxy object

serialization

server-activated object

Simple Object Access Protocol (SOAP)
formatter

SingleCall object

Singleton object

`System.MarshalByRefObject`

`System.Runtime.Remoting`

TCP channel

XML configuration files

Review Questions

1. What best describes the trade-offs that must be considered when deciding whether to use a TCP channel or an HTTP channel?

    A. The TCP channel is faster but offers less security.

    B. The HTTP channel is faster but offers less security.

    C. The TCP channel can be configured to use Secure Sockets Layer (SSL) but can use only the binary formatter.

    D. The HTTP channel can be configured to use Secure Sockets Layer (SSL) but can use only the SOAP formatter.

2. When registering a channel, how should you select a port number?

    A. You are restricted to using port numbers 0 through 1023.

    B. .NET Remoting works only with port numbers 1433 and 1434.

    C. .NET Remoting works only with port numbers in the 8000–8999 range.

    D. You can assign any port number, but be careful that you do not conflict with the port numbers that are conventionally used by other applications.

3. When registering a channel in your code, which System DLL should you set a reference to?

    A. `System.Web.Services.dll`

    B. `System.ServiceProcess.dll`

    C. `System.Runtime.Remoting.dll`

    D. `System.Runtime.EnterpriseServices.dll`

4. You have a class in your .NET Remoting application that requires that its complete object state be sent to the calling client code. What are two ways that this can be specified? (Choose two.)

    A. Mark the class with the `<Serializable>` attribute.

    B. Mark the class with the `<MarshalByValue>` attribute.

    C. Implement the `IMarshal` interface in your class and create a custom marshalling method.

    D. Implement the `ISerializable` interface in your class and create a custom serialization method.

5. You would like your .NET Remoting application to create a proxy object on the client side when the client instantiates a remote object but not necessarily to contact the server until the client accesses the object. How do you create classes that support this behavior?

    A. Your classes must inherit from `MarshalByValue`.

    B. Your classes must inherit from `MarshalByRefObject`.

    C. Your classes must implement `ISerializable`.

    D. Your classes must implement `IMarshal`.

6. You want to create a server-activated object that will remain in memory while the host application is running and that will service multiple requests from multiple clients. This type of object is defined by setting the `WellKnownObjectMode` property to what?

    A. `SingleUse`

    B. `SingleCall`

    C. `Singleton`

    D. `SingleInstance`

7. You want to create a server-activated object that holds unique data for each caller. After a method call is complete, the object will no longer be needed and the server memory it was using must be released as quickly as possible. This type of object is defined by setting the `WellKnownObjectMode` property to what?

    A. `SingleUse`

    B. `SingleCall`

    C. `Singleton`

    D. `SingleInstance`

8. When an object's lifetime lease expires, what happens?

    A. The client receives an exception.

    B. The object is marked as available for garbage collection.

    C. The client receives an event notification to extend the lease.

    D. The object is immediately removed from memory.

9. What should you do to make a custom setting for the `InitialLeaseTime` property in your code?

    A. In the client code, call the `Lease.Renew` method at the end of every method call.

    B. In the client code, change the `RenewOnCallTime` property at the end of every method call.

    C. In the server code, override the `GetLifetimeService` method and change the property setting.

    D. In the server code, override the `InitializeLifetimeService` method and change the property setting.

10. What should you do to change the setting for the `CurrentLeaseTime` property in your code?

    A. In the client code, get a reference to the remote object's lease object by calling the `GetLifetimeService` method. Then call the `Renew` method of the lease object.

    B. In the client code, get a reference to the remote object's lease object by calling the `InitializeLifetimeService` method. Then call the `Renew` method of the lease object.

    C. In the server code, call the `Lease.Renew` method at the end of every method call.

    D. In the server code, change the `RenewOnCallTime` property at the end of every method call.

11. When designing a class that will be used in a remote server as a part of a .NET Remoting application, why should you start by defining and compiling an interface DLL?

    A. It is a requirement of the .NET Framework that all classes are defined by an interface.

    B. It is a requirement of .NET Remoting that all classes are defined by an interface.

    C. So that the complete implementation DLL does not need to be deployed on every client computer.

    D. So that the complete implementation DLL does not need to be deployed on the remote server computer.

12. What is one of the main advantages of using XML configuration files to set .NET Remoting properties?

    A. Improved performance

    B. Easier maintenance

    C. Increased security

    D. Greater scalability

13. What is one of the most common errors that is made when working with XML configuration files?

    A. Putting the configuration file in the wrong directory

    B. Giving the configuration file an invalid filename

    C. Forgetting to compile the configuration file

    D. Incorrect use of uppercase and lowercase letters in the XML tag names

14. What is the main advantage of calling remote methods asynchronously?

    A. The user interface of the client application remains responsive, and the developer can provide status messages to the user.

    B. The method call will automatically be repeated if you cannot connect to the server on the first try.

    C. The user is notified by the .NET Remoting infrastructure that they will have to wait for their results.

    D. The client's results will be stored on the server until the client application requests them.

15. When calling a remote method asynchronously, which set of methods should you use?

    A. `CallStart` and `CallComplete`

    B. `BeginMethod` and `EndMethod`

    C. `BeginInvoke` and `EndInvoke`

    D. `MethodStart` and `MethodComplete`

Answers to Review Questions

1.   A.   The TCP channel transmits data faster than HTTP. However, HTTP (the "higher-level" protocol) supports various security features such as SSL. The third and fourth answers are incorrect. The default is for the TCP channel to use the binary formatter and the HTTP channel to use the SOAP formatter; however, they can be configured to use either formatter. Custom formatters can also be created to extend these basic classes provided by the .NET Framework.

2.   D.   Although you can use any port number, numbers up to 1023 are widely used by common applications (such as port 80 for web browsers and servers), so you should select port numbers greater than 1024. Microsoft SQL Server commonly uses port numbers 1433 and 1434. You should be aware of other applications that are using ports on your server and choose port numbers that do not conflict.

3.   C.   To use the `ChannelClass` and other important .NET Framework classes in a .NET Remoting project, set a reference to `System.Runtime.Remoting.dll`.

4.   A, D.   By adding the `<Serializable>` attribute to your class, you can use the built-in .NET Framework serialization capabilities to send all the data that completely describes the object's state to another component. By implementing the `ISerializable` interface, you can create a custom method for controlling how the object's data is transcribed. This is useful for serializing complex objects or for using application-specific knowledge of the data to reduce the amount of data transferred.

5.   B.   In order for the .NET Remoting infrastructure to create proxy objects on the client, the server classes must inherit from `MarshalByRefObject`. Marshal-by-value objects are those that implement `ISerializable` or make use of the `<Serializable>` attribute to transcribe the complete object state to the client.

6.   C.   A Singleton object can remain in memory on the server for an indefinite period of time and service multiple requests from multiple clients. A SingleCall object is created and destroyed for each method call. The others are not valid `WellKnownObjectMode` types.

7.   B.   A SingleCall object is created and destroyed for each method call and serves only a single caller. The object can hold unique data for the caller while it is in memory. A Singleton object remains in memory and is reused for each method call by multiple callers. The others are not valid `WellKnownObjectMode` types.

8.   B.   When the object's lifetime lease expires, it is marked as available for garbage collection by the CLR.

9.   D.   The `InitialLeaseTime` property can be changed only from the default in the `MarshalByRefObject.InitializeLifetimeService` method. To make a custom setting, you must override this method and change the property setting in your code.

10. A.   The CurrentLeaseTime property can be changed by accessing the remote object's associated lease object (which is created and maintained by the .NET Remoting infrastructure). The GetLifetimeService method returns a reference to a lease object. You can then call Lease.Renew. The InitializeLifetimeService method is executed only when the object is created. Lease.Renew should be called by the client, not in the server code. You do not need to change the RenewOnCallTime property; it will automatically extend the object's lifetime by the specified time (the default is 2 minutes) after every client call on the object.

11. C.   The interface DLL contains the minimum information that the .NET Remoting infrastructure on the client side needs to create a proxy for the remote class. By providing the interface, you do not need to distribute the complete implementation DLL to client computers.

12. B.   XML configuration files make ongoing maintenance and support of applications easier because changes can be made directly to the configuration file. Developers do not have to change the original source code and recompile.

13. D.   XML parsers require that all XML tag names exactly match their definitions, including exact matches of uppercase and lowercase characters. Because a configuration file can be named anything, as long as it matches the name referenced in the code, that is not a common error. A configuration file does not need to be compiled.

14. A.   Asynchronous method calls enable the client application's user interface to remain responsive, so that the developer can provide status information to the user.

15. C.   The Delegate object provides the BeginInvoke and EndInvoke methods that enable you to create asynchronous callback functions in your applications.

Chapter

4

Creating and Managing XML Web Services

MICROSOFT EXAM OBJECTIVES COVERED IN THIS CHAPTER:

✓ **Create and consume an XML Web service.**

- Control characteristics of Web methods by using attributes.
- Control XML wire format for an XML Web service.
- Instantiate and invoke an XML Web service.
- Create asynchronous Web methods.
- Create and use SOAP extensions.

XML Web services are one of the most talked about aspects of .NET development. They enable you to expose your application's functionality to the widest possible range of users. XML Web services can be used when it is impossible to use .NET Remoting—because your XML Web services application runs on a web server accessible to the Internet, users do not have to be on the same platform or part of the same network to access your application. XML Web services are based on Internet standards, such as HTTP, XML, and SOAP, which enable your application to be visible and accessible to users on any platform. XML Web services give your applications the ability to access resources over the Internet with the ease that has made the World Wide Web so popular for searching and browsing.

This chapter covers the basics of creating and calling XML Web services by using Visual Studio .NET. You will learn how the .NET Framework enables attributes to be assigned to XML Web services and methods, how to call Web methods asynchronously, and how to extend basic Simple Object Access Protocol (SOAP) processing with custom SOAP headers and SOAP extensions.

Introduction to XML Web Services

XML Web services are designed for interoperability with clients and other web services running on many different platforms. To accomplish this goal, XML Web services have been built using underlying technologies that are widely accepted standards in the computing industry. As you work with XML Web services, you will see references to the features of these underlying technologies over and over again. Here is a brief description of each of these important technologies that XML Web services are built on:

Hypertext Transfer Protocol *Hypertext Transfer Protocol (HTTP)* is an application-level protocol by which text and other types of data can be transferred over the Internet. HTTP is supported on all platforms. HTTP traffic is usually allowed to move through corporate firewalls with little interference on well-known port 80. These factors make it a good choice for XML Web services, because no special access or proprietary formats need to be in place in order to communicate with clients and other web services.

Extensible Markup Language *Extensible Markup Language (XML)* is a markup language that enables you to add tags and attributes to a data file; these tags and attributes serve to describe the meaning and structure of the data items. Although individual applications might use any tag names and organization of data they find appropriate, XML defines a few simple rules that ensure consistency among all XML documents. These rules include case-sensitivity, a uniquely named root element that encloses all the data, strict matching of start and end tags, proper nesting of elements within the hierarchy, and a few others. XML documents that are in compliance with all these rules are said to be "well-formed." A well-formed XML document can be processed by any standard software tool that can parse XML markup.

XML Schema Definition   *XML Schema Definition* (also referred to as *XSD Schema*) is a standard way to define an exact format for a specific XML document. Flexibility of the XML format is useful in some situations. However, when exchanging information between applications, the ability to validate against a specific XML format is important in ensuring data integrity and avoiding processing errors.

Simple Object Access Protocol   *Simple Object Access Protocol (SOAP)* is a standardized XML format that is used to exchange method calls and associated data between web services clients and servers. The SOAP protocol defines a set of XML tag names that form an "envelope" for your message. Header tag names are defined for routing information. The Body section contains information about the method call, parameters, and return values. The Fault section contains error information on return from a method call, if a method call does not complete.

Universal Description, Discovery, and Integration   *Universal Description, Discovery, and Integration (UDDI)* is a service for locating XML Web services by consulting online registries, such as uddi.microsoft.com, which contain information about available web services. You can publish information about web services that your organization wants to make available, including the information or functionality that the service offers, contact information for support, technical details of your service, and more. If you are looking for a particular service, you can manually search the UDDI registry sites. There is a programmatic application programming interface (API) to access a UDDI registry server from your application. For example, if the server that you usually connect to is down, your application can search the registry at runtime, find another server that offers the same service, and connect to that one instead.

UDDI is discussed in more detail in Chapter 11, "Deploying and Securing XML Web Services."

In the .NET Framework, XML Web services are implemented as ASP.NET applications that run with Microsoft Internet Information Server (IIS). XML Web service files are indicated by an .asmx file extension. XML Web services use attributes to identify that classes and methods should be exposed to clients as a part of the XML Web service interface. Additionally, XML Web service classes must inherit from *System.Web.Services.WebService*, and your project must reference *System.Web.Services.dll*. After you have created your source code in Visual Studio .NET, you will compile your code into a DLL. This is the file that must be deployed to a web server and will handle all incoming requests for the service.

Creating an XML Web Service

In this section, you are going to see how easy it is to create an XML Web service in Visual Studio .NET. The ASP.NET Web service project template handles most of the steps described in the preceding paragraph. In Exercise 4.1, you will put together a simple service that performs two calculations. You can test the web service directly from your web browser. After the exercise, we will discuss the items that are created automatically for you by Visual Studio .NET in more detail.

Because XML Web services that you create with Visual Studio .NET run on Microsoft Internet Information Server (IIS) with ASP.NET, make sure that you know the location of the development web server that you will be using to complete the exercises in this chapter. The exercises specify localhost as the web server name. This assumes that you are running a local copy of IIS on your development computer (the same computer that you are running Visual Studio .NET on). If you are connecting to a different web server, over the network, please substitute the appropriate computer name for localhost.

EXERCISE 4.1

Creating and Testing a Simple XML Web Service

Creating the Web Service:

1. Start Visual Studio .NET and create a new project by using the ASP.NET Web Service template. In the Location text box, specify **http://localhost/SquareRootService**.

    This creates a virtual root directory on your web server. This example uses localhost as the server name. This indicates that the web server is running on the same computer as Visual Studio .NET. You can substitute a different server name for localhost if it is appropriate to your environment.

2. In the Solution Explorer, change the name of the file Service1.asmx to **Square.asmx**.

3. Right-click the file Square.asmx and choose View Code.

4. Change the name of the class from Service1 to **Square**. Notice the text and sample code that is commented out. Visual Studio .NET is providing an example of a simple Web method. You will follow this example and create two simple methods for your web service.

EXERCISE 4.1 *(continued)*

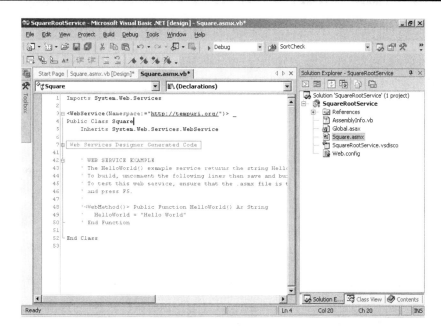

5. Add the `Name` and `Description` parameters to the `WebService` attribute for the class definition. Your code should look like this:

```
<WebService(Namespace:="http://tempuri.org/", _
    Name:="SquareRootService", _
    Description:="Performs square and square root calculations.")> _
```

6. Add the following code within the class to create the first Web method, called `GetSquare`:

```
<WebMethod(Description:="Get the square of a number")> _
 Public Function GetSquare(ByVal inputVal As Double) As Double
    Return inputVal * inputVal
End Function
```

Notice that an `Imports` statement for the `System.Web.Services` namespace has been automatically added to the code.

7. The next method that you are going to create uses the `sqrt()` function from the `System.Math` namespace. You need to add another `Imports` statement. Your code should look like this:

```
Imports System.Web.Services
Imports System.Math
```

8. Add the following code within the class to create the second Web method, called GetSquareRoot:

    ```
    <WebMethod(Description:="Get the square root of a number")> _
     Public Function GetSquareRoot(ByVal inputVal As Double) As Double
        Return sqrt(inputVal)
    End Function
    ```

9. Make sure that the Square.asmx page is set as the start page for the project. To do this, right-click Square.asmx in the Solution Explorer and then choose Set As Start Page.

10. Save your work. Use the Build ➢ Build SquareRootService menu option to create a compiled DLL for your web service.

Testing the Web Service:

11. Start your web browser and type the following URL:

    http://localhost/SquareRootService/Square.asmx

    A standard test page is generated by Visual Studio based on the methods it finds in your Web service code. It should look like the following screen.

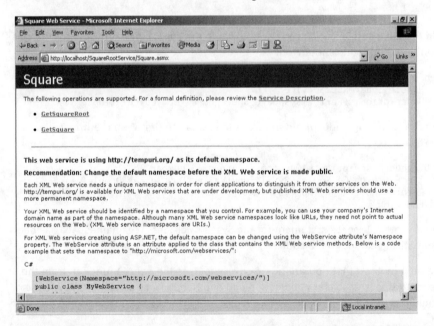

12. Click the hyperlink for the GetSquareRoot method. You will see a second test page, which shows the parameter required when calling the GetSquareRoot method and an Invoke button to run the test. Type a value (in this case, **144**) into the text box provided on the page and click the Invoke button.

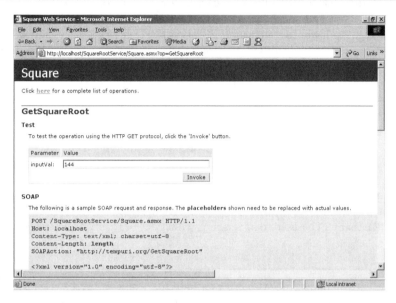

The results of the test are displayed in a new browser window. The results are returned as an XML document, as shown here. After you have reviewed the results, you can close this browser window.

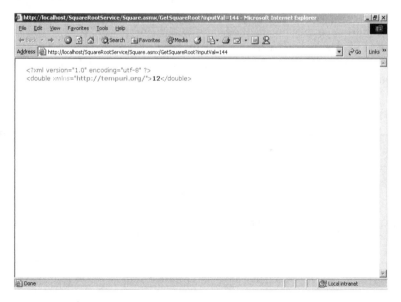

13. Click the Back button on your web browser to return to the first test page. Click the hyperlink for the GetSquare method. Test this method in the same way.

As you can see from Exercise 4.1, creating an XML Web service in Visual Studio .NET is simple. That's because Visual Studio .NET takes care of several steps that you would otherwise have to perform manually. First of all, references to `System.Web` and `System.Web.Services` have been added to the project. An `Imports` statement for `System.Web.Services` is also added. Each class in a Web service project is marked to inherit from the `System.Web.Services.WebService` class and the class declaration is marked with an attribute called `WebService`.

The *WebService attribute* is shown with a parameter used to declare a unique namespace for your web service. The value assigned to the `Namespace` parameter is in the form of a *Uniform Resource Identifier (URI)*. A URI is defined as any unique string that is used to identify the publisher of a particular web service. By default, this is set to `http://tempuri.org/`. It is OK to use this string during development, but you should replace it with your own identifier when the web service is made available on the Internet, in order to make sure that the namespace and web service name combination uniquely identifies your web service. Although the namespace URI is conventionally taken from an organization's Internet domain name, it is not meant to be a *Uniform Resource Locator (URL)*, that is, it does not need to be set to the URL that will be used to access the web service or to any other specific web page location.

 If you point your web browser to `http://tempuri.org`, Visual Studio .NET will display a Help page that has more information about namespaces and URIs.

Each method that you want to expose as a part of the public interface of your service is marked with a *WebMethod attribute*. You can have private methods included in the class that can be called only from your public methods, not by the end users of your web service. Any procedure without the `WebMethod` attribute will not be visible to your users. A complete list of Web service attributes is shown in Table 4.2 in the next section. Table 4.1 shows the parameters that are available for the `WebMethod` attribute.

TABLE 4.1   Parameters of the *WebMethod* Attribute

Parameter	Description
BufferResponse	Gets or sets whether the response for this request is buffered before being sent down to the client. Defaults to True.
CacheDuration	Gets or sets the number of seconds the response should be held in the cache. A value of 0 disables caching for the method.
Description	Describes the purpose of the XML Web service method. This text is printed on the service Help page.
EnableSession	Shows whether session state is enabled for an XML Web service method. Defaults to False.

TABLE 4.1   Parameters of the *WebMethod* Attribute *(continued)*

Parameter	Description
MessageName	Specifies the message name, which is used to call the method. This parameter will be specified most commonly when you overload a method with different implementations for different data types, because it provides a way for the user to call the method implementation appropriate for the type of data they are providing. Defaults to the method name.
TransactionOption	Provides the transaction support of an XML Web service method. Defaults to TransactionOption.Disabled.

Listing 4.1 shows the complete code for the SquareRootService project that you created in Exercise 4.1.

Listing 4.1: The Complete Code for the SquareRootService

```
Imports System.Web.Services
Imports System.Math


<WebService(Namespace:="http://tempuri.org/", _
    Name:="SquareRootService", _
    Description:="Performs square and square root calculations.")> _
  Public Class Square
    Inherits System.Web.Services.WebService

'Region " Web Services Designer Generated Code "

    ' WEB SERVICE EXAMPLE
    ' The HelloWorld() example service returns the string Hello World.
    ' To build, uncomment the following lines then save and build the project.
    ' To test this web service, ensure that the .asmx file is the start page
    ' and press F5.
    '
    '<WebMethod()> Public Function HelloWorld() As String
    ' HelloWorld = "Hello World"
    ' End Function

    <WebMethod(Description:="Get the square of a number")> _
     Public Function GetSquare(ByVal inputVal As Double) As Double
        Return inputVal * inputVal
    End Function
```

```
<WebMethod(Description:="Get the square root of a number")> _
 Public Function GetSquareRoot(ByVal inputVal As Double) As Double
     Return sqrt(inputVal)
 End Function
End Class
```

 Real World Scenario

Google Web Services Interface

In the folklore of the computer industry, for a new technology to capture attention and quickly gain widespread acceptance, there must be a "killer app" that makes use of it. This "killer" application provides new and powerful capabilities that are so compelling that the technology quickly becomes a new standard. The killer app for XML Web services has not yet been identified, but one of the most significant advancements for XML Web services is the Google web service API. In early 2002, Google announced that they would make their search services available through a web service interface.

As of this writing, this is not yet a commercial application; it is offered for testing and demonstration purposes. There is no fee; however, users must register and use a special license key provided by Google when accessing the service. Each license key is limited to a certain number of connections per day. You can download sample code for Visual Studio .NET, and other languages too, at: http://www.google.com/apis/.

Here is the Object Browser view of the Google web class.

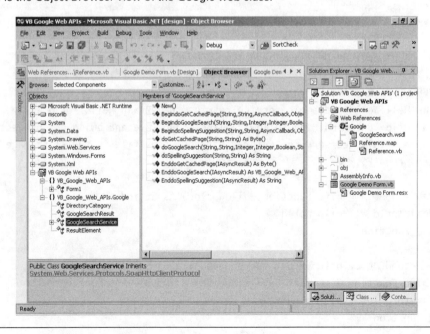

The following code snippet shows a call to the doGoogleSearch method:

```
Dim r As Google.GoogleSearchResult = s.doGoogleSearch(txtLicenseKey.Text, _
    txtSearchTerm.Text, 0, 1, False, "", False, "", "", "")


'Extract the estimated number of results for the search and display it
Dim estResults As Integer = r.estimatedTotalResultsCount
lblSearchResults.Text = CStr(estResults)
```

The method call passes the user's license key, the term to be searched for, and several other parameters to the service. This method does not return actual URLs; it displays only the total number of matches found for the current search term. Other methods available in the demo programs offer other features.

By having services such as this available, developers can greatly extend the possibilities for what they can deliver in their applications. Other web services are available that provide weather information, address and zip code searches, and many more. Rather than having to develop functionality from scratch and maintain databases on this information, you can use the Internet to connect to a service that is already offering the information you need and integrate that data seamlessly into your applications. Another use for the web service interface is to automate a process that otherwise might require a user to manually look up information over and over again. A web service application could monitor a stock quote server—for example, checking the price every few minutes, but only notifying the user if a change occurred.

Take a look at some of the sample services that are offered; it's fun to connect to other people's applications over the Internet and see what kind of uses you can find for the data they are making available. Other websites where you can find XML Web services for learning and testing are http://www.gotdotnet.com and http://www.xmethods.com.

As you can see from completing Exercise 4.1, Visual Studio .NET makes working with XML Web services easy by doing a lot of the underlying work for you. If you are creating XML Web services that will be used by other platforms, you might need to make some adjustments to the format of the SOAP messages that your application is sending, to meet the other platform's particular needs. Next, you'll learn how to use attributes to change the way that the XML markup of the SOAP message is formatted.

Using Attributes to Control XML Wire Format

In addition to the WebService and WebMethod attributes shown earlier, there are additional attributes that you can add to your XML Web service code to control how the XML/SOAP messages are formatted when they are serialized and sent over the Internet (or the "wire"). For example, you can determine what XML tag names are created for your methods and their parameters, and how those tags are nested in relation to one another. Table 4.2 shows attributes that can be applied to the classes and methods that make up an XML Web service.

TABLE 4.2   Attributes That Can Be Used with XML Web Services

Attribute	Description
WebMethod	Indicates a method to be exposed to users of the XML Web service.
WebService	Indicates a class that implements an XML Web service; parameters for this attribute include the default XML namespace.
WebServiceBinding	Indicates a class that implements an XML Web service or a proxy class that specifies the bindings, similar to interfaces, implemented by the XML Web service that are outside of the default namespace.
SoapDocumentMethod	Indicates that an XML Web service method or a method of a proxy class expects document-based SOAP messages.
SoapDocumentService	Indicates that by default XML Web service methods within the class expect document-based SOAP messages.
SoapRpcMethod	Indicates that an XML Web service method or a method of a proxy class expects RPC-based SOAP messages.
SoapRpcService	Indicates that by default XML Web service methods within the class expect RPC-based SOAP messages.
SoapHeader	Indicates that an XML Web service method or a method of a proxy class can process a specific SOAP header.
SoapExtension	Indicates that a SOAP extension should execute when the XML Web service method executes.
MatchAttribute	Indicates a regular expression for using text pattern matching. Valid only for XML Web service clients.

According to the SOAP specification (http://www.w3.org/TR/SOAP/), there are two styles of mapping the Web service method's parameters to XML elements in the SOAP message that is generated. ASP.NET is capable of processing both formats. However, when accessing XML Web services that are hosted on other platforms, you might find that you are required to specify one or the other.

The two types of mapping are called *RPC encoding* and *Document encoding*. ASP.NET is capable of processing both formats, but uses Document encoding by default. These attributes can be applied to the individual methods of an XML Web service class and also to the methods of a proxy class. Alternatively, you can mark an entire XML Web services class with the SoapDocumentService or SoapRpcService attribute.

Remote Procedure Call encoding (RPC encoding) uses general rules from the SOAP specification and generates a format of XML with an element whose tag name matches the method name. Nested inside that element are additional elements matching the parameter names for the method. The SOAP specification does not require that these parameters appear in any particular order. An application that is receiving the SOAP request must be able to handle these variations in formatting.

By using Document encoding, you can use the Web Services Description Language (WSDL) information for your web service which strictly describes the exact format of XML that will be created in the SOAP message (see the section later in this chapter titled Using Web Services Description Language).

The following code snippet shows the use of the `SoapDocumentMethod` attribute:

```
<SoapDocumentMethod(Use:=SoapBindingUse.Literal, _
    ParameterStyle:=Wrapped), WebMethod()> _
    Public Function GetSquare(ByVal inputVal As Double) As Double
        Return inputVal * inputVal
End Function
```

The `Use` parameter of the attribute is set to either `Encoded` or `Literal`. `ParameterStyle` determines whether the parameters are encapsulated within a single message part following the body element (`Wrapped`) or whether each parameter is an individual message part (`Bare`). The following is an example of the format of the SOAP message that is created:

```
<soap:Envelope namespaces>
    <soap:Body>
        <GetSquare xmlns="http://tempuri.org/">
            <inputVal>12</inputVal>
        </GetSquare>
    </soap:Body>
</soap:Envelope>
```

You will also look at the `SoapHeader` and `SoapExtension` attributes later in this chapter, in the section titled "Creating and Using SOAP Headers and SOAP Extensions."

Consuming XML Web Services

Now that you have seen how Visual Studio .NET helps you to create and publish an XML Web service, you are ready to learn how to create client applications. In this section, Exercise 4.2 shows how to create a Windows application that calls a web service. Exercise 4.3 creates a web page application.

Before you create the client applications, it is important to understand the mechanisms used by client applications to locate and see the methods that an XML Web service offers. The two technologies that are used to do this are *discovery*, for locating a web service, and *Web Services Description Language (WSDL)* for describing its functions.

Using Discovery

A discovery document enables clients to obtain information about which XML Web services are available at a given endpoint (or on a web server). This is an XML document with a specific set of tag names. You can create this document manually and place it in a directory on the web server; make sure you use the filename extension `.disco`. If you are running your XML Web service on Microsoft Internet Information Server (IIS) with ASP.NET, however, a discovery document will be generated whenever a request for it is made by a client. For example, a client can request the following URL for the XML Web service you created in Exercise 4.1:

```
http://localhost/SquareRootService/square.asmx?disco
```

The resulting discovery document will look like Listing 4.2.

Listing 4.2: The .disco File for the SquareRootService

```
<?xml version="1.0" encoding="utf-8"?>
<discovery xmlns:xsd="http://www.w3.org/2001/XMLSchema"
        xmlns:xsi="http://www.w3.org/2001/XMLSchema-instance" xmlns="http://
           schemas.xmlsoap.org/disco/">
  <contractRef ref="http://localhost/SquareRootService/square.asmx?wsdl"
     docRef="http://localhost/SquareRootService/square.asmx"
        xmlns="http://schemas.xmlsoap.org/disco/scl/" />
  <soap address="http://localhost/SquareRootService/square.asmx"
       xmlns:q1="http://tempuri.org/" binding="q1:SquareSoap"
        xmlns="http://schemas.xmlsoap.org/disco/soap/" />
</discovery>
```

The `<contractRef>` tag in Listing 4.2 is particularly important because it gives the location of the WSDL document, or the contract that states how your Web service works.

Using this type of `.disco` file is called *static discovery*. It requires that the client has some prior knowledge about the URL for your web service. Visual Studio .NET also supports something called *dynamic discovery*. In dynamic discovery, the client is allowed to search all the directories on the web server until it locates an available XML Web service. In this case, there is a `.vsdisco` file in either the default website directory or in one of your application's virtual directories. When you install Visual Studio .NET, a file called `Default.vsdisco` is placed into the default website directory, and a `ServiceName.vsdisco` file is placed in the project directory. These files are used by Visual Studio .NET, and you can leave them in place on development servers. However, when deploying a publicly available XML Web service to a production server, you should remove these files and use static discovery.

Listing 4.3 shows the contents of the `SquareRootService.vsdisco` file that was added by default to the XML Web service project. The default file lists those directories (marked with `<exclude>` tags) that should remain private on the web server and not be searched by client applications.

Listing 4.3: The SquareRootService.vsdisco File

```
<?xml version="1.0" encoding="utf-8" ?>
<dynamicDiscovery xmlns="urn:schemas-dynamicdiscovery:disco.2000-03-17">
<exclude path="_vti_cnf" />
<exclude path="_vti_pvt" />
<exclude path="_vti_log" />
<exclude path="_vti_script" />
```

```
<exclude path="_vti_txt" />
<exclude path="Web References" />
</dynamicDiscovery>
```

Using Web Services Description Language

Web Services Description Language (WSDL) is another defined format of XML tags that are used to describe the contract between the publisher of a web service and their clients. As you saw in the preceding code, the generated discovery document for a web service contains a reference to its WSDL document for further information. A WSDL document shows all the methods of the web service, the arguments that are passed when a method is called, the data types for the arguments, and the data type of the return value of the method call. In the same way that Visual Studio .NET generated the `.disco` file, Visual Studio .NET will also generate a WSDL document to describe your web service. For example, request the following URL for the XML Web service you created in Exercise 4.1:

`http://localhost/SquareRootService/square.asmx?wsdl`

The resulting discovery document will look like Figure 4.1. Figure 4.1 shows the partial listing. Test this with the `SquareRootService` project that you created in Exercise 4.1 to see the full WSDL that is generated.

FIGURE 4.1 The WSDL document for the `SquareRootProject`

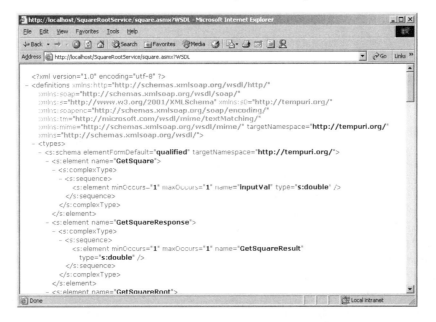

In conversation, many people pronounce the acronym WSDL as "wiz-dull" rather than spelling it out.

Notice that the methods of the **SquareRootService**—**GetSquare** and **GetSquareRoot**—are shown. You can also see the parameter name, **inputVal**, and data type, which is **Double**. The WSDL document contains all the information that a client application needs in order to call methods of the XML Web service.

A Visual Studio .NET client application interacts with a web service by reading the WSDL information and then using this information to create a *proxy class* in the client project. The client application programmer can then access a Web service in the same way as they access any local object. In Visual Studio .NET, this proxy class code is generated automatically for you when you add a Web reference to an XML Web service to your client project. If you are not using Visual Studio .NET, a command-line tool called *wsdl.exe* can be used to generate the proxy class from the WSDL file. Figure 4.2 shows the partial code for a proxy class in a client application that consumes the **SquareRootService**. When you are working on Exercises 4.2 and 4.3, you will be able to see the complete code.

FIGURE 4.2   The proxy class for the SquareRootProject

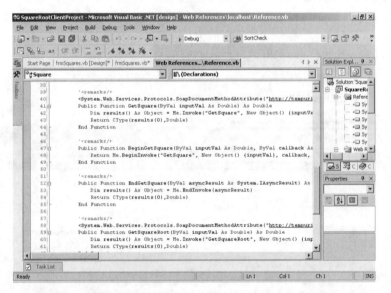

After the proxy class is added to your project, you can instantiate objects from the class and call their methods, just as though the web service code was running on your local computer. The code in the proxy class, the runtime, and ASP.NET take care of the details of contacting the XML Web services across the Internet. One thing that you will notice when you get to step 10 in Exercise 4.2 is that the web service proxy has its own namespace. In Visual Studio .NET projects, when you declare or instantiate the web service object, you will need to refer to it by its fully qualified name, like this:

```
Dim objSquare As SquareRootService.Square = _
    New SquareRootService.Square()
```

After the object is instantiated, you can call its methods just like any other local object:

```
webResult = objSquare.GetSquare(inputValue)
```

In Exercise 4.2, you will create a Windows form application that consumes the SquareRoot-Service XML Web service.

EXERCISE 4.2

Using an XML Web Service from a Windows Application

1. Create a new Visual Studio .NET project by using the Windows Application project template. Select an appropriate project directory and name the project **SquareRootClientProject**.

2. Rename the default Form1.vb to **frmSquares.vb**.

3. Create a user interface for the form that looks like the following graphic. Create two text boxes and two command buttons. Name the controls as follows:

    -   TextBox1: **txtValue**
    -   TextBox2: **txtResult**
    -   Button1: **btnSquare**
    -   Button2: **btnRoot**

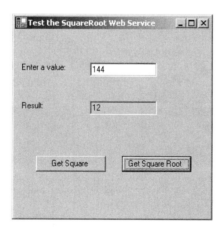

4. Add a Web reference to the SquareRootService. Right-click the SquareRootClientProject in the Solution Explorer and choose Add Web Reference. Type the URL for the SquareRoot-Service: **http://localhost/SquareRootService/Square.asmx.**

5. Click the Go button. Displayed in the left pane of the Add Web Reference dialog box, you will see the same test page that you saw when testing the Web service at the end of Exercise 4.1. In the right pane, there are two links. Click the View Contract link to view the WSDL. Click the View Documentation link to redisplay the test page. You might have to click the blue Back button in the toolbar to return to a page containing the View Documentation link.

6. Click the Add Reference button to add the Web reference to your project.

EXERCISE 4.2 *(continued)*

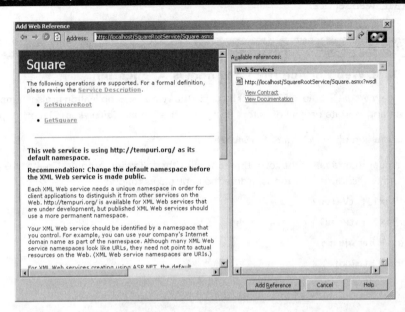

7. You will now see a node for Web references added to the Solution Explorer window. Click the Show All Files toolbar button to display all the files. (The Show All Files button is at the top of the Solution Explorer window. It is highlighted in the graphic below.)

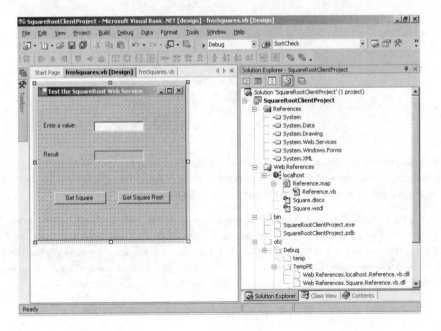

8. Right-click the localhost node (with the globe icon) and choose Rename. Change the name to **SquareRootService**.

9. You can now view the proxy class that was created. In the Solution Explorer window, under the Web References node, expand the SquareRootService node. You will see a node called Reference.map. You may have to expand the Reference.map node further to see Reference.vb. Right-click Reference.vb and choose View Code. Review this code.

10. Use the Visual Studio .NET menus to choose View ➢ Other Windows ➢ Object Browser. Expand the SquareRootClientProject node and then expand SquareRootClient-Project.SquareRootService and click the Square class. You can see the available methods of the Web service class in the panel on the right, as shown in the following graphic. Close the Object Browser window when you are finished.

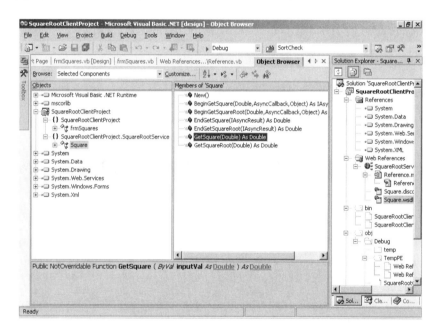

11. Now you can add code to the Windows form to call the methods of the SquareRootService. Create a procedure for the Click event of the Get Square command button. Your code should look like this:

```
Private Sub btnSquare_Click(ByVal sender As System.Object, _
        ByVal e As System.EventArgs) Handles btnSquare.Click
```

```
Dim objSquare As SquareRootService.Square = _
    New SquareRootService.Square()
Dim inputValue As Double
Dim webResult As Double

inputValue = CType(txtValue.Text, Double)
webResult = objSquare.GetSquare(inputValue)
txtResult.Text = webResult.ToString
objSquare = Nothing
```

End Sub

12. Create a similar procedure for the Get Square Root command button, this time calling the GetSquareRoot method.

13. Save your work. Test the client application by choosing Debug ➤ Start from the menu. Type in a value and click one of the buttons. After you have clicked the button, you will notice a slight delay on the first request while ASP.NET loads and compiles the web service, but all subsequent requests will be much faster.

The procedure for creating an ASP.NET Web application that consumes an XML Web service is substantially the same as using a Windows application. Exercise 4.3 shows an example but provides less detail. If any of the steps are unclear, review Exercise 4.2.

EXERCISE 4.3

Using an XML Web Service from an ASP.NET Web Application

1. Create a new Visual Studio .NET project by using the ASP.NET Web Application project template. Create the new project at **http://localhost/SquareRootClientWeb**.

Use localhost as the server name if you are running a web server on your development machine; otherwise, replace it with an appropriate server name.

2. Rename the default WebForm1.aspx to **SquareClient.aspx**. Right-click this file and choose Set As Start Page.

3. Create a user interface for the form that looks like the next graphic. Create three TextBox Web Forms controls and an HTML Submit button. Name the TextBox controls as follows:

- **txtValue**
- **txtSquare**
- **txtRoot**

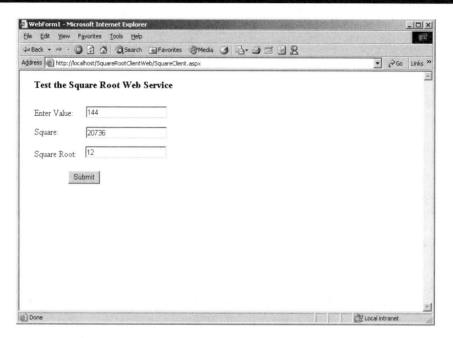

4. Add a Web reference to your project by following the same procedures as in Exercise 4.2. Change the name of the Web reference from localhost to **SquareRootService**.

5. Add code to the Page_Load event in SquareClient.aspx.vb to instantiate the object and call its methods. Notice that this code is slightly different from that in Exercise 4.2. Rather than allowing the user to select which method to call, it always runs both on the input value. Your code should look like the following:

```
Private Sub Page_Load(ByVal sender As System.Object, _
    ByVal e As System.EventArgs) Handles MyBase.Load

        If Page.IsPostBack Then
            Dim objSquare As SquareRootService.Square = _
                New SquareRootService.Square()
            Dim inputValue As Double
            Dim webResult1 As Double, webResult2 As Double

            inputValue = CType(txtValue.Text, Double)

            webResult1 = objSquare.GetSquare(inputValue)
            txtSquare.Text = webResult1.ToString

            webResult2 = objSquare.GetSquareRoot(inputValue)
```

```
            txtRoot.Text = webResult2.ToString
            objSquare = Nothing
        End If
    End Sub
```

6. Save your work. Test the client application by choosing Debug ➤ Start from the menu. Type a value in the Value textbox and click the Submit button. The square and square root of the value that you input should be displayed.

Now that you understand the basics of creating and consuming XML Web services we can look at a way to call those methods asynchronously. When making calls over the Internet or even a busy Intranet, asynchronous calls will allow you to manage calls that do not seem to be getting through to their intended destination or taking a long time to complete. You can also provide status messages to your users to let them know that the method call is still in progress. The next section shows how to call Web methods asynchronously.

Creating Asynchronous Web Methods

If you look at the proxy class that was created in the SquareRootClient projects, you will see that it offers more than a simple, synchronous method call for each of the methods exposed by the XML Web service. For each of the web service methods, there is also a set of proxy methods called Begin*methodname* and End*methodname*. These methods enable you to use *asynchronous callbacks*—that is, your application can make a Web service request and continue with its own activities, without having to wait for the Web service request to complete.

When calling XML Web services over the Internet, you might find that the response time can vary. Instead of having your client application wait for the results to be returned from the web service and appear to be unresponsive to the user, use the asynchronous calls to enable your user interface to remain responsive and provide status information to the user. Listing 4.4 shows the methods from the proxy class that provides synchronous and asynchronous access to the GetSquareRoot method of your SquareRootService.

Listing 4.4: The Methods That Are Automatically Generated in the Proxy Class

```
<System.Web.Services.Protocols.SoapDocumentMethodAttribute( _
    "http://tempuri.org/GetSquareRoot", _
    RequestNamespace:="http://tempuri.org/", _
    ResponseNamespace:="http://tempuri.org/", _
    Use:=System.Web.Services.Description.SoapBindingUse.Literal, _
    ParameterStyle:=System.Web.Services.Protocols.SoapParameterStyle.Wrapped)> _
Public Function GetSquareRoot(ByVal inputVal As Double) As Double
```

```
        Dim results() As Object = Me.Invoke("GetSquareRoot", _
            New Object() {inputVal})
                Return CType(results(0),Double)
End Function


Public Function BeginGetSquareRoot(ByVal inputVal As Double, _
    ByVal callback As System.AsyncCallback, _
    ByVal asyncState As Object) As System.IasyncResult

        Return Me.BeginInvoke("GetSquareRoot", _
            New Object() {inputVal}, callback, asyncState)
End Function


Public Function EndGetSquareRoot(ByVal asyncResult As _
    System.IAsyncResult) As Double

        Dim results() As Object = Me.EndInvoke(asyncResult)
            Return CType(results(0),Double)
End Function
```

The code in Listing 4.5 shows how to use a .NET Framework class called `AsyncCallback` with the `BeginGetSquareRoot` and `EndGetSquareRoot` methods that are included in the proxy class.

Listing 4.5: Calling an XML Web Service Method Asynchronously

```
Private Sub asyncSquare()
    Dim objSquare As SquareRootService.Square =↵
        New SquareRootService.Square()
    Dim inputValue As Double

    sBar.Text = "Beginning async Web Service call . . ."
    inputValue = CType(txtValue.Text, Double)

    'create the callback delegate
    Dim myCallBack As AsyncCallback
    myCallBack = New AsyncCallback(AddressOf Me.GetResult)
    objSquare.BeginGetSquareRoot(inputValue, myCallBack, objSquare)
End Sub


Private Sub GetResult(ByVal ar As System.IAsyncResult)
    Dim webResult As Double
```

```
Dim objSquare As SquareRootService.Square = _
    CType(ar.AsyncState, SquareRootService.Square)

webResult = objSquare.EndGetSquareRoot(ar)

sBar.Text = "Returned from async Web Service call . . ."
txtResult.Text = webResult.ToString
End Sub
```

Here we have two procedures. The first one, `asyncSquare`, is responsible for calling the `BeginGetSquareRoot` method from the proxy class and setting up the `AsyncCallback` delegate. When instantiating an `AsyncCallback` object in Visual Basic .NET, the object's constructor requires that the `AddressOf` operator is used to assign a reference to the procedure that will be called when the `BeginSquareRoot` method is complete. If you look at the code in the `BeginGetSquareRoot` method in the proxy class, you see that all it is doing is calling `GetSquareRoot` and passing along the reference to the `AsyncCallback` object. When the `BeginSquareRoot` method is complete, execution goes to the `GetResult` method. `GetResult` receives state information about the currently executing asynchronous operation and completes it by calling `EndGetSquareRoot`. The `EndGetSquareRoot` method is responsible for calling `EndInvoke` on itself and passing the results back to the client code.

In Exercise 4.4, you will test the asynchronous method call by modifying the project that you completed in Exercise 4.2.

EXERCISE 4.4

Calling an XML Web Service Method Asynchronously

1. Open the Visual Studio .NET project, called `SquareRootClientProject`, that you created in Exercise 4.2.

2. Create two new procedures in the code for `frmSquares.vb` by using the code in Listing 4.5.

3. Comment out the code that is currently in the `btnRoot_Click` subprocedure and add a call to the `asyncSquare` procedure, as shown in this code snippet:

   ```
   Call asyncSquare()
   ```

4. Save and test your work. Set a breakpoint in the `GetResult` procedure and verify that it is hit when the response from the Web service is completed.

Calling Web methods asynchronously adds an important level of control and sophistication to your applications. In the next section you will learn how to further extend your Web services and client applications by creating custom SOAP headers to send additional information along with your method call, and by using SOAP Extensions to cause procedures to run each time a SOAP message is sent or received.

Creating and Using SOAP Headers and SOAP Extensions

Now that you understand the basics of creating and using XML Web services, you will learn about two techniques that enable you to add customized behavior: SOAP headers and SOAP extensions. SOAP headers enable you to add custom fields to the Header section of the SOAP messages that are passed back and forth between the client and the web service. SOAP extensions enable you to add custom processing each time a SOAP message is sent or received—for example, you can write code to encrypt your data before it is sent over the Internet and decrypt it on the receiving end.

SOAP Headers

Earlier in this chapter, we discussed the SOAP message format, which consists of the SOAP Envelope, Header, and Body sections. The SOAP Body contains the information about the Web method that you are calling and any parameters that must be passed with the method call. The Header section of the SOAP message typically contains routing information that is used by the web service application when it receives a request. The SOAP specification does not make exact requirements about what items must appear in this section, so you can create customized SOAP headers that are meaningful to your application. A common use of customized SOAP headers is to pass along user identification.

Custom SOAP headers are created by adding a class to your original XML Web services project. This class must inherit from the *System.Web.Services.Protocols.SoapHeader class*. This class then defines one or more public variables that will become the custom header items. Each Web method in the XML Web service class that will use the custom headers must then be marked with the *SoapHeader attribute*. The code in your XML Web service would look like Listing 4.6. The bold text shows what we have added to the original web service code.

Listing 4.6: Adding the SoapHeader Class and Attributes to XML Web Service Code

```
Imports System.Web.Services
Imports System.Web.Services.Protocols
Imports System.Math

<WebService(Namespace:="http://tempuri.org/")> _
  Public Class Square
  Inherits System.Web.Services.WebService

  Public custID As UserIDHeader

  <WebMethod(Description:="Get the square of a number"), _
   SoapHeader("custID", Required:=False)> _
```

```
    Public Function GetSquare(ByVal inputVal As Double) As Double
        Return inputVal * inputVal
  End Function
  <WebMethod(Description:="Get the square root of a number"), _
   SoapHeader("custID", Required:=False)> _
      Public Function GetSquareRoot(ByVal inputVal As Double) As Double
          Return Sqrt(inputVal)
  End Function
End Class


Public Class UserIDHeader
    Inherits SoapHeader
    Public userID As String
End Class
```

Adding the SoapHeader attributes to the XML Web service will change how the WSDL document and the proxy classes are generated. They will also show the attribute and a public variable, UserIDHeaderValue, that will be added to the proxy class, as shown in Listing 4.7. Don't forget that if you make these changes to the original XML Web services project from Exercise 4.1 and recompile it, you must delete the Web reference from your client project(s) and add them again to regenerate the proxy class with these updates.

Listing 4.7: Additions to the Auto-Generated Proxy Class
```
Public UserIDHeaderValue As UserIDHeader

<System.Web.Services.Protocols.SoapHeaderAttribute( _
   "UserIDHeaderValue", Required:=false)> _
   Public Function GetSquare(ByVal inputVal As Double) As Double

      Dim results() As Object = Me.Invoke("GetSquare", _
          New Object() {inputVal})


              Return CType(results(0),Double)
End Function
```

So we have added a class derived from SoapHeader and the SoapHeader attributes to the original XML Web service code. The next step is to modify the client application to provide the value for the custom Header field when calling the Web service method. Listing 4.8 shows the client application code. The lines in bold show the new code that was added to the procedure since Exercise 4.2. First, declare and instantiate a local variable of type UserHeaderID, as defined in our XML Web service. Set the userID property of the object to the desired value. Assign the UserIDHeaderValue property of the Web service Square object to the local object that we just created and populated with values.

Listing 4.8: Setting a Value for the SOAP Header in Client Code

```
Private Sub btnSquare_Click(ByVal sender As Object, _
    ByVal e As System.EventArgs) Handles btnSquare.Click

    Dim objSquare As SquareRootService.Square = _
        New SquareRootService.Square()

    Dim custID As SquareRootService.UserIDHeader = _
        New SquareRootService.UserIDHeader()
    custID.userID = "X75042"
    objSquare.UserIDHeaderValue = custID

    Dim inputValue As Double
    Dim webResult As Double

    inputValue = CType(txtValue.Text, Double)
    webResult = objSquare.GetSquare(inputValue)
    txtResult.Text = webResult.ToString
    objSquare = Nothing
End Sub
```

Finally, let's add code to the XML Web service to read the user ID that is passed with the method call. In Listing 4.9, the bold lines have been added to access the header information and take appropriate action based on the value that is found. The variable shown here, custID, is the new public variable that was added to the Web service code in Listing 4.6.

Listing 4.9: Modifying the XML Web Service Code to Retrieve the SOAP Header Value

```
<WebMethod(Description:="Get the square of a number"), _
 SoapHeader("custID", Required:=False)> _
        Public Function GetSquare(ByVal inputVal As Double) As Double
        If custID.userID = "X75042" Then
            Return inputVal * inputVal
        Else
            Return 0
        End If
    End Function
```

This technique shows how to pass user information by using custom SOAP headers. This example is intended to demonstrate how to use SOAP headers to pass additional information with your Web service request. By themselves, SOAP headers are not a secure communication, so extra steps to encrypt the user information would be required in a production XML Web service. Security options for XML Web services are discussed in Chapter 9, "Overview of Security Concepts," and Chapter 11.

In Exercise 4.5, you will create customized SOAP headers by modifying the projects that you completed in Exercises 4.1 and 4.2.

EXERCISE 4.5

Using Customized SOAP Headers

1. Open the Visual Studio .NET XML Web service project, called SquareRootService, that you created in Exercise 4.1. Add another Imports statement to the top of the Square.asmx code module:

   ```
   Imports System.Web.Services.Protocols
   ```

2. Create a new class in Square.asmx as shown in this code snippet:

   ```
   Public Class UserIDHeader
       Inherits SoapHeader
       Public userID As String
   End Class
   ```

3. Add the SoapHeader attribute to both of your Web methods as shown:

   ```
   <WebMethod(Description:="Get the square of a number"), _
    SoapHeader("custID", Required:=False)> _
       Public Function GetSquare(ByVal inputVal As Double) As Double
   ```

4. Declare a class-level variable of type UserIDHeader:

   ```
   Public custID As UserIDHeader
   ```

   Refer to Listing 4.6 to see what the complete code should look like.

5. Modify the code inside of each Web method to read the custom value:

   ```
   <WebMethod(Description:="Get the square of a number"), _
    SoapHeader("custID", Required:=False)> _
       Public Function GetSquare(ByVal inputVal As Double) As Double
           If custID.userID = "X75042" Then
               Return inputVal * inputVal
           Else
               Return 0
           End If
       End Function
   ```

6. Save your work and build the SquareRootService.

Now you will modify the Windows client application that you created in Exercise 4.2 to set the value of the custom SOAP header when calling the Web service method.

7. Open the Visual Studio .NET project, called SquareRootClientProject, that you created in Exercise 4.2.

8. Delete the existing Web reference to the SquareRootService; then add a reference to the newly modified version. Rename the web reference from localhost to **SquareRootService** the same way that you did in Exercise 4.2. This will cause Visual Studio .NET to generate a new proxy class in your project that contains the SOAP header information.

9. Add the following code to the btnSquare_Click event procedure, before calling the Web service method. See Listing 4.8 to see what the complete code should look like.

```
Dim custID As SquareRootService.UserIDHeader = _
    New SquareRootService.UserIDHeader()
custID.userID = "X75042"
objSquare.UserIDHeaderValue = custID
```

10. Save your work and test the client application.

SOAP Extensions

A SOAP extension is a custom procedure that runs during a specified stage of SOAP message processing. When a client creates a SOAP request, the data from the client application must be serialized, or written out to the SOAP XML format, so that it can be sent to the Web service over HTTP. You might want to insert a SOAP extension in the AfterSerialize stage of the extension's SoapExtension.ProcessMessage method to encrypt all application data before sending to the Web service. When the SOAP message reaches the Web service, there is a BeforeDeserialize stage in the extension's SoapExtension.ProcessMessage method, during which a decryption procedure could be run to decrypt all data. This is an example of when both the client and the XML Web service must each run a SOAP extension in order for the process to work. Also, it's important to synchronize when your extension processing occurs—if you are doing encryption or compression after serializing the data on one side, make sure you decrypt or decompress before deserializing on the other side. Conversely, if you are selectively encrypting or compressing at the BeforeSerialize stage, the other side of your connection should apply the same selective techniques at the AfterDeserialize stage. Other examples—for example, when you are logging incoming requests to the web service—would require SOAP extensions to be added only at the web server side.

Working with SOAP extensions is similar to the process outlined in the preceding section on SOAP headers. You begin by creating a class that inherits from System.Web.Services.Protocols.SoapExtension. This is where the working code of the extension is located. This class must override methods defined by the *SoapExtension base class*. These methods are listed here:

GetInitializer   This method runs the first time an XML Web service or a particular method is called. Values that are initialized in this procedure are cached and can be used for all future method calls on the service.

Initialize   This method is called for every method call to the web service and is automatically passed the data that was stored in cache during the GetInitializer method.

ChainStream   This method enables you to store the incoming SOAP message (in a Stream object) and create a new Stream object to hold output from the extension. During subsequent processing of the extension code, you should read data from the incoming stream and write data to the new output stream.

ProcessMessage   This method is where you perform the desired processing on the SOAP message. Typically, you will test the Stage property of the incoming message and use conditional logic in the procedure to determine the appropriate action to take. The Stage property will be one of the following: BeforeSerialize, AfterSerialize, BeforeDeserialize, AfterDeserialize.

Summary

In this chapter, you learned about creating and managing XML Web services. We covered the following topics:

- An introduction to how XML Web services work. XML Web services are nonproprietary and cross-platform.
- The underlying technologies that support XML Web services are HTTP, XML, XSD, and SOAP.
- UDDI is a mechanism for locating available XML Web services via an online registry system. It can be searched manually or through a programmatic interface.
- The properties and methods of the .NET Framework System.Web.Services base class, from which all XML Web services application classes must inherit.
- How to use Visual Studio .NET to quickly create an XML Web service. How to test XML Web services directly from a web browser.
- .NET Framework attributes are defined to mark WebService classes and WebMethods.
- Other attributes, such as SoapDocumentMethod and SoapRpcMethod, can determine how the XML wire format of the SOAP message is created.
- How static and dynamic discovery documents are generated, so that clients can locate XML Web services on a server.
- How Web Services Description Language (WSDL) provides clients with information on available Web methods, parameter requirements, and return values.
- How to use Visual Studio .NET to create both Windows and web-based client applications to consume XML Web services.
- How to call Web methods asynchronously from your client applications by using the AsyncCallback class.
- How to create and use custom SOAP headers to pass application-specific data along with an XML Web service request.
- How to create and use SOAP extensions to run custom processing code at different stages of SOAP message transmission.

Exam Essentials

Know how to create and consume an XML Web service.   Visual Studio .NET offers you a built-in template that makes setting up XML Web services easy. XML Web service applications inherit from the `System.Web.Services` namespace. Client applications use a proxy class, generated when a reference is added to the client project, in order to communicate with an XML Web service as though it were a local class. After the Web reference is added, local objects that represent the Web service can be instantiated and method calls on these proxy objects are forwarded to the XML Web service.

Be familiar with the attributes that are available for the `System.Web.Services.WebService` class.   Know how to use the `WebService` and `WebMethod` attributes. Know how to control the way that the XML wire format for the SOAP message is created by using the `SoapDocument-Method` and `SoapRpcMethod` attributes.

Know how to instantiate and invoke an XML Web service.   Use Visual Studio .NET to set web references to XML Web services in your client applications. Understand how a proxy class is generated so that you can call XML Web service methods, just as if you were calling methods on a local object.

Know how to create client applications that call Web methods asynchronously.   Use the `Begin`*methodname* and `End`*methodname* procedures that are automatically generated in the proxy class code to initiate and complete asynchronous calls. Use the .NET Framework `AsyncCallback` class to enable this behavior.

Understand how custom SOAP headers enable you to pass application-specific identifiers as a part of the SOAP message.   Know how to add a class to your XML Web service project that has public variables to handle the custom SOAP header fields. Instantiate an instance of this class in your client project to set values for the custom SOAP header fields. Retrieve the custom SOAP header values that are passed to your Web method code.

Understand how to add custom processing while sending and receiving SOAP messages by using SOAP extensions.   Know how to add a class to your XML Web services project that inherits from the `SoapExtension` base class and overrides the base methods for `GetInitializer`, `Initialize`, `ChainStream`, and `ProcessMessage`.

Key Terms

Before you take the exam, be certain you are familiar with the following terms:

asynchronous callbacks	dynamic discovery
discovery	Extensible Markup Language (XML)
document encoding	Hypertext Transfer Protocol (HTTP)

proxy class

RPC encoding

Simple Object Access Protocol (SOAP)

`SoapDocumentMethod` attribute

`SoapExtension` base class

`SoapHeader` attribute

`SoapHeader` class

`SoapRpcMethod` attribute

`static discovery`

`System.Web.Services.dll`

`System.Web.Services.WebService`

`System.Web.Services.Protocols`
`.SoapHeader` class

Uniform Resource Identifier (URI)

Uniform Resource Locator (URL)

Universal Description, Discovery, and
Integration (UDDI)

Web Services Description Language (WSDL)

`WebMethod` attribute

`WebService` attribute

`wsdl.exe`

XML Schema Definition (XSD Schema)

XML Web services

Review Questions

1. Which item is a message-based protocol that enables applications to call each other's methods over the Internet or other network?

A. HTTP

B. UDDI

C. XML

D. SOAP

2. When creating an XML Web service application in the .NET Framework, what filename extension is used for your main source code pages?

A. `.aspx`

B. `.wsdl`

C. `.asmx`

D. `.disco`

3. When creating an XML Web service class, which one of the .NET Framework system classes do you need to inherit from?

A. `System.Web.Services.WebServices`

B. `System.Web.Protocols.SoapMessage`

C. `System.WebServices`

D. `System.Web.Services.WebServiceAttribute`

4. When you need to specify the exact format for the way that the XML tags in a SOAP message are created, which attribute should you add to your Web methods?

A. `SoapDocumentMethod`

B. `SoapRpcMethod`

C. `SoapHeader`

D. `SoapExtension`

5. What does a WSDL document contain?

A. The source code for your Web service

B. A list of directories on your web server that contain XML Web services applications

C. A description of your Web service's methods, parameters, and return values

D. An HTML page so that users can test your web service

6. When using Visual Studio .NET to create a client application that calls an XML Web service, how do you get information at design time about the web service's interface?

    A. By reading the WSDL file.

    B. From documentation provided by the owner of the XML Web service.

    C. When you add a web reference to your Visual Studio .NET project, a proxy class is added to your project.

    D. By adding a reference to `System.Web.Services`.

7. You are creating a web services client application. You want to make an asynchronous call on a Web method called `GetCustomerID`. What should you do?

    A. Add a method to the proxy class called `GetCustomerIDAsync`.

    B. Add a method to the your application code called `BeginGetCustomerID`.

    C. Call the method `GetCustomerIDAsync` from the proxy class.

    D. Call the method `BeginGetCustomerID` from the proxy class.

8. What is the purpose of using a SOAP extension?

    A. To add custom fields to the Body section of the SOAP message

    B. To perform custom processing each time a SOAP message is sent or received

    C. To enable SOAP messages to be read by operating systems other than Windows

    D. To enable SOAP messages to be read by programs written in languages other than Visual Basic .NET

9. What is the purpose of an XSD document?

    A. It contains a description for an exact format of XML markup that an application requires.

    B. It contains a list of directories on your web server that contain XML Web services applications.

    C. It contains a description of your web service's methods, parameters, and return values.

    D. It is an HTML page so that users can test your web service.

10. What is the purpose of UDDI?

    A. To provide a searchable, centralized registry of available XML Web services.

    B. To provide a list of directories on your web server that contain XML Web services applications.

    C. To describe a web service's methods, parameters, and return values.

    D. It is an Internet network protocol.

11. You are creating the source code for an XML Web service. What will be the result if you do not mark some of the procedures in your code with the `WebMethod` attribute?

    A. You will receive a compilation error when you try to build your project.

    B. You will receive an HTTP error when you try to test your web service.

    C. Users of your web service will receive an unhandled exception if they try to call that method.

    D. That method will not be visible to users of your web service.

12. When Visual Studio .NET creates a new ASP.NET Web services project from the template, it assigns a default namespace URI of `http://tempuri.org/`. Should you change this value?

    A. No, it is required that all XML Web services use this namespace.

    B. Yes, you should change it to an identifier that is unique to your own organization.

    C. Yes, you should change it to the URL where you will be deploying the XML Web service.

    D. Yes, you should change it to a new domain name that is registered strictly for that XML Web service.

13. You want to add custom SOAP headers to your XML Web services project. Which of these code segments is correct?

    A.
```
Public Class myCustomHeader
Inherits SoapHeader
Public userID As String
Public userName As String
End Class
```

    B.
```
Private Class myCustomHeader
Inherits SoapHeader
Private userID As String
Private userName As String
End Class
```

    C.
```
Public Class myCustomHeader
Inherits SoapExtension
Public userID As String
Public userName As String
End Class
```

    D.
```
Public Class myCustomHeader
Inherits WebService
Public userID As SoapHeader
Public userName As SoapHeader
End Class
```

14. When you are creating a SOAP extension, your code must override certain methods of the base `SoapExtension` class. Which of these is the method where the main functionality of the extension is carried out?

A. `Initialize`

B. `ProcessMessage`

C. `InputMessage`

D. `OutputMessage`

15. You have developed an XML Web services application and you have created a client project for testing the web service. Since you first created the test client, you have added new methods to the web service, but you cannot access the new methods from your test client. How can you most easily solve this problem?

A. After rebuilding your XML Web service project, add the new methods to the proxy class in your client project.

B. After rebuilding your XML Web service project, delete the existing Web reference in the client project and then add a new Web reference to regenerate the proxy class to match the updated web service.

C. After rebuilding your XML Web service project, stop and restart the web server.

D. After rebuilding your XML Web service project, you will have to create a new test client project. The old one will no longer work.

Answers to Review Questions

1. D. Simple Object Access Protocol (SOAP) is a message-based means for applications to communicate over the Internet or a network. HTTP is a lower-level protocol that can send text and other data types over the Internet. XML is a markup language that describes data. UDDI is a registry system for XML Web services.

2. C. When working with ASP.NET-based XML Web services, `.asmx` is the filename extension used for your source code pages. The extension `.aspx` is used for standard ASP.NET pages. The `.wsdl` and `.disco` files contain XML documents that provide discovery and Web Services Description Language information.

3. A. The `System.Web.Services` namespace contains the `WebServices` class, which is the base class for all XML Web services.

4. A. `SoapDocumentMethod` specifies that the XML tags should be created in the exact format specified by the XSD Schema information that is in a Web service's WSDL document. `SoapRpc-Method` follows the generic encoding rules from the SOAP specification. The `SoapHeader` and `SoapExtension` attributes are not directly related to encoding format.

5. C. The WSDL file contains a complete description of your web service, including all the available methods, the name and data type of all parameters, and return values. Source code for a web service is in an `.asmx` file. If you wish to provide a list of searchable directories on your server, you use a `.disco` or `.vsdisco` file. An HTML page is not required for web services. Visual Studio .NET provides a default test page that works with all web services.

6. C. Visual Studio .NET makes it easy to create web service clients, because it can use the WSDL information to generate a proxy class. After the proxy class is added to your project, you can take advantage of Intellisense in Visual Studio .NET. Although it is possible to read the WSDL document, and some web service creators might provide documentation, the proxy class is the easiest and most direct way to interact with the web service. A client application does not need to reference `System.Web.Services`.

7. D. When Visual Studio .NET generates the proxy class, the `Begin`*methodname* and `End`*method-name* methods (to be used for asynchronous calls) are automatically created for each method exposed by the web service. All you need to do is call `BeginGetCustomerID` (and later `EndGet-CustomerID`) from the proxy class. You do not need to add any methods manually. There is no method with the name `GetCustomerIDAsync` automatically defined.

8. B. SOAP extensions enable you to include custom processing on the client, server, or both, each time a SOAP message is sent or received. SOAP headers enable you to add items to the message itself. SOAP is a nonproprietary standard that uses XML and text files; these can be read by any operating system or programming language.

9. A. An XSD Schema document contains a description for an exact format of XML markup. Visual Studio .NET includes XSD information in the WSDL documents that describe a web service interface. XSD Schema can be used for processing all types of XML documents, however—not just in relation to XML Web services. If you wish to provide a list of searchable directories on your server, you use a `.disco` or `.vsdisco` file. An HTML page is not required for web services. Visual Studio .NET provides a default test page that works with all web services.

10. A. Universal Description, Discovery, and Integration (UDDI) is a system for establishing searchable, central registries of available XML Web services. If you wish to provide a list of searchable directories on your server, you use a `.disco` or `.vsdisco` file. An individual web service's methods, parameters, and return values are described in a WSDL file. HTTP is the primary Internet protocol used by XML Web services.

11. D. Any methods that are not marked with the `WebMethod` attribute will not be a part of the public interface of the web service; therefore, users will not be able to call the methods. They are considered private methods and can be called from other code inside the web service. This is valid code and should not, by itself, cause any errors to occur.

12. B. The default namespace should be set to an identifier that uniquely identifies the organization publishing the XML Web service. Conventionally an organization's Internet domain name is used, but the value can be any unique string; it does not need to be a valid URL. It is not necessary to register a domain name for an individual XML Web service.

13. A. Define custom SOAP headers by adding a public class to your XML Web service project. This class must inherit from `System.Web.Services.Protocols.SoapHeader` and must include public variables to hold the data items for the custom headers.

14. B. `ProcessMessage` is the name of the `SoapExtension` class method where the main processing is carried out. `Initialize` is also a valid method, used to read in any necessary initialization data. `InputMessage` and `OutputMessage` are not methods defined by the base class.

15. B. After making changes to the web service, you must drop the existing Web reference and create a new one so a proxy class can be generated that matches the current version of the web service. This is all that is necessary to update the client project. The first option is feasible, but you should avoid adding code to the proxy class manually. ASP.NET does not require you to stop and restart the server to update applications.

Chapter

5

Working with the .NET Data Providers

MICROSOFT EXAM OBJECTIVES COVERED IN THIS CHAPTER:

✓ Access and manipulate data from a Microsoft SQL Server database by creating and using ad hoc queries and stored procedures.

The task of data access is common to almost every business application that you will develop. Accordingly, this topic is emphasized in the certification exams. To thoroughly cover all the new capabilities for working with data in the .NET Framework classes, this book divides the overall topic of data access into three chapters.

This chapter and Chapter 6, "Working with the DataSet," cover the classes found in the `System.Data` namespace, what we know as ADO.NET. ADO.NET is Microsoft's newest object model for data access. The classic ADO object model, introduced about five years ago, offered relatively few objects to work with, but each of those objects had long lists of properties and parameters that enabled the developer to fine-tune their behavior for different tasks. ADO.NET offers a larger number of classes, but each is designed to perform a specific task.

Chapter 7, "Working With XML Data," shows both the XML capabilities of ADO.NET and the classes in the `System.Xml` namespace. You will see where the functionality overlaps and learn which classes to choose to get your work accomplished.

Within the `System.Data` namespace, you will find many new objects, the examples in the chapter will help you understand the differences between the old ADO model and the new ADO.NET model, and how to choose which of the new classes to use for a specific task. This book makes the distinction between objects that operate directly against the database—such as Connections, Commands, and the DataReader—and the new ADO.NET DataSet object, which is a disconnected data store providing considerable functionality to your applications for working with data.

This chapter covers direct database access. It begins with a discussion of the differences between the .NET data providers. Then you will learn about connecting to a database. You will learn how to use the versatile Command object to create a DataReader; to send SQL insert, update, and delete instructions; and to call stored procedures with parameters. The chapter concludes with some of the other classes in the new ADO.NET model, including the `Transaction`, `Exception`, and `Error` classes.

Consuming and Manipulating Data with ADO.NET

The *System.Data namespace* in the .NET Framework class library provides the classes that you need to work with data and databases. The primary distinction to be made among the ADO.NET objects is whether the objects directly connect to a specific type of database (as the Connection, Command, or DataAdapter objects do) or whether the objects are used by the client application in a disconnected manner. The DataSet object is meant to be used as a disconnected data store. The DataSet is similar to the disconnected recordset in the classic ADO object model, but it has even greater functionality. The `System.Data` namespace directly contains the `DataSet` class and its supporting objects, such as DataTables, DataRows, DataColumns, DataViews, and others.

The DataSet and the related classes are the subject of Chapter 6, which covers working with disconnected data in detail.

The `System.Data` namespace contains additional, more specialized namespaces such as *System.Data.SqlClient* and *System.Data.OleDb*. Their classes are designed to connect directly to different categories of databases. The differences between these specialized namespaces are discussed in the next section. For the most part, each namespace contains an equivalent set of classes, which work the same way. There are a few minor differences in the way that the classes have been implemented. One detail that you might notice right away is that the objects are named differently. When you use the class names in your code, you will actually use either a *SqlConnection* object or an *OleDbConnection* object. As you read the rest of this chapter, keep in mind that in general discussion we use a generic name of Connection or Command, but in code examples or when discussing a specific class, we use their proper names.

After you are familiar with using the classes in the `System.Data.SqlClient` namespace, for example, it should not be difficult to write an application that targets a database other than Microsoft SQL Server 2000 and requires the use of the `System.Data.OleDb` classes. The examples in this chapter use the `System.Data.SqlClient` classes for consistency.

Working with .NET Data Providers

The `System.Data.SqlClient` and `System.Data.OleDb` namespaces provide classes that are optimized to use a specific database access API. Database access is accomplished through one of the .NET data providers. .NET data providers are the Common Language Runtime (CLR) equivalent of the OleDb providers that were used with classic ADO for the Win32/COM platform.

Your first step is to determine which one of the .NET data providers (and which namespace) is appropriate for the database you are using. The .NET data providers are as follows:

- `System.Data.SqlClient`
- `System.Data.OleDb`
- `System.Data.Odbc`
- Any .NET data providers from a third party

If your application targets Microsoft SQL Server 7, SQL Server 2000, or later versions, you can use classes in the `System.Data.SqlClient` namespace. These are optimized to provide the best performance by using SQL Server's native Tabular Data Stream (TDS) protocol.

If your application must support older versions of Microsoft SQL Server, Microsoft Access databases, Oracle, or others, then you must use the `System.Data.OleDb` classes.

The Open DataBase Connectivity (ODBC) data provider is not installed as part of the Visual Studio .NET package but can be downloaded from the Microsoft website. You will need the classes in this library if you are supporting legacy systems that cannot be accessed with the OleDb data provider.

It is expected that as the .NET development platform grows in popularity, third-party database software vendors will create custom data providers for their own products.

If you are working in Visual Studio .NET, a reference will automatically be set to the `System.Data.dll` for most project types. If not, you must add this reference manually. The `System.Data.dll` assembly supports both `System.Data.SqlClient` and `System.Data.OleDb`. If you install the ODBC data provider or any third-party providers, you will have to set references to the appropriate assemblies.

Connecting to a Data Source

After you have decided which of the .NET data providers you need to use, your next step is to declare and instantiate a Connection object. Listing 5.1 shows a simple example using the SqlClient data provider. This section will also discuss how to handle usernames and passwords, how connection pooling is used, where to store connection string information and the importance of closing connections promptly.

Listing 5.1: A Typical SqlClient Connection String

```
Imports System.Data
Imports System.Data.SqlClient

Public Sub GetDataList()

    Dim strConnect as String = _
      "Data Source=localhost;Initial " & _
      "Catalog=pubs; Integrated Security=SSPI; "

    Dim myConn As SqlConnection = _
       New SqlConnection(strConnect)
    myConn.Open()

     'continue with the work of this function

    myConn.Close()
End Sub
```

First, the `Imports` statements are placed at the top of the code module. This enables you to declare the objects with their short type names, rather than having to specify a fully qualified reference every time you use them in your code. Without the `Imports` statements, your declaration for the `SqlConnection` object would look like the following code:

```
Dim myConn As System.Data.SqlClient.SqlConnection = New _
    System.Data.SqlClient.SqlConnection(strConnect)
```

We are taking advantage of the `SqlConnection` object's parameterized constructor to set the *ConnectionString property* directly, at the same time as it is instantiated. Another option is to use the default constructor and then later set the `ConnectionString` property in a separate line of code, as shown here:

```
Dim myConn As SqlConnection = New SqlConnection()
myConn.ConnectionString = _
    "Data Source=localhost; Initial " & _
    "Catalog=pubs; Integrated Security=SSPI; "
```

The connection string in this example is simple and contains the minimum information required to make a connection. The connection string must always be set before the connection is opened, and it cannot be changed after the connection is open.

Let's examine each part of the connection string:

Data source   This is the machine name of the computer that is running SQL Server. In this case, our application is running on the same machine as SQL Server (common for web applications and server components), so we can use the generic reference `localhost` to indicate that.

Initial catalog   This is the name of the specific database that we want to access.

Integrated security   This indicates that the current user's Windows credentials are being used to access SQL Server. We will discuss this further in the next section, "Protecting Usernames and Passwords."

Many other settings can be passed as a part of the connection string. You can use these to control the way that connection pooling works, the length of the time-out period, and security options. Some of these connection string options, particularly those that have to do with connection pooling, will be discussed later in this chapter. Connection strings require exact syntax, including spacing and case sensitivity in some cases. Take care when creating them. In Chapter 6, you will see some Visual Studio .NET tools that will help you create connection strings.

Working with the `OleDbConnection` object is similar to using the `SqlConnection` object. However, because the OleDb .NET data provider can be used to connect to several types of databases, you must specify a provider name in the connection string. These provider names will be the same ones that were used with earlier versions of ADO. Here is an example of a connection string for a Microsoft Access database:

```
Dim myConn As OleDbConnection = New _
    OleDbConnection()
myConn.ConnectionString = _
    "Provider=Microsoft.Jet.OLEDB.4.0; Data " & _
    "Source=C:\data\northwind.mdb; User ID=guest; " & _
    "Password=p5n7u!N"
```

While this example provides a valid connection string, putting usernames and passwords directly into your source code can provide problems both with security and maintenance. In the next section we will talk about other strategies for storing this sensitive information.

Protecting Usernames and Passwords

Exposing username and password information in your connection string code is one of the greatest database security vulnerabilities. Anyone with access to your source code can take this information and use it to access the database via their own programs, perhaps getting to data that they should not be able to see or modify.

A better option is to use *Windows Integrated Security*. This is a more secure method and is considered a security "best practice" when your application is running in an environment enabling you to take advantage of it—that is, when all users running your application are connected to the same local network. A connection string that specifies Windows Integrated Security would look like this:

```
myConn.ConnectionString = _
    "Data Source=localhost; Initial " & _
    "Catalog=pubs; Integrated Security=SSPI; "
```

Windows Integrated Security also provides benefits in terms of ongoing security maintenance. A Windows group can be created specifically for users who are authorized to run the application (and to see any sensitive data that the application might be processing). Network administrators are responsible for adding new authorized users and removing those who no longer are allowed access. The SQL Server administrator can simply add the group to the list of authorized users in the application database and set the appropriate permissions.

If users of web applications are connecting to your server through the public Internet, you will have to prompt them for username and password information when they connect to your site. You can verify their credentials in a variety of ways (see Chapter 9, "Overview of Security Concepts," for more information on security considerations). After you have established that they are valid users of your service, you can have the application connect to the database by using a designated Windows login and password for the application.

 **Real World Scenario**

Security Considerations: Blank Passwords and SQL Injection Attacks

In the discussion of databases in general and Microsoft SQL Server in particular, there are two common security risks that you should be aware of.

The first is that SQL Server is often installed with default settings. It is not at all uncommon to find servers that allow applications to connect with a login name of sa (system administrator) and a blank password. Any client program that can access your SQL Server database, including those run on unknown hosts around the Internet if your server is Internet-accessible, can access the database if they know the login name and password used.

The second security-related problem is that developers often accept user input and then pass that input string directly into a SQL query, without performing any checks for validity. Some developers think that this doesn't matter because the application is coded to access only certain data and run specific queries, so users won't be able to do any harm. However, attackers have found a way to exploit this lack of security. Your code might be asking the user to supply something innocent such as a name to search for, but the attacker can send additional instructions along with the innocent data. For example, your code might accept user input and build a query something like this:

```
SELECT * FROM Customers WHERE LastName LIKE userinput
```

This works fine for regular users who will enter only plausible data. But it leaves an open opportunity for the attacker who will try to inject additional SQL instructions along with the simple data. An attacker might try to send something like this as an input string:

```
Smith; DROP TABLE importantTable
```

Your innocuous query will execute, finding matching customer names, but the semicolon character indicates to SQL Server that a second command is to be performed—and the attacker has sent along an additional, destructive command. If the connection is made under a highly privileged account, such as sa, the attacker could be successful in destroying valuable data.

Another SQL injection approach is for the attacker to add instructions to set their own username, password, and permissions, so they can access your complete database later on, at their convenience.

It's the combination of leaving defaults in place, running code under highly privileged accounts, and not checking user input that makes you vulnerable to this type of attack.

Using Connection Pooling to Optimize Performance

Connection pooling is a mechanism that maintains a group of already initialized connections to the database. When a user requests a connection, an existing one in the pool can be made available more quickly than if it were being initialized at the user's request. When the user releases the connection, it can be returned to the pool and recycled for the next user.

One disadvantage of Integrated Security is that each connection to the database is made under an individual username. This defeats the connection pooling mechanism of the .NET data providers. If your application needs to take advantage of the performance enhancement of connection pooling, every connection to the database must use exactly the same connection string. This requires a model in which individual users are authorized by the application as necessary, but a single username and password for the application are used in the connection string for every access to the database.

You can also make settings such as minimum and maximum pool size and connection lifetime. Use these settings to optimize performance. If you don't maintain enough connections in the pool, users will have to wait for a connection to be created or to become available. If the connection string's Connect Timeout period expires before a connection is available, an error occurs. If you create too many connections, you will be using memory unnecessarily. Some additional items that can be added to the connection string to control connection pooling behavior are listed in Table 5.1.

TABLE 5.1   Additional Connection String Properties to Control Connection Pooling

Property	Descriptions
Connection Lifetime	Determines how long a connection will be maintained in the pool. A value of zero (0), the default, will cause pooled connections to have the maximum time-out.
Connection Reset	Determines whether the database connection is reset when being removed from the pool. If the connection is not reset, the next user might inherit some properties that were set by the previous user. The default is True.
Enlist	Determines whether the connection will be enlisted in the current transaction. The default is True.
Max Pool Size	Determines the maximum number of connections allowed in the pool. The default is 100.
Min Pool Size	Determines the minimum number of connections maintained in the pool. The default is 0.
Pooling	Determines whether pooling is enabled. The default is True.

Storing Connection String Information

Connection strings are considered sensitive data because they contain server names (or worse, IP addresses!), database names, usernames, and passwords. Because of security concerns, this information must be in a secure location where those who might try to break into your database cannot read it.

Connection strings also require ongoing maintenance because over time, and in different installations, this information might need to be changed. Because of the ongoing maintenance requirements, it is preferable to store the information outside of compiled code, in a location where the application can read it at runtime. This is usually accomplished by putting the information into an application's configuration file. Information specific to configuring various types of components can be found in Chapter 10, "Deploying, Securing, and Configuring Windows-based Applications," and Chapter 11, "Deploying and Securing XML Web Services."

Closing Connections

When working with data providers, it is important to make sure that you explicitly call the Connection object's Close or Dispose method when you have completed your work with the database.

Ideally, you will open and close a connection within the scope of one method call. Doing this releases the user's connection to the database (which in some cases might be limited to a specific number of concurrent users due to licensing) and enables other users to access this resource.

Sending Commands to a Data Source

In this section we will see how to use methods of the Command object to send different types of commands to the data source. The most commonly used commands are likely to be SQL SELECT queries, which will return rows of data to your application. We will see how to use a DataReader object to access the data that is retrieved from this type of command. We will discuss important parameters that can modify the Command object's behavior when executing commands. Finally, we will learn how to use the Command object to send queries to the database that do not return rows of data. These may be SQL INSERT, UPDATE, and DELETE queries, or queries that perform calculations.

The SqlCommand and OleDbCommand objects have a few important properties. These are shown in Table 5.2.

TABLE 5.2 Selected Properties of the Command Object

Property	Description
CommandText	Gets or sets the SQL statement or stored procedure name to execute at the data source.
CommandTimeout	Gets or sets the wait time before terminating the attempt to execute a command and generating an error. The default is 30 seconds.
CommandType	Gets or sets a value indicating how the CommandText property is to be interpreted (Text, Stored Procedure, or TableDirect). The default is CommandType.Text.
Connection	Gets or sets the connection used by this command.
Parameters	Gets the ParameterCollection.
Transaction	Gets or sets the transaction in which the command executes.

The *CommandText property* and *CommandType property* indicate the type of instruction that you will be sending to the database. There are three possibilities:

- If you would like to build a SQL statement in your code and submit this query to the database, the CommandType property is set to Text (that is, CommandType.Text), and the corresponding CommandText property to a string that contains your SQL statement.

- If you would like to call a stored procedure, the CommandType property is set to Stored-Procedure, and the CommandText property is set to a string that contains the name of the stored procedure as defined in the database.

- If you would like to access an entire table (recommended small tables only, such as a list of categories), the CommandType property is set to TableDirect, and the CommandText property is set to a string that contains the name of the table as defined in the database.

You must also set the command's Connection property to reference an existing Connection object that you have already created in your code.

As with most ADO.NET objects, SqlCommand and OleDbCommand have a set of overloaded constructor methods that enable you to create the objects in your code in various ways. With the Command objects, you can use the default constructor, with no parameters, to instantiate the objects and then set properties in separate lines of code. Listing 5.2 shows an example of this, by expanding on the code from Listing 5.1 (which showed how to create a connection).

Listing 5.2: Creating a Connection and Command

```
Imports System.Data
Imports System.Data.SqlClient

Public Sub GetDataList()
  Dim myConn As SqlConnection = New SqlConnection()
  Dim myQuery As SqlCommand = New SqlCommand()

  myConn.ConnectionString = _
    "Data Source=localhost; Initial " & _
    "Catalog=pubs; Integrated Security=SSPI; "
  myConn.Open()

  With myQuery
     .Connection = myConn
     .CommandType = CommandType.Text
     .CommandText = "SELECT * FROM publishers"
  End With


  'continue working with the data from the database
  myConn.Close()
End Sub
```

The other constructor methods for the Command object enable you to accomplish some of the property settings shown in Listing 5.2 all in one step, at the time you declare and instantiate the object. One of the constructors accepts a single string argument that contains the CommandText property. Another accepts two arguments: CommandText and a reference to the Connection object. Yet another constructor accepts three arguments: the text string, the Connection object, and a reference to an ADO.NET Transaction object. (Transaction objects are introduced later in this chapter, in the section titled "Understanding New Objects in the ADO.NET Object Model.") The following code example creates a Command object that is equivalent to the longer code in Listing 5.2:

```
Dim myQuery As SqlCommand = New SqlCommand( _
    "SELECT * FROM publishers", con)
myQuery.CommandType = CommandType.Text
```

After you have created a Command object and set its properties to define how it will work, the next step is to use one of the command methods to carry out your instruction against the database. Table 5.3 lists those methods.

TABLE 5.3 Methods of the *SqlCommand* and *OleDbCommand* Objects

Method	Description
Cancel	Cancels the execution of a command.
CreateParameter	Creates a new instance of a Parameter object.
ExecuteNonQuery	Executes a Transact-SQL statement against the connection and returns the number of rows affected, but not resultset data. Primarily used with SQL INSERT, UPDATE and DELETE statements.
ExecuteReader	Creates a DataReader based on the CommandText property. The DataReader is used to access the resultset data.
ExecuteScalar	Executes the query and returns a single value.
ExecuteXmlReader	Creates an XmlReader object based on the CommandText property. This method is available only for the SqlClient object and is used with queries that include the SQL Server 2000 FOR XML clause.
Prepare	Creates a prepared version of the command on the data source.
ResetCommandTimeout	Resets the CommandTimeout property to its default value.

Often your command will retrieve rows of data from the database, but there are other methods available for issuing other types of commands. The *ExecuteReader method* creates a DataReader object to retrieve rows of data, and the *ExeuteNonQuery method* and *ExecuteScalar method* issue commands that do not return rows of data. These latter two methods can be used with SQL INSERT, UPDATE, and DELETE statements or with SQL statements that calculate and aggregate values, such as a sum, count, or average.

The *ExecuteXMLReader method* is supported only by SqlDataReader for use with the special FOR XML clause of a SQL query that is unique to Microsoft SQL Server 2000. Executing this method returns data from the database in the form of an XML document rather than as a rowset. This method will create an object of type System.Xml.XMLTextReader to enable you to work with the data. The XMLTextReader object and working with XML data are covered in Chapter 7.

Using the DataReader

The *SqlDataReader class* and the *OleDbDataReader class* provide the similar functionality that was available in the original ADO object model by using a *forward-only*, *read-only recordset*. This is the object typically used when you are retrieving the data from the database only for the purpose of displaying that data for the user. When you use a DataReader, you can access each row in the resultset only once. The DataReader holds the connection to the database open until you have completed your work with the data, and then you must explicitly close the Data-Reader and the connection. The DataReader is always created by using the ExecuteReader method of a Command object. You cannot instantiate a DataReader by using the New keyword.

Before you look at an example of the DataReader, let's review the properties and methods that you will use while working with it. The properties of both the SqlDataReader and the OleDbDataReader are the same. Table 5.4 lists these properties.

TABLE 5.4   Properties of the *SqlDataReader* and the *OleDbDataReader*

Property	Description
Depth	Gets a value indicating the depth of nesting for the current row.
FieldCount	Gets the number of columns in the current row.
IsClosed	Indicates whether the DataReader is closed.
Item	Gets the value of a column in its native format.
RecordsAffected	Gets the number of rows changed, inserted, or deleted by execution of the SQL statement. This property will always return −1 for SQL SELECT statements.

Some of the methods for the SqlDataReader and the OleDbDataReader classes are different from one another. Table 5.5 lists those methods that they have in common. The SqlDataReader adds methods that work with Microsoft SQL Server 2000 native data types as discussed later in this section.

TABLE 5.5   Methods That Are Common to *SqlDataReader* and *OleDbDataReader*

Methods	Description
Read	Reads the next row of the DataReader.
Close	Closes the DataReader object.
IsDBNull	Gets a value indicating whether a specific column (by ordinal) is DBNull.

TABLE 5.5 Methods That Are Common to *SqlDataReader* and *OleDbDataReader (continued)*

Methods	Description
NextResult	Advances the DataReader to the next resultset, when reading the results of batch SQL statements.
Get*DataType*	Gets the value of the specified column as a specific .NET Framework data type, such as GetString, GetDateTime, etc.
GetBytes	Reads a stream of bytes, used primarily for binary large objects (BLOB data).
GetChars	Reads a stream of characters, used primarily for binary large objects (BLOB data).
GetDataTypeName	Gets the name of the source data type.
GetFieldType	Gets the type that is the data type of the object.
GetName	Gets the name of the specified column (by ordinal).
GetOrdinal	Gets an integer value that represents the column position when the column name is supplied.
GetSchemaTable	Returns a DataTable that describes the column metadata of the DataReader.
GetValue	Gets the value of a specific column (by ordinal) as a .NET Framework data type.
GetValues	Gets the values for all the columns in the current row as an Object array.

The Read and Close methods are used every time you work with a DataReader. The IsDBNull method enables you to test individual columns to see if their value is null. The NextResult method is used only when a single DataReader is used to retrieve the results of multiple SQL queries—for example, if you call a stored procedure that performs SELECT statements on multiple tables. Unlike the prior versions of ADO, you do not need to use any recordset navigation methods to iterate through all the rows. An example of this is shown in Listing 5.3.

Notice that to retrieve individual column values from a given row, you will use a method designed to retrieve the specific data type that each column contains (GetString or GetDateTime, for example). For the sake of brevity, we have summarized the set of Get*DataType* methods into one entry in Table 5.5. Please consult the Visual Studio .NET documentation for a complete list of all data type methods that are available.

The SqlDataReader class has an additional set of GetSql*DataType* methods. The methods that are supported by both DataReader classes are based on the data types that are defined by the .NET Framework. The GetSql*DataType* methods return values in the form of the native data types defined by SQL Server. Consult the Visual Studio .NET documentation for a complete listing of these under System.Data.SqlTypes.

In addition to the methods designed to retrieve a specific data type there are also methods that enable you to retrieve column data without knowing the data type in advance: GetValue and GetValues. Both of these return values as the .NET Framework type Object. The GetValues method will return all of the column values from a row at once, as an array of Object types. At first it might seem more convenient to use these methods rather than the methods that are specific to a particular data type. Keep in mind that you will most likely have to write additional code to test each value's data type and then do an explicit conversion before you can do any work with it.

Now that you have learned about the important methods of the SqlDataReader and OleDbDataReader objects, and some of the differences between the two, you are ready to see how they are used. Assuming that we are using the same Connection and Command objects that were shown in Listing 5.2, Listing 5.3 shows a section of code that creates and reads the data from a DataReader.

Listing 5.3: Creating a DataReader and Retrieving Column Values

```
Dim myReader As SqlDataReader
Dim outString As String

'use the existing Command object to create the DataReader
myReader = myQuery.ExecuteReader()

'set up a simple loop
Do While myReader.Read
   outString = myReader.GetString(0) & _
      myReader.GetString(1) & "<BR>"
   Response.Write(outString)
Loop

myReader.Close()
myConn.Close()
```

The ExecuteReader method of the existing Command object named myQuery will create the SqlDataReader. Then we will set up a loop. At the beginning of each iteration through the loop, the SqlDataReader object's Read method is called. This method will return True as long as there are more data rows available to read. Each time through the loop, we are simply building and outputting a string that consists of the values from the first two columns in the resultset. When we reach the end of the resultset and there are no more rows of data available, The Read method will return False and the code will exit the loop. Remember to use the SqlDataReader object's Close method when you are finished reading all the data and to also use the SqlConnection object's Close method when you have completed all your work with the database.

Modifying Command Behavior

The ExecuteReader method has an optional parameter called *CommandBehavior*. The most common use for this parameter is to take advantage of the CloseConnection option. This ensures that the connection will be closed at the same time that the DataReader is closed. You will see this option used in the examples in Exercise 5.1, where you will pass a SqlDataReader back from a function; then it is up to the code in the procedure that called the function to close the SqlDataReader when it is through using the data. Table 5.6 shows all the possible values for the CommandBehavior parameter. CommandBehavior values can be combined.

TABLE 5.6 The *Command.ExecuteReader (CommandBehavior)* Enumeration

Value	Description
CloseConnection	The associated Connection object is closed when the DataReader object is closed.
Default	No parameters are set.
KeyInfo	The query returns column and primary key information. The query is executed without any locking on the selected rows.
SchemaOnly	The query returns column information only and does not affect the database state.
SequentialAccess	Provides an efficient way for the DataReader to handle rows that contain columns with binary large objects (BLOB).
SingleResult	The query returns a single resultset.
SingleRow	The query is expected to return a single row. Some .NET data providers might, but are not required to, use this information to optimize the performance of the command.

Exercise 5.1 creates a simple web page application that retrieves and displays data in ASP.NET server controls. ASP.NET server controls can simply use data binding to read the values from the DataReader. Unfortunately, this ability in not available in Windows forms controls. Exercise 5.1 shows an example of data binding to controls and also has an example similar to Listing 5.3, which reads the individual values from the DataReader.

The exercises in this chapter use the Microsoft SQL Server 2000 sample database called pubs.

EXERCISE 5.1

Using Connection, Command, and DataReader Objects

1. Start Visual Studio .NET and open a new ASP.NET Web application project. Set the location to **http://localhost/DataReaderExamples**. Use your own web server name in place of localhost if appropriate.

2. Change the name of WebForm1.aspx to **default.aspx**.

3. Use the Properties window to change the pageLayout property of the document to **FlowLayout**.

4. Using the Visual Studio .NET Toolbox, drag the Web Forms DropDownList, Label, and Data-Grid controls to the design surface of default.aspx. Use the Properties window to set the AutoPostBack property of the DropDownList control to **True**. Your page should look like the following screen.

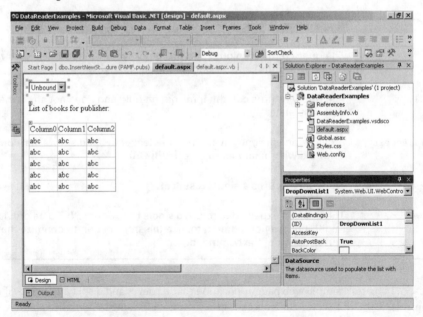

5. Right-click default.aspx in the Solution Explorer and choose View Code. Add the **Imports System.Data.SqlClient** statement at the top of the code module.

6. Create a Function procedure called **GetPublisherList**. This function will return a SqlDataReader object to the calling procedure. Add the following code to create and open a SqlConnection object:

```
Public Function GetPublisherList() As SqlDataReader
    Dim myConn As SqlConnection = New SqlConnection()
    myConn.ConnectionString = "Data Source=localhost; Initial " & _
        "Catalog=pubs; Integrated Security=SSPI; "
    myConn.Open()
```

7. Complete this function by writing the code to create SqlCommand and SqlDataReader objects to retrieve rows from the Publishers table and to return the DataReader to the calling procedure:

```
    Dim myPublishers As SqlCommand = New SqlCommand( _
        "SELECT pub_ID, pub_name FROM publishers", myConn)
    myPublishers.CommandType = CommandType.Text

    Dim myPubReader As SqlDataReader
    myPubReader = myPublishers.ExecuteReader(CommandBehavior.CloseConnection)

    Return myPubReader
End Function
```

8. In the Page_Load procedure for default.aspx, write the code to call the GetPublisherList function and display the data from the Publishers table in the DropDownList1 control:

```
Private Sub Page_Load(ByVal sender As System.Object, _
    ByVal e As System.EventArgs) Handles MyBase.Load

    Dim pubReader As SqlDataReader

    If Not Page.IsPostBack Then
        pubReader = GetPublisherList()

        With DropDownList1
            .DataSource = pubReader
            .DataValueField = "pub_ID"
            .DataTextField = "pub_name"
            .DataBind()
            .SelectedIndex = 0
        End With
        pubReader.Close()
    End If

End Sub
```

9. Save and test your work. You should see the DropDownList control populated with the names of eight publishers. You will not see the DataGrid yet.

EXERCISE 5.1 *(continued)*

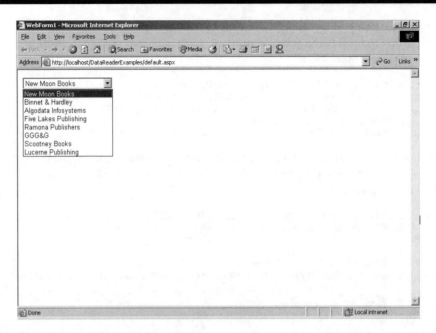

10. Create the `GetTitleList` function to retrieve data from the Titles table, based on publisher ID. This function takes one argument, the publisher ID, and will also return a `SqlDataReader`:

```
Public Function GetTitleList(ByVal pubID As String) As SqlDataReader

    Dim myConn As SqlConnection = New SqlConnection()
    myConn.ConnectionString = "Data Source=localhost; Initial " & _
        "Catalog=pubs; Integrated Security=SSPI; "
    myConn.Open()

    Dim sqlString As String = _
        "SELECT title, price, pubdate FROM titles " & _
            "WHERE pub_id = " & pubID

    Dim myTitles As SqlCommand = New SqlCommand(sqlString, myConn)
    myTitles.CommandType = CommandType.Text

    Dim myTitleReader As SqlDataReader
    myTitleReader = myTitles.ExecuteReader( _
        CommandBehavior.CloseConnection)

    Return myTitleReader

End Function
```

11. Declare a class level variable named pubID.

```
Private pubID As String
```

12. With the Page_Load procedure, declare another local variable as type `SqlDataReader`. Then, directly after the code from step 8, determine the ID value of the publisher that is currently selected in `DropDownList1` and store it in a variable. Then call the `GetTitleList` function, passing the publisher ID from the DropDownList selection.

```
'at the top of the page_load procedure
   Dim titleReader As SqlDataReader

'directly after the code from step 8
   pubID = DropDownList1.SelectedItem.Value
   titleReader = GetTitleList(pubID)
```

13. Write the code to display information from the Titles table in the DataGrid.

```
With DataGrid1
    .DataSource = titleReader
    .DataBind()
End With
TitleReader.Close()
```

14. Save and test your work. The complete code for the Page_Load event procedure is shown in Listing 5.4. Your finished page should look like the following graphic. Each time you change the publisher name that is selected in the DropDownList, a post back to the web application will occur, the `GetTitleList` function will be called, and the DataGrid will display the results of the new query. Not all publishers in the list have associated books in the Titles table.

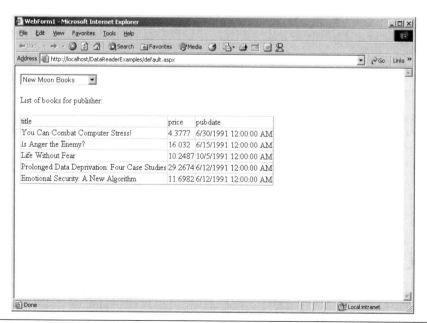

Listing 5.4: The Complete Code for the Page_Load Event Procedure for Exercise 5.1

```
Private Sub Page_Load(ByVal sender As System.Object, _
    ByVal e As System.EventArgs) Handles MyBase.Load

    Dim pubReader As SqlDataReader
    Dim titleReader As SqlDataReader

    If Not Page.IsPostBack Then
    'this code runs only the first time the page is loaded
        pubReader = GetPublisherList()
        With DropDownList1
            .DataSource = pubReader
            .DataValueField = "pub_ID"
            .DataTextField = "pub_name"
            .DataBind()
            .SelectedIndex = 0
        End With
        PubReader.Close()
    End If

    pubID = DropDownList1.SelectedItem.Value
    titleReader = GetTitleList(pubID)

    With DataGrid1
        .DataSource = titleReader
        .DataBind()
    End With
    titleReader.Close()
End Sub
```

Now you are familiar with the basics of using a Command object and the very useful Data-Reader for retrieving and displaying data from the database. There are other types of queries that you might need to perform against your database. You might want to issue SQL INSERT, UPDATE, or DELETE queries. You might want to execute a query that returns a single value, such as a count of rows in a table or a count of rows that match a SQL WHERE clause in your query. You can even use ADO.NET commands to issue Data Definition Language (DDL) queries that are used to make changes to the database structure. Next, you will look at other methods of the Command object.

Using Queries That Don't Return Rows

The Command object has two other methods you can use when you want to issue an instruction against your database that does not return rows of data: the ExecuteNonQuery method and the ExecuteScalar method.

ExecuteNonQuery is used for SQL statements that don't return rows. This method can also be used for calling stored procedures that return data via the Command object's Parameter collection (you will learn about stored procedures and parameters in the next section). ExecuteNonQuery will return the number of rows that were changed in the database as a result of your SQL instruction. You can check the RecordsAffected property after the query is run to verify that the operation completed as expected.

ExecuteScalar is used when you are performing a query that will return a single value, such as one of the aggregate functions (Count, Sum, Average) or perhaps a stored procedure that does some calculations.

Listing 5.5 shows an example of using the ExecuteNonQuery method to perform a SQL UPDATE statement.

Listing 5.5: Using the ExecuteNonQuery Method

```
Private Function DoUpdate() As Integer
    Dim recsUpdated As Integer

    Dim myConn As SqlConnection = New SqlConnection()
    myConn.ConnectionString = _
        "Data Source=localhost; Initial " & _
        "Catalog=pubs; Integrated Security=SSPI; "
    myConn.Open()

    Dim sqlString As String = "UPDATE titles SET " & _
        "price = price * 1.1"

    Dim myUpdate As SqlCommand = _
        New SqlCommand(sqlString, myConn)
    myUpdate.CommandType = CommandType.Text

    recsUpdated = myUpdate.ExecuteNonQuery()

    myConn.Close()

    Return recsUpdated

End Function
```

We have a function that performs an update on the database and returns the number of records affected. First we create a SqlConnection object. We have a SQL UPDATE statement that will change the value of the price column for every row in the database. Each price value will be increased by 10 percent. Now we can create the SqlCommand object. We need an integer variable to hold the return value of the ExecuteNonQuery method, which will tell us how many rows in the database were changed.

Listing 5.6 shows how to use ExecuteScalar to return the average price of a book in the Titles table.

Listing 5.6: Using the ExecuteScalar Method

```
Private Function GetAveragePrice() As Decimal
    Dim objPrice As Object
    Dim avgPrice As Decimal

    Dim myConn As SqlConnection = New SqlConnection()
    myConn.ConnectionString = _
        "Data Source=localhost; Initial " & _
        "Catalog=pubs; Integrated Security=SSPI; "
    myConn.Open()

    Dim sqlString As String = _
        "SELECT Avg(price) FROM titles"

    Dim myCalc As SqlCommand = _
        New SqlCommand(sqlString, myConn)
    myCalc.CommandType = CommandType.Text
    objPrice = myCalc.ExecuteScalar()

    myConn.Close()
    avgPrice = CType(objPrice, Decimal)
    Return avgPrice

End Function
```

This procedure is similar to Listing 5.5, which uses the ExecuteNonQuery method. The main difference is that ExecuteScalar returns an Object type. We need to declare a variable of type Object to hold the return value and then we need to convert the value to the appropriate data type before we can use it. In this example, we are calculating an average on a column that is defined as a SQL Server money data type, which is compatible with the .NET Framework data type of decimal. In Exercise 5.2 you will create an application that uses the ExecuteNonQuery method to update values in the database and the ExecuteScalar method to run a query that returns a single result.

EXERCISE 5.2

Using Queries That Don't Return Rows

1. Start Visual Studio .NET and create a new Windows Application project named **NoRowSetExample**.

2. Change the name of the default Form1.vb to **frmNoRowset.vb**.

3. Add two TextBox controls and two Command Button controls to the form. Name them:

   - txtUpdate

   - txtAverage

   - btnUpdate

   - btnAverage

   Your form should look like this:

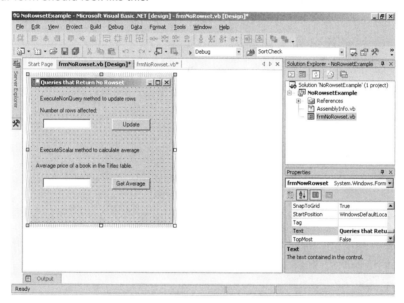

4. Right-click frmNoRowset.vb in the Solution Explorer and choose View Code.

5. At the top of the code module for the form, add an Imports statement:

   Imports System.Data.SqlClient

6. Create a new function named GetAveragePrice. This function will run a SQL query to cal-culate the average price of items in the Titles table of the pubs sample database. Your code should look like this:

```
Private Function GetAveragePrice() As Decimal
    Dim objPrice As Object
    Dim avgPrice As Decimal

    Dim myConn As SqlConnection = New SqlConnection()
    myConn.ConnectionString = "Data Source=localhost; Initial " & _
        "Catalog=pubs; Integrated Security=SSPI; "
    myConn.Open()
```

EXERCISE 5.2 *(continued)*

```
Dim sqlString As String = "SELECT Avg(price) FROM titles"
Dim myCalc As SqlCommand = New SqlCommand(sqlString, myConn)
myCalc.CommandType = CommandType.Text
objPrice = myCalc.ExecuteScalar()

myConn.Close()
avgPrice = CType(objPrice, Decimal)
Return avgPrice
```

```
End Function
```

7. Create a new function named DoUpdate. This function will run a SQL UPDATE query that will increase the price of every item in the Titles table by ten percent. Your code should look like this:

```
Private Function DoUpdate() As Integer
    Dim recsUpdated As Integer
    Dim myConn As SqlConnection = New SqlConnection()

    myConn.ConnectionString = "Data Source=localhost; Initial " & _
        "Catalog=pubs; Integrated Security=SSPI;"
    myConn.Open()

    Dim sqlString As String = _
        "UPDATE titles SET price = price * 1.1"

    Dim myUpdate As SqlCommand = New SqlCommand(sqlString, myConn)
    myUpdate.CommandType = CommandType.Text

    recsUpdated = myUpdate.ExecuteNonQuery()

    myConn.Close()

    Return recsUpdated

End Function
```

8. In the Form Load event procedure for the form, add code to call the GetAveragePrice function and display the return value in txtAverage:

```
Private Sub frmNowRowset_Load(ByVal sender As System.Object, _
    ByVal e As System.EventArgs) Handles MyBase.Load

    txtAverage.Text = CType(GetAveragePrice(), String)

End Sub
```

9. In the Button Click event procedure for btnAverage, add code to call the GetAveragePrice function and display the return value in txtAverage:

```
Private Sub btnAverage_Click(ByVal sender As System.Object, _
    ByVal e As System.EventArgs) Handles btnAverage.Click

    txtAverage.Text = CType(GetAveragePrice(), String)

End Sub
```

10. In the Button Click event procedure for btnUpdate, add code to call the DoUpdate function and display the return value in txtUpdate:

```
Private Sub btnUpdate_Click(ByVal sender As System.Object, _
    ByVal e As System.EventArgs) Handles btnUpdate.Click

    txtUpdate.Text = CType(DoUpdate(), String)

End Sub
```

11. Save and test your work. Once the form loads, you will see the average price displayed in txtAverage.

12. Click the Update button. You will see the number of records that were updated displayed in txtUpdate.

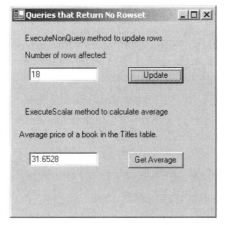

13. Click the Get Average button to see a new value displayed in txtAverage. Because we used the DoUpdate function to increase the price of every book, the calculated average price increased as well.

Calling Stored Procedures

A *stored procedure* is any *Structured Query Language (SQL)* statement or set of statements that are saved on the database server along with the database definition. The Microsoft SQL Server database uses its own programming language, called *Transact-SQL* (or T-SQL for short), to write these queries. Transact-SQL is based on the American National Standards Institute (ANSI) and the International Organization for Standardization (ISO) standard SQL language published in 1992 (Microsoft SQL Server 2000 supports the Entry Level of SQL-92). T-SQL also includes programming features beyond just standard SQL instructions, such as conditional logic, standard operators, variables, built-in functions, and system variables, so stored procedures can be quite complex.

There are a lot of advantages to using stored procedures as an alternative to generating all SQL statements in your application code:

- When you send a SQL string from your application code, the database server must check the syntax of the SQL statement, verify that table and field names are correct, and then create a plan before each execution of the query. Stored procedures are compiled the first time they are run, and this information is saved, so subsequent calls to them run quickly.

- Stored procedures can be a security improvement as well. The database administrator (DBA) grants permission to execute the stored procedures, rather than granting full access to the underlying database tables. Users of your application can run the stored procedures, but cannot access the data in any other way.

- Maintenance can be improved too. Because stored procedures are all located in one place, any changes that need to be made can be done once, and applications that call the stored procedures can continue to use the revised procedures without having to recompile or redeploy the application.

Although you can use the tools that come with Microsoft SQL Server to create and maintain stored procedures, Visual Studio .NET gives you the ability to do this as well. The Server Explorer enables you to access any SQL Server installation on your development workstation, or on your network (assuming you have the appropriate permissions to do so). Figure 5.1 shows the Server Explorer, the pubs sample database, and the listing of stored procedures in pubs.

We will be working with the stored procedure called byroyalty in the upcoming examples.

FIGURE 5.1   Viewing stored procedures with the Server Explorer

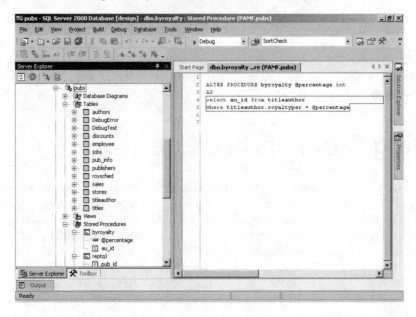

When you are using the Server Explorer, just expand the Servers node, expand the computer name that you are interested in, and then continue drilling down through SQL Servers. You should see the database names, and by expanding those you can see the database tables and columns. If you right-click one of the table names, the menu offers choices such as Retrieve Data from Table and Design Table. When you expand the Stored Procedures node, you will see a list of all procedures. When you expand one of the procedure names, you see a list of the parameters that the procedure accepts and the list of data fields that it will return.

You can edit the stored procedure directly from the Server Explorer. Using the pubs sample database, right-click the byroyalty stored procedure name and choose Edit Stored Procedure from the menu. This is a simple procedure that returns the Author ID (au_id) column from the TitleAuthor table. It accepts one input parameter that is used in the SQL WHERE clause. The WHERE clause selects only those authors who have a value matching the input parameter, in their Royalty Percentage (royaltyper) column. Notice that Transact-SQL uses the single @ character in front of the names of local variables and parameters. Listing 5.7 shows the complete code of this procedure.

Listing 5.7: The byroyalty Stored Procedure from the pubs Sample Database

```
ALTER PROCEDURE byroyalty @percentage int
AS
SELECT au_id from titleauthor
WHERE titleauthor.royaltyper = @percentage
```

You can also test the stored procedure. Right-click the procedure name and choose Run Stored Procedure from the menu. Because the byroyalty stored procedure requires an input parameter in order to run, a dialog box pops up requesting you to fill in the value for the percentage parameter. Figure 5.2 shows the Run Stored Procedure dialog box.

FIGURE 5.2   The Run Stored Procedure dialog box

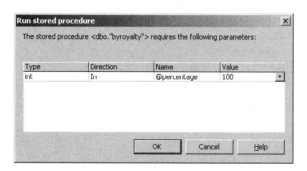

Type in a value (some valid values are 100, 50, 25) and click OK. The results of the stored procedure can be viewed in the Output window. If this window doesn't display automatically after the procedure runs, choose View ➢ Other Windows ➢ Output from the menu to display it. Figure 5.3 shows the results of the query displayed in the Output window.

FIGURE 5.3   Query results in the Output window

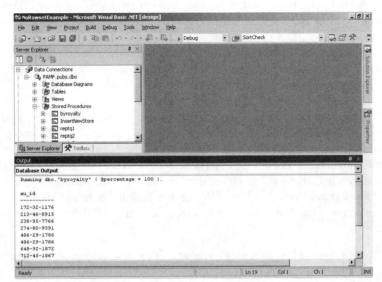

When you want to call a stored procedure from your code, you can create a Command object. In the following example, we set the CommandText property to the name of the stored procedure and set the CommandType property to **StoredProcedure**. Then we add parameters to the Command object's Parameters collection, setting the properties for each parameter as we add it. Table 5.7 lists the properties of the Parameter object. Most properties are supported by both the *SqlParameter object* and *OleDbParameter object*; those that are not are noted in the table.

Listing 5.8 shows how to create the parameter and then how to set the Value property.

TABLE 5.7   Properties of *SqlParameter* and *OleDbParameter*

Property	Description
DbType	Gets or sets the data type of the parameter.
Direction	Gets or sets a value indicating whether the parameter is Input, Output, InputOutput, or a stored procedure ReturnValue.
IsNullable	Gets or sets a value indicating whether the parameter accepts null values.
Offset	Gets or sets the offset to the Value property—SqlParameter only.
OleDbType	Gets or sets the OleDbType of the parameter—OleDbParameter only.
ParameterName	Gets or sets the name of the Parameter object.
Precision	Gets or sets the maximum number of digits used to represent the Value property.

TABLE 5.7   Properties of *SqlParameter* and *OleDbParameter (continued)*

Property	Description
Scale	Gets or sets the number of decimal places to which Value is resolved.
Size	Gets or sets the maximum size, in bytes, of the data within the column.
SourceColumn	Gets or sets the name of the source column.
SourceVersion	Gets or sets the DataRowVersion to use when loading Value.
SqlDbType	Gets or sets the SqlDbType of the parameter—SqlParameter only.
Value	Gets or sets the value of the parameter.

Listing 5.8: Calling a Stored Procedure with an Input Parameter

```
Private Function GetAuthorsByRoyalty(ByVal percentRoyalty _
    As Integer) As SqlDataReader

    Dim myConn As SqlConnection = New SqlConnection()
    myConn.ConnectionString = _
        "Data Source=localhost; Initial " & _
        "Catalog=pubs; Integrated Security=SSPI; "
    myConn.Open()

    Dim myProc As SqlCommand = _
        New SqlCommand("byroyalty", myConn)
    myProc.CommandType = CommandType.StoredProcedure

    myProc.Parameters.Add("@percentage", _
        SqlDbType.Int).Value= percentRoyalty

    Dim myProcReader As SqlDataReader
    myProcReader = myProc.ExecuteReader( _
        CommandBehavior.CloseConnection)
    Return myProcReader

End Function
```

The Value property is set when the parameter is added to the parameters collection. The final step is to add the SqlParameter to the *SqlCommand.Parameters collection.* Then we are ready to execute the command.

Exercise 5.3 gives you an opportunity to create a new stored procedure in the pubs sample database and then write code to call that procedure.

Creating and Calling Stored Procedures

Setting Up the Project:

1. Start a new Visual Studio .NET ASP.NET Web Application project. Set the location to **http://localhost/StoredProcedureExamples**. Use your own web server name in place of localhost if appropriate.

2. Change the name of WebForm1.aspx to **default.aspx**.

3. Use the Properties window to change the pageLayout property of the document to **FlowLayout**.

4. Using the Visual Studio .NET Toolbox, drag a Web Forms Label, DataGrid, and HyperLink controls to the design surface of default.aspx. Your page should look like the following screen.

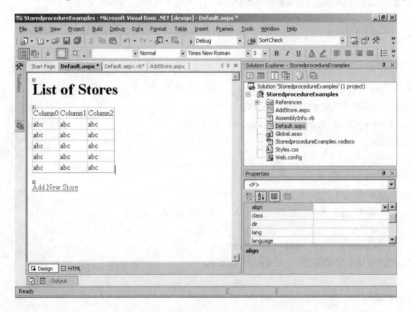

5. Right-click default.aspx in the Solution Explorer and choose View Code. Add the Imports statement at the top of the code module.

```
Imports System.Data.SqlClient
```

6. Create a function procedure called GetStoreList. Add code to connect to the pubs sample database and issue a SQL command to retrieve all the data in the Stores table. This function will return a SqlDataReader. Here is the code to do this:

```
Private Function GetStoreList() As SqlDataReader
    Dim myConn As SqlConnection = New SqlConnection()
```

```
Dim myQuery As SqlCommand = _
   New SqlCommand("SELECT * FROM stores", myConn)
myQuery.CommandType = CommandType.Text
myConn.ConnectionString = _
   "Data Source=localhost; Initial " & _
   "Catalog=pubs; Integrated Security=SSPI; "
myConn.Open()

Dim myReader As SqlDataReader
myReader = myQuery.ExecuteReader( _
   CommandBehavior.CloseConnection)

Return myReader

End Function
```

7. Call the GetStoreList function from the Page_Load event procedure and bind the returned SqlDataReader to the DataGrid:

```
Private Sub Page_Load(ByVal sender As System.Object, _
   ByVal e As System.EventArgs) Handles MyBase.Load

   Dim localReader As SqlDataReader
   localReader = GetStoreList()
   DataGrid1.DataSource = localReader
   DataGrid1.DataBind()
   LocalReader.Close()
End Sub
```

8. Save and test your work. You project should look something like the following.

Creating a New Stored Procedure:

9. Open the Server Explorer window and expand nodes until you can see the pubs database stored procedures. Right-click Stored Procedures and choose New Stored Procedure from the menu.

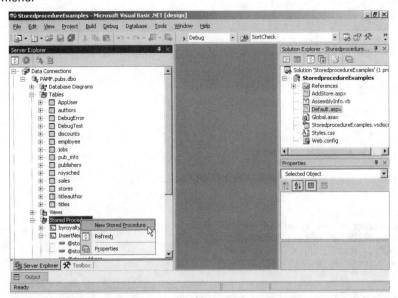

You will see a basic format for Transact-SQL stored procedures in the Code Editor window. You will create a stored procedure to insert a new entry into the Stores table. Write the code as shown:

```
CREATE PROCEDURE dbo.InsertNewStore
    (
        @storeid char(4),
        @storename varchar(40),
        @storeaddress varchar(40),
        @city varchar(20),
        @state char(2),
        @zip char(5)
    )
AS
INSERT stores
(stor_id, stor_name, stor_address, city, state, zip)
VALUES
(@storeid, @storename, @storeaddress, @city, @state, @zip);

GRANT EXECUTE ON InsertNewStore TO public
```

Notice that after you have saved the procedure for the first time, the statement on the first line changes from CREATE PROCEDURE to ALTER PROCEDURE. The statement on the last

EXERCISE 5.3 *(continued)*

line is necessary so that your sample application will have permission to run the stored procedure:

```
GRANT EXECUTE ON InsertNewStore TO public
```

10. Right-click your new procedure and choose Run Stored Procedure to test it. Fill in appropriate values in the Run Stored Procedure dialog box.

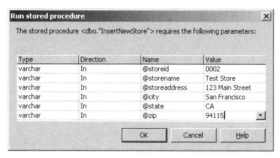

11. Right-click the Stores table and choose Retrieve Data From Table to view the data and verify that your new item has been added.

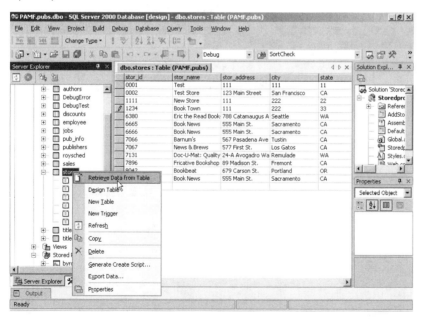

Note: After the first time you test the stored procedure, remove the GRANT statement and save the procedure.

EXERCISE 5.3 *(continued)*

Creating a Web Page for User Input and Calling the Stored Procedure:

12. In the Solution Explorer window, right-click your project name and choose Add Web Form. Name the new form **AddStore.aspx**.

13. Use the Properties window to change the pageLayout property of the document to **FlowLayout**.

14. Using the Visual Studio .NET Toolbox, drag six Web Forms TextBox controls and an HTML Submit button to the design surface of default.aspx. Use the following names for the TextBox controls:

   - **txtID**

   - **txtName**

   - **txtAddress**

   - **txtCity**

   - **txtState**

   - **txtZip**

15. Add descriptive Label controls. Your page should look like the following.

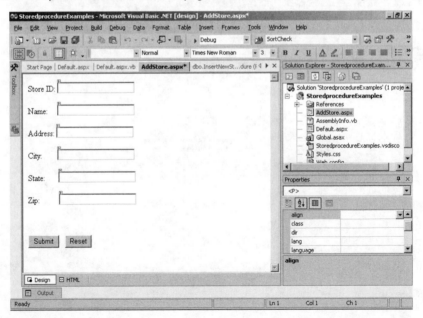

16. Right-click AddStore.aspx in the Solution Explorer and choose View Code. Add the Imports statement at the top of the code module.

```
Imports System.Data.SqlClient
```

17. Add code to the Page_Load event procedure for AddStore.aspx:

```
Private Sub Page_Load(ByVal sender As System.Object, _
    ByVal e As System.EventArgs) Handles MyBase.Load

    If Page.IsPostBack Then
        Dim recsAdded As Integer
        Dim myConn As SqlConnection = New SqlConnection()
        Dim myProc As SqlCommand = _
            New SqlCommand("InsertNewStore", myConn)
        myProc.CommandType = CommandType.StoredProcedure
        myConn.ConnectionString = _
            "Data Source=localhost; Initial " & _
            "Catalog=pubs; Integrated Security=SSPI; "
        myConn.Open()

        myProc.Parameters.Add("@storeid", _
            SqlDbType.Char, 4).Value= txtID.Text
        myProc.Parameters.Add("@storename", _
            SqlDbType.VarChar, 40).Value = txtName.Text
        myProc.Parameters.Add("@storeaddress", _
            SqlDbType.VarChar, 40).Value = txtAddress.Text
        myProc.Parameters.Add("@city", _
            SqlDbType.VarChar, 20).Value = txtCity.Text
        myProc.Parameters.Add("@state", _
            SqlDbType.Char, 2).Value = txtState.Text
        myProc.Parameters.Add("@zip", _
            SqlDbType.Char, 5).Value = txtZip.Text

        recsAdded = myProc.ExecuteNonQuery()

        If recsAdded = 1 Then
            Response.Redirect("default.aspx")
        Else
            Response.Write("Record could not be added.")
        End If
        MyConn.Close()
    End If
End Sub
```

Your code will:

- Connect to the database.

- Create a SqlCommand.

- Create the six parameters that are required to send the value from the text boxes to the stored procedure.

- Call the stored procedure.

- Check the return value of the SqlCommand.ExecuteNonQuery method.

- If the return value is something other than 1, you give an error message.

- If the return value is 1, you redisplay the default.aspx page.

18. Back on the design surface of default.aspx, set the Text property of the Hyperlink control to **Add New Store** and the NavigateURL property to **AddStore.aspx**.

19. Save and test your work. You will be adding to this project in Exercise 5.5.

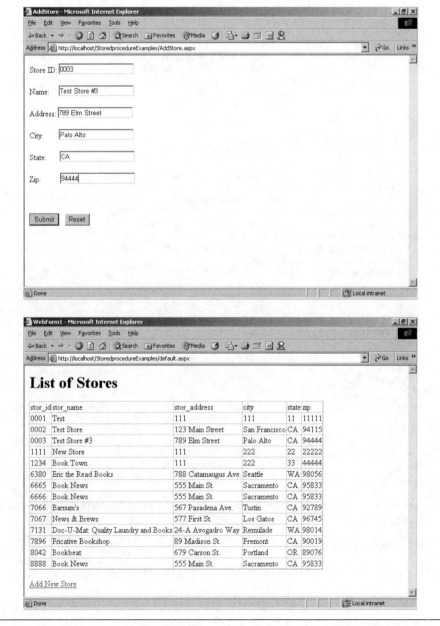

In Exercise 5.4, you will call a stored procedure that returns multiple results and use the `DataReader.NextResult` method to access all of the data.

Accessing Multiple Resultsets

1. Start a new Visual Studio .NET ASP.NET Web Application project. Set the location to **http://localhost/MutilpleResultExamples**. Use your own web server name in place of localhost if appropriate.

2. Change the name of WebForm1.aspx to **default.aspx**.

3. Use the Properties window to change the pageLayout property of the document to **FlowLayout**.

4. Use the Server Explorer to locate the stored procedure called reptq1 in the pubs sample database. Remove the two COMPUTE statements at the end of the procedure and replace them with SELECT statements. Your stored procedure should look like this:

```
ALTER PROCEDURE reptq1 AS
SELECT pub_id, title_id, price, pubdate
from titles
where price is NOT NULL
order by pub_id

SELECT avg(price) from titles
```

5. Run the stored procedure and view the results in the Output window.

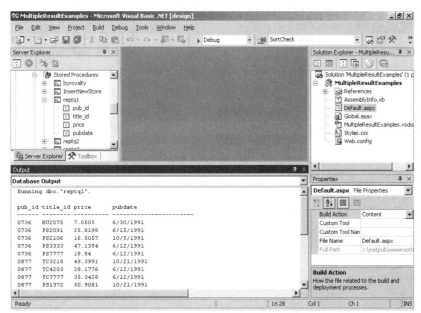

EXERCISE 5.4 *(continued)*

6. Right-click AddStore.aspx in the Solution Explorer and choose View Code. Add the Imports statement at the top of the code module.

   Imports System.Data.SqlClient

7. Add code to the Page_Load event procedure of default.aspx to call the stored procedure and display the results. After you loop through the first resultset and display the rows of data that were returned for the first SELECT statement, you can call the NextResult method and move to the average price value that is returned from the second SELECT statement in the stored procedure. Here is the code:

```
Private Sub Page_Load(ByVal sender As System.Object, _
    ByVal e As System.EventArgs) Handles MyBase.Load

    Dim myConn As SqlConnection = New SqlConnection()
    myConn.ConnectionString = _
        "Data Source=localhost; Initial " & _
        "Catalog=pubs; Integrated Security=SSPI; "
    myConn.Open()

    Dim myProc As SqlCommand = _
        New SqlCommand("reptq1", myConn)
    myProc.CommandType = CommandType.StoredProcedure

    Dim myProcReader As SqlDataReader
    myProcReader = myProc.ExecuteReader()
    Do While myProcReader.Read()
        Response.Write(myProcReader.GetString(0) & ", " & _
            myProcReader.GetString(1) & ", " & _
            myProcReader.GetDecimal(2).ToString & ", " & _
            myProcReader.GetDateTime(3) & "<BR>")
    Loop

    myProcReader.NextResult()
    myProcReader.Read()
    Response.Write("The Average price of a book is: " & "<BR>")
    Response.Write(myProcReader.GetDecimal(0).ToString)
    myProcReader.Close()
    myConn.Close()
End Sub
```

EXERCISE 5.4 *(continued)*

8. Save and test your work. Your results should look like the following.

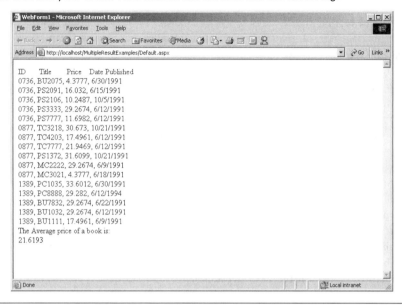

Understanding New Objects in the ADO.NET Object Model

In this section, you will learn about some additional objects that are new in the ADO.NET object model. These include transactions, exceptions, and errors.

Transactions

Sometimes your application must coordinate two separate database operations—for example, you might want to delete an entry from one table and add it to a different one. In this case, you want to be sure that if an error occurs during either operation, both operations are cancelled. It would be a problem for most applications if the record was deleted from the first table and then because an error occurred it did not get added to the second one. The information would be lost. You want to be assured that if an error occurs during any part of your processing, all the operations that are running within the same transaction are cancelled, or rolled back. If all operations are able to complete successfully, then you want to commit those changes to the database permanently.

If you were trying to do this yourself, you would have to write a lot of code to buffer the temporary results and perhaps undo your changes. Fortunately, you do not have to worry about this. Several options are available to .NET Framework programmers for transaction management.

In Chapter 2, "Creating and Managing Serviced Components," we discussed the capability of .NET Enterprise Services to manage distributed transactions. These are useful if your transactions involve multiple databases or database servers. If you need to handle only local transactions, such as multiple operations on different tables in the same database, then you can use the ADO.NET Transaction class to handle this for you. (A third option is to use the transaction control statements in Transact-SQL when you are writing stored procedures.)

In earlier versions of ADO, transactions were managed by using methods of the Connection object. This is not the case in ADO.NET. There is now a Transaction class. The *Sql-Transaction object* or the *OleDbTransaction object* is first created by calling the *Connection .BeginTransaction method*. All commands that participate in the transaction must use the same connection. A common way of using transactions is to place a call to the *Transaction.Commit method* at the end of the procedure, following all of the database operations, and to place a call to the *Transaction.Rollback method* in your error handler. If a runtime error occurs, the entire transaction will be rolled back. If all database operations complete without runtime errors, then the transaction will be committed and the changes will be made permanent in the database. Table 5.8 lists the properties and methods of the Transaction object, and Table 5.9 lists the enumerated values for the IsolationLevel *property*.

T A B L E   5.8   Properties and Methods of *SqlTransaction* and *OleDbTransaction*

Properties	Description
Connection	Provides a reference to the Connection object associated with the transaction.
IsolationLevel	Specifies the isolation level for this transaction. Isolation levels are listed in Table 5.9.
Methods	**Description**
Commit	Commits the database transaction.
Dispose	Releases the unmanaged resources used by the Transaction object and optionally releases the managed resources.
Rollback	Rolls back (cancels) a transaction from a pending state.
SqlTransaction Only	**Description**
Save	Creates a named savepoint that can be used to roll back a portion of the transaction.

TABLE 5.9 Enumeration Values of the *IsolationLevel* Property

Level	Description
Serializable	The greatest level of isolation, preventing other users from updating or inserting rows into the resultset until the transaction is complete.
RepeatableRead	Locks are placed on all data that is used in a query, preventing other users from updating the data. Prevents nonrepeatable reads but phantom rows are still possible.
ReadCommitted	Shared locks are held while the data is being read to avoid dirty reads, but the data can be changed before the end of the transaction, resulting in nonrepeatable reads or phantom data.
ReadUncommitted	A dirty read is possible, meaning that no shared locks are issued and no exclusive locks are honored.
Chaos	The pending changes from more highly isolated transactions cannot be overwritten.
Unspecified	A different isolation level than the one specified is being used, but the level cannot be determined.

The Save method is available only for the SqlTransaction object. This takes advantage of a capability of Microsoft SQL Server to roll back to a specific point in a complex transaction. The *IsolationLevel property* can be set to request that the database server place a high level of isolation, or protection, against other users changing (or even reading) the same data that your transaction is working with, until your transaction completes. The interaction between your code and the database server's internal mechanisms for determining how locks are held on the data can be quite complex and can affect your application's performance. You should test this carefully in each individual situation to determine the optimal setting.

Listing 5.9 shows a procedure that uses ADO.NET transactions along with error-handling code. This example extends the code from Exercise 5.3.

Listing 5.9: ADO.NET Transactions

```
Public Sub UpdateTwoTables()

   Dim myConn As SqlConnection = New SqlConnection()
   myConn.ConnectionString = _
      "Data Source=localhost; Initial " & _
      "Catalog=pubs; Integrated Security=SSPI; "
   Dim myTrans As SqlTransaction
```

```
Try
    myConn.Open()
    myTrans = myConn.BeginTransaction()

    Dim myProc As SqlCommand = _
        New SqlCommand("InsertNewStore", myConn)
    myProc.CommandType = CommandType.StoredProcedure
    myProc.Transaction = myTrans

    myProc.Parameters.Add("@storeid", _
        SqlDbType.Char, 4).Value = txtID.Text
    myProc.Parameters.Add("@storename", _
        SqlDbType.VarChar, 40).Value = txtName.Text
    myProc.Parameters.Add("@storeaddress", _
        SqlDbType.VarChar, 40).Value = txtAddress.Text
    myProc.Parameters.Add("@city", _
        SqlDbType.VarChar, 20).Value = txtCity.Text
    myProc.Parameters.Add("@state", _
        SqlDbType.Char, 2).Value = txtState.Text
    myProc.Parameters.Add("@zip", _
        SqlDbType.Char, 5).Value = txtZip.Text
    myProc.ExecuteNonQuery()

    Dim mySecondProc As SqlCommand = _
        New SqlCommand("InsertStoreSales", myConn)
    mySecondProc.CommandType = CommandType.StoredProcedure
    mySecondProc.Transaction = myTrans

    mySecondProc.Parameters.Add("@storeid", _
        SqlDbType.Char, 4).Value = txtID.Text
    mySecondProc.Parameters.Add("@ordernumber", _
        SqlDbType.VarChar, 20).Value = txtNum.Text
    mySecondProc.Parameters.Add("@orderdate", _
        SqlDbType.DateTime).Value = txtDate.Text
    mySecondProc.Parameters.Add("@qty", _
        SqlDbType.Int).Value = txtQty.Text
    mySecondProc.Parameters.Add("@payment", _
        SqlDbType.VarChar, 12).Value = txtPay.Text
```

```
    mySecondProc.Parameters.Add("@titleid", _
        SqlDbType.VarChar, 6).Value = txtTitle.Text
    mySecondProc.ExecuteNonQuery()

    myTrans.Commit()

  Catch e As Exception
    myTrans.Rollback()
    'additional error handling here
  Finally
    myConn.Close()
  End Try
End Sub
```

In this example, we have two stored procedures, the `InsertNewStore` procedure from Exercise 5.3 and a new one called `InsertStoreSales` for inserting data into the Sales table. We need to make sure that we can successfully complete the first operation, adding the new store, before we try to insert sales information for that store ID. The statements that show the use of the Transaction object and the error-handling code are shown in bold. Notice that we start with the `SqlConnection.BeginTransaction` method. Then we must set the `Transaction` property of the Command object to reference the newly created `SqlTransaction` object. After the second stored procedure call is the `SqlTransaction.Commit` method call. If both stored procedures are executed correctly, we are ready to make our changes permanent. The `Catch` block of the error handler contains the call to `SqlTransaction.Rollback`. If a runtime error occurred, neither statement's results would be written to the database. In the `Finally` block of the error handler, we can close the connection. Code that is in the `Finally` block will execute whether an error occurred or not, so we know for sure that our connection to the database will always be terminated at the end of the procedure, no matter what the outcome.

Understanding the Exception Class and the Error Class

If an error occurs when you are executing a statement against the database, the database server will send the error information to the .NET data provider. This error information might consist of one or more messages. The .NET data provider will raise an exception that can be caught by error-handling code in your procedures.

The Exception object has an *Errors collection*. By iterating through it, you can examine all the messages that the database server has sent. For the Exception object itself, and each Error object in the `Errors` collection, you can examine several properties that give you information about the problem that occurred at the database server. Table 5.10 lists the properties for the Exception and Error objects.

TABLE 5.10   Properties of *SqlException, SqlError, OleDbException,* and *OleDbError*

SqlException and SqlError	Description
Class	Gets the severity level of the error returned from the SQL Server .NET data provider.
LineNumber	Gets the line number within the Transact-SQL command batch or stored procedure that generated the error.
Message	Gets the text describing the error.
Number	Gets a number that identifies the type of error.
Procedure	Gets the name of the stored procedure or Remote Procedure Call (RPC) that generated the error.
Server	Gets the name of the computer running an instance of SQL Server that generated the error.
Source	Gets the name of the provider that generated the error.
State	Gets a numeric error code from SQL Server that represents an error, warning, or no data found message. For more information, see SQL Server Books Online.

OleDbException	Description
ErrorCode	Gets the HRESULT of the error.
Message	Gets the text describing the error.
Source	Gets the name of the OLE DB provider that generated the error.

OleDbError	Description
Message	Gets a short description of the error.
NativeError	Gets the database-specific error information.
Source	Gets the name of the provider that generated the error.
SQLState	Gets the five-character error code following the ANSI SQL standard for the database.

SqlException and OleDbException Only	Description
Errors	Gets a collection of one or more Error objects that give detailed information about exceptions generated by the .NET data provider.

There is a significant difference between the properties that are available for the SqlClient data provider and those available for the OleDb data provider. In Table 5.10, notice that the *OleDbException object* and *OleDbError object* have different sets of properties. However, the *SqlException object* and *SqlError object* have identical properties (except for the SqlException .Errors collection). If you ask for the properties of the SqlException object, you will see the same values as the properties of the first SqlError in its Errors collection.

Exercise 5.5 adds error-handling code to the StoredProcedureExamples project that you created in Exercise 5.3.

EXERCISE 5.5

Adding Error Handling

1. Open the Visual Studio .NET project called StoredProcedureExamples that you created in Exercise 5.3.

2. Add an error handler to the Page_Load event procedure in AddStore.aspx.vb. Remove the If Then Else block at the end of the procedure. Place the instruction to redirect back to the default.aspx page directly after the call to execute the stored procedure. Your code should look like this:

```
recsAdded = myProc.ExecuteNonQuery()
Response.Redirect("default.aspx")
```

3. Add a Try statement immediately before the call and open the connection. Add Catch, Finally, and End Try statements at the end of the procedure. Add the code to examine the SqlException and Errors collection in the Catch block. Add the instruction to close the connection in the Finally block. Here is what your code should look like (bold lines indicate code that you need to add):

```
Private Sub Page_Load(ByVal sender As System.Object, _
    ByVal e As System.EventArgs) Handles MyBase.Load

  If Page.IsPostBack Then
      Dim recsAdded As Integer
      Dim myConn As SqlConnection = New SqlConnection()

      Dim myProc As SqlCommand = _
          New SqlCommand("InsertNewStore", myConn)
      myProc.CommandType = CommandType.StoredProcedure

      myConn.ConnectionString = _
          "Data Source=localhost; Initial " & _
          "Catalog=pubs; Integrated Security=SSPI; "

      Try
          myConn.Open()
          myProc.Parameters.Add("@storeid", _
              SqlDbType.Char, 4).Value = txtID.Text
          myProc.Parameters.Add("@storename", _
              SqlDbType.VarChar, 40).Value = txtName.Text
```

```
                myProc.Parameters.Add("@storeaddress", _
                    SqlDbType.VarChar, 40).Value = txtAddress.Text
                myProc.Parameters.Add("@city", _
                    SqlDbType.VarChar, 20).Value = txtCity.Text
                myProc.Parameters.Add("@state", _
                    SqlDbType.Char, 2).Value = txtState.Text
                myProc.Parameters.Add("@zip", _
                    SqlDbType.Char, 5).Value = txtZip.Text
                recsAdded = myProc.ExecuteNonQuery()

                Response.Redirect("default.aspx")

            Catch ex As SqlException
                Dim myErrors As SqlErrorCollection = ex.Errors

                Response.Write("Class: " & ex.Class & "<BR>")
                Response.Write("Error #" & ex.Number & " " & _
                    ex.Message & _
                    " on line " & ex.LineNumber & "<BR>")
                Response.Write("Error reported by " & _
                    ex.Source & _
                    " while connected to " & ex.Server & "<BR>")

                Response.Write("Errors collection contains " & _
                    myErrors.Count & " items:<BR>")

                Dim err As SqlError
                    For Each err In myErrors
                        Response.Write("Class: " & _
                            err.Class & "<BR>")
                        Response.Write("Error #" & _
                            err.Number & " " & err.Message & _
                            " on line " & err.LineNumber & "<BR>")
                        Response.Write("Error reported by " & _
                            err.Source & _
                            " while connected to " & err.Server & "<BR>")
                    Next

            Finally
                myConn.Close()
            End Try
        End If
    End Sub
```

4. Save and test your work. When you enter the data to add a new store, use a store ID number that already exists in the database. This will cause an error because you are not allowed to have duplicate values in the primary key column. The error messages will be written directly to the web page and should look like the following.

EXERCISE 5.5 *(continued)*

This example is designed to teach you about the error information that you will receive from ADO.NET. In a real production application, you would never display this kind of detailed information to the users of your web pages. Chapter 8, "Testing and Debugging", will explain how to log error information safely. Error messages that are displayed to users, should general in nature and should not include information such as database table and field names or server names.

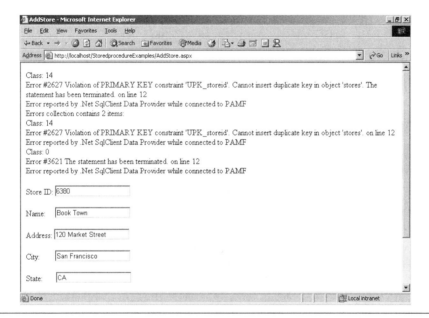

Summary

In this chapter, you learned about ADO.NET data providers and some of the objects in the System.Data Framework classes. We covered the following topics:

- How to select the correct .NET data provider for your database.
- How to create a Connection object with an appropriate connection string and how to control connection pooling.
- How to create Command objects and how to use appropriate methods for different types of database queries.

- How to use a DataReader to access rows of data returned from a database query. How to move through the data in a forward-only, read-only fashion and how to retrieve individual column values. How to access multiple resultsets in a single DataReader.

- How to use the `ExecuteNonQuery` and `ExecuteScalar` methods to run queries that do not return rows of data.

- How to use Visual Studio .NET to create, edit, and test stored procedures.

- How to call stored procedures with the ADO.NET Command object, using the `Parameters` collection to pass input parameters and retrieve output parameters and return values.

- How to use the new ADO.NET Transaction object to coordinate multiple database updates in the same procedure.

- How to handle data access exceptions when an error occurs.

Exam Essentials

Know how to select a .NET data provider.   The SqlClient data provider is used with Microsoft SQL Server 7 and 2000. Older versions of Microsoft SQL Server must use the OleDb data provider. The OleDb data provider is also used with other types of databases, such as Oracle and Access. Use the ODBC data provider for legacy systems.

Know how to use the ADO.NET Connection object.   Understand how connection pooling works and how to create a connection string. Understand the differences between appropriate values for the `SqlConnection.ConnectionString` and the `OleDbConnection.ConnectionString`.

Understand the different methods of the Command object.   Use the `ExecuteReader` method to create a DataReader to access rows of data returned from the database. Use `ExecuteNonQuery` to run a SQL `UPDATE`, `INSERT`, or `DELETE` statement, or other type of query that does not return rows of data. `ExecuteNonQuery` returns the number of records affected by the operation. Use the `ExecuteScalar` method when your query will return a single value, such as the result of a sum, count, or average calculation. Use the `ExecuteXmlReader` method with SQL Server 2000 when writing queries that use the `FOR XML` clause.

Know how to access data with a DataReader.   Understand the `Read` and `Close` methods and how to retrieve column data by using the `GetDataType` methods. Remember that the Data-Reader provides only forward-only, read-only access to data. The DataReader maintains an open connection to the database while you are accessing its data. Understand the `CommandBehavior` parameters and how they can be used to optimize your application. Know how to access multiple resultsets with a single DataReader. Remember to close the DataReader as soon as possible after you have used the data and to close the DataReader after each ExecuteReader method if you are using it for multiple operations.

Know how to work with stored procedures.   Use the Visual Studio .NET Server Explorer window to create, edit, and test SQL Server stored procedures. Use the Command object to call stored procedures from your code. Create a `Parameters` collection that passes input parameters to the stored procedure and can retrieve output parameters and return values after the stored procedure has completed.

Know how to use ADO.NET transactions. Use the `BeginTransaction` method to create a Transaction object. Set the `Transaction` property of the Command object that will participate in the same transaction. Use the `Commit` and `Rollback` methods to control transaction outcome. Understand the differences between the `IsolationLevel` property values.

Know how to use Exception and Error objects. The Exception object is fired by the .NET data provider if an error occurs at the database. The Exception object has an `Errors` collection that contains one or more Error objects. Exception and Error objects have properties that enable you to retrieve error information such as error number and messages.

Key Terms

Before you take the exam, be certain you are familiar with the following terms:

ADO.NET data providers

`CommandBehavior`

`CommandText` property

`CommandType` property

connection pooling

`Connection.BeginTransaction` method

`ConnectionString` property

`Errors` collection

`ExeuteNonQuery` method

`ExecuteReader` method

`ExecuteScalar` method

`ExecuteXMLReader` method

forward-only, read-only recordset

`IsolationLevel` property

`OleDbCommand`

`OleDbConnection`

`OleDbDataReader` class

`OleDbError` object

`OleDbException` object

`OleDbParameter` object

OleDbTransaction object

property

SqlCommand

SqlCommand.Parameters collection

SqlConnection

SqlDataReader class

SqlError object

SqlException object

SqlParameter object

SqlTransaction object

stored procedure

Structured Query Language (SQL)

System.Data namespace

System.Data.OleDb

System.Data.SqlClient

Transaction.Commit method

Transaction.Rollback method

Transact-SQL

Windows Integrated Security

Review Questions

1. Which of the following is the appropriate connection string for logging onto a Microsoft SQL Server 6.5 database?

   A. myConn.ConnectionString = _
   "Provider=MSSQL; Data Source=(local); " & _
   "Initial Catalog=pubs" & _
   "User ID=guest; Password=p5n7u!N"

   B. myConn.ConnectionString = _
   "Data Source=(local); Initial Catalog=pubs" & _
   "User ID=guest; Password=p5n7u!N"

   C. myConn.ConnectionString = _
   "Provider=MSSQL; Data Source=pubs; " & _
   "Initial Catalog=(local) " & _
   "User ID=guest; Password=p5n7u!N"

   D. myConn.ConnectionString = _
   "Provider=MSSQL; Data Source=SSPI; " & _
   "Initial Catalog=(local) " & _
   "User ID=guest; Password=p5n7u!N"

2. Your Windows forms application uses Windows Integrated Security and allows users of your application to connect to the SQL Server database by using their own Windows username. Users sometimes report that database operations are very slow. What action might improve data access time?

   A. Change the SQL Server security mode to mixed mode.

   B. Allow your application to log in as the system administrator.

   C. Create a single application login so that a single connection pool can serve all users of your application.

   D. Rewrite your application's SQL queries.

3. Your application will be using ADO.NET Command objects to call stored procedures. Which Command property settings should you use?

   A. Set the CommandType property to StoredProcedure and the CommandText property to the name of the procedure.

   B. Set the CommandText property to StoredProcedure and the CommandType property to the name of the procedure.

   C. Set the CommandType property to Database and the CommandText property to StoredProcedure.

   D. Set the CommandType property to StoredProcedure and the CommandText property to the value of the input parameter.

4. You are using an ADO.NET Command object to run a SQL query that requests a count of rows in a database table. Which command method should you use?

A. ExecuteNonQuery

B. ExecuteReader

C. ExecuteXMLReader

D. ExecuteScalar

5. You are using an ADO.NET Command object to run a SQL query that will delete a row in the database. Which command method should you use?

A. ExecuteNonQuery

B. ExecuteReader

C. ExecuteXMLReader

D. ExecuteScalar

6. You have created a DataReader object to read customer information from the database. What instruction should you use to retrieve the customer's name from the first column in a Data-Reader's resultset?

A. myString = myReader.GetChars(0)

B. myString = myReader.GetChars(1)

C. myString = myReader.GetString(0)

D. myString = myReader.GetString(1)

7. In order to read all the rows from a DataReader, which method should you call?

A. myReader.NextResult()

B. myReader.MoveNext()

C. myReader.Read()

D. myReader.GetValues()

8. You need to be sure that the database connection is closed immediately when its associated DataReader object is closed by the consumer. How can you most easily accomplish this?

A. With the DataReader.Dispose method.

B. With the DataReader.Close method.

C. When the DataReader is created by the Command.ExecuteReader method, pass a parameter called CommandBehavior.SequentialAccess.

D. When the DataReader is created by the Command.ExecuteReader method, pass a parameter called CommandBehavior.CloseConnection.

9. When creating an ASP.NET web application, how can you quickly display information from a DataReader, called `myReader`, in a Web Forms DataGrid control?

    A. Set the `DataSource` property of the DataGrid to reference the `myReader` and then call the `DataGrid.DataBind` method.

    B. Set the `DataReader` property of the DataGrid to reference the `myReader` and then call the `DataGrid.DataBind` method.

    C. Set up a loop to read through the DataReader and assign values to the rows and columns of the DataGrid.

    D. Set up special template columns for the DataGrid and then use the `GetDataType` methods of the DataReader to display each row of data.

10. You are using an ADO.NET Command object to run a SQL query that will update selected rows in the database, based on the criteria specified in your SQL statement's `WHERE` clause. Your call to the `ExecuteNonQuery` method looks like this:

    `x = myCommand.ExecuteNonQuery()`

    What will the variable `x` contain after the query is run?

    A. −1

    B. True or False, indicating whether or not any errors occurred while processing the data

    C. A status code from the data base server

    D. The number of rows that were updated

11. You are using an ADO.NET Command object to run a SQL query that will return a single calculated value. Your call to the `ExecuteScalar` method looks like this:

    `x = myCommand.ExecuteScalar()`

    What data type should you use when you declare your variable named `x`?

    A. `Integer`

    B. `Object`

    C. `Variant`

    D. `Decimal`

12. Your procedure needs to perform two separate database queries. You need to debit an amount in the first database table and credit that amount in another table. You want to make sure that both operations are successful. If one of the instructions fails, no partial changes should be written to the database. Which ADO.NET objects should you use?

    A. Use the Connection object's `BeginTrans`, `CommitTrans`, and `Rollback` methods.

    B. Instantiate a new Transaction object and call its methods to commit or roll back the transaction.

    C. Use the Connection object to create a new Transaction object and then use methods of the Transaction object to commit or roll back the transaction.

    D. Create a new Transaction object and add it to the `Connection.Transactions` collection.

13. You are using the ADO.NET Transaction object to coordinate database operations in your code. You would like to make a setting indicating to the database server that you would like the highest level of database locking to be applied while your transaction is running. Which value should you use for the `Transaction.IsolationLevel` property?

A. `ReadCommitted`

B. `Serializable`

C. `ReadUncommitted`

D. `RepeatableRead`

14. You are creating error handling for your ADO.NET application that will use the SqlClient data provider. You are interested in processing only data access errors with this `Catch` block. How should you specify the `Catch` block portion of your error handler?

A. `Catch ex As Exception`

B. `Catch ex As SqlException`

C. `Catch ex As SqlError`

D. `Catch ex as SqlException.Errors`

15. Code in your error handler does not access the `SqlException.Errors` collection to read error messages, but rather reads the `Message` property directly from the `SqlException` object. What effect does this have on your application?

A. You will not see any error messages.

B. You will see the same message as the first `SqlError` object in the `Errors` collection.

C. You will see a message warning you to read the `Errors` collection.

D. You will see a generic message.

Answers to Review Questions

1. A. Version 6.5 and older of Microsoft SQL Server must use the OleDb data providers; therefore, they need to specify a provider name in the connection string. The Data Source should be set to the computer name of the database server (or local machine), and the Initial Catalog is the name of the database.

2. C. When users log into the database with unique login names, connection pooling cannot work efficiently because each user will get their own connection pool. Changing to a single application login will enable users to get existing connections from the pool, which is quicker than creating new connections for each user. Changing SQL Server to mixed mode will not improve performance and will introduce new security considerations, as will allowing your application to log in as an administrator. Rewriting your SQL queries might or might not have any effect on application performance.

3. A. The CommandType property indicates what kind of operation the command will be performing. There are three valid values: Text (a SQL statement provided in your code), StoredProcedure, or TableDirect. The CommandText property is a string value that is a SQL statement provided in your code, the name of a stored procedure, or the name of a table. Parameter values are handled by the Command.Parameters collection.

4. D. Use the ExecuteScalar method when running a query that returns a single value. Use the ExecuteReader method when running a query that returns rows of data. Use the ExecuteNonQuery method when running a query such as a SQL INSERT, UPDATE, or DELETE statement. The ExecuteXMLReader returns an XML document object and is for use only with the SqlClient data provider and SQL Server 2000 FOR XML queries.

5. A. Use the ExecuteNonQuery method when running a query such as a SQL INSERT, UPDATE, or DELETE statement. Use the ExecuteScalar method when running a query that returns a single value. Use the ExecuteReader method when running a query that returns rows of data. The ExecuteXMLReader returns an XML document object and is for use only with the SqlClient data provider and SQL Server 2000 FOR XML queries.

6. C. The GetString method should be used because you know that the field that contains the customer name is defined as a string or character data type. The GetChars method is used to read database columns that hold large binary data objects (BLOB). The first column in the DataReader's resultset is at ordinal position zero (0), not 1.

7. C. The Read method is used to advance the DataReader to the next row of data. The NextResult method is used when several SQL queries were run as a batch and there are multiple resultsets in a single DataReader. The MoveNext method was used with older versions of the ADO recordset and is not used in ADO.NET. The GetValues method is for retrieving column data.

8. D. Although you can write code to create this behavior, it is most easily accomplished by simply setting the CommandBehavior.CloseConnection parameter when creating the DataReader.

9. A. ASP.NET Web Forms controls are able to use automatic data binding to access data through a DataReader. Windows Forms controls cannot do this. Just set the DataSource property of the DataGrid to reference the DataReader instance and call the DataGrid.DataBind method. You do not need to loop through the rows in the DataReader or write code to work with individual column values.

10. D.   The ExecuteNonQuery method returns an integer value showing the number of records that were affected by the query. When working with a DataReader, the RecordsAffected property always returns –1 for SQL SELECT statements. Error information and status codes are accessed through the Exception and Error objects.

11. B.   Because the ExecuteScalar method can return different types of data, it returns an Object data type. You can then write code to convert to a more specific data type. The data type of Variant was used in Visual Basic 6 and is not one of the .NET Framework data types.

12. C.   The ADO.NET Transaction object cannot be instantiated with the New keyword. It is created by the Connection.BeginTransaction method. After the object is created, you can call methods of the Transaction object to commit or roll back the transaction. In older versions of ADO, the Connection object was used to control transactions and did have BeginTrans, CommitTrans, and Rollback methods. There is no Connection.Transactions collection.

13. B.   Serializable provides the highest level of isolation and ensures that no other operations can change or even read the data until your transaction is committed. The other settings provide lower levels of protection.

14. B.   Specify a SqlException object in the Catch block. Inside the Catch block, you can then access the SqlError objects that make up the SqlException.Errors collection. If you specify System.Exception in the Catch block, you will receive all types of runtime errors.

15. B.   The SqlException object's property values will be the same as the first SqlError object in the Errors collection.

Chapter

6

Working with the DataSet

MICROSOFT EXAM OBJECTIVES COVERED IN THIS CHAPTER:

✓ **Create and manipulate DataSets.**
  - Manipulate a DataSet schema.
  - Manipulate DataSet relationships.
  - Create a strongly typed DataSet.

Chapter 5, "Working with the .NET Data Providers," covered some of the classes found in the System.Data namespace that work in a connected fashion with the database—primarily the Connection, Command, and DataReader classes. This chapter covers the ADO.NET objects that work in a disconnected fashion, taking data from the database and enabling a client to work with it locally and to submit updates at a later time. You will still be using Connection and Command objects to initially retrieve data from the database and to finally submit changes, but you have some new objects to consider, starting with the DataAdapter and DataSet, that manage data after it is sent to the client.

This chapter introduces you to the DataAdapter and DataSet objects, as well as other classes in the System.Data namespace including the DataView, DataColumn, DataRelation, and Constraint classes. The DataView object provides customized views of the tables in the DataSet by using Sort, Filter, and Find operations. The DataColumn object describes the type and size of data to be stored in each column in a table and is important for determining the structure of a DataTable. DataRelation and Constraint objects define data integrity rules for the DataSet, to mirror those conditions that have been set in the database itself.

This chapter also includes an example of how to use Visual Studio .NET components to add ADO.NET objects, such as the Connection, Command, and DataSet objects, to your application simply by dragging and dropping them from the Toolbox. Visual Studio .NET will then automatically generate the code to instantiate and configure those objects. You can also ask Visual Studio .NET to generate a strongly typed DataSet, which is an extension of the basic DataSet object. The strongly typed DataSet defines the data structure in advance, and enforces that structure by using XML Schema definition language (XSD) and by creating a class in your application to supply custom properties and methods based on the data definition.

Additional methods of the DataSet that provide easy reading and writing of XML data are covered in Chapter 7, "Working with XML Data."

Creating and Manipulating DataSets

Before you can begin working with DataSets, you must understand how to retrieve data from the database and load it into the DataSet. To do this you must learn how the DataAdapter is used. The DataAdapter handles the job of retrieving data from the database and filling the DataSet. The DataAdapter is also responsible for sending updates back to the database when the client has made changes to the data in the DataSet. The *DataSet object* is a disconnected local data store that can be used by client applications to work with data locally, or easily pass data from one component to another. Data stored in the DataSet is further broken down into DataTable and DataRow objects, which you will also look at in this chapter. The DataAdapter and DataSet objects must be used together. The DataAdapter has the necessary information to connect to a specific database and run a query to retrieve data. The DataAdapter `Fill` method then loads that data into a DataSet. The DataSet can be much more complex than the RecordSet object that you might be familiar with from previous versions of ADO. The DataSet can hold data from multiple sources, can manage client updates, and has many other features.

Like the SqlConnection or OleDbConnection objects that were discussed in the previous chapter, the SqlDataAdapter and OleDbDataAdapter objects are responsible for connecting to a specific database, so the DataAdapter is implemented in each data-provider-specific namespace: `System.Data.SqlClient` and `System.Data.OleDb`.

The *SqlDataAdapter object* and the *OleDbDataAdapter object* are responsible for connecting to the database and retrieving the data that will be stored in the DataSet. They are also responsible for submitting updates back to the database when the local client is finished making changes to the data inside a DataSet.

> Aside from the SqlDataAdapter and OleDbDataAdapter, all the other objects discussed in this chapter belong to the `System.Data` namespace itself. Because they are not specific to a particular provider, we do not need to qualify their names with a reference to the data provider. For simplicity, in the rest of the chapter we refer to the DataAdapter class generically, unless we are providing a specific code sample.

Working with the DataSet requires the use of many cooperating classes. In the following sections, you will see how these classes are used together to perform common tasks, such as retrieving data from the database and submitting updates to the database.

Using DataAdapter Objects

The DataAdapter object is used to fill a DataSet. It is responsible for connecting to the database and retrieving information via its `SelectCommand` property. Then the DataAdapter can also send updates back to the database via its `InsertCommand`, `UpdateCommand`, and `DeleteCommand` properties. These properties can also be set to reference an existing Command object.

Similarly, the DataAdapter can be associated with an existing Connection object or can use a connection string that is passed to its constructor method. If you are not using an explicit Connection object that you created in your code, then the DataAdapter creates and uses an implicit Connection object (with the connection string you supply). The DataAdapter can also implicitly open and close an existing connection, or it can detect that the referenced Connection object is already open and can make use of it.

Table 6.1 lists all properties and methods that apply to both the SqlDataAdapter and OleDbDataAdapter classes.

TABLE 6.1 Important Properties and Methods of the *SqlDataAdapter* and *OleDbDataAdapter* Classes

Property	Description
SelectCommand	Defines the SQL statement or stored procedure used to retrieve records from the data source.
DeleteCommand	Defines the SQL statement or stored procedure used to delete records from the data source.
InsertCommand	Defines the SQL statement or stored procedure used to insert new records into the data source.
UpdateCommand	Defines the SQL statement or stored procedure used to update records in the data source.
AcceptChanges-DuringFill	Indicates whether AcceptChanges is called on a DataRow after it is added to the DataTable.
ContinueUpdate-OnError	Specifies whether to generate an exception, or skip the row in error and continue with the rest of the updates. The default is False.
TableMappings	Provides access to a collection that provides the master mapping between a source table and a DataTable.
MissingMappingAction	Specifies the action to take when incoming data does not have a matching table or column in the DataSet mappings collection. The default action is to create the table or column, but you can choose to ignore the data or force an exception.
MissingSchemaAction	Specifies the action to take when existing DataSet schema does not match incoming data. The default action is to add the new information to the schema. You can also choose to add the columns with primary key information, ignore the extra columns, or force an exception.

Method	Description
Fill	Adds, or refreshes (when the AddWithKey property is True), rows in the DataSet to match those in the data source.
FillSchema	Adds a DataTable to a DataSet and configures the schema to match that in the data source.
GetFillParameters	Provides access to the parameters set by the user when executing a SQL SELECT statement.
Update	Calls the appropriate INSERT, UPDATE, or DELETE statement for each row in the DataSet that was changed by the user.

The most important properties of the DataAdapter are those that control how data is retrieved and updated. The *SelectCommand*, *DeleteCommand*, *InsertCommand*, and *UpdateCommand* properties can be set to string values, which are the SQL statements that define what data is retrieved by the DataAdapter and how changes are submitted back to the database.

The most common DataAdapter methods are `Fill` and `Update`. The *Fill method* will connect to the database and execute the SQL statement (or Command object) associated with the Data-Adapter's `SelectCommand` property, loading the records that are returned to a specified DataSet. After the DataSet is filled, the connection to the database is closed and your code can work with the data locally.

When you call the *Update method*, a new connection to the database is opened and each row in the DataSet that has been added, changed, or deleted by the client application is automatically submitted back to the database by using the appropriate `DeleteCommand`, `InsertCommand`, or `UpdateCommand` SQL instruction.

Listing 6.1 shows how to set up a simple DataAdapter to fill a DataSet. We are using the `Fill` method with two parameters. The first parameter is a reference to the DataSet object, and the second parameter assigns a name for the DataTable that will be created to hold the results of this operation. A DataSet object can consist of multiple DataTable objects, each receiving their data from a different DataAdapter instruction.

Listing 6.1: Using a DataAdapter to Fill a DataSet

```
Public Sub GetData()
    Dim connectString As String
    Dim sqlSelect As String

    connectString = "Data Source=localhost; Initial " & _
        "Catalog=pubs; Integrated Security=SSPI; "

    sqlSelect = "SELECT pub_id, pub_name, city, state, " & _
        "country FROM publishers"

    Dim pubAdapter As SqlDataAdapter = New _
        SqlDataAdapter(sqlSelect, connectString)

    Dim pubSet As DataSet = New DataSet()

    pubAdapter.Fill(pubSet, "Publishers")

    'continue working with the DataSet

End Sub
```

We will continue working with the DataAdapter and show you how to use its other properties and methods later in this chapter, in the section titled "Using DataSets to Manage Updates to Data-bases." But first we are going to discuss the structure, properties, and methods of the DataSet object.

Working with the DataSet's Constituent Objects

A DataSet is a complex, in-memory store for data that can mimic many of the features of the database engine itself. The *DataSet* object can be used as a simple container for holding data, perhaps for passing information between components, but it has many additional capabilities. The DataSet itself is made up of many other types of objects. As you saw in Listing 6.1, even a simple DataSet will contain a *DataTable object*.

The default behavior of the `DataSet` class is to create and configure the objects necessary to perform its work even if the user does not explicitly specify all the details. For example, in Listing 6.1 the parameters passed to the `Fill` method indicated that we wanted to assign the name of Publishers to the DataTable. If we had not specified this, the DataTable would still be created and we could access it through the `DataSet.Tables` collection, as shown by this code snippet:

```
DataGrid1.DataSource = pubSet.Tables(0)
```

When you want to use the DataSet to perform more complex tasks, or to generate the entire data structure at runtime from your code, you can work directly with the constituent objects to control exactly how they will operate. Table 6.2 lists the main classes that make up the internal structure of a DataSet.

TABLE 6.2   Classes in *System.Data* Namespace That Make Up the Internal Structure of the DataSet

Class	Description
DataTable	A DataSet is made up of one or more DataTables.
DataTableCollection	The `DataSet.Tables` collection provides access to the DataTable objects.
DataColumn	A DataTable is made up of one or more DataColumns. DataColumn properties describe characteristics of the column such as name, data type, and size. DataColumns do not provide access to data values.
DataColumnCollection	The `DataTable.Columns` collection provides access to the DataColumn objects.
DataRow	Each DataTable is made up of one or more DataRows.
DataRowCollection	The `DataTable.Rows` collection provides access to the DataRow object. By accessing the `Item` collection of a DataRow, you can read or change data values.
Constraint	Constraints are applied to an individual DataColumn, including the derived types `ForeignKeyConstraint` and `UniqueConstraint`.
ConstraintCollection	The `DataTable.Constraints` collection provides access to the Constraint objects.

TABLE 6.2   Classes in *System.Data* Namespace That Make Up the Internal Structure of the DataSet *(continued)*

Class	Description
DataRelation	A DataRelation is created by specifying the parent/child relationship between a DataColumn that contains the primary key in one DataTable and a DataColumn with the matching ForeignKey in the related table.
DataRelationCollection	The DataSet.Relations collection provides access to the Relation objects.
DataView	The DataView creates a custom view of the data in a table by applying sort, filter, or search criteria.

Table 6.3 lists the properties and methods of the DataSet class. Some of these properties and methods also apply to constituent objects (such as DataTables and DataRows) so they can be applied at different levels of scope. In the examples and exercises that follow, you will see the most common of these properties and methods demonstrated.

TABLE 6.3   Selected Properties and Methods of the *DataSet* Class

Property	Description
CaseSensitive	Indicates whether string comparisons within DataTable objects are case-sensitive.
DataSetName	The name of the current DataSet.
DefaultViewManager	Allows filtering, searching, and navigating by using a custom DataViewManager.
EnforceConstraints	Indicates whether constraint rules are followed when attempting any update operation. A ConstraintException is generated if an update would violate a constraint.
ExtendedProperties	Retrieves the collection of custom user information.
HasErrors	Indicates whether there are errors in any of the rows in any of the tables of this DataSet.
Locale	Sets or retrieves the locale information used to compare strings within the table.
Namespace	The namespace of the DataSet.

TABLE 6.3   Selected Properties and Methods of the *DataSet* Class *(continued)*

Property	Description
Prefix	An XML prefix that aliases the namespace of the DataSet.
Relations	Retrieves the collection of relations that link tables and allow navigation from parent tables to child tables.
Tables	Retrieves the collection of tables contained in the DataSet.

Method	Description
AcceptChanges	Commits all the changes made to this DataSet since it was loaded or since the last time AcceptChanges was called.
Clear	Clears the DataSet of any data by removing all rows in all tables.
Clone	Copies the structure of the DataSet, including all DataTable schemas, relations, and constraints. Does not copy any data.
Copy	Copies both the structure and data for this DataSet.
GetChanges	Gets only the rows of the DataSet that have changed since the DataSet was last loaded or since AcceptChanges was called.
GetXml	Gets the XML representation of the data stored in the DataSet.
GetXmlSchema	Gets the XSD schema for the XML representation of the data stored in the DataSet.
HasChanges	Indicates whether the DataSet has changes, including new, deleted, or modified rows.
InferXmlSchema	Infers the XML schema from the specified TextReader or file into the DataSet.
Merge	Merges this DataSet with a specified DataSet.
ReadXml	Reads XML schema and data into the DataSet.
ReadXmlSchema	Reads an XML schema into the DataSet.
RejectChanges	Rolls back all the changes made to the DataSet since it was created, or since the last time AcceptChanges was called.
Reset	Resets the DataSet to its original state.

TABLE 6.3   Selected Properties and Methods of the *DataSet* Class *(continued)*

Method	Description
WriteXml	Writes XML data, and optionally the schema, from the DataSet.
WriteXmlSchema	Writes the DataSet structure as an XML schema.

Table 6.4 lists properties and methods that can be used with the individual DataTable objects that make up a DataSet.

TABLE 6.4   Selected Properties and Methods of the *DataTable* Class

Property	Description
CaseSensitive	Indicates whether string comparisons within the table are case-sensitive.
ChildRelations	Retrieves the collection of child relations for this DataTable.
Columns	Retrieves the collection of columns that belong to this DataTable.
Constraints	Retrieves the collection of constraints maintained by this DataTable.
DataSet	Retrieves the DataSet that this DataTable belongs to.
DefaultView	Retrieves a customized view of the DataTable, which might include a filtered view, or a cursor position.
DisplayExpression	The expression that will return a value used to represent this Data-Table in the user interface.
ExtendedProperties	Retrieves the collection of customized user information.
HasErrors	Retrieves a value indicating whether there are errors in any of the rows in any of the tables of the DataSet to which the DataTable belongs.
Locale	The locale information used to compare strings within the table.
MinimumCapacity	The initial starting size for this table.
Namespace	The namespace for the XML representation of the data stored in the DataTable.
ParentRelations	Retrieves the collection of parent relations for this DataTable.
Prefix	The namespace for the XML representation of the data stored in the DataTable.

TABLE 6.4   Selected Properties and Methods of the *DataTable* Class *(continued)*

Property	Description
PrimaryKey	An array of columns that function as primary keys for the DataTable.
Rows	Retrieves the collection of rows that belong to this DataTable.
TableName	The name of the DataTable.

Method	Description
AcceptChanges	Commits all the changes made to this table since it was created or since the last time AcceptChanges was called.
BeginInit	Begins the initialization of a DataTable that is used on a form or used by another component. The initialization occurs at runtime.
BeginLoadData	Turns off notifications, index maintenance, and constraints while loading data.
Clear	Clears the DataTable of all data.
Clone	Clones the structure of the DataTable, including all DataTable schemas and constraints.
Compute	Computes the given expression on the current rows that pass the filter criteria.
Copy	Copies both the structure and data for this DataTable.
EndInit	Ends the initialization of a DataTable that is used on a form or used by another component. The initialization occurs at runtime.
EndLoadData	Turns on notifications, index maintenance, and constraints after loading data.
GetChanges	Creates a copy of the DataTable containing all changes made to it since it was loaded or since AcceptChanges was called.
GetErrors	Creates an array of DataRow objects that contain errors.
ImportRow	Copies a DataRow into a DataTable, preserving any property settings, as well as original and current values.
LoadDataRow	Finds and updates a specific row. If no matching row is found, a new row is created by using the given values.

TABLE 6.4   Selected Properties and Methods of the *DataTable* Class *(continued)*

Method	Description
NewRow	Creates a new DataRow with the same schema as the table.
RejectChanges	Rolls back all changes that have been made to the table since it was loaded or since the last time AcceptChanges was called.
Reset	Resets the DataTable to its original state.
Select	Retrieves an array of DataRow objects.

It is often useful to work at the level of the *DataRow object*. By working at this level, you can retrieve and change the column data values for a specific DataRow object and can add new data to the DataSet object programmatically. Table 6.5 lists the properties and methods that can be used with a DataRow object.

TABLE 6.5   Selected Properties and Methods of the *DataRow* Class

Property	Description
HasErrors	Retrieves a value indicating whether errors exist in a row
Item	Reads or writes the data stored in a specified column
ItemArray	Reads or writes all of the values for this row through an array
RowError	Reads or writes the custom error description for a row
RowState	Retrieves the current state of the row in regard to its relationship to the DataRowCollection
Table	Retrieves the DataTable for which this row has a schema

Method	Description
AcceptChanges	Commits all the changes made to this row since it was created or since the last time AcceptChanges was called
BeginEdit	Begins an edit operation on a DataRow object
CancelEdit	Cancels the current edit on the row

TABLE 6.5 Selected Properties and Methods of the *DataRow* Class *(continued)*

Method	Description
ClearErrors	Clears the errors for the row, including the RowError and errors set with SetColumnError
Delete	Deletes the DataRow
EndEdit	Ends the edit occurring on the row
GetChildRows	Retrieves the child rows of a DataRow
GetColumnError	Retrieves the error description for a column
GetColumnsInError	Retrieves an array of columns that have errors
GetParentRow	Retrieves the parent row of a DataRow
GetParentRows	Retrieves the parent rows of a DataRow
HasVersion	Indicates whether a specified version exists
IsNull	Indicates whether the specified column contains a null value
RejectChanges	Rejects all changes made to the row since AcceptChanges was last called
SetColumnError	Sets the error description for a column
SetParentRow	Sets the parent row of a DataRow

Using DataSets to Manage Updates to Databases

It is important to understand how the DataAdapter and DataSet process updates and how they store data while a user is working with it. Changes are managed at the DataRow level. When the DataAdapter.Update method is called, only the rows that have been added, changed, or marked for deletion are processed. The DataSet contains multiple versions of the data items. The original values (the values that were retrieved from the database when the DataSet was filled) are available until the AcceptChanges method is called. The new values that the user has entered (or changed) are available as well.

The DataRow versions go through a transition when the user begins to edit. The new data is considered the proposed value, but the current value (the one that is likely to be displayed) is still the same as the original value. At the end of the edit, the current value is replaced with the proposed value, but the original value is still available.

> In Exercise 6.1, you will be working with the Windows forms DataGrid control to edit data. The control enables you to transition through the editing and updating phases transparently as you navigate the grid and make changes to data. It is also possible to control these states in your code by responding to objects' events and calling BeginEdit and EndEdit methods. Having both the updated and original values of the data available is very useful. In Listing 6.2, you will see an example of how to retrieve the original value of a column.

These different versions of data exist only while the user is working with the data. After the *AcceptChanges method* or *RejectChanges method* is called, all values are set to an identical state. When AcceptChanges is called, all versions are set to the new, user-provided values, and the original values are no longer available. When RejectChanges is called, all user-provided values are discarded and the original values are restored.

The AcceptChanges and RejectChanges methods are supported by the DataSet, Data-Table, and DataRow objects, giving you control over the scope of the operation. AcceptChanges also has the effect of changing the *DataRow.RowState property*. When a user (or your code) makes a change to a data value, the RowState property is changed to indicate that the row has been modified. When an Update method is called, only those rows with a RowState of Modified will be submitted to the database. Remember, calling AcceptChanges immediately before an Update method will result in no user changes being sent back to the database, even though they are visible at the client. After database updates have been processed successfully, you can call AcceptChanges to keep the local DataSet in sync with the database.

Table 6.6 lists the enumerated values that are valid for the RowState property and for other properties and methods, such as DataRow.HasVersion, that use the RowVersion enumeration.

TABLE 6.6 *RowState* and *RowVersion* Enumerations

DataRowVersion Enumerated Value	Description
Current	The row contains current values.
Default	The default row version (Current, Default, or Original), according to the current DataRowState. For most DataRowStates, the default row version is Current. The default row version for a deleted row is Original. The default row version for a detached row is Proposed.

TABLE 6.6 *RowState* and *RowVersion* Enumerations *(continued)*

DataRowVersion Enumerated Value	Description
Original	The row contains its original values.
Proposed	The row contains its proposed values. Exists during an edit operation.

DataRowState Enumerated Value	Description
Added	The row has been added to a DataRowCollection, and AcceptChanges has not been called.
Deleted	The row was deleted by using the Delete method of the DataRow, and AcceptChanges has not been called.
Detached	The row has been created but is not part of any DataRowCollection. A DataRow is in this state immediately after it has been created and before it is added to a collection, or if it has been removed from a collection.
Modified	The row has been modified, and AcceptChanges has not been called.
Unchanged	The row has not changed since AcceptChanges was last called.

In order to use the Update method to send the local changes that have been made to the DataSet to the database, you must add the additional SQL statements to perform Delete, Insert, and Update operations and assign them to the DataAdapter's properties. Listing 6.2 shows how to configure the InsertCommand, UpdateCommand, and DeleteCommand properties. This code assumes that you have previously created a valid SqlConnection object named myConn that we are referencing as we configure the DataAdapter.

Listing 6.2: Configuring a DataAdapter to Update Data

```
Public Sub GetData()

Dim pubAdapter As SqlDataAdapter = New SqlDataAdapter()
Dim pubSet As DataSet = New DataSet()

    pubAdapter.SelectCommand = New SqlCommand( _
        "SELECT pub_id, pub_name, city, state, " & _
        "country FROM publishers", myConn)
```

```
pubAdapter.UpdateCommand = New SqlCommand( _
    "UPDATE publishers SET pub_name = @pub_name, " & _
    "city = @city, state = @state, " & _
    "country = @country WHERE pub_id = " & _
     "@original_id", myConn)

pubAdapter.UpdateCommand.Parameters.Add( _
    "@pub_name", SqlDbType.VarChar, 40, "pub_name")
pubAdapter.UpdateCommand.Parameters.Add( _
    "@city", SqlDbType.VarChar, 20, "city")
pubAdapter.UpdateCommand.Parameters.Add( _
    "@state", SqlDbType.Char, 2, "state")
pubAdapter.UpdateCommand.Parameters.Add( _
    "@country", SqlDbType.VarChar, 30, "country")
pubAdapter.UpdateCommand.Parameters.Add( _
    "@original_id", SqlDbType.Char, 4, "pub_id" _
    ).SourceVersion = DataRowVersion.Original

pubAdapter.Fill(pubSet, "Publishers")

'continue working with the DataSet
```

End Sub

The SQL statement that determines how the update is performed contains parameters, such as @pub_name and @city. The parameters in the SQL statement represent the *DataRowVersion .Current value* (including user input) of the data items in the row of the DataTable that is being processed. The last parameter in Listing 6.2 shows how to access the *DataRowVersion.Original value*. This parameter is used in the WHERE clause of the SQL Update statement because we want to make sure that the user didn't accidentally try to change the pub_id (primary key) value, and that we are selecting the correct row in the database, based on the primary key that was originally retrieved.

 Real World Scenario

DataSet versus DataReader

As a software developer, you probably enjoy discussions with fellow developers about the merits of different design choices. One issue that has been frequently discussed on Internet mailing lists and newsgroups is when to use a DataReader versus a DataSet, and which object will provide better performance. Performance of course is a relative term, based on exactly what you are measuring. Also, consider what is most important to the success of your application: is it raw speed, or is a sophisticated user interface, enabling extensive user interaction with the data, preferable?

Remember that the DataSet object provides a local, in-memory store of data that can be nearly as complex as the database structure itself. Users can sort, filter, and change data as much as they want. Users have some measure of control over when their updates will be sent to the database. Although this provides a nice user experience, it creates problems for the developer who has to manage update conflicts. It also requires powerful resources on the client computers and adds to network traffic.

The DataReader object provides fast forward-only, read-only access to your data. Users have no ability to interact with the data; it is good only for display. This behavior works well for web applications, which cannot depend on an uninterrupted connection to the server and database. As a developer, you will have to plan an additional strategy to capture new information or changes from users and communicate those back to the database, perhaps by using ADO.NET commands or stored procedures.

Your selection of one class over the other can greatly affect your application's effectiveness and should be considered carefully.

In Exercise 6.1, you will create a Windows application that uses a DataAdapter to fill a DataSet. Your user interface will use a Windows forms DataGrid control to display this data and to enable the users to edit and add new data to the pubs sample database.

 The exercises in this chapter (as well in Chapter 7) use the Microsoft SQL Server 2000 sample database called pubs. This sample database is a part of the default installation of SQL Server 2000.

EXERCISE 6.1

Creating the DataSet and Updating the Database

Creating the DataSet:

1. Start a new Windows application project in Visual Studio .NET. Name the project **DataSetExample**.

2. Change the name of the form to **frmJobs**. Add a DataGrid and two Command Button controls to the form. Name the command buttons **btnSave** and **btnRejectChanges**. Your form should look something like this:

EXERCISE 6.1 *(continued)*

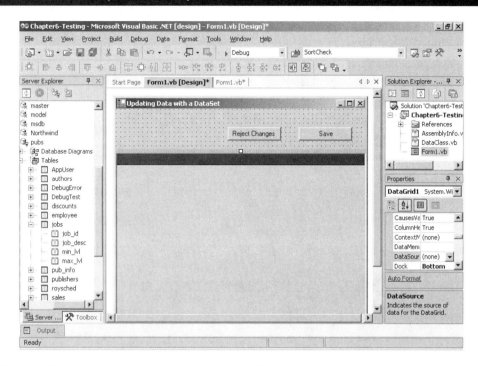

3. Add the following Imports statements to the form's code module:

```
Imports System.Data
Imports System.Data.SqlClient
```

4. Declare class-level variables for the SqlConnection, SqlDataAdapter, and DataSet objects:

```
Public Class frmJobs
    Inherits System.Windows.Forms.Form

Private myConn As SqlConnection = New SqlConnection( _
        "Data Source=localhost; Initial " &
        "Catalog=pubs; Integrated Security=SSPI;")

Private jobAdapter As SqlDataAdapter = New SqlDataAdapter()

Private jobSet As DataSet = New DataSet()
```

5. In the frmJobs_Load event procedure, add code to set the SelectCommand property of the SqlDataAdapter:

```
jobAdapter.SelectCommand = New SqlCommand( _
    "SELECT job_id, job_desc, min_lvl, max_lvl " & _
    "FROM jobs", myConn)
```

EXERCISE 6.1 *(continued)*

6. Call the `Fill` method to retrieve data into the DataSet, and set the data binding for the DataGrid control to display this data:

```
Try
    jobAdapter.Fill(jobSet, "Jobs")
    DataGrid1.SetDataBinding(jobSet, "Jobs")
```

7. Add a simple error handler to help you diagnose any errors that might occur:

```
Catch exp As Exception
    MessageBox.Show(exp.Message)
End Try
```

8. Save and test your work. The form should display the data from the `jobs` table of the pubs sample database.

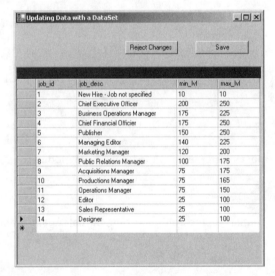

Updating the Database:

Remember that you can use the Server Explorer to find information about the database, such as the field names, data types, and field sizes that are used in the code after step 9.

Although the DataGrid control enables you to edit the information displayed on the screen, you have not yet added any code to perform updates so that these changes are saved permanently to the database. In the rest of this exercise, you are going to add code to create the SqlDataAdapter's `InsertCommand`, `UpdateCommand`, and `DeleteCommand` properties. The code described in steps 9 through 12 should be added to the `frmJobs_Load` event procedure. Listing 6.3 shows the complete code for this procedure.

9. Create the new Command object. Write a SQL statement that will insert the data. Create three Parameter objects, which will map to the three columns in the DataTable that contain the new information you are sending to the database: `job_desc`, `min_lvl`, and `max_lvl`.

Because the job_id column is defined in the database as an Identity column (autonumber), you do not have to supply any data for that column.

Here is the code to do this:

```
jobAdapter.InsertCommand = New SqlCommand( _
    "INSERT INTO jobs (job_desc, " & _
    "min_lvl, max_lvl) VALUES " & _
    "(@job_desc, @min_lvl, @max_lvl)", myConn)

jobAdapter.InsertCommand.Parameters.Add( _
    "@job_desc", SqlDbType.VarChar, 50, "job_desc")
jobAdapter.InsertCommand.Parameters.Add( _
    "@min_lvl", SqlDbType.TinyInt, 1, "min_lvl")
jobAdapter.InsertCommand.Parameters.Add( _
    "@max_lvl", SqlDbType.TinyInt, 1, "max_lvl")
```

10. Create the UpdateCommand. This command has four parameters: the three columns that contain the changed data and a new parameter, called @original_id. This new parameter is set to the DataRowVersion.Original value, which is the value that was present when the data was retrieved from the database, before any user changes. The SQL statement used for the UpdateCommand uses this parameter in the WHERE clause to make sure that you are updating the correct row. You will notice that the SQL statement does not allow changes to the job_id column. Because this is an Identity column and the primary key for the table, it would not be a good idea to allow the user to change it. Here is what your code should look like:

```
jobAdapter.UpdateCommand = New SqlCommand( _
    "UPDATE jobs SET job_desc = @job_desc, " & _
    "min_lvl = @min_lvl, max_lvl = @max_lvl " & _
    "WHERE job_id = @original_id", myConn)

jobAdapter.UpdateCommand.Parameters.Add( _
    "@job_desc", SqlDbType.VarChar, 50, "job_desc")
jobAdapter.UpdateCommand.Parameters.Add( _
    "@min_lvl", SqlDbType.TinyInt, 1, "min_lvl")
jobAdapter.UpdateCommand.Parameters.Add( _
    "@max_lvl", SqlDbType.TinyInt, 1, "max_lvl")
jobAdapter.UpdateCommand.Parameters.Add( _
    "@original_id", SqlDbType.SmallInt, 2, "job_id" _
    ).SourceVersion = DataRowVersion.Original
```

11. Create the DeleteCommand. This command has only one parameter, the @original_id. The SQL statement used for the DeleteCommand uses this parameter in the WHERE clause to make sure that you are deleting the correct row. Here is what your code should look like:

```
jobAdapter.DeleteCommand = New SqlCommand( _
    "DELETE FROM jobs WHERE job_id = @original_id", myConn)

jobAdapter.DeleteCommand.Parameters.Add( _
    "@original_id", SqlDbType.SmallInt, 2, "job_id" _
    ).SourceVersion = DataRowVersion.Original
```

EXERCISE 6.1 *(continued)*

---

12. Add code to the Command Button control's Click event procedures to either save the user's changes or to cancel them:

```
Private Sub btnSave_Click(ByVal sender As System.Object, _
    ByVal e As System.EventArgs) Handles btnSave.Click

    Try
        jobAdapter.Update(jobSet, "Jobs")
        MessageBox.Show("Changes successfully made to the database.")
    Catch ex As Exception
        MessageBox.Show(ex.Message)
    End Try
End Sub

Private Sub btnReject_Click(ByVal sender As System.Object, _
    ByVal e As System.EventArgs) Handles btnRejectChanges.Click

    jobSet.RejectChanges()
End Sub
```

13. Save your project. You will be adding to it in future exercises in this chapter.

14. Test your `UpdateCommand`, `InsertCommand`, and `DeleteCommand` properties by changing some of the data.

15. Add a few new entries at the blank row at the bottom of the DataGrid control. For each row, leave the first column (`job_id`) blank, enter a text description (such as "Administrative Assistant") to the `job_desc` column, and enter numeric values between 1 and 250 to the `min_lvl` and `max_lvl` columns.

16. Click on the left margin of any row to select the row and then press the Delete key to delete it.

17. Click the Reject Changes button. Your changes will disappear, and the data will be returned to its original state.

18. Click the Save button. Your changes will be sent to the database.

19. Shut down the project and restart it, or open the table in the Server Explorer, to verify that your changes and new rows are in the database.

The complete listing for the `frmJobs_Load` procedure from Exercise 6.1 is shown in Listing 6.3.

Listing 6.3: The Complete frmJobs_Load Procedure from Exercise 6.1

```
Private Sub FrmJobs_Load(ByVal sender As System.Object, _
    ByVal e As System.EventArgs) Handles MyBase.Load

        jobAdapter.SelectCommand = New SqlCommand( _
            "SELECT job_id, job_desc, min_lvl, max_lvl " & _
            "FROM jobs", myConn)
```

```
    jobAdapter.InsertCommand = New SqlCommand( _
        "INSERT INTO jobs (job_desc, " & _
        "min_lvl, max_lvl) VALUES " & _
        "(@job_desc, @min_lvl, @max_lvl)", myConn)

    jobAdapter.InsertCommand.Parameters.Add( _
        "@job_desc", SqlDbType.VarChar, 50, "job_desc")
    jobAdapter.InsertCommand.Parameters.Add( _
        "@min_lvl", SqlDbType.TinyInt, 1, "min_lvl")
    jobAdapter.InsertCommand.Parameters.Add( _
        "@max_lvl", SqlDbType.TinyInt, 1, "max_lvl")

    jobAdapter.UpdateCommand = New SqlCommand( _
        "UPDATE jobs SET job_desc = @job_desc, " & _
        "min_lvl = @min_lvl, max_lvl = @max_lvl " & _
        "WHERE job_id = @original_id", myConn)

    jobAdapter.UpdateCommand.Parameters.Add( _
        "@job_desc", SqlDbType.VarChar, 50, "job_desc")
    jobAdapter.UpdateCommand.Parameters.Add( _
        "@min_lvl", SqlDbType.TinyInt, 1, "min_lvl")
    jobAdapter.UpdateCommand.Parameters.Add( _
        "@max_lvl", SqlDbType.TinyInt, 1, "max_lvl")
    jobAdapter.UpdateCommand.Parameters.Add( _
        "@original_id", SqlDbType.SmallInt, 2, "job_id" _
        ).SourceVersion = DataRowVersion.Original

    jobAdapter.DeleteCommand = New SqlCommand( _
        "DELETE FROM jobs WHERE job_id = @original_id", myConn)

    jobAdapter.DeleteCommand.Parameters.Add( _
        "@original_id", SqlDbType.SmallInt, 2, "job_id" _
        ).SourceVersion = DataRowVersion.Original

Try
    jobAdapter.Fill(jobSet, "Jobs")
    DataGrid1.SetDataBinding(jobSet, "Jobs")

Catch exp As Exception
    MessageBox.Show(exp.Message)
End Try
End Sub
```

Now that you understand the basics of creating a DataSet and using the DataAdapter to retrieve and update data, you are ready to look at some of the additional capabilities that you have available for working with the DataSet. First you will consider error handling, and then see how to use DataViews to sort, search, and filter data in a DataSet. Finally, you will look at using Constraints and DataRelations to enforce data integrity in the local DataSet.

Handling DataExceptions

As a developer, you know that robust error handling is one of the most important aspects of creating high-quality applications. In addition to handling general application errors by using System.Exception, the System.Data namespace provides the DataException class. The *DataException class* inherits from System.Exception and defines specific kinds of errors that are likely to occur when you are working with ADO.NET objects. Your error-handling scheme should include provisions for dealing with these common data-related exceptions.

Table 6.7 lists the specific DataException types that are available.

TABLE 6.7   Derived Types of the *System.Data.DataException* Class

Type	Description
ConstraintException	This exception is thrown when an attempted update violates a database constraint.
DeletedRowInaccessible-Exception	This exception is thrown when you try to access a DataRow that has previously been deleted.
DuplicateNameException	This exception is thrown when you attempt to add objects to a DataSet with duplicate names.
InRowChangingEventException	This exception is thrown when you try to call EndEdit at an invalid time.
InvalidConstraintException	This exception is thrown when a relation is found to be invalid.
InvalidExpressionException	This exception is thrown when a DataColumn expression is invalid.
MissingPrimaryKeyException	This exception is thrown when no primary key has been specified.
NoNullAllowedException	This exception is thrown when attempting to add a null value to a column that does not allow nulls.
ReadOnlyException	This exception is thrown when attempting to change a read-only column.
RowNotInTableException	This exception is thrown when the DataRow cannot be found in the specified DataTable.

TABLE 6.7   Derived Types of the *System.Data.DataException* Class *(continued)*

Type	Description
StrongTypingException	This exception is thrown when a null value is used with a strongly-typed DataSet.
TypedDataSetGenerator-Exception	This exception is thrown when duplicate names are found when generating a strongly typed DataSet.
VersionNotFoundException	This exception is thrown when the requested DataRowVersion is no longer available.

Other Data-related exceptions Derived from System.Exception	Description
DBConcurrencyException	This exception is thrown when the DataAdapter Update operation cannot update a row in the database.

Listing 6.4 shows how to use multiple Catch blocks to vary your error handling based on the type of error that has occurred.

Listing 6.4: Handling DataExceptions

```
Private Sub btnTest_Click(ByVal sender As System.Object, _
ByVal e As System.EventArgs) Handles btnTest.Click

    Try
        MessageBox.Show(CType(jobSet.Tables( _
            "Jobs").Rows(14)("job_desc"), String))

    Catch deletedEx As DeletedRowInaccessibleException
        MessageBox.Show( _
            "That row has been deleted from the DataSet.")
    Catch dbConEx As DBConcurrencyException
        MessageBox.Show("Error at the database.")
    Catch dataEx As DataException
        MessageBox.Show("Data Exception")
    Catch ex As Exception
        MessageBox.Show("Generic Exception: " & ex.Message)
    End Try
End Sub
```

In this example, there are three specific types of exceptions that we are interested in. The DeletedRowInaccessibleException occurs when a row is deleted from the local DataSet but other code tries to access it. The `DBConcurrencyException` will occur when an update fails at the database. The `DataException` will catch any of the special types of exceptions shown in Table 6.7. The generic `Exception` will catch any type of exception that occurs in the application, whether data related or not.

The DataAdapter has a property named *ContinueUpdateOnError*. When this property is set to `False` (which is the default), the first error that occurs during a DataAdapter `Update` operation will cause an exception to be fired and the process to stop. Any further updates that might be required for the rest of the data in the DataSet will not be submitted. When the property is set to `True`, no exception will be fired and all updates will be processed and sent to the database. Any rows that could not be updated because of an error (perhaps the user typed an invalid data value for the column as defined in the database) will have a `RowError` property setting of `True`. Because no exception occurs, you will not know whether any errors occurred unless your code actively tests the `HasErrors` property of the DataSet and uses the `GetErrors` method of the DataTable to programmatically identify the rows that failed to update at the database. You will have an opportunity to test this behavior in Exercise 6.2.

In Exercise 6.2, you will add code to the `DataSetExamples` project from Exercise 6.1, and then test several scenarios and see which errors are fired.

EXERCISE 6.2

Testing DataExceptions

1. Open the project that you created in Exercise 6.1 named `DataSetExamples`.

2. Add two Command Button controls to the form, named **btnTest** and **btnHasErrors**. It should look like this:

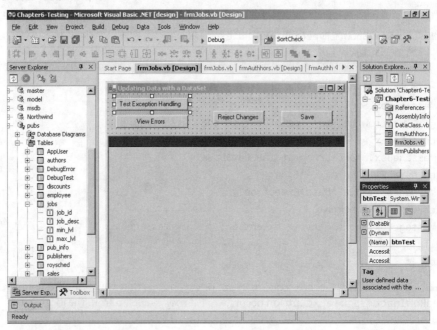

3. Add the following code to the Click event procedure of btnTest:

```
Try
    'try to access the data in the deleted row
    MessageBox.Show(CType(jobSet.Tables("Jobs").Rows(14) _
        ("job_desc"), String))

Catch ex As Exception
    MessageBox.Show("Generic Exception: " & ex.Message)

Catch deletedEx As DeletedRowInaccessibleException
    MessageBox.Show("That row has been deleted from the DataSet.")

Catch dbConEx As DBConcurrencyException
    MessageBox.Show("Error at the database.")

Catch dataEx As DataException
    MessageBox.Show("Data Exception")
End Try
```

4. Save your work and run the application. Depending on changes that you have made to the jobs table in Exercise 6.1, your data might look a little different. The original sample data has 14 numbered entries in the table.

5. Add or delete as many rows as necessary so that you have a total of 14 rows, and click the Save button.

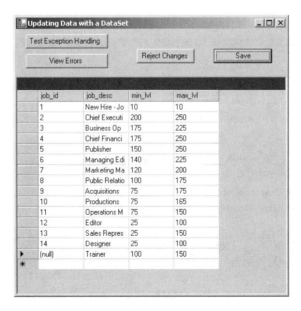

6. Click the Test button. Your code will try to access the 15th row (index value 14) and read data. You should see the generic exception message, informing you the row was deleted.

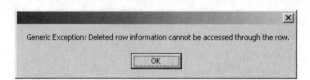

7. To see why you received the generic exception and not the `DeletedRowInaccessible-Exception`, close the application, set a breakpoint at the beginning of the procedure, and try this test again. Step through the code in the procedure. Because the generic `Catch ex as Exception` was listed first in the code, that syntax will catch any error that occurs. That error handler is used, and the others are ignored.

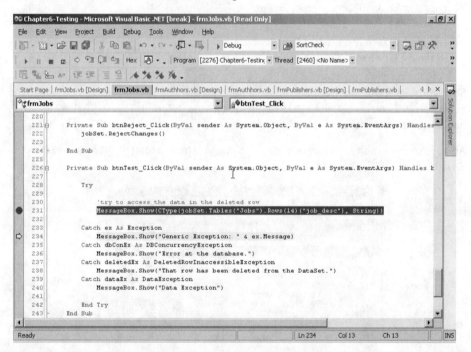

8. Change the code so that the `Catch` blocks are listed in this order: `DBConcurrencyException`, `DeletedRowInaccessibleException`, `DataException`, and `Exception`:

```
Try
    MessageBox.Show(CType(jobSet.Tables("Jobs").Rows(14) _
        ("job_desc"), String))

Catch dbConEx As DBConcurrencyException
    MessageBox.Show("Error at the database.")

Catch deletedEx As DeletedRowInaccessibleException
    MessageBox.Show("That row has been deleted from the DataSet.")
```

```
Catch dataEx As DataException
   MessageBox.Show("Data Exception")

Catch ex As Exception
   MessageBox.Show("Generic Exception: " & ex.Message)
End Try
```

9. With the breakpoint from step 7 still in your code, run the application again and, if necessary, delete items so that there are only 14 items in the list.

10. Click the Test button. Step through the code, and you will see that `DeletedRowInaccessible-Exception` is caught. Although the row has been marked as deleted, and you are not allowed to access its data, it still exists in the DataSet.

11. Click the Save button. This will make the change permanent in the database.

12. Click the Test button again. You should see the generic `Exception`, informing you that there is no item at position 14. You receive the generic exception because after making the change permanent to the database, the deleted row is completely gone from the DataSet.

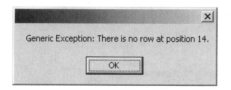

13. Add another new row of data so you can try another test. Click the Save button to update the database. Close the application.

14. Change the error-handling code for the `btnSave` Click event procedure to this:

```
Catch dbex As DBConcurrencyException
   MessageBox.Show("DBC: " & dbex.Message)
Catch ex As Exception
   MessageBox.Show("Generic: " & ex.Message)
End Try
```

15. Save and run your application.

16. Using Windows Explorer, locate the `DataSetExamples.exe` executable in the `\bin` sub-directory of your project. Double-click the filename to run a second instance of your application. You should see the same data in both instances.

17. In the first instance of the application, delete the last row and then click the Save button.

18. The local DataSet in the second instance still displays the row that you deleted in the previous step. In the second instance of the application, make a change to one of the data items in the row that was deleted in the previous step and click the Save button. You should see a DBConcurrency error.

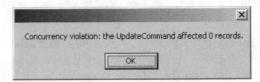

The Update command failed because it could not find a row with that primary key value in the database. Notice that the DataGrid control displays a red exclamation point icon to the left of the row that was in error.

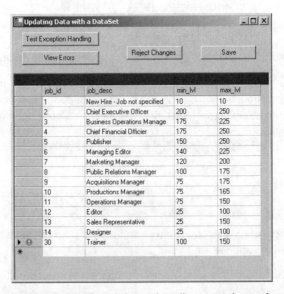

You can change the way that the DataAdapter handles errors by setting its ContinueUpdate-OnError property. This is set to False by default, so any time an error occurs, no updates are written to the database and an exception is generated.

19. Change the ContinueUpdateOnError property to True by adding this line of code before the DataAdapter Update method call in the btnSave Click event procedure:

    ```
    jobAdapter.ContinueUpdateOnError = True
    ```

20. Save your application and run the test as described in steps 16–18 again. This time, notice that the "success" message box is displayed, but the row is still marked with the error icon in the DataGrid.

21. Change some data in other rows and click the Save button. The other rows will be updated successfully.

22. Verify your updates by opening the jobs table with the Server Explorer. The Continue-UpdateonError property enables the successful updates to the database to complete and lets you handle the error rows later.

23. Although the DataGrid control provides a convenient user interface to see which rows had an error, at times you will want to access this information through code. To do this, implement the btnHasErrors Click event procedure to test for errors and display error information programmatically:

```
Private Sub btnHasErrors_Click(ByVal sender As System.Object, _
    ByVal e As System.EventArgs) Handles btnHasErrors.Click

        If jobSet.HasErrors Then

            Dim row As DataRow

            For Each row In jobSet.Tables("Jobs").GetErrors
                MessageBox.Show(row.RowError)
            Next
        End If
End Sub
```

24. Repeat the test again. Click the btnHasErrors button to test your code.

25. Save your work. You will be adding to this project in the remaining exercises in this chapter.

Working with DataView Objects

The strength of the DataSet object is that it enables you to retrieve data once from the database and enables local clients to work with the data for as long as they need to without having to keep a connection open to the database. When users are viewing large amounts of data, it is a common requirement that the user interface allow them to sort the information in various ways, to filter out subsets of data based on some selection criteria, or to search for a specific value. The *DataView object* enables your application to create these different ways to view the data in a DataSet, without changing the underlying data and without having to make additional queries to the database server. This can improve the performance of your user interface and provide a powerful tool for your users.

The DataView has a *Sort property* that changes the order in which data is displayed, and a *RowFilter property* that determines what subset of the data is displayed. The *RowStateFilter property* lets you filter the data in the table based on the status of the row: original, changed, added, deleted, and so on. The DataView also has a *Find method* that searches through the data in specified columns. After you have created a DataView, you can work with it just as if it were the table itself.

Sort, RowFilter, and RowStateFilter are the most common operations that you will be performing with the DataView. Table 6.8 shows the complete list of properties and methods of the DataView class.

The DataView has other related objects that you can make use of, such as the *DataView-Manager*, to make settings for all DataViews associated with a DataSet and the Data-RowView.

You will see examples of using these objects in Exercise 6.3.

The most common use of the DataView is to provide the user with customized subsets of all the data contained in a DataSet by applying different filter and sort keys. This code snippet shows an example:

```
authViewMan.DataViewSettings("Authors").Sort = "au_lname"
```

```
authViewMan.DataViewSettings("Authors").RowFilter = _
    "state = 'CA'"
```

You can sort in reverse order by using the DESC modifier in the sort string:

```
authViewMan.DataViewSettings("Authors").Sort = "au_lname DESC"
```

A DataView is also useful when using the Find method to locate a specific row in a DataTable in the DataSet. You will see an example of this in Exercise 6.4. This code snippet shows the basic syntax:

```
findView.Sort = "pub_id"
rowIndex = findView.Find("9999")
```

To use the Find method, first you set the sort key to the column that contains the data that you want to search, and then you specify the value to search for. The Find method returns an integer value that indicates the row index in the DataTable of the matching row.

You can also search multiple columns by providing an array of strings to the Find method:

```
findView.Sort = "au_lname, au_fname"
```

```
Dim objValues(1) As Object
objValues(0) = "Green"
objValues(1) = "Marjorie"
```

```
rowIndex = findView.Find(objValues)
```

Table 6.8 lists the properties and methods of the DataView class.

TABLE 6.8   Properties and Methods of the *DataView* Class

Property	Description
AllowDelete	Indicates whether deletes are allowed.
AllowEdit	Indicates whether edits are allowed.
AllowNew	Indicates whether the new rows can be added by using the AddNew method.
ApplyDefaultSort	Indicates whether to use the default sort.
Count	Retrieves the number of records in the DataView after RowFilter and RowStateFilter have been applied.
DataViewManager	Retrieves the DataViewManager associated with this view.
Item	Retrieves a row of data from a specified table.
RowFilter	The expression used to filter which rows are viewed in the DataView.
RowStateFilter	The row state filter used in the DataView.
Sort	The sort column or columns, and the sort order for the DataTable.
Table	The source DataTable.

Method	Description
AddNew	Adds a new row to the DataView.
BeginInit	Begins the initialization of a DataView that is used on a form or used by another component. The initialization occurs at runtime.
CopyTo	Copies items into an array. Only for Web forms interfaces.
Delete	Deletes a row at the specified index.
EndInit	Ends the initialization of a DataView that is used on a form or used by another component. The initialization occurs at runtime.
Find	Finds a row in the DataView by the specified sort key value.
FindRows	Retrieves an array of DataRowView objects whose columns match the specified sort key value.
GetEnumerator	Gets the index value for this DataView.

In Exercise 6.3, you will work with the DataView and the DataViewManager classes to sort and filter data in a DataSet.

Sorting and Filtering with the DataView and DataViewManager

1. Open the DataSetExamples project that you originally created in Exercise 6.1 and added to in Exercise 6.2. Add a new Windows form to the project and name it **frmAuthors**.

2. Add a DataGrid, a ComboBox, and a Command Button control to the form. Name the command button **btnDisplayAll**. Your form should look like this:

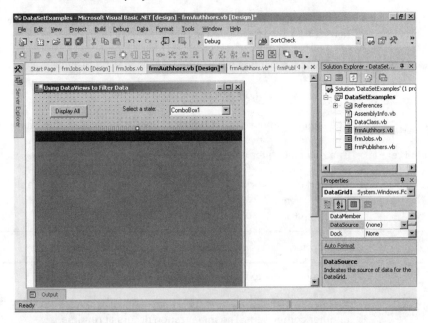

3. Add Imports statements at the top of the code module for the form:

```
Imports System.Data
Imports System.Data.SqlClient
```

4. Declare class-level variables for a SqlConnection, two SqlDataAdapters, and a DataSet:

```
Public Class frmAuthors
    Inherits System.Windows.Forms.Form

Private myConn As SqlConnection = New SqlConnection( _
    "Data Source=localhost; Initial " & _
    "Catalog=pubs; Integrated Security=SSPI;")

Private authAdapter As SqlDataAdapter = New SqlDataAdapter()
Private stateAdapter As SqlDataAdapter = New SqlDataAdapter()

Private authSet As DataSet = New DataSet()
```

5. In the frmAuthors_Load event procedure, do the following:

    ▪ Set up the SelectCommand properties for the two SqlDataAdapters.

    ▪ Open the connection.

    ▪ Fill the DataSet by adding two tables—Authors and States—to the DataSet.

    ▪ Open the connection explicitly, rather than letting the SqlDataAdapter do it implicitly, because you have more than one Fill method to execute.

    ▪ Bind the Authors table to the DataGrid and bind the States table to the ComboBox.

    ▪ Add simple error handling for this procedure and make sure to close the connection in the Finally block of the error handler.

6. Your code should look like this:

```
Private Sub frmAuthors_Load(ByVal sender As System.Object, _
    ByVal e As System.EventArgs) Handles MyBase.Load

    Try
        stateAdapter.SelectCommand = New SqlCommand( _
            "SELECT DISTINCT state " & _
            "FROM authors", myConn)

        authAdapter.SelectCommand = New SqlCommand( _
            "SELECT au_id, au_lname, au_fname, state " & _
            "FROM authors", myConn)

        myConn.Open()
        authAdapter.Fill(authSet, "Authors")
        stateAdapter.Fill(authSet, "States")

        DataGrid1.SetDataBinding(authSet, "Authors")
        ComboBox1.DataSource = authSet.Tables("States")
        ComboBox1.DisplayMember = "state"

    Catch exp As Exception
        MessageBox.Show(exp.Message)
    Finally
        myConn.Close()
    End Try
End Sub
```

7. In the Solution Explorer, right-click the DataSetExample project and choose Properties from the menu. Set the startup object for the project to **frmAuthors**.

8. Save and test your work. The DataGrid should display all the authors from the pubs sample database Authors table, and the ComboBox should display a list of United States state code abbreviations.

EXERCISE 6.3 *(continued)*

9. In the `ComboBox1_SelectedIndexChanged` event procedure, create a DataViewManager for the DataSet that will change the `RowFilter` property each time the user changes the selection in the ComboBox. Then, change the data binding of the DataGrid control to bind to the filtered DataView instead of the entire table. Here is the code to do this:

```
Private Sub ComboBox1_SelectedIndexChanged(ByVal sender _
    As System.Object, ByVal e As System.EventArgs) _
    Handles ComboBox1.SelectedIndexChanged

    Dim authViewMan As DataViewManager = New _
        DataViewManager(authSet)

    authViewMan.DataViewSettings("Authors").Sort = "au_lname"

    authViewMan.DataViewSettings("Authors").RowFilter = _
        "state = '" & ComboBox1.Text & "'"

    'Bind to a DataGrid.
    DataGrid1.SetDataBinding(authViewMan, "Authors")

    End Sub
```

EXERCISE 6.3 *(continued)*

10. Add code to the `btnDisplayAll_Click` event procedure to restore the data bindings of the DataGrid control to the complete DataSet and display all authors:

```
Private Sub btnDisplayAll_Click(ByVal sender As System.Object, _
    ByVal e As System.EventArgs) Handles btnDisplayAll.Click

    DataGrid1.SetDataBinding(authSet, "Authors")

End Sub
```

11. Run the application. You will see only California authors at first. When you change the selection in the ComboBox, you will see a different list of authors displayed in the DataGrid.

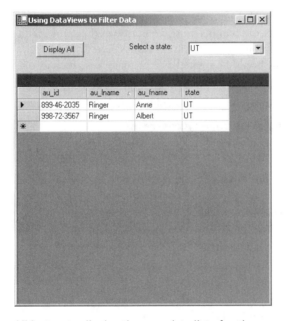

12. Click the Display All button to display the complete list of authors.

13. Save your work. You will be adding to this project in later exercises in this chapter.

Configuring DataSet Constraints and DataRelations

When you are working with a full-featured database engine such as Microsoft SQL Server 2000, you can take advantage of features to maintain consistency between related data in multiple tables when data is changed, and make sure related child records are deleted when a parent record is deleted. Maintaining this consistency between related data is an important aspect of maintaining the data integrity of the database. Depending on the needs of your application, it is sometimes desirable to enforce these same data integrity rules on data in a DataSet. By enforcing the rules on the DataSet, and therefore catching and fixing any data integrity violations locally, before updates are attempted at the database, you can eliminate unnecessary traffic back and forth to the database server.

DataSet Constraints and DataRelations are used to enforce data integrity rules. These settings often match those that are defined in the source database. They might also be used to enforce constraints specific to the application that do not apply to all data in the database.

There are two types of Constraints that can be applied to a DataSet:

ForeignKeyConstraint   The *ForeignKeyConstraint* specifies how rows in a related table are deleted or changed (`Cascade`), or the row values are set to null (`SetNull`), or the values are set to a default value (`SetDefault`), or not changed (`None`). This behavior is based on the values that are set for the `AcceptRejectRule`, `DeleteRule`, and `UpdateRule` properties of the Constraint.

UniqueConstraint   The *UniqueConstraint* requires that each value in a column or combination of values in a specified set of columns must be unique in that table. This constraint can apply to one column or to a combination of column values. The `IsPrimaryKey` property indicates that the column value(s) should be treated as a primary key, such as they are in the database.

Listing 6.5 shows how to create a `ForeignKeyConstraint` by defining DataColumn objects that reference the specific parent and child columns in the related tables.

Listing 6.5: Creating a ForeignKeyConstraint

```
Dim parentColumn As DataColumn
Dim childColumn As DataColumn
Dim pubKey As ForeignKeyConstraint

parentColumn = pubSet.Tables("Publishers").Columns("pub_id")
childColumn = pubSet.Tables("Titles").Columns("pub_id")
pubKey = New ForeignKeyConstraint("PubTitleFKConstraint", _
    parentColumn, childColumn)


pubKey.DeleteRule = Rule.SetNull
pubKey.UpdateRule = Rule.Cascade
pubKey.AcceptRejectRule = AcceptRejectRule.Cascade


pubSet.Tables("Publishers").Constraints.Add(pubKey)
pubSet.EnforceConstraints = True
```

The constructor method for the `ForeignKeyConstraint` class accepts three parameters: a string name for the constraint, and the two object references to the parent and child Data-Column objects. Values are set for the rule properties that determine whether changes (or deletions) to the parent table affect the child table. Finally, the constraint must be added to the `DataSet.Constraints` collection of the DataTable.

As already noted, a UniqueConstraint can be added to a column in a DataTable to ensure that each row has a unique value for that column or set of columns. This will prevent users from entering duplicate data and guard against sending inaccurate information back to the database. Listing 6.6 shows how to create a UniqueConstraint.

Listing 6.6: Creating a UniqueConstraint

```
Dim idColumn As DataColumn
idColumn = pubSet.Tables("Publishers").Columns("pub_id")

Dim pubUniqueConst As UniqueConstraint = New _
   UniqueConstraint("PubIDConstraint", idColumn)

pubTable.Constraints.Add(pubUniqueConst)
```

Now you have seen an example of creating a Constraint for a particular DataColumn. Table 6.9 lists the complete set of properties and methods for the Constraint class.

TABLE 6.9   Properties of the *Constraint* Class

Property	Description
ConstraintName	The name of a constraint in the DataSet.Constraints.
ExtendedProperties	Returns the collection of user-defined constraint properties.
Table	Returns the DataTable to which the constraint applies. For ForeignKeyConstraint, it returns the child table. For Unique-Constraint, it returns the original DataTable.
ForeignKeyConstraint only	
AcceptRejectRule	Indicates the action that should take place across this constraint when AcceptChanges is invoked: either None or Cascade.
Columns	Retrieves the child columns of this constraint.
DeleteRule	Retrieves or sets the action that occurs across this constraint when a row is deleted: Cascade, None, SetDefault, or SetNull.
RelatedColumns	The parent columns of this constraint.
RelatedTable	Retrieves the parent table of this constraint.
UpdateRule	Indicates the action that occurs across this constraint when a row is updated: Cascade, None, SetDefault, or SetNull.

TABLE 6.9   Properties of the *Constraint* Class *(continued)*

Property	Description
UniqueConstraint only	
Columns	Retrieves the array of columns that this constraint affects.
IsPrimaryKey	Indicates whether the constraint is on a primary key.

The *DataRelation object* is used to model the same parent/child relationships that are defined in the database itself. Specifying DataRelations in the DataSet can be useful in locating related records in two tables.

Exercise 6.4 shows an example of using a DataRelation to create DataViews based on related records.

The basic syntax for creating a DataRelation is shown in Listing 6.7.

Listing 6.7: Creating a DataRelation Object

```
Dim pubRelation As DataRelation

pubRelation = bookSet.Relations.Add("PubTitles", _
    bookSet.Tables("Publishers").Columns("pub_id"), _
    bookSet.Tables("Titles").Columns("pub_id"))
```

This code declares a DataRelation object and then uses the DataSet.Relations.Add method to add the new DataRelation to the DataSet's collection. The parameters for the Add method are a string name for the DataRelation and two column references. These column references represent the matching columns in the parent and child tables. Table 6.10 lists the properties of the DataRelation class.

TABLE 6.10   Properties of the *DataRelation* Class

Property	Description
ChildColumns	Retrieves the child DataColumn objects of this relation
ChildKeyConstraint	Retrieves the ForeignKeyConstraint for the relation
ChildTable	Retrieves the child table of this relation
DataSet	Retrieves the DataSet to which the DataRelation belongs
ExtendedProperties	Retrieves the collection that stores customized properties
Nested	Indicates whether DataRelation objects are nested

TABLE 6.10   Properties of the *DataRelation* Class *(continued)*

Property	Description
ParentColumns	Retrieves an array of DataColumn objects that are the parent columns of this DataRelation
ParentKeyConstraint	Retrieves the UniqueConstraint that ensures values in the parent column of a DataRelation are unique
ParentTable	Retrieves the parent DataTable of this DataRelation
RelationName	The name used to retrieve a DataRelation from the DataRelation-Collection

Exercise 6.4 will review what you learned earlier about using the DataView Find method to locate a selected row in the data. You will also create a DataRelation that defines the parent/child relationship between two tables in the DataSet. After you have selected a row from the Publishers table, you will use the DataView.CreateChildView method to locate related records in the Titles table.

EXERCISE 6.4

Using a DataRelation and Creating a ChildView

1. Open the DataSetExamples project that you originally created in Exercise 6.1 and modified in Exercises 6.2 and 6.3. Add a new Windows form to the project. Name it **frmPublishers**.

2. Add a ComboBox and a ListBox control to the form. Your form should look like this:

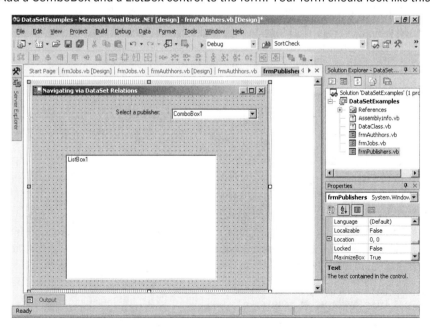

3. Add Imports statements at the top of the code module for the form:

```
Imports System.Data
Imports System.Data.SqlClient
```

4. Declare class-level variables for a SqlConnection, two SqlDataAdapters, and a DataSet:

```
Public Class frmPublishers
    Inherits System.Windows.Forms.Form

Private myConn As SqlConnection = New SqlConnection( _
    "Data Source=localhost; Initial " & _
    "Catalog=pubs; Integrated Security=SSPI;")

Private pubAdapter As SqlDataAdapter = New SqlDataAdapter()
Private titleAdapter As SqlDataAdapter = New SqlDataAdapter()

Private bookSet As DataSet = New DataSet()
```

5. In the frmPublishers_Load event procedure, add code to set up the SelectCommand properties for the two SqlDataAdapters, open the connection, and fill the DataSet. Add two tables—Publishers and Titles—to the DataSet. Open the connection explicitly, rather than letting the SqlDataAdapter do it implicitly, because there is more than one Fill method to execute. Here is the code to do this:

```
myConn.Open()

pubAdapter.SelectCommand = New SqlCommand( _
    "SELECT pub_id, pub_name " & _
    "FROM publishers", myConn)

titleAdapter.SelectCommand = New SqlCommand( _
    "SELECT title_id, pub_id, title, price " & _
    "FROM titles", myConn)
Try
    pubAdapter.Fill(bookSet, "Publishers")
    titleAdapter.Fill(bookSet, "Titles")
```

6. Create a DataRelation to link the Publishers and Titles tables by using the pub_id column that exists in each table:

```
Dim pubRelation As DataRelation

pubRelation = bookSet.Relations.Add("PubTitles", _
    bookSet.Tables("Publishers").Columns("pub_id"), _
    bookSet.Tables("Titles").Columns("pub_id"))
```

7. Bind the Publishers table to the ComboBox. There is also simple error handling for this procedure, so make sure to close the connection in the Finally block of the error handler. Your code should look like this:

```
ComboBox1.DataSource = bookSet.Tables("Publishers")
ComboBox1.DisplayMember = "pub_name"
```

EXERCISE 6.4 *(continued)*

```
ComboBox1.ValueMember = "pub_id"

Catch exp As Exception
    MessageBox.Show(exp.Message)
Finally
    myConn.Close()
End Try
```

8. In the Solution Explorer, right-click the `DataSetExamples` project and choose Properties from the menu. Set the startup object for the project to **frmPublishers**.

9. Save and test your work. The application should display a list of publisher names in the ComboBox.

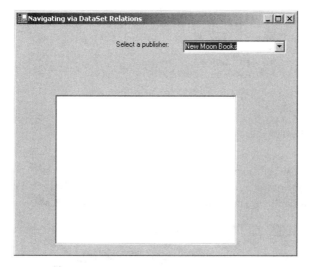

   Add code in the `ComboBox_SelectedIndexChanged` event procedure to locate a selected publisher ID when the user changes the ComboBox selection.

10. First, declare variables:

```
Dim rowIndex As Integer

Dim childView As DataView

Dim findView As DataView = New _
    DataView(bookSet.Tables("Publishers"))
```

11. Set the `DataView.Sort` property to the column you want to search. Then call the `DataView.Find` method, which will return an integer value that gives you the row index of the row you are looking for. Here is the code to do this:

```
Try
    findView.Sort = "pub_id"
    rowIndex = findView.Find(ComboBox1.SelectedValue)
```

12. If the rowIndex value is zero or greater, then you know you have located a matching row. If so, create another DataView that contains child rows from the titles table. The Create-ChildView method takes the name of the DataRelation that you defined in step 6 as an argument. Then you can loop through all the rows in the child view and add the name of the book to the ListBox control.

13. Your code should look like this:

```
'test to see if the Find method was successful
If rowIndex > -1 Then

    childView = findView(rowIndex).CreateChildView("PubTitles")

    Dim row As DataRowView

    ListBox1.Items.Clear()
        For Each row In childView
            'add names to list box
            ListBox1.Items.Add(row.Item(2))
        Next
End If

Catch exp As Exception
    MessageBox.Show(exp.Message)
End Try
```

14. Save and test your work. The application should display a list of book names in the ListBox when you select one of the publisher names in the ComboBox. Note that not all publishers have matching book titles. The complete code for this exercise is shown in Listing 6.8.

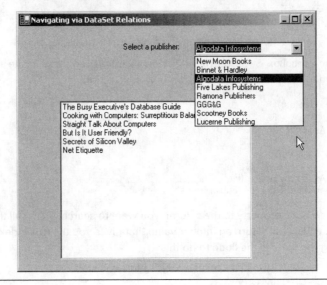

Listing 6.8: The Complete Code for Exercise 6.4

```
Option Strict On
Imports System.Data
Imports System.Data.SqlClient

Public Class frmPublishers
    Inherits System.Windows.Forms.Form
    Private myConn As SqlConnection = New SqlConnection( _
        "Data Source=localhost; Initial " & _
        "Catalog=pubs; Integrated Security=SSPI;")

    Private pubAdapter As SqlDataAdapter = _
        New SqlDataAdapter()
    Private titleAdapter As SqlDataAdapter = _
        New SqlDataAdapter()
    Private bookSet As DataSet = New DataSet()

' Windows Form Designer generated code

Private Sub frmPublishers_Load(ByVal sender As _
    System.Object, ByVal e As System.EventArgs) _
    Handles MyBase.Load
        myConn.Open()

        pubAdapter.SelectCommand = New SqlCommand( _
            "SELECT pub_id, pub_name " & _
            "FROM publishers", myConn)

        titleAdapter.SelectCommand = New SqlCommand( _
            "SELECT title_id, pub_id, title, price " & _
            "FROM titles", myConn)
        Try
            pubAdapter.Fill(bookSet, "Publishers")
            titleAdapter.Fill(bookSet, "Titles")

            Dim pubRelation As DataRelation

            pubRelation = bookSet.Relations.Add("PubTitles", _
                bookSet.Tables("Publishers").Columns("pub_id"), _
                bookSet.Tables("Titles").Columns("pub_id"))
```

```vb
        ComboBox1.DataSource = bookSet.Tables("Publishers")
        ComboBox1.DisplayMember = "pub_name"
        ComboBox1.ValueMember = "pub_id"

    Catch exp As Exception
        MessageBox.Show(exp.Message)
    Finally
        myConn.Close()
    End Try
End Sub

  Private Sub ComboBox1_SelectedIndexChanged( _
      ByVal sender As System.Object, _
      ByVal e As System.EventArgs) _
      Handles ComboBox1.SelectedIndexChanged

        Dim rowIndex As Integer
        Dim childView As DataView
        Dim findView As DataView = New _
            DataView(bookSet.Tables("Publishers"))

        Try
            findView.Sort = "pub_id"
            rowIndex = findView.Find( _
                ComboBox1.SelectedValue)

            If rowIndex > -1 Then
                childView = findView( _
                    rowIndex).CreateChildView("PubTitles")

                Dim row As DataRowView

                ListBox1.Items.Clear()

                For Each row In childView
                    'add names to list box
                    ListBox1.Items.Add(row.Item(2))
                Next
            End If
        Catch exp As Exception
            MessageBox.Show(exp.Message)
```

```
        End Try
    End Sub
End Class
```

Using Visual Studio .NET Components and Working with Strongly Typed DataSets

Now that you have a solid introduction to working with DataAdapters and DataSets (as well as the other related classes in the `System.Data` namespace), we will show you how Visual Studio .NET can make working with these classes much easier. In the examples that you have seen so far, we have written the code that is necessary to declare, instantiate, and set the properties for our ADO.NET objects. In this section, you are going to use the Visual Studio .NET data components to create an application.

These components are found in the Visual Studio .NET Toolbox and can be added to your project simply by dragging and dropping them onto a form, just like the standard TextBox or Command Button controls that you are used to using. After the controls are added to the project, Visual Studio .NET will generate the majority of the code that is required to use them, based on the settings that you make by using dialog boxes. These components behave exactly the same way as the ADO.NET objects that you create manually. After the code has been generated, you can modify it or add additional code of your own for further customization.

In this section, you will also learn about strongly typed DataSets. The second goal of this section is to demonstrate their use. A *strongly typed DataSet*, also referred to simply as a typed DataSet, is an object whose definition is provided at design time and expressed in the form of an XML Schema Definition (XSD) document. Visual Studio .NET will also generate a class in your project that expresses the definition in terms of object properties, methods, and events.

All of the examples so far in this chapter relied on the ADO.NET DataSet object's ability to create appropriate columns automatically as data is being loaded. Although this is convenient, it can lead to errors if you use data types inappropriately when your application is running. A typed DataSet has all column names and data types defined in advance, so while you are writing code, the compiler can check whether you are using data types correctly and ensure that you are not making any invalid type conversions while working with the data. Another advantage of typed DataSets is that you can see column name information in Intellisense while you are working in the Visual Studio .NET code editor. Using the Visual Studio .NET Toolbox data components is one of the easiest ways to create a typed DataSet, although they can be created in other ways. For example, you can add an XSD Schema file to your project, or can drag and drop a stored procedure definition from the Server Explorer.

We cover specifics about XSD in Chapter 7. This section concentrates on creating the typed DataSet and working with it in your code. After having completed the first four exercises in this chapter, you will appreciate the time savings that Visual Studio .NET provides by generating much of the repetitive code for you.

Using the Toolbox Components

Just as you did when you first began learning about ADO.NET in Chapter 5, you will begin by creating and configuring a Connection object to access the database. Then you will see how to add a DataAdapter component to the application and use the Data Adapter Configuration Wizard to set its properties. After you have configured the DataAdapter, you can use the Generate DataSet menu option to create a strongly typed DataSet that will be automatically configured according to the settings that you have previously specified for the DataAdapter.

ADO.NET Toolbox components can easily and quickly be added to your project in Visual Studio .NET. To add a component, go to the Data tab in the Toolbox and click on the item you want to add. Then, drag it onto the form design surface, just as you would add a standard Windows forms control such as a TextBox or Command Button. The components will not appear on the design surface itself, but in the "tray" area directly below it. The ADO.NET-equivalent components that are available from the Visual Studio .NET Toolbox are as follows:

- DataSet

- OleDbDataAdapter, SqlDataAdapter

- OleDbConnection, SqlConnection

- OleDbCommand, SqlCommand

- DataView

Figure 6.1 shows the Visual Studio .NET Toolbox and data components added to the tray area below the form design surface.

FIGURE 6.1 The Visual Studio .NET data components

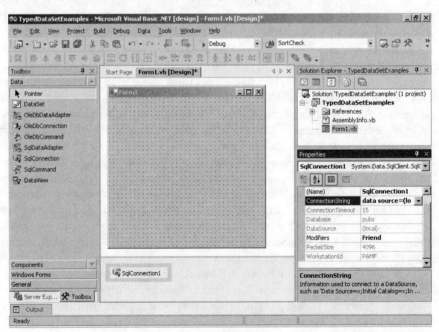

After you drag a Connection component onto the form, you can then go to the Properties window to begin configuring the `ConnectionString` property. When you select `<NewConnection>`, you will see the familiar Data Link Properties dialog box, shown in Figure 6.2, to select a server, login information, and a database.

FIGURE 6.2   The Data Link Properties dialog box

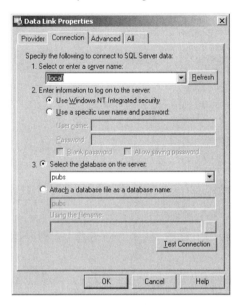

If you expand the Windows Form Designer Generated region of your form's code module, you will see the `SqlConnection1` object declared as `Friend` and `WithEvents`, and then instantiated, as shown in this code snippet for the Connection component:

```
Friend WithEvents SqlConnection1 As _
    System.Data.SqlClient.SqlConnection
Me.SqlConnection1 = New _
    System.Data.SqlClient.SqlConnection()
```

The `ConnectionString` property is set with the values that you set in the Data Link Properties dialog box:

```
Me.SqlConnection1.ConnectionString = _
    "data source=(local);initial catalog=pubs;" & _
    "integrated security=SSPI;persist security " & _
    "info=False;workstation id=COMP1;packet size=4096"
```

When you add a DataAdapter component, Visual Studio .NET automatically starts up the *Data Adapter Configuration Wizard.*

You will go through the steps of using the Data Adapter Configuration Wizard in detail in Exercise 6.5.

This wizard helps you to configure the `SelectCommand` property of the DataAdapter component by using a visual query builder, and then automatically generates matching `InsertCommand`, `UpdateCommand`, and `DeleteCommand` SQL statements. The wizard gives you the option of creating SQL statements that will be added to your source code or calling stored procedures. While configuring a DataAdapter to create a simple `SelectCommand` to retrieve data from the `jobs` table (just as you did in Exercise 6.1), the visual query builder would look like Figure 6.3.

FIGURE 6.3   The Query Builder

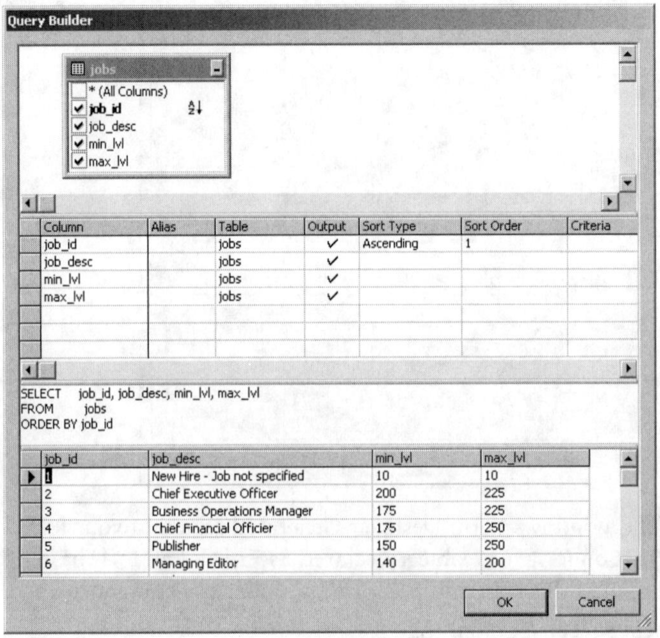

The Data Adapter Configuration Wizard then generates code, which is also found in the Windows Form Designer generated code region of the form's code module.

For the DataAdapter component, the `SelectCommand` property is generated based on your query builder selections. Matching `InsertCommand`, `UpdateCommand`, and `DeleteCommand` statements are also generated. However, this is done differently from the way that you created them in Exercise 6.1. Visual Studio .NET creates a complex `WHERE` clause, which requires every column value for that row in the database to match the corresponding original value stored in the DataSet. Any mismatches that are found indicate that another user made changes to the same record in the database since the time that the data was retrieved to your local DataSet. Rather than have your update overwrite another user's changes, the Visual Studio .NET–generated code, by default, will not allow the update to go through and will show that row to be in error.

This is the safest way to create the SQL updates and it protects against inadvertently overwriting another user's changes. It does, however, create some complex SQL statements. If you prefer, you can change these statements to use a time stamp or row version column to check whether intermediate changes were made, in order to simplify your code. Keep in mind that if you change the generated code and then have to run the Data Adapter Configuration Wizard again, your changes will be replaced by new wizard-generated code. Also, keep in mind that one of the options is to call stored procedures; you might prefer to create your own stored procedures and then let the wizard generate ADO.NET code to call only your procedures.

Listing 6.9 shows what the generated code looks like for the `SelectCommand` and `Update-Command` properties. The `DeleteCommand` property uses similar logic to make sure you do not delete a record if another user has changed it since you first retrieved the data.

Listing 6.9: The Wizard-Generated SQL Statements

```
'SqlSelectCommand1
Me.SqlSelectCommand1.CommandText = _
   "SELECT job_id, job_desc, " & _
   "min_lvl, max_lvl FROM jobs ORDER BY job_id"
Me.SqlSelectCommand1.Connection = Me.SqlConnection1


'SqlUpdateCommand1

Me.SqlUpdateCommand1.CommandText = _
   "UPDATE jobs SET job_desc = @job_desc, " & _
   "min_lvl = @min_lvl, max_lvl = @max_lvl " & _
   "WHERE (job_id = @Original_job_id) AND " & _
   "(job_desc = @Original_job_desc) AND (max_lvl = " & _
   "@Original_max_lvl) AND " & __
   "(min_lvl = @Original_min_lvl); " & _
   "SELECT job_id, job_desc, min_lvl, max_lvl " & _
   "FROM jobs WHERE (job_id = @job_id) ORDER BY job_id"

Me.SqlUpdateCommand1.Connection = Me.SqlConnection1
Me.SqlUpdateCommand1.Parameters.Add(New _
   System.Data.SqlClient.SqlParameter( _
   "@job_desc", System.Data.SqlDbType.VarChar, & _
   50, "job_desc"))

Me.SqlUpdateCommand1.Parameters.Add(New _
   System.Data.SqlClient.SqlParameter( _
   "@min_lvl", System.Data.SqlDbType.TinyInt, _
   1, "min_lvl"))

Me.SqlUpdateCommand1.Parameters.Add(New _
   System.Data.SqlClient.SqlParameter( _
   "@max_lvl", System.Data.SqlDbType.TinyInt, _
   1, "max_lvl"))
```

```
Me.SqlUpdateCommand1.Parameters.Add(New _
    System.Data.SqlClient.SqlParameter( _
    "@Original_job_id", System.Data.SqlDbType.SmallInt, _
    2, System.Data.ParameterDirection.Input, _
    False, CType(0, Byte), CType(0, Byte), _
    "job_id", System.Data.DataRowVersion.Original, Nothing))

Me.SqlUpdateCommand1.Parameters.Add(New _
    System.Data.SqlClient.SqlParameter( _
    "@Original_job_desc", System.Data.SqlDbType.VarChar, _
    50, System.Data.ParameterDirection.Input, False, _
    CType(0, Byte), CType(0, Byte), "job_desc", _
    System.Data.DataRowVersion.Original, Nothing))

Me.SqlUpdateCommand1.Parameters.Add(New _
    System.Data.SqlClient.SqlParameter( _
    "@Original_max_lvl", System.Data.SqlDbType.TinyInt, 1, _
    System.Data.ParameterDirection.Input, False, _
    CType(0, Byte), CType(0, Byte), "max_lvl", _
    System.Data.DataRowVersion.Original, Nothing))

Me.SqlUpdateCommand1.Parameters.Add(New _
    System.Data.SqlClient.SqlParameter( _
    "@Original_min_lvl", System.Data.SqlDbType.TinyInt, 1, _
    System.Data.ParameterDirection.Input, False, _
    CType(0, Byte), CType(0, Byte), "min_lvl", _
    System.Data.DataRowVersion.Original, Nothing))

Me.SqlUpdateCommand1.Parameters.Add(New _
    System.Data.SqlClient.SqlParameter( _
    "@job_id", System.Data.SqlDbType.SmallInt, 2, "job_id"))
```

Generating the Typed DataSet

After you have finished the DataAdapter configuration, you can generate a typed DataSet based on the SelectCommand that you created for your DataAdapter. This feature is available from the Visual Studio .NET Data ➤ *Generate DataSet menu*, or by right-clicking the SqlDataAdapter component in the tray.

Give your DataSet a descriptive name. The name you choose here will be the name given to the files that are generated and used for the class name. By default, the component that is added to your project will be called `DataSet1`, the same way that a TextBox control that you add to your form is called `TextBox1` by default. This is the name that you will use in your code when working with the component. For this example, the component is named `jobSet`. Figure 6.4 shows `JobSet1` in the tray, and the `jobSet.xsd` file (which is the XSD document) and the `jobSet.vb` class in the Solution Explorer.

FIGURE 6.4   The typed DataSet is added to the project.

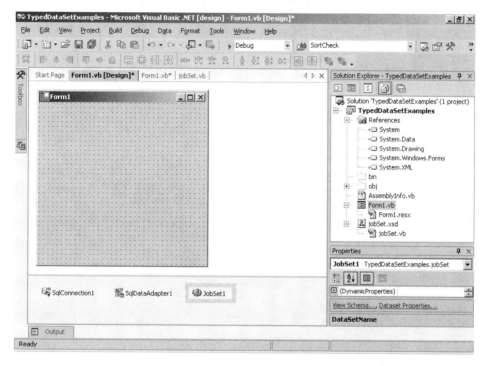

If you review the code in the generated class file, you will find overridden methods for constructors, and other methods and event procedures of the ADO.NET `DataSet` class. There are also property accessor procedures for all of the columns. The following code snippet shows the property procedure for the `job_desc` column:

```
Public Property job_desc As String
    Get
        Return CType(Me(Me.tablejobs.job_descColumn),String)
    End Get
    Set
        Me(Me.tablejobs.job_descColumn) = value
    End Set
End Property
```

After you have created the typed DataSet, it is easier to access its tables and columns. The table and column names show up in Intellisense. The next code snippet shows how to retrieve a field value, and Figure 6.5 shows how Intellisense provides the column names.

```
txtDescription.Text = JobSet1.jobs(0).job_desc
```

FIGURE 6.5   Typed DataSet column names in Intellisense

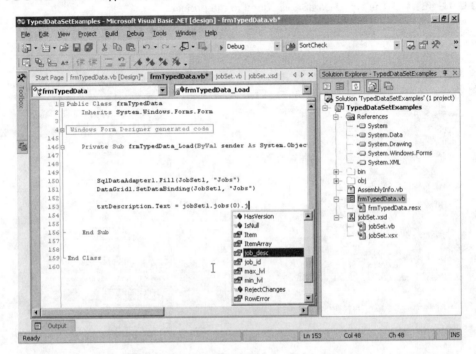

As you've seen, the XSD document that is generated to describe the typed DataSet contains information about the original table and column names and data types in the database, and also reflects the jobSet class name that we assigned.

Listing 6.10 shows the XSD document for the typed DataSet named jobSet.

Listing 6.10: The jobSet XSD Document

```xml
<?xml version="1.0" standalone="yes" ?>
<xs:schema id="jobSet" targetNamespace="http://www.tempuri.org/jobSet.xsd"
    xmlns:mstns="http://www.tempuri.org/jobSet.xsd"
    xmlns="http://www.tempuri.org/jobSet.xsd"
    xmlns:xs="http://www.w3.org/2001/XMLSchema"
    xmlns:msdata="urn:schemas-microsoft-com:xml-msdata"
    attributeFormDefault="qualified" elementFormDefault="qualified">

    <xs:element name="jobSet" msdata:IsDataSet="true">
        <xs:complexType>
```

```
            <xs:choice maxOccurs="unbounded">
                <xs:element name="jobs">
                    <xs:complexType>
                        <xs:sequence>
                            <xs:element name="job_id"
                                msdata:ReadOnly="true"
                                msdata:AutoIncrement="true"
                                type="xs:short" />
                            <xs:element name="job_desc"
                                type="xs:string" />
                            <xs:element name="min_lvl"
                                type="xs:unsignedByte" />
                            <xs:element name="max_lvl"
                                type="xs:unsignedByte" />
                        </xs:sequence>
                    </xs:complexType>
                </xs:element>
            </xs:choice>
        </xs:complexType>
        <xs:unique name="Constraint1" msdata:PrimaryKey="true">
            <xs:selector xpath=".//mstns:jobs" />
            <xs:field xpath="mstns:job_id" />
        </xs:unique>
    </xs:element>
</xs:schema>
```

If you are not using Visual Studio .NET to create your applications, you can use the command-line tool xsd.exe to use an XSD document, such as the one shown in Listing 6.10, to generate the class module that can then be compiled along with your other source code.

Exercise 6.5 gives you an opportunity to try using the Visual Studio .NET Toolbox DataAdapter component and to see how strongly typed DataSets are used.

EXERCISE 6.5

Creating a Typed DataSet and Using Visual Studio .NET Components

1. Start a new Windows application project in Visual Studio .NET. Name the project **TypedDataSetExample**.

2. Change the name of the form to **frmTypedData**. Add a DataGrid control. Your form should look something like this.

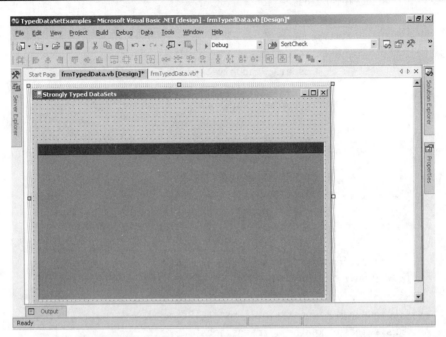

3. From the Toolbox, click the Data tab and then drag a SqlDataAdapter component to the form design surface. The Data Adapter Configuration Wizard will run. Click the Next button.

4. The next screen asks you to choose a connection. Click the New Connection button.

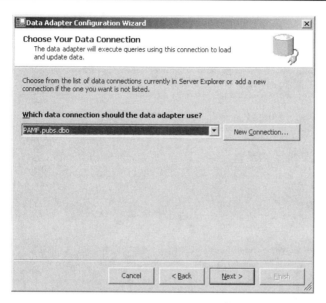

5. Fill in the Data Link Properties dialog box with the server name. Use **(local)** if you are running SQL Server on your development machine, or use the appropriate server name for your environment. Set the login information to Use Windows NT Integrated Security (or provide appropriate username and password information for your environment), and select the pubs sample database. Click the Test Connection button. Then click OK.

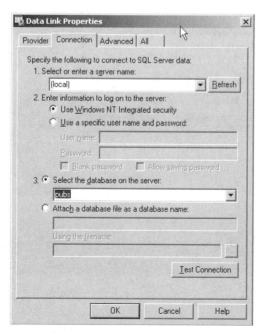

EXERCISE 6.5 *(continued)*

6. The next screen asks you to select a query type. Click the Use SQL Statements radio button to select it. Click Next.

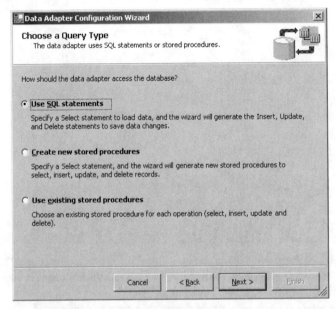

7. The next screen asks you to provide a SQL SELECT statement. Click the Query Builder button.

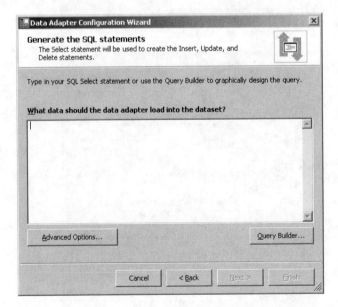

8. Select the jobs table and click Add. Then click Close.

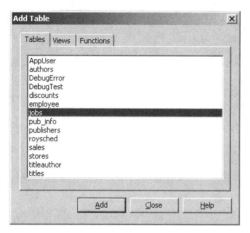

9. Use the query builder to design a query that looks like the following graphic. Right-click in the query builder window and choose Run from the menu to test your query.

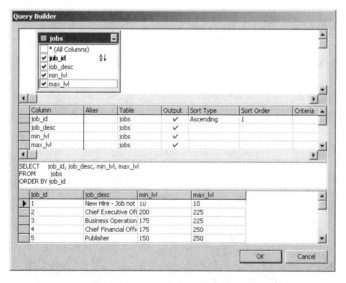

10. Click OK to close the query builder and click Advanced Options. This screen gives you options as to how the DataAdapter `Insert`, `Update`, and `Delete` command statements will be coded. Notice that all options are selected by default. Click OK to close the Advanced SQL Generation Options dialog box. Then click Next.

EXERCISE 6.5 *(continued)*

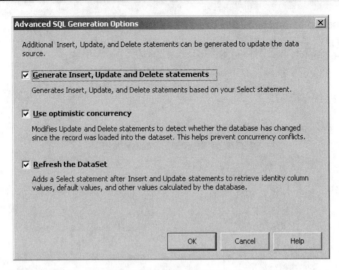

11. The last screen is a summary of what the wizard has created. Click Finish.

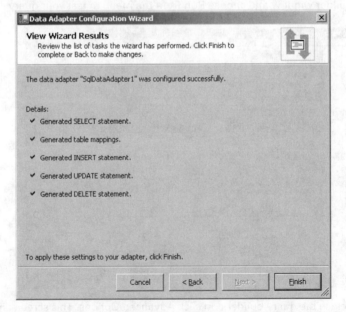

12. Open the code module for `frmTypedData` and expand the Windows Form Designer generated code region. Examine the code that was generated to create and configure the Connection and DataAdapter components.

13. Right-click the `SqlDataAdapter1` component in the tray area. Choose Generate DataSet from the menu. Change the DataSet name to **jobSet** and click OK.

EXERCISE 6.5 *(continued)*

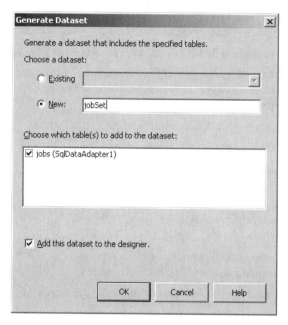

You will see the JobSet1 component added to the tray.

14. Review the files jobSet.xsd and jobSet.vb that have been added to your project. You might have to click the Show All Files toolbar button at the top of the Solution Explorer to see these files.

15. Even though you have created and configured the components, you still need to write code to fill the DataSet and bind to the DataGrid. Add the following code to the frmTypedData_Load procedure:

```
SqlDataAdapter1.Fill(JobSet1, "Jobs")
DataGrid1.SetDataBinding(JobSet1, "Jobs")
```

16. Save and test your work.

Summary

In this chapter, you learned about working with disconnected data by using the DataSet and many other related ADO.NET classes. We covered the following topics:

- How to create and configure a DataAdapter to fill a DataSet

- How to configure a DataAdapter to submit inserts, updates, and deletes from the local DataSet back to the database

- How to work with the DataTable, DataRow, and DataColumn objects that make up the internal structure of the DataSet

- How the DataSet maintains both current values and original values of the data and keeps track of the state (modified, unchanged, deleted, and so on) of each row

- How the AcceptChanges and RejectChanges methods affect row version and row state, and which updates are sent to the database

- What specific types of DataExceptions are available and how to write error-handling code to catch different types of exceptions

- How to use DataViews to sort, filter, and find data in the DataSet

- How to use a DataViewManager to manage settings for all DataViews associated with a DataSet

- How to apply ForeignKeyConstraints and UniqueConstraints to DataSets and DataTables

- How DataRelations enable navigation between parent and child records in related tables in the DataSet

- How to use Visual Studio .NET Toolbox data components to add ADO.NET objects to your project and automatically generate code to create and configure the objects

- How to use the Data Adapter Configuration Wizard to generate SQL commands

- How to automatically generate a strongly typed DataSet

- The advantages of working with strongly typed DataSets

Exam Essentials

Know how to create a DataSet and manipulate disconnected data.   A DataSet is made up of a complex internal structure that includes DataTable, DataRow, and DataColumn objects.

Know how to create and configure a DataAdapter to fill a DataSet and later submit changes back to the database.   Understand how to code DataAdapter.SelectCommand, InsertCommand, UpdateCommand, and DeleteCommand SQL statements, or call stored procedures.

Understand how the DataSet schema can be created and how it describes the column and data types a table contains.   A schema can be added to a DataSet when it is filled, or a schema can be generated when creating a strongly typed DataSet.

Know how to use Constraints and DataRelations to enforce data integrity rules in the DataSet.   ForeignKeyConstraints and UniqueConstraints define rules for cascading or prohibiting changes that would affect parent/child data relationships. DataRelations define parent/child relationships between tables and can be used to navigate from a parent row to its related child rows in another table.

Understand the advantages of using strongly typed DataSets.   Strongly typed DataSets have the table and column names and column data types defined in advance. The compiler can warn against invalid data type conversions, preventing runtime errors. Object names are available through Intellisense when you are writing code. Referencing objects by their defined names provides a more direct way to access data values.

Key Terms

Before you take the exam, be certain you are familiar with the following terms:

AcceptChanges method

ADO.NET Toolbox components

ContinueUpdateOnError

Data Adapter Configuration Wizard

DataException class

DataRelation object

DataRow object

DataRow.RowState property

DataRowVersion.Current value

DataRowVersion.Original value

DataSet

DataTable object

DataView object

DataViewManager

ForeignKeyConstraint

Generate DataSet menu

InsertCommand

OleDbDataAdapter object

RejectChanges method

RowFilter property

RowStateFilter property

SelectCommand

Sort property

SqlDataAdapter object

strongly typed DataSet

UniqueConstraint

Update method

UpdateCommand

Review Questions

1. How can you access the data in a DataTable if you do not explicitly assign a name to the DataTable when it is added to the DataSet by the Fill method?

    A. You cannot access the data unless you assign a name.

    B. You will receive a runtime error if you do not assign a name.

    C. You can reference the DataTable by using the DataSet.Tables collection, table index value.

    D. You can reference the DataTable by asking for the DataSet.DefaultTable.

2. Which statement best describes the structure of a DataSet?

    A. A DataSet contains a set of records returned from the database.

    B. A DataSet has a collection of DataTable objects. In turn, each DataTable has a collection of DataViews and DataRows.

    C. A DataSet has a collection of DataTable objects. In turn, each DataTable has a collection of DataColumns and DataRows.

    D. A DataSet contains collections of DataTables, DataColumns, and DataRows. Relationships between these objects are defined by DataRelations.

3. What will happen when you call the DataSet.AcceptChanges method?

    A. Changes that the user has made to the data in the DataSet will be sent to the database.

    B. The user will receive a message asking them to confirm their changes.

    C. Rows that the user changed in the DataSet will no longer have a row state of Modified. The original values will still be available.

    D. Rows that the user changed in the DataSet will no longer have a row state of Modified. The original values will no longer be available.

4. When you send a SQL Update instruction to the database with a DataAdapter.Update method call, how should you make sure that your statement will identify the correct record to update?

    A. Specify the original DataRow version of the primary key column in the WHERE clause of the SQL statement.

    B. Specify the current DataRow version of the primary key column in the WHERE clause of the SQL statement.

    C. Specify the default DataRow version of the primary key column in the WHERE clause of the SQL statement.

    D. Specify the proposed DataRow version of the primary key column in the WHERE clause of the SQL statement.

5. You want to create custom error handling to determine when an update conflict has occurred at the database and to handle this appropriately. Which `Catch` block should you use?

A. `Catch ex As Exception`

B. `Catch ex As DataException`

C. `Catch ex as DBConcurrencyException`

D. `Catch ex as DuplicateNameException`

6. What is a common use of a DataView?

A. To send updates to the database.

B. To pass data from one procedure to the next.

C. To provide a sorted or filtered subset of the data in a DataTable.

D. A DataView is a Windows forms control that displays data.

7. You would like to use a DataView to create a subset of data that shows all rows that the user has deleted from a DataTable. Which property setting would you make?

A. `myView.RowFilter = DataViewRowState.Deleted`

B. `myView.RowStateFilter = DataViewRowState.Deleted`

C. `myView.RowFilter = "Deleted"`

D. `myView.RowStateFilter = "Deleted"`

8. You have created a `ForeignKeyConstraint` object in your DataSet. You want to allow the user to delete a row in the parent table and make sure that any child rows in a related table are also deleted. How can you accomplish this?

A. Make sure the `DeleteRule` property of the constraint is set to `Cascade`.

B. Make sure the `DeleteRule` property of the constraint is set to `SetDefault`.

C. Make sure the `RelatedColumns` property of the constraint is set to `Delete`.

D. Make sure the `RelatedColumns` property of the constraint is set to `Cascade`.

9. You want to create a `UniqueConstraint` for your DataTable to make sure that duplicate primary keys are not entered by the user. The primary key for the data you are working with is made up of two columns. How can you specify this when creating the constraint?

A. Create two constraints, one for each column.

B. Create a new column in the DataTable and combine both values into that column.

C. Create references to both DataColumns and pass them as an array of DataColumn objects when creating the constraint.

D. It is impossible to create a `UniqueConstraint` for multiple columns.

10. A function in your application must create and return a new, empty DataSet object that has the same structure as the DataSet that is passed in. How can you accomplish this?

   A. Use the `DataSet.Copy` method.

   B. Use the `DataSet.Merge` method.

   C. Use the `DataSet.Clear` method.

   D. Use the `DataSet.Clone` method.

11. You would like to use the Data Adapter Configuration Wizard to help you generate code for your application, but your database administrator allows access to data only through existing stored procedures. What should you do?

   A. Run the wizard in the standard fashion, and change the code manually to call stored procedures.

   B. Ask the database administrator to create appropriate stored procedures; you can then tell the wizard to generate code to call them.

   C. You will not be able to use the features of the wizard because the DataAdapter can call only stored procedures that it created.

   D. You will not be able to use the features of the wizard because the DataAdapter cannot call stored procedures.

12. Your Windows application uses a DataSet object to allow users access to all of the data in your inventory table. Most users are interested in viewing information about only one category of inventory items at a time. How can you easily enable your users to restrict their viewing to a selected category?

   A. Provide a user interface element that enables a user to select from a list of categories. Then create a DataTable object that contains only rows that match the user's selection.

   B. Provide a user interface element that enables a user to select from a list of categories. Then create a DataRow object that contains only rows that match the user's selection.

   C. Provide a user interface element that enables a user to select from a list of categories. Then set the `Filter` property of the DataTable object to show only rows that match the user's selection.

   D. Provide a user interface element that enables a user to select from a list of categories. Then set the `Filter` property of a DataView object to show only rows that match the user's selection.

13. You are creating an application that will be used by customer service representatives, working on your company's local area network, to track service history and customer complaints. Your users will need to view customer history information, update the status of pending service calls, and input new service requests. What model would provide the most flexibility for your users?

   A. Use a DataSet to create a web page that displays customer information and link to other pages that enable the representative to input data.

   B. Use a DataReader to create a web page that displays customer information and link to other pages that enable the representative to input data.

   C. Create a DataSet that contains all pertinent customer information. The representative can review data, make changes, add new information, and submit updates after completing the call.

   D. Create a DataReader that contains all pertinent customer information. The representative can review data, make changes, add new information, and submit updates after completing the call.

14. You are using a DataAdapter to send changes to the database from your DataSet. Sometimes an error will occur at the database, and a row cannot be updated because of a conflict. You would like all other updates from the DataSet to complete. How can you ensure this behavior?

   A. Set a property of the DataSet that controls this behavior.

   B. Set a property of the DataAdapter that controls this behavior.

   C. If an error occurs, remove the row that has the error from the DataSet and try the update again.

   D. Call `RejectChanges` and try the update again.

15. You have set the `ContinueUpdateOnError` property to `True`. All of your update operations seem to complete successfully, but some changes are not showing up in the database. How can you determine which rows failed to update?

   A. Iterate through the `DataSet.GetErrors` collection.

   B. Iterate through the collection created by the `DataTable.GetErrors` method.

   C. Iterate through the `DataSet.HasErrors` collection.

   D. Iterate through the collection created by the `DataTable.HasErrors` method.

Answers to Review Questions

1. C.   You do not have to explicitly assign a table name. It will not cause an error. You can reference all the DataTables in a DataSet by iterating through the `DataSet.Tables` collection. `DefaultTable` is not a valid property of the DataSet.

2. C.   A DataSet contains a collection of DataTables. The DataTable in turn contains the Data-Columns and DataRows collections. The DataSet, not the DataTable, also contains the collection of DataViews, available through the DataViewManager. The first option describes a RecordSet object from the older ADO object model.

3. D.   The `AcceptChanges` method does not update the database or prompt the user. All changed, deleted, or inserted rows in the DataSet will be marked as unchanged. The original values will be set to match the current values in the DataSet—that is, the original values from the database will no longer be available locally in the DataSet.

4. A.   The `DataRowVersion.Original` setting will return the value that was originally retrieved from the database. Specify this version in the SQL `WHERE` clause to ensure that you are updating the correct record in the database, even if the user inadvertently changed the primary key field.

5. C.   The `DBConcurrencyException` is a specialized type of exception that will fire if `DataAdapter.Update` cannot send a change to the database because of a conflict. `Exception` will catch any type of runtime error in your application. `DataException` defines exceptions that are fired by ADO.NET objects. The `DuplicateNameException` would occur when filling a DataSet, not during a database update.

6. C.   The DataView object is commonly used for its `Sort` and `Filter` properties that provide a customized view of the data, and its `Find` method to locate specific items in a DataTable. The Data-Adapter is responsible for sending updates to the database. The DataSet is most appropriate for passing data from one procedure (or component) to another. The DataGrid is a Windows forms control that displays data.

7. B.   Use the `RowStateFilter` property to filter rows based on the `RowState` values, such as `Deleted`, `Added`, `Unchanged`, and so on. Use `RowFilter` to set a string to match data in a column.

8. A.   The `DeleteRule` property controls what happens to child rows when a parent row is deleted. A setting of `Cascade` will pass deletion of (or changes to) the parent row to the child rows. The `RelatedColumns` property gets a reference to the parent column of the constraint.

9. C.   The `UniqueConstraint` constructor can accept a single column reference or an object array of multiple column references. Creating two constraints would require uniqueness in each column, but would not act as a combined key. Combining the values into a new column would not be effective.

10. D.   `DataSet.Clone` creates a new DataSet object that contains all of the same structural elements as the original but no data. `Copy` creates a new DataSet with all of the same structural elements, plus a copy of the original DataSet's data. `Clear` will remove all data from the original DataSet. `Merge` is used to combine two DataSets.

11. B. The Data Adapter Configuration Wizard is flexible enough to generate SQL statements in your source code, generate stored procedures, or create code that calls existing stored procedures. The first option would result in unnecessary work.

12. D. Only the DataView object provides a `Filter` property. DataViews are the best way to filter, sort, or search data in a DataSet.

13. C. In a local area network application or Windows application, you can take advantage of client processing to maintain a local DataSet with all necessary information. The DataSet enables the user to scroll back and forth through data, and to edit and add new information. The Data-Reader object provides a forward-only, read-only view of the data that is suitable for display on a web page or report.

14. B. The DataAdapter object has a property called `ContinueUpdateOnError` that controls this behavior. Set this property to `True`, and updates for all rows that are not in error will go through. The property is `False` by default. The third option would be impractical, and the last option would remove all changes from the DataSet, so that no updates would go through.

15. B. The DataTable has a `GetErrors` method that returns a collection of DataRow objects with a value in their `RowError` property. The DataSet does not have a `GetErrors` method. The `HasErrors` property is available for the DataSet, DataTable, and DataRow objects, but it returns only a Boolean value that indicates whether there are any errors at all for the object.

Working with XML Data

MICROSOFT EXAM OBJECTIVES COVERED IN THIS CHAPTER:

- ✓ **Create and manipulate DataSets.**
  - ▪ Manipulate a DataSet schema.
- ✓ **Access and manipulate XML data.**
  - ▪ Access an XML file by using the Document Object Model (DOM) and an XmlReader.
  - ▪ Transform DataSet data into XML data.
  - ▪ Use XPath to query XML data.
  - ▪ Generate and use an XSD schema.
  - ▪ Write a SQL statement that retrieves XML data from a SQL Server database.
  - ▪ Update a SQL Server database by using XML.
  - ▪ Validate an XML document.

Chapter 5, "Working with the .NET Data Providers," and Chapter 6, "Working with the DataSet," examined the ADO.NET System.Data classes in detail. This chapter begins with a discussion of the XML processing capabilities of the ADO.NET DataSet and then moves on to the System.Xml namespace and the many other classes that the .NET Framework provides to work with XML data.

As you will see in this chapter, the .NET Framework classes make it easy to generate XML data files and schemas. This chapter covers the basics of the XML format and how schemas can be used to define a specific XML format. You will look at the methods provided by ADO.NET to work with XML data. You will also look at classes in the System.XML namespace and learn about using them to work with the XML Document Object Model (DOM), XML Schema Definition (XSD) language validation, and Extensible Stylesheet Language (XSL) and XSL Transformations (XSLT), and to search for data with XPath. This chapter concludes with a look at how to return XML data from SQL Server 2000 queries and how to update a database with XML data.

Introduction to XML Data

Extensible Markup Language (XML) is a language for marking up (or tagging) data so that the meaning of the data items and the overall structure and relationships between data is easy to understand. XML markup can be read and understood by users, but it is equally easy to use any of a wide range of software tools to parse and process the data. XML data files are simple text documents that can be read by software on any computing platform and travel over the Internet via the HTTP protocol.

Because XML was designed and its specification is maintained by the *World Wide Web Consortium (W3C)*, www.w3.org, it is primarily thought of as an Internet or web technology. (The W3C is an international standards body that oversees Internet application standards such as HTML and XML.) However, XML is also useful in application integration. Because the XML format is not platform or programming language specific, it provides a quick way to pass data between applications with a minimal amount of conversion code.

The .NET Framework uses XML as the format for its configuration files and as a means to serialize object state when passing an object to a remote component. In this section, you will first learn about the basic rules for creating well-formed XML data files and see how a schema defines a particular format of XML. You will then learn the basics of working with XML data and the XSD language.

Understanding XML Basics

XML markup uses angle brackets (<. . .>) to enclose tag names that describe each data item, very much like HTML does. Matching pairs of tags enclose the data. These are called *elements*. The closing element tag begins with the forward slash (/) character.

Here is an example of a simple XML element that contains data, or what is called text content.

```
<job>Chief Executive Officer</job>
```

Elements can also contain data in the form of *attributes*. Attributes are enclosed inside the angle brackets and always take the form of a name/value pair. The value is enclosed in quotes.

Here is an example of an XML element that has an attribute named id, with a value of 1.

```
<job id="1">Chief Executive Officer</job>
```

Because one of the goals of XML is to be a universal medium for data exchange, XML files must follow some standard rules, resulting in a document that is said to be *well formed*. These rules are part of a W3C specification. Computer programs that read XML data are called *XML parsers* and they depend on XML data files to be well formed in order to interpret their content correctly. The standard behavior for an XML parser is to stop reading a file and report an error at the first point that it finds an incorrect character. If your XML data file conforms to the rules, and therefore is well formed, then any standard parser can read the data. Microsoft Internet Explorer (version 5 and later) is capable of parsing XML data and then displaying it with special formatting. Figure 7.1 shows a simple XML data file displayed in Internet Explorer.

FIGURE 7.1   An XML data file displayed in Internet Explorer

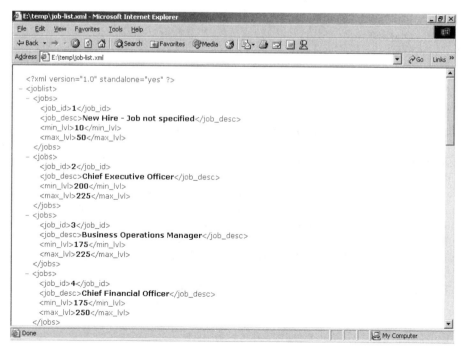

The rules for creating well-formed XML files are as follows:

- Every XML document must have a uniquely named root element that encloses all of the data.
- Every element must have matching opening and closing tags.
- Elements at each level of the document hierarchy must be completely nested inside their parent elements (opening and closing tags of different elements cannot overlap).
- Element tag names and attribute names are case sensitive (`<Job>` and `</job>` are not considered a match).
- All attribute values must be enclosed in quotes (either single or double quotes).
- Attribute names cannot repeat for a single element.

Listing 7.1 shows an XML data file that follows these rules.

Listing 7.1: An XML Data File

```
<?xml version="1.0" encoding="UTF-8" standalone="yes" ?>
<!-- This is a comment -->
<joblist>
  <jobs id="1">
    <job_desc>New Hire - Job not specified</job_desc>
    <min_lvl>10</min_lvl>
    <max_lvl>50</max_lvl>
  </jobs>
  <jobs id="2">
    <job_desc>Chief Executive Officer</job_desc>
    <min_lvl>200</min_lvl>
    <max_lvl>225</max_lvl>
  </jobs>
</joblist>
```

You can see that a *uniquely named root element* `<joblist>` is at the beginning of the data and that its matching closing tag `</joblist>` is the last line in the file.

The first line in the file is a *processing instruction*, indicated by the `<?` syntax. This is a special processing instruction, called the XML declaration, and is always the first line of an XML data file. Processing instructions provide information that the parser can use while processing the file. The XML declaration indicates three attribute values: the version of the XML language that we are using, the encoding (for interpreting any extended characters), and the stand-alone attribute, which indicates (when set to `yes`) that no other files are needed to process this document. Other processing instructions can be included anywhere in the XML data file. They can contain information that is widely understood (such as a stylesheet instruction), or useful only to a custom parser.

Following the processing instruction is a comment. This uses the same `<!--` syntax that HTML comments use.

Now that you understand the basics of XML markup language, you will see variations in the basic format as you work through the examples in this chapter. Next you'll learn how schema definition language can be used to define and validate a specific format for XML markup.

Understanding XML Schema Definition

XML inherently enables you to create any element and attribute names that best describe your data and offers lots of flexibility in defining the hierarchical structure of a data file. This flexibility is useful, but when you are designing a format for XML that will be processed by your application code, or trying to conform to the format requirements of a system you want to exchange data with, you need a way to verify that data files are in the correct format.

When XML first became popular, the only means to validate the format of a data file was the *Document Type Definition (DTD)*. DTD was inherited from an older markup language version. DTD was limited in what it could validate and used an unfamiliar syntax. Most of the tools in the .NET Framework that can validate by using XSD schema can also validate by using DTD. This enables you to support legacy data that uses DTD.

 We will not cover DTD in detail here, but information about that technology is available in most XML reference books.

To improve on the shortcomings of DTD, the W3C designed and standardized what we now know as *XML Schema Definition (XSD)* language, or XSD. You might sometimes see references to an intermediate version called *XML Data Reduced (XDR)* that was used before the W3C finalized XSD. Although there are some similarities between XDR and XSD, XSD is much more sophisticated. Most of the tools available in the .NET Framework that perform validation provide support for the older technologies as well as XSD.

Listing 7.1 showed a simple XML data file with data from the jobs table of the pubs sample database. Listing 7.2 shows the XSD that describes this format.

Listing 7.2: The XSD Schema for the jobs Table

```
<?xml version="1.0" standalone="yes"?>
<xs:schema id="joblist" xmlns=""
   xmlns:xs="http://www.w3.org/2001/XMLSchema"
   xmlns:msdata="urn:schemas-microsoft-com:xml-msdata">

  <xs:element name="joblist" msdata:IsDataSet="true">
    <xs:complexType>
      <xs:choice maxOccurs="unbounded">
        <xs:element name="jobs">
          <xs:complexType>
            <xs:sequence>
              <xs:element name="job_id"
                  type="xs:short" minOccurs="0" />
```

```
            <xs:element name="job_desc"
                type="xs:string" minOccurs="0" />
            <xs:element name="min_lvl"
                type="xs:unsignedByte" minOccurs="0" />
            <xs:element name="max_lvl"
                type="xs:unsignedByte" minOccurs="0" />
          </xs:sequence>
        </xs:complexType>
      </xs:element>
    </xs:choice>
  </xs:complexType>
</xs:element>
</xs:schema>
```

The first thing to notice about this XSD file is that it is a well-formed XML document. This file can be parsed or processed by any program that can parse a well-formed XML data file. This enables the standard XML processing tools in the .NET Framework, as well as your custom code, to read, change, or create schema information programmatically. An XSD file is also a valid XML document because the element and attribute names are defined by the XSD specification. If you were to enter a tag name incorrectly (using uppercase letters in place of lowercase, for example) or to add a tag name that was not recognized, your parser would report an error and do no further processing on the files.

The schema file contains a standard XML declaration as its first line. This is followed by the root element `<xs:schema>` that has several namespace declarations. *XML namespaces* are used much the same way that they are used in your .NET Framework applications, although the syntax is different. In XML, the namespace is defined once and assigned prefix characters. As you read through the XML file, all element names using the prefix characters belong to that namespace. A colon character separates the prefix from the tag name. Namespaces are used to add another level of qualification to an element name—either to resolve naming conflicts (by distinguishing one element name from another of the same name originating in another namespace, or simply to indicate where a particular element name is defined. This schema snippet first shows the namespace defining the `xs:` prefix, by using a Uniform Resource Identifier (URI) that references the W3C, and then shows a tag name of `element` that is prefixed by `xs:`, to indicate that it is part of that namespace:

```
xmlns:xs="http://www.w3.org/2001/XMLSchema"
  <xs:element name="joblist" msdata:IsDataSet="true">
```

All element tag names that begin with the `xs:` prefix are defined by the W3C XSD definition.

Another namespace prefix that is defined is `msdata:`. Elements prefixed with `msdata:` contain information that is specific to a schema created and used by Microsoft .NET Framework tools, and can be ignored by parsers on other platforms. The following code snippet shows the namespace declaration and an attribute that is added to the definition of the `<joblist>` element. The attribute with the msdata: prefix shows that the origin of this item of data was an ADO.NET DataSet:

```
xmlns:msdata="urn:schemas-microsoft-com:xml-msdata">
```

```
<xs:element name="joblist" msdata:IsDataSet="true">
```

The rest of the schema file contains an `<xs:element>` definition for each of the element tag names that occur in the data. These element definitions are nested inside each other in the same way that they are shown in the data file. First is the `<xs:joblist>` definition of the unique root element. That is followed by an `<xs:complexType>` element. `<xs:complexType>` indicates that the `<joblist>` element contains a hierarchy of child elements or attributes. This is followed by an `<xs:choice maxOccurs="unbounded">` element. This indicates that the `<joblist>` root element can contain any number of child elements, although our example contains only one, the `<jobs>` element.

The `<jobs>` element is a direct child of the `<joblist>` root element and it is also a complex type. The `<jobs>` element has four child elements, which are listed inside a set of `<xs:sequence>` tags. The `<xs:sequence>` tag means that the child elements listed must always appear in the same order as shown in the schema. These elements do not contain any further child elements or attributes, only text content (the data). They are known as simple types. Their definition includes a name attribute, which is taken from the column name in the DataSet, and a data type attribute, which enables you to verify that appropriate data types are being used. The attributes of `minOccurs` (minimum number of occurrences) and `maxOccurs` (maximum number of occurrences) are also in this definition. By default, the ADO.NET methods create schema that sets all the `minOccurs` attributes to zero (see Listing 7.2). A setting of `minOccurs="0"` indicates that the element is optional (that is, if the child element is missing from any of the `<jobs>` elements, the data file will still be considered valid). You might want to change the value to 1 to indicate that the element is required. You might also want to specify a `maxOccurs` value (use the value of `unbounded` to indicate that the element can be repeated any number of times) for some of your elements when it is compatible with your format to have repeating elements and data, as seen here:

```
<xs:element name="job_id" type="xs:short" minOccurs="1" />
<xs:element name="job_desc" type="xs:string" minOccurs="1"
    maxOccurs="unbounded" />
<xs:element name="min_lvl" type="xs:unsignedByte"
    minOccurs="1" />
<xs:element name="max_lvl" type="xs:unsignedByte"
    minOccurs="1" />
```

Notice that these simple type elements are defined on one line. Their tags carry all pertinent data as attribute values so they do not need opening and closing tags to enclose any data. In this case, you can use a short version of the closing tag. Simply place the / character at the end of the opening tag.

Much more information can be added to an XSD schema to describe your data. This simple example is designed to show you the basics and help you understand the XSD files that are created for your applications in Visual Studio .NET. You can learn more about XSD schemas in the Visual Studio .NET documentation or at `http://msdn.Microsoft.com/xml`.

In the next section, you will learn how to create XML data files and XSD schemas directly from your ADO.NET DataSets.

ADO.NET *DataSets* and XML

Chapter 6 covered the basic use of the `DataSet` to retrieve and edit data from a database. In this chapter, you will look at the additional capabilities of the `DataSet` class to work with XML data. The `DataSet` can be loaded directly with data that is already stored as an XML file on disk, or with XML data that is stored in a `Stream` object, a `String` variable, a `TextReader`, or an `XmlReader`. The `DataSet` can also write its data into XML format by using any of those same mechanisms. The `DataSet` XML methods all work with or without a specific schema and can generate a schema if none is provided. You can capture a representation of the `DataSet` that includes user changes and the original values of data that were modified, by requesting the `DiffGram` option when saving data as XML. Table 7.1 lists the methods of the `DataSet` that work with XML data.

TABLE 7.1   XML Methods of the *DataSet*

Method	Description
GetXml	Returns the XML representation of the data stored in the DataSet
GetXmlSchema	Returns the XSD schema for the XML representation of the data stored in the DataSet
InferXmlSchema	Generates the XML schema from the specified TextReader or file into the DataSet
ReadXml	Reads XML schema and data into the DataSet
ReadXmlSchema	Reads an XML schema only, no data, into the DataSet
WriteXml	Writes XML data, and optionally the schema, from the DataSet
WriteXmlSchema	Writes the DataSet structure as an XML schema

In this section, you will see examples of filling a `DataSet` by using an XML file, writing XML files with `DataSet` data, and creating `DiffGram` output.

Reading XML Data into a *DataSet*

The *ReadXml method* and *ReadXmlSchema method* enable you to load your DataSet directly from XML data—no database required. Anytime you fill a DataSet, a schema is created that describes the contents of the DataSet. Even if you fill the DataSet from a database query, you can ask to view the schema by using the GetXmlSchema method. When you are working with XML data rather than a database as your data source, it is likely that you will have a schema defined and will want to use that information to verify that your data is valid.

The schema for your XML data will either be in-line, that is stored in the same file as the data itself, or stored in a separate file (usually with a .xsd extension). If you would like to load schema information only, use the ReadXmlSchema method. This method can be used either with in-line schemas—in which case the data will not be loaded—or with a separate XSD file. One approach is to load the schema information first, from a known schema file, and then when the data is loading, the DataSet will validate it against the specified schema.

This code shows how to load a DataSet from an XML data file:

```
Dim xmlSet As DataSet = New DataSet()
xmlSet.ReadXml("C:\path\titles.xml")
```

Here is an example of loading a DataSet by using an XmlTextReader:

```
Dim xmlSet As DataSet = New DataSet()
Dim fsXml As New System.IO.FileStream _
  ("C:\path\titles.xml", System.IO.FileMode.Open)

Dim xmlReader As New System.Xml.XmlTextReader(fsXml)

xmlSet.ReadXml(xmlReader, XmlReadMode.ReadSchema)

'process the XML data

xmlReader.Close()
```

The ReadXml method has different behaviors based on its optional *XmlReadMode parameter* (Auto, DiffGram, Fragment, IgnoreSchema, InferSchema, and ReadSchema). The default behavior is to use an XmlReadMode value of Auto, which attempts to determine the format of the XML file automatically and use the appropriate behavior. If the DataSet already has a schema or the file has an in-line schema, the ReadSchema behavior will be used. If there is no DataSet schema and no in-line schema, the InferSchema behavior will be used and a schema will be created based on the contents of the XML data.

There are subtle differences among three of the XmlReadMode choices: ReadSchema, IgnoreSchema, and InferSchema. It's important to understand the differences, because using them incorrectly could result in a failure to load data (either partially or completely) or a runtime error. The ReadSchema choice requires that schema information be available (either already loaded in the DataSet or in-line with the data) or the ReadXml method will fail to load data. If the DataSet has a schema defined, you can add new tables to the DataSet via an in-line schema, but if the in-line schema information duplicates what is already in the DataSet, an error will occur. The IgnoreSchema choice will disregard any in-line schema and use the previously defined DataSet schema. Any data that does not match the existing schema will not be loaded. If there is no schema established for the DataSet, then no data will be loaded. There is a subtle difference in the behavior of InferSchema: this choice also ignores any in-line schema, but will load data and create schema information for any data that does not match the existing DataSet schema.

Using the DataSet.InferXmlSchema method is similar to using ReadXml with the InferSchema parameter. The InferXmlSchema method offers the extended functionality of being able to specify one or more namespaces in the incoming data that should be ignored when creating the schema for the DataSet.

The *GetXml method* and *GetXmlSchema method* can be used when you simply want to display or to pass the data or the schema stored in a DataSet in an XML format. Both of these methods return a string value. Exercise 7.2 later in this section demonstrates how to use these methods.

Now let's look at how to write XML data from a DataSet.

Writing XML Data from a *DataSet*

Writing the contents of a DataSet to an XML disk file, a Stream object, a TextWriter, or an XmlWriter is simple. Call the DataSet *WriteXml method* and specify a filename or the object that will hold the data. The WriteXml method has an optional *XmlWriteMode parameter* that determines what output is created. The values for the XmlWriteMode parameter are WriteSchema, IgnoreSchema, and DiffGram.

The WriteSchema choice for this parameter adds the schema information, in-line with the data, as a single output. WriteSchema is the default and this is what you will get if no value is specified for the parameter. Another choice is IgnoreSchema; only the data will be written. The third option is DiffGram; this format includes information about user modifications to the data in the DataSet and also includes the original values from the database. DiffGrams are explained further in the section titled "Creating DiffGram Output." You will work with the DiffGram format in Exercise 7.3.

The WriteXmlSchema method can be used when you want to output only schema information, separate from the data. WriteXmlSchema can be used to create the same types of output as the WriteXml method (disk file, string, TextWriter, or XmlWriter). This method has no additional parameters.

The following code shows how to use the WriteXml and WriteXmlSchema methods to create two disk files, one that contains the XML data and one that contains the schema definition. By convention, the .xml filename extension is used for XML data files, and the .xsd extension is used for schemas.

```
xmlSet.WriteXml("C:\path\job-list.xml", XmlWriteMode.IgnoreSchema)


xmlSet.WriteXmlSchema("C:\path\job-schema.xsd")
```

The DataSet provides methods to easily create XML output in a default format. Sometimes you will need to have greater control over the exact format of XML that is created. You can do this by setting properties of the DataColumns that contain the data that will be output.

Controlling XML Format with Column Mappings

By default, the DataSet.WriteXml method creates a format of XML that uses only elements, not attributes. The element hierarchy for a simple table would be as follows: first, a root element, which takes its name from the DataSet, followed by an element that represents each row in the table, which takes its name from the DataTable. Nested inside the table-level element is a set of elements that contain data from each column in the table. This default behavior of the DataSet.WriteXml method with the IgnoreSchema creates a format of XML that is shown in Listing 7.3.

Listing 7.3: Default XML Format for the DataSet.WriteXml Method

```
<?xml version="1.0" standalone="yes"?>
<NewDataSet>
  <Jobs>
    <job_id>1</job_id>
    <job_desc>New Hire - Job not specified</job_desc>
    <min_lvl>10</min_lvl>
    <max_lvl>10</max_lvl>
  </Jobs>
  <Jobs>
    <job_id>2</job_id>
    <job_desc>Chief Executive Officer</job_desc>
    <min_lvl>200</min_lvl>
    <max_lvl>225</max_lvl>
  </Jobs>
</NewDataSet>
```

If you need to create a different format that uses attributes, or if you need to change the default names, you can set properties of the DataColumn to do this. If you do not provide a value for the DataSet.Name property (either when you are instantiating it or later), the default name NewDataSet will be used. The DataTable name that was assigned when you filled the DataSet will be used as an element tag name that occurs for each row in the table, and the database column names will be used as element tag names for each data item.

Keep in mind that XML element tag names are strictly case sensitive, so the names that you assign in your code—or the database column names—must match any defined schema. Otherwise, any code that consumes the XML data will experience parsing errors.

The *ColumnMapping property* of the DataColumn object controls whether a column is output as an XML element or as an attribute. The ColumnMapping property can be specified as either Element, Attribute, Hidden (that column will not be included in the XML output), or SimpleContent (the column data will be output as the text content of the row element). Additionally, you can set the DataColumn.ColumnName property to change the element or attribute name that is used in the output. This code snippet shows how to assign a DataSet name and a DataTable name, and then set the ColumnMapping and ColumnName properties for the job_id column:

```
Dim jobSet As DataSet = New DataSet("joblist")
jobAdapter.Fill(jobSet, "jobs")

Dim dt As DataTable
dt = jobSet.Tables("jobs")
dt.Columns("job_id").ColumnMapping = MappingType.Attribute
dt.Columns("job_id").ColumnName = "id"
```

Listing 7.4 shows the XML output that was created by the preceding code.

Listing 7.4: Changing the Format of XML Output

```xml
<?xml version="1.0" standalone="yes"?>
<joblist>
  <jobs id="1">
    <job_desc>New Hire - Job not specified</job_desc>
    <min_lvl>10</min_lvl>
    <max_lvl>50</max_lvl>
  </jobs>
  <jobs id="2">
    <job_desc>Chief Executive Officer</job_desc>
    <min_lvl>200</min_lvl>
    <max_lvl>225</max_lvl>
  </jobs>
</joblist>
```

In Exercise 7.1, you will create a simple console application that will write XML data and schema files from a DataSet (again, you will be using the sample pubs database from SQL Server 2000). You will use the files that you create in this exercise to complete Exercise 7.2, in which you will load a DataSet from the XML files.

EXERCISE 7.1

Writing *DataSet* Data to an XML File

1. Start Visual Studio .NET and create a new Console Application project called **SaveXML**.

2. You will be using the same pubs sample database that you did in Chapters 5 and 6. You are going to set up SqlConnection, SqlDataAdapter, and DataSet objects that are very similar to the examples used in Chapter 6. Feel free to cut and paste some of the code from those exercises if you have it available. Place the Imports statements at the top of the code module and place the rest of the code inside the Sub Main procedure. Notice in the following code that the lines shown in bold are new or different for this exercise. Your code should look like this (note that where the code shows C:*path*, you should specify the same directory that you specified when you created this project):

```
Option Strict On
Imports System.Data
Imports System.Data.SqlClient

Module Module1

    Sub Main()

        Dim myConn As SqlConnection = New SqlConnection( _
            "Data Source=localhost; Initial " & _
            "Catalog=pubs; Integrated Security=SSPI;")

        Dim jobAdapter As SqlDataAdapter = New SqlDataAdapter()

        Dim jobSet As DataSet = New DataSet("joblist")

        jobAdapter.SelectCommand = New SqlCommand( _
            "SELECT job_id, job_desc, min_lvl, max_lvl " & _
            "FROM jobs", myConn)

        Try
            jobAdapter.Fill(jobSet, "jobs")

            ' column mapping code will be added here later
            jobSet.WriteXml("C:\path\job-list.xml", _
                XmlWriteMode.IgnoreSchema)
            jobSet.WriteXmlSchema("C:\path\job-schema.xsd")
            Console.WriteLine("Files have been created.")
        Catch exp As Exception
            Console.WriteLine(exp.Message)
        Finally
            Console.ReadLine()
        End Try
    End Sub
End Module
```

3. Save and test your work. Select the project name in the Solution Explorer and click the Show All Files button on the Solution Explorer toolbar.

4. Open the file named job-list.xml. It will be displayed in the code editor. Review the contents of the file. When Visual Studio .NET displays an XML file, it shows you two views: first the XML markup and, alternatively, a table display. To switch to the table display, click the Data tab at the bottom of the window. The two views of the XML data file should look like the following images.

EXERCISE 7.1 *(continued)*

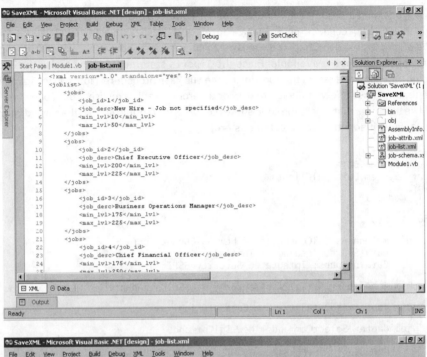

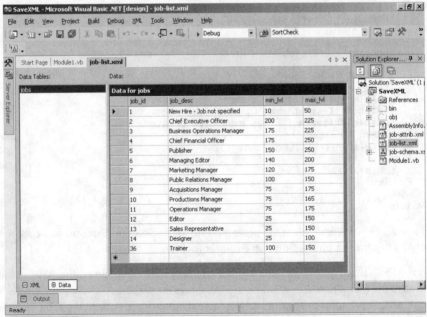

5. Double-click the `job-schema.xsd` file in the Solution Explorer to open it. When Visual Studio .NET displays a schema file, it shows you two views: the DataSet view (which

shows a table that lists elements and attributes and their data types) and the XSD view. To
see the XSD, click the XML tab at the bottom. The schema file should look like the following.

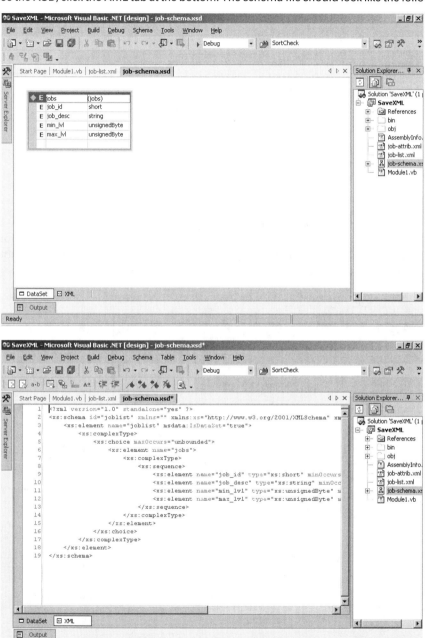

6. Create a different format of XML. Use the `DataColumn.ColumnMapping` property to completely change the format of XML that is created. Insert the following code after the call to `jobAdapter.Fill`:

```
Dim dt As DataTable
dt = jobSet.Tables("jobs")
dt.Columns("job_id").ColumnMapping = MappingType.Attribute
dt.Columns("job_id").ColumnName = "id"
dt.Columns("job_desc").ColumnMapping = MappingType.Attribute
dt.Columns("job_desc").ColumnName = "description"
dt.Columns("min_lvl").ColumnMapping = MappingType.Attribute
dt.Columns("min_lvl").ColumnName = "min"
dt.Columns("max_lvl").ColumnMapping = MappingType.Attribute
dt.Columns("max_lvl").ColumnName = "max"
```

7. Comment out the calls to `jobSet.WriteXml` and `jobSet.WriteXmlSchema` and add this line:

```
jobSet.WriteXml("C:\path\job-attrib.xml")
```

8. Save and test your work. Review the files that are created; the new XML file `job-list.xml` should contain a `<joblist>` root element and repeating `<jobs>` element, each with four attributes and no nested elements. The complete file will look like the next screen shot. A single row would look like this:

```
<jobs id="2" description="Chief Executive Officer"
      min="200" max="225" />
```

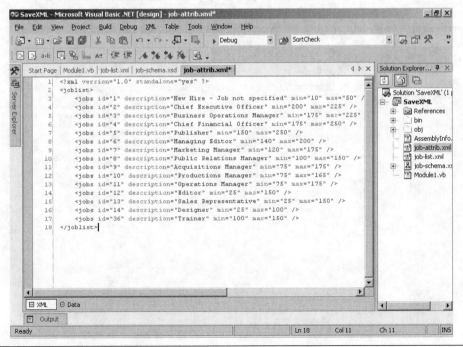

Exercise 7.1 showed you that it is easy to read XML data into an ADO.NET DataSet. Now, in Exercise 7.2, you will practice how to create XML output from a DataSet.

EXERCISE 7.2

Reading XML Data into a DataSet

1. Start Visual Studio .NET and create a new Windows Application project called **ReadXML**.

2. Add a TextBox and two Command Button controls to the form. Name them **txtDisplay**, **btnShowXML**, and **btnShowSchema**, respectively. Set the Multiline property of txtDisplay to **True**. Change the form name to **frmReadXML**. Your form should look like the following one.

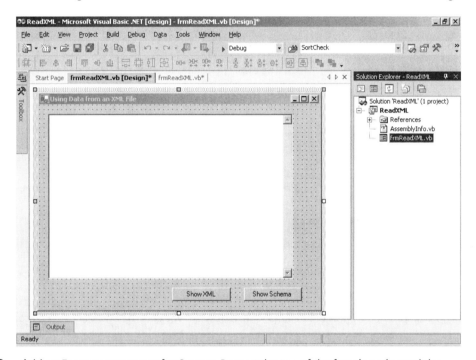

3. Add an Imports statement for System.Data at the top of the form's code module:

   ```
   Imports System.Data
   ```

4. Add a class-level declaration to instantiate a DataSet:

   ```
   Dim jobSet As DataSet = New DataSet("joblist")
   ```

5. In the Form_Load event procedure, load the DataSet from the XML file that you created in Exercise 7.1 (substitute the correct path and filename for the files on your computer) and add a simple error handler. Here is the code to do this:

   ```
   Try
       jobSet.ReadXml("C:\path\job-list.xml")
   ```

```
Catch exp As Exception
   MessageBox.Show(exp.Message)
End Try
```

6. Add code to the btnShowXML_Click procedure to call the GetXml method of the DataSet and display the data in the text box:

```
txtDisplay.Clear()
txtDisplay.Text = jobSet.GetXml()
```

7. Add code to the btnShowSchema_Click procedure to call the GetXmlSchema method of the DataSet and display the schema in the text box:

```
txtDisplay.Clear()
txtDisplay.Text = jobSet.GetXmlSchema()
```

8. Save the project and test your work. The application should show the data as follows.

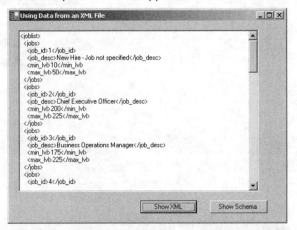

9. The application should show the schema as follows when you click the Show Schema button.

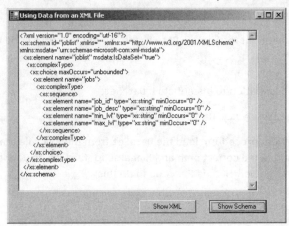

10. Test some variations on the ReadXml method to see how schemas can be used to control how data is loaded. Add the XmlReadMode.ReadSchema parameter to the code that loads the DataSet:

```
jobSet.ReadXml("C:\path\job-list.xml", XmlReadMode.ReadSchema)
```

11. Test your application. Click the Show XML button. No data will be loaded because there has been no schema established for the DataSet and there is no in-line schema in the XML file.

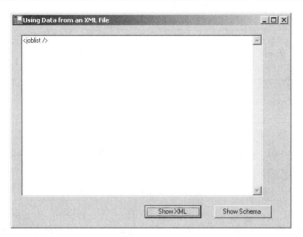

12. Click the Show Schema button. A default schema outline will be displayed, but no specific elements are defined.

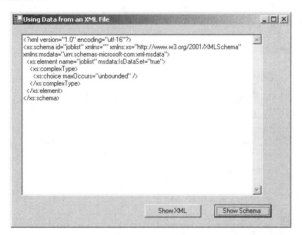

13. Add a call to ReadXmlSchema to load a schema, before loading the data:

```
jobSet.ReadXmlSchema("C:\path\job-schema.xsd")
jobSet.ReadXml("C:\path\job-list.xml", XmlReadMode.ReadSchema)
```

14. Test this version. It should work exactly like the first test when no XmlReadMode parameter was specified. The first test worked because the default behavior uses the InferSchema

EXERCISE 7.2 *(continued)*

option and generates a schema for the DataSet if none is provided. This test worked because the schema was explicitly provided.

15. Test the behavior of the IgnoreSchema option. To do this, add some additional XML elements to the XML data file. Open the XML file, job-list.xml, in Visual Studio .NET or any text editor. Add a new XML element to the first two or three <jobs> elements (make sure you don't break the rules for a well-formed XML document):

```
<jobs>
    <job_id>1</job_id>
    <job_desc>New Hire - Job not specified</job_desc>
    <min_lvl>10</min_lvl>
    <max_lvl>50</max_lvl>
    <test>100</test>
</jobs>
```

16. Save the job-list.xml file.

17. Change the code in your project that loads the DataSet to use the IgnoreSchema parameter:

```
jobSet.ReadXmlSchema("C:\path\job-schema.xsd")
jobSet.ReadXml("C:\path\job-list.xml", XmlReadMode.IgnoreSchema)
```

18. Test your project. The original data is loaded correctly, but the new elements you added were not loaded. This is because they are not described in the schema, so they are ignored.

19. Comment out the call to ReadXmlSchema and test the application again. No data will be loaded. Just like the ReadSchema parameter, the IgnoreSchema parameter will not load any data if no schema is present.

20. Change the parameter value to **InferSchema**.

```
jobSet.ReadXml("C:\path\job-list.xml", XmlReadMode.InferSchema)
```

21. Test the application. You should see that the new items that you added are loaded and displayed in the XML data.

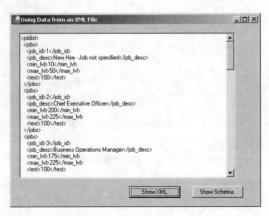

22. The description of a <test> element has also been added to the schema.

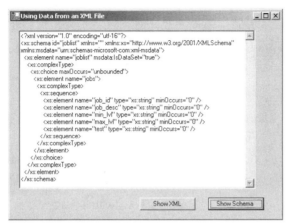

23. Save this project. You will be using it in future exercises. Remove the test items that you added to job-list.xml to return it to its original state.

Creating *DiffGram* Output

As discussed earlier, the DataSet.WriteXml method has an optional parameter called XmlWriteMode. This parameter has three possible settings. The WriteSchema and IgnoreSchema choices determine whether an in-line schema is included in the output file. The third choice, *DiffGram*, creates a completely different type of output.

A DiffGram file contains additional attributes that indicate which of the items in the DataSet have been modified, inserted, or deleted. Following the XML output of the data rows, the DiffGram contains a section of XML that retains the original values of the modified records. The new section of XML output begins with a <diffgr:before> element. If any of the data rows have an error, that information will be noted in another section of the output file starting with a <diffgr:errors> element.

The element and attribute names that are added to the data when creating DiffGram output, called annotations, are defined as part of the diffgr: namespace. There are also annotations defined by the DataSet itself; these are part of the msdata: namespace. The annotations are listed in Table 7.2. Listing 7.5 shows a partial DiffGram output file; in Exercise 7.3 you will create your own DiffGram output and you can examine a complete file.

TABLE 7.2   Element and Attribute Names Used in *DiffGram* Output

Name	Type	Description
<diffgr:diffgram>	Element	Indicates the root element for the output file.
<diffgr:before>	Element	Begins the section that shows original values.

TABLE 7.2 Element and Attribute Names Used in *DiffGram* Output *(continued)*

Name	Type	Description
`<diffgr:errors>`	Element	Begins the section that shows error information.
`diffgr:id`	Attribute	Creates a unique sequential ID value. Matches elements in the main output section with the corresponding information in the `<diffgr:before>` and `<diffgr:errors>` blocks.
`diffgr:parentId`	Attribute	Identifies the parent element of an element, when a DataSet has multiple, related tables.
`diffgr:hasChanges`	Attribute	Identifies a modified row as either inserted, modified, or descent (a modification was made in a child row).
`diffgr:hasErrors`	Attribute	Identifies a row with a RowError.
`diffgr:Error`	Attribute	Contains the text of the RowError, used in the `<diffgr:errors>` block.
`msdata:rowOrder`	Attribute	Indicates the row order of the original data in the DataTable.
`msdata:hidden`	Attribute	A column in the DataTable that had its ColumnMapping property set to hidden.

Listing 7.5: An XML DiffGram Data File

```
<?xml version="1.0" standalone="yes"?>
<diffgr:diffgram
    xmlns:msdata="urn:schemas-microsoft-com:xml-msdata"
 xmlns:diffgr="urn:schemas-microsoft-com:xml-diffgram-v1">
  <joblist>
    <jobs diffgr:id="jobs1" msdata:rowOrder="0"
        diffgr:hasChanges="modified">
      <job_id>1</job_id>
      <job_desc>New Hire - Job not specified</job_desc>
      <min_lvl>10</min_lvl>
      <max_lvl>75</max_lvl>
    </jobs>
</joblist>
  <diffgr:before>
    <jobs diffgr:id="jobs1" msdata:rowOrder="0">
```

```
      <job_id>1</job_id>
      <job_desc>New Hire - Job not specified</job_desc>
      <min_lvl>10</min_lvl>
      <max_lvl>50</max_lvl>
    </jobs>
  </diffgr:before>
</diffgr:diffgram>
```

EXERCISE 7.3

Creating *DiffGram* Output

1. Open the ReadXML project that you created in Exercise 7.2. Add a new form to the project and name it **frmDiff**.

2. Add a DataGrid control and a Command Button control to the form. Name the button **btnMakeDiff**. Your form should look like the following one.

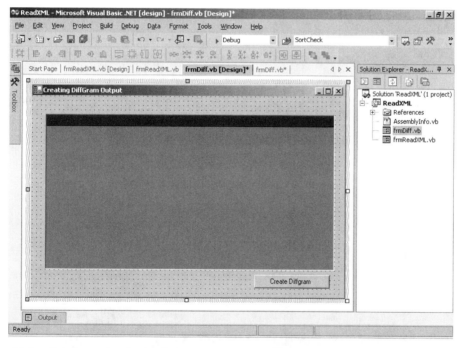

3. Right-click the project in the Solution Explorer and choose Properties from the menu. Set the new frmDiff to be the startup object.

4. Add an Imports statement for System.Data at the top of the form's code module:

```
Imports System.Data
```

EXERCISE 7.3 *(continued)*

5. Add a class-level declaration to instantiate a DataSet:

```
Private jobSet As DataSet = New DataSet("joblist")
```

6. In the Form_Load event procedure, load the DataSet from the XML file that you created in Exercise 7.2 (substitute the correct path and filename for the files on your computer). Call the DataSet.AcceptChanges method; otherwise, all entries will show up as newly inserted. Set the data binding for the DataGrid to use data from the DataSet. Add a simple error handler. Here is the code to do this:

```
Try
    jobSet.ReadXml("C:\path\job-list.xml")
    jobSet.AcceptChanges()
    DataGrid1.SetDataBinding(jobSet, "jobs")

Catch exp As Exception
    MessageBox.Show(exp.Message)
End Try
```

7. Add code to the btnMakeDiff_Click procedure to call the WriteXml method of the DataSet, with the XmlWriteMode.DiffGram parameter:

```
jobSet.WriteXml("C:\path\diffgram.xml", XmlWriteMode.DiffGram)
```

8. Save and run the application. It should look like this one.

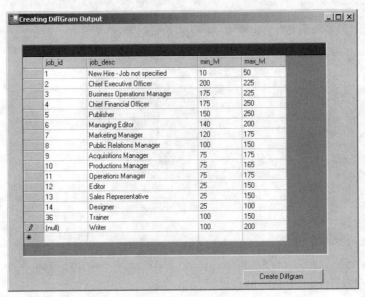

9. Add one or two new items to the DataSet by entering them on the last line of the DataGrid. Make changes to the values of some of the existing rows.

10. Click the Create DiffGram button.

11. Use Windows Explorer or Visual Studio .NET to open the resulting XML file. Additional attributes that belong to the `diffgr:` namespace are added to the code, such as the hasChanges attribute that marks the rows you inserted or modified. You will see items that look like this:

```
<jobs diffgr:id="jobs1" msdata:rowOrder="0"
      diffgr:hasChanges="modified">
  <job_id>1</job_id>
  <job_desc>New Hire - Job not specified</job_desc>
  <min_lvl>10</min_lvl>
  <max_lvl>75</max_lvl>
</jobs>
<jobs diffgr:id="jobs16" msdata:rowOrder="15"
      diffgr:hasChanges="inserted">
  <job_desc>Writer</job_desc>
  <min_lvl>100</min_lvl>
  <max_lvl>200</max_lvl>
</jobs>
```

At the end of the file, a section of XML marked `<diffgr:before>` has the `<jobs>` element for all of the new or changed items. These elements contain the original values, as shown in the following screen shot.

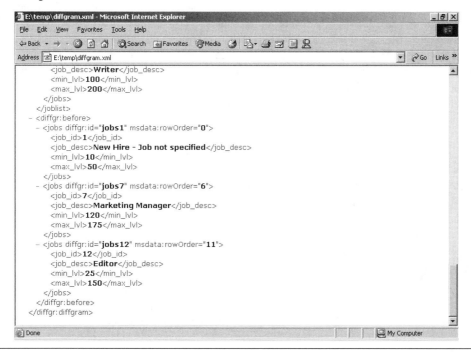

XML Classes in the .NET Framework

Now that you have had an introduction to working with XML data by using the familiar DataSet class, you can look at additional classes in the .NET Framework *System.XML namespace* that enable you to have programmatic access to XML data. You will learn about working with the XML Document Object Model (DOM). The XML DOM is another W3C standard, which specifies a set of classes and their properties and methods, that provides an object model for programming against XML data structures. The classes in System.Xml are the .NET Framework implementation of this standard. You will also learn how to do validation, how to apply XSLT stylesheets to transform XML from one format to another, and how to locate specific nodes in your XML data with the XPath language. This section will finish with an introduction to the XmlDataDocument class, which enables you to load relational data from a database and work with it as if it were loaded into an XmlDocument.

Using the *XMLReader* and *XMLWriter* Classes

The *XmlReader class* and *XmlWriter class* are the XML equivalent of the DataReader that you learned about in Chapter 5. XmlReader provides forward-only, read-only access to your data. XmlWriter provides simple output. Both of these classes are abstract base classes that cannot be instantiated directly in your code.

The System.XML namespace also contains the *XmlTextReader*, *XmlNodeReader*, and *XmlValidatingReader* classes that are derived from the XmlReader base class. Each of these implementations provides slightly different functionality. You can also create your own derived class based on XmlReader if you would like to include additional methods for special processing of the incoming XML data that your own application requires.

Table 7.3 lists the properties and methods of the XmlReader base class and its derived classes. The XmlTextReader and XmlValidatingReader each have some extended properties and methods that support their unique behavior; these are noted in the table. Also noted are methods that are not available for some of the derived classes.

TABLE 7.3 Properties and Methods of the *XmlReader* Base Class and Derived Classes

Property	Description
AttributeCount	The number of attributes on the current node.
BaseURI	The base URI of the current node.
CanResolveEntity	Indicates whether this reader can parse and resolve entities.
Depth	The depth of the current node in the XML document.
Encoding	The encoding of the document (XmlTextReader only).

TABLE 7.3 Properties and Methods of the *XmlReader* Base Class and Derived Classes *(continued)*

Property	Description
EntityHandling	Indicates how entity references are expanded (XmlValidatingReader only).
EOF	Indicates whether the reader is positioned at the end of the stream.
HasAttributes	Indicates whether the current node has any attributes.
HasValue	Indicates whether the current node can have a value.
IsDefault	Indicates whether the current node is an attribute that was generated from the default value defined in the DTD or schema.
IsEmptyElement	Indicates whether the current node is an empty element (for example, <element/>).
Item	The value of the attribute.
LineNumber	The current line number (XmlTextReader only).
LinePosition	The current character position on the line (XmlTextReader only).
LocalName	The local name of the current node.
Name	The qualified name of the current node.
Namespaces	Indicates whether to do namespace support (XmlTextReader and XmlValidatingReader only).
NamespaceURI	The namespace URI of the node on which the reader is positioned.
NameTable	The XmlNameTable associated with this implementation.
NodeType	The type of the current node (element, attribute, text, processing instruction, etc.).
Normalization	Indicates whether to normalize white space and attribute values (XmlTextReader only).
Prefix	The namespace prefix of the current node.
QuoteChar	The quotation mark character used to enclose the value of an attribute node.
Reader	Reference to the reader used to construct this XmlValidatingReader (XmlValidatingReader only).

TABLE 7.3 Properties and Methods of the *XmlReader* Base Class and Derived Classes *(continued)*

Property	Description
ReadState	The state of the reader (closed, endoffile, error, initial interactive).
Schemas	The collection of schemas to be used for validation (XmlValidating-Reader only).
SchemaType	The schema type of the current node (simpleType or complexType) (XmlValidatingReader only).
ValidationType	The type of validation performed (Auto, DTD, None, Schema, XDR) (XmlValidatingReader only).
Value	The text value of the current node.
WhitespaceHandling	Indicates how white space is handled (maintained or removed) (XmlTextReader only).
XmlLang	The current xml:lang scope.
XmlResolver	Used for resolving references to external DTD or schema files (XmlTextReader only).
XmlSpace	The current xml:space scope.

Method	Description
Close	Sets the ReadState to Closed.
GetAttribute	Gets the value of an attribute.
IsName	Gets a value indicating whether the string argument is a valid XML name (not available for XmlNodeReader or XmlValidatingReader).
IsNameToken	Gets a value indicating whether the string argument is a valid XML name token (not available for XmlNodeReader or XmlValidatingReader).
IsStartElement	Returns true if the current content node is a start tag.
LookupNamespace	Resolves a namespace prefix in the current element's scope.
MoveToAttribute	Moves to the specified attribute.
MoveToContent	Moves to the next content node (non-white space text, CDATA, Element, EndElement, EntityReference, or EndEntity). It skips over ProcessingInstruction, DocumentType, Comment, Whitespace, or SignificantWhitespace nodes.

TABLE 7.3   Properties and Methods of the *XmlReader* Base Class and Derived Classes *(continued)*

Method	Description
MoveToElement	Moves to the element that contains the current attribute node.
MoveToFirstAttribute	Moves to the first attribute.
MoveToNextAttribute	Moves to the next attribute.
Read	Reads the next node from the stream.
ReadAttributeValue	Parses the attribute value into one or more Text, EntityReference, or EndEntity nodes.
ReadBase64	Returns decoded Base64 (XmlTextReader only).
ReadBinHex	Returns decoded BinHex (XmlTextReader only).
ReadChars	Buffers very long text strings (XmlTextReader only).
ReadElementString	Reads simple text-only elements.
ReadEndElement	If the current content node is an end tag, moves to the next node.
ReadInnerXml	Reads all node content, including markup, as a string.
ReadOuterXml	Reads the content, including markup, representing this node and all its children.
ReadStartElement	If the current node is an element, moves to the next node.
ReadString	Reads the contents of an element or text node as a string.
ResetState	Resets the reader to ReadState.Initial (XmlTextReader only).
ResolveEntity	Resolves the entity reference for EntityReference nodes.
Skip	Skips over the children of the current node.

When working with data in a DataSet, we are used to thinking about moving through data one row at a time, with a row consisting of a set of columns. Relational data tables have a symmetrical row and column structure, and all rows in a given table have the same number of columns. The structure of XML data is not limited to a simple row and column format. XML data is best thought of as a hierarchical, or tree, structure. Each XML document has a root. Each element that is a direct child of the root can, in turn, have its own child elements, a set of attributes, and text content. This nesting of child elements (each containing their own child elements, attributes, and text content) can continue as many levels deep as required by the complexity of the data you are working with.

The XmlReader classes work by moving through the data one node at a time (rather than one row at a time, the way a DataReader does). XmlReader classes are typically used by setting up a loop. Each time through the loop, you have access to a single node. It is usually desirable to test the NodeType property to know whether you are currently processing an element, attribute, or text node. All other valid items in an XML data file, such as processing instructions and comments, also have a specific node type. After you have identified the type of node you are currently processing, you can retrieve its data (such as its name and value) or do other work with it (such as checking to see whether an element node has attributes or further levels of child elements).

Listing 7.6 creates and loads an XmlTextReader and then loops through the data, looking for a specific element and retrieving its data. You will learn about using the XmlValidatingReader later in this chapter, in the section titled "Validating XML Data."

Listing 7.6: Using an XmlTextReader

```
Private Sub GetJobTitles()
    Dim jobReader As XmlTextReader = New _
        XmlTextReader("C:\path\job-list.xml")

    While jobReader.Read()
        If jobReader.NodeType = XmlNodeType.Element Then
            If jobReader.Name = "job_desc" Then
                lstJobTitle.Items.Add(jobReader.ReadInnerXml())
            End If
        End If
    End While
End Sub
```

The base class of XmlWriter and its derived class, XmlTextWriter, enable you to create a new XML data file (or Stream object) by explicitly writing each item that should appear in the file. As you review the list of methods for these classes in Table 7.4, you will notice many of the methods begin with the verb "Write." You will use these methods to output the different types of nodes that make up an XML data file.

TABLE 7.4   Properties and Methods of the *XmlWriter* Base Class and Derived *XmlTextWriter* Class

Property	Description
BaseStream	Gets the underlying Stream object (XmlTextWriter only).
Formatting	Indicates how the output is formatted (XmlTextWriter only).
Indentation	The number of IndentChars to write for each level in the hierarchy when Formatting is set to Formatting.Indented (XmlTextWriter only).

TABLE 7.4 Properties and Methods of the *XmlWriter* Base Class and Derived
XmlTextWriter Class *(continued)*

Property	Description
IndentChar	The character to use for indenting when Formatting is set to Formatting.Indented (XmlTextWriter only).
Namespaces	Indicates whether to provide namespace support (XmlText-Writer only).
QuoteChar	The character to use to quote attribute values (XmlText-Writer only).
WriteState	The state of the writer.
XmlLang	The current xml:lang scope.
XmlSpace	An XmlSpace representing the current xml:space scope.

Method	Description
Close	Closes this stream and the underlying stream.
Flush	Flushes whatever is in the buffer to the underlying streams and also flushes the underlying stream.
LookupPrefix	Returns the closest prefix defined in the current namespace scope for the namespace URI.
WriteAttributes	Writes all the attributes found at the current position in the XmlReader.
WriteAttributeString	Writes an attribute with the specified value.
WriteBase64	Encodes the specified binary bytes as Base64 and writes the resulting text.
WriteBinHex	Encodes the specified binary bytes as BinHex and writes the resulting text.
WriteCData	Writes a <![CDATA[...]]> block containing the specified text.
WriteCharEntity	Creates a character entity for the specified Unicode character value.
WriteChars	Writes text a buffer at a time.

TABLE 7.4 Properties and Methods of the *XmlWriter* Base Class and Derived *XmlTextWriter* Class *(continued)*

Method	Description
WriteComment	Writes a comment <!--...--> containing the specified text.
WriteDocType	Writes the DOCTYPE declaration with the specified name and optional attributes.
WriteElementString	Writes an element containing a string value.
WriteEndAttribute	Closes the previous WriteStartAttribute call.
WriteEndDocument	Closes any open elements or attributes and puts the writer back in the Start state.
WriteEndElement	Closes one element and pops the corresponding namespace scope.
WriteEntityRef	Writes an entity reference as follows: & name;.
WriteFullEndElement	Closes one element and pops the corresponding namespace scope.
WriteName	Writes the specified name.
WriteNmToken	Writes the specified name, ensuring it is a valid NmToken.
WriteNode	Copies everything from the reader to the writer and moves the reader to the start of the next sibling.
WriteProcessingInstruction	Writes a processing instruction with a space between the name and text as follows: <?name text?>.
WriteQualifiedName	Writes the namespace-qualified name. This method looks up the prefix that is in scope for the given namespace.
WriteRaw	Writes characters literally to the XML output from a string. Does not perform entity substitutions.
WriteStartAttribute	Writes the start of an attribute.
WriteStartDocument	Writes the XML declaration.
WriteStartElement	Writes the specified start tag.
WriteString	Writes the given text content.

TABLE 7.4 Properties and Methods of the *XmlWriter* Base Class and Derived *XmlTextWriter* Class *(continued)*

Method	Description
WriteSurrogateCharEntity	Creates and writes the surrogate character entity for the surrogate character pair. Use this method if you are concerned about correctly converting characters from UTF-8 to UTF-16 encoding.
WriteWhitespace	Writes a specified string of space characters to the XML output.

You can begin creating a new XML data file by calling the `WriteDocumentStart` method and can continue calling the appropriate `Writexxx` method for each element, attribute, text node, comment, or processing instruction that will appear in your data file. The `WriteAttributeString` and `WriteElementString` methods provide a shortcut by enabling you to create an attribute or simple element by using one method call, rather than three calls (`WriteStartElement`, `WriteString`, `WriteEndElement`).

Listing 7.7 shows an example of using an `XmlTextWriter`.

To create formatted data files, set the `XmlTextWriter.Formatting` property to `Indented`. The data file will have line breaks after each item, and nested elements indented below their parent elements. This is useful when the XML data will be displayed to end users. In other situations, it's not necessary—for example, if you are creating an XML `Stream` object that will be passed to another procedure.

Listing 7.7: Creating an XML Data File with an XmlTextWriter
```
Private Sub CreateXMLFile()

   Private newWriter As XmlTextWriter = New _
      XmlTextWriter("C:\path\new-employees.xml", Nothing)

   newWriter.Formatting = Formatting.Indented
   newWriter.WriteStartDocument(True)
   newWriter.WriteStartElement("newemployees")

      newWriter.WriteStartElement("employee")
      newWriter.WriteAttributeString( _
         "emp_id", CType(counter, String))
         newWriter.WriteStartElement("jobtitle")
         newWriter.WriteString( _
            lstJobTitle.SelectedItem.ToString)
         newWriter.WriteEndElement()
```

```
        newWriter.WriteElementString( _
            "firstname", txtFirst.Text)
        newWriter.WriteElementString( _
            "lastname", txtLast.Text)
      newWriter.WriteEndElement()

   'close the root element
   newWriter.WriteEndElement()
   newWriter.Close()
End Sub
```

Exercise 7.4 demonstrates how to instantiate an XMLTextReader and load it from an XML data file. You will also read through the data, identify node types and names, and retrieve data. Then you will use the XmlTextWriter to create unique XML output.

EXERCISE 7.4

Using the *XmlTextReader* and *XmlTextWriter*

1. Start Visual Studio .NET and create a new Windows Application project called **XMLReaderWriter**. Name the form **frmTextReader**.

2. Add a ListBox, two TextBoxes, and two Command Button controls to the form. Name them **lstJobTitle**, **txtFirst**, **txtLast**, **btnEnterEmp**, and **btnSaveFile**, respectively. Your form should look like this:

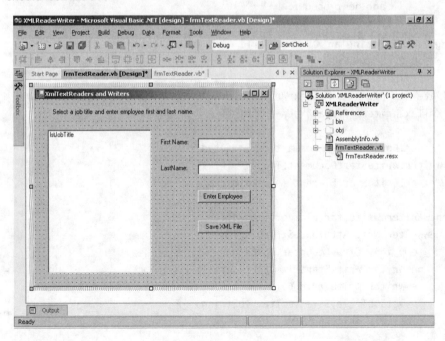

3. Add an Imports statement for System.Xml at the top of the form's code module:

```
Imports System.Xml
```

4. Add a class-level counter variable:

```
Private counter As Integer = 1
```

Using an XmlTextReader:

5. In the Form_Load event procedure, instantiate an XmlTextReader and set up a loop to read data. Your code will also test each node to see whether it is an XmlNodeType.Element and then test to see whether the element node's name is job_desc. When a matching element node is found, the text will be added to the ListBox control.

6. Here is the code to do this (substitute the correct path and filename for your computer):

```
Private Sub frmTextReader_Load(ByVal sender As System.Object, _
    ByVal e As System.EventArgs) Handles MyBase.Load

    Dim jobReader As XmlTextReader = New _
        XmlTextReader("C:\path\job-list.xml")

    While jobReader.Read()
        If jobReader.NodeType = XmlNodeType.Element Then

            If jobReader.Name = "job_desc" Then
                lstJobTitle.Items.Add(jobReader.ReadInnerXml())
            End If

        End If
    End While
End Sub
```

7. Save and test your work. The application should display a list of job titles in the ListBox control.

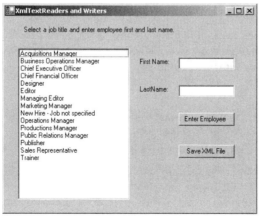

Using the XmlTextWriter:

8. Instantiate a class level XmlTextWriter to create a new XML file based on user input (use an appropriate path and filename for your computer):

```
Private newWriter As XmlTextWriter = New _
    XmlTextWriter("C:\path\new-employees.xml", Nothing)
```

9. Create an event procedure for the btnEnterEmp_Click event procedure. This code will write XML elements and attributes with the data values taken from user input. If the counter variable has a value of 1, then you will start a new document and create an XML entry. If the counter is greater than 1, you will create another XML entry. Increment the counter variable at the end of the procedure.

10. Here is the code to do this:

```
Private Sub btnEnterEmp_Click(ByVal sender As System.Object, _
    ByVal e As System.EventArgs) Handles btnEnterEmp.Click

    If counter = 1 Then
        newWriter.Formatting = Formatting.Indented
        newWriter.WriteStartDocument(True)
        newWriter.WriteStartElement("newemployees")
    End If

    newWriter.WriteStartElement("employee")
    newWriter.WriteAttributeString("emp_id", _
        CType(counter, String))
    newWriter.WriteStartElement("jobtitle")
    newWriter.WriteString(lstJobTitle.SelectedItem.ToString)
    newWriter.WriteEndElement()
    newWriter.WriteElementString("firstname", txtFirst.Text)
    newWriter.WriteElementString("lastname", txtLast.Text)
    newWriter.WriteEndElement()

    counter += 1
End Sub
```

11. Create an event procedure for the btnSaveFile_Click event procedure. This code will write the final closing tag for the XML file and close the XmlTextWriter. At the end of the procedure, reset the counter variable to 1.

12. Here is the code to do this:

```
Private Sub btnSaveFile_Click(ByVal sender As System.Object, _
    ByVal e As System.EventArgs) Handles btnSaveFile.Click

    newWriter.WriteEndElement()
    newWriter.Close()

    counter = 1
End Sub
```

13. Save and test your work. Select a job title from the list box, type a first and last name into the text boxes, and click the Enter Employee button. Repeat this procedure to enter names for two or three more employees and then click the Save XML File button. Use Windows Explorer to locate the `new-employees.xml` file that your application just created. Examine the contents. The format of XML that was created should look like this:

```xml
<?xml version="1.0" standalone="yes"?>
<newemployees>

  <employee emp_id="1">
    <jobtitle>Editor</jobtitle>
    <firstname>John</firstname>
    <lastname>Smith</lastname>
  </employee>

  <employee emp_id="2">
    <jobtitle>Productions Manager</jobtitle>
    <firstname>Liz</firstname>
    <lastname>Jones</lastname>
  </employee>

  <employee emp_id="3">
    <jobtitle>Marketing Manager</jobtitle>
    <firstname>Susan</firstname>
    <lastname>Wilson</lastname>
  </employee>
</newemployees>
```

The `XmlReader` and `XmlWriter` classes are useful when your goal is simple input and output of XML data. When you need to perform more complex operations with XML data in your program code, you will need to use the .NET Framework classes that implement the W3C XML Document Object Model (DOM). These are discussed in next.

Programming with the XML Document Object Model

The *XML Document Object Model (DOM)* offers complete programmatic access to XML data. When working with the DOM, you approach your XML data as a tree of nodes, which starts from the root element and continues for as many levels of depth as your data structure requires. In this section, you will learn about the properties and methods of the DOM that enable you to navigate the DOM tree structure, read and change data, and also generate new XML structures in your application code.

There are two ways to navigate the XML document hierarchy. One option is to move through the node hierarchy from parent node to child nodes, for as many levels of nesting as the data contains. The other option is to use methods such as `GetElementsByTagName`, `SelectNodes`, or `SelectSingleNode` to directly locate nodes that match a selection criteria. `SelectNodes` and `SelectSingleNode` use XPath expressions to specify selection criteria. This is covered later in this chapter, in the section titled "Selecting Nodes with XPath."

Each node in a document is one of the specialized types of nodes defined by the DOM. A node can represent the document itself, or an element, an attribute, text content, a processing instruction, a comment, or any of the other items that are valid in an XML file. The base class of XmlNode defines the basic set of properties and methods for all types of nodes. Each specialized type of node, which is a class derived from the XmlNode base class, has some additional properties and methods that are unique to that node type's characteristics.

Also important in the XML DOM are two collection classes: the *NodeList collection class* and the *XmlNamedNodeMap collection class*. The NodeList collection class can be used to iterate through a set of related nodes. A set of related nodes can be based on the hierarchy—for example, all the child nodes of a selected element. A NodeList collection can also consist of a set of nodes that match a selection criteria, such as all nodes with a specific element tag name or matching value. The NodeList collection can be navigated by index value in an ordered fashion. The XmlNamedNodeMap collection class is a collection of name/value pairs and is typically used to access sets of XML attributes. The .NET Framework has a class called *XmlAttribute-Collection* that extends the base class XmlNamedNodeMap's functionality.

Table 7.5 lists the properties and methods of the *XmlNode base class*. Table 7.6 through Table 7.9 list the extended properties and methods of the classes that inherit from XmlNode.

The next set of Tables (Table 7.5 through Table 7.9) shows the properties and methods of classes that implement the XML DOM. Table 7.5, which lists the properties and methods of the XmlNode base class and is, of course, the longest list. The rest of the tables show the extended properties and methods of each of the classes that inherit from XmlNode. The derived classes also support all of the base class properties and methods. In some of the derived classes, the base class methods have been overridden to customize the behavior of the derived class.

TABLE 7.5   Properties and Methods of the *XmlNode* Base Class

Property	Description
Attributes	An XmlAttributeCollection containing the attributes of this node
BaseURI	The base URI of the current node
ChildNodes	A collection of the children of the node
FirstChild	References the first child of the node
HasChildNodes	Indicates whether this node has any child nodes
InnerText	The concatenated values of the node and all its children
InnerXml	The markup representing just the children of this node

TABLE 7.5   Properties and Methods of the *XmlNode* Base Class *(continued)*

Property	Description
IsReadOnly	Indicates whether the node is read-only
Item	References the specified child element
LastChild	References the last child of the node
LocalName	Writes the name of the node with the prefix removed
Name	The qualified name of the node
NamespaceURI	The namespace URI of this node
NextSibling	References the node immediately following this node
NodeType	The type of the current node
OuterXml	The markup representing this node and all its children
OwnerDocument	References the XmlDocument to which this node belongs
ParentNode	References the parent of this node (for nodes that can have parents)
Prefix	The namespace prefix of this node
PreviousSibling	References the node immediately preceding this node
Value	The value of the node

Method	Description
AppendChild	Adds the specified node to the end of the list of children of this node
Clone	Creates a duplicate of this node
CloneNode	Creates a duplicate of the node
CreateNavigator	Creates an XPathNavigator for navigating this object
GetEnumerator	Provides support for each style iteration over the nodes in the XmlNode
GetNamespaceOfPrefix	Looks up the closest xmlns declaration for the given prefix that is in scope for the current node and returns the namespace URI in the declaration

TABLE 7.5 Properties and Methods of the *XmlNode* Base Class *(continued)*

Method	Description
GetPrefixOfNamespace	Looks up the closest xmlns declaration for the given namespace URI that is in scope for the current node and returns the prefix defined in that declaration
InsertAfter	Inserts the specified node immediately after the specified reference node
InsertBefore	Inserts the specified node immediately before the specified reference node
Normalize	Puts all XmlText nodes in the full depth of the subtree underneath this XmlNode into a "normal" form, where only markup (that is, tags, comments, processing instructions, CDATA sections, and entity references) separates XmlText nodes, that is, there are no adjacent XmlText nodes
PrependChild	Adds the specified node to the beginning of the list of children of this node
RemoveAll	Removes all the children and/or attributes of the current node
RemoveChild	Removes the specified child node
ReplaceChild	Replaces the child node oldChild with newChild node
SelectNodes	Selects a list of nodes matching the XPath expression
SelectSingleNode	Selects the first XmlNode that matches the XPath expression
Supports	Tests whether the DOM implementation implements a specific feature
WriteContentTo	Saves all the children of the node to the specified XmlWriter
WriteTo	Saves the current node to the specified XmlWriter

The *XmlDocument class* has functionality that governs the document as a whole.

TABLE 7.6 Extended Properties and Methods of the *XmlDocument* Class

Property	Description
DocumentElement	References the root XmlElement for the document
DocumentType	References the node containing the DOCTYPE declaration

TABLE 7.6 Extended Properties and Methods of the *XmlDocument* Class *(continued)*

Property	Description
Implementation	The XmlImplementation object for the current document
NameTable	The XmlNameTable associated with this implementation
PreserveWhitespace	Indicates whether to preserve white space
XmlResolver	Sets the XmlResolver to use for resolving external resources

Method	Description
CreateAttribute	Creates an XmlAttribute with the specified name
CreateCDataSection	Creates an XmlCDataSection containing the specified data
CreateComment	Creates an XmlComment containing the specified data
CreateDocumentFragment	Creates an XmlDocumentFragment object. This object represents an incomplete XML document and is useful for creating sections of XML that will be inserted into another document.
CreateDocumentType	Returns a new XmlDocumentType object
CreateElement	Creates an XmlElement
CreateEntityReference	Creates an XmlEntityReference with the specified name
CreateNode	Creates an XmlNode
CreateProcessingInstruction	Creates an XmlProcessingInstruction with the specified name and data
CreateSignificantWhitespace	Creates an XmlSignificantWhitespace node that can be used to add spacing or carriage return/line feed characters to the XML output (limited to the &#20;  and 	 characters)
CreateTextNode	Creates an XmlText with the specified text
CreateWhitespace	Creates an XmlWhitespace node that can be used to add spacing or carriage return/line feed characters to the XML output
CreateXmlDeclaration	Creates an XmlDeclaration node with the specified values
GetElementById	Gets the XmlElement with the specified ID
GetElementsByTagName	Returns an XmlNodeList containing a list of all descendant elements that match the specified name

TABLE 7.6 Extended Properties and Methods of the *XmlDocument* Class *(continued)*

Method	Description
ImportNode	Imports a node from another document to the current document
Load	Loads the XML documents from an object or stream
LoadXml	Loads the XML document from a string
ReadNode	Creates an XmlNode object based on the information in the XmlReader. The reader must be positioned on a node or attribute
Save	Saves the XML document to the specified location—a file, stream, or object

An important property of the XmlDocument class is DocumentElement, which gets a reference to the root element of the document. This is a common starting point for procedures that navigate the tree structure. The XmlDocument also supports methods such as *CreateElement* and *CreateAttribute* to programmatically create new sections of XML data that can be appended or inserted into the document's tree structure. Also important is the *Load method* for populating your XmlDocument from a disk file or other object, and the *LoadXML method* for populating your XmlDocument from a string. The *Save method* enables you to persist your XmlDocument to disk or to a Stream object that can be passed to another procedure.

Listing 7.8 shows two ways to load an XmlDocument: first from a disk file and then by using a string variable that you have created in your application code.

Listing 7.8: Loading an XmlDocument

```
    Dim empDocument As XmlDocument = New XmlDocument()
    Dim newDocument As XmlDocument = New XmlDocument()
Private Sub LoadDoc()

Try
        'load the first XmlDocument from a disk file
        empDocument.PreserveWhitespace = True
        empDocument.Load("C:\path\new-employees.xml")
        txtDisplay.Text = empDocument.InnerXml

        'load the second XmlDocument from a string
        newDocument.PreserveWhitespace = True
```

```vb
        newDocument.LoadXml(("<employeelist>" & _
            "<employee id='1' job='Editor'>" & _
            "<name>John Smith</title>" & _
            "</employee></employeeelist>"))

        'Save the document to a file.
        newDocument.Save("C:\path\new-data.xml")

    Catch xex As XmlException
        MessageBox.Show(xex.Message)
    Catch ex As Exception
        MessageBox.Show(ex.Message)
    End Try
End Sub
```

Another important function of the XmlDocument is to create new items of XML data that can be added into an existing XML tree structure. After the new items are created, they must be added to a specific place in the tree structure by using the AppendChild, PrependChild, InsertBefore, InsertAfter, or ReplaceChild methods. Listing 7.9 shows an example of adding a new element and data to an XmlDocument.

Listing 7.9: Creating a New Element

```vb
Private Sub AddElement()
    Try
        Dim newElement As XmlElement = _
            newDocument.CreateElement("salary")
        Dim newText As XmlText = _
            newDocument.CreateTextNode(txtSalary.Text)
        Dim empList As XmlNodeList
        Dim empnode As XmlElement

        empList = _
            newDocument.GetElementsByTagName("employee")
        empnode = CType(empList(0), XmlElement)

        empnode.AppendChild(newElement)
        empnode.LastChild.AppendChild(newText)

        newDocument.Save("C:\path\new-data.xml")

    Catch xex As XmlException
        MessageBox.Show(xex.Message)
```

```
   Catch ex As Exception
      MessageBox.Show(ex.Message)
   End Try
End Sub
```

Table 7.7 lists the extended properties and methods of the *XmlElement class* mostly have to do with working with an element's attributes collection. There are methods to add, remove, and change the value of attributes.

TABLE 7.7   Extended Properties and Methods of the *XmlElement* Class

Property	Description
HasAttributes	Indicates whether or not the current node has any attributes.
IsEmpty	Indicates the tag format of the element.

Method	Description
GetAttribute	Indicates the attribute value for the specified attribute.
GetAttributeNode	References the specified XmlAttribute.
GetElementsByTagName	Returns an XmlNodeList containing a list of all descendant elements that match the specified name.
HasAttribute	Indicates whether the current node has the specified attribute.
RemoveAllAttributes	Removes all specified attributes from the element. Default attributes, as defined in the schema, are not removed.
RemoveAttribute	Removes the specified attribute.
RemoveAttributeAt	Removes the attribute node with the specified index from the element.
RemoveAttributeNode	Removes an XmlAttribute.
SetAttribute	Sets the value of the specified attribute.
SetAttributeNode	Adds a new XmlAttribute.

Listing 7.10 shows how to change an attribute value by using the SetAttribute method. The listing also provides an example of changing the text value of an XmlElement.

Listing 7.10: Changing Attribute and Element Values by Using the XmlElement Class
```
Private Sub ChangeValues()
   Dim empList As XmlNodeList
```

```
Dim empNode As XmlElement
Dim nameNode As XmlElement
Dim nameList As XmlNodeList

'get a reference to the first employee element
empList = newDocument.GetElementsByTagName("employee")
empNode = CType(empList(0), XmlElement)

'change the attribute value, based on user input
If txtID.Text <> "" Then
   empNode.SetAttribute("id", txtID.Text)
End If

'get a reference to the name element, change the InnerText property
If txtName.Text <> "" Then
   nameList = empNode.GetElementsByTagName("name")
   nameNode = CType(nameList(0), XmlElement)
   nameNode.InnerText = txtName.Text
End If

'Save the document to a file.
newDocument.Save("C:\path\new-data.xml")
End Sub
```

The *XmlAttribute class* has little in the way of extended properties. These are listed in Table 7.8.

TABLE 7.8   Extended Properties and Methods of the *XmlAttribute* Class

Property	Description
OwnerElement	References the XmlElement to which the attribute belongs
Specified	Indicates whether the attribute value was explicitly set

The OwnerElement property returns a reference to the parent element. The Specified property indicates whether the attribute value was supplied when the attribute was created or whether it is a default value supplied in a DTD or schema.

The *XmlText class* inherits many of its extended properties and methods from the XmlCharacterData class, which stands in the inheritance chain between XmlNode and XmlText. These properties and methods (listed in Table 7.9) are useful for manipulating the data of the XmlText node.

TABLE 7.9   Extended Properties and Methods of the *XmlCharacterData* and *XmlText* Class

Property	Description
Data	The data of the node
InnerText	The concatenated values of the node and all the children of the node
Length	The length of the data, in characters

Method	Description
AppendData	Appends the specified string to the end of the character data of the node
DeleteData	Removes a range of characters from the node
InsertData	Inserts the specified string at the specified character offset
ReplaceData	Replaces the specified number of characters, starting at the specified offset with the specified string
SplitText	Splits the node into two nodes at the specified offset, keeping both in the tree as siblings
Substring	Retrieves a substring, of the full string, from the specified range

Although there are many other related classes that represent the other items that you can find in an XML document, the XmlDocument, XmlElement, XmlAttribute, and XmlText classes are likely to be the ones that you will work with most frequently. After you understand how to use these classes, you can use the Visual Studio .NET documentation to find information about other classes that you might need to use from time to time.

You have looked at several of the most commonly used functions of XML DOM programming. Exercise 7.5 will put this all together in an application that loads XML data from a file, creates a new XmlDocument, loads it with a string that is created by incorporating user input, and then saves that file to disk. You will also learn about parsing errors that can occur when loading XmlDocuments, how to edit the data in an XmlDocument, and how to add new elements and attributes to existing XmlDocuments. This exercise uses the XML data file new-employees.xml that you created in Exercise 7.4.

EXERCISE 7.5

XML DOM Programming

1. Start Visual Studio .NET and create a new Windows Application project called DOMProgrammingExamples. Rename the default form to frmDOMCode.

2. Add a TextBox control to the form named **txtDisplay**, and set its Multiline property to True and its ScrollBars property to Both.

3. Add four more TextBox controls and name them **txtID**, **txtJobTitle**, **txtName**, and **txtRegion**.

4. Add two Command Button controls to the form. Name them **btnSaveXML** and **btnEditXML**. Your form should look like the following one.

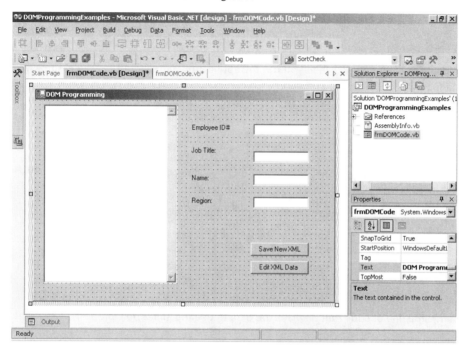

5. Add an Imports statement to the top of the form's code module:

```
Imports System.Xml
```

6. Add two class-level variables for XmlDocuments:

```
Private empDocument As XmlDocument = New XmlDocument()
Private newDocument As XmlDocument = New XmlDocument()
```

Loading XML Data:

7. In the frmDomCode_Load event procedure, add code to load the XmlDocument from a text file. Display the markup and data from the XmlDocument in txtDisplay. Also, add some simple error handling. Your code should look like this (use an appropriate drive and filename path for your computer):

```
Private Sub frmDOMCode_Load(ByVal sender As System.Object, _
    ByVal e As System.EventArgs) Handles MyBase.Load
```

```
    Try
        empDocument.PreserveWhitespace = True
        empDocument.Load("C:\path\new-employees.xml")

        txtDisplay.Text = empDocument.InnerXml

    Catch xex As XmlException
        MessageBox.Show(xex.Message)
    Catch ex As Exception
        MessageBox.Show(ex.Message)
    End Try
End Sub
```

8. Save and test your work. When you run the application, you should see the entire XML data file, with both markup and data.

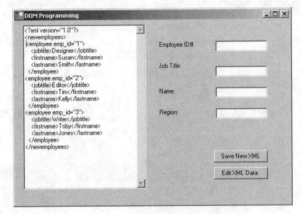

9. Change the line of code that displays the data to use the `InnerText` property:

```
txtDisplay.Text = empDocument.InnerText
```

10. Test the application again. You will see only data, and no markup in the text box.

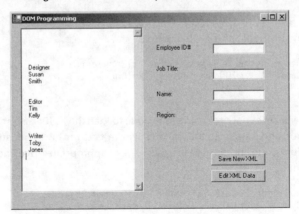

Creating New XML Data in Your Application:

Create a new XmlDocument and load it with XML that you will build manually in code combining XML tags with data from user input. Use a StringBuilder object to create the XML data string.

11. Add another Imports statement to the top of the module for the StringBuilder object:

```
Imports System.Text
```

12. In the btnSaveXml_Click event procedure, write code to create the StringBuilder, and append XML markup and user input values from the TextBoxes. Use the LoadXML method to load the string data into the new XmlDocument, save the document, and display it.

13. Here is what your code should look like (use an appropriate path and filename for your computer):

```
Private Sub btnSaveXML_Click(ByVal sender As System.Object, _
    ByVal e As System.EventArgs) Handles btnSaveXML.Click

    Dim xmlBuilder As StringBuilder = _
        New StringBuilder("<employees>")

    Try
        xmlBuilder.Append(Environment.NewLine)
        xmlBuilder.Append("<employee id='")
        xmlBuilder.Append(txtID.Text)
        xmlBuilder.Append("' job='")
        xmlBuilder.Append(txtJobTitle.Text)
        xmlBuilder.Append("'>")
        xmlBuilder.Append(Environment.NewLine)
        xmlBuilder.Append("<name>")
        xmlBuilder.Append(txtName.Text)
        xmlBuilder.Append("</name>")
        xmlBuilder.Append(Environment.NewLine)
        xmlBuilder.Append("<region>")
        xmlBuilder.Append(txtRegion.Text)
        xmlBuilder.Append("</region>")
        xmlBuilder.Append(Environment.NewLine)
        xmlBuilder.Append("</employee>")
        xmlBuilder.Append(Environment.NewLine)
        xmlBuilder.Append("</employees>")
```

```
            newDocument.PreserveWhitespace = True
            newDocument.LoadXml(xmlBuilder.ToString)

            'Save the document to a file.
            newDocument.Save("C:\path\new-data.xml")

            txtID.Clear()
            txtJobTitle.Clear()
            txtRegion.Clear()
            txtName.Clear()
            txtDisplay.Clear()

            txtDisplay.Text = newDocument.InnerXml

        Catch xex As XmlException
            MessageBox.Show(xex.Message)
        Catch ex As Exception
            MessageBox.Show(ex.Message)
        End Try
    End Sub
```

14. Save and test your work. Fill in a value in each of the four text boxes and then click the Save New XML button. You should see the newly created XML data displayed. Use Windows Explorer to verify that the disk file has also been saved.

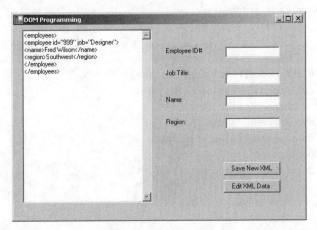

Editing XML Data:

Next, implement code to change the data in the newDocument XmlDocument.

15. Add code to the btnEditXML_Click event procedure that will use the GetElementsByTagName method to identify the first <employee> element. You can then change the values for the id and job attributes by using the SetAttribute method. Change the values of the <name> and <region> elements by navigating to the node and then changing the InnerText property.

16. Here is what your code should look like (use an appropriate path and filename for your computer):

```
Private Sub btnEditXML_Click(ByVal sender As System.Object, _
  ByVal e As System.EventArgs) Handles btnEditXML.Click

    Dim empList As XmlNodeList
    Dim empNode As XmlElement
    Dim nameNode As XmlElement
    Dim nameList As XmlNodeList
    Dim regionNode As XmlElement
    Dim regionList As XmlNodeList

    Try
        empList = newDocument.GetElementsByTagName("employee")
        empNode = CType(empList(0), XmlElement)

        If txtID.Text <> "" Then
          empNode.SetAttribute("id", txtID.Text)
        End If

        If txtJobTitle.Text <> "" Then
            empNode.SetAttribute("job", txtJobTitle.Text)
        End If

        If txtName.Text <> "" Then
            nameList = empNode.GetElementsByTagName("name")
            nameNode = CType(nameList(0), XmlElement)
            nameNode.InnerText = txtName.Text
        End If

        If txtRegion.Text <> "" Then
          regionList = empNode.GetElementsByTagName("region")
          regionNode = CType(regionList(0), XmlElement)
          regionNode.InnerText = txtRegion.Text
        End If

        newDocument.Save("C:\path\new-data.xml")
        txtDisplay.Clear()
        txtDisplay.Text = newDocument.InnerXml
    Catch xex As XmlException
        MessageBox.Show(xex.Message)
    Catch ex As Exception
        MessageBox.Show(ex.Message)
    End Try
End Sub
```

17. Save and test your application. Run the application and type values into the four text boxes. Click the Save New XML button.

18. Change one or more of the text box values and click the Edit XML Data button. You should see the data in the XML display. Use Windows Explorer to verify that the disk file was saved and that it contains your changes.

EXERCISE 7.5 *(continued)*

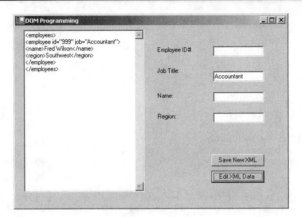

Now you are going to create a brand new element (`<salary>`) to change the format of the XML file that you created in step 12 of this exercise.

19. Update the user interface by adding another TextBox named **txtSalary** and another Command Button named **btnAddElement**.

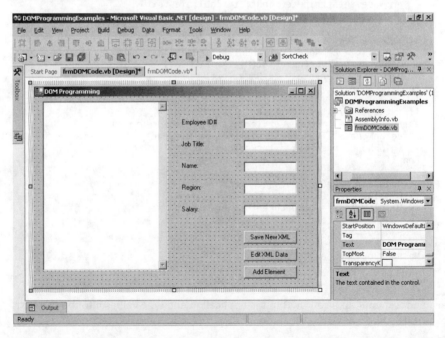

20. Add code to the `btnAddElement_Click` event procedure that will use `XmlDocument`'s `CreateElement` and `CreateTextNode` to create the new nodes. Then add the `AppendChild` method to add the new element as the last item in the `<employee>` element, and again to append the value from the TextBox to the element.

21. Your code should look like this (use an appropriate path and filename for your computer):

```
Private Sub btnAddElement_Click(ByVal sender As System.Object, _
    ByVal e As System.EventArgs) Handles btnAddElement.Click

    Dim empList As XmlNodeList
    Dim empnode As XmlElement

    Try
        'Create new element and text nodes
        Dim newElement As XmlElement = _
            newDocument.CreateElement("salary")
        Dim newText As XmlText = _
            newDocument.CreateTextNode(txtSalary.Text)

        'identify the node we want to append to
        empList = newDocument.GetElementsByTagName("employee")
        empNode = CType(empList(0), XmlElement)

        'append the new nodes
        empnode.AppendChild(newElement)
        empnode.LastChild.AppendChild(newText)

        txtDisplay.Clear()
        txtDisplay.Text = newDocument.InnerXml
        newDocument.Save("C:\path\new-data.xml")

    Catch xex As XmlException
        MessageBox.Show(xex.Message)
    Catch ex As Exception
        MessageBox.Show(ex.Message)
    End Try
End Sub
```

22. Save and test your application. Run the application and type values into the first four text boxes. Click the Save New XML button.

23. Type a value into the Salary text box and click the Add Element button. You should see the new data in the XML display. Use Windows Explorer to verify that the disk file was saved and that it contains your changes.

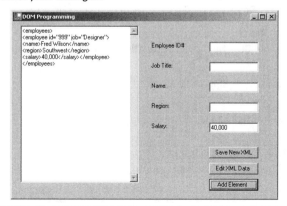

Now you have had a chance to work with the XML DOM to programmatically create and change both the data values and the structure of your XML data files. As you have seen in the tables in this section, many more methods can be explored. Exercise 7.5 demonstrated some of the most common operations.

In the rest of this section, you will learn about other tools that are used to manipulate XML data. First, you will look at XPath expressions.

Selecting Nodes with XPath

The XPath language enables you to locate nodes in your XML data that match specific criteria you are searching for. An *XPath expression* can specify criteria by evaluating either the position of a node in the document hierarchy, data values of the node, or a combination of both. For example, this expression will locate all last-name nodes:

```
//employee/lastname
```

But this expression will match only a node with the specific emp_id attribute value of 1:

```
//employee[@emp_id=1]/lastname
```

XPath queries can be quite complex. This is a simple introduction to creating XPath expressions; there is much more to the language. For more information, consult the Microsoft Developer Network (MSDN) Library, Microsoft XML SDK 3.0 documentation. Remember that XPath expressions are used with many different XML processing tools. The examples shown in Exercise 7.6 use the special classes in System.Xml.XPath, but you can use the same expression language with DOM programming and XSLT stylesheets.

The *SelectNodes method* and the *SelectSingleNode method* of the XmlNode class use XPath instructions to locate a node or nodeset in your XML data. You can use these methods interchangeably with the *GetElementsByTagName method* that was demonstrated in Exercise 7.5.

Listing 7.11 shows how to use these methods. SelectNodes will return a NodeList collection of all nodes in the document that match your criteria. You can then iterate through the collection to retrieve data. SelectSingleNode returns a reference to a single node, the first match that is located.

Listing 7.11: Using the DOM Methods SelectNodes and SelectSingleNode
```
Private Sub FindXML()
    Dim doc As XmlDocument = New XmlDocument()
    Dim myNode As XmlNode
    Dim myNodeList As XmlNodeList

    Try
        doc.Load("C:\path\new-employees.xml")
```

```
        myNode = doc.SelectSingleNode( _
            "//employee[@emp_id=1]/lastname")

        txtSingleNode.Text = myNode.InnerXml

        Dim node As XmlNode
        Dim nameString As String = _
            "Employee Names: " & Environment.NewLine

        myNodeList = doc.SelectNodes("//employee/lastname")
            For Each node In myNodeList
                nameString &= node.InnerText & _
                Environment.NewLine
            Next
        txtNodeList.Text = nameString

    Catch ex As Exception
        MessageBox.Show(ex.Message)
    End Try
End Sub
```

Another way to use XPath to query your XML data is to create and use an XPathNavigator object. This object is instantiated by calling the XmlDocument.CreateNavigator method. The XPathNavigator class has methods such as Select, Compile, and Evaluate to perform queries on your XML data by using XPath expressions.

The *System.Xml.XPath* namespace includes the *XPathNavigator class* and several other classes that you can use along with the XPathNavigator to optimize performance when you are working with XPath queries. These classes are the *XPathDocument class*, *XPathExpression class*, and the *XPathNodeIterator class*. Table 7.10 lists all the XPathNavigator class's properties and methods.

TABLE 7.10 Properties and Methods of the *System.Xml.XPath.XPathNavigator* Class

Property	Description
BaseURI	The base URI for the current node
HasAttributes	Indicates whether the element node has any attributes
HasChildren	Indicates whether the current node has child nodes
IsEmptyElement	Indicates whether the current node is an empty element (for example, <MyElement/>)

TABLE 7.10 Properties and Methods of the *System.Xml.XPath.XPathNavigator* Class *(continued)*

Property	Description
LocalName	The name of the current node without the namespace prefix
Name	The qualified name of the current node
NamespaceURI	The namespace URI (as defined in the W3C Namespace Specification) of the current node
NameTable	The XmlNameTable associated with this implementation
NodeType	The type of the current node
Prefix	The prefix associated with the current node
Value	The text value of the current node
XmlLang	The xml:lang scope for the current node

Method	Description
Clone	Creates a new XPathNavigator positioned at the same node as this XPathNavigator
ComparePosition	Compares the position of the current navigator with the position of the specified XPathNavigator
Compile	Compiles a string representing an XPath expression and returns an XPathExpression object
Evaluate	Evaluates the given expression and returns the typed result
GetAttribute	Gets the value of the attribute with the specified LocalName and NamespaceURI
GetNamespace	Returns the value of the namespace node corresponding to the specified local name
IsDescendant	Determines whether the specified XPathNavigator is a descendant of the current XPathNavigator
IsSamePosition	Determines whether the current XPathNavigator is at the same position as the specified XPathNavigator
Matches	Determines whether the current node matches the specified XPath pattern

TABLE 7.10 Properties and Methods of the *System.Xml.XPath.XPathNavigator* Class *(continued)*

Method	Description
MoveTo	Moves to the same position as the specified XPathNavigator
MoveToAttribute	Moves to the attribute with matching LocalName and NamespaceURI
MoveToFirst	Moves to the first sibling of the current node
MoveToFirstAttribute	Moves to the first attribute
MoveToFirstChild	Moves to the first child of the current node
MoveToFirstNamespace	Moves the XPathNavigator to the first namespace node of the current element
MoveToId	Moves to the node that has an attribute of type ID whose value matches the specified string
MoveToNamespace	Moves the XPathNavigator to the namespace node with the specified local name
MoveToNext	Moves to the next sibling of the current node
MoveToNextAttribute	Moves to the next attribute
MoveToNextNamespace	Moves the XPathNavigator to the next namespace node
MoveToParent	Moves to the parent of the current node
MoveToPrevious	Moves to the previous sibling of the current node
MoveToRoot	Moves to the root node to which the current node belongs
Select	Selects a node set by using the specified XPath expression
SelectAncestors	Selects all the ancestor element nodes of the current node matching the selection criteria
SelectChildren	Selects all the child nodes of the current node matching the selection criteria
SelectDescendants	Selects all the descendant nodes of the current node matching the selection criteria

Listing 7.12 shows how to create an XPathDocument object and load data into it, compile an XPath expression string into an XPathExpression object, and use the XPathNodeIterator when your XPath expression returns an XmlNodeList collection.

Listing 7.12: Creating an XPathNavigator

```
Private Sub ListJobs()
    Dim xpDoc As XPathDocument = _
        New XPathDocument("C:\path\job-list.xml")
    Dim xpNav As XPathNavigator = xpDoc.CreateNavigator()

    Dim xpExpr As XPathExpression
    xpExpr = xpNav.Compile("//job_desc")

    Dim xpIterator As XPathNodeIterator = _
        xpNav.Select(xpExpr)
      While (xpIterator.MoveNext())
        Dim xpNav2 As XPathNavigator = _
            xpIterator.Current.Clone()
        xpNav2.MoveToFirstChild()
        MessageBox.Show("Job title:  " & xpNav2.Value)
      End While
End Sub
```

As Table 7.10 points out, the XPathNavigator also has a set of MoveToxx methods—such as MoveToFirstChild, MoveToNext, MoveToParent—which give you to opportunity to explicitly position the XPathNavigator at a specific node. For example, you might use an XPath expression to locate a particular employee node by matching the job_id attribute value. After you have located the node you are interested in, you can use the MoveToFirstChild method to get to a particular data item.

Exercise 7.6 shows you how to use the objects in the System.Xml.XPath namespace. You will create an XPathDocument and XPathNavigator. You will use an XPath expression to identify all matching nodes in the data file and then use an XPathNodeIterator to process each matching node. You will be using the file new-employees.xml that you created in Exercise 7.5.

EXERCISE 7.6

Using XPath Expressions and the *XPathNavigator*

1. Start Visual Studio .NET and create a new Windows Application project called **XPath-Examples**. Rename the default form to **frmXPath**.

2. Add a ComboBox control and a ListBox to the form named frmXPath. Name them **cboSelect** and **lstDisplay**. Your form should look like the following.

EXERCISE 7.6 *(continued)*

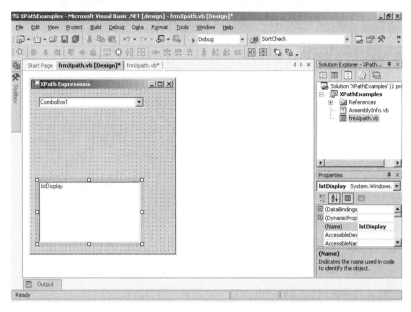

3. Add Imports statements to the top of the form's code module:

```
Imports System.Xml
Imports System.Xml.XPath
```

4. Add two module-level variables for an XPathDocument and an XPathNavigator (use the appropriate path and filename for your computer):

```
Private navDocument As XPathDocument = New _
    XPathDocument("C:\path\new-employees.xml")
Dim xpNav As XPathNavigator
```

5. In the frmXPath_Load event procedure, add code to create the XPathNavigator and to fill the ComboBox with a set of different XPath expressions for testing:

```
Private Sub frmXPath_Load(ByVal sender As System.Object, _
   ByVal e As System.EventArgs) Handles MyBase.Load

    xpNav = navDocument.CreateNavigator()

    cboSelect.Items.Add("//employee/lastname")
    cboSelect.Items.Add("//employee[@emp_id=1]/lastname")
    cboSelect.Items.Add("//employee/firstname")
    cboSelect.Items.Add("//employee[@emp_id=2]/firstname")
    cboSelect.Items.Add("//employee/jobtitle")
    cboSelect.Items.Add("//employee[@emp_id=3]/jobtitle")
    cboSelect.Items.Add("//employee[@emp_id<3]/jobtitle")
    cboSelect.Items.Add("//employee[3]/jobtitle")
    cboSelect.SelectedIndex = 0

End Sub
```

EXERCISE 7.6 *(continued)*

6. In the `cboSelect_SelectedIndexChanged` event procedure, add code to retrieve the text of the selected XPath expression from the ComboBox. Then compile the expression and create an `XpathNodeIterator` to move through the set of nodes that match your XPath query. A second `XPathNavigator` is used to move from the matching element node to its first child node, which is a text node. The value of the text node is then displayed in the ListBox.

7. Your code should look like this:

```
Private Sub cboSelect_SelectedIndexChanged( _
    ByVal sender As System.Object, _
    ByVal e As System.EventArgs) _
    Handles cboSelect.SelectedIndexChanged

    Dim selectString As String = cboSelect.Text
    Dim xpExpr As XpathExpression

    xpExpr = xpNav.Compile(selectString)

    Dim xpIterator As XPathNodeIterator = xpNav.Select(xpExpr)

    lstDisplay.Items.Clear()

    While (xpIterator.MoveNext())
        Dim xpnav2 As XPathNavigator = xpIterator.Current.Clone()
        xpnav2.MoveToFirstChild()
        lstDisplay.Items.Add(xpnav2.Value)
    End While
End Sub
```

8. Save and test your work. When the application starts, you will see a list of last names. These match the first item in the ComboBox list. Try the other combo box selections to see what data is returned.

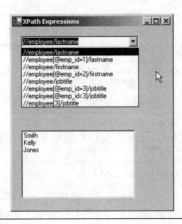

Next, you will learn how to validate XML data with a schema.

Validating XML Data

In the beginning of this chapter, you learned the basics of creating an XSD schema document to describe the exact format for an XML data file. Although XML data files must be well formed to be used by any of the XML-aware classes in the .NET Framework, validating your XML data file against a specified schema adds another level of confidence that the data is going to be of the appropriate types and in the correct format. After you have validated your data file, you can use it in your application and you will be far less likely to encounter errors caused by using data types incorrectly. Validation is especially important when you are receiving XML data files from outside sources.

To perform validation while working with XML data in your application, you will use the XmlValidatingReader, one of the derived classes of the XmlReader base class that was discussed earlier in this chapter. The XmlValidatingReader class can be used to validate XML data that you are processing either with an XmlTextReader or with an XmlDocument.

To validate data in an XmlTextReader, create the XmlTextReader and load the XML data from a disk file or Stream object. Then create the XmlValidatingReader class and pass it a reference to the XmlTextReader. If your XML data has an in-line schema, that is all you have to do. If you are using a schema that is stored in a separate location, then you must create an object from the *XmlSchemaCollection class* and load the schema file into the collection.

 Although XSD Schema is the most current technology available for validating your XML data, the .NET Framework classes also support validation against older DTD and XDR technologies. Set the XmlValidatingReader.Validation-Type property to specify which version should be used.

If you would like to use the XML DOM to programmatically access the data after it has been validated, you will still need to use the XmlTextReader to load the data from its original source (disk file or Stream object). Then pass the reference to the XmlTextReader to a new instance of the XmlValidatingReader. If validation is successful, then you can use the XmlDocument.Load method to populate the XmlDocument object, as shown in this code snippet:

```
Dim xmlDoc as XmlDocument = New XmlDocument()
Dim txtReader as XmlTextReader = _
    New XmlTextReader("C:\path\data.xml")
Dim valReader as XmlValidatingReader = _
    New XmlValidatingReader(tr)
xmlDoc.Load(valReader)
```

If a validation error occurs, an XmlException (for parsing errors) or an XmlSchemaException (validation error) will be fired. You can write error-handling code to processes these errors.

Listing 7.13 shows how to validate XML data by using an XmlTextReader and Xml-ValidatingReader, how to add an external schema file to the XmlSchemaCollection, and how to set up an error handler in case validation is not successful.

Listing 7.13: Validating by Using an XmlValidatingReader
```
Private Sub ValidateData()
    Dim valReader As XmlValidatingReader
```

```
    Dim txtReader As XmlTextReader
    Dim xscSchemas As New XmlSchemaCollection()

    Try
        xscSchemas.Add(Nothing, _
            New XmlTextReader("C:\path\title-schema.xsd"))
        txtReader = New XmlTextReader( _
            "C:\path\title-list.xml")
        valReader = New XmlValidatingReader(txtReader)

        valReader.Schemas.Add(xscSchemas)
        valReader.ValidationType = ValidationType.Schema

        While valReader.Read()
            If valReader.NodeType = XmlNodeType.Element Then
                If valReader.Name = "title" Then
                    lstTitles.Items.Add( _
                        valReader.ReadInnerXml())
                End If
            End If
        End While

    Catch e As Exception
        MessageBox.Show(e.ToString())
    Finally
        valReader.Close()
        txtReader.Close()
    End Try
End Sub
```

In Exercise 7.7, you will set up an XmlValidatingReader to test the validity of an XML data file.

 Exercise 7.7 uses an XML file called title-list.xml and a schema called title-schema.xml that can be found on the CD included with this book.

EXERCISE 7.7

Validating with the *XmlValidatingReader* and XSD Schema

1. Start Visual Studio .NET and create a new Windows Application project called **ValidationExamples**. Rename the default form to **frmValid**.

2. Add a ListBox control and name it **lstTitles**. Your form should look like this:

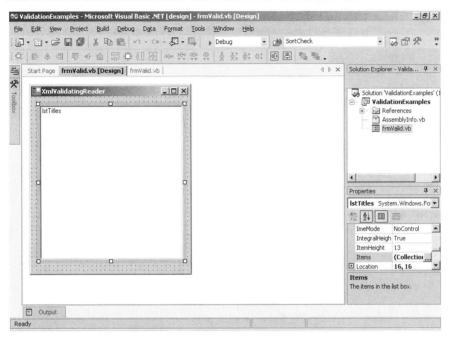

3. Add Imports statements to the top of the form's code module:

```
Imports System.Xml
Imports System.Xml.Schema
```

4. In the frmValid_Load event procedure, add code to add the schema file to the schema collection, create the readers, and read through the data. Also, add error handling to catch any schema validation errors. Here is the code to do this (use the appropriate path and filename for your computer):

```
Private Sub frmValid_Load(ByVal sender As System.Object, _
    ByVal e As System.EventArgs) Handles MyBase.Load

    Dim valReader As XmlValidatingReader
    Dim txtReader As XmlTextReader
    Dim xscSchemas As New XmlSchemaCollection()

    Try
        xscSchemas.Add(Nothing, New _
            XmlTextReader("C:\path\title-schema.xsd"))
        txtReader = New XmlTextReader("C:\path\title-list.xml")
        valReader = New XmlValidatingReader(txtReader)

        valReader.Schemas.Add(xscSchemas)
        valReader.ValidationType = ValidationType.Schema
```

```
        While valReader.Read()
            If valReader.NodeType = XmlNodeType.Element Then
                If valReader.Name = "title" Then
                    lstTitles.Items.Add(valReader.ReadInnerXml())
                End If
            End If
        End While

    Catch schemaExp As XmlSchemaException
        MessageBox.Show(schemaExp.ToString())
    Catch ex As Exception
        MessageBox.Show(ex.ToString())
    Finally
        valReader.Close()
        txtReader.Close()
    End Try
End Sub
```

5. Save and test your work. The first time, this application should not throw any exceptions and a list of book titles should be displayed.

6. Open the file `title-schema.xsd` in Notepad or any other text editor. Here is what the schema file looks like:

```
<?xml version="1.0" standalone="yes"?>
<xs:schema id="NewDataSet" xmlns=""
    xmlns:xs="http://www.w3.org/2001/XMLSchema"
    xmlns:msdata="urn:schemas-microsoft-com:xml-msdata">
  <xs:element name="NewDataSet" msdata:IsDataSet="true">
    <xs:complexType>
      <xs:choice>
        <xs:element name="titles" maxOccurs="unbounded">
          <xs:complexType>
            <xs:sequence>
              <xs:element name="title_id" type="xs:string"
                  minOccurs="1" />
              <xs:element name="title" type="xs:string"
                  minOccurs="1" />
```

```
            <xs:element name="type" type="xs:string"
                minOccurs="1" />
            <xs:element name="pub_id" type="xs:string"
                minOccurs="1" />
            <xs:element name="price" type="xs:decimal"
                minOccurs="0" />
            <xs:element name="advance" type="xs:decimal"
                minOccurs="0" />
            <xs:element name="royalty" type="xs:int"
                minOccurs="0" />
            <xs:element name="ytd_sales" type="xs:int"
                minOccurs="0" />
            <xs:element name="notes" type="xs:string"
                minOccurs="0" />
            <xs:element name="pubdate" type="xs:dateTime"
                minOccurs="0" />
        </xs:sequence>
      </xs:complexType>
    </xs:element>
  </xs:choice>
  </xs:complexType>
 </xs:element>
</xs:schema>
```

7. Change the `minOccurs="0"` attribute (highlighted in bold in the preceding code) for the price element to **minOccurs="1"**. Save the schema file and run the application again. You should see the following error message.

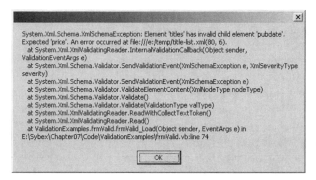

Here is an example for the format of XML in the `title-list.xml` file.

```
<?xml version="1.0" standalone="yes"?>
<NewDataSet>
  <titles>
    <title_id>BU1032</title_id>
    <title>The Busy Executive's Database Guide</title>
    <type>business</type>
    <pub_id>1389</pub_id>
    <price>29.2674</price>
    <advance>5000</advance>
    <royalty>10</royalty>
    <ytd_sales>4095</ytd_sales>
```

```
<notes>An overview of available database systems with
       emphasis on common business applications.
       Illustrated.</notes>
<pubdate>1991-06-12T00:00:00.0000000-07:00</pubdate>
  </titles>
</NewDataSet>
```

8. Open the file in Notepad and remove the first `<title_id>` element. Save the file and test the application again. You will now see the following error message.

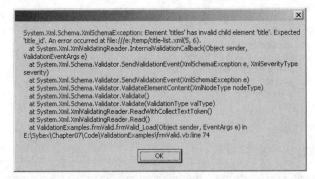

Experiment with other changes to the files and see what other types of error messages you receive.

Performing XSLT Transformations

Extensible Stylesheet Language (XSL) and XSL Transformations (XSLT) is a technology that can be applied to XML data files when you need to take an existing format of XML data and change it into a new format of output. The two primary uses for this are to take XML data and apply HTML formatting tags so that the data can be displayed on a web page and to change the format of the XML markup (while retaining the data values) so that the XML file can be sent to another application or consumer that requires the new format.

These are only the most commonly used scenarios. You can use XSLT to produce any application-specific output that you require.

Designing XSLT stylesheets is a complex topic and is outside the scope of the 70-310 exam and therefore this book. A sample stylesheet and accompanying XML data file (`title-list.xml` and `title-style.xsl`) are included on the CD that comes with this book so that you can complete Exercise 7.8.

XSLT stylesheets have some things in common with XSD schemas in that they are also valid and well-formed XML documents, and the elements and attributes that make up a stylesheet must adhere to a standard that is recommended by the W3C. XSLT stylesheets consist of a set of templates describing the output that is produced when each node in the source XML data file is processed. XSLT stylesheets are used in conjunction with an XSLT processor. Microsoft Internet Explorer (version 5 and later) is capable of performing XSLT processing. If you open an XML data file that contains an XSL processing instruction, Internet Explorer will process the stylesheet and display the formatted data.

When working with classes in the System.Xml namespace (XmlDocument, XmlDataDocument, and the XPathDocument), you can use the *XslTransform class* from the *System.Xml.Xsl namespace* to perform the stylesheet processing. If you are concerned only with XSLT processing— and do not need to do other processing on the data—the XPathDocument is optimized for the best performance during XSLT processing.

The XslTransform class has a simple interface. Its single property, XmlResolver, is used to locate external stylesheet files. The Load method is used to read the XSLT file into the object, and the Transform method is used to perform the stylesheet processing. An XmlReader object is used to hold the results of the XSLT transformation. You can then use the methods of the XmlReader to access your data.

Listing 7.14 shows you how to use the XslTransform class to do stylesheet processing in your code.

Listing 7.14: Performing XSLT Transformations

```
Dim objTransform As XslTransform = New XslTransform()
objTransform.Load(Server.MapPath("title-style.xsl"))

Dim objData As New XPathDocument( _
   Server.MapPath("title-list.xml"))

Dim objReader As XmlReader

objReader = objTransform.Transform(objData, Nothing)
```

Exercise 7.8 shows you how to take an XML data file and apply stylesheet transformation to produce a nicely formatted HTML page. You can do this in an ASP.NET page and send XML data directly to the browser.

EXERCISE 7.8

Displaying XML Data as HTML

1. Start Visual Studio .NET and create a new ASP.NET Web Application project called **TransformationExample**.

2. In the Form Designer for WebForm1.aspx, click the HTML tab near the bottom left of the screen to display the HTML for the page. Inside the <form> tags, type in a <div> tag that will be used to display the data:

   ```
   <div id="divOutput" runat="server"></div>
   ```

EXERCISE 7.8 (continued)

3. Your HTML should look like this graphic:

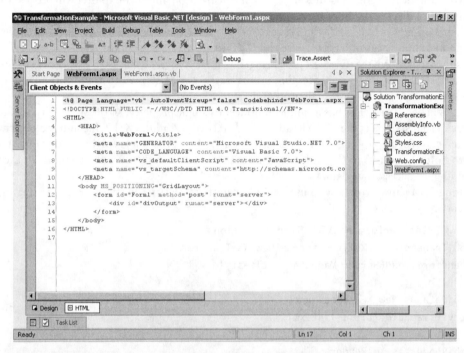

4. Right-click WebForm1.aspx in the Solution Explorer and choose View Code from the menu.

5. Add Imports statements to the top of the form's code module:

    ```
    Imports System.Xml
    Imports System.Xml.XPath
    Imports System.Xml.Xsl
    ```

6. In the Page_Load event procedure, add code to do the following:

    - Create an XslTransform object and load an XSLT stylesheet file
    - Create an XPathDocument and load an XML data file
    - Create an XmlReader object to hold the results of the transformation
    - Call the Transform method
    - Display the results in a <div> control

    Your code should look like this:

    ```
    Private Sub Page_Load(ByVal sender As System.Object, _
        ByVal e As System.EventArgs) Handles MyBase.Load

        Dim objTransform As XslTransform = New XslTransform()
            objTransform.Load(Server.MapPath("title-style.xsl"))
    ```

EXERCISE 7.8 *(continued)*

```
Dim objData As New XPathDocument( _
    Server.MapPath("title-list.xml"))

Dim objReader As XmlReader

objReader = objTransform.Transform(objData, Nothing)
objReader.MoveToContent()

divOutput.InnerHtml = objReader.ReadOuterXml
End Sub
```

7. Locate the files `title-list.xml` and `title-style.xsl` in the Chapter 7 folder on the CD that is included with this book. Copy these files to the project directory, which should be located at `C:\Inetpub\wwwroot\TransformationExample` (or the appropriate path and directory for your web server). Use Notepad to review the contents of these files.

8. Save and test your work. Run the application. Your web page should look like the following one.

Synchronizing *XMLDataDocuments* and *DataSets*

The *XmlDataDocument class* is a member of the System.Xml namespace that brings the best capabilities of a DataSet and an XmlDocument together. You can create a DataSet by retrieving data from a database and then create the XmlDataDocument by referencing the DataSet. This is called synchronizing the DataSet and the XmlDataDocument.

After you have established that these two objects should remain synchronized, you can use the properties and methods of the DataSet to work with the data as relational tables and, when needed, use the properties and methods of the XmlDocument to work with the data as a hierarchy of nodes.

The XmlDataDocument inherits most of its properties and methods from either the XmlNode base class or the XmlDocument class, all of which have already been explained in this chapter. Following are some code examples that show how to synchronize the two objects.

The following shows how to start with a DataSet created from database data, and then create and synchronize the XmlDataDocument:

```
Dim myDataSet As DataSet = New DataSet

MyDataAdapter.Fill(myDataSet)

Dim xmlDoc As XmlDataDocument = _
    New XmlDataDocument(myDataSet)
```

This code shows how to start with an XmlDataDocument and load it with an XML data file, and then create and synchronize the DataSet:

```
Dim xmlDoc As XmlDataDocument = New XmlDataDocument
Dim myDataSet As DataSet = xmlDoc.DataSet

myDataSet.ReadXmlSchema("schema.xsd")

xmlDoc.Load("XMLDocument.xml")
```

One constraint of working with XMLDataDocuments is that the DataSet you are synchronizing with must have a schema established. In the first example, this could be accomplished by allowing the DataSet to infer a schema when data is loaded from the database. In the last example, you should explicitly load a schema file into the DataSet before synchronizing with the XmlDataDocument.

Now that you have the seen major classes in the .NET Framework that work with XML data in your applications, the final section of this chapter will deal with some special capabilities of Microsoft SQL Server 2000 for handling XML data.

Using XML with SQL Server 2000

The Transact-SQL (T-SQL) query language for Microsoft SQL Server 2000 enables you to use special SQL syntax to return XML data directly from your database queries rather than the more standard row and column resultset. This is done by using the System.Data.SqlCommand .ExecuteXmlReader method that was mentioned in Chapter 5. Chapter 5 covered the SqlCommand object thoroughly, so in this section we will concentrate on the new syntax options for T-SQL queries that return XML data directly.

Please review Chapter 5 if you need more information on ADO.NET and the SqlCommand object. This section also discusses how to send XML data to SQL Server 2000.

In this section, you will look at T-SQL FOR XML queries and how to update SQL Server tables with XML.

Retrieving XML Data from T-SQL Queries

Returning XML data instead of a traditional database resultset is easy. All you need to do is to add a *FOR XML clause* to the end of your standard SQL query. There are also a few modifiers and options that enable you to vary the format of the XML output that is produced.

Here's a standard SQL query that returns a database resultset:

```
SELECT * FROM jobs
```

Add the FOR XML clause with one of the three modifiers—RAW, AUTO, or EXPLICIT—to return XML data.

This SQL query uses the RAW modifier and produces the format of XML shown. Here is an example:

```
SELECT * FROM jobs FOR XML RAW

<row job_id="1" job_desc="New Hire - Job not specified"
    min_lvl="10" max_lvl="50"/>
<row job_id="2" job_desc="Chief Executive Officer"
    min_lvl="200" max_lvl="225"/>
```

Each row of data is returned as a <row> element with a set of attributes. The attribute names match the database column names, and the attribute values represent the data.

Using the AUTO modifier produces an XML format in which each row is returned as an element with a tag name that matches the table name. Here is an example:

```
SELECT * FROM jobs FOR XML AUTO

<jobs job_id="1" job_desc="New Hire - Job not specified"
    min_lvl="10" max_lvl="50"/>
<jobs job_id="2" job_desc="Chief Executive Officer"
    min_lvl="200" max_lvl="225"/>
```

The EXPLICIT modifier is used when you are constructing a query that must retrieve data from multiple tables.

The other optional parameters that can be added to the query are XMLDATA, which is used to include an in-line schema in your output; ELEMENTS, which is used to produce an XML format with nested elements instead of all data being held as attribute values; and BINARY BASE64, which is used if you need to include BLOB data in your output.

Here's an example of a query that uses the ELEMENTS modifier, and the output:

```
SELECT * FROM jobs FOR XML AUTO, ELEMENTS
```

```
<jobs>
   <job_id>1</job_id>
   <job_desc>New Hire - Job not specified</job_desc>
   <min_lvl>10</min_lvl>
   <max_lvl>50</max_lvl>
</jobs>
```

Keep in mind that XML data produced by SQL Server 2000 does not have a root element, so it is considered an XML fragment, not a complete, well-formed, XML document. In order to work with the XML, you should add code to create the unique root element when processing the XML data that is returned from the SQL query.

Now that you understand how to write XML queries, you can use them with an ADO.NET SqlCommand to return XML data to your application. Listing 7.15 gives an example of this.

Listing 7.15: Using the SqlCommand.ExecuteXMLReader Method

```
Private Sub GetXMLData()
   Dim myConn As SqlConnection = New SqlConnection()
   myConn.ConnectionString = _
      "Data Source=localhost; Initial " & _
      "Catalog=pubs; Integrated Security=SSPI;"
   myConn.Open()

   Dim sqlString As String = _
       "SELECT * from jobs FOR XML AUTO"

   Dim myXMLCommand As SqlCommand = _
      New SqlCommand(sqlString, myConn)
   myXMLCommand.CommandType = CommandType.Text

   Dim myXmlReader As XmlReader
   myXmlReader = myXMLCommand.ExecuteXmlReader()

   While myXmlReader.Read()
       'process the XML data
   End While

   myXmlReader.Close()
   myConn.Close()
End Sub
```

Next you will learn how to take XML data and use it to update SQL Server 2000 tables.

Updating SQL Server Tables with XML

In order to send XML directly to SQL Server 2000, you must use stored procedures. First you will call a system stored procedure that parses the XML data and loads it into memory:

```
sp_xml_preparedocument @document
```

Then your stored procedure will use a SQL INSERT, UPDATE, or DELETE statement in conjunction with the special *OPENXML clause* to direct the XML elements and attributes into the appropriate tables and columns. This example selects job_id, job_desc, min_lvl, and max_lvl from each record in the XML data file and inserts it into the jobs table:

```
INSERT jobs
SELECT * FROM OPENXML (@document, 'job', 1)
WITH (job_id, job_desc, min_lvl, max_lvl)
```

This procedure is then completed by calling another system stored procedure to release the memory that is being used by the XML data file:

```
sp_xml_removedocument @document
```

The OPENXML queries can become quite complex when the data in an XML file must be separated into several different tables in the database.

Exercise 7.9 demonstrates how to use the ExecuteXmlReader method of the SqlCommand class.

EXERCISE 7.9

Using *SqlCommand.ExecuteXmlReader*

1. Start Visual Studio .NET and create a new Windows Application project called **SQL-XML-Example**. Rename the default form to **frmQuery**.

2. Add a TextBox control and name it **txtDisplay**. Set the Multiline property to True and the ScrollBars property to Both. Your form should look like the following one.

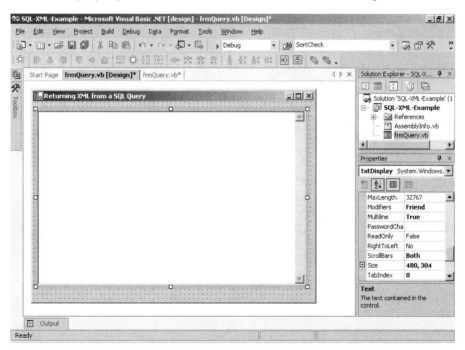

EXERCISE 7.9 *(continued)*

3. Add `Imports` statements to the top of the form's code module:

    ```
    Imports System.Xml
    Imports System.Data.SqlClient
    ```

4. In the `frmQuery_Load` event procedure, add code to create a `SqlConnection` and open the connection:

    ```
    Dim myConn As SqlConnection = New SqlConnection()
    myConn.ConnectionString = _
        "Data Source=localhost; Initial " & _
        "Catalog=pubs; Integrated Security=SSPI;"
        myConn.Open()
    ```

5. Set up the `SqlCommand` object, declare the `XmlReader`, and call the `ExecuteXmlReader` method:

    ```
    Dim sqlString As String = "SELECT * from jobs FOR XML AUTO"
    Dim myXMLCommand As SqlCommand = New SqlCommand(sqlString, myConn)
    myXMLCommand.CommandType = CommandType.Text

    Dim myXmlReader As XmlReader

    myXmlReader = myXMLCommand.ExecuteXmlReader()
    ```

6. Declare a string variable to hold the output and set up a loop to read through the data in the `XmlReader`:

    ```
    Dim str As String

    While myXmlReader.Read()
        Select Case myXmlReader.NodeType
            Case XmlNodeType.Element
                str &= "<" & myXmlReader.Name

                While myXmlReader.MoveToNextAttribute()
                    str &= " " & myXmlReader.Name & "='" & _
                        myXmlReader.Value & "'"
                End While

                str &= "/>" & Environment.NewLine
        End Select
    End While
    ```

7. Display the output and close the `XmlReader` and the `SqlConnection`:

    ```
    txtDisplay.Text = str
    myXmlReader.Close()
    myConn.Close()
    ```

8. Save and test your work. The running application should look like this:

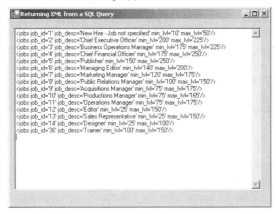

9. Change the SQL statement in your code to use the RAW modifier:

   ```
   SELECT * from jobs FOR XML RAW
   ```

10. Test the application again and observe how the output has changed.

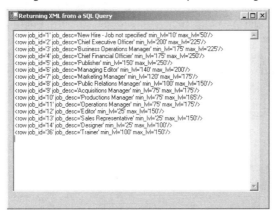

 **Real World Scenario**

XML for Application Integration

You are a software developer for a company that still runs most of its daily transaction processing on legacy mainframe applications. The day-to-day business operations are handled reliably by these applications, and your company has no plans to replace any of the applications in the foreseeable future. However, the applications provide only a few basic reports and have no easy interface to access the proprietary data storage format to create new reports. Your business manager and marketing department frequently request that you provide them with more detailed information than the legacy apps make available. Two maintenance programmers are responsible for making sure that the legacy mainframe applications keep running and for fixing any problems that occur. They have no time to code additional reports.

The only way that they will provide data to you is in the form of Comma Separated Value (CSV) text files. You find these files tedious to work with. Anytime there is a change in either your application or the legacy application, the CSV files have to be changed to accommodate the changes. Then you have to do extensive testing of even the smallest changes to either system, because even a small mistake when parsing those CSV files will make resulting reports incorrect.

A colleague has suggested that you should request that the mainframe team provide data in XML format. When you first mentioned this to the mainframe team, they expressed the opinion that "XML is just the latest silver bullet technology that has gotten too much hype." After doing a little research, you gave a presentation explaining how simple the XML format is, and they agreed that it would not be too difficult for them to meet your request. After a couple more meetings, you were able to agree on a schema that they would follow to produce their output.

Now that you have the data in XML format, your job is much easier. You quickly learned to use the new .NET Framework classes to work with XML data just as if you were working with a database table. Other tools, such as XSLT, took a little longer to learn, but now you can quickly produce different formats from the data files and post them to the company intranet for direct access by management. Best of all, you discovered that the latest version of Microsoft Excel can load XML data files directly into a spreadsheet. Marketing analysts can use this data on their own without requiring you to do any coding at all.

A simple change in data exchange format has reduced the turnaround time for new data report requests by several weeks. That should look good on your next annual review.

Summary

In this chapter, you learned about using XML data in the .NET Framework. We covered the following topics:

- An introduction to the basics of XML data formats
- An introduction to the basics of the XML Schema Definition (XSD) language
- How an ADO.NET DataSet object can read and write XML data
- How to control XML formats with the ColumnMapping property when writing XML data from a DataSet
- How to create DiffGram XML output that shows the user changes that have been made to DataSet data along with the original values

- Classes in the System.Xml namespace of the .NET Framework

- How to use XmlReader and its derived classes XmlTextReader, XmlNodeReader, and XmlValidatingReader to process a forward-only, read-only stream of XML data

- How to use the XmlTextWriter to create XML output

- How to have complete programmatic access to an XML data file by using the XML Document Object Model (DOM)

- The base classes of the DOM: XmlNode, XmlNodeList, and XmlNamedNodeMap, and the derived classes such as XmlDocument, XmlElement, XmlAttribute, and XmlText

- How XPath expressions use a common format to select matching nodes that can be used with DOM programming, XSLT stylesheets, and other XML technologies

- How to use classes in the System.Xml.XPath namespace, such as XPathNavigator and XPathDocument, to optimize performance when using XPath expressions and doing XSLT transformations

- How to use an XmlValidatingReader to validate an XML data file against a specific schema

- How to handle XmlSchemaExceptions

- How to use classes in the System.Xml.Xsl namespace to perform XSLT transformations on XML data to create different formats of output from your XML data

- How to use the XmlDataDocument to access both relational and hierarchical views of the same data

- How to use special SQL syntax, the FOR XML clause, and the SqlCommand object's ExecuteXmlReader method to retrieve XML data directly from a SQL Server 2000 database

- How to use special SQL syntax, the OPENXML clause, and SQL Server 2000 system stored procedures to read data from an XML data file and store it into SQL Server tables

Exam Essentials

Know how to use XSD schemas with a DataSet.   Understand that if no schema is provided, the DataSet can construct one based on the data that is loaded. If a schema is explicitly provided, then you have the choice of either restricting the DataSet to loading only data that matches the schema, or adjusting the schema to accommodate new data. Understand how to call the GetSchema method to retrieve the schema that has been generated by the DataSet.

Know how to access data in XML files.   XML data can be loaded directly into a DataSet with the ReadXml method. The .NET Framework also has other classes that can access XML data, such as the XmlReader, XmlDocument, and XmlDataDocument.

Understand how to use the XmlReader and XmlWriter classes for XML input and output operations.   The XmlReader and its three derived classes (XmlTextReader, XmlNodeReader, and XmlValidatingReader) provide forward-only, read-only access to XML data. The

XmlReader classes parse an XML document and enable you to read data values sequentially. The XmlTextWriter enables you to create XML output by specifying each item (element, attribute, or text) that should be included, in sequential order, in the output.

Understand how to load XML data into an XML DOM document.   The DOM XmlDocument enables you to access the entire XML tree structure in memory. The XML DOM has properties and methods that provide programmatic access to navigate the tree structure, to read and change data values, to create or remove XML nodes, and to change the XML document structure.

Understand how to use XPath expressions to query your XML files to locate specific nodes or sets of nodes.   XPath expressions can locate nodes based on their position in a document tree structure, or based on selection criteria that evaluates data values, or a combination of both.

Understand when validating XML data against a schema is important and how to use an XmlValidatingReader to parse a document.   Validation can be done with in-line schemas or by using external schema files. Understand the difference between a parsing error (which occurs because of an error in the basic rules of XML markup) and a validation error (which occurs when the data in an XML data file does not match the tag and attribute names, parent/child relationship, element sequence, data types, required/optional settings, or other formatting that can be specified by using XSD schema).

Understand how XSLT can be used to transform XML data from one format to another. XSLT can be used to create HTML-formatted output from XML data. XSLT can also be used when exchanging data with other applications that require variations in the XML format (such as changing a tag name or changing the order of elements) while maintaining data values. XSLT can also be used to create any other text-based output formats that your applications might require.

Understand how to use special SQL syntax to retrieve XML data from SQL Server 2000. The FOR XML clause can be added to standard queries to output XML data. The AUTO, RAW, EXPLICIT, and ELEMENTS modifiers can be used to change the output format. When executing a FOR XML query against SQL Server 2000, use an ADO.NET SqlCommand with the ExecuteXml-Reader method to populate an XmlReader with the results from the query.

Understand the features that are available for submitting data to SQL Server 2000 in XML format.   These include using an OPENXML clause in a SQL INSERT, UPDATE, or DELETE query.

Key Terms

Before you take the exam, be certain you are familiar with the following terms:

attributes	DiffGram
ColumnMapping property	Document Type Definition (DTD)
CreateAttribute	elements
CreateElement	Extensible Markup Language (XML)

Extensible Stylesheet Language (XSL) and XSL Transformations (XSLT)

`FOR XML` clause

`GetElementsByTagName` method

`GetXml` method

`GetXmlSchema` method

Load method

`LoadXML` method

`NodeList` collection class

`OPENXML` clause

processing instruction

`ReadXml` method

`ReadXmlSchema` method

Save method

`SelectNodes` method

`SelectSingleNode` method

`System.XML` namespace

`System.Xml.Xpath`

`System.Xml.Xsl` namespace

uniquely named root element

well formed

World Wide Web Consortium (W3C)

`WriteXml` method

XML Data Reduced (XDR)

XML Document Object Model (DOM)

XML namespaces

XML parsers

XML Schema Definition (XSD)

`XmlAttribute` class

`XmlAttributeCollection`

`XmlDataDocument` class

`XmlDocument` class

`XmlElement` class

`XmlNamedNodeMap` collection class

`XmlNode` base class

`XmlNodeReader`

`XmlReader` class

`XmlReadMode` parameter

`XmlSchemaCollection` class

`XmlText` class

`XmlTextReader`

`XmlValidatingReader`

`XmlWriteMode` parameter

`XmlWriter` class

XPath expression

`XPathDocument` class

`XpathExpression` class

`XPathNavigator` class

`XpathNodeIterator` class

`XslTransform` class

Review Questions

1. XML data files must follow some simple rules in order to be called "well formed" and to be used by standard XML parsers. Which one of these choices is *not* one of the rules?

   A. Each file must have a uniquely named root element.

   B. Element tag names and attribute names are case sensitive.

   C. Only element tag names that are defined in the schema can be used.

   D. Each opening tag must have a matching closing tag.

2. Several technologies have been developed for validating the contents of XML files against a defined set of element and attribute names and other formatting specifics. Which of these is the most up-to-date technology?

   A. XDR

   B. XSD

   C. DTD

   D. XSLT

3. You are creating an application that loads data from XML data files into a `DataSet`. The XML data file contains several items that you do not want to load for this particular application. How can you most easily accomplish this?

   A. You will have to write custom DOM code to remove the data that you do not want.

   B. You will have to use XSLT to transform the data file to the new format.

   C. Read the schema file into the data that establishes your desired data format. Read in the XML data with the `XmlReadMode` parameter set to `InferSchema`.

   D. Read the schema file into the data that establishes your desired data format. Read in the XML data with the `XmlReadMode` parameter set to `IgnoreSchema`.

4. You would like to output a copy of the current `DataSet` schema to a disk file, to use for performing validation in another part of your application. How can you quickly accomplish this?

   A. `myDataSet.WriteXml(filename, _`
      `XmlWriteMode.WriteSchema )`

   B. `myDataSet.GetXmlSchema()`

   C. `myDataSet.WriteXmlSchema(filename)`

   D. `myDataSet.InferXmlSchema(filename)`

5. You would like to create XML output from your `DataSet`. When you call the `WriteXml` method, the resulting XML output looks like this:

```
<jobs>
    <id>1</id>
    <job_desc>New Hire - Job not specified</job_desc>
    <min_lvl>10</min_lvl>
    <max_lvl>50</max_lvl>
</jobs>
```

The application that will be consuming your data requires this format:

```
<jobs id="2" description="Chief Executive Officer"
    min="200" max="225" />
```

How can you create this output?

A. Set the `DataSet.ColumnMapping` property to `Element`.

B. Set the `DataSet.ColumnMapping` property to `Attribute`.

C. Set each `DataColumn.ColumnMapping` property to `Element`.

D. Set each `DataColumn.ColumnMapping` property to `Attribute`.

6. After allowing your user to edit the data in a `DataSet`, you would like to pass an XML file to a business logic component for verification. The verification logic requires that records changed by the user are easily identifiable, and that any user changes that violate business rules must be reset to the original value. Which feature of the ADO.NET `DataSet` enables you to capture this information in an XML document?

A. `DiffGram`.

B. `UpdateGram`.

C. You must clone the `DataSet` before the user makes any changes.

D. You must copy the `DataSet` before the user makes any changes.

7. Which statement best describes the way that an `XmlTextReader` works?

A. The `XmlTextReader` enables you to load an XML data file in memory and have complete programmatic access to the data.

B. The `XmlTextReader` enables to you to process each node in an XML file sequentially.

C. The `XmlTextReader` enables you to work with your XML data as either a relational table or a hierarchical tree of nodes.

D. The `XmlTextReader` enables you to convert text files into XML data.

8. The XML Document Object Model (DOM) has only three base classes at its core. Which of the following is one of the base classes?

   A. XmlElement

   B. XmlAttribute

   C. XmlNodeList

   D. XmlDocument

9. The XML DOM has two similar methods, SelectNodes and SelectSingleNode. What makes these methods similar?

   A. Both methods return a NodeList collection.

   B. Both methods return a NamedNodeMap collection.

   C. Both methods select nodes based on tag name.

   D. Both methods select nodes based on XPath expressions.

10. You are using XML DOM programming in order to create a new structure of XML nodes in your application code. You have created a root node <employeelist> and an <employee> node. As you create the next set of nodes, you would like each new node to be added as the last child of the <employee> node. Which method should you call?

    A. myElement.InsertBefore(newNode, lastNode)

    B. myElement.InsertAfter(newNode, lastNode)

    C. myElement.AppendChild(childNode)

    D. myElement.PrependChild(childNode)

11. You're writing a function that processes XML data. The procedures that call your function pass in a Stream object that contains the XML data. Which method do you call to populate and XmlDocument object?

    A. XmlDocument.LoadXml

    B. XmlDocument.Load

    C. XmlDocument.ImportNode

    D. XmlDocument.ReadNode

12. What is an advantage of learning to use XPath expressions?

    A. XPath expressions are the fastest way to locate data in an XML document.

    B. XPath expression syntax is a common notation that is used by several XML processing technologies.

    C. XPath is the only way to locate nodes in an XML data file.

    D. XPath is a special capability of the .NET Framework classes.

13. Your application must do extensive searching through large XML data files. Which option is likely to give you the best performance?

    A. Use XmlDataDocument objects. If your XPath queries do not work, you can always fall back on SQL queries.

    B. Use an XPathDocument and the SelectNodes method.

    C. Use an XPathDocument and the Compile method.

    D. Use an XmlDocument and the SelectNodes method.

14. You are developing an application that processes business transactions from many e-commerce trading partners, in the form of XML documents. At what point, or points, in the data flow is it most important to perform XSD schema validation on the data files that you are exchanging with your business partners?

    A. Anytime XML data is read or written by your program code, validation is necessary.

    B. Validation is most important to ensure that your application is sending valid XML data to your business partners.

    C. Validation is most important to ensure that your application is receiving valid XML data from your business partners.

    D. Validation is important only if you notice a large number of errors when the data from XML input files are processed.

15. You are writing a SQL query to retrieve XML data from Microsoft SQL Server 2000. You would like each column value from the table to be in the form of *columnname*="*value*" and you would like the element name to reflect the name of the database table. Which SQL query would you use?

    A. SELECT * FROM *table* FOR XML AUTO

    B. SELECT * FROM *table* FOR XML RAW

    C. SELECT * FROM *table* FOR XML EXPLICIT

    D. SELECT * FROM *table* FOR XML ELEMENTS

Answers to Review Questions

1. **C.** A uniquely named root element, case sensitivity, and matching opening and closing tags are some the rules that define a well-formed XML data file. The third choice is incorrect because validation against a schema is a separate step beyond the rules for well-formed XML.

2. **B.** DTD was the original means for validating XML data. XDR was an interim technology, mostly used on the Microsoft platform before the W3C finalized XSD. XSLT is used for creating stylesheets for formatting XML data; it does not perform validation.

3. **D.** The first two choices could be used to create the desired result, but either option would result in writing a considerable amount of code. The last option is correct because the IgnoreSchema parameter will not load any data from the source file that doesn't match the current DataSet schema. Using the InferSchema parameter will cause all the data items to be loaded and will change the schema to include the new data as well.

4. **C.** The third option is correct because this produces a disk file with only the schema information. The first option would produce a disk file with both an in-line schema and the data. The second option returns the schema information as a string, so additional programming would be required to save the information to a disk file. The last option is used to input schema information into a DataSet.

5. **D.** The ColumnMapping property of each DataColumn determines whether the value for that column is output as an XML element or attribute. The DataSet class does not have a ColumnMapping property.

6. **A.** DiffGram is correct. DiffGram output adds a hasChanges attribute to any modified, inserted, or deleted rows. The original values of the data are in a separate <diffgr:before> section of the XML output. UpdateGrams are used to send updates to SQL Server 2000 in the form of XML data files. The DataSet Copy method would retain a record of the original values, but would require more coding to compare the two versions. The DataSet Clone method copies only the structure of the DataSet, not data.

7. **B.** The XmlTextReader provides forward-only, read-only access to XML data. The XML DOM XmlDocument provides complete programmatic access to XML data. The XmlDataDocument enables you to treat your data as either a relational table or a hierarchical tree of nodes. There is no class that automatically converts text files to XML.

8. **C.** The base classes of the XML DOM are XmlNode, and two collection classes, XmlNodeList and XmlNamedNodeMap. XmlElement, XmlAttribute, and XmlDocument (along with many other classes) are derived from the XmlNode base class.

9. **D.** Both methods use XPath expressions to select matching nodes. SelectNodes returns a NodeList collection, and SelectSingleNode returns a reference to the first matching node. These methods can include a tag name in the selection criteria but they can evaluate much more sophisticated patterns that match a node's position in the document hierarchy or specific data values.

10. **C.** The AppendChild method will add the new node as the last child node of the parent (myElement). PrependChild adds the new element as the first child of the parent. The InsertBefore and InsertAfter methods require you to specify a reference node and do not automatically add the new element as a child of the current node.

11. B.   The Load method can read data from a disk file or Stream object. The LoadXml method loads data from a string variable. The ImportNode method reads information from one XmlDocument into another. The ReadNode method reads node information from the current node of an XmlReader object.

12. B.   After you understand XPath expression syntax, you can use it in XML DOM programming, XSLT processing, and other XML-related technologies. XPath expression queries can be optimized for performance if you use XPathDocument and compiled XPathExpression objects, but might not always be the fastest method of locating data. Other methods are available for locating specific nodes, such as the GetElementsbyTagName method and using an XmlReader and testing each node for type and name as it is processed. The last option is incorrect because the XPath specification (like most other XML related technologies) is managed by the W3C and is not proprietary to any single software platform.

13. C.   The XPathDocument (and also some classes in the System.Xml.Xsl namespace) is optimized to perform XPath queries. When you compile an XPath expression, repeated searches with the same expression are further optimized. The XPath document does have a SelectNodes method. The other options are functional but might not provide the best performance.

14. C.   It is most important to validate incoming data files, before you use the information in your own applications or store the information in your database. After you have thoroughly tested your own applications that produce XML output, you should be reasonably sure that the XML output created is in the correct format. Because validation requires extra processing overhead, it is not necessary to validate XML data at every step of processing. The last option is incorrect because validation of XML input files will notify you in advance of trying to process them that the data might be invalid.

15. A.   The first choice is correct because it will create a format of XML output that uses the table name as the element name for each row, and creates an attribute name/value pair for each column name and its data value. The second choice would use the generic <row> element tag name for each data row in the resultset. The third choice creates a custom XML output when a query retrieves data from multiple tables. The last choice is incorrect because it should actually state SELECT * FROM table FOR XML AUTO, ELEMENTS and this would result in a format of XML with no attributes; columns would be written as child elements of the <table> element.

Chapter

8

Testing and Debugging

MICROSOFT EXAM OBJECTIVES COVERED IN THIS CHAPTER:

- ✓ **Create a unit test plan.**
- ✓ **Instrument and debug a Windows service, a serviced component, a .NET Remoting object, and an XML Web service.**
  - ▪ Configure the debugging environment.
  - ▪ Create and apply debugging code to components and applications.
  - ▪ Execute tests.
  - ▪ Provide multicultural test data to components and applications.
- ✓ **Log test results.**
  - ▪ Resolve errors and rework code.
  - ▪ Control debugging in the web.config file.
  - ▪ Use SOAP extensions for debugging.
- ✓ **Use interactive debugging.**
- ✓ **Implement tracing.**
  - ▪ Configure and use trace listeners and trace switches.
  - ▪ Display trace output.

The first four chapters of this book taught you how to create Windows services, serviced components, .NET Remoting applications, and XML Web services. Chapters 5 through 7 showed you how to use .NET Framework classes in the `System.Data` namespace and the `System.Xml` namespace to access data in your applications. This chapter begins the last section of the book, which covers testing and debugging, security considerations, deploying applications, and configuring applications in a production environment.

This chapter introduces you to Visual Studio .NET debugging capabilities and to the .NET Framework classes in the *System.Diagnostics namespace* that enable you to instrument your applications by using tracing. You will learn how to control debugging in the `web.config` file for ASP.NET applications and how to use SOAP extensions to debug XML Web services. However, first you will look at some recommendations for creating a testing strategy for your projects.

Planning a Testing Strategy

To produce applications that are reliable and do not fail when your users are depending on them, you must make sure that all code is thoroughly tested before releasing it. The best testing strategy requires that code be tested in various ways throughout the development phase and not just when the application is completed and ready to be deployed. By testing early, you can often catch defects while they are still easy to fix and do not affect other parts of the application code. Many organizations prefer to defer testing to the end of a project. They look at testing as an activity that adds a burden of time to the project schedule (and money to the project budget), when they would prefer to move quickly ahead with the coding. Most experts in the field of software project management disagree with this viewpoint and point out that it is several times more costly to wait until the application is complete to begin identifying defects and fixing them.

If your project team has done a good job of analyzing the requirements for the project and writing a good functional specification, then that information can be used directly when designing your test strategy. Each item in a functional specification should be documented in such as way that the resulting code can be tested to determine that it does, in fact, satisfy the requirements set forth in the functional specification.

Design goals for a software project often include specifications for performance, reliability, and other desirable characteristics. When testing your application, you should keep these goals in mind. Here are some testing recommendations for common design goals:

Availability   Availability means that the application is available when users need it and that it does not experience downtime resulting in a loss of time, money, or opportunity for the business. Testing for availability should include tests of external resources (such as database servers and network bandwidth) to make sure they can handle the demands of your application. You should also test maintenance procedures and disaster recovery procedures to determine how long the application will be offline.

Manageability   Manageability means that maintenance and ongoing monitoring of application performance can be carried out easily. Testing for manageability should include testing on different hardware configurations and testing any code in the application that provides instrumentation for performance monitoring.

Performance   Performance measures include response times or number of transactions performed per time unit that were part of the original functional specifications for your application. Testing for performance includes determining baseline performance and then "stress testing" your application to see at what point greater levels of demand will cause your application to fail.

Reliability   Reliability means that your application produces consistent results under any conditions. Testing for reliability includes testing each component with a variety of input data and with peak usage demands. Equally important is testing the system as a whole with the same type of stresses. Reliability testing requires testing in a real-world environment, reflecting actual use conditions. Reliability tests are often designed to find a way to make the application fail.

Scalability   Scalability describes the application's ability to serve increasing numbers of users or to perform increasing numbers of transactions, while still maintaining acceptable performance measurements. Testing for scalability includes many of the same activities as performance testing.

Securability   Securability addresses your application's resistance to exploitation by those who are interested in breaking into your systems. Testing for securability includes making sure that code runs at the lowest level of privilege necessary, that user input is validated, and that your code cannot be used to perform destructive operations, such as overwriting disk files.

With these larger goals in mind, you can begin writing test cases for your application. Because it is good practice to test throughout application development, in this section you will look at three types of testing that you can include at different phases of the application development cycle: unit testing, integration testing, and regression testing. In addition, you will also learn about how to test for globalization.

Unit Testing

The application developer typically carries out unit testing on his or her own code. *Unit testing* determines whether a single set of code, perhaps a single class or a component that contains a few related classes, is correctly performing its tasks. Code should be tested with a range of data, representing both valid input values and invalid ones. The code should return consistent results on valid data and handle error conditions caused by the invalid test data.

After you have created a test application that can test your modules by calling the methods with all of the different test data, this test can be reused, and tests should be run each time the module is changed in any way. This way, you can be sure that subsequent changes to the module do not cause new errors.

The functional specifications for the application should provide information for generating test data. The specifications should include information about valid input and output values for each method that you code.

Unit testing is cost-effective because it will catch defects at the very earliest point in the development cycle. Defects are less costly and easier to fix when you are focusing on only one small section of code at a time.

Integration Testing

After individual modules or components have been verified as working to specification, they can be put into service by other developers who are working on other parts of the application. For example, you might develop a component to calculate tax information that will be used by ASP.NET web developers. The ASP.NET developers are mostly concerned with creating a user interface but will call your component, and others, to perform complex calculations. *Integration testing* makes sure that calls are being made correctly to your component and that the return results are in the correct format.

As your application becomes more complex, data might be passed through several components to achieve the final results. Integration testing should begin by testing the interaction between each pair of components. After that has been verified as working correctly, you can test the interactions between multiple components as they will actually occur when the application is in production.

Regression Testing

Regression testing is done when changes or additions are made to your application. In addition to testing the code that was changed or is new, regression testing tests all of the previously tested parts of the application to make sure the new code has not inadvertently caused an error to occur in another part of the system.

Regression testing can be automated and will most likely consist of running the test cases developed during unit and integration testing. The goal of regression testing is to make sure that all code that was working correctly before the change is still working correctly afterwards.

Testing for Globalization

You might be required to run your application in an environment that uses different locale settings from those that it was originally developed with. In other scenarios, you might be exchanging data that was created on a computer running under a different locale. In these cases, it is important to test your application with *multicultural test data* to make sure that those items that vary from culture to culture, such as dates, currency, and separator characters in numbers, are interpreted correctly by your application.

If your application's user interface is going to be localized, you also need to make sure that all text string information is contained in a resource file and that strings that will be displayed to the user are not coded into the source code. Be aware that the length of string data might change greatly when the text is translated into another language, so make sure that your code and your user interface can accommodate strings of varying lengths.

 **Real World Scenario**

FxCop: Enforcing Coding Standards

You are a software developer for an organization that is cautiously moving to the .NET platform. Your manager is concerned that inexperience with the platform will lead to mistakes in design. Management is also concerned that developers will overlook important considerations that will cause problems down the road, such as security vulnerabilities or problems interoperating with existing applications. Standard testing and debugging procedures can provide confidence that your code is performing correctly, but they can't tell you if you are missing important features.

Your manager also wants the team to do a better job of following a set of standard naming conventions across all projects. After all, because everyone is learning a new programming platform and languages, this is a perfect time to instill some good habits.

You have been assigned the tasks of researching standards and best practices for developing on the .NET platform, and recommending procedures that your team can use to make sure that their first attempts are successful, and ensuring that best practices and coding standards are enforced. Your web research pays off quickly when you read some comments on a developer forum about FxCop. FxCop is tool from Microsoft that checks your assemblies and verifies the code against a set of rules based on the Microsoft .NET Framework Design Guidelines. Each of these rules verifies that your code includes important .NET Framework features, such as security permission requests, or does not include common errors that could slow performance. The FxCop program includes a comprehensive set of rules that cover such areas as:

- COM interoperability
- Class design
- Globalization
- Naming conventions
- Performance
- Security

You can also create new rules that apply to your own projects, or choose to exclude some of the existing rules when analyzing your code. Here is a screen shot of the FxCop analysis provided for the TimeServer.dll that was a part of the Chapter 3, "Creating and Managing .NET Remoting Objects," exercise.

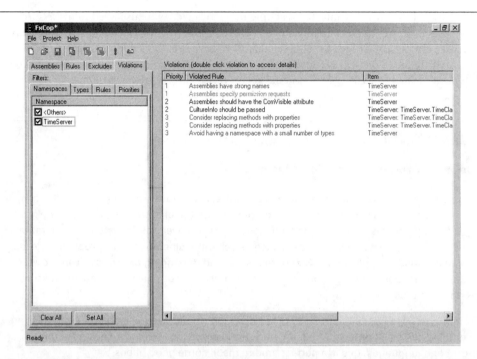

FxCop supports many other features that will help you to create an automated process to make sure that all of your team's code is checked regularly. You can save sets of rules and exclusions on a per-project basis. You can also save analysis reports as XML (or plain text) files, so management can review them.

FxCop is available for free download on the www.gotdotnet.com site: http://www.gotdotnet .com/team/libraries/.

If you want to learn more about the .NET Framework Design Guidelines, you can find that information at http://msdn.microsoft.com/library/default.asp?url=/library/en-us/ cpgenref/html/cpconnetframeworkdesignguidelines.asp.

Configuring the Debugging Environment

The Visual Studio .NET IDE provides much more control over the debugging process than what was available in Visual Basic 6. Although some features will be familiar, others have been enhanced, and there are new features to learn about.

This section covers Visual Studio .NET settings and tools to use during debugging, and specific considerations for debugging special types of applications.

The first change you will notice in the Visual Studio .NET IDE is the drop-down list on the main toolbar that enables you to select whether you want a *Debug configuration* or a *Release configuration* when you build your application.

The Debug configuration creates a PDB (program database) file that contains what are called *debugging symbols* for your executable. This file is found in the project's \bin directory along with the executable file, and will have a .pdb filename extension. A Debug build will also cause extra information to be added to the executable file so that the debugger can stop at breakpoints and let you step through your executing code. The ability to do these things is necessary during the development phase, and you will typically use the Debug build throughout the development of your application.

When you are ready to create a version of the application that will be installed in a production environment, you should change this option and create a Release build. This type of build does not include the extra overhead needed to work with the debugger. If your solution is complex and consists of multiple projects, the Configuration Manager dialog box enables you to select Debug and Release build options on a project-by-project basis. Figure 8.1 shows the Visual Studio .NET IDE displaying the Configuration Manager dialog box. Also, note the toolbar for setting a Debug or Release build.

FIGURE 8.1   The Configuration Manager

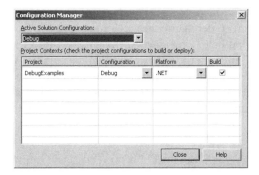

Other settings that control debugging behavior for your Visual Studio .NET projects are found on the project Property Pages dialog box, shown in Figure 8.2. To access this dialog box, right-click the project name in the Solution Explorer and choose Properties from the menu.

FIGURE 8.2   The project Property Pages dialog box

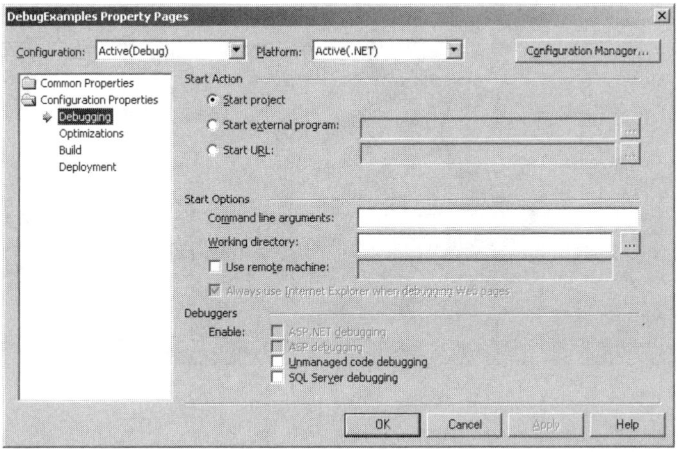

If you click Configuration Properties and Debugging in the left pane of this dialog box, you will see several items in the right pane:

Start Action   This has three options. The Start Project option is used for standard Windows forms or console applications, which start up on their own. The Start External Program option enables you to specify another program, such as a testing application, to start running and make calls on your component. The Start URL option is used for XML Web services and enables you to specify a start URL.

Start Options   This section enables you to type in any arguments that would normally be entered at the command line for console applications, to specify a working directory, to specify that you are debugging on a remote server, or to specify that you want to use Internet Explorer instead of the Visual Studio .NET internal web browser when debugging web applications.

Debuggers   This section enables you to include debugging for ASP.NET applications, unmanaged code, or SQL Server stored procedures.

Other settings pertinent to debugging are also found on the Configuration Properties, Build portion of this dialog box (see Figure 8.3). These include an output path for your executable and PDB file, and whether your compiled executable will include DEBUG and TRACE constants that determine whether output from `Debug.Write` and `Trace.Write` statements in your code are included in the compiled executable. `Debug` and `Trace` statements are covered in detail in the next section of this chapter, "Implementing Instrumentation and Tracing."

FIGURE 8.3   The Build portion of the project Property Pages dialog box

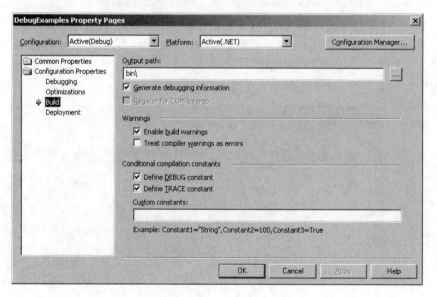

Now let's look at some of the features that are available while you are using the debugger from within the Visual Studio .NET IDE.

Configuring Debugging in ASP.NET Applications

For ASP.NET applications and XML Web services, the setting that controls whether debugging symbols are included in your compiled code is made in the `web.config` file. The following code snippet shows how this setting is formatted in the `web.config` file:

```
<configuration>
  <system.web>
    <compilation defaultLanguage="VB"
      debug="true"
      numRecompilesBeforeAppRestart="15">
    </compilation>
  </system.web>
</configuration>
```

Be sure to set this to `debug="false"` when your application is ready to go into production, because enabling the debugging capability can adversely affect performance.

Running the Visual Studio .NET Debugger

The Visual Studio .NET debugger is running whenever you start your application from within the Visual Studio .NET IDE with a Debug build selected. While running within the IDE, your application will go into Break mode automatically whenever a runtime error is encountered. Alternatively, you can set breakpoints at specific locations in your code to control exactly when your application will enter Break mode.

While in Break mode, execution of your application is suspended at a specific line of code (the line where you set a breakpoint, or the line where an error occurred). You can use the debugging tools provided by Visual Studio .NET to find out detailed information about the state of your application, such as the current call stack or values of variables. When in Break mode, the Debug menu and toolbar give you access to these tools.

Next, you will learn about the debugging tools provided by Visual Studio .NET.

Setting Breakpoints

Breakpoints are an important debugging tool, by setting a breakpoint at a specific line of code you can control exactly at what point in program execution the debugger will go into Break mode. In Visual Studio .NET, *breakpoints* have been enhanced to provide more functionality than was available in the Visual Basic 6 IDE. Breakpoints can be saved with your solution (information about breakpoints is one type of information that is stored in the solution `.suo` file).

Breakpoints can also be conditional. In Visual Basic 6, when you set a breakpoint, it was hit every time that line of code was executed. In Visual Studio .NET, you can set conditions on each breakpoint that cause it to be hit (and program execution suspended), only if the condition is met. You can evaluate variable values or just specify that you want to break on the *n*th time that the line of code executes.

You can set breakpoints in various ways: by using the menu, toolbar, or keystroke short-cuts. The most direct way is to click on the left margin of the code editor window, next to the line of code where you want to set the breakpoint. A line of code with a breakpoint will be highlighted in the code editor. You can set breakpoints only on an executable line of code. You cannot set them on a comment or a simple variable declaration. Breakpoints can also be disabled, so that they will not be hit when code is executing, without removing them completely from the project.

After you have set the breakpoint, you can set conditions. Right-click on that line of code and select Breakpoint Properties from the menu. Figure 8.4 shows the Breakpoint Properties dialog box.

FIGURE 8.4   The Breakpoint Properties dialog box

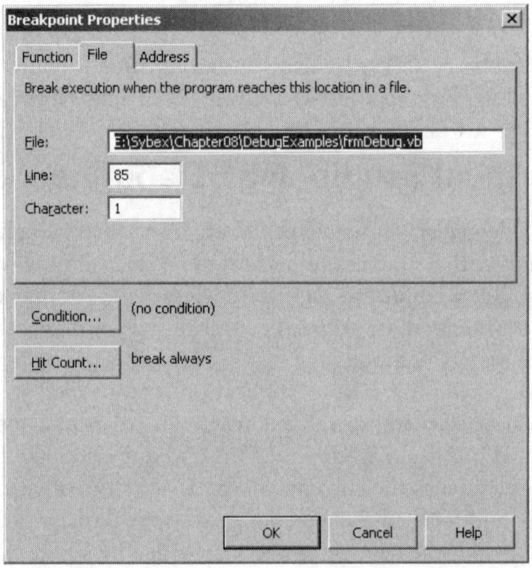

You can then set a condition by entering an expression to evaluate or a variable name and specifying that the breakpoint will be hit if the condition is True or when the value changes. When working with loops or subroutines that are executed many times, you might want to specify a hit count. Rather than breaking each time the line of code is executed, it will break only at a specific count, or every 10 times (a multiple), or when the hit count reaches or exceeds a specified number.

Use the Breakpoint window to see the status of all breakpoints in your project. You can access this window by choosing Debug ➢ Windows ➢ Breakpoints from the Visual Studio .NET menu.

You will practice setting breakpoints in Exercise 8.1.

Using Debugging Tools

Other tools that are available to you in Break mode are accessed through the Debug menu and toolbar. These include the following:

Resuming/stopping program execution   The Debug menu and toolbar include commands to continue application execution at the current line of code, to stop debugging (and end application execution), to break all (similar to pressing Ctrl+Break when the application is executing), and to restart the application execution from its startup code. When not in Break mode, the Debug menu also offers an option called Start Without Debugging, which enables you to test your application's behavior without the debugger running.

Stepping through code one line at a time, stepping over or out of procedures   When you enter Break mode, the next line of code that will be executed is highlighted. You can use the Step Into instruction to execute code line by line. Step Over will execute a subprocedure or function without stepping line by line. Step Out will finish executing a subprocedure or function and take you back to the line of code following the one that called the subprocedure.

Status windows, such as Memory, Registers, Call Stack, Threads, Modules, and Disassembly   You can access detailed information about how your application is executing, such as viewing the contents of memory and registers. You can view the call stack to see which procedures are currently executing and see how many active threads are running. The Modules window shows you information about assemblies that are loaded, such as the `mscorlib.dll`, `system.dll`, and any others that your application references, as well as your application's executable. The Disassembly window shows you the assembly language code that has been compiled from your source code.

Status windows, such as Watch, Locals, Autos, and Me   These status windows show information about variables and objects in your application. You can use the Watch window to change the value of a variable in Break mode and then resume application execution. The Locals window shows the value of variables in the current procedure. The Autos window also shows values from previously executed procedures. The Me window shows the status of your Windows form and its controls.

Command window   The Command window is similar to the Immediate window in Visual Basic 6. When this window is set to Immediate mode, you can use it to evaluate expressions, query the value of variables, and execute lines of code. By switching to Command mode (type **>cmd** in the window and type **>immed** to return to Immediate mode), you can type commands to control Visual Studio .NET, such as starting and stopping your application, or to run Visual Studio .NET macros.

Figure 8.5 shows the Debug toolbar and the options that are available on the Debug menu when you are in Break mode. You will test many of these options in Exercise 8.1.

FIGURE 8.5   The Debug menu and toolbar

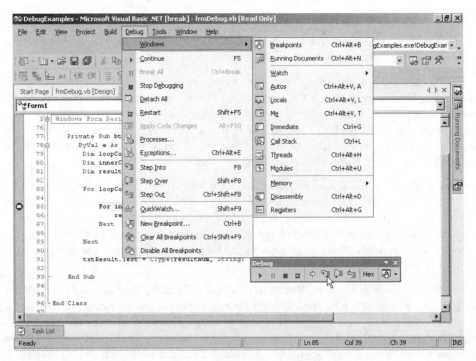

In Exercise 8.1, you will set breakpoints and use the Command window and some of the other Visual Studio .NET debugging tools.

Setting Conditional Breakpoints and Using the Debugging Tools

1. Start Visual Studio .NET and begin a new Windows application. Name the project **DebugExamples**.

2. Change the name of the default Form1.vb to **frmDebug.vb**.

3. Add a Command Button and a TextBox to the form. Name them **btnStart** and **txtResult**. Your form should look like the following one.

EXERCISE 8.1 *(continued)*

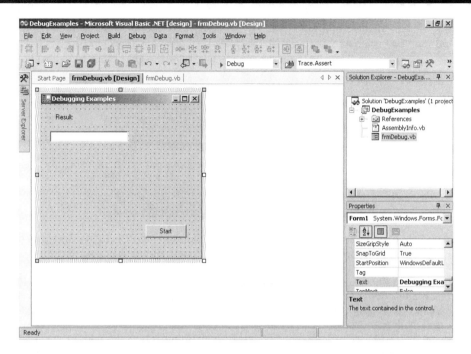

4. Create a Click event procedure for btnTest. This code will perform some simple calculations in a loop so you can test the Debug features. You code should look like this:

```
Private Sub btnStart_Click(ByVal sender As System.Object, _
    ByVal e As System.EventArgs) Handles btnStart.Click

    Dim loopCounter As Int32
    Dim innerCounter As Int32
    Dim resultNum As Int32

    For loopCounter = 1 To 10

        For innerCounter = 1 To 10
            resultNum = loopCounter * innerCounter
        Next

    Next

    txtResult.Text = CType(resultNum, String)

End Sub
```

5. Set a breakpoint on the line of code that reads For innerCounter = 1 To 10 by clicking in the left margin of the code editor. The line of code will be highlighted.

6. Right-click on the breakpoint and choose Breakpoint Properties from the menu. Click the Condition button and a second dialog box will open. Type **loopCounter=5** in the text box. Make sure that the Is True option is selected. Click the OK button to close each dialog box.

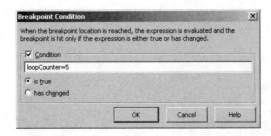

7. On the Debug menu, choose Debug ➢ Windows ➢ Breakpoints. The Breakpoints window displays at the bottom of the screen and shows information about the breakpoint you just set.

8. Save and run the application. Click the Start button. When your application goes into Break mode, choose Debug ➢ Windows ➢ Locals to display the Locals window and view the values of your variables. Verify that loopCounter is equal to 5.

9. Use the Step Into toolbar button to step line by line through the code. Watch the variable values change in the Locals window. After you have observed the values changing, stop the application.

10. Remove the breakpoint on the line of code that reads For innerCounter = 1 To 10 by clicking again in the left margin of the code editor. The highlight will go away.

11. Set a breakpoint on the line of code that reads resultNum = loopCounter * innerCounter by clicking in the left margin of the code editor. That code line will be highlighted.

12. Right-click on the breakpoint and choose Breakpoint Properties from the menu. Click the Hit Count button and then choose Break When The Hit Count Is Equal To from the drop-down list. Type a value, such as 35, in the text box.

13. Run the application again. Click Start, and when it goes into Break mode, display the Locals window. Examine the value of your variables.

14. Display the Command window. The window should be in Immediate mode, the title bar should display "Command Window - Immediate."

15. Type **? loopCounter** in the Command window. Press the Enter key. You should see the value of loopCounter, which should be 4.

16. Type **loopcounter = 7**. Press the Enter key. Verify in the Locals window that the value has been changed.

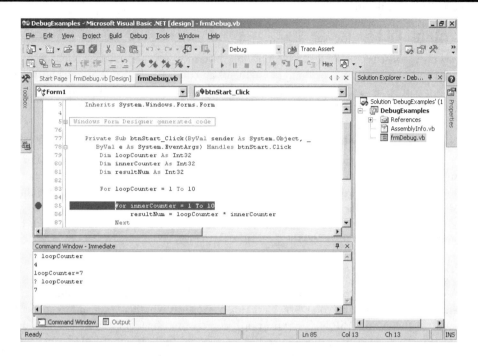

17. Click the Continue button on the Debug toolbar to resume application execution.

Debugging Other Types of Applications

When you are working on standard applications in the Visual Studio .NET IDE, you have all the source code loaded into Visual Studio .NET and are working on a single computer. As you work with other types of applications, such as Windows services, .NET Remoting objects, or XML Web services, debugging can become more complex. You might need to debug code that is running on a different computer. This section covers some of the special considerations for debugging.

Debugging Windows Services

As we discussed in Chapter 1, "Creating and Managing Windows Services," a Windows service cannot be started by running it in the Visual Studio .NET IDE. It must first be installed as a Windows service and then started with the Service Control Manager. After the service is running, you can attach the Visual Studio .NET debugger to the process. This is done by choosing Debug ➢ Processes from the menu, locating your service in the list of processes running on your computer, and then attaching to that process. Chapter 1 explains this procedure in more detail.

Debugging DLLs

If your project consists of only DLLs with no user interface or other startup code, you can still debug these applications by specifying the name of a project (such as a Windows Form application) that will be used to test the DLL. This information is entered in the Project Properties dialog box under Configuration Properties ➤ Debugging, Start External Program.

Debugging Remote Components

If you need to debug an application that is running on a different computer across the network, you must make sure that either Visual Studio .NET or the remote components are installed on the remote machine. The remote components are installed by using the Visual Studio .NET setup disk. You will see the option to install remote components on the first screen. To debug remotely, you must be a member of the Windows Debugger Users group and an Administrator on the remote machine.

Just-in-Time Debugging

When your .NET Framework applications are running outside of the Visual Studio .NET environment and an error occurs, you will see a dialog box asking whether you want to debug them. For Windows forms and ASP.NET applications, you can use the Common Language Runtime debugger; for classic ASP applications and other script-based applications, use the Script debugger. There is also a native debugger available for C++ applications.

Debugging XML Web Services

When debugging an XML Web service, you can step from code in a test client, into the code of the Web service (assuming the Web service was created with Visual Studio .NET and you have the source file and debugging symbols file, .pdb, available). You do not have to load the Web service project into Visual Studio .NET. You can load the test client, set a breakpoint on the line of code that makes a call to the Web service, and then watch as you step from your test client into the code module of the Web service. Remember that your Visual Studio .NET test project contains a proxy class that hides some of the details involved in calling Web service methods. By default, this class is marked with a <DebuggerStepThrough()> attribute. This means that when stepping though the code, you typically do not see the code in the proxy class executing. If you remove the attribute, you will step from the client code, to the proxy class, and then into the Web service code.

Debugging SQL Server Stored Procedures

Visual Studio .NET not only gives you the ability to view and run SQL Server stored procedures from the Server Explorer, but also provides the ability to debug them. Expand the Server Explorer to display your database's stored procedure, right-click the procedure name, and choose Step Into Stored Procedure from the menu. Please consult the Visual Studio .NET documentation for more information about components that need to be installed for SQL Server and permissions that are required to debug this way.

Debugging with Command-Line Debuggers

The .NET Framework includes two command-line debugging utilities. The *CLR Debugger (DbgCLR.exe)* provides debugging services with a graphical interface when the .NET Framework is installed but Visual Studio .NET is not present. The *Runtime Debugger (Cordbg.exe)* is a command-line debugger.

Implementing Instrumentation and Tracing

Instrumentation is the process of adding features to your applications that provide the ability to measure performance and to track and troubleshoot errors. There is a need during testing, as well as after the application is running in a production environment, to have some means of tracking how the application is performing and what type of errors are encountered. Instead of relying on users to report errors accurately, you can make use of the Trace classes to make sure that accurate information is recorded every time that an error occurs. This information can be written to a log file, or even the system event log, and reviewed periodically to make sure that your applications are running reliably and up to their specifications.

The .NET Framework offers a set of classes that enable you to easily add these features to your applications. This section covers how the Debug class differs from the familiar Visual Basic 6 Debug object and also covers the new .NET Framework Trace, TraceListener, BooleanSwitch, and TraceSwitch classes. These classes are all part of the System.Diagnostics namespace.

The Debug.Write and Trace.Write statements can be placed directly in your code at every point where you would like status information about what is happening at runtime. Output from the Debug.Write and Trace.Write statements is displayed in the Output window when you are running your application in the Visual Studio .NET IDE. The Output window is usually displayed when you start your application in Visual Studio .NET. You can access it by choosing View ➢ Other Windows ➢ Output from the Visual Studio .NET menu.

In general, it makes sense to use Debug.Write statements for your own information during testing and troubleshooting in the development phase. By default, Debug statements are not included in your compiled executable when you create a Release build.

Trace.Write statements can be added to your application to add permanent instrumentation to the compiled executable. The behavior of Trace statements can be controlled by using them in conjunction with TraceListeners and TraceSwitches.

The TraceListeners determine where the output from Trace.Write statements are directed at runtime (the console, a text file, or the event log).

TraceSwitches enable you to turn tracing on and off. You might not need to produce trace output every time your application runs, but only when a problem is reported and you need to troubleshoot. TraceSwitches can also have a priority level that determines whether all Trace.Write messages are output, or only those above the specified priority level. Settings for TraceSwitches can be made directly in your source code or in an *application configuration file*. Visual Studio .NET defines a standard XML format for the application configuration files. The application configuration file is created by Visual Studio .NET with default settings, you can customize these for your application. Using a configuration file also enables settings to be changed by an administrator as frequently as required after the application is deployed, without having to recompile and redistribute the application executables.

You will look at `TraceListeners` and `TraceSwitches` in more detail later in this chapter.

If you want debugging and tracing code to be included in your compiled executables, the *DEBUG compiler directive* and the *TRACE compiler directive* must be set to `True` before compiling your application. When you are using Visual Studio .NET, these settings are handled automatically for you. When you build your application by using a Debug configuration (see the previous section, "Configuring the Debugging Environment," for an explanation of Debug versus Release builds), both the `DEBUG` and `TRACE` directives will be set to `True`. When you change the configuration setting to create a Release build, only the `TRACE` directive will be enabled. If you would like to manage these settings yourself or to view the settings made by Visual Studio .NET, go to the project Property Pages dialog box (go to Project ➤ Properties menu, click Configuration Properties, and then click Build). In this dialog box, you will see check boxes to enable either of the `DEBUG` and `TRACE` constants. Figure 8.6 shows the Project Properties dialog box displaying these choices.

FIGURE 8.6   DEBUG and TRACE compiler directives in the project Property Pages dialog box

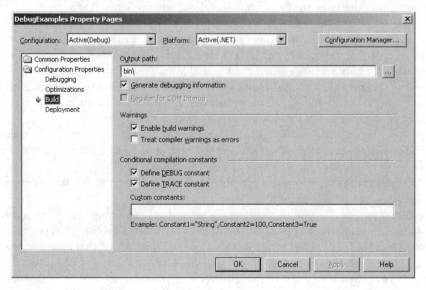

You can also control DEBUG and TRACE settings by declaring the constants at the top of your source code modules:

```
#Const DEBUG = True
#Const TRACE = True
```

If you are not using Visual Studio .NET and are compiling by using the vbc.exe command-line compiler, you can use command-line switches to include or omit the tracing and debugging code in your executable (these settings are case sensitive):

```
C:\path\vbc.exe /r:System.dll /d:TRACE=TRUE /d:DEBUG=FALSE MySource.vb
```

Next, you will learn about the methods and properties of the Debug and Trace classes.

Writing Messages with *Debug* and *Trace*

Both the *Debug class* and the *Trace class* work the same way and have the same set of properties and methods. As discussed in the previous section, the main difference is that the Debug class is more suitable for providing information to the developer during development and testing using the Visual Studio .NET IDE. The Trace class is more suitable for permanently adding instrumentation to applications because Trace statements can be controlled by TraceSwitch settings. The properties and methods of the Debug and Trace classes are listed in Table 8.1.

TABLE 8.1 Properties and Methods of the *Debug* and *Trace* Classes

Property	Description
AutoFlush	Indicates whether the Flush method should be called on the listeners after every write
IndentLevel	Indicates the indent level
IndentSize	Indicates the number of spaces in an indent
Listeners	Provides access to the collection of listeners that is monitoring the trace output

Method	Description
Assert	Checks for a condition and displays a message if the condition is false
Close	Flushes the output buffer and then closes the listeners
Fail	Emits an error message
Flush	Flushes the output buffer and causes buffered data to be written to the listeners
Indent	Increases the current IndentLevel by one
Unindent	Decreases the current IndentLevel by one

TABLE 8.1 Properties and Methods of the *Debug* and *Trace* Classes *(continued)*

Method	Description
Write	Writes information to the trace listeners in the Listeners collection
WriteIf	Writes information to the trace listeners in the Listeners collection if a condition is true
WriteLine	Writes information to the trace listeners in the Listeners collection, with a line-terminating character at the end of each message.
WriteLineIf	Writes information to the trace listeners in the Listeners collection if a condition is true, with a line-terminating character at the end of each message.

As you can see, there are four variations of the *Write method*. Write simply outputs a text string. The *WriteLine method* outputs the string with a line-ending character at the end. The *WriteIf method* and the *WriteLineIf method* will produce output only if a specified conditional statement evaluates to True.

Output messages are written to the Output window in Visual Studio .NET and to all Trace-Listeners. The Write and WriteLine methods have overloaded constructors that can accept a single parameter (the message text) or two parameters (the message text and a category description). The WriteIf and WriteLineIf methods require either two or three parameters. The first parameter is always an expression that can resolve to a Boolean (True or False) result. Output messages will be written only if the expression resolves to True. Following that, you can specify a message, or a message and category description. The category descriptions and message text are left to the developer to define. You should plan and document the information that your debug and trace messages output, to best aid those who are responsible for the ongoing maintenance of your application.

Listing 8.1 shows some examples of outputting messages with the Debug and Trace classes.

Listing 8.1: Writing Debug and Trace Messages

```
Dim crucialValue As Integer = 5001

Debug.Write("Debug message")
Trace.Write("Trace message")

Debug.WriteLine("Debug message", "Category=GeneralError")
Trace.WriteLine("Trace message", "Category=GeneralError")

Debug.WriteIf(crucialValue >= 5000, "Debug message")
Trace.WriteIf(crucialValue >= 5000, "Trace message")

Debug.WriteLineIf(crucialValue >= 5000, "Debug message", _
    "Category=GeneralError")
Trace.WriteLineIf(crucialValue >= 5000, "Trace message", _
    "Category=GeneralError")
```

Using Assertions

Both the Debug and Trace classes offer an *Assert method*. When you write an Assert statement, you provide an expression that you expect to evaluate to True, while your application is running as expected. Assertions are useful when debugging, because they enable your application to run normally and interrupt only if an expected value turns out to be false. When the test expression evaluates to False, the Assert method causes an error dialog box to be displayed, along with writing messages to the Output window. This is fine during the development and testing stages, but is not acceptable for a Release version of the executable.

Listing 8.2 is an example of code using a Debug.Assert statement to test an assertion while your application is running. Figure 8.7 shows the error message that is displayed when the Assert statement fails.

Listing 8.2: Using Assertions

```
Dim crucialValue As Integer = 1003


Trace.Assert(crucialValue <= 1000, "Crucial value has exceeded 1000")
```

FIGURE 8.7   The message box that is displayed when an Assert method call fails

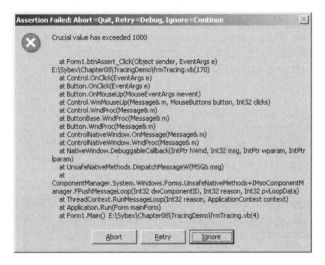

During application testing and debugging, the Trace.Assert method's default behavior of displaying the detailed error message causing the debugger to go into Break mode is useful to developers. But if you would like the Assert statements to remain in your application and have the application run without interruption, then you can add an element to the <system .diagnostics> section of your application configuration file to disable the message box and send the output to a text file instead.

```
<assert assertuienabled="false" logfilename="C:\path\errorLog.txt"/>
```

After your Trace statements are in place, you can control their output by using TraceListeners and TraceSwitches. You will learn about these next.

Using *TraceListeners*

Now that you have seen how to add debug and trace messages to your code, let's look at how to direct their output by using `TraceListeners`. There is a .NET Framework class called *DefaultTraceListener* that is automatically added to the `Trace.Listeners` collection. This is the mechanism that is responsible for writing to the Visual Studio .NET Output window, by default.

If you are using debug and trace messages only for development purposes, it is fine to allow these statements to display in the Output window and nowhere else. When you are adding `Trace` statements to your code that will remain for ongoing performance monitoring and troubleshooting, you will want to direct the output to a persistent store, such as a text file or, in some cases, to the Windows event log. `TraceListeners` provide this capability.

After you have added `Trace` or `Debug Write` statements (or any of the variations) to your application code, you should add one or more `Trace.Listener` objects to direct the output messages to the appropriate location. This location can be a text file or a Windows event log entry. When you are adding listeners to your application, you will choose one of the derived classes of the `TraceListener` class, the *TextWriterTraceListener class*, or the *EventLogTraceListener class*.

The `TextWriterTraceListener` class can write output to any .NET Framework `Stream` object, such as a text file. The `EventLogTraceListener` class is designed to write to a Windows event log. To further customize your application's tracing capability, you can inherit from the `TraceListener` class and override its methods to create a custom output source for your trace messages.

Custom `TraceListeners` are outside the scope of the 70-310 exam and this book.

Here are some code examples showing how to create standard `TraceListeners`. First the `TextWriterTraceListener`:

```
Dim myFileWriter As New TextWriterTraceListener("c:\path\errorLog.txt")
Trace.Listeners.Add(myFileWriter)
```

The constructor method creates the `TextWriterTraceListener` and assigns a filename that it should write to. The second line of code adds the new listener to the `Listeners` collection. This is important because unless the listener is added to the collection, it will not receive the trace messages.

During application execution, the `TextWriterTraceListener` holds trace messages in its buffer. To cause this information to be written to the specified text file, you must call the *Flush method*, usually at the end of a procedure that includes trace messages. At the end of application execution, you can call the *Close method* to release the file. Here is an example:

```
myFileWriter.Flush()
myFileWriter.Close()
```

The `EventLogTraceListener` will write to a Windows event log. By default, it uses the application log. You can add a source name for event log entries when you create the listener. This is usually the application or component name (in the following example, you are using `TracingApp`). This will show up in the event log in the Source column. This code adds an `EventLogTraceListener` to your application:

```
Dim myLogger As EventLogTraceListener = New EventLogTraceListener("TracingApp")
Trace.Listeners.Add(myLogger)
```

Table 8.2 lists the properties and methods available for `TraceListeners`.

TABLE 8.2 Properties and Methods of the *TextWriterTraceListener* and the *EventLogTraceListener* Classes

Property	Description
IndentLevel	The indent level
IndentSize	The number of spaces in an indent
Name	The name for this TraceListener
EventLog	The EventLog object to write output to (EventLogTraceListener only)
Writer	The TextWriter object to write output to (TextWriterTraceListener only)

Method	Description
Close	Closes the output stream so it no longer receives tracing or debugging output
Fail	Sends error messages to the listener
Flush	When overridden in a derived class, flushes the output buffer
Write	Writes a message and category name to the listener
WriteLine	Writes a message and category name to the listener, followed by a line terminator

`TraceListeners` are important because they direct the output from your debug and trace messages to a persistent source, rather than just the Visual Studio .NET Output window. If you add more than one listener to the `Listeners` collection, messages will be sent to all listeners.

Using *TraceSwitches*

Although trace output is useful in monitoring your applications, when everything is running satisfactorily, you might prefer to turn off the trace messages to improve application performance. `TraceSwitches` enable you to manage the settings that determine when trace output is created via configuration files.

There are two types of trace switches: the *BooleanSwitch class* and the *TraceSwitch class*. The `BooleanSwitch` class has a simple on/off behavior. The `TraceSwitch` class can be set to one of five levels; output is produced only when a conditional test shows that the level is appropriate.

A setting of 0 (zero) means that the switch is set to Off (the available settings for the Level property are listed in Table 8.4). A setting of 1 means that only the most severe error messages should be output. The remaining three settings enable you to further categorize your messages as to their priority level. When you set the Level property to a setting of 2 or higher, the TraceListeners will output all messages of that level or lower. That is, a setting of 2 will cause both error and warning messages to be output, whereas a setting of 4 will cause all messages in your application to be output.

TraceSwitches have no unique methods (other than those inherited from the System.Object class, such as ToString, and supported by all .NET Framework classes), so Table 8.3 lists only properties. Table 8.4 lists the enumerated values that are used to set the TraceSwitch.Level property.

TABLE 8.3   Properties of the *BooleanSwitch* and *TraceSwitch* Classes

Property Inherited from the *Switch* Class	Description
Description	A description of the switch
DisplayName	A name used to identify the switch (in configuration files)

Property of the *BooleanSwitch* Class	Description
Enabled	Specifies whether the switch is enabled or disabled

Property of the *TraceSwitch* Class	Description
Level	Indicates the trace level that specifies the messages to output for tracing and debugging
TraceError	Indicates whether the Level property is set to Error, Warning, Info, or Verbose
TraceInfo	Indicates whether the Level property is set to Info or Verbose
TraceVerbose	Indicates whether the Level property is set to Verbose
TraceWarning	Indicates whether the Level property is set to Warning, Info, or Verbose

TABLE 8.4   Enumerated Values of the *TraceSwitch.Level* Property

Setting	Integer	Type of Message Output
Off	0	None (the switch is Off)
Error	1	Only error messages

TABLE 8.4   Enumerated Values of the *TraceSwitch.Level* Property *(continued)*

Setting	Integer	Type of Message Output
Warning	2	Warning messages and error messages
Info	3	Informational messages, warning messages, and error messages
Verbose	4	Verbose messages, informational messages, warning messages, and error messages

TraceSwitches are usually declared at the class level, like this:

```
Private boolSwitch As New BooleanSwitch( _
   "BSwitch", "TestCode")
```

```
Private lvlSwitch As New TraceSwitch( _
   "LSwitch", "TestCode")
```

It is possible to include the switch settings in your source code, as shown here:

```
boolSwitch.Enabled = False
lvlSwitch.Level = TraceLevel.Warning
```

However, using the *application configuration file* to manage the settings gives you more flexibility in adjusting your tracing behavior after the application has been deployed. The advantage of using the configuration file is that an administrator can change the settings whenever needed, without having to request a change to the source code and having to reinstall the application.

Notice that in the configuration file, you will refer to the switch by the name that was specified when you instantiated the switch. The name is the first argument that you supplied to the constructor method, in the preceding code snippet. Here is an example of using an XML configuration file to make the same settings as shown in the code snippet.

```
Private boolSwitch As New BooleanSwitch( _
   "BSwitch", "TestCode")
```

```
Private lvlSwitch As New TraceSwitch( _
   "LSwitch", "TestCode")
<configuration>
<system.diagnostics>
   <switches>
      <add name="BSwitch" value="0" />
      <add name="LSwitch" value="2" />
   </switches>
</system.diagnostics>
</configuration>
```

If you will be using TraceSwitches with your application, you will need to write your Trace statements differently from the simple examples that you have seen so far. Before each message is output, your code should test either the *BooleanSwitch.Enabled property* or the *TraceSwitch .Level property* to see whether it is appropriate to write the message based on the current settings in the configuration file. This can be done with the WriteIf and WriteLineIf methods of the Trace object, or just by wrapping your Trace statement in an If block.

Here is an example of using WriteLineIf to test whether the BooleanSwitch is enabled and the TraceSwitch is set to level 1:

```
Trace.WriteLineIf(boolSwitch.Enabled, "Trace message")
Trace.WriteLineIf(lvlSwitch.TraceWarning, _
    "An event of Error or Warning status has occurred")
```

Here is similar code using If blocks:

```
If boolSwitch.Enabled Then
    Trace.WriteLine("Trace message")
End If


If lvlSwitch.TraceWarning Then
    Trace.WriteLine( _
        "An event of Error or Warning status has occurred ")
End If
```

Using the WriteIf and WriteLineIf methods can incur performance overhead in your application. This is because both arguments of the method (both the property test and the message itself) must be evaluated when the statement is encountered. If the property test indicates that tracing is not required at this time, any work that was done to evaluate the second argument would have been unnecessary. If your second argument (the message) is complex, this might cause noticeable performance delays. To avoid this problem, use the explicit If blocks in your code.

In Exercise 8.2, you will write trace messages to log files and the Windows application event log. You will learn how to add TraceSwitches to control when output is produced and how to change these settings in an application configuration file.

EXERCISE 8.2

Instrumenting Your Application with Tracing

Creating and Using TraceListeners:

1. Start Visual Studio .NET and begin a new Windows application. Name the project **TracingDemo**.

2. Change the name of the default Form1.vb to **frmTracing.vb**.

3. Add five Command Buttons—btnTextTrace, btnEventLog, btnBoolSwitch, btnLevel, and btnAssert—and three TextBoxes—txtMessage (set the Multiline property to True), txtMessage2 (set the Multiline property to True), and txtAssertValue—to the form. Your form should look like the following one.

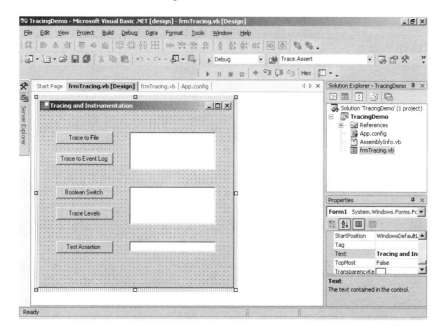

4. Double-click the Trace To File button to create a Click event procedure in the code module. You will add code to this procedure to create and use a TextWriterTraceListener (when setting the path and filename for the errorLog.txt file, use an appropriate directory on your computer):

```
Private Sub btnTextTrace_Click(ByVal sender As System.Object, _
    ByVal e As System.EventArgs) Handles btnTextTrace.Click

    Dim myLogFile As String = "C:\path\errorLog.txt"
    Dim myFileWriter As New TextWriterTraceListener(myLogFile)

    Trace.Listeners.Add(myFileWriter)

    Trace.WriteLine("Log error into a text file " & Now())

    txtMessage.Text = _
        "Message has been logged check the text file: " & _
        Environment.NewLine & myLogFile

    myFileWriter.Flush()
    myFileWriter.Close()
    Trace.Listeners.Remove(myFileWriter)

End Sub
```

5. Create a Click event procedure for btnEventLog. You will add code to this procedure to create and use an EventLogTraceListener:

```
Private Sub btnEventLog_Click(ByVal sender As System.Object, _
    ByVal e As System.EventArgs) Handles btnEventLog.Click

    Dim myLogger As EventLogTraceListener = New _
        EventLogTraceListener("TracingApp")

    Trace.Listeners.Add(myLogger)

    Trace.WriteLine("Log error to the event log " & Now())

    txtMessage.Text = _
        "Message has been logged check the Application Event Log"

    Trace.Listeners.Remove(myLogger)

End Sub
```

6. Save and test your work. Click the Trace To File button. You should see a confirmation message in the text box. Click the button a few more times. The application should look like the following.

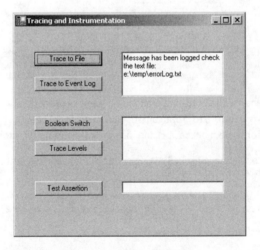

7. Use Windows Explorer to locate the directory that you specified for the errorLog.txt file. Open this file in Notepad and review the contents. You should see the messages that were produced by the Trace.WriteLine method:

```
Log error into a text file 3/11/2003 9:53:27 AM
Log error into a text file 3/11/2003 9:53:28 AM
Log error into a text file 3/11/2003 9:53:30 AM
Log error into a text file 3/11/2003 9:53:31 AM
```

8. Now click the Trace To Event Log button. You should see a confirmation message in the text box. Access the Windows Event Viewer by choosing Start ➤ Programs ➤ Administrative Tools ➤ Event Viewer (or the equivalent procedure for your operating system version). Select the Application Log. You should see an entry with TracingApp in the Source column. This was the name that you assigned to the EventLogTraceListener in the code in step 5.

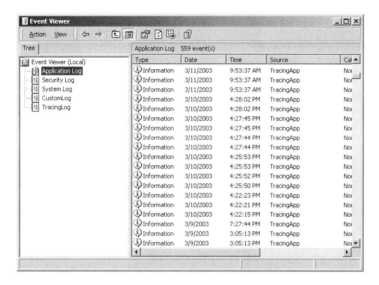

9. Double-click the entry to open the Event Properties dialog box and see the message produced by the Trace.WriteLine method in the Description field.

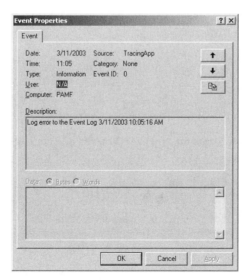

EXERCISE 8.2 *(continued)*

Creating and Using TraceSwitches:

10. Create two class-level variables to declare and instantiate a `BooleanSwitch` and a `TraceSwitch`. Notice that the first argument in each case is the name that you are assigning to the switch; this is how you refer to it in the configuration file. The second argument is a description.

11. Here is the code to do this:

```
Private boolSwitch As New BooleanSwitch("BSwitch", "TestCode")

Private lvlSwitch As New TraceSwitch("LSwitch", "TestCode")
```

12. Create a Click event procedure for `btnBoolSwitch`. You will add code to this procedure to create and use a `BooleanSwitch`:

```
Private Sub btnBoolSwitch_Click(ByVal sender As System.Object, _
    ByVal e As System.EventArgs) Handles btnBoolSwitch.Click

    Dim myLogFile As String = "C:\path\errorLog.txt"
    Dim myFileWriter As New TextWriterTraceListener(myLogFile)

    Trace.Listeners.Add(myFileWriter)

    If boolSwitch.Enabled = True Then
        Trace.WriteLine("Log error into a text file " & _
            "when tracing is enabled " & Now())

        txtMessage2.Text = "Tracing is enabled. " & _
            "Message has been logged, " & _
            "check the text file: " & _
            Environment.NewLine & myLogFile
    Else
        txtMessage2.Text = "Tracing is NOT enabled. " & _
            "No message logged."

    End If

    myFileWriter.Flush()
    myFileWriter.Close()
    Trace.Listeners.Remove(myFileWriter)
End Sub
```

13. Create a Click event procedure for `btnLevel`. You will add code to this procedure to create and use a `TraceSwitch`:

```
Private Sub btnLevel_Click(ByVal sender As System.Object, _
    ByVal e As System.EventArgs) Handles btnLevel.Click

    Dim myLogFile As String = "C:\path\errorLog.txt"
    Dim myFileWriter As New TextWriterTraceListener(myLogFile)
```

EXERCISE 8.2 *(continued)*

```
Trace.Listeners.Add(myFileWriter)

If lvlSwitch.Level = TraceLevel.Warning Then

    Trace.WriteLine("Log error into a text file when Level " & _
        "is greater than 2 (Warning) " & Now())

    txtMessage2.Text = "Level is 2 or greater. " & _
        "Message has been logged, check the text file: " & _
        Environment.NewLine & myLogFile
Else
    txtMessage2.Text = "Level is less than 2 (Warning). " & _
        "No message logged."
End If

myFileWriter.Flush()
myFileWriter.Close()
Trace.Listeners.Remove(myFileWriter)
End Sub
```

14. Add an application configuration file to your project. Right-click the project name in the Solution Explorer and choose Add ➢ Add a New Item from the menu. Select Application Configuration File from the Add New Item dialog box.

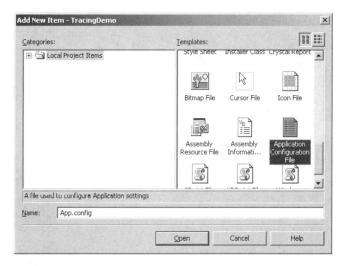

15. Review this file in Visual Studio .NET and you will see only the XML declaration and `<configuration>` tags:

```
<?xml version="1.0" encoding="utf-8" ?>
<configuration>
</configuration>
```

EXERCISE 8.2 *(continued)*

16. Add a `<system.diagnostics>` section and `<switches>` section to this file:

```
<?xml version="1.0" encoding="utf-8" ?>
<configuration>
<system.diagnostics>
    <switches>
        <add name="BSwitch" value="0" />
        <add name="LSwitch" value="1" />
    </switches>
</system.diagnostics>
</configuration>
```

17. Remember that the XML element and attribute names in the configuration file are case sensitive and must be typed exactly as shown. Otherwise, you will get an error when you try to run the project. Notice that you are adding two switches, using the names that were assigned in your code when you instantiated the objects: `BSwitch` and `LSwitch`. You are setting the value of `BSwitch` to zero (0), which means that the switch is not enabled for your application. You are setting the value of the second switch to 1, which indicates a level of `Error`.

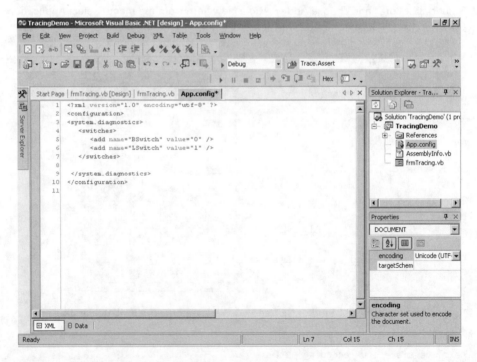

18. Save and test your work. When you build the project, a file called `TracingDemo.exe.config` will be created in the `\bin` subdirectory of your project directory.

19. Run the application and click the Boolean Switch button. Because you have set BSwitch as not enabled, the Trace.WriteLine method will be skipped. You will see a message in the text box that tracing is not enabled.

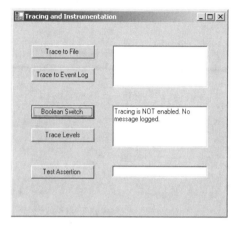

20. Click the Trace Levels button—you have set the level for this switch to 1 (Error) in the configuration, and your code tests for a level of 2 (Warning). So the Trace.WriteLine method is skipped. The message in the text box confirms this.

21. Stop the application. In the application configuration file, change the value of BSwitch to 1 and the value of LSwitch to 2 (or higher). Run the application again and click the buttons. You should see messages in the text box confirming that the error was logged.

22. Use Windows Explorer to open the errorLog.txt file in Notepad and review the contents. You should see a message similar to this one added to the file.

```
Log error into a text file when Level is greater than 2 (Warning) 3/11/2003
   11:00:58 AM
```

Testing Assertions:

23. Create a Click event procedure for btnAssert. You will add code to this procedure to create and test a Trace.Assert statement:

```
Private Sub btnAssert_Click(ByVal sender As System.Object, _
   ByVal e As System.EventArgs) Handles btnAssert.Click

   Dim crucialValue As Integer = CType(txtAssertValue.Text, Integer)

   Trace.Assert(crucialValue <= 1000, _
      "Crucial value has exceeded 1000")

End Sub
```

24. Save and test your work. Run the application. Type a number greater than 1000 into the txtAssertValue text box and click the Test Assertion button. Because your Trace.Assert statement tests for a value that is less than or equal to 1000, the assertion will fail. You will see a message box with the assert error message. Close the application.

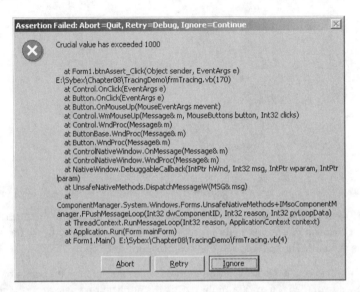

25. In the application configuration file, add a new element to control how the Trace.Assert error messages are displayed. Your application configuration file should look like this (the line shown in bold is the line you need to add here):

```xml
<?xml version="1.0" encoding="utf-8" ?>
<configuration>
<system.diagnostics>
    <switches>
        <add name="BSwitch" value="1" />
        <add name="LSwitch" value="2" />
    </switches>
<assert assertuienabled="false" logfilename="C:\path\errorLog.txt"/>
</system.diagnostics>
</configuration>
```

26. Save and test your work. Run the application again, type in a value greater than 1000, and click the Test Assertion button. This time your application will not be interrupted. Use Windows Explorer to open errorLog.txt in Notepad and examine the contents. You should see output added to the file that provides the same information that was displayed in the message box in step 22.

```
errorLog.txt - Notepad                                                    _ 8 x
File  Edit  Format  Help
Log error into a text file 3/11/2003 9:53:27 AM
Log error into a text file 3/11/2003 9:53:28 AM
Log error into a text file 3/11/2003 9:53:30 AM
Log error into a text file 3/11/2003 9:53:31 AM
Log error into a text file when tracing is enabled 3/11/2003 11:00:56 AM
Log error into a text file when Level is greater than 2 (Warning) 3/11/2003 11:00:58
AM
---- DEBUG ASSERTION FAILED ----
---- Assert Short Message ----
Crucial value has exceeded 1000
---- Assert Long Message ----

    at Form1.btnAssert_Click(Object sender, EventArgs e)
E:\Sybex\Chapter08\TracingDemo\frmTracing.vb(170)
    at Control.OnClick(EventArgs e)
    at Button.OnClick(EventArgs e)
    at Button.OnMouseUp(MouseEventArgs mevent)
    at Control.WmMouseUp(Message& m, MouseButtons button, Int32 clicks)
    at Control.WndProc(Message& m)
    at ButtonBase.WndProc(Message& m)
    at Button.WndProc(Message& m)
    at ControlNativeWindow.OnMessage(Message& m)
    at ControlNativeWindow.WndProc(Message& m)
    at NativeWindow.DebuggableCallback(IntPtr hwnd, Int32 msg, IntPtr wparam, IntPtr
lparam)
    at UnsafeNativeMethods.DispatchMessageW(MSG& msg)
    at
ComponentManager.System.Windows.Forms.UnsafeNativeMethods+IMsoComponentManager.FPushMe
ssageLoop(Int32 dwComponentID, Int32 reason, Int32 pvLoopData)
    at ThreadContext.RunMessageLoop(Int32 reason, ApplicationContext context)
    at Application.Run(Form mainForm)
    at Form1.Main()  E:\Sybex\Chapter08\TracingDemo\frmTracing.vb(4)
```

Using SOAP Extensions for Debugging

Earlier in this chapter, we briefly discussed some special considerations for debugging XML Web services. The debugging tools supplied by Visual Studio .NET are useful for making sure that the code inside your Web methods is working correctly. Sometimes it is also necessary to view the SOAP messages that are created and sent back and forth between the Web service and the client application.

In the standard course of operations, SOAP messages are not directly visible, because the components in the .NET Framework that make it easy to create Web services generate the messages automatically. In this section, you are going to learn how to use *SOAP extensions*. SOAP extensions are classes that you create with your own application-specific processing. Your custom code will run each time a SOAP message is received or sent by a Web service.

In Exercise 8.3, you will see an example of how to capture the complete SOAP message and store it in a text file. You could use SOAP extensions for other types of logging and debugging purposes as well.

You can create custom SOAP extensions by creating your own `Extension` classes that inherit from `System.Web.Services.Protocols.SoapExtension`. You must also create a class that inherits from `SoapExtensionAttribute`. The `SoapExtension` class contains the code that will run when a SOAP message is processed. The *SoapExtensionAttribute class* provides a means to mark a Web method, so that your SOAP extension will be called when the method is invoked. You will then compile these classes into a DLL that will be referenced by your XML Web service.

When you create a class that inherits from `SoapExtension`, you must override the methods of the base class with your own custom methods. When you create a class that inherits from `SoapExtensionAttribute`, you must override the property procedures defined by the base class.

Here are the methods of the `SoapExtension` class that will be implemented:

GetInitializer   This method runs the first time an XML Web service or a particular method is called. Values that are initialized in this procedure are cached and can be used for all future method calls on the service.

Initialize   This method is called for every method call to the Web service and is automatically passed the data that was stored in cache during the `GetInitializer` method.

ChainStream   This method enables you to store the incoming SOAP message (in a `Stream` object) and create a new `Stream` object to hold output from the extension. During subsequent processing of the extension code, you should read data from the incoming stream and write data to the new output stream.

ProcessMessage   This method performs the desired processing on the SOAP message. Typically, you will test the `Stage` property of the incoming message and use conditional logic in the procedure to determine the appropriate action to take. The `Stage` property will be one of the following: `BeforeSerialize`, `AfterSerialize`, `BeforeDeserialize`, `AfterDeserialize`.

The SOAP message is made available to your extension class in the `ChainStream` method (see Listing 8.3). Your code in the `ChainStream` method merely copies the incoming message into a `Stream` object (`soapStream`) and creates a new empty `Stream` object (`myStream`) to hold output. These `Stream` objects are declared as class-level variables so they will be available to all the methods of the `SoapExtension` class.

The `ProcessMessage` method is the most interesting because that is where you specify the custom code to be run and also at which stage it should be run. The base class version of `ProcessMessage` contains a `Select Case` statement that includes options for each of the stages that a SOAP message goes through as it is processed.

In Exercise 8.3, you will capture incoming messages in the `BeforeDeserialize` stage and capture the outgoing results in the `AfterSerialize` stage. These are the two stages where you can examine the XML markup of the SOAP message that is being transmitted. After you have determined the current message stage, you can call your own custom procedures (`CopyStream` and `WriteStream`) to create the log file entries. Listing 8.3 shows some of the code that you will use in Exercise 8.3 (for the full code listing, including the custom procedures, see the exercise).

Listing 8.3: The ChainStream and ProcessMessage Methods

```
Private soapStream As Stream
Private myStream As Stream
```

```vb
Public Overrides Function ChainStream(ByVal  _
    stream As Stream) As Stream

    soapStream = stream
    myStream = New MemoryStream()
    Return myStream
End Function

Public Overrides Sub ProcessMessage(ByVal _
    message As SoapMessage)

    Select Case message.Stage
        Case SoapMessageStage.BeforeDeserialize
            CopyStream(soapStream, myStream)
            WriteStream(Environment.NewLine & _
                "***** Sent to Web service at " & _
                Now.ToString & "*****" & Environment.NewLine)

        Case SoapMessageStage.AfterDeserialize

        Case SoapMessageStage.BeforeSerialize

        Case SoapMessageStage.AfterSerialize
            WriteStream(Environment.NewLine & _
                "***** Returned from Web service at " & _
                Now.ToString & "*****" & Environment.NewLine)
            CopyStream(myStream, soapStream)
    End Select
End Sub
```

To create the SoapExtensionAttribute class, you should override the ExtensionType and Priority properties. The code in Listing 8.4 shows these property procedures.

Listing 8.4: Properties of the SoapExtensionAttribute

```vb
Public Overrides ReadOnly Property ExtensionType() As Type
    Get
        Return GetType(DebugExtension)
    End Get
End Property

Public Overrides Property Priority() As Integer
    Get
        Return m_Priority
    End Get
```

```
    Set(ByVal Value As Integer)
        m_Priority = Value
    End Set
End Property
```

The `ExtensionType` property returns the type of your derived `SoapExtension` class (called `DebugExtension` here). The `Priority` property determines the order in which multiple SOAP extensions would be processed (0 is the highest priority level). (Exercise 8.3 will also include another custom property to hold the filename for the log file.)

After you have created the classes derived from `SoapExtension` and `SoapExtension-Attribute`, you can compile them into a DLL. That DLL is then placed in the `\bin` directory of the XML Web service application that will use the SOAP extension.

When you create your XML Web service project, you will set a reference to the SOAP extension DLL. There are two ways to specify that the SOAP extension is to be invoked when the methods of the Web service are invoked. You can use an attribute to mark each method, as shown here:

```
<WebMethod(Description:="Get the square of a number"), _
    DebugExtension.DebugExtension( _
        LogFile:="C:\path\DebugInfo.txt", Priority:= "1")> _
    Public Function GetSquare(ByVal _
        inputVal As Double) As Double
        Return inputVal * inputVal
End Function
```

Or you can add the information to the `web.config` file:

```
<configuration>
 <system.web>
   <webServices>
     <soapExtensionTypes>
       <add type="DebugExtension.DebugExtension"
            Priority="1"
            LogFile="C:\path\DebugInfo.txt" />
     <soapExtensionTypes>
     <webServices>
 <system.web>
<configuration>
```

After you have marked your methods with the SOAP extension attribute, your custom code will be invoked each time a method of your Web service is called by a client, and again when the Web service sends a result back to the client.

Exercise 8.3 contains a comprehensive example of creating a SOAP extension that captures the XML markup of incoming and outgoing SOAP messages; you can extend the custom code in the class to log many different types of information about your Web service's performance and usage. This exercise consists of three Visual Studio .NET projects:

- A Class Library project that includes the `SoapExtension` and `SoapExtensionAttribute` classes

- An ASP.NET Web service project
- A Windows application project that will be used to test the Web service

EXERCISE 8.3

Using SOAP Extensions to Log SOAP Messages to a File

Creating the SOAP Extension DLL:

1. Start Visual Studio .NET and create a new Class Library project called **DebugExtension**.

2. Remove the declaration for the default `Class1`.

3. Set a reference to the `System.Web.Services.dll` and add the following `Imports` statements to the top of the module:

```
Imports System.IO
Imports System.Web.Services.Protocols
```

4. You will add two classes to this project, one that inherits from `SoapExtension` and one that inherits from `SoapExtensionAttribute`. In each of your derived classes, you will provide customized implementations of the base class methods. You will create the `DebugExtension` class, which is derived from `SoapExtension` in step 5 of this exercise. The code for the `DebugExtensionAttribute` class should look like this:

```
<AttributeUsage(AttributeTargets.Method)> _
Public Class DebugExtensionAttribute

    Inherits SoapExtensionAttribute

    Private m_LogFile As String
    Private m_Priority As Int32

    Public Overrides ReadOnly Property ExtensionType() As Type
        Get
            Return GetType(DebugExtension)
        End Get
    End Property
    Public Overrides Property Priority() As Integer
        Get
            Return m_Priority
        End Get
        Set(ByVal Value As Integer)
            m_Priority = Value
        End Set
    End Property

    Public Property LogFile() As String
        Get
            Return m_LogFile
        End Get
        Set(ByVal Value As String)
            m_LogFile = Value
        End Set
    End Property
End Class
```

EXERCISE 8.3 *(continued)*

5. Now add the DebugExtension class:

```
Public Class DebugExtension
    Inherits SoapExtension

    Private soapStream As Stream
    Private myStream As Stream
    Private LogFile As String

    'this initializer is used with a configuration file
    Public Overloads Overrides Function GetInitializer( _
        ByVal serviceType As System.Type) As Object

        Return serviceType
    End Function

    'this initializer is used with an attribute
    Public Overloads Overrides Function GetInitializer( _
        ByVal methodInfo As LogicalMethodInfo, _
        ByVal attribute As SoapExtensionAttribute) As Object

        Return attribute
    End Function

    Public Overrides Sub Initialize(ByVal initializer As Object)
        LogFile = CType(initializer, DebugExtensionAttribute).LogFile
    End Sub


    Public Overrides Function ChainStream(ByVal stream _
        As Stream) As Stream

        soapStream = stream
        myStream = New MemoryStream()

        Return myStream
    End Function

    Private Sub CopyStream(ByVal inputStream As Stream, ByVal outputStream As
        Stream)
        Dim txtReader As TextReader = New StreamReader(inputStream)
        Dim txtWriter As TextWriter = New StreamWriter(outputStream)
        txtWriter.WriteLine(txtReader.ReadToEnd())
        txtWriter.Flush()
    End Sub

    Private Sub WriteStream(ByVal title As String)
        myStream.Position = 0
        Dim myReader As New StreamReader(myStream)
        Dim myWriter As New StreamWriter(LogFile, True)
        myWriter.WriteLine(title)
        myWriter.WriteLine(myReader.ReadToEnd)
        myWriter.Close()
        myStream.Position = 0
    End Sub
```

```
      Public Overrides Sub ProcessMessage(ByVal message As SoapMessage)
         Select Case message.Stage
            Case SoapMessageStage.BeforeDeserialize
               CopyStream(soapStream, myStream)
               WriteStream(Environment.NewLine & _
                  "***** Sent to Web service at " & _
                  Now.ToString & "*****" & Environment.NewLine)

            Case SoapMessageStage.AfterDeserialize
            Case SoapMessageStage.BeforeSerialize

            Case SoapMessageStage.AfterSerialize
               WriteStream(Environment.NewLine & _
                  "***** Returned from Web service at " & _
                  Now.ToString & "*****" & Environment.NewLine)
               CopyStream(myStream, soapStream)
         End Select
      End Sub
   End Class
```

6.   Save your work. Build the `DebugExtension` class library.

Creating the XML Web Service:

7.   Start Visual Studio .NET and create a new ASP.NET Web service application at **http://localhost/DebugSOAP**.

8.   Change the name of `Service1.asmx` to **DebugService.asmx**.

9.   View the code for `DebugService.asmx` and change the class name from `Service1` to **DebugService**. Add an `Imports` statement:

```
Imports System.Math
```

10.   Copy the `DebugExtension.dll` file to the `\bin` directory of the `DebugExtension` project.

11.   Right-click the project name in the Solution Explorer and choose Add Reference from the menu. Click the Browse button and locate `DebugExtension.dll` in the project `\bin` directory. Click the Select button and then click OK.

12.   Create two Web methods for your class, similar to the ones that you created in Exercise 4.1 in Chapter 4, "Creating and Managing XML Web Services." In addition to the basic function of these methods, you will add an additional attribute specifying the SOAP extension that will be invoked each time the Web method itself is invoked and the filename for the log file that should be used (use an appropriate path and filename for your computer).

13.   Your code should look like this:

```
<WebMethod(Description:="Get the square of a number"), _
   DebugExtension.DebugExtension( _
      LogFile:="C:\path\DebugInfo.txt")> _
```

EXERCISE 8.3 *(continued)*

```
Public Function GetSquare(ByVal inputVal As Double) As Double

    Return inputVal * inputVal

End Function

<WebMethod(Description:="Get the square root of a number"), _
    DebugExtension.DebugExtension( _
        LogFile:="C:\path\DebugInfo.txt")> _
    Public Function GetSquareRoot(ByVal inputVal As Double) As Double

    Return Sqrt(inputVal)

End Function
```

14. Save your work and build the DebugSOAP project.

Creating the Client Application:

15. Create a new Windows application project named **DebugExtensionClient**.

16. Add two TextBox controls—txtInputValue and txtResult—and two Command Button controls—btnGetSquare and btnGetSquareRoot. Your form design should look like the following.

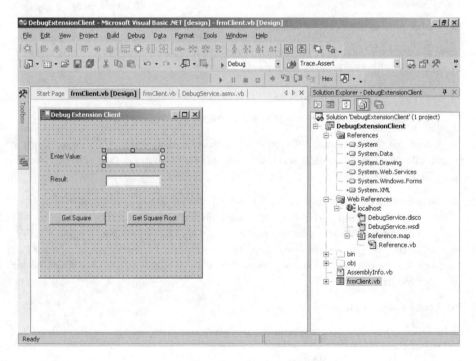

17. Right-click the project name in the Solution Explorer and choose Add Web Reference from the menu. In the Add Web Reference dialog box, type the URL for the Web service in the Address bar at the top of the dialog box:

```
http://localhost/DebugSOAP/DebugService.asmx
```

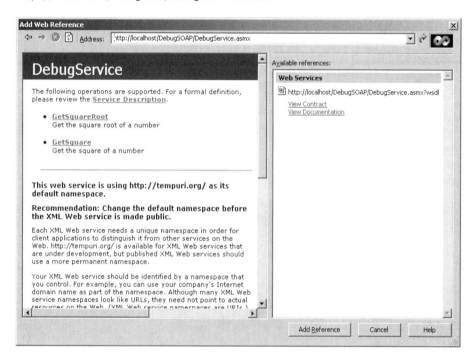

18. Create button click procedures for the two command buttons. In these procedures, you will call the GetSquare and GetSquareRoot methods of the Web service.

19. Your code should look like this for btnGetSquare:

```
Private Sub btnGetSquare_Click(ByVal sender As System.Object, _
    ByVal e As System.EventArgs) Handles btnGetSquare.Click

    Dim inputValue As Double = CType(txtInputValue.Text, Double)

    Dim webResult As Double

    Dim objSquare As localhost.DebugService = New localhost.DebugService()
    webResult = objSquare.GetSquare(inputValue)

    txtResult.Text = CType(webResult, String)

End Sub
```

20. Your code should look like this for btnGetSquareRoot:

```
Private Sub btnGetSquareRoot_Click(ByVal sender As System.Object, _
    ByVal e As System.EventArgs) Handles btnGetSquareRoot.Click

    Dim inputValue As Double = CType(txtInputValue.Text, Double)
    Dim webResult As Double

    Dim objSquare As localhost.DebugService = _
        New localhost.DebugService()

    webResult = objSquare.GetSquareRoot(inputValue)

    txtResult.Text = CType(webResult, String)

End Sub
```

21. Save and test your work. Run the application and type a value into txtInputValue. Click the Get Square button, then the Get Square Root button. You will see the results displayed in txtResult.

22. Use Windows Explorer to locate the log file. The contents of the file should look something like this:

```
***** Sent to Web service at 3/23/2003 8:48:38 AM*****

<?xml version="1.0" encoding="utf-8"?>
<soap:Envelope xmlns:soap="http://schemas.xmlsoap.org/soap/envelope/"
    xmlns:xsi="http://www.w3.org/2001/XMLSchema-instance"
    xmlns:xsd="http://www.w3.org/2001/XMLSchema">
<soap:Body>
    <GetSquare xmlns="http://tempuri.org/">
        <inputVal>4</inputVal>
    </GetSquare>
</soap:Body>
</soap:Envelope>

***** Returned from Web service at 3/23/2003 8:48:38 AM*****
```

EXERCISE 8.3 *(continued)*

```
<?xml version="1.0" encoding="utf-8"?>
<soap:Envelope xmlns:soap="http://schemas.xmlsoap.org/soap/envelope/"
    xmlns:xsi="http://www.w3.org/2001/XMLSchema-instance"
    xmlns:xsd="http://www.w3.org/2001/XMLSchema">
<soap:Body>
    <GetSquareResponse xmlns="http://tempuri.org/">
        <GetSquareResult>16</GetSquareResult>
    </GetSquareResponse>
</soap:Body>
</soap:Envelope>
```

Summary

In this chapter, you learned about testing and debugging Visual Studio .NET applications. We covered the following topics:

- An introduction to testing strategy, including unit testing, integration testing, and regression testing

- Considerations for testing applications in a multicultural environment

- How to configure the Visual Studio .NET debugging tools, including Debug versus Release builds

- How to configure Debug versus Release builds for ASP.NET applications in the web.config file

- How to set project options that control the Visual Studio .NET debugging tools

- How to set breakpoints in your code and how to set breakpoint conditions

- How to use debugging tools, such as step-by-step execution of code while in Break mode

- How to use the various windows that display information about your application in Break mode

- How to use the Command window to assess the value of variables and execute code while in Break mode

- Considerations for debugging special types of applications, such as Windows services, XML Web services, remote components, and others

- How to instrument your applications for ongoing troubleshooting and performance monitoring by using Trace statements

- How to use assertions to test conditions while your application is executing

- How to control debug and trace output with TraceListeners

- How to turn tracing on and off by using TraceSwitches and the application configuration file

- How to use SOAP extensions to add custom processing each time a SOAP message is sent or received by an XML Web service

Exam Essentials

Know how to plan application testing.   Understand the differences between the goals of unit testing, integration testing, and regression testing, and at which phases in the application development cycle they are carried out.

Be familiar with multicultural testing issues.   Understand that data such as dates, numbers, and currency might be interpreted differently if the application is running under different locale settings. Understand that text strings embedded in the user interface might make it difficult to localize applications and that errors might occur due to different sized text strings during localization.

Know the differences between Debug and Release builds.   Know how to configure Visual Studio .NET to produce Debug and Release builds selectively. Know where debugging symbol files are located. Know how to configure Debug versus Release builds in ASP.NET applications by using settings in the `web.config` file.

Know what options in the Project Properties affect debugging.   Know how to select options for application startup during debugging for different types of applications.

Know how to use breakpoints to enter Break mode during debugging.   Know how to set breakpoints and use the new breakpoint conditions to locate problems in your applications.

Be familiar with the Visual Studio .NET debugging tools.   Know how to perform step-by-step debugging through your code. Understand the many windows that are available to give you status information while in Break mode. Know how to use the Command window to run code, query variable values, and give Visual Studio .NET commands.

Be familiar with special considerations for debugging different types of applications.   Know that Windows service applications cannot be run from within Visual Studio .NET. They must be started by the Service Control Manager, and then the Visual Studio .NET debugger can attach to the running process. DLLs can be debugged by specifying an external startup application; XML Web services can be debugged by calling them from a client application. Debugging on a remote computer requires installation of remote components and special permissions on the remote machine. Just-in-Time debugging enables you to attach one of the Visual Studio .NET debuggers to a script-based application when an error occurs during application execution.

Know how to add Debug and Trace statements to your code to instrument the application for monitoring.   Know how to set compiler directives to make sure that `Debug` and `Trace` statements are included in the build. Understand the difference between the `Write`, `WriteLine`, `WriteIf`, and `WriteLineIf` methods. Know how to view output from the `DefaultTraceListener` in the Visual Studio .NET Output window.

Know how to add TraceListeners to your application to direct the output to persistent storage.   Understand that the `TextWriterTraceListener` can write to a text file and that the `EventLogTraceListener` can send output to the event log. If more than one `TraceListener` is present in your application, output will be directed to all `TraceListeners`.

Know how to produce trace output selectively by using TraceSwitches.   `BooleanSwitches` have an on/off behavior (using the `Enabled` property), so that trace output can be turned on only when a problem appears and you need to troubleshoot. `TraceSwitches` have a `Level` property and will produce output only when the `Level` property is set to the specified level. Switch settings can be set in the source code, but it is often more useful to maintain the settings in the application configuration file. This way, the settings can be changed as often as required without having to change source code. Know how to use conditional statements in your code to test switch settings.

Know how to use SOAP extensions to add custom processing for XML Web services.   Create a class that inherits from `SoapExtension` and overrides the methods of the base class. In the `ProcessMessage` method, you select the appropriate stage for your custom code to run. Use `BeforeDeserialize` or `AfterDeserialize` for processing incoming SOAP requests. Use `BeforeSerialize` or `AfterSerialize` for processing outgoing SOAP responses. Your SOAP extension assembly should also contain a class that inherits from `SoapExtensionAttribute`. In this class, you will override properties defined by the base class and add new properties for your custom extension. Use your `SoapExtensionAttribute` to mark all Web methods that should run your extension code.

Key Terms

Before you take the exam, be certain you are familiar with the following terms:

application configuration file	regression testing
`Assert` method	Release configuration
`BooleanSwitch` class	Runtime Debugger (`Cordbg.exe`)
`BooleanSwitch.Enabled` property	SOAP extensions
breakpoints	`SoapExtensionAttribute` class
`Close` method	`System.Diagnostics` namespace
CLR Debugger (`DbgCLR.exe`)	`TextWriterTraceListener` class
`Debug` class	`Trace` class
`DEBUG` compiler directive	`TRACE` compiler directive
Debug configuration	`TraceSwitch` class
`DefaultTraceListener`	`TraceSwitch.Level` property
`EventLogTraceListener` class	unit testing
`Flush` method	`Write` method
instrumentation	`WriteIf` method
integration testing	`WriteLine` method
multicultural test data	`WriteLineIf` method

Review Questions

1. As a developer on a large team, you are required to perform unit testing on all of your code before other developers can work with it. What is the goal of unit testing?

   A. To make sure that all methods of the class return accurate results with a range of valid input values and that they handle errors correctly when given invalid input data

   B. To create performance benchmarks for each of your functions, to make sure they meet performance targets set forth in the functional specification

   C. To make sure that any changes or fixes that you make in one component do not cause problems in other parts of the application

   D. To test the interfaces between each set of components that will exchange data, to make sure that correct values are being passed and return values are interpreted correctly

2. After you check in a component that you have completed, your testers perform integration testing with related components. What is the goal of integration testing?

   A. To make sure that all methods of the class return accurate results with a range of valid input values and that they handle errors correctly when given invalid input data

   B. To create performance benchmarks for each of your functions, to make sure they meet performance targets set forth in the functional specification

   C. To make sure that any changes or fixes that you make in one component do not cause problems in other parts of the application

   D. To test the interfaces between each set of components that will exchange data, to make sure that correct values are being passed and return values are interpreted correctly

3. You are a tester on a large team that is in the later phases of developing a complex application. The team is currently occupied in fixing bugs that have been discovered by beta testers. You are performing regression testing on the application as each bug fix is completed. What is the goal of regression testing?

   A. To make sure that all methods of the class return accurate results with a range of valid input values and that they handle errors correctly when given invalid input data

   B. To create performance benchmarks for each of your functions, to make sure they meet performance targets set forth in the functional specification

   C. To make sure that any changes or fixes that you make in one component do not cause problems in other parts of the application

   D. To test the interfaces between each set of components that will exchange data, to make sure that correct values are being passed and return values are interpreted correctly

4. When testing your application for localization considerations, which one of these is *not* something that you need to be concerned about?

   A. Making sure that text strings are not embedded in the source code

   B. Stress testing the application for maximum user load

   C. Making sure that dates are interpreted correctly

   D. Making sure that the user interface can handle text strings of varying lengths

5. You need to debug a component that is running on your web server. You have installed the Visual Studio .NET remote components on the server, but you are still getting error messages and are unable to debug the remote component. What is the most likely cause?

   A. You must have a copy of Visual Studio .NET on the remote machine in order to do debugging.

   B. You must have a copy of the type library for the component on your local machine.

   C. You are not a member of the Debugger Users group on the remote server.

   D. You are not a member of the Everyone group on the remote server.

6. You are debugging your XML Web service code by using a test client application. When you step through your code in Break mode, you would like to see what code in the Web service proxy class is being executed. How can you cause Visual Studio .NET to step into the proxy class?

   A. Set the test application as the startup project.

   B. Set the XML Web service as the startup project.

   C. Add a `<DebuggerStepInto()>` attribute to the proxy class.

   D. Remove the `<DebuggerStepThrough()>` attribute from the proxy class.

7. You have placed `Trace.Write` statements in your application to write output to a text file, but you notice that the text file is difficult to read because all the messages run together. How can you quickly fix this problem?

   A. Use `Trace.Warn` to highlight important messages.

   B. Use `Trace.WriteLine` to separate messages.

   C. Use `Trace.WriteLineIf` to separate messages.

   D. Use `Trace.AutoFlush = True` to separate messages.

8. When you are developing applications, you frequently use `Trace.Assert` statements in your code to alert you when there are unexpected conditions during application execution. These statements cause a problem during automated testing—they cause the application to go into Break mode and display a message box. How can you get the information provided by these `Trace.Assert` messages and still allow your applications to run uninterrupted?

   A. Uncheck the Define TRACE Constant check box in the project Property Pages dialog box.

   B. Add the `#Const TRACE = True` declaration to your application.

   C. Add an `<assert>` tag with appropriate value settings to the application configuration file.

   D. Add a `<trace>` tag with appropriate value settings to the application configuration file.

9. During development of your application, you are content to allow debug and trace output to be written to the `DefaultTraceListener`. Where should you look for this output in the Visual Studio .NET menus?

    A. Debug ➢ Windows ➢ Immediate

    B. Debug ➢ Windows ➢ Watch

    C. View ➢ Other Windows ➢ Output

    D. View ➢ Other Windows ➢ Command Window

10. You have added a `TextWriterTraceListener` to your application and have `Trace.Write` statements in most procedures to track application execution. You run your application to test various features, but when you look at the error log text file, it is blank. What is the most likely cause of this problem?

    A. You did not call the `WriteLine` method of the `TextWriterTraceListener`.

    B. You did not call the `Flush` method of the `TextWriterTraceListener`.

    C. You did not call the `Close` method of the file.

    D. You did not call the `Dispose` method of the file.

11. What happens when you set the `Level` property of a `TraceSwitch` to `TraceError`?

    A. Output will be written only if there is a runtime error in the application.

    B. Output will be written only if the `Trace.Write` statement is in an error handler.

    C. All output messages will be written as message boxes that force the application to end.

    D. Only the most severe tracing messages will be output.

12. You would like to add instrumentation to your application for performance monitoring, and to log significant errors that might occur while your application is in use. Which would best describe a good strategy for this?

    A. Use `Trace.Write` statements in your code to log messages during application execution, use a `TraceListener` to direct output to a log, and use a `TraceSwitch` to control when output is produced.

    B. Use `Trace.Assert` statements in your code to log messages during application execution, use a `TraceSwitch` to direct output to a log, and use a `TraceListener` to control when output is produced.

    C. Use `Trace.Write` statements in your code to keep track of the performance information and use `Debug.Write` statements to log errors.

    D. Use `Debug.Write` statements in your code to keep track of the performance information and use `Trace.Write` statements to log errors.

13. You have created a component (DLL) that will be used by ASP.NET developers. Before releasing this component for others to use, you need to debug it to resolve some intermittent errors. How should you set up the Visual Studio .NET IDE to debug a DLL?

   A. You cannot debug the DLL; the ASP.NET developers will have to do that when they debug their ASP.NET pages.

   B. Set a breakpoint and start the application normally; you will go into Break mode at the appropriate line of code.

   C. Use the project Property Pages dialog box to specify ASP.NET debugging.

   D. Use the project Property Pages dialog box to designate an external program that references and will call functions in the DLL.

14. In order to capture the XML markup of a SOAP message, you need to have SOAP extension code run at the appropriate stage of processing. At which stages should you run your code?

   A. Capture incoming SOAP requests in the `AfterDeserialize` stage, and outgoing SOAP responses in the `BeforeSerialize` stage.

   B. Capture incoming SOAP requests in the `BeforeDeserialize` stage, and outgoing SOAP responses in the `AfterSerialize` stage.

   C. Capture incoming SOAP requests in the `AfterSerialize` stage, and outgoing SOAP responses in the `BeforeDeserialize` stage.

   D. Capture incoming SOAP requests in the `BeforeSerialize` stage, and outgoing SOAP responses in the `AfterDeserialize` stage.

15. The `SoapExtensionAttribute.Priority` property is used for what purpose?

   A. To determine at which stage of SOAP message processing the extension code is run.

   B. To determine whether a SOAP message should be written to a log file.

   C. When you have specified multiple SOAP extensions for a single Web method, it determines the order in which the extensions are run.

   D. When you have specified multiple SOAP extensions for a single Web method, it determines which one of the extensions is run.

Answers to Review Questions

1. A. The goal of unit testing is to make sure that each component performs correctly before it is put into use by other developers. This is typically done by testing the functions with a range of valid and invalid input values. Unit testing finds and fixes defects at the earliest possible point in the development cycle.

2. D. The goal of integration testing is to test the interfaces between each set of components to make sure values are being passed correctly. By testing the interaction between each pair of components, it is easier to determine where a problem is occurring.

3. C. The goal of regression testing is to make sure that any changes or bug fixes made to one component in the application do not cause errors to occur in other parts of the application. Regression testing involves retesting the entire application after changes are made to make sure that no new errors have been introduced. Creating performance benchmarks and testing performance is a separate form of testing.

4. B. Testing for maximum user load is part of testing for scalability. Localization requires translating your user interface from one language to another. Therefore, strings should not be hard-coded; they should be stored in a resource file, and the user interface should be able to accommodate text strings of varying lengths. You should also make sure that dates, numbers, and currency indicators are interpreted correctly.

5. C. Remote debugging requires that you install the Visual Studio .NET remote components on the remote machine and that you are a member of the Debugger Users group on the remote machine. Being a member of the Everyone group would not grant sufficient privileges to debug on the remote server, in most cases you must also be a member of the Administrators group. You do not need a full copy of Visual Studio .NET or a type library on the remote server for debugging.

6. D. The <DebuggerStepThrough()> attribute causes code in the proxy class to be skipped over during debugging. You can remove this attribute to step into the proxy class. Setting either of the applications as the startup project will have no effect on the debugging behavior, as concerns the proxy class. <DebuggerStepInto()> is not a valid attribute name.

7. B. Trace.WriteLine will automatically place a line-ending character after each message. Trace.WriteLineIf is used when you want to evaluate a conditional expression to determine whether the message should be output. Trace.Warn is not a valid method of the Trace class. The Trace.AutoFlush property does not affect message formatting.

8. C. Add an <assert> tag to the application configuration file that has the appropriate values set. This will redirect the Assert message to a text log file. Unchecking the Define TRACE Constant check box will suppress all trace messages in your application, producing no output. Adding the #Const TRACE = True is unnecessary in Visual Studio .NET because this option is set automatically. The <trace> tag in a configuration file does not control the output of the Assert method.

9. C. Output from the DefaultTraceListener is sent to the Output window.

10. B.   You must call the Flush and/or Close methods of the TextWriterTraceListener to cause the output to be written to the file and for the file to be released. You do not need to create a separate file object for the trace listener, so you do not need to call any methods on the file itself.

11. D.   You can test for the Level property of a TraceSwitch and use that information to determine which messages should be output. Trace statements can be placed in an error handler or anywhere else in code. Trace statements are output during the normal course of application execution, not only if a runtime error occurs. Message boxes that force the application to break are the typical behavior of Trace.Assert statements.

12. A.   Trace.Write statements will output messages to a TraceListener, which determines where the output is sent. TraceSwitches are used to turn output on and off, or to filter messages based on a priority level. Trace.Assert statements are used to test conditions during application execution; they do not work with TraceListeners or TraceSwitches. It is preferred to use Trace statements for instrumentation that will remain in the application; Debug statements are for the developer's use and are not included in the compiled executable when a Release build is produced.

13. D.   A DLL (created by a Visual Studio .NET Class Library project) can be debugged in Visual Studio .NET by using the project Property Pages dialog box to specify an external program that will reference and use the DLL. This can be any type of client application, either a Windows form, WebForm, or console application. A DLL project cannot be started directly in Visual Studio .NET.

14. B.   To capture the XML markup of incoming SOAP requests, you must run code in the BeforeDeserialize stage, while it is still in its XML wire format. For outgoing messages, the correct stage is AfterSerialize.

15. C.   The SoapExtensionAttribute.Priority property determines the order in which extension code is run, when there are multiple SOAP extensions specified for a single Web method.

Chapter 9

Overview of Security Concepts

MICROSOFT EXAM OBJECTIVES COVERED IN THIS CHAPTER:

- ✓ Implement security for a Windows service, a serviced component, a .NET Remoting object, and an XML Web service.

- ✓ Configure security for a Windows service, a serviced component, a .NET Remoting object, and an XML Web service.

- ✓ Configure authentication type. Authentication types include Windows authentication, Microsoft .NET Passport, custom authentication, and none.

- ✓ Configure and control authorization. Authorization methods include file-based authorization and URL-based authorization.

- ✓ Configure and implement identity management.

Recently, the software industry has experienced a push for improved application security. Although in prior years features were emphasized over security, the tide has begun to turn. For instance, in Windows Server 2003, many services turned on by default in prior Windows server operating systems are now disabled by default. This new emphasis on security occurred for a variety of reasons, including the IT industry's frustration with the sheer number of critical patches required for software installed on corporate servers and desktops. In addition software vendors pushed the security issue so that they could minimize legal repercussions in the event that their software were involved in a breach of security at a customer site.

Given this new emphasis on secure coding, it should be no surprise that Microsoft has asked developers to concentrate more on security than they have in the past. Proper use of .NET security features can substantially reduce the vulnerability of these applications, and the systems that host them, to unauthorized and even malicious use.

In this chapter, you will look first at basic security concepts and security features of the .NET Framework. From there, you will delve into the code security models provided by the .NET Framework, which include brand new models such as .NET Framework role-based security and code-access security, as well as a model borrowed from earlier technologies such as COM+. Additionally, you will examine various ways to implement encryption by using the .NET Framework, a concept vital to ensuring secure transmission of data across insecure networks.

Chapter 10, "Deploying, Securing, and Configuring Windows-Based Applications," and Chapter 11, "Deploying and Securing XML Web Services," delve further into the selection and implementation of appropriate security for production components and services.

Introduction to Security Concepts

Before presenting the details of .NET Framework security features, this section describes some basic security capabilities you might want to implement in your applications. It also provides a brief look at a Microsoft security threat model illustrating the types of issues you should keep in mind as a component or service developer. Because the terms introduced in this section are used in discussing the implementation of security in Visual Basic .NET applications in this and later chapters, make sure that you are familiar with them.

Identifying Basic Security Capabilities

Application platforms typically provide several standard security features, which developers can take advantage of to implement security for their applications. Some of the capabilities commonly provided include the following:

Authentication   *Authentication* is the process of demonstrating who you are, to the system. It can be accomplished in Visual Basic .NET applications in a variety of ways, which are discussed later in this chapter, in the "CLR and .NET Framework Security Features" section. Many applications require callers to authenticate to the system in order to prove that they are entitled to access a particular application or assembly, or to determine what functions of the application are available to them.

Permissions   *Permissions* describe categories of activities that can be performed, such as reading from or writing to the file system, creating files in a certain directory, accessing network resources, reading environment variables, and creating user interface elements. The .NET Framework also includes the concept of a permission set, which is a collection of permissions that can be manipulated as a unit, for programmer and administrator convenience.

Authorization   *Authorization* is the process of verifying that a process has the required permissions to perform specified system actions. It is closely connected with authentication in that the identity of the user running the process often determines what the process is authorized to do. When using the .NET Framework, authorization is provided by a combination of the Common Language Runtime's (CLR's) code access security and role-based security mechanisms.

Impersonation   Authorization is also connected with *impersonation*, in which a process can temporarily take on the identity of another user, whose authorization to perform certain tasks might be different from the user identity under which the process was created. The ASP.NET subsystem can automatically perform impersonation for a service depending on how the service is configured.

Security policies   *Security polices* are used to determine what permissions apply to particular code groups and users. Typically, they are set outside the application itself. The security policies can be set by either a custom administration tool provided with the application or by a standard tool on the platform, such as the `caspol.exe` utility provided with Visual Studio .NET and the .NET Framework. Security policies are discussed further in Chapters 10 and 11.

Cryptography   *Cryptography* is the process of encoding data to an unrecognizable form, known as ciphertext, for the sake of secrecy, and decoding it to obtain the original data, known as plaintext. It is often employed to securely persist data to media such as hard disks or tape, as well as to allow for secure transmission of information across insecure networks such as the Internet. It is important in the realms of network-oriented Windows services and Web services, because these processes are often accessed by clients across the Internet and might sometimes store data (temporarily or permanently) on a server accessed by many thousands of unrelated users. Because "good," difficult-to-break encryption algorithms are difficult to create, computing platforms often include a selection of encryption capabilities.

We discuss some of these security capabilities in the context of Visual Basic .NET in more detail throughout this chapter.

Understanding the STRIDE Model of Security Threats

Secure coding attempts to minimize the risk of threats turning into actual security incidents. Microsoft uses the acronym *STRIDE* to describe common types of threats. *STRIDE* stands for the following:

Spoofing identity   Spoofing is the compromise and unauthorized use of a user's identity. It might result from an attacker gaining access to that user's physical credentials (such as login, password, or smart card) or virtual credentials (such as authentication "cookies"). You can guard against spoofing by safeguarding credentials and choosing strong authentication methods.

Tampering with data   Tampering with data is the intentional destruction or modification of data while it is being transmitted or stored. You can protect data from tampering by using encryption, resource permissions, and physical security measures.

Repudiation   Repudiation is the ability to deny that something happened because absolute proof that it did is not available. For example, often a user can deny sending a particular e-mail message, because popular e-mail protocols alone do not have the ability to prove the origin of a message. A measure of nonrepudiation can often be gained by using digital signatures to "stamp" data such as an assembly or e-mail message with information attesting to the sender's identity.

Information disclosure   Information disclosure is the dissemination of data to unauthorized individuals. Information disclosure is the "read"-oriented version of the "write"-oriented data tampering threat, and many of the same types of actions protect against it.

Denial of service   Denial of service (DoS) is an attack that makes system resources and applications unavailable to authorized users. Although many DoS attacks occur at levels of the operating system below those that solution developers can control, others are based on taking advantage of application coding errors that enable an attacker to use up system resources such as memory or disk space over time. You can protect your applications from higher-level DoS attacks through careful assignment of privileges to applications and their users, and the use of development platforms such as Visual Studio .NET, which allow for some runtime verification of code operations.

Elevation of privilege   Elevation of privilege occurs when an attacker obtains and uses higher levels of privileges (and thus potentially obtains access to additional system resources) than he is authorized to have. As with DoS attacks, privilege elevation is often accomplished by exploiting improperly written code. To reduce this threat, applications and services should be configured to run with the minimum privilege level that is absolutely required. Additionally, the .NET Framework's managed code runtime environment helps minimize the potential security consequences of many types of coding errors by detecting and disallowing operations that appear dangerous.

You will see in the following sections how Visual Basic .NET enables you to make use of these security-related features and more to address the threats described by the STRIDE model.

Implementing Security on the .NET Platform

When we talk about the .NET platform, we are referring to the combination of the Common Language Specification that enables code written in many languages to interoperate, the .NET Framework's class libraries, the Common Language Runtime (CLR), and the Windows operating system (such as Windows 2000, Windows XP, or Windows Server 2003) on which .NET applications run. Figure 9.1 shows an illustration of the .NET Framework.

FIGURE 9.1   Diagram of OS/CLR/.NET Framework classes

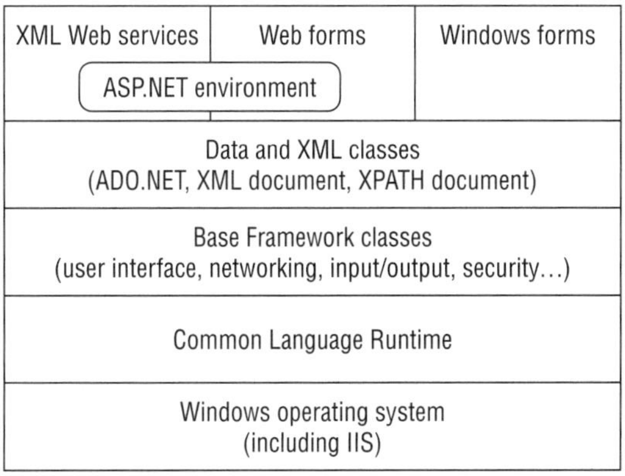

Each of these aspects of the .NET platform provides features that can be used by .NET services to implement security—for example, restricting access to functionality based on user identity, encrypting data sent from a client to a Web service, and customizing the data displayed by an application based on a user's assigned organizational role. Because a thorough understanding of how to secure services on .NET depends on details at both the NET Framework level and the operating system level, we will now present the features provided by each.

CLR and .NET Framework Security Features

The Common Language Runtime (CLR) is the lowest-level portion of the .NET Framework that is not considered part of the operating system. The CLR provides virtual machine-related capabilities to .NET applications, including the following:

▪ Memory management (including garbage collection)

- Type checking via code verification
- Code isolation via application domains (appdomains) and assemblies
- Authorization via code-access security
- Authorization via role-based security

Because the designers of the CLR had the advantage of considering security problems inherent in previous approaches to application platforms, they were able to incorporate new security features to help protect .NET applications and services from some common vulnerabilities that had plagued applications in the past.

Managed code, such as a compiled Visual Basic .NET project, runs in close cooperation with the CLR and can take advantage of the protections it provides.

The CLR's automatic memory garbage collection functionality guards against a programmer allocating memory and then forgetting to release it (by, for example, setting an object to `Nothing`). This type of error would result in a program gradually using up more and more memory, until it (or the server itself) stopped operating correctly. The CLR's garbage collector can determine when an object is no longer used and can free the memory it was using, without explicit instructions by the programmer.

A type of vulnerability frequently found in both desktop and network applications is a buffer overflow, which enables a malicious user to supply data to the application that causes it to behave in unexpected ways. Programs are susceptible to buffer overflows due to (sometimes very obscure) errors in their logic. Because buffer overflows can be exploited, even from across the Internet, to run the attacker's code of choice on the server, they can make for a major hole in your application's (and entire server's) security. Managed code runs in a type-safe execution environment that verifies compatible data types and sizes when data is copied from one location to another, performs bounds-checking on array elements, and takes other precautions to minimize the occurrence of buffer overflow conditions.

In older architectures, security restrictions tended to be enforced process by process. The .NET platform features a new application architecture paradigm, introducing the concepts of the assembly and application domain (or appdomain).

The assembly is the basic building block for applications, analogous to a DLL in Win32. Assemblies have many security features, including the ability to be assigned a *strong name*, which gives the assembly a unique identity and ensures that the correct assembly is loaded when requested by an application. Instead of an application's DLLs and EXEs being scattered around the file system (some in the application directory, some in Windows, some in `Windows\System32`, and so on), a .NET application's assemblies are usually stored together within the application's directory, or if assigned a strong name, optionally in a global cache of assemblies. This provides the advantage of allowing multiple versions of the same application to coexist, with less ambiguity about versioning than there has been in the past. The simple XCOPY installation process advocated by Microsoft eliminates the problems that can occur as a result of invalid or incomplete installations. The XCOPY technique to install an application is accomplished by simply copying the source directory from the installation location to the target computer, and to uninstall an application you simply remove that directory from the target computer. There is no longer a need, when not working with COM InterOp, to register application information in the registry or to add .dll's to the shared system directory.

 If you use the Global Assembly Cache (GAC) for shared assemblies; you cannot use the XCOPY installation process.

.NET code is self-describing, which means that information about data types, method parameters, and so on, used by an assembly is available directly in the assembly file itself. Therefore, COM-style component registration is no longer required—and it's no longer possible for component registration information and the component itself to get out of sync when new versions are deployed.

 Deployment-related security features and concerns are discussed in more detail in Chapters 10 and 11.

All managed code runs within an *application domain*, which is a logical segment of a process at the operating system level. More than one application domain can be hosted within each operating system–level process. Each application domain within a process is isolated from the others, so that it cannot access resources in other application domains, and a failure in one application domain will not affect any other application domain.

The .NET Framework implements two major types of security models:

Code-access security   With *code access security*, the CLR takes advantage of security policies to determine when code is allowed to run and what it is allowed to do, based on evidence such as the origin of the code, its publisher, and (for components) the assembly that has called the code. Much like the Internet Explorer browser, the CLR can classify code as trusted or nontrusted and assign different permissions based on the location (or zone) of the module being executed, as well as other criteria such as the code's publisher, strong name, and URL. Permissions granted to code can be easily configured by the administrator without the need to recompile.

Role-based security   With *role-based security*, the identity of the user running the code is used to determine what the code can do. The .NET Framework includes two versions of role-based security: a COM+ style model as well as a new .NET Framework–native implementation.

It is possible to combine code access security and role-based security within the same application. All of these models are discussed in more detail in the "Using Code Security Models" section later in this chapter.

The .NET Framework class libraries include many objects related to security, which the .NET programmer can incorporate into service code. Table 9.1 lists the namespaces that contain security features.

TABLE 9.1   Security-Related Namespaces in .NET

Namespace	Contents
System.Security	Helper types for handling security exceptions, persisting security objects, improving code performance, and working with permissions and policies
System.Security.Cryptography	Types used to encrypt and decrypt data, and supporting functionality such as generation of hash values to uniquely identify sets of data
System.Security.Permissions	Types used to apply and verify permission attributes
System.Security.Policy	Types used to apply and verify policies
System.Security.Principal	Types used to manage role-based security
System.Web.Security	Types related to web-based security, such as passport authentication

The .NET Framework also includes a variety of authentication mechanisms, which determine how the calling user's identity is determined and verified. These are summarized in Table 9.2. The implications of the different types of authentication for different types of processes (such as XML Web services and .NET Remoting objects) are discussed in Chapter 11. Not all authentication mechanisms are available for all types of processes.

TABLE 9.2   Selected .NET Authentication Mechanisms

Authentication Mechanism	Description
Forms authentication	Unauthenticated requests are redirected to an HTML form. The user inputs credentials and submits the form. If the application properly authenticates the request, the client machine is sent back a cookie containing a credentials identifier. This cookie is then sent in the request header of future HTTP requests.
Passport authentication	Authentication is provided by a centralized service, which offers participating applications the ease of use of "single sign on," enabling users to authenticate once and have their credentials subsequently passed to other applications participating in passport-based authentication.
Client certificate authentication	Clients are authenticated based on the content of the client's digital certificate. This avoids the exchange of user/password information across the network.

TABLE 9.2   Selected .NET Authentication Mechanisms *(continued)*

Authentication Mechanism	Description
Anonymous authentication	Users are not authenticated by ASP.NET. Processes run as the specified user. In IIS6, this is configured by using the Internet Services Manager. In IIS5, code runs as the user defined in the machine.config file in the system.web section under the <processModel> element.
Windows authentication	Clients are authenticated by one of the mechanisms built into IIS (ASP.NET).
IIS Basic authentication	A specific type of Windows authentication in which user credentials are sent from the client to the server in plain text. Although sending user and password information unencrypted sounds like a bad idea, Basic authentication can work well when used in conjunction with SSL.
IIS Digest authentication	A specific type of Windows authentication in which client-supplied passwords are encrypted with a weak algorithm prior to transmission. Digest authentication is somewhat more secure than Basic authentication, but less secure than Integrated Windows authentication.
IIS Integrated Windows authentication	A specific type of Windows authentication formerly known as NTLM authentication or Windows NT Challenge/Response authentication. This mechanism provides for a higher level of security by using computed challenge/response communication to authenticate, rather than passing encrypted or unencrypted user and password data across the network. Whereas Basic and Digest authentication work over an HTTP or HTTPS connection, Integrated Windows authentication directly uses the Windows operating system's authentication features and requires communication over additional ports that might not be open on a corporate firewall, so this option might not always be available.

Modern Windows Operating System Security Features

The .NET security features discussed previously are layered on top of the features provided by the Windows operating system. It is important to note that many Windows security features appearing in Windows 2000, XP, and Server 2003 are not available in older consumer versions such as Windows 98. Therefore, for optimal security, it is recommended that .NET applications be deployed on one of these more full-featured editions of Windows.

Some Windows security features include the following:

- User accounts and groups
- User rights

- File permissions

- Policies

User accounts include built-in accounts, such as Administrator and LocalSystem, as well as custom accounts created at a site for each user, such as Tsmith or Bdawson. Built-in accounts ship with Windows-defined default permissions and are often used to run Microsoft-supplied services at a relatively high level of privilege. Individual user accounts have a lower level of permission that is sufficient for typical nonadministrative use of the network. You saw when discussing Windows services that code might sometimes require a higher level of permission than that provided by a standard user account, to perform required tasks (for instance, to run as a Windows service). Fortunately, that is not necessarily the case for other types of services that might be developed with Visual Studio .NET.

For ease of administration, accounts are often combined into sets known as groups. Assigning permissions and rights at the group level rather than the user level reduces the amount of system administration effort required to keep security settings up to date as staff join the organization, leave it, or are transferred to positions with other duties. This advantage of operating system–level groups is also found in role-based security mechanisms employed by .NET. In fact, one of the role-based security models supplied with .NET directly uses these Windows groups as roles.

User rights are privileges that can be granted to users. For instance, standard users typically have the right to log on locally to network desktop computers. They usually do not have higher-level rights (such as the right to back up files), which are typically enjoyed only by administrators and staff with network operator duties. User rights are the lowest level at which the administrator can control the basic activities that the user is allowed to perform on the system.

To set user rights effective on the local system only, use the Local Security Policy applet (available at Start ➢ Settings ➢ Control Panel ➢ Administrative Tools in Windows 2000 Professional) and choose Security Settings ➢ Local Policies ➢ User Rights Assignment. User rights applicable to all computers in the domain can be set by using the Domain Security Policy applet. Figure 9.2 shows the interface used to set user rights on the local system.

FIGURE 9.2   Local security policy user rights

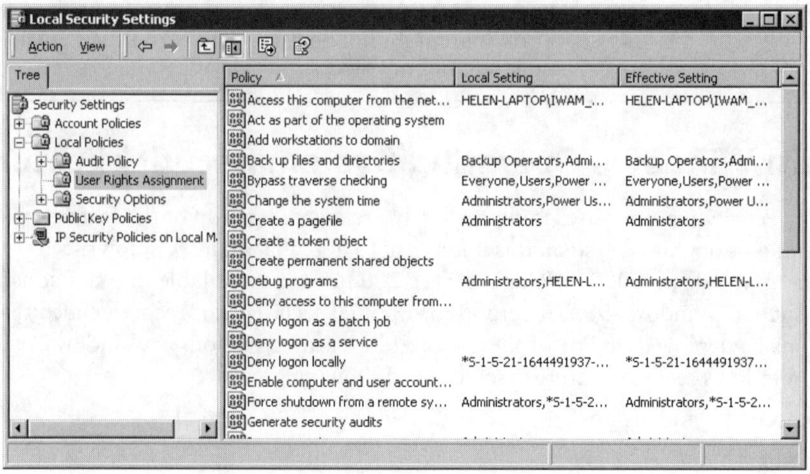

Additionally, you might further restrict access to individual resources on the system, by group and user, through the use of access control lists (ACLs) on resources such as files. For example, if your application writes certain text files to the folder C:\myapp\exportdata, but you don't wish to allow nonadministrative users to view the names of files in that folder, you can use an ACL to deny that type of access. To do that, navigate to the C:\myapp folder in Windows Explorer, right-click the exportdata folder, choose Properties, and select the Security tab. Click the Deny check box for List Folder Contents to select it, click Apply, and then click OK. The dialog box you will see looks similar to Figure 9.3.

FIGURE 9.3   Setting file access permissions

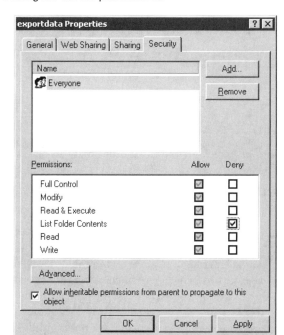

The permissions that a .NET application has when running are a layered combination of those granted at the .NET Framework level (via code access security and role-based security) and those granted the user under whose identity the application is running, at the operating system level (via resources, ACLs, and user rights.)

The application cannot be granted permissions at the .NET Framework level that the user is not authorized to have at the operating system level. For example, if the user cannot access files in the C:\PrivateAdmins folder with a standard system application such as Notepad, you will not be able to give an application running under that user's identity permission to access those files within your Visual Basic .NET application. Assigning permissions under the various security models available on the .NET platform is covered in the next section of this chapter.

Policies are groups of configuration settings that customize Windows in line with the operational policies of an organization. Policies can be set on various levels, including for the entire enterprise, particular machines, particular users, and particular groups of users. As you will see later in this chapter, the concept of policies makes an appearance in the .NET Framework.

Now that you have had the opportunity to look at some of the features available to implement security in .NET services, you're ready to take a closer look at some of them, such as permissions, code security models, and support for cryptography.

Configuring Authorization via Permissions

The CLR determines whether an application can access resources and perform certain actions based on the permissions granted to it and its callers. The .NET Framework uses Permission objects to represent three types of permissions:

- *Code-access permissions*, which are the capabilities that can be granted to applications
- *Identity permissions*, which describe the identity and origin of the code
- *Role-based security permissions*, which describe the groups that the caller of the code might, or might not, be a member of

Most of these permissions are organized within the System.Security.Permissions namespace. As you will see from the partial list in Tables 9.3 and 9.4, the .NET Framework enables you to grant or examine permissions on a very granular level. For instance, you might wish to restrict your service from accessing environment settings or the system Registry, because if an attacker devised a way to exploit your service, you would not want them to be able to find out the details about your server that are exposed in those locations.

Knowledge of how permissions work is important for understanding how they are used to implement two of the three .NET platform security models, so next you will look at them in greater detail before learning more about the security models themselves.

Introduction to Permissions

Code-access permissions, which are part of the code access security model discussed later in this chapter, tend to focus on controlling access to specific system resources. They specify the types of actions that the code is permitted to perform. The CodeAccessPermission class is defined within the System.Security namespace. Each class derived from the CodeAccessPermission class has one or more public properties through which you can customize the behavior of that permission. For example, you can selectively allow access to areas of the file system, the Clipboard, and certain types of user interface windows, the default printer or all printers, and so forth. Table 9.3 lists some of the most common code access permission classes you might encounter as a .NET platform service developer.

TABLE 9.3   Common .NET Code Access Permission Classes

Permission	Gives Permission To...
EnvironmentPermission	Read and/or write environment variables.
FileDialogPermission	Display the file dialog, which if displayed, can enable the user to see files in directories and navigate the file system.
FileIOPermission	Read, write, and/or append to files or folders.
IsolatedStoragePermission	Read and/or write files in a specially isolated area of the file system, enabling the application to save data to the file system without giving it access to the entire file system. You can also set a quota governing the maximum amount of isolated storage that can be used by the application.
PrintingPermission	Print. (This permission is found in the System.Drawing .Printing namespace.)
RegistryPermission	Read and/or write to the system Registry.
SecurityPermission	Manipulate the security subsystem, such as asserting permissions, electing to skip code verification, and allowing the assembly to call unmanaged code.
SQLClientPermission	Access SQL databases as a client.
UIPermission	Create user interface elements. (This is an example of a right that a service will generally not require.)

Because it is useful for developers to be able to perform actions in standardized ways, the permission concept is also used to express information about the origin and identity of code. Table 9.4 lists common identity permissions, which are also found in the System.Security .Permissions namespace.

TABLE 9.4   Common .NET Framework Identity Permission Objects

Permission	Contains
PublisherIdentityPermission	Code publisher's digital signature
SiteIdentityPermission	Site from which the code originated

TABLE 9.4 Common .NET Framework Identity Permission Objects *(continued)*

Permission	Contains
StrongNameIdentityPermission	Assembly's strong name
URLIdentityPermission	URL from which the code originated
ZoneIdentityPermission	Zone from which the code originated

Most of these permissions should be self-explanatory. The ZoneIdentityPermission object's possible values parallel the zones offered in Internet Explorer: Local Intranet, Trusted Sites, Internet, Restricted Sites, and Local Machine.

There is only one role-based permission, PrincipalPermission. By passing identity information (username and/or role), a PrincipalPermission object can be used to verify the identity currently in effect or to verify that identity is a member of a specified role.

The permissions listed in Tables 9.3 and 9.4 are just a subset of the types of permissions available in .NET. For ease of use, permissions can be grouped into *permission sets*, which specify a collection of one or more types of permissions, as you learned earlier in this chapter. Permission sets can be named or unnamed. The .NET Framework furnishes a number of conveniently named permission sets, listed in Table 9.5, which feature useful combinations of permissions. The permissions assigned to these named sets are fixed, though if you like, you can create your own named permission sets and define custom combinations of permissions specific to your application.

TABLE 9.5 Common .NET Named Permission Sets

Permission Set	Description
Execute	Permission to execute (but not any other .NET permissions).
Everything	All built-in permissions.
FullTrust	All built-in permissions plus all user-defined permissions.
Internet	Permissions useful for trusted Internet-based applications. (Check the .NET Framework version on which you are deploying for specifics, as the permissions in this set have changed with new releases.) Granted by default to code in the Trusted_Zones code group.

TABLE 9.5   Common .NET Named Permission Sets *(continued)*

Permission Set	Description
LocalIntranet	Permissions useful for trusted intranet-based applications. Currently includes all Internet permissions as well as the ability to discover the local user identity, read files from the application's directory, and access the event log. Again, you might wish to verify the current LocalIntranet permission set in the version of the .NET Framework that you are using. Granted by default to code in the LocalIntranet_Zone code group.
Nothing	Granted by default to all code, and includes no permissions.

Understanding How Permission-Checking Works

Each executing .NET managed code process has an associated call stack, which contains information about all methods that have been called and have not yet ended, including the permissions granted to that method (or stack frame). To determine the code access permissions in effect at the current time, the CLR performs a *stack walk*. That is, it examines the permissions granted to the current stack frame and then starts traveling upward on the stack, examining the permissions granted at successively higher levels of the call stack, for all method calls currently executing. In most cases, if a permission is not granted at all higher levels of the call stack, the permission is not considered to be in effect, even if it has been granted to the currently executing code.

Let's take a look at an analogy to show how this might work in everyday business. Suppose the chief executive officer of the company you work for places no restrictions on who can travel first class on business trips. However, the chief technical officer reporting to that CEO is carefully minding her budget and specifies that all staff in her area of the organization must travel coach or business class. She passes this policy down to employees who report directly to her, including the director of the application development group. Meanwhile, the project managers reporting to the director haven't heard about the new policy yet and are still encouraging their staff to travel first class on long business trips. One day, you find yourself needing to travel to a client site to debug a challenging application configuration problem. You submit your first-class travel plans to your project manager, who approves them and passes them up the line to the director of application development. The director calls your manager to let him know that the request is being denied because of policy, and very soon your manager lets you know that the request was not approved. Unbeknownst to you, somewhere above you in the organizational hierarchy "stack," the permission had been denied. This situation is illustrated in Figure 9.4.

Now, relate this example to coding. Say you have an application that is granted all permissions by default, which calls a component that is explicitly denied permission to modify the value of the Path environment variable. That component might call a third-party component that in some cases tries to modify the Path's value, because it was written by a developer who did not anticipate it would ever be called by a method that did not want its Path's value modified.

When the third-party component attempts to modify the value of the Path, a security exception is thrown, because the component does not have permission to do so. Figure 9.5 summarizes how this works.

FIGURE 9.4 A corporate stack walk

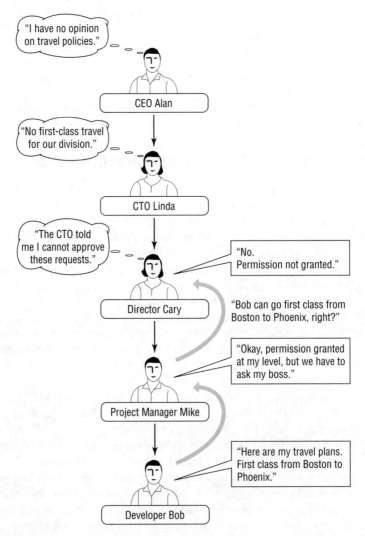

Why base effective permissions on those granted to callers as well as those granted to the currently executing method? Such a mechanism supports flexible configuration for modern, network-based components and reflects the notion that not all callers of a method are trusted equally. .NET handles permissions in this way so that the same code can run with different permissions depending on the caller. For example, a method might opt to write only to small areas of isolated storage if called from a process across the Internet, and write to other areas of the file system if called from a process on the local intranet, because it trusts the intentions of local callers more than it trusts those of random Internet users.

FIGURE 9.5   A stack walk in code

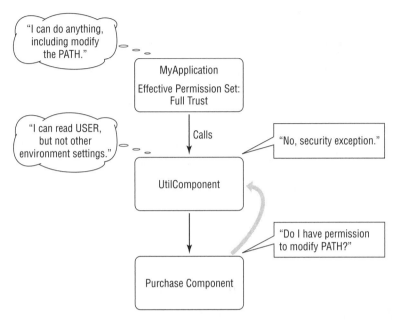

Now that you understand what permissions are and how .NET evaluates them to enforce security, next you'll see how they are used in .NET applications.

Using Permissions in Code

.NET programmers can interact with permissions by using *declarative* (attribute-based) and *imperative* (traditional code-based) techniques. Why have two styles of working with security permissions? Attribute-based programming is convenient, enabling the developer to make use of a lot of .NET functionality without having to write additional lines of procedural code. Applying attributes to assemblies and methods also aids in documentation—the permissions required by that code are clearly noted. However, not all permission interaction can be accomplished via attributes (for example, choosing between two program behaviors based on the permissions currently in effect at runtime can be accomplished only imperatively), and not all programmers prefer notating their code with attributes to explicitly writing code to perform functions. Conversely, there are also some permission-related functions available via declarative notation that are not available in imperative code, so sometimes the attribute-based method of permission manipulation is required.

You are free to combine declarative and imperative methods of working with permissions, so that you can implement the desired functionality in the most convenient way. For example, you might want to use an attribute to declaratively demand permission for your assembly to read a file, but at runtime, use imperative method calls to restrict the writing of that file to users in the Administrator role. You'll now look at what you can do with permissions, first through examples in the imperative style, then in the declarative style.

 Real World Scenario

Declarative Permissions, Classes, and Methods

Be aware that if you assign declarative permissions to a method, these override any conflicting declarative permissions assigned for the class that contains the method. Possible security actions are defined by the SecurityAction enumeration in the System.Security.Permissions namespace.

For example, if you demand, via attributes at the class-level permission, to access the Registry and then demand, via attributes on a method, permission to read a certain file, the demand for Registry access will not be in effect for that method—it has been replaced by the demand for Read permission on a file.

Because this is somewhat confusing, it is recommended that you not mix class and method permission attributes.

Methods Common to All Permission Objects

There are many ways in which .NET applications can interact with permissions. Table 9.6 lists methods available to all types of Permission objects.

TABLE 9.6 Selected .NET Permission Object Methods

Method	Description
Demand	Verifies that all callers higher in the call stack have been granted this permission; if not, a security exception is generated.
Intersect	Creates a Permission object that contains the permissions common to both the specified permission and the current permission.
IsSubsetOf	Determines whether the current permission is a subset of the specified permission.
Union	Creates a Permission object that contains the permissions in the specified permission and the current permission.

It is good programming practice to specifically check for the permissions in code before they are needed. Using the Permission.Demand method, the programmer can verify that the currently executing code has the permission(s) to perform the anticipated functions and, if the code does not have the appropriate permission(s), to fail gracefully. The developer can even check which permissions are available and vary the code path, based on the current permissions. By varying the code path you are increasing the flexibility of your application with regard to the permissions that are required for the code to run. Another reason to use Demand is to verify that the required permissions for an action performed late in a method call are present before you perform resource-intensive setup code.

Listing 9.1 demonstrates the imperative use of the Demand method.

Listing 9.1: Imperative Use of the Permission.Demand Method

```
Imports System
Imports System.Security
Imports System.Security.Permissions


Public Class Example1


Private Sub WriteToLog()
Dim LogFilePermission as New FileIOPermission _
      (FileIOPermissionAccess.Write, "C:\example1.log")


Try
   LogFilePermission.Demand()
Catch
   ' handle exception here
End Try


End Sub


End Class
```

Now that you've seen how to implement Permission.Demand via imperative method calls, look at the declarative attribute-based technique in Listing 9.2. Notice that the name of the attribute is the permission name plus Attribute. The first argument is the Demand action, and the second is the permission property being verified.

Listing 9.2: Declarative Use of the Permission.Demand Method

```
Imports System
Imports System.Security
Imports System.Security.Permissions


Public Class Example1


<FileIOPermissionAttribute(SecurityAction.Demand, _
      Write:="C:\example1.log")> _
Private Sub WriteToLog()
```

End Sub

End Class

The Intersect, IsSubsetOf, and Union methods all allow manipulation of Permission objects for additional flexibility, because some permissions are actually subsets or supersets of other permissions, and possession of one of the higher-level permissions implies possession of lower ones.

Methods Available to Code Access Security Permission Objects

Code access Permission objects have additional methods, described in Table 9.7. These methods are used to alter the stack-walk behavior when the CLR is checking code access security permissions.

TABLE 9.7   Selected .NET Code-Access Permission Object Methods

Method	Description
Assert	Asserts that this permission is granted even if callers higher in the stack do not possess it, as long as the executing code has been granted the specified permission. By default, only code in the intranet zone and fully trusted code can call Assert.
Deny	Causes any Demand method that passes through this stack frame (via a stack walk) for a specific permission in the current permission set to fail.
PermitOnly	Causes any Demand method that passes through this stack frame for a permission that is not a subset of the current permission set to fail.
RevertAll	Removes any permission overrides for the current frame.
RevertAssert	Causes any previous Assert method for the current frame to be removed.
RevertDeny	Causes any previous Deny method for the current frame to be removed.
RevertPermitOnly	Causes any previous PermitOnly method for the current frame to be removed.

Some programmers, upon seeing the Assert method, might be tempted to confuse it with Demand. However, its functionality is different. Whereas Demand causes the system to walk up the call stack verifying that code has a certain permission, the Assert method states that the code is permitted to access the resource specified by the current permissions of the calling code, even if callers higher in the stack haven't directly been granted permission to access the resource, thus no stack walk is required.

To understand how this works in practice, let's revisit our analogy regarding travel permissions. Suppose your project manager doesn't want to bother the busy director by asking her to approve your request for first-class travel, and simply rubber-stamps it approved and hands it back to you. Your project manager has taken upon himself the responsibility that those reporting to him will use the permission to travel in first class responsibly (for example, by using it only when traveling on flights longer than three hours). In .NET Framework terms, he asserts that those below him in the hierarchy should be given this permission, regardless of the views or restrictions put in place by those above him. Figure 9.6 shows this in graphical form.

FIGURE 9.6   Asserting permission

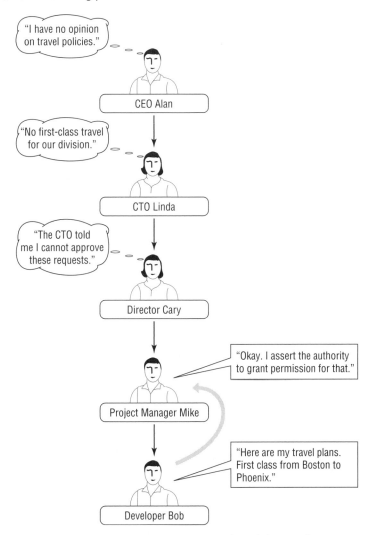

The use of Assert results in an increase in security vulnerability, in that you've just increased the chances that this code, when called from an untrusted process, can be used to do more than the programmer might have anticipated. Therefore, consider the implications carefully before using Assert in your code. Although both Assert and Demand will fail if the code in question doesn't possess the specified permission, only Demand will fail if the code's callers don't possess the permission.

To assert a particular permission, you might use imperative code such as the following:

```
Dim LogFilePermission as New FileIOPermission _
    (FileIOPermissionAccess.Write, "C:\example1.log")


Try
    LogFilePermission.Assert()
Catch
    ' handle exception here
End Try
```

Alternatively, you could use declarative notation:

```
<FileIOPermissionAttribute(SecurityAction.Assert, _
    Write:="C:\example1.log")> _
Private Sub WriteToLog()

End Sub
```

The Deny method performs a function similar to Assert, but in the other direction. Whereas Assert indicates that the indicated permission should be considered granted, Deny indicates that the specified permission should be considered disallowed. To go back to our travel example, the chief technical officer is issuing a real-world denial of first-class travel permission to those reporting to him when he sends out the policy memo. It can be useful to deny any permissions that are not absolutely required before calls to a third-party class library, to help ensure that any implementation flaws in that library don't compromise the security of your code. To deny a permission imperatively, you would use code like the following:

```
Dim LogFilePermission as New FileIOPermission _
    (FileIOPermissionAccess.Write, "C:\example1.log")


Try
    LogFilePermission.Deny
Catch
    ' handle exception here
End Try
```

And to deny declaratively, you would use code similar to this:

```
<FileIOPermissionAttribute(SecurityAction.Deny, _
    Write:="C:\example1.log")> _
Private Sub WriteToLog()

End Sub
```

Similarly, the `PermitOnly` method applies the stack-walk-avoiding idea to the concept of explicitly specified permissions. The effect of `PermitOnly` is to deny all permissions except those explicitly included in the specified permission. Because only one `PermitOnly` is allowed per frame, `PermitOnly` is most likely to be used with PermissionSet objects rather than an individual Permission object, because code generally needs more than a single permission for proper operation. For example, it might require both file access permissions and environment access permissions.

The `Assert`, `Deny`, and `PermitOnly` methods can be used to increase the efficiency of code because they reduce the amount of time spent performing stack walks when explicitly testing permissions with `Demand` or attempting to execute code requiring permissions. However, as previously mentioned, because they prevent the CLR from considering security-related evidence that might be provided by the code's callers, they should be used with care.

Normally, the effects of these functions last only until the stack frame is removed (for example, when the method finishes execution). The *Revert* methods listed in Table 9.7 can be used to "turn off" any `Assert`, `Deny`, or `PermitOnly` calls that have been made before that point, if desired. If you want to permanently deny a specific permission to an assembly and all of the code it calls, note that a specific permission is required for proper application operation. Or if you want to request that a specific permission be made available for the assembly, you must use declarative security at the assembly level. For example, to deny an assembly the permission to read drive C:, you would include the following attribute within the assembly's code:

```
<Assembly: FileIOPermissionAttribute _
    (SecurityAction.RequestRefuse, _
    Read:="C:\") >
```

To require permission to read drive C:, you could include an attribute such as the following within the assembly's code:

```
<Assembly: FileIOPermissionAttribute _
    (SecurityAction.RequestMinimum, _
    Read:="C:\") >
```

To optionally request (but not require) Read access to drive C:, you could use the following attribute:

```
<Assembly: FileIOPermissionAttribute _
    (SecurityAction.RequestOptional, _
    Read:="C:\") >
```

Now that you've seen the basics of interacting with individual permissions, let's take a look at interacting with permission sets.

Using Permission Sets

The Permission object's methods, displayed in Table 9.8, and the Permission object's attributes in the previous examples are also available for PermissionSet objects, and their use is similar.

In addition, PermissionSet objects feature several other methods for manipulating collections of permissions, as listed Table 9.8.

TABLE 9.8   Selected .NET Framework PermissionSet Object Methods

Method	Description
AddPermission	Adds a specified permission to the PermissionSet
RemovePermission	Removes a specified permission from the PermissionSet
SetPermission	Sets a permission in the PermissionSet, replacing any permission of the same type

To build a permission set, you can call AddPermission repeatedly to fill the permission set with your desired permissions. The following code creates a permission set allowing only user interface element, environment, and file access. Notice that the permission set starts out empty, and that a permission set can contain multiple types of permissions.

```
Dim myPermissionSet as New PermissionSet( _
        PermissionState.None)
Dim myEnvPerm as new EnvironmentPermission( _
        PermissionState.Unrestricted)
Dim myFilePerm as new FileIOPermission( _
        PermissionState.Unrestricted)
Dim myUIPerm as New UIPermission( _
        PersmissionState.Unrestricted)
myPermissionSet.AddPermission(myEnvPerm)
myPermissionSet.AddPermission(myFilePerm)
myPermissionSet.AddPermission(myUIPerm)
myPermissionSet.PermitOnly()
```

Because some permissions might be required for only a short time, you can use Remove-Permission to take a specific permission out of the permission set. For example, if you no longer needed permission to access the environment, you could use the following code to remove that permission:

```
MyPermissionSet.RemovePermission(myEnvPerm)
```

You can also use SetPermission to replace an existing Permission object in the permission set, with a new one of the same type.

Using Code Security Models

Code security models are logical frameworks for designing and implementing application security. They define the conditions under which certain actions might, or might not, be taken in code.

The .NET Framework provides three code security models, which can be combined within a single application or service to implement the appropriate security for your application:

- CLR role-based security
- .NET code access security
- .NET Enterprise services role-based security

The first two are new to the .NET Framework, while the third is an adaptation of the COM+ role-based security model that might already be familiar to you. In this section, we discuss each in turn.

CLR Role-Based Security

CLR role-based security (sometimes called .NET role-based security) grants permissions based on the identity of the user running the code and the roles to which that user is assigned are assigned. It is often used to check whether a specific Windows user is authorized to access a particular system or network resource.

The two primary objects used in this security model are the Identity and Principal objects. An *Identity object* contains information about the identity of the user (such as their user ID) and the authentication provider used to determine and verify that identity, as well as some Boolean fields that can be checked to see whether the identity represents an Anonymous, Guest, or System user. The available Identity types are as follows:

- `FormsIdentity`
- `GenericIdentity` (for custom authentication methods)
- `PassportIdentity`
- `WindowsIdentity` (which allows for impersonation)

A *Principal object* contains an Identity object as well as information about the roles for which the user with that identity is authorized. The available Principal types are as follows:

- `GenericPrincipal` (based on an identity that does not correspond to a Windows user)
- `WindowsPrincipal` (based on an identity that is a Windows user)
- `CustomPrincipal` (application-defined)

To select which of these types of Principal objects is used in CLR role-based security checks, you would use the `SetPrincipalPolicy` method of the current application domain.

In addition to these objects, there is the concept of a *role*, which is often thought of as corresponding to the user's role(s) in the organization. Because users can be assigned multiple roles within an organization, they can also be assigned multiple roles in CLR role-based security. For Windows Principal objects, the Windows groups to which the user is assigned are considered to be their roles. This enables an administrator to add and delete users from application roles simply by changing the users' Windows group memberships. When specifying a Windows group in the context of role-based security, the group must be specified with its fully qualified name. For example, a local group called Friends on a machine named Linda would have a fully qualified name of `Linda\Friends`. The built-in groups such as Administrators and Users would have fully qualified names of BUILTIN\Administrators and BUILTIN\Users, respectively. You could also refer to them in your code as Linda\Administrators or Linda\Users, hard-coding the machine name. However, using the generic BUILTIN designation instead enables the code to be deployed to any machine, with the security checks performed against the groups defined on the current machine.

In role-based security, the code evaluates whether the current Principal object is in a specific role (or is a specific user), and allows or disallows certain functionality based on the result of the check. For example, a class that returns employee data might return the employee's social security number if called by an application running with a Principal object that is assigned the role of Personnel-Administrator. But it might return a string of asterisks in place of the social security number if called by an application whose Principal object is assigned the role of NetworkAdministrator.

The .NET Framework provides several ways to perform this role membership verification, including these three:

- Imperatively demanding the permission corresponding to the role
- Imperatively verifying that the user is in a role, by using the IsInRole method
- Declaratively demanding the permission corresponding to the role

You will look at each of these options next.

Imperatively demanding the permission corresponding to the role or user identity is performed in much the same way as any other imperative permission demand. If the Demand method is not satisfied, an exception is thrown. In addition to using this method to demand membership in a particular role, you can also use it to check the current user's identity. To do this, instead of using the following:

```
Dim RolePermission as New PrincipalPermission _
      (Nothing, "BUILTIN\Administrators", True)
```

you would use a principal permission declaration, such as this:

```
Dim UserPermission as New PrincipalPermission _
      ("CORPDOMAIN\Linda", Nothing, True)
```

For example, to demand that the principal is a member of the group BUILTIN\Administrators, you would use code like that in Listing 9.3.

Listing 9.3: Imperative Demand of Role Membership via Permission

```
Imports System
Imports System.Threading
Imports System.Security.Principal
Imports System.Security.Permission


Public Class RoleExample


Private Sub CheckRole()
Dim RolePermission as New PrincipalPermission _
      (Nothing, "BUILTIN\SystemOperators", True)
```

```
Try
    RolePermission.Demand()
Catch
    ' handle exception here
End Try

End Sub

End Class
```

Imperatively verifying whether a particular principal belongs to a role is done via a method call to the Principal object's IsInRole function, using code like that in Listing 9.4.

Listing 9.4: Imperative Query of Role Membership via Principal.IsInRole

```
Imports System
Imports System.Threading
Imports System.Security.Principal

Public Class RoleExample

Private Sub CheckRole()

AppDomain.CurrentDomain.SetPrincipalPolicy _
    (PrincipalPolicy.WindowsPrincipal)

If (Thread.CurrentPrincipal.IsInRole _
  ("BUILTIN\SystemOperators")) then
    ' perform action for users in SystemOperators group
Else
    ' perform action for users not in SystemOperators
End If

End Sub

End Class
```

Note that in this listing, we supply a string consisting of the fully qualified role (or Windows group) name, and that a failure returns a Boolean False rather than throwing an exception as with permission demands. You also have the option of specifying some built-in group names by using predefined enumerated values, such as WindowsBuiltInRole.SystemOperator and WindowsBuiltInRole.Administrator.

Finally, as with other types of permissions, you can use the declarative attribute syntax to demand that the caller's identity have a specific role. An example of this is shown in Listing 9.5.

Listing 9.5: Declarative Demand of Role Membership via Permission

```
Imports System
Imports System.Threading
Imports System.Security.Principal
Imports System.Security.Permissions

Public Class RoleExample

<PrincipalPermissionAttribute(SecurityAction.Demand, _
    Role = "BUILTIN\SystemOperators")> _
Private Sub CheckRole()
    ' perform whatever actions require SystemOperators role
End Sub

End Class
```

 Real World Scenario

Developing under the Administrator Account

Suppose you are a developer writing a serviced component that will be accessed by many accounts payable data-entry operators in your organization to update vendor information in a centralized database. You develop the component, test it, and turn it over to the quality assurance person on your team.

Within a day, you see an e-mail message from the quality assurance person, addressed to all project team members, noting that the component is generating an exception when invoked by the data-entry application. You test it again on your computer, just to be sure, and then send back the infamous developer reply that causes quality assurance and end-user personnel the world over to wince: "It works for me; I don't know why it's failing for you." Several hours later, after you've paid a personal visit to the QA person, seen the code fail, and had him come back to your office with you so that he could log in on your Visual Studio .NET–equipped workstation and you could trace through the code, you discover that his account is missing a permission required by your component. Because you had been developing under an account in the Administrators group, which had been granted that permission by default, you had not noticed that it would be necessary to add this permission to typical application user accounts.

Actually, you were fortunate, because the code went through a quality assurance department. Instead, you could have found yourself working with an end user—possibly on the other side of the globe, in a time zone whose work hours perfectly overlap with your usual sleep hours—to troubleshoot the failure.

The solution is for developers to make a habit out of developing and testing under a user account with "normal" system privileges (those that apply to the Everyone group, for example) rather than Administrator, so that these problems could often be detected and avoided earlier in the development cycle.

Many developers see logging into an account with Administrator privileges and doing all of their development from that account to be the path of least resistance. However, this practice has often led to code that fails out in the field when run by non-Administrators or that results in hastily updated installation instructions requesting (usually in very small print, in the middle of a paragraph) that all users be assigned certain high-level Windows permissions manually, so that the code will run correctly for them. Discovering and solving permission-related problems during development, rather than during external testing or live production use, contributes favorably to application usability and quality.

Exercise 9.1 gives you hands-on experience in the use of role-based security. Because the exercise demonstrates the effect of testing whether the user is in the Administrators built-in group, you should ideally have access to at least one user who is in that group, and at least one who is not.

EXERCISE 9.1

Using CLR Role-Based Security

1. Create a new Visual Studio .NET project by using the Windows Application project template. Name this project **RoleBasedExample**.

2. In the Solution Explorer, right-click the project name and choose Add Reference. In the Add Reference dialog box, select System.Security.

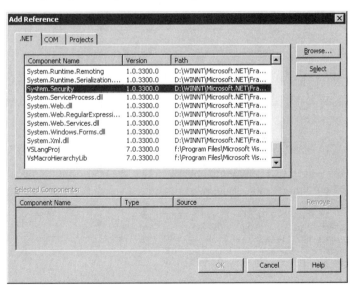

3. Switch to the Code View for the form and add the following Imports statements to the top of the module as follows, to support working with CLR role-based security:

```
Imports System
Imports System.Threading
Imports System.Security.Principal
```

4. Add the following controls to the form, with the following properties set:

   - Control Type: **Button**

   - Name: **btnCheckRole**

   - Text: **Check Result**

   - Control Type: **Textbox**

   - Name: **txtResult**

   - Text: (blank)

     a. Your form should look something like this:

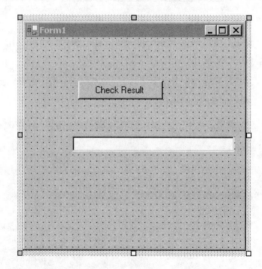

5. Add code to the button's Click event to check whether the user running the application is a member of the Administrators built-in group:

```
Private Sub btnCheckRole_Click (ByVal sender as _
        System.Object, ByVal e As System.EventArgs) _
        Handles btnCheckRole.Click
   AppDomain.CurrentDomain.SetPrincipalPolicy _
       (PrincipalPolicy.WindowsPrincipal)
```

```
If Thread.CurrentPrincipal.IsInRole _
    ("BUILTIN\Administrators") Then
    txtResult.Text = "User is a member of Administrators"
Else
    txtResult.Text = "User is NOT a member of Administrators"
End If

End Sub
```

6. Save, build, and run the application. Click the Check Result button on the form. The application will report whether the current user is a member of the Administrators group.

7. Close the application.

8. Log off that user account and log onto the other account (in Administrators if your original account was not in the group, or not in the group if your original account was).

9. Run the application again. Once more, the application will report whether the current user is a member of Administrators.

10. Close the application.

.NET Code Access Security

Prior to the advent of code access security, all code run under the same user ID ran with the same permissions, regardless of the origin or trustworthiness of the code. The reality of the component- and network-oriented computing world we live in today is that all code is not equally trustworthy. You have no way of knowing whether someone has maliciously modified the code located on an Internet server you don't control. You might not want intranet-based code accessing certain privileged resources of your local PC (such as its hard disk). That third-party class library might have latent bugs waiting to be discovered. Or a certain software publisher might be known for calling Beta version 3, Release 1.0. Any of these pieces of code might be calling your code and might be able to lure it into performing some action you never anticipated. For example, suppose you wrote a component that displays the most recent 100 lines in one of several log files and can optionally delete lines from the files. The name of the log file is a parameter passed to the component. You might want to allow local intranet-based callers of this component access to full functionality, but restrict the functionality available to Internet-based callers. That is, you might want to allow Internet-based callers to view the most recent 100 lines of only one of the log files but might want to deny them permission to use the deletion function.

Code-access security facilitates restricting the operation of code in these scenarios and more, based on what the CLR knows about the calling code. Code-access security is implemented by combining .NET permissions with the concepts of evidence, security policies, and code groups.

Evidence

.NET code-access security complements user and role-based security mechanisms by granting permissions to managed code based on evidence. *Evidence* is information identifying the code and its origin. Common types of evidence considered when evaluating (or administering) code-access security are listed in Table 9.9.

TABLE 9.9   Selected Evidence Used by Code Access Security

Evidence	Description
ApplicationDirectory	Directory containing the application
Publisher	Publisher (Authenticode signature) of the application
Site	Website of origin for an assembly that was loaded directly from a website
StrongName	Strong name of the assembly (as generated by sn.exe -k)
Url	URL of origin for the assembly (note that Site and Url are relevant only for applications run directly from a website, not those downloaded and then run locally)
Zone	Security zone from which the code originates (Trusted Sites, LocalIntranet, etc.)

Security Policies

How is this evidence connected to the permissions assigned to managed code? Permissions are granted via .NET security policies, which are administered by the .NET Framework Configuration tool (see Figure 9.7). This is accessed by choosing Start ➤ Settings ➤ Control

Panel ➢ Administrative Tools ➢ Microsoft .NET Framework Configuration, in Windows 2000, or by using command-line utilities such as `caspol.exe`.

FIGURE 9.7   The Microsoft .NET Framework Configuration tool

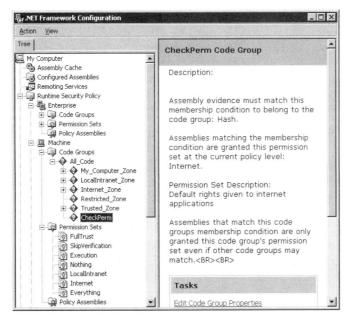

When a demand is made for a permission, the evidence is run through the security policy. A permission set is produced, which can be searched for the permission being demanded.

.NET provides four levels of policy, so that application behavior and security options can be customized at the appropriate granularity, and applications can be configured to behave differently from enterprise to enterprise or from machine to machine. The available policy levels are listed in Table 9.10.

TABLE 9.10   .NET Security Policy Levels

Level	Description
Enterprise	Affects all machines in an organization
Machine	Affects all users on the machine
User	Affects all appdomains in programs run by that user (user or administrator controlled)
ApplicationDomain	Affects a single appdomain (programmer controlled, not persisted to disk nor visible in the configuration tools that are used to maintain the other policy levels)

Each policy level has several components: a named `PermissionSet` collection, a code group hierarchy, and a list of assemblies. The named `PermissionSet` collection includes system-supplied permission sets such as those listed in Table 9.5, and additional user-defined permission sets. When policy settings at different levels conflict, the most restrictive setting takes effect. For example, if a machine-level policy disallows access to the system environment settings, and a user-level policy allows access to the environment, assemblies to which both of those policies apply will not have permission to access the system environment settings.

Code Groups

Within each security policy level are one or more code groups. These *code groups* (such as `All_Code`—) are used to indicate the evidence that must be present in order for the permissions listed for that code group to be granted to the assembly. They are used to organize and simplify permission assignments in much the same way as Windows groups are used to simplify permission assignments to multiple users. Code groups are organized into hierarchies, and each code group has a membership condition (a defined list of the evidence that must be present for code to be considered a member of that group), a permission set name, and additional attributes. If the membership condition is satisfied, then the rights listed in the named permission set are granted to the code.

In Exercise 9.2, you will explore code access security. By default, code originating locally is fully trusted. In order to create a situation in which some code access permissions will fail, you will create a code group specific to this assembly, by setting the code group's membership criteria to be "those assemblies having a hash code (that is, a statistically unique identifier) equal to the hash code of this assembly." Then you will assign that code group `Internet` rather than `FullTrust`. This will be sufficient to create conditions under which a demand for Write access to files on drive C: will fail, because the `Internet` permission set allows only restricted access to the local disk.

EXERCISE 9.2

Using Code-Access Security

1. Create a new Visual Studio .NET project by using the Windows Application project template. Name this project **CodeAccessSecurityExample**.

2. In the Solution Explorer, right-click the project name and choose Add Reference. In the Add Reference dialog box, select `System.Security`.

3. Switch to the Code View of the form and add `Imports` statements to the top of the module as follows, to support working with code access security permissions:

```
Imports System
Imports System.Security
Imports System.Security.Permissions
```

4. Add an additional Imports statement and assembly attribute following those Imports statements, to support strong-naming:

```
Imports System.Reflection
<Assembly: AssemblyKeyFile("C:\myKey.snk")>
```

5. Add the following controls to the form, with the following properties set:

    ▪ Control Type: **Button**

    ▪ Name: **btnCheckFileIOPermission**

    ▪ Text: **Check Permission**

    ▪ Control Type: **Textbox**

    ▪ Name: **txtResult1**

    ▪ Text: (blank)

    ▪ Control Type: **Textbox**

    ▪ Name: **txtResultBoth**

    ▪ Text: (blank)

    a. Your form should look something like this:

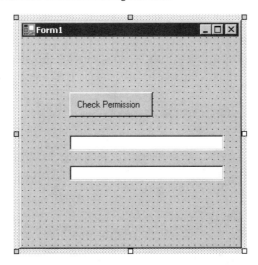

6. Add code to the button's Click event handler to perform two permission checks. You'll verify that the code can access a single file, c:\Ex92a.txt, for writing, and you'll verify that the code can access both c:\Ex92a.txt and c:\Ex92b.txt for writing. The following example

demonstrates how to issue the Demand method for multiple permissions by combining them via the Union method:

```
Private Sub btnCheckFileIOPermission_Click(ByVal sender as _
        System.Object, ByVal e As System.EventArgs) _
        Handles btnCheckFileIOPermission.Click

  Dim WritePermission1 As New FileIOPermission _
      (FileIOPermissionAccess.Write, "C:\Ex92a.txt")
  Dim WritePermission2 As New FileIOPermission _
      (FileIOPermissionAccess.Write, "C:\Ex92b.txt")

  Try
      WritePermission1.Demand()
      txtResult1.Text = "Demand of WritePermission1 succeeded."
  Catch
      txtResult1.Text = "Demand of WritePermission1 failed."
  End Try

  Try
      WritePermission1.Union(WritePermission2).Demand()
      txtResultBoth.Text = "Demand of both permissions succeeded."
  Catch
      txtResultBoth.Text = "Demand of both permissions failed."
  End Try
End Sub
```

7. Open a Visual Studio .NET command prompt and navigate to the C:\ directory. Use the strong-name utility to generate a key pair:

   C:\> sn.exe -k myKey.snk

8. Save, build, and run the application. Click the Check Permission button on the form. You should see results like the following, which report that both permission demands succeeded:

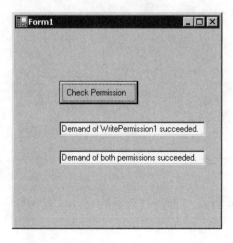

9. Close the running application.

10. Open the .NET Framework Configuration tool by choosing Start ➤ Settings ➤ Control Panel ➤ Administrative Tools ➤ Microsoft .NET Framework Configuration in Windows 2000 Professional. Create a new code group and assign it the appropriate permissions. To do this, expand Runtime Security Policy ➤ Machine ➤ Code Groups ➤ All_Code.

11. Right-click All_Code and choose New. Name the new code group **CheckPerm** and click the Next button.

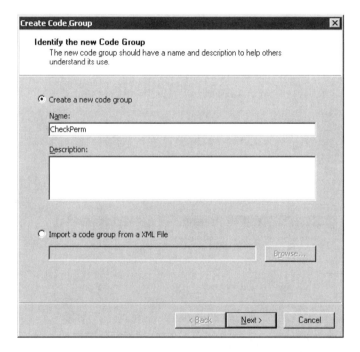

12. Choose Hash as the condition type, so you can easily set permissions that will apply to only a single assembly.

13. Select the SHA1 hashing algorithm, click Import, and browse to the assembly (EXE file) for this project, which should be in the project's \bin directory.

14. Click the Open button. The hash code should now be displayed. Before continuing, verify that your code group is configured as in the next graphic, and then click Next.

EXERCISE 9.2 *(continued)*

Note: Your hash code will vary from the one displayed in the following graphic.

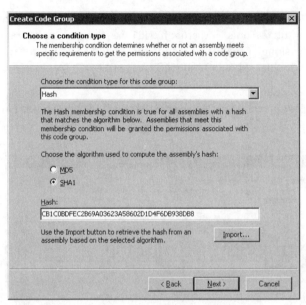

15. Select the Internet permission set to restrict what the app can do.

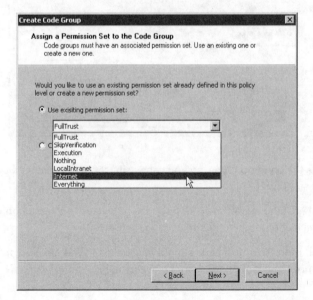

16. Click Finish.

EXERCISE 9.2 *(continued)*

17. Right-click the CheckPerm node and choose Properties.

18. On the General tab, select the check box labeled "This policy level will only have the permissions from the permission set associated with this code group" to restrict this assembly's permissions to only those specified here. Then click OK.

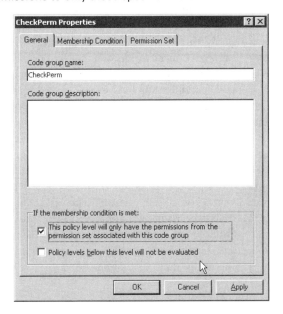

19. Run the application again. You should see results like the following, which indicate that both demands failed:

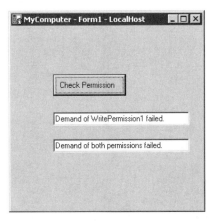

20. Save and close your project in Visual Studio .NET.

.NET Enterprise Services Role-Based Security

In addition to the role-based security implemented at the CLR level, .NET provides a second role-based security mechanism. This one is inherited from COM+ and defined in the `System .EnterpriseServices` namespace, which includes COM+ functionality for .NET Framework–based applications, as discussed in Chapter 2, "Creating and Managing Serviced Components."

This *.NET Enterprise Services role-based security* mechanism provides compatibility with legacy code, as well as an easy way to implement role-based security when roles are not defined as Windows groups. In this security model, roles are independently defined for each application, with each role representing a logical grouping of Windows groups and users that is meaningful to the application. Role names do not need to be unique across components, nor do they need to correspond to Windows group names. For example, both the QueryAPVendor and the QueryARCustomer components can define a Supervisors role, and each can include a different set of users and groups. The Supervisors role in the Accounts Payable application might include only Accounts Payable supervisors, and the Supervisors role in the Accounts Receivable application might include only Accounts Receivable supervisors. These roles and the list of Windows groups and users participating in them are stored in the COM+ catalog.

The CLR's role-based security can be extended to implement security based on criteria other than Windows group membership by using the `GenericPrincipal` object to manually code your own security checks. However, you should consider using the facilities built into .NET Enterprise Services instead of inventing your own application-specific role-based security. .NET Enterprise Services already allow for checking role assignments that do not correspond to Windows groups, and include useful features such as the Component Services tool (see Figure 9.8), which can be used to view and maintain the role memberships.

FIGURE 9.8 The Component Services tool

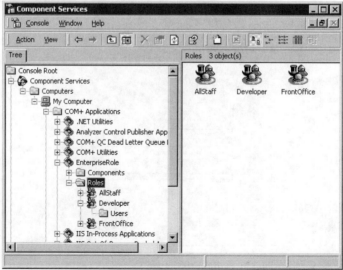

This tool is accessed by choosing Start ➤ Settings ➤ Control Panel ➤ Administrative Tools ➤ Component Services in Windows 2000 Professional.

In the Component Services tool, navigate down the tree in the left-hand pane and select the COM+ application whose roles you wish to configure. You can perform the following actions:

- Add and remove roles recognized by that application, using the `Roles` node

- Add and remove Windows groups and users from any role, using the `Users` node under that role

To use .NET Enterprise Services features, including role-based security, your component must derive from the `ServicedComponent` base class. Security-related methods are available in the `System.EnterpriseServices.ContextUtil` class. To check whether .NET Enterprise Services' role-based security is enabled, check the value of the Boolean `ContextUtil`.`IsSecurityEnabled` property. The calling user's role membership can be checked either imperatively, via the `ContextUtil.IsCallerInRole` method, or declaratively, via attributes.

For example, to imperatively verify that the calling user is in the role HRstaff, you might use the code in Listing 9.6.

Listing 9.6: .NET Enterprise Services Role-Based Security

```
Imports System
Imports System.EnterpriseServices

Public Class EnterpriseRoleExample
    Inherits ServicedComponent

Private Sub CheckRole()
   If (ContextUtil.IsSecurityEnabled) Then
    If (ContextUtil.IsCallerInRole ("HRstaff")) Then


        ' perform whatever actions require HRstaff role
      End If
   End If

End Sub


End Class
```

Alternatively, you can check the .NET Enterprise Services role membership declaratively. To require the caller to be in the HRstaff role, simply notate the assembly or method with a security role attribute: `SecurityRoleAttribute`. The first parameter of this attribute is the name of the role, and the second parameter is a Boolean indicating whether the built-in group Everyone is automatically added to the members included in that role. For example:

```
<SecurityRoleAttribute("HRstaff", False)> _
Private Sub CheckRole
...
```

Using .NET Framework Cryptography

When writing services that communicate over the network or that persist data to servers accessed by potentially thousands of Internet users, you might want to protect the confidentiality of some or all of that data by using cryptography. Although this is the traditional purpose for encryption, it is not the only reason to employ cryptography. In addition to preserving data confidentiality, cryptography can also provide message integrity (proof that the message has not been altered since it was sent) and authentication (proof that the person who claims to be the message sender really did send the message).

In this section, we discuss types of cryptographic algorithms available in the .NET Framework and criteria for deciding how and when to use encryption in your application.

Understanding the Types of Cryptographic Algorithms

Three major varieties of algorithms are used in cryptography:

- Symmetric encryption
- Asymmetric encryption
- Hashing algorithms

Traditional encryption algorithms use *symmetric cryptography*, with the same key being used to encrypt and decrypt data. Any user possessing the shared key can use it to encrypt or decrypt messages.

Newer algorithms often use *asymmetric cryptography*, sometimes called public key cryptography, which uses different keys to encrypt and decrypt data. Each user is issued one or more pairs of keys. One key in the pair is kept private to that user, and the other key is made available publicly to others. A characteristic of asymmetric encryption algorithms is that either the private key or the public key can be used to encrypt data, and once encrypted, the data can be decrypted only by providing the other key. Users can encrypt data with the intended receiver's public key, and know that the only person who can decrypt it is the one holding the private key from that pair. This ensures that the content of the message cannot be discovered by unauthorized individuals.

Additionally, a user can encrypt data with the private key from their key pair, and then that data can be decrypted by anyone with that user's public key. Although this does not provide confidentiality (because anyone and everyone could have the user's public key), it does provide another benefit not available with symmetric encryption—a way for the receiver of the data to verify that the data originated with the person who claims to be the source of it. If the recipient can successfully decrypt the data by using the sender's public key, the recipient knows that the data had to have been encrypted using the sender's private key and has not been changed since originally encrypted. This newer style of cryptography is the technology that enables the .NET platform's strong names and Authenticode signatures to identify the origin of an assembly and verify that the file containing the code has not been altered since originally created. The downside to asymmetric cryptography is that it is much less efficient to perform than symmetric cryptography, thus necessitating that developers find creative ways to gain the advantages of asymmetric cryptography without vastly increasing encryption/decryption overhead.

Hashing algorithms are not truly encryption algorithms, because unlike symmetric and asymmetric cryptography, hashing algorithms are one-way doors. You send a large set of data through a hashing algorithm, and it quickly produces a statistically unique "signature" consisting of a smaller amount of data. For instance, a hashing algorithm run over an assembly might produce a hash result only 128 or 160 bits long, depending on the algorithm employed. Because multiple sets of data might hash to the same result, it is not possible to "decrypt" a hash value into its original larger set of data. Because it is unlikely that other sets of data that happened to hash to the same result would appear to be valid assemblies, hashing algorithms can be used as a shortcut in the computation of digital signatures for items such as assemblies—it's necessary only to encrypt the hash value, rather than the entire assembly file, using asymmetric encryption. Typically, the hash value for a set of data is computed before the data is distributed and then sent with the data to its intended recipients. Before the data is used, the recipient computes the hash value for the received data and verifies that it is identical to the original hash value supplied by the sender. Hash values are used as a unique identifier for assemblies, as you saw in Exercise 9.2 when using an assembly's SHA1 hash value to uniquely identify it for a code group. They are also used frequently for authentication, so that the system can avoid transmitting or storing actual passwords.

Choosing an Encryption Algorithm

Many criteria can come into play when choosing which type of encryption and which particular algorithm of that type to employ. Some of these criteria are related to business guidelines (your organization might have lists of approved cryptographic algorithms), and some are related to what makes the best sense technically.

For example, encryption algorithms are available in various strengths, generally measured by the estimated length of time required for someone to break the encryption and find some way of decrypting the data. There is generally a trade-off between performance and strength—the stronger the algorithm or longer the key length, the longer it takes to encrypt the data.

Be aware that some cryptographic algorithms such as TripleDES are available only if the high encryption pack has been installed on the system on which the encryption is being performed. The AES (also called by its original name, Rijndael) algorithm is available on any system on which the .NET Framework is installed.

Designing an Encryption Strategy

There are several ways to use cryptography from within .NET applications. One way is to take advantage of .NET's built-in support for *Secure Sockets Layer (SSL)* encryption. You can run XML Web services, .NET Remoting, and anything else that can be tunneled via HTTP (such as custom communications protocols) over an SSL-encrypted HTTP connection, with very little extra programmer effort.

 The details of using encryption with different types of services are covered in Chapters 10 and 11.

To use SSL, the server must have a digital certificate, obtained from a certificate authority such as VeriSign, and this certificate must be installed into IIS through the website properties dialog. If your server hosts virtual sites and you want to use SSL on those virtual sites, you must first obtain and install a digital certificate for the system's default website and then install the certificates for the virtual sites.

If you require more control over how and when the encryption is performed (perhaps for performance reasons, you want to encrypt only a subset of the data to be transported), can't use SSL due to firewall or political restrictions (the HTTPS port might be blocked at your organization), or want to encrypt data for storage rather than network transmission, it is necessary to use the .NET Framework's cryptography methods, discussed next. For example, when designing your encryption approach for an XML Web service, you might choose to encrypt selected fields transmitted in SOAP headers, or the body of the message, or the body of only the messages carrying sensitive information such as credit card number, and so on.

Using *System.Security.Cryptography*

The .NET Framework provides a rich selection of symmetric encryption, asymmetric encryption, and hashing abstract algorithm classes, each with one or more physical implementations. The algorithm classes are listed in Table 9.11.

TABLE 9.11 Selected Cryptographic Algorithms Available in the .NET Framework

Algorithm	Type
SHA1	Hashing
SHA256	Hashing
MD5	Hashing
TripleDES	Symmetric
RC2	Symmetric
DES	Symmetric
Rijndael	Symmetric
RSA	Asymmetric
DSA	Asymmetric

Several classes from the System.Security.Cryptography namespace are useful in implementing cryptography in your applications. They are summarized in Table 9.12.

TABLE 9.12   Cryptography-Related Classes and Interfaces Available in the .NET Framework

Class	Type
cryptoprovider	One of the classes that exists for each type of cryptographic algorithm supported by the .NET Framework—for example, RijndaelManaged or DESCryptoServiceProvider
ICryptoTransform	The interface through which encryption and decryption is performed
CryptoStream	The class associating your data with the ICryptoTransform function you wish to perform

The object corresponding to the specific cryptographic algorithm class of interest, such as TripleDES, is necessary because that object is the basic one required to perform cryptography by using the specified algorithm. The Encryptor object associated with the algorithm class is used to obtain the actual encryption functions (conversely, the Decryptor object is used to obtain the decryption functions). Finally, the *CryptoStream* object links the output stream and Encryptor to the input stream, and when the CryptoStream.Write method is called, results in encrypted text being written to the specified output stream.

The use of the asymmetric encryption functions is beyond the scope of the exam. However, you should be familiar with the basic steps in using a symmetric algorithm to encrypt an incoming plaintext string into an outgoing ciphertext string, which can then be sent over the network, persisted to the system's hard disk, and so on. Here is the general procedure to follow:

1. Create an instance of the Cryptographic Service Provider (CSP).

2. Create a stream to hold the output of the encryption (file or memory stream, as needed).

3. Create an Encryptor object (the encryption-oriented CryptoTransform) by using the Create-Encryptor method of the object you created in step 1. Pass it your desired key and algorithm initialization vector (also known as IV, which is used to modify the behavior of the encryption algorithm) to control the encrypted output.

4. Create a CryptoStream object that can write encrypted data. Pass it the output ciphertext stream and Encryptor objects created in steps 2 and 3.

5. Call the CryptoStream.Write method, passing to it the plaintext data to be encrypted as a byte array, the transform to be used (if any), and the length of the data.

6. Call the CryptoStream.FlushFinalBlock method to ensure that all encrypted data is written to the CryptoStream object, if required.

7. Convert the output stream into the desired form (string, byte array, or other form).

    You will use the cryptography capabilities of the .NET Framework in Chapter 11 when exploring SOAP data encryption.

Summary

In this chapter, you learned about the security features available on the .NET platform. We covered the following topics:

- An introduction to security concepts
- Security features provided by the CLR and .NET Framework, including the security-related namespaces and authentication mechanisms available in .NET
- Security features provided at the operating system level
- The three types of permissions (code access, identity, and role-based) and how to work with common permissions
- Common named permission sets and how to work with permission sets
- The three code security models provided by .NET: CLR role-based security, .NET code access security, and .NET Enterprise Services role-based security
- Details about CLR role-based security, such as its use of Identity and Principal objects in determining whether the user running the application is a member of the specified role, ways to check role membership, and use of Windows groups as roles
- Details about code access security—for example, that it grants permissions based on evidence provided by the code assembly and the code's host, and the contents of security policies, which include code groups and permission lists
- Details about .NET Enterprise Services role-based security
- Cryptography, including when to use explicitly-coded encryption instead of SSL, and the steps required to implement symmetric encryption of an input plaintext string

Exam Essentials

Be familiar with the types of authentication offered in .NET. Know the characteristics of the most popular authentication methods. Know that Basic, Digest, and Integrated Windows Security are authentication methods supplied by IIS.

Know how to work with Permission and PermissionSet objects. Know the three types of permissions (code access, identity, and role-based). Know how to demand permissions by using both declarative and imperative code. Know how and why to assert, deny, and permit only code access permissions. Know how to combine permissions with the Union and Intersect methods. Know how to use AddPermission, RemovePermission, and SetPermission methods to manipulate permission sets.

Understand and know how to work with the three code security models provided by .NET. Know how CLR role-based security uses Identity and Principal objects to determine role membership, and how to check role membership via imperative Demand, imperative IsInRole, and declarative Demand. Know that code access security grants permissions by examining evidence and comparing that to the evidence indicated for security policies, and that the permissions granted to code are the most restrictive of those granted at all policy levels combined. Know that .NET Enterprise Services role-based security requires your class to inherit from the `Serviced-Component` class, how to use the IsSecurityEnabled property of the `SecurityCallContextObject` to verify that .NET Enterprise Services role-based security is enabled, and how to check role membership via `IsCallerInRole` or declaratively, via attributes.

Understand the basics of the cryptographic features provided or used by .NET and know how to work with them.   Know how to decide when to use SSL-based encryption and when to use explicitly coded encryption. Know the steps required to encrypt a data item.

Key Terms

Before you take the exam, be certain you are familiar with the following terms:

asymmetric cryptography	permissions
authentication	Principal object
authorization	role
CLR role-based security	role-based security
code access permissions	role-based security permissions
code access security	security policies
code groups	Secure Sockets Layer (SSL)
cryptography	stack walk
`CryptoStream` class	STRIDE
declarative	strong name
evidence	symmetric cryptography
Identity object	`System.Security` namespace
identity permissions	`System.Security.Cryptography` namespace
imperative	`System.Security.Permissions` namespace
impersonation	`System.Security.Policy` namespace
.NET Enterprise Services role-based security	`System.Security.Principal` namespace
permission sets	

Review Questions

1. What is the term used to describe the act of presenting user-furnished credentials to the system, which evaluates them and assigns an identity?

   A. Authorization

   B. Permission

   C. Authentication

   D. Integration

2. Which of the following approaches to security in .NET uses the `Thread.CurrentPrincipal` `.IsInRole` method to verify that the current principal is a member of a specific role?

   A. CLR role-based security

   B. .NET Enterprise Services security

   C. Thread safety security

   D. Code access security

3. To automatically have a method verify that it has permission to access the system environment settings, and throw a security exception if it does not, which of the following attributes would you apply to the method?

   A. `<EnvironmentPermission(SecurityAction.Assert, Unrestricted = True)>`

   B. `<EnvironmentPermissionAttribute (SecurityAction.RequestMinimum, Unrestricted = True)>`

   C. `<EnvironmentPermissionAttribute(SecurityAction.Demand, Unrestricted = True)>`

   D. `<EnvironmentPermission(SecurityAction.Demand, Unrestricted = True)>`

4. You are designing an XML Web service that requires passing custom authentication information from the client to the server. The service includes a method that returns a small amount of sensitive data to the client and several methods that return a large amount of nonconfidential data. Which approach to encryption might offer the best performance, while preserving the confidentiality of sensitive information?

   A. Use a custom approach, encrypting the custom authentication headers and the bodies of the messages that return sensitive data.

   B. Use a custom approach, encrypting just the authentication headers.

   C. Use SSL, to automatically encrypt all traffic related to the Web service.

   D. No special approach is required. Sensitive data is automatically encrypted when sent as part of a SOAP message.

5. Which of the following authentication types presents the user with a web page requesting his credentials and then evaluates the credentials furnished by the user when the page is submitted?

A. Basic authentication

B. HTML authentication

C. Integrated Windows authentication

D. Forms authentication

6. Which of the following best describes .NET Enterprise Services role-based security?

A. It is no longer used, because it has been superseded by the CLR's role-based security mechanism.

B. It requires that users be assigned to Windows groups, to specify the roles to which they belong.

C. It can be used only when you are using other Enterprise Services such as transactions.

D. It requires that classes using it inherit from the `ServicedComponent` class.

7. Which of the following is not a typical step in the encryption of a data item's .NET cryptographic functions?

A. Call the `CryptoStream.Write` method to perform the data encryption.

B. Call the `CryptoStream.Encrypt` method to perform the data encryption.

C. Use the cryptographic algorithm class's `CreateEncryptor` method to create an Encryptor object.

D. Ensure that all data is processed by the encryption algorithm and sent to the output stream by calling the `CryptoStream.FlushFinalBlock` method.

8. You are designing a class that uses code access security permissions to verify that the code has permission to perform certain operations, such as calling a small amount of unmanaged code (because that functionality is not available natively in .NET). This class can be called from a wide variety of sources, some more trusted than others, but it must always have permission to call the unmanaged code even if its callers do not have permission to call unmanaged code themselves. How can this be accomplished?

A. Ensure that all possible calling code acquires the permission to call unmanaged code.

B. Use the `<TrustedClassAttribute>` to indicate that permissions granted (or not granted) to methods higher in the call stack should not affect the permissions in effect for this class.

C. This cannot be done, because code access security permissions are always the intersection of all permissions granted to the current stack frame and all other active method stack frames.

D. Ensure that this assembly is granted the right to call unmanaged code and then use the `CodeAccessPermission.Assert` method to indicate to the code access security system that its demands for that right are to succeed regardless of caller permissions.

9. Which of the following tools are used to administer .NET code access security polices?

   A. Microsoft .NET Framework Configuration tool

   B. User Manager for Domains

   C. Component Services tool

   D. `secutil.exe`

10. Which of the following is a feature of .NET that helps guard against buffer overflow vulnerabilities?

   A. Authentication

   B. Cryptographic classes

   C. Code verification

   D. Role-based security

11. Which method of the `CodeAccessPermission` class would you use to specify that the code can access only the specified printer and no others?

   A. `RevertDeny`

   B. `Permit`

   C. `Subset`

   D. `PermitOnly`

12. You are developing a `serviced component` that performs some sensitive database operations. You have assigned some users to a role called DBA, and all users to a role called AllUsers in the Component Services tool. You do not have access to Windows groups administration, and no Windows group by the name of DBA exists. You want to ensure that only users assigned the DBA role can access the component methods that you consider sensitive. How would you implement this protection?

   A. Place the attribute `<SecurityRoleAttribute("DBA", False)>` on the methods considered sensitive.

   B. Place the attribute `<SecurityRole ("DBA", True)>` on the methods considered sensitive.

   C. Remove all roles except DBA from the component by using the Component Services tool.

   D. Call `Permission.Demand`, requesting DBA role membership, at the beginning of each sensitive method call.

13. Which of the following statements are true about the `Principal` object? (Choose all that apply.)

   A. Available principal types include `GenericPrincipal`, `WindowsPrincipal`, and `CustomPrincipal`.

   B. It is contained within an Identity object.

   C. It contains information about the roles for which the user is authorized.

   D. It contains an Identity object.

14. What is a hashing algorithm used for?

    A. It provides secure encryption of data.

    B. It generates a statistically unique signature of data.

    C. It decrypts data, when given the proper key string.

    D. It is used to encrypt private keys used in asymmetric cryptography.

15. Which of the following statements are true regarding the effective permissions for an assembly? (Choose all that apply.)

    A. If the assembly asserts permission to access a data file, the access is allowed even if it is disallowed at the Windows operating system level by ACLs that deny access to the file.

    B. If `PermitOnly` is called twice within a stack frame, the second call to `PermitOnly` adds to the effective permissions.

    C. They might depend on the origin of the assembly from which the current assembly was called.

    D. If the assembly asserts permission to access a data file, and access is disallowed at the Windows operating system level by ACLs, attempts to access the file in that assembly will not succeed.

Answers to Review Questions

1. **C.** Authentication is the process of presenting user-supplied credentials to the system, which evaluates them and assigns an identity based on the information provided. A permission is a specific right held by the application. Authorization is used to verify that an application has been granted permission to perform a specific action. Integration is not a .NET security term.

2. **A.** CLR role-based security can use the `IsInRole` method or demand a specific `Principal-Permission` to verify that the current principal is a member of a role. .NET Enterprise Services security uses the `InCallerInRole` method to check role membership. Code access security is used to check security based on the characteristics and origin of an assembly, not roles. Thread safety security is not a .NET security model.

3. **C.** The `Demand` method can be used in a method attribute to verify that the method has a particular code access permission. Code access security attribute names are of the format *Permission*`Attribute`, so the first and last answers cannot be correct. `RequestMinimum` can be used at the assembly level to require permissions.

4. **A.** You should use a custom approach in which the authentication-related headers and bodies of the messages containing confidential data would be the most efficient. Encrypting just the authentication headers would not preserve the confidentiality of any message data. Using SSL to encrypt all components of every message is not the most efficient approach because SSL can be resource intensive, and one of the messages returns a large amount of data that is not considered sensitive. Sensitive data is not automatically encrypted when sent as part of a SOAP message.

5. **D.** Forms authentication is a .NET authentication method presenting the user with a web page requesting credentials, and evaluating those credentials when the page is submitted. Basic authentication is a Windows authentication method that requests user credentials via a dialog and transmits them across the network to the domain controller in unencrypted form (unless being run over SSL to encrypt it) for validation. Integrated Windows authentication is another Windows authentication method, which is an improvement over Basic authentication because it does not send unencrypted credentials across the network when requesting that the domain controller validate them. There is no such thing as HTML authentication.

6. **D.** .NET Enterprise Services role-based security requires that classes using it inherit from the `ServicedComponent` class, as with any class taking advantage of Enterprise Services such as transactions and message queuing. It does not require that the programmer access any other .NET Enterprise Services in their code. It peacefully coexists with the newer CLR role-based security model; each has advantages and disadvantages that make one or the other the best choice in a specific circumstance. Unlike the CLR role-based security model, .NET Enterprise Services role-based security enables users to be assigned to roles that do not correspond to Windows groups.

7. **B.** Encryption is performed via the `CryptoStream.Write` method, not its `Encrypt` method. The first step in encrypting data is usually to create an instance of your selected cryptographic algorithm class. Next, use that class's `CreateEncryptor` method to create an Encryptor object. Then create a `CryptoStream` object, passing the cryptographic algorithm object and Encryptor object as parameters. Then call the `CryptoStream.Write` method, passing the plaintext, to encrypt it. Finally, call the `CryptoStream.FlushFinalBlock` method to finalize the encryption.

8.   D.   Ensure that the assembly is granted the permission to call unmanaged code; then use the `CodeAccessPermission.Assert` method to indicate that its demands for that right should succeed, regardless of callers' permissions.

9.   A.   The Microsoft .NET Framework Configuration tool is used to view and update .NET code access security policies. User Manager for Domains is used to manage users and group memberships. The Component Services tool is used to administer application roles for .NET Enterprise Services role-based security. The command-line utility `secutil.exe` is used to extract public-key information from an assembly; although this is a .NET security function somewhat related to code access security (because it accesses evidence), it is not used to administer code access security policies.

10.   C.   Code verification ensures assembly integrity and performs runtime checking of data types when assignments are made, to minimize opportunities for buffer overflows to occur. Cryptographic classes help ensure data privacy, sender authentication, and data integrity, but do not protect against buffer overflows. Authentication is used to verify the identity of the caller; although this helps keep unauthorized users out of your system and thus might reduce opportunities for malicious attacks, it offers no guarantees that an authorized user won't accidentally trigger a buffer overflow. Role-based security involves checking the effective identity and the roles to which it belongs, and deciding to run, or not run, code based on the results of that check.

11.   D.   The `PermitOnly` method is used to indicate the only permissions that are granted to the frame. `RevertDeny` removes any deny requests currently in effect for the frame. `Permit` and `Subset` are not valid methods of the `CodeAccessPermission` class.

12.   A.   Place the `<SecurityRoleAttribute("DBA", False)>` attribute on sensitive methods. There is no such attribute as `SecurityRole`. If you removed the AllUsers role from the component, users not assigned to the DBA role would not be able to access any features of the component. Because the scenario calls for the use of COM+ style role-based security, rather than the newer CLR-based implementation, you cannot use `Permission.Demand` to verify role membership.

13.   A, C, D.   `GenericPrincipal`, `WindowsPrincipal`, and `CustomPrincipal` are all valid principal types. A `Principal` object contains information about the roles for which the user is authorized. It also contains an Identity object. It is not contained within an Identity object.

14.   B.   A hashing algorithm is used to generate a statistically unique signature, called a hash value, for a set of data. The signature is normally much smaller in size than the data for which the hash value was computed. It does not encrypt or decrypt data. Because a hashing algorithm is not an encryption algorithm, it is not used for the encryption of private keys.

15.   B, C.   If the assembly asserts permission to access a data file, and access to that data file is disallowed at the Windows operating system level by ACLs, attempts to access the file in that assembly will not succeed. Effective permissions can be influenced by many types of evidence provided at runtime, including the origin of the assembly's caller. Permissions asserted in a Visual Basic .NET program cannot override permissions denied at the Windows operating system level. `PermitOnly` can be called only once within a stack frame.

Chapter

10

Deploying, Securing, and Configuring Windows-Based Applications

---

MICROSOFT EXAM OBJECTIVES COVERED IN THIS CHAPTER:

✓ Plan the deployment of and deploy a Windows service, a serviced component, and a .NET Remoting object.

✓ Create a setup program that installs a Windows service, a serviced component, a .NET Remoting object.

  ▪ Register components and assemblies.

✓ Implement versioning.

✓ Plan, configure, and deploy side-by-side deployments and applications.

✓ Configure security for a Windows service, a serviced component, and a .NET Remoting object.

  ▪ Configure authentication type. Authentication types include Windows authentication, Microsoft .NET Passport, custom authentication, and none.

  ▪ Configure and control authorization. Authorization methods include file-based authorization and URL-based authorization.

  ▪ Configure and implement identity management.

After you have designed, created, and successfully tested your application, you will need to deploy and configure it for the production environment. A finished application should be easy to install for the administrator or user deploying your application. This will make your life easier because you might not be there or might not want to have to step users of your application through the install process.

Creating a deployment package can vary because your application might consist of Windows services, serviced components, .NET Remoting objects, or XML Web services. In this chapter, you will look at deploying and configuring Windows services, serviced components, and .NET Remoting objects. You will also look at specific security considerations and configurations for each of these technologies.

XML Web services are covered in Chapter 11, "Deploying and Securing XML Web Services."

Creating a Setup Project by Using Visual Studio .NET

You can have complete control over the deployment of an application to a user's computer by creating a *Windows Installer setup project*, or Windows Installer project for short. A Windows Installer project uses Visual Studio .NET to create a setup file and a *Microsoft Installer file* (.msi) that will install with Windows Installer (msiexec.exe). This is the customary way to package and install a Windows application on Windows, but you can also use it to package and deploy an ASP.NET application to a web server or group of web servers.

MSI files can also be published to Add/Remove Programs in the Control Panel console and deployed by using Active Directory software deployment policies. If they are wrapped in a cabinet file (.cab), you can deploy them via Internet Explorer. Creating a Microsoft Installer file gives you full control over the location of files and what needs to be put into the global assembly cache (GAC) or the Registry.

You can use the Windows Installer project to install, repair, or uninstall applications. This is the most effective way to make sure your users can install and uninstall an application that has shortcuts, Start menu items, Registry entries, and assemblies installed in the GAC. Your applications and controls written with Visual Studio .NET require that the .NET Framework is installed on any computer to which you distribute them.

In this section you will learn to configure a Windows Installer project and then look at the editors that you will use to build a setup project.

Choosing Setup Templates and Configuring Properties

You create a Windows Installer project in Visual Studio .NET in a way similar to creating code projects in Visual Studio .NET. There are templates for each of the projects that you can create in the Setup And Deployment Projects section of the Visual Studio .NET Project Templates dialog box, which is shown in Figure 10.1. They are as follows:

Setup Project   The *Setup Project* template is the standard project that will create the familiar deployment package with a `setup.exe` file that the user can run to start the install. This installation option will generate MSI files by default for packaging the application files. The application will install into a folder under the `Program Files` folder on the system. You can also specify any Registry settings and location of Start menu and Desktop shortcuts, install components in the GAC, install other files or setup projects that might be needed, and even do conditional installs based on the operating system. This is the option that you will use to deploy a Windows application to a client computer.

FIGURE 10.1   Setup and Deployment Projects templates in Visual Studio .NET

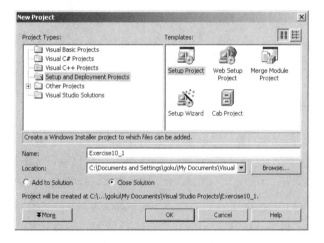

Web Setup Project   The *Web Setup Project* template is similar to the Setup Project template except that the Web Setup Project installs in a virtual directory under the `Virtual Root` directory on a web server as opposed to the file system. It is used to generate packages for installing web applications.

Merge Module Project   The *Merge Module Project* template packages assemblies that might be shared by other setup projects. When this project is built, it will generate an `.msm` file that can be added to other setup projects. The MSM file contains all the files and Registry settings and the setup configuration for installing the assemblies. They must be used from within a setup project and cannot be run alone. Merge modules should never be modified after they are distributed because this can lead to dependency and versioning problems. You should create a new merge module for each version of your assembly.

Setup Wizard   The Setup Wizard template helps you get started by providing a wizard that generates a setup project.

Cab Project   The Cab Project template enables you to package ActiveX controls for downloading into Internet Explorer. This is used to support legacy applications or to wrap an MSI file for distribution via Internet Explorer.

After you decide which project you will use, you need to set the deployment project properties to tell Visual Studio .NET how to build the deployment project. This is done in the deployment project Property Pages dialog box, shown in Figure 10.2. To open this dialog box, right-click the deployment project name in the Solution Explorer window and choose Properties.

FIGURE 10.2   The deployment project Property Pages dialog box

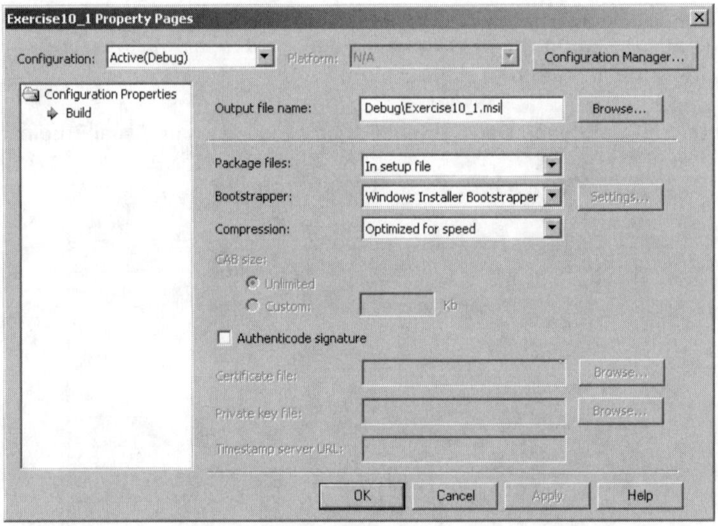

In the deployment project Property Pages dialog box, you can set the following:

Output File Name   This is the name and location of the Windows Installer file that will be built from the deployment project. By default, this is the debug\projectname.msi or .msm, depending on whether it is a setup project (Web or Windows) or merge module, respectively.

Package Files   This is the type of packaging you want for Windows Installer. The options are as follows:

As Loose Uncompressed Files   The application's files are copied to the directory along with the MSI file.

In Setup File   The application's files are put inside the MSI file.

In Cabinet File(s)   The application's files are put into one or more cabinet files that can be distributed across multiple disks.

Bootstrapper   Visual Studio .NET uses Windows Installer 2, which comes with Windows XP. If you plan to install the application to an older version of Windows, you will need to include a bootstrapper. A bootstrapper will first install Windows Installer 2 and then install the application that was packaged in the Windows Installer files. The options are as follows:

None   Don't deploy a bootstrapper.

Windows Installer Bootstrapper   Include the bootstrapper in this install.

Web Bootstrapper   Include a version of the bootstrapper that can be installed from a web server with the install.

Settings   This will become available if you select Web Bootstrapper in the Bootstrapper list box. This enables you to set the location of where the Windows Installer's files and your application's files are downloaded.

Compression   This indicates the amount of compression you want for the In Setup File or In Cabinet File(s) options under the Package Files section. The options are as follows:

Optimized For Speed   Results in less compression, meaning that the files will be larger but the install will go more quickly.

Optimized For Size   Results in more compression, meaning the files will be smaller but the install will go more slowly.

None   Results in no compression being applied to the files.

CAB Size   Use this option for deploying the application from multiple disks. You can set the maximum size for each cabinet file generated and then copy them to each disk. The options are as follows:

Unlimited   Only one cabinet file is created.

Custom   The maximum size of each cabinet file in kilobytes (KB).

Authenticode Signature   This determines whether the files in the deployment project are signed. This provides the client with a mechanism for determining if the code came from a certain company or individual. The signature will aid them in determining how much to trust the package.

Certificate File   Set this to the Authenticode certificate file (.spc), which can be obtained from a certificate authority. You can obtain a certificate from your own certificate authority by setting up a certificate server on Windows 2000 Server or Windows 2003 Server (best for an intranet or extranet situation), or from a third-party certificate authority such as VeriSign whose public key is already shipped with each Internet browser (best for some extranets or the Internet). A certificate is basically a public key and some contact information that has been signed by the certificate authority, which is trusted by the end user. The public key in the certificate can then be used to verify that the file really came from the vendor who claims to be shipping the application.

Private Key File Set this to the private key file (.pvt) that will be used to sign the package. This must be the private key that matches the public key contained in the Authenticode certificate file.

Timestamp Server URL This is the server providing the timestamp used to sign the setup files.

Using the Setup Project Editors

After you configure your setup application, you need to tell the installer how to install the application on the system. Visual Studio .NET provides six setup project editors to configure your Windows Installer project. You can switch editors by using the toolbar at the top of the Solution Explorer window or the View option in the pop-up menu for the setup project shown in Figure 10.3, or by selecting the icon for each editor at the top of the Solution Explorer window while your setup project is selected.

FIGURE 10.3 Using the View option to select an editor

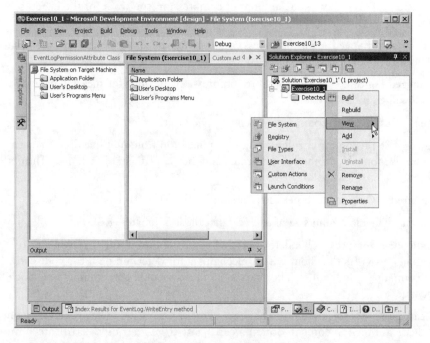

Use any of the following six editors to add to or modify the contents of the setup project and to control where you want the files of your application to be placed:

File System Editor Lets you create the directories and place files where they will be installed. You can also choose to install files in special locations such as the desktop or GAC.

Custom Actions Editor Lets you create code called custom actions to be run during the installation or in response to four stages of the install.

File Types Editor   Lets you create associations for file extensions that your application will use. For example, if you create an application that uses .xyz extensions, you can associate all files with .xyz extensions with your application's executable.

Launch Conditions Editor   Lets you set conditions that have to be met before the application will install on a computer. For example, if your application depends on another application or on a specific version of an application, you can search for files and Registry keys specific to the application; if they are not found, the associated launch condition will present an error message.

Registry Editor   Lets you specify the Registry keys and values that your application will write to the Registry on installation.

User Interface Editor   Lets you customize the appearance of the Installation Wizard. For example, you could customize the install screens with your company's logo.

Using the File System Editor

The default editor is the File System Editor, so we'll cover it first. By using the File System Editor, you can add new folders, project outputs (such as source files, the DLLs generated by the project, debug symbols, or all content files), files, or assemblies to the setup project. Figure 10.4 shows the File System Editor.

FIGURE 10.4   The File System Editor

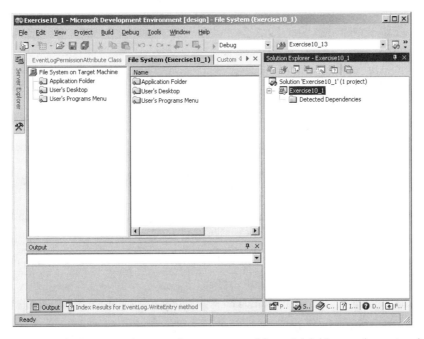

If you are using the Setup Project template, you can add special folders to the project by right-clicking the File System On Target Machine node on the project tree and choosing Add Special Folder ➢ *special_folder_name*. Figure 10.5 shows this pop-up menu choice. Special folders represent various locations in the Windows operating system—for example, the GAC or the Start menu. You can then put files in these folders to have the installer deploy them there.

FIGURE 10.5   The pop-up menu for the special folders

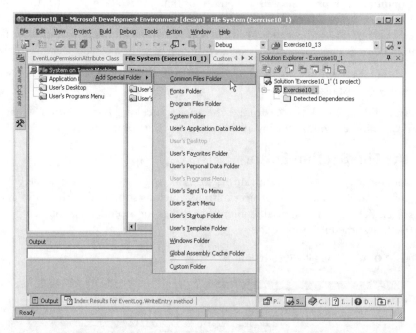

Table 10.1 lists the special folders and their typical locations on a Windows XP machine.

TABLE 10.1   The Special Folders

Folder	Description
Application Folder	The application's folder; usually located in the C:\Program Files folder, but the user can specify another folder on install.
Common Files Folder	The application's folder for components between applications, usually located in the C:\Program Files\Common folder.
Fonts Folder	The folder containing the system fonts, usually located in C:\Windows\fonts.
Module Retargetable Folder	The alternative custom folder you want a merge module to install into.
Program Files Folder	The program files folder, which represents the location that Microsoft recommends for installing software on Windows. It is usually located at C:\Program Files.

TABLE 10.1 The Special Folders *(continued)*

Folder	Description
System Folder	The Windows system folder, where shared DLLs and files are installed, usually located in C:\Windows\System32.
User's Application Data Folder	A per-user folder that can store application data, usually located in C:\Documents and Settings*user_name*\Application Data.
User's Desktop	The per-user folder representing the Windows Desktop, usually located in C:\Documents and Settings*user_name*\Desktop.
User's Favorites Folder	A per-user folder representing the user's Favorites folder, usually located in C:\Documents and Settings*user_name*\Favorites.
User's Personal Data Folder	A per-user folder representing the user's My Documents folder, usually located in C:\Documents and Settings*user_name*\My Documents.
User's Programs Menu	A per-user folder representing the user's Programs in the Start menu, usually located in C:\Documents and Settings*user_name*\Start Menu\Programs.
User's Send To Menu	A per-user folder representing the user's Send To pop-up menu item, usually located in C:\Documents and Settings*user_name*\SendTo.
User's Start Menu	A per-user folder representing the user's Start menu, usually located in C:\Documents and Settings*user_name*\Start Menu.
User's Template Folder	A per-user folder representing a folder that contains the user's document templates, usually located in C:\Documents and Settings*user_name*\Templates.
Windows Folder	The system's root directory, usually located in C:\Windows.
Custom Folder	A folder that you want created on the target system.

Using the Custom Actions Editor

The Custom Actions Editor, shown in Figure 10.6, enables you to create code to respond to four events:

- Install
- Commit
- Rollback
- Uninstall

FIGURE 10.6 The Custom Actions Editor

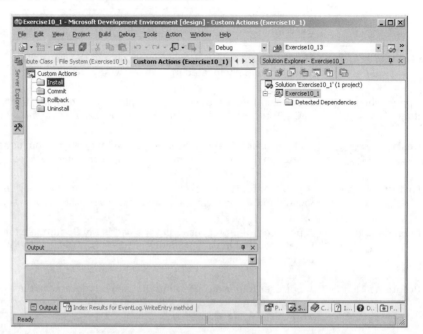

You can require code in a DLL, EXE, VBScript, or JScript file to run for any one of these events, or for each one. The Install event happens after the installation of the application is completed, but before the installation is committed on the computer. The Commit event executes the code after the installation is committed on the computer. Code in the Rollback event executes if the installation fails or is canceled and needs to be undone. The code in the Uninstall event section executes when the application is uninstalled from the computer.

After you add the action to the event, you can right-click the event and select the Properties window option to set the condition for executing this action, the entry point for a DLL (the function in the DLL that will be executed for the action), or the custom data that you want to pass into your action.

Using the File Types Editor

The File Types Editor, shown in Figure 10.7, enables you to link file types to your application. This means that when a user double-clicks the data file, your application will launch and load the data file automatically. For example, if you double-click a file with a .doc extension, Microsoft Word will generally launch and load the document you clicked. You can add a new file type by right-clicking File Types On Target Machine and choosing Add File Type. In the Properties window for the file type, you can set the command or application to run when the file type is double-clicked, the description for the file type, the file extension, the icon to use for files with the extension, and the MIME type to associate with this extension.

FIGURE 10.7   The File Types Editor

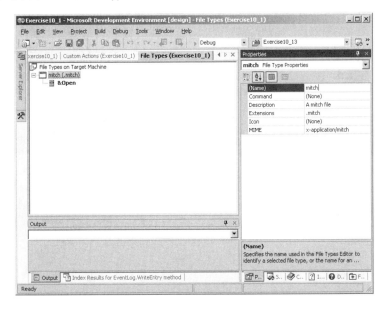

Using the Launch Conditions Editor

The Launch Conditions Editor, shown in Figure 10.8, enables you to check whether files, Registry keys, and Windows Installer components exist before the installation will proceed. You can check whether a specific version of Windows is installed or the .NET runtime exists on the machine.

FIGURE 10.8   The Launch Conditions Editor

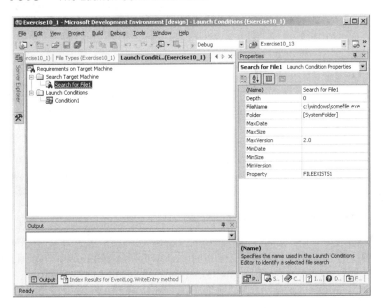

You set up launch conditions in two steps with this editor. First, you add a search condition by right-clicking the Search Target Machine category and choosing a file, Registry, or Windows Installer search condition. You then configure the properties of the specific search condition you want to search out. For example, you can specify the filename, the minimum date of the file, the Registry key, and so forth. After you have set up your Search Target Machine section, you can configure the Launch Conditions Editor to set the error message for the specific search condition created, as shown in Figure 10.9.

FIGURE 10.9 Setting the Launch Conditions for a specific search target

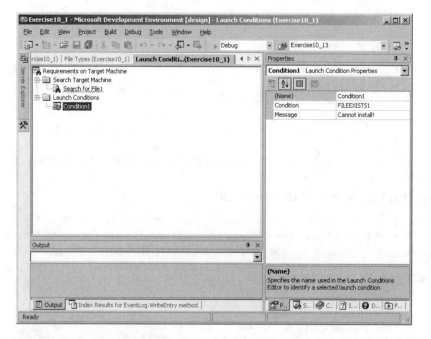

Using the Registry Editor

The Registry Editor, shown in Figure 10.10, is where you can create Registry keys and the name/value pairs that you want to add to the Registry when the application is installed. You simply navigate to the location where you want to add the key or value in the editor. You then right-click and choose New ➢ Item you want to add from the pop-up menu.

You can set many properties on the keys and values in the Properties window—such as a condition to be met for this key to be added to the Registry, or whether you would like to remove this key when the application is uninstalled.

Using the User Interface Editor

The User Interface Editor, shown in Figure 10.11, enables you to insert custom dialog boxes for the Installation Wizard that the user will step through when installing your application. You can customize messages and graphics presented to the user during installation. This is where you would add your own splash screens and installation instructions.

FIGURE 10.10   The Registry Editor

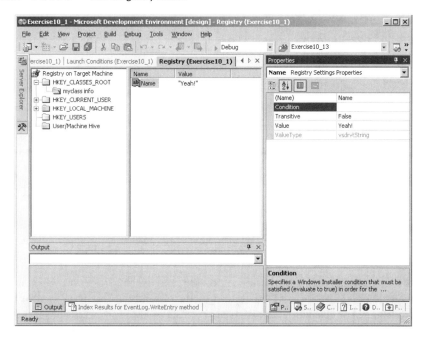

FIGURE 10.11   The User Interface Editor

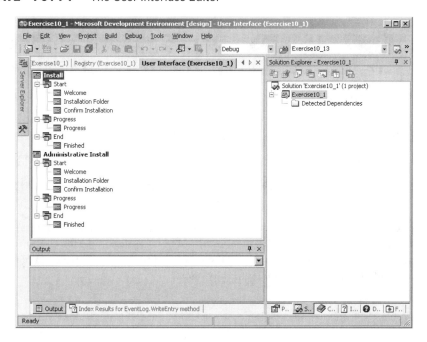

You right-click on the installation step and choose Add Dialog from the pop-up menu to add a new dialog box (see Figure 10.12).

FIGURE 10.12   Add Dialog dialog box

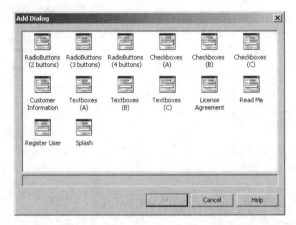

After you select which dialog box you want to add, you use the Properties window to set the bitmap image you want on the dialog box and the labels and names of the various controls (mostly CheckBoxes) on the dialog box. You can then access these properties programmatically, by using an action setup in the Custom Actions Editor to process the user's choices.

In Exercise 10.1, you will create and explore the options of a Windows setup project to familiarize yourself with it.

EXERCISE 10.1

Creating and Exploring a Windows Setup Project in Visual Studio .NET

1. Create a new Visual Studio .NET project by choosing File ➢ New ➢ Project from the main menu.

2. Under Project Types, choose Setup And Deployment Projects and under Templates, choose Setup Project.

3. Name the setup project **WindowsSetup** and click the OK button.

4. Right-click File System On Target Machine in the rightmost pane and choose Add Special Folder to reveal the special folders you can add to a project.

5. In the Solutions Explorer window, right-click WindowsSetup and choose View to reveal the various setup project editors. Click the Custom Actions option to switch to the Custom Actions Editor. Try switching to some of the other editors. You can also use the toolbar buttons at the top of the Solution Explorer window.

6. Right-click WindowsSetup and choose Properties from the pop-up menu. This reveals the setup project's Property Pages dialog box. Click the Cancel button to close the dialog box.

Deploying a Windows Service

After you create a Windows service with Visual Studio .NET, you need to deploy it. You can use a Framework utility called the *.NET Framework Installation utility* (*InstallUtil.exe*) or a Windows Installer file to install or uninstall a Windows service. This section walks you through both processes. (You could also just set the proper Registry keys if you wanted, though this is not as easy.)

Using the Installation Utility

The Installation utility executes the installers that are contained in the Windows service's .NET assembly. The installers can be turned on and off via the `RunInstaller` attribute. When the attribute is set to `True`, the installer will be executed. Setting it to `False` will disable the installer after a recompile of the project. The following code snippet shows the creation of the installer class called `ProjectInstaller` and the `RunInstaller` attribute:

```
<RunInstaller(True)> Public Class ProjectInstaller
    Inherits System.Configuration.Install.Installer
```

Installers contain the code necessary to update the Windows Registry with appropriate information for the application. In the case of a Windows service application, they update the Registry based on the properties of two classes:

ServiceProcessInstaller The *ServiceProcessInstaller* class encapsulates the functionality necessary for all services. It is used by the installation utility (`InstallUtil.exe` or Windows Installer) to write entries to the Registry. There is only one instance of this class per assembly.

ServiceInstaller The *ServiceInstaller* class updates the HKEY_LOCAL_MACHINE\System\ CurrentControlSet\Services subkeys in the Registry. There is an instance of this class for each service that might be included in the assembly.

These classes contain properties, methods, and events that let you set the values that will be written to the Registry or control what happens when the service is installed, committed, rolled back, or uninstalled as part of the install process.

After you create the Installer classes, you need to add them to the Installer collection of the `InstallerComponent` class. For example, the following code snippet updates the Registry with the service account information:

```
'ServiceProcessInstaller1
'
Me.ServiceProcessInstaller1.Password = "p@ssw0rd"
Me.ServiceProcessInstaller1.Username = "servacct"

'ServiceInstaller1
'
Me.ServiceInstaller1.ServiceName = "MyServiceName"
```

The `ServiceInstaller.ServiceName` and the `ServerBase.ServiceName` (set in your service's code) need to be the same because the `ServiceInstaller` uses this name to locate the service in the assembly.

You then add the Installer classes to the Installer collection in the `System.Configuration.Install.Installer` class, as the following code snippet shows:

```
Me.Installers.AddRange(New _
    System.Configuration.Install.Installer() _
    {Me.ServiceProcessInstaller1, Me.ServiceInstaller1})
```

If you set the password and username to `Nothing` for the service account, you will be prompted for this information during the install of the Windows service.

For a simple component, you might not even override any of the methods on the Installer class because defaults are usually sufficient for installing services.

The Installer utility works in a transacted manner, so if the install for one assembly fails, all the assemblies listed will fail.

You can create your own installer by using these classes, as Listing 10.1 shows.

Listing 10.1: Using the ServiceInstaller and ServiceProcessInstaller Classes to Create an Installer

```
Imports System
Imports System.Collections
Imports System.ServiceProcess
Imports System.ComponentModel


' Set the RunInstallerAttribute to True to enable the installer
<RunInstallerAttribute(True)> _
Public Class ProjectInstaller
Inherits System.Configuration.Install.Installer
Private pi As ServiceProcessInstaller
Private si As ServiceInstaller

Public Sub New()
' Create instances of the installers
pi = New ServiceProcessInstaller()
si = New ServiceInstaller()
```

```
' Run this service under the local system account, you could specify
' the username and password properties to set this to a domain account
pi.Account = ServiceAccount.LocalSystem

' The services will be started manually.
si.StartType = ServiceStartMode.Manual

' ServiceName must equal those on ServiceBase derived classes.
si.ServiceName = "My Service"

' Add the installers to the collection, order does not matter.
Installers.Add(si)
Installers.Add(pi)
End Sub
End Class
```

Visual Studio .NET makes it easy to create an installer for a service. When you are in Design view of the service, just right-click on a blank area of the Visual Designer screen and choose Add Installer from the pop-up menu, as shown in Figure 10.13. This will generate a new class called `Project-Installer` that will contain `ServiceProcessInstaller` and `ServiceInstaller` classes.

FIGURE 10.13   Adding an installer to a Windows Service in Visual Studio .NET

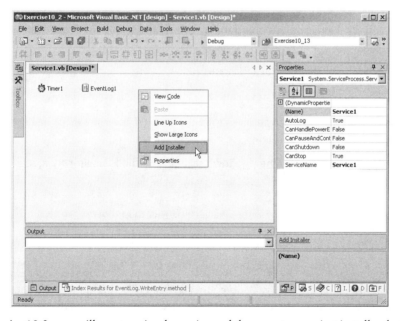

In Exercise 10.2, you will create a simple service and then create a project installer that you will explore. Finally you will use the `InstallUtil.exe` utility to install and uninstall the service.

Windows services run only on Windows NT–based operating systems such as Windows 2000 and Windows XP. The exercises dealing with Windows services, COM+, and remoting through IIS section will not work on Windows 9x or Windows ME. You can, however, go through the motions and see the options in a Windows Installer project or look at the code involved in generating an installer. You cannot, however, install and test the service.

EXERCISE 10.2

Installing a Windows Service

1. Create a new project by choosing File ➤ New ➤ Project from the main menu.

2. Select Visual Basic Projects from the Project Types and choose Windows Service from the Templates.

3. Name the project **TimerService** and click the OK button.

4. Select the Toolbox toolbar and click on the Components section.

5. Drag a Timer and EventLog component to the Service1.vb [Design] window.

6. Right-click the Timer1 component and choose Properties from the pop-up menu.

7. Set the Interval property to **5000**. This is the number of milliseconds that the timer will wait. In this case, you are going to log a message to the Windows event log every 5 seconds.

8. Right-click EventLog1 and choose Properties.

9. Set the Log property to **Application** and the Source property to **Service1**.

10. From the solution explorer, right-click the Service1.vb [Design] window and choose View Code from the pop-up menu.

11. In the OnStart() method for the Windows service, add the following code:

    ```
    Timer1.Start()
    ```

12. In the OnStop() method for the Windows service, add the following code:

    ```
    Timer1.Stop()
    ```

13. In the Class Name drop-down list box (the list box on the top left), choose Timer1.

14. In the Method Name drop-down list box (the list box on the top right of the source window), choose Elapsed to add a Timer1_Elapsed event handler to your code.

EXERCISE 10.2 *(continued)*

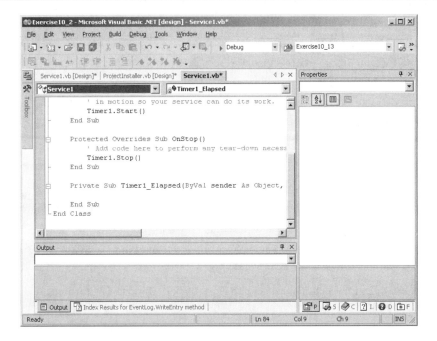

15. Add the following code to the `Timer1_Elapsed` event handler:

    ```
    EventLog1.WriteEntry("Your time is up, logging!")
    ```

16. Switch back to the Service1.vb [Design] window, right-click on a blank area, and choose Add Installer.

17. Right-click on a blank spot of the ProjectInstaller.vb [Design] window and choose View Code.

18. Expand the Component Designer Generated Code region to reveal the installer code. You are looking at the components that create a `ServiceProcessInstaller` and `ServiceInstaller`.

19. Scroll down until you locate the following code:

    ```
    Me.ServiceProcessInstaller1.Password = Nothing
    Me.ServiceProcessInstaller1.Username = Nothing
    ```

20. Set the *ComputerName*\Username properties to an account that has local administrative rights so that the service can write to the Registry. (Normally you don't want your service running as an account with administrative rights. However, we don't want to focus on setting up security in this exercise.)

21. Build the solution by choosing Build ➤ Build Solution from the main menu.

22. Launch a Visual Studio .NET command prompt by choosing Start ➤ Programs ➤ Microsoft Visual Studio .NET ➤ Visual Studio .NET Tools ➤ Visual Studio .NET Command Prompt.

23. Use the InstallUtil.exe utility to install the service by typing the following at the command prompt:

    ```
    installutil "C:\Documents and Settings\your_username\My Documents\Visual Studio↩
    Projects\TimerService\bin\TimerService.exe"
    ```

    The path should be the path to the executable that you compiled.

24. You should get a successful install message. If you get an error, you probably have a typo in the username or password.

25. Test the service by going to the Service Controller applet in Start ➤ Settings ➤ Control Panel ➤ Administrative Tools ➤ Services.

26. Find Service1 in the list of services and right-click it. Choose Start from the pop-up menu.

27. Wait about 10 or 15 seconds and then stop the service.

28. Open the Event Viewer tool by choosing Start ➤ Settings ➤ Control Panel ➤ Administrative Tools ➤ Event Viewer. You should see a message from the Service1 source that says, "Your time is up!"

29. Uninstall Service1 by typing the following at a Visual Studio .NET command prompt:

    ```
    installutil /u "C:\Documents and Settings\your_username\My Documents\Visual↩
    Studio Projects\TimerService\bin\TimerService.exe"
    ```

30. Save this project because you will use it in the next exercise.

Using the Windows Installer

A better way to distribute your service into production environments is to use a Windows Installer project. This project can be used to install and uninstall the application (much like InstallUtil.exe) but can also benefit from being able to be pushed out via software policies in Active Directory and is the standard way to install software on the Windows platform so administrators and users will be familiar with it.

You can create a Windows Installer project by adding the primary output of the project that you used to create your service. You then need to add the project output for the service to the Custom Actions Editor, as shown in Figure 10.14.

FIGURE 10.14 Adding the project output to the Custom Actions Editor

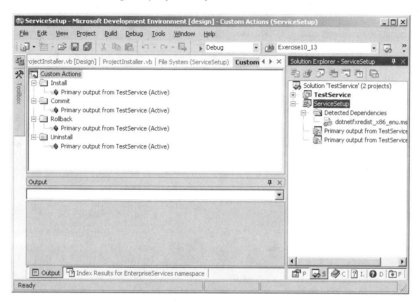

The Windows Installer project will then use the code generated by the ServiceProcess-Installer and the ServiceInstaller classes to instruct the Windows Installer project on how to install, commit, roll back, or uninstall the Windows service.

In Exercise 10.3, you will create a Windows Installer project for the simple service created in Exercise 10.2 and install and uninstall the service.

EXERCISE 10.3

Creating a Windows Installer Project to Install the Service

1. Open the TimerService project if it is not already open.

2. Add a new project to the solution by right-clicking Solution 'TimerService' and choosing Add ➢ New Project from the pop-up menu.

3. Select Setup And Deployment Projects in the Project Type window and select Setup Project in the Template window.

4. Type **TimerInstall** for the project name and click the OK button.

5. Right-click the project name, TimerInstall, and choose Add ➢ Project Output.

6. Choose Primary Output from the Add Project Output dialog box and click OK.

7. Switch to the Custom Actions Editor by right-clicking the setup project name (TimerInstall) and choosing View ➢ Custom Actions.

EXERCISE 10.3 *(continued)*

8. Right-click Custom Actions and choose Add Custom Action from the pop-up menu.

9. Select the Application Folder in the dialog box and then double-click the Primary Output From TimerService to add the actions to each of the events.

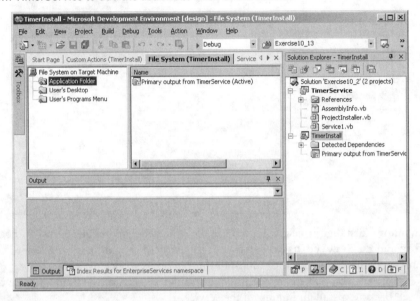

10. Build your setup project by choosing Build ➢ Build TimerInstall from the main menu.

11. Test the install of the service by navigating to the \debug directory for `TimerInstall` and double-clicking the `TimerInstall.msi` file.

12. Verify that the service is registered with the Service Controller applet by choosing Start ➢ Settings ➢ Control Panel and then double-clicking the Service Controller applet.

13. Uninstall the service by using Add/Remove programs in Control Panel.

14. Verify that the service is removed from the Service Controller applet.

Deploying a Serviced Component

You can deploy a *serviced component* (also known as a *COM+ application*) written with .NET to Windows 2000 or Windows XP computers or to Windows Server 2003 servers that have the Framework installed. There are many ways to do this—from something as simple as copying the application to the server, to something as complex as generating a Windows Installer project. In this section, you will look at the ways to deploy a serviced component and their strengths and weaknesses.

Deploying Serviced Components by Using Dynamic Registration

You might be developing or prototyping a serviced component. The simplest way to deploy a serviced component is to copy the application to the required location and run it. The first time a client tries to use an unregistered serviced component, the Common Language Runtime will check whether it is registered. If not, it will dynamically register the assembly and type library of the component in the Registry. It will also add information to the COM+ catalog based on the values of various attributes contained in the System.EnterpriseServices namespace, as listed in Table 10.2.

TABLE 10.2 A Sample of Attributes Used for Dynamic Registration

Attribute	Description
ApplicationAccessControlAttribute	Configures security at the library or server-application level in the COM+ application containing this assembly
ApplicationActivationAttribute	Tells COM+ service whether this component runs in the creators process (library application) or whether it runs in a new process (server application)
ApplicationIDAttribute	Specifies the GUID that identifies this application
ApplicationNameAttribute	Sets the name of the COM+ application used when the application is installed into the COM+ catalog
ApplicationQueuingAttribute	Marks this assembly as supporting queued (support messaging) or gives the assembly the ability to read from the queue
AutoCompleteAttribute	Sets a method to automatically commit the transaction if there is no error and to automatically roll back if an error is encountered
ComponentAccessControlAttribute	Configures security checks at the component level in the COM+ application
ConstructionEnabledAttribute	Marks the assembly as supporting the object construction string set in the Component Services tool
DescriptionAttribute	Sets the description of the COM+ application, component, interface, or method
JustInTimeActivationAttribute	Tells the COM+ services to create the component as needed and to destroy the component when it is no longer useful

TABLE 10.2   A Sample of Attributes Used for Dynamic Registration *(continued)*

Attribute	Description
LoadBalancingSupportedAttribute	Marks the application as supporting component load balancing if the COM+ container supports it
MustRunInClientContextAttribute	Makes the assembly marked with this attribute be created in the calling assembly's container
ObjectPoolingAttribute	Marks this object as being able to support object pooling, which is the opposite of just-in-time activation
SecurityRoleAttribute	Specifies a security role for an application (assembly) or component (class)
TransactionAttribute	Sets the transaction type for the object by using the TransactionOption enumeration

The Common Language Runtime will register each version of a component only once if it is not registered. Although this is the simplest way to deploy a serviced component, it will usually not be your first choice for deploying an application into production. You cannot use dynamic registration in certain situations. For example:

- You can't use dynamic registration if you need to test COM+ registration, because it does not raise an error message if your component violates COM+ settings. The component just does not activate. You need to manually register the component by using the Component Services tool to see the error message.

- This method will not install the component in the global assembly cache if it needs to be a shared component.

- The user of the application must be a member of the local Administrators group (by default or a member of the Administrators role of the COM+ system application) to write into the COM+ catalog. This will preclude most users and web or ASP.NET applications because they generally run as accounts that are not members of the local Administrators group.

- Not all COM+ configuration properties are available as attributes of the System .EnterpriseServices namespace. For example, you cannot set up role membership or tell a serviced component to run as a service by using attributes.

In Exercise 10.4, you will deploy a serviced component by using dynamic registration.

 This exercise assumes that you are logged in as a local administrator or are a member of the Administrators role of the COM+ system application and you are running Windows 2000 or Windows XP.

EXERCISE 10.4

Deploying a Serviced Component by Using Dynamic Registration

1. Create a new Visual Basic project by choosing File ➤ New ➤ Project. Select the Class Library template.

2. Name the project **DynReg** and click the OK button.

3. Add a reference to the System.EnterpriseServices assembly by right-clicking Reference and choosing Add Reference.

4. Replace the code for Class1 with the following code to the class:

```
Imports System.EnterpriseServices

<Assembly: ApplicationName("DynRegApp")>
<Assembly: ApplicationActivation(ActivationOption.Server)>
<Assembly: Description("A simple serviced component" & _
 "created to test the various install options")>

Namespace ComPlusStuff
    Public Interface IHelloMessage
        Function Message() As String
    End Interface

    <Transaction(TransactionOption.Required)> _
    Public Class DynReg
        Inherits ServicedComponent
        Implements IHelloMessage
'The message makes more sense in conjunction with exercise 10.11
        Public Function Message() As String Implements IHelloMessage.Message
            Return "Well isn't somebody on an ego trip!"
        End Function
    End Class
End Namespace
```

This code creates an application name for the component, sets it to be a library application, and sets the component to require a transaction.

5. Add a new project to the solution by right-clicking the solution and choosing Add ➤ New Project.

6. Choose a Windows application and call the project **TestDynReg** and click the OK button.

7. Add a reference to the DynReg project.

8. Set the TestDynReg project as the startup project by right-clicking TestEx10_4 and choosing Set As Startup Project.

9. Drag a button and a Textbox control to the Windows form of the TestDynReg project.

EXERCISE 10.4 (continued)

10. Double-click the button and add the following code to the `Button1` event handler:

```
Try
    Dim obj As New DynReg.ComPlusStuff.DynReg()
    TextBox1.Text = obj.Message()
Catch exp As Exception
    MessageBox.Show(exp.Message)
End Try
```

11. Use the Strong-Named (`sn.exe`) utility at the Visual Studio .NET command prompt to generate a key pair file as follows:

```
sn -k c:\keyfile.snk
```

            The Strong-Named utility is covered in detail later in this chapter.

12. Add the following attribute to the `AssemblyInfo.vb` file in DynReg:

```
<Assembly: AssemblyKeyFile("c:\keyfile.snk")>
```

13. Build the solution. This should install the component in the COM+ catalog. Verify this by choosing Start ➤ Settings ➤ Control Panel ➤ Administrative Tools ➤ Component Services.

14. Navigate to the `DynRegApp` application, right-click it, and choose Properties.

15. Click the Transactions tab. Verify that the component requires a transaction and verify the settings for library type on the Activation tab.

16. Use the Component Services tool to delete the COM+ application by right-clicking the application name and choosing Delete.

17. Save this project because you will be using it in the Exercises 10.5–10.7 for COM+.

Using the Services Registration Utility and the *RegistrationHelper* Class

You can get around some of the limitations of dynamic registration by using the *.NET Framework Services Registration utility* (*regsvcs.exe*) command-line utility or the *RegistrationHelper* class. These tools can be run by someone with local administration privileges to configure the COM+ catalog and to register the component and type library in the Registry. They also provide better error messages than simply not activating the component—which makes testing and debugging easier for you, the developer of the component.

The `regsvcs.exe` utility will register the serviced component in the Registry as if you ran `regasm.exe`. It will then generate a COM type library as if you ran `tlbexp.exe` on the assembly.

Finally, it will use the APIs in the System.Reflection namespace to look at the metadata and set the appropriate attribute settings for the application in the COM+ catalog.

You use regsvcs.exe by issuing the following at a Visual Studio .NET command prompt:

```
regsvcs yourAssembly.dll
```

There are additional options you can issue to the regsvcs utility to define, for example, the COM+ application name or type library to use. Table 10.3 lists the command-line switches for the regsvcs utility:

TABLE 10.3   Command Switches for *regsvcs.exe*

Switch	Description
/appname:*name*	Specifies the name of the serviced component. This option is used in conjunction with /c, /exapp, or /fc options.
/c	Creates the application specified by the /appname switch or by the name of the assembly set with the AssemblyName attribute (usually in the AssemblyInfo.vb file) and will generate an error if it already exists.
/componly	Configures the components only and ignores the configuration on methods or interfaces.
/exapp	Specifies that the application name is an existing application in the COM+ catalog.
/extlb	Uses an existing type library.
/fc	Finds or creates the application. This is the default option.
/help	Displays the Help screen listing these options.
/noreconfig	Tells the installer not to reconfigure the application.
/nologo	Tells regsvcs.exe not to display the full name, version, and copyright information, but to still print errors to the console.
/parname:*IdOrName*	Specifies the name or ID of the target partition in a serviced component (Windows XP and Windows Server 2003 only).
/reconfig	Reconfigures an existing application. This is a default setting.
/tlb:*tlbname*	Sets the name of the type library file to use for the install.
/u	Uninstalls the application specified in the /appname switch.
/quiet	Suppresses the output of the logo and success information.
/?	Displays the Help screen listing these options.

The `RegistrationHelper` class in the `System.EnterpriseServices` namespace provides the same functionality as the `regsvcs.exe` utility through a programmatic interface. This means that you can create your own install application or extend the administration tool of your application to support installing components. All you need to do is create an instance of the `RegistrationHelper` class and call the `InstallAssembly` method to install the assembly as a COM+ application or `UninstallAssembly` to uninstall the assembly.

The `InstallAssembly` method takes four parameters:

- The path to the assembly.

- The application name. (By default, the value of the `AssemblyName` attribute will be used.)

- The type library for the assembly specified in the path.

- An `InstallationFlags` enumeration option to indicate whether you want to create a new application or update an existing application.

The following code is an example of using the `RegistrationHelper` class:

```
Dim AppName As String = Nothing
Dim TypeLib As String = Nothing

Dim rh As New RegistrationHelper()
Try
    rh.InstallAssembly("C:\MyAppDir\MyComponent.dll", _
      AppName, TypeLib, _
      InstallationFlags.CreateTargetApplication)
Catch Ex As Exception
   Console.WriteLine("Registration failed!");
End Try)
```

In Exercise 10.5, you will use the `regsvcs` utility to install and uninstall a serviced component and then use the `RegistrationHelper` class to create code that will install and uninstall the same serviced component.

EXERCISE 10.5

Using *regsvcs.exe* and the *RegistrationHelper* Class

Using the regsvcs Utility:

1. Open a Visual Studio .NET command prompt by clicking Start ➢ Programs ➢ Microsoft Visual Studio .NET ➢ Visual Studio .NET Tools ➢ Visual Studio .NET Command Prompt.

2. Type the following at the command prompt to register the assembly you created in Exercise 10.4 with `regsvcs.exe`:

   ```
   regsvcs "c:\Document and Settings\My Documents\↵
   your_user_name\Visual Studio Projects\bin\↵
   DynReg.dll"
   ```

3. Verify that the application was installed by navigating to the Component Services tool in the Administrative Tools folder of Control Panel (or any other way you are more familiar with).

4. Expand the following nodes to get to your application: Component Services, Computers, My Computer, COM+ Applications.

5. Look for the COM+ application named DynRegApp and right-click it and choose properties from the pop-up menu.

6. Verify that the application contains the settings specified by the attributes added to the assembly.

7. Uninstall the application by using the following command:

```
regsvcs /u "c:\Document and Settings\My Documents\↵
your_user_name\Visual Studio Projects\bin\↵
debug\DynReg.dll"
```

Using the RegistrationHelper Class:

8. Open Visual Studio .NET and create a new Visual Basic .NET console application called RegHelp.

9. Set a reference to the System.EnterpriseServices.dll file.

10. Add the following Imports statement to the top of the source code (above the Module statement):

```
Imports System.EnterpriseServices
```

11. Add the following code to the Sub Main() procedure of the console application:

```
Dim AppName As String = Nothing
Dim TypeLib As String = Nothing

Dim rh As New RegistrationHelper()
Try
    rh.InstallAssembly("c:\Document and Settings\" & _
      "My Documents\your_user_name\Visual Studio" & _
      " Projects\bin\debug\DynReg.dll ",  _
      AppName, TypeLib, _
      InstallationFlags.CreateTargetApplication)
    Console.WriteLine("Registration failed!")
Catch Ex As Exception
    Console.WriteLine("Registration succeeded for " & TypeLib)
End Try
```

12. Build the solution.

13. Run the application and verify that the COM+ application was created with the Component Services tool.

14. Leave the DynRegApp COM+ application installed for the next exercise.

Using the Component Services Tool to Export a Service Component to an MSI File

The most flexible and complete way to deploy a COM+ application is by using the Windows Installer. You can package all the application's files, COM+ catalog attributes, and COM registration information in a single MSI file. This file can then be deployed on CD, from a network share, through Active Directory, or (if you wrap it as a CAB file) via Internet Explorer. All you need to do is double-click the MSI file or `setup.exe` if a bootstrapper was generated.

Fortunately, you do not need to create your own Windows Install setup project to generate the MSI file. All you need to do is use the *Component Services tool* in Computer Management or under the Administrative Tools Start menu option (Figure 10.15). This tool will package all of the necessary settings and files into an MSI for deployment; it will even provide the CAB file that is needed to deploy the component via Internet Explorer.

FIGURE 10.15 Component Services Tool

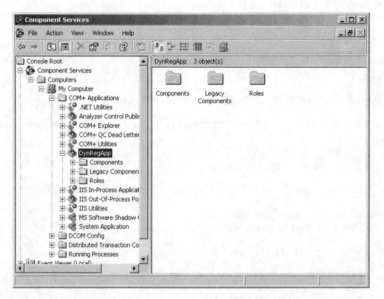

> The Component Services tool will create only a Windows Installer file for the COM+ application. If you have other DLLs that this application is dependent upon, you will need to add them to the Windows Installer file with the Windows Installer authoring tool.

You will need to install and configure your serviced component first either manually or through one of the methods already described. You then will use the Component Services tool to export the COM+ application. The COM+ Application Export Wizard will start. You want to make sure that you choose Sever Application on the Application Export Information page's Export As option, as shown in Figure 10.16.

FIGURE 10.16   The Application Export Information page

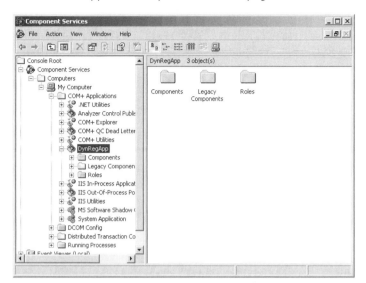

This will generate an MSI file in the location specified that will install the assemblies and type libraries associated with the COM+ application, register them, and configure the COM+ application based on the current settings. This means that you can use the Component Services tool to set additional attributes on your COM+ application that cannot be set with the EnterpriseServices namespace's attributes.

In Exercise 10.6, you will use the Component Services tool to generate an MSI file and test it for the COM+ component you created in Exercise 10.4.

EXERCISE 10.6

Creating a Windows Installer File with the Component Services Tool

1.   Open the Component Services tool in the Administrative Tools folder of Control Panel.

2.   Expand the following nodes to get to your application: Component Services, Computers, My Computer, COM+ Applications.

3.   Right-click DynRegApp and choose Export from the pop-up menu to launch the COM+ Application Export Wizard.

4.   Click the Next button to move past the first screen of the COM+ Application Export Wizard.

5.   Type the following to create the folder and name of the MSI file that should be created:

    c:\complusinstall\ExportDynRegApp.msi

6.   Make sure that the Server Application check box is selected to create an install file for the complete COM+ application and not just a proxy.

7. Select the Export User Identities With Roles check box to export to the MSI file all Windows accounts and groups that are mapped to roles. This would be useful if you are installing the component to multiple computers in the same domain, as in a component load balancing situation.

8. Click the Next button to generate the MSI and CAB files to perform the install. The CAB file is provided so you can install the application by using Internet Explorer.

9. Click the Finish button to complete the export process.

10. Navigate to the `C:\complusinstall` folder to view the MSI and CAB files.

11. Double-click the MSI file to start the install.

Deploying COM+ Proxies

Up to now, you have looked at deploying only the COM+ application. Typically, client computers will not have the full COM+ application installed locally or might not even possess the COM+ services in the case of Windows 9*x*, ME, or NT but still might need to interact with a COM+ application. In these cases, you will want to deploy a COM+ proxy.

COM+ *proxies* are wrappers that mimic the interface of the COM+ component locally, but contain only the code necessary to make a call to the COM+ application in another process, or more likely on another computer. You can use the Component Services tool to create a Windows Installer file for the proxy in a similar fashion to how you created a package for the COM+ application in Exercise 10.6. The only change is that you select the Application Proxy option on the Application Export Information page. This will then generate an MSI file that installs the proxy only.

By default, the application proxy will point to the server that you exported the COM+ application's proxy from. This could be problematic because this might be a development or staging server. Fortunately, you can change the name by setting the *Application Proxy RSN* (Remote Server Name) option before exporting the MSI file. That way, the proxy will point to the desired server (instead of the developer's laptop) when installed. This can be accomplished by performing the following steps:

1. Right-click the computer container in the Component Services tool for the computer from which you are exporting applications.

2. Choose Properties from the pop-up menu.

3. Click the Options tab in the Properties dialog box.

4. Type the name of the remote COM+ server computer you want the proxies to use in the Application Proxy RSN box, and then click the OK button.

Another more flexible option would be to use the Windows Installer utility (`msiexec.exe`) and set the REMOTESERVERNAME property override as follows:

```
Msiexec -I REMOTESERVERNAME=MyNewServer MyProxy.msi
```

The application proxy will need to be installed in each calling application's private directory unless you register it as a shared assembly (this can be accomplished by installing the assembly in the GAC, which is discussed later in this chapter, in the section "Deploying to the GAC").

In Exercise 10.7, you will export a proxy.

EXERCISE 10.7

Exporting a Proxy

1. Open the Component Services tool in the Administrative Tools folder of Control Panel.

2. Expand the following nodes to get to your application: Component Services, Computers, My Computer, COM+ Applications.

3. Right-click DynRegApp and choose Export from the pop-up menu to launch the COM+ Application Export Wizard.

4. Click the Next button to move past the first screen of the COM+ Application Export Wizard.

5. Type the following to create the folder and name of the MSI file that should be created:

    `C:\complusinstall\ProxyDynRegApp.msi`

6. Make sure that the Application Proxy RSN check box is selected to create an install file for the complete COM+ application and not just a proxy.

7. Check the Export User Identities With Roles to export to the MSI file all Windows accounts and groups that are mapped to roles. This would be useful if you are installing the component to multiple computers in the same domain, as in a component load balancing situation.

8. Click the Next button to generate the MSI and CAB files to perform the install. The CAB file is provided so you can install the application by using Internet Explorer.

9. Click the Finish button to complete the export process.

10. Navigate to the C:\complusinstall folder to view the MSI and CAB file.

11. You then just need to double-click the MSI file to start the install.

If the component's class identifier (CLSID), type library identifier (TypeLibId), or interface identifier (IID) change after you export the application and install the proxy on the client machines, you must export the application proxy again and install it on the client machines.

Deploying a .NET Remoting Object

You have seen how to deploy a Windows service and a serviced component (a COM+ application written in .NET). The principles you learned also apply to deploying a .NET Remoting object because it is usually implemented as a Windows service or a serviced component. There are a few other options for deploying .NET Remoting objects.

You can deploy them as stand-alone executables, which must be started manually. This requires copying the executable and the application configuration file to the server and manually executing the file. You can improve upon this by using a scheduler or file watcher to make sure the application is executing, but it is not going to be as robust as a Windows service or COM+ application.

The other option you have for deploying your .NET Remoting object is using IIS as a host for it. This enables you to take advantage of the authentication and encryption services built into IIS. This also cuts down on the amount of code you need to develop to provide these services.

 Real World Scenario

Hosting .NET Remoting Objects in IIS

You are developing an application that keeps track of patient information for a hospital. The requirements state that you need to make sure the application is secure and performs well. You have decided to implement an object called PatientInfo that can be used to read and write various patient data. This object could have a need to be called in process, in another application domain or most likely on another server. You have no need for interoperability with this application, but need to make sure it is secure and performs well. In addition, you have a very tight deadline for delivery of this component of the application.

You decide to implement the object by using .NET Remoting and to use an HTTP for the protocol. This will enable you to host the application under Internet Information Server, which means you can save development time by taking advantage of the authentication (Basic or Windows Integrated) and encryption (SSL) services that are built into IIS. You also decide to use the binary formatter to serialize the object data that is moved between server and client. This performs much better than the SOAP formatter and can be used when interoperability is not an issue.

Hosting a .NET Remoting object in IIS is straightforward. You create a virtual directory on the server, add a web.config file with the necessary configuration information for remoting, and then deploy the compiled assembly containing the remoting type to the \bin directory in the virtual directory you created for a private application or register it in the GAC to make it shared among all applications. There are, however, a few points to consider:

- You cannot specify the application name of the Remoting object when deploying to IIS. The virtual directory name that you create is the name of the application.

- You must use the `HttpChannel`, but you have your choice for `Formatters`, either `Binary` or `Soap`.

- You cannot use the `<debug>` element in a `web.config` file, which is used to alert you of errors in your configuration file as soon as the assembly is loaded.

- You cannot use the `<client>` element in the `web.config` file to configure your client web application automatically. This can be done by using the `RemotingConfiguration` class in the `global.asax` files's `Application_Start` event.

- You can configure the `HttpChannel` in the `web.config`, but you do not specify a port because this is done in IIS.

In Exercise 10.8, you will deploy a .NET Remoting object to a virtual directory in IIS and connect to it with a client.

EXERCISE 10.8

Deploying a .NET Remoting Object in Internet Information Server

1. Create a new Visual Basic Project Class Library project called **HWRemote**.

2. Add a reference to your project for `System.Runtime.Remoting`.

3. Replace the code in the class with the following code to create the .NET Remoting server object:

```
Imports System.Runtime.Remoting

Public Class HWServer
     Inherits MarshalByRefObject
Public Function Message() As String
   Return "Hello World!"
End Function
End Class
```

4. Build the project.

5. Add a new Visual Basic .NET Windows Application project to the solution by right-clicking on the solution and choosing Add ➢ New Project.

6. Name the project **HWClient**.

7. Add a reference to the HWRemote project by right-clicking References in the Solution Explorer and choosing Add References. Click the Project tab on the Add References dialog box and select HWRemote project; then click the Select button and click OK.

8. Add a Button control and a TextBox control to the form.

9. Set a reference to the `System.Runtime.Remoting` assembly. Add the following `Imports` to the top of the source file:

```
Imports System.Runtime.Remoting
Imports System.Runtime.Remoting.Channels
Imports System.Runtime.Remoting.Channels.Http
Imports HWRemote
```

10. Double-click the Button control and add the following to the Button1_Click event:

```
ChannelServices.RegisterChannel(New HttpChannel())

Dim hws As HWRemote.HWServer = _
CType(Activator.GetObject(GetType(HWRemote.HWServer), _
    "http://localhost/RemoteHello/HwServer.rem"), HWRemote.HWServer)

TextBox1.Text = hws.Message()
```

11. Build the project to make sure it is compiles.

12. Create a new directory on the C: drive called **RemoteHello**. Create a directory in the RemoteHello directory called **bin**.

13. Right-click the RemoteHello directory and choose Properties from the pop-up menu.

14. Click the Web Sharing tab of the RemoteHello Properties dialog box.

15. Select the option Share The Folder. The Edit Alias dialog box appears.

16. Click the OK button to accept the defaults.

17. Click the OK button of the RemoteHello Properties dialog box.

18. Open the Internet Services Manager console by navigating to the Administrative Tools folder of Control Panel.

19. Expand Your Computer Name, then expand the Default Web Site node.

20. Right-click the RemoteHello virtual directory and choose Properties from the pop-up menu.

21. Click the Configuration button on the Virtual Directory tab of the RemoteHello Properties dialog box.

22. Click the OK button.

23. Close the Internet Services Manager console.

24. Navigate to the C:\RemoteHello folder. Right-click in the folder and create a new text document called **web.config**.

25. Add the following to the text document:

```
<?xml version="1.0" encoding="utf-8" ?>
<configuration>
<system.runtime.remoting>
<application>
<service>
<wellknown mode="SingleCall"
    type="HWRemote.HWServer, HWRemote"
    objectUri="HWServer.rem" />
</service>
<channels>
<channel ref="http" />
</channels>
</application>
</system.runtime.remoting>
</configuration>
```

26. Copy the assembly, `HWServer.dll`, from the `My Documents\Visual Studio Projects\` `HWRemote\bin` directory to the `\bin` directory of the `C:\RemoteHello` folder.

27. Set the `HWClient` project as the startup project.

28. Run the client to test the application. You should see "Hello World!" printed in the text box.

Considering Other Deployment Issues

You have looked at using the Windows Installer setup project and the specifics of installing and deploying a Windows service, serviced component, and .NET Remoting object. Now you need to consider other deployment issues, such as registering COM components and .NET assemblies or adding components to the global assembly cache. In this section, you will look at registering components and assemblies, working with strong-named assemblies, deploying the GAC, and implementing component versioning.

Registering Components and Assemblies

The *.NET Framework Assembly Registration utility* (*regasm.exe*) enables you to register an assembly in the Registry for use by COM+ objects. You should give any assembly that you want used by COM+ a strong name. The assembly is not what COM+ interacts with, but you will notice that the `mscoree.dll` (the Common Language Runtime) is registered as the `InprocServer32` for the class identifier (CLSID). The assembly is specified in another key, called `assembly`, that is used by the CLR to load the assembly.

In Exercise 10.9, you will register an assembly in the Registry by using `regasm`.

Using *regasm* and the Registry Editor in a Windows Installer Project

1. Start a Visual Studio .NET command prompt.

2. Use the .NET Framework Assembly Registration utility to register the assembly that you created in Exercise 10.4 by typing the following:

```
regasm "c:\Document and Settings\My Documents\_
your_user_name\Visual Studio Projects\DynReg\bin\_
DynReg.dll"
```

3. Verify that the assembly was registered by searching the Registry for `DynReg.dll`. Notice how the `InProcServer32` points to the `mscoree.dll`, which is the Common Language Runtime. This is the COM+ object that is loaded; then the assembly key specifies the DLL or EXE of the assembly to load.

Working with Strong-Named Assemblies

A *strong-named assembly* is an assembly that has been signed by using a public key/private key pair generated by the `sn.exe` utility. A strong name uniquely identifies an assembly by generating a hash of the assembly's manifest and then encrypting the hash with the private key. The encrypted hash is a signature and is stored in the manifest of the assembly. It is verified by the assembly's client by using the public key of the key pair that is also included in the assembly's manifest. Strong-named assemblies provide the following benefits:

- They enable applications to run with the version of the assembly to which they were built. The signature along with the name, version, and culture ID of the assembly is recorded in the calling assembly's manifest. This guarantees that your application will always use the right version of the assembly, unless the `<assemblyBinding>` configuration option overrides this.

- They provide a strong code integrity check. The hash of the assembly computed at compile time is checked at runtime. If the result of the runtime check is different, then the assembly has been tampered with and it will not load. The strong name can also be used as evidence for code access security.

- They make it possible to share assemblies. Only assemblies that have been signed can be registered in the GAC where they are shared. The strong name provides for strong binding to a specific version of the assembly and enables multiple versions of the same DLL to be installed and even loaded into an application domain at the same time. The strong name helps prevent a problem known as DLL Hell that plagued Windows and COM for years.

- A strong-named assembly has more deployment options than a private assembly because you can place it in the GAC, which makes it available as a shared component on the system. Strong-named assemblies can also be used by COM components, and a serviced component must be strong named.

You create a strong-named assembly by using the `sn.exe` utility to generate a public key/private key pair in a file and then referencing the key file with the `AssemblyKeyFile` attribute from within the assembly. This attribute is located in the `System.Reflection` namespace. The following is an example of using the `AssemblyKeyFile` attribute to make a strong-named assembly:

```
Imports System.Reflection
<Assembly: AssemblyKeyFile("c:\mykeyfile.snk")>
Public Class Customer
...
End Class
```

There is a file named `AssemblyInfo.vb` that is associated with each project that you create in Visual Studio .NET. This file contains all of these assembly-level attributes. It is compiled into the resultant assembly of the project and should be used for noting the author, version, keyfile, and so forth of the assembly.

 Remember that serviced components must be strong named.

Deploying to the GAC

A shared assembly is a strong-named assembly that is installed in the *global assembly cache (GAC)*. The GAC is a code collection that is shared with all applications on the machine. Because it is shared by multiple applications, you must sign your assemblies so they can be uniquely identified and versioned. This prevents versioning issues by making sure the version of the assembly that you built—and more importantly, tested your application with—is the one that you bind to. An assembly is verified when it is installed in the GAC, and will not be installed if the hash does not match the encrypted version in the signature.

You can install an assembly in the GAC by using the Windows Installer project, the .NET Framework Configuration tool, the Global Assembly Cache tool (`gacutil.exe`), or Windows Explorer.

Using Windows Installer is the recommended way to deploy assemblies to the GAC in a production environment because it provides for assembly reference counting, which means it will keep track of the number of applications using the shared assembly and can remove it when it is no longer in use. Windows Installer packages also support installation through Active Directory software policies, giving users of your application an automated deployment option.

The `gacutil.exe` is a utility included in the .NET Framework to install strong-named assemblies in the GAC. It is run from a Visual Studio .NET command prompt, and although it has many options, here are the three most useful:

-i installs a strong-named assembly in the GAC.

-l lists the assemblies in the GAC.

-**u** uninstalls an assembly from the GAC.

The following example shows how to install an assembly in the GAC with `gacutil.exe`, assuming it has a strong name:

```
gacutil -i TestAssembly.dll
```

The .NET Framework Configuration tool is an Microsoft Management Console (MMC) snap-in that enables you to configure many aspects of your applications and the .NET Framework. You can add an assembly to the GAC by clicking Assembly Cache in the tree pane and then clicking the Add An Assembly To The Assembly Cache link in the right-hand pane. This will launch the Add Assembly To The Assembly Cache Wizard.

You can use Windows Explorer to drag and drop or to copy the assembly to the assembly cache that is represented as a directory called `assembly` under the `Windows` directory.

You can install the assemblies that you use for Windows services, serviced components, and Remoting objects in the GAC also. The main criteria you should use is whether this is a server-level resource or one just local to the application.

Serviced components hosted in a COM+ server application require registration in the GAC, whereas COM+ library applications do not. It is recommended that COM+ library applications be installed in the GAC also, because COM+ applications are generally server-level resources.

In Exercise 10.10, you will add the assembly that you created in Exercise 10.4 to the GAC by using the `gacutil.exe` utility.

EXERCISE 10.10

Installing an Assembly in the Global Assembly Cache

1. The assembly already has been given a strong name. Run the following command in a Visual Studio .NET command prompt:

    ```
    gacutil /i "c:\Document and Settings\My Documents\_
    your_user_name
    \Visual Studio Projects\DynReg\bin\_
    DynReg.dll"
    ```

2. Verify the installation by navigating to the following path, %windir%\assembly, and looking for the assembly in the Windows directory.

3. You can also verify that it was installed by typing the following:

    ```
    gacutil /l DynReg
    ```

4. Use the following command to uninstall the assembly from the global assembly cache:

    ```
    gacutil /u DynReg
    ```

Implementing Component Versioning

Any assembly registered in the GAC is versioned. Whenever you build an assembly, it binds to a specific version of any shared assembly (an assembly registered in the GAC) that you use. If the user installs a newer version of the assembly on their computer, your assembly will still use the version it was compiled against. This strict version-binding can be overridden by a developer or administrator by using the `<assemblyBinding>` tag in the configuration files for the application.

The GAC can store multiple versions of the same assembly, which is called side-by-side deployment. The runtime checks the GAC first for a strong-named assembly before it begins probing directories for the assembly if it does not exist in the GAC.

You can control the version of your assembly by modifying the `<Assembly: Assembly-Version(1.0.*)>` attribute in the `AssemblyInfo.vb` file. The `AssemblyVersion` attribute takes the following format for the version string: *major.minor.build.revision*. At a minimum, you need to specify the major portion of the version number. You can have part of the version number automatically populated if you use an asterisk (*), although you need to specify at least the major and minor portions of the version number.

Microsoft recommends specifying the version number by hand, but this can be a pain to do with every build in development, so they provided you with the asterisk (*). When you create a Release build, you should set the version number manually. If you use an asterisk, the build number will be set to the number of days since January 1, 2000 local time and the revision will be set to the number of seconds since midnight local time modulo 2. You can use an asterisk for just the revision number if you want, which will set it to the number of seconds since midnight local time modulo 2.

The following are examples of valid version numbers: 1, 1.1, 1.1.*, 1.1.1.*, 1.1.1, 1.1.1.1.

> ### ⊕ Real World Scenario
>
> #### Using Versioning in .NET
>
> You create an assembly called `ABCGUI.dll` that contains custom GUI interface components. These will be used by four applications that your company will be shipping. These applications will be released at different intervals over the next three years. Because of changing requirements on the applications, some of the GUI components might need to change in the `ABCGUI.dll`. You need to make sure that changes to the GUI components will not affect the applications that are already released if the `ABCGUI.dll` assembly changes.
>
> You decide to take advantage of the side-by-side installation feature of the GAC. You give `ABCGUI.dll` a strong name. You add the `AssemblyVersion` attribute to the assembly and change the version for each build of the component by hand. You have the assembly being used by each application register in the GAC with a Windows Installer project used to install each application. You release the first application with the 1.0.0.0 version of the `ABCGUI.dll`. During the development of the second application, there are some major modifications made to the `ABCGUI.dll` assembly so it is released with version 2.0.0.0 of `ABCGUI.dll`. You test the install of both applications on the same machine; running ildasm.exe on the applications shows that the first application is using 1.0.0.0 of `ABCGUI.dll` and the second uses 2.0.0.0. Both assemblies exist in the GAC. This reduces the possibility of version conflicts between versions.

Ensuring Security in Windows-Based Services

Securing Windows-based services involves the standard set of security options that you learned about in Chapter 9, "Overview of Security Concepts." You need to make sure that users are authenticating against your service and are authorized to do the minimum needed to accomplish the task at hand. Visual Studio .NET's role-based security makes this easier to accomplish by grouping users under common functions. You will also want to take advantage of code access security to make sure the code running is trusted and limited to only what it needs to do; that way if someone finds a hole in your application that enables them to elevate their permissions, your code can do no more than it is allowed to do. You also should remember that data you receive should not be trusted and should be verified to make sure it is what your application expects. You can use regular expression as a powerful tool to accomplish this task. Data you send over a network is also potentially vulnerable to snooping. You should consider using encryption on any sensitive data sent over a network (after all, the network protocol analyzer (sniffer) Ethereal is a free download).

In addition to these generic principles, each type of application can have some specific security considerations, which you will look at in this section.

Securing Windows Services

A Windows service runs with a service account. This account is used by the service when accessing the file system or database services, or even when logging onto another machine remotely. You need to make sure that you don't elevate the permissions of the service by linking it to an account that has more permissions than the service needs.

For example, you could create a service that looks for a file in a specific directory and then updates a database table with the information in the file. If you set this up to use an account with Administrator privileges, the service could have Full Control permissions on any directory on the whole computer and maybe have access to many more databases and the accompanying tables and stored procedures and commands (such as the Data Definition Language commands of DROP, CREATE, and ALTER). This service would need permissions only to read from a directory and write to a specific table in a database, no more, no less. You should then create an account and give it these permissions. Otherwise, your service might have a bug in it, and a user might accidentally or purposely exploit the bug. If you used the least privileges principle, you could avoid extensive damage.

> You should also use declarative attributes to state which types of permissions your code is requesting, as discussed in Chapter 9.

Securing Serviced Components

COM+ applications use a role-based security mechanism to simplify the security features provided by DCOM and authenticated Remote Procedure Call, which COM+ is built upon. The COM+ role-based security model is one in which the individual identity of the user is not important, but the logical role that the user can assume is important.

There are three levels at which you can apply role-based security to a COM+-based component: component, interface, and method. The role you apply at one level automatically propagates to the lower levels. For example, if you assign a role to the component level, then members of the role can call into any interface and method on the component. You would need to add the role to the interface or methods for more fine-grained control.

You can implement role-based security on a serviced component declaratively with various attributes that are contained in the `System.EnterpriseServices` namespace. You just need to apply them at the proper level in your code.

You can also check security imperatively in a serviced component. This is useful if you require doing security checks at a finer level than the method. You use two methods to use imperative security: `IsCallerInRole` and `IsSecurityEnabled`.

The `IsCallerInRole` method has the following signature:

`IsCallerInRole(String_Value)`

This is used to check whether the current COM+ security context is in the role that is passed to the method. The *String_Value* is the name of the role allowed to perform the action. It is part of the `ContextUtil` object in the `System.EnterpriseServices` namespace.

The `IsSecurityEnabled` method will test whether security is turned on for this COM+ application. The administrator could turn off security by using the Component Services tool. If security is turned off, then `IsCallerInRole` will always return `True`.

The following is an example of imperative security:

```
Public Function GetSSN(ByVal PatientID As Integer)As String
If Not ContextUtil.IsSecurityEnabled Then
   Return "Must have security " & "enabled to call this method"
End If
If ContextUtil.IsCallerInRole("AdminManager") Then
   Return SSN
End If
End Function
```

The .NET Framework and COM+ role-based security models use different mechanisms and are independent of each other. COM+ uses the Windows token to identify the user. The Windows token and the COM+ role are associated with the context of the serviced component through a security descriptor. The .NET Framework associates the security context with the current thread. This context is based on the Identity and Principal objects and does not necessarily rely on a Windows token. The `WindowsIdentity` and `WindowsPrincipal` objects are associated with a Windows token. This means that if you use the .NET Framework role-based security, the security context is not available to the serviced component. If you use COM+ role-based security, the security properties of the serviced component are not available to the .NET assembly outside of the current process or newly created threads without extra work on your part.

In Exercise 10.11, you will configure a serviced component to use role-based security.

EXERCISE 10.11

Configuring Serviced Components to Use Role-Based Security

1. Open the project called DynReg in Visual Studio .NET.

2. Add the following attributes just above the `Public Class DynReg` statement:

   ```
   <Transaction(TransactionOption.Required), _
       ComponentAccessControl(), SecureMethod()> _
   Public Class DynReg
   ```

3. Add the following attributes just above the `Message` function:

   ```
   <SecurityRole("GuruDeveloper")> _
   Public Function Message() As String
   ```

4. Add the following assembly-level directives to the `AssemblyInfo.vb` file in the project:

   ```
   <assembly: ApplicationAccessControl(AccessChecksLevel= _
       AccessChecksLevelOption.ApplicationComponent)>
   <assembly: SecurityRole("GuruDeveloper")>
   <assembly: SecurityRole("JustADeveloper")>
   <assembly: SecurityRole("User")>
   <assembly: SecurityRole("SeniorManager")>
   ```

   At the top of the `AssemblyInfo.vb` file add the following Imports statement to the top:

   ```
   Imports System.EnterpriseServices
   ```

EXERCISE 10.11 *(continued)*

5. Build the solution.

6. Install the component in the GAC by using the following command at a Visual Studio .NET command prompt:

    ```
    gacutil -i path_to_MyDocuments\Visual Studio↵
    Projects\DynReg\bin\DynReg.dll
    ```

7. Register the component in the COM+ catalog by typing the following line:

    ```
    regsvcs path_to_MyDocuments\Visual Studio↵
    Projects\DynReg\bin\DynReg.dll
    ```

8. Verify that the component is installed by opening the Component Services tool.

9. Expand Component Services, Computers, My Computer, COM+ Applications.

10. Right-click DynReg and choose Properties.

11. Click the Security tab and verify that Enforce Access Checks For This Application is selected and that the security level is set for the process and component level.

12. Click OK to close the Properties dialog box.

13. Expand the DynReg application, the Components folder, and the DynReg class, IHelloMessage interface.

14. Right-click the Message method and click Properties.

15. Click the Security tab and verify that the GuruDeveloper role is associated with the method.

16. Click the OK button to close the dialog box.

17. Expand the Roles folder under the DynReg application and verify the roles were added that you specified in the SecurityRole attributes of the file.

Securing .NET Remoting Objects

Security can become an issue with .NET Remoting objects when the object is moved into another application domain with lesser permissions or especially when the object is moved to a different server. For example, the object might work fine opening secure files and reading them on your workstation because they are being loaded in the same executable (for example, client.exe) and thus are running under your security context. But when you move the object to a server and try the same thing through remoting, it will fail. This happens because the server is not running in the client's security context that is authorized to access the files.

You should realize that this will be the case with Remoting objects that are running in a different process or server. What you need is for the server to impersonate the client. You need to consider a mechanism to authenticate the user, impersonate the user, and make sure the data that is moving between the server and the client is secure. (You might interact with the Secure Support Provider Interface APIs of Windows in conjunction with the `CryptoStream` objects of .NET to do this.) Otherwise, you can also use the services provided by IIS for authenticating the user and encrypting the traffic over the network as we discussed earlier in the "Deploying a .NET Remoting Object" section to make this easier.

If the .NET Remoting object is part of a Windows service or COM+ application (which it usually is), you should follow the security procedures already outlined for each of these services above.

Summary

In this chapter, you learned about deploying, securing, and configuring Windows-based applications. We covered the following topics:

- How to create a Windows Installer file (`.msi`) with Visual Studio .NET to install an application along with all of its settings

- How to register, version, and share the components that you create through the use of `regasm.exe`, .NET versioning of strong-named assemblies, and the GAC

- The utilities and deployment options for installing Windows services, serviced components (COM+ components created with .NET), and .NET Remoting objects

- How to use the MSI file to deploy each of these types of solutions

- How to deploy .NET Remoting objects to an Internet Information Server process and the flexibility that affords you with authentication and encrypting data

- The specific security issues that arise when working with Windows services, serviced components, and .NET Remoting

Exam Essentials

Remember that a Windows Installer file (`.msi`) is generally the most flexible and appropriate way to deploy an application to production. A Windows Installer file provides control over the location of the files, a friendly user interface that can be customized, the ability to add items to the Registry or the global assembly cache, and the ability to package all the necessary files together in one package file that can be installed and uninstalled.

Understand how to use the `ServiceProcessInstaller` and the ServiceInstaller classes. These classes are used by either `InstallUtil.exe` or a Windows Installer project to control what happens during the install, commit, rollback, and uninstall phases of an installation of a Windows service.

Know how to use the `InstallUtil.exe` utility to install a service. You can pass more than one assembly to the utility and they will all install as one transaction. So if one fails, they all will not install.

Know how to install .NET Remoting objects in an IIS process. This is very useful for providing access to objects through a firewall via the HTTP protocol and for having IIS authenticate the user and provide encryption of data through the use of SSL (HTTPS).

Remember that a serviced component must be strong named. You don't need to install the component in the GAC if you don't want it to be shared, but you do need to make it strong named. A strong name is used to uniquely identify any assembly that is used by COM (which allows for interaction with the COM+ services).

Understand how COM+ security roles work. Know how you would manipulate them through attributes and programmatically.

Key Terms

Before you take the exam, be certain you are familiar with the following terms:

.NET Framework Assembly Registration utility

`regasm.exe`

.NET Framework Installation utility

`RegistrationHelper`

.NET Framework Services Registration utility

`regsvcs.exe`

Application Proxy RSN

serviced component

COM+ application

`ServiceInstaller`

COM+ proxies

`ServiceProcessInstaller`

Component Services tool

setup project

global assembly cache (GAC)

strong-named assembly

`InstallUtil.exe`

web setup project

merge module Project

Windows Installer setup project

Microsoft Installer file

Review Questions

1. You create a .NET Remoting object named Account that exposes a client's financial information. The business requirements state that you must ensure that this confidential data is secure. Your design calls for client applications to connect to Account over a secure communication channel. You need the application to perform as well as possible. You also want to accomplish this task by writing the minimum amount of code. What should you do?

   A. Install Account in an Internet Information Services (IIS) virtual directory called VAccount. Configure Account to use an HttpChannel and a SoapFormatter. Configure IIS to use SSL. Enable SSL on VAccount.

   B. Create a Windows service to host the application. Configure Account to use an HttpChannel and a BinaryFormatter. Use a CryptoStream object to encrypt the content traveling over the wire.

   C. Install Account in an Internet Information Services (IIS) virtual directory called VAccount. Configure Account to use an HttpChannel and a BinaryFormatter. Configure IIS to use SSL. Enable SSL on VAccount.

   D. Create a Windows service to host the application. Configure Account to use an HttpChannel and a SoapFormatter. Use a CryptoStream object to encrypt the content traveling over the wire.

2. You create three Windows services named MyServiceA, MyServiceB, and MyServiceC. You want to install all three services on a computer named Server1 by using the .NET Installer utility (InstallUtil.exe). You open a Visual Studio .NET command prompt and run the following command:

   ```
   installutil.exe MyServiceA MyServiceB MyServiceC
   ```

   During the installation process, MyServiceC throws an installation error and then the installation process completes. How many of the three services are now installed on Server1?

   A. None

   B. One

   C. Two

   D. Three

3. You create a COM+ application named Goals by using Visual Basic .NET. Goals consists of a series of components used to track incentive compensation for a sales staff of over 500 people in your company. You need to deploy the application to a number of regional servers that the sales staff will connect to from their Goals client and from another sales client application on their workstations and laptops to track how they are doing in meeting goals and to update information used by Goals to track progress to incentives. The business people can also use Goals from their client application to run "what if" scenarios for various incentive programs.

The clients run on a variety of Windows platforms, including Windows 98 and Windows NT Workstation. Each client needs to connect to the server in their region because of bandwidth requirements for the application. What should you do to deploy the application? (Choose the best answer.)

A. Generate an application proxy Windows Installer file by using the Component Services tool. On install, you will be prompted for the server name you need to connect to. Enter the server name for the region that the salesperson or manager is in.

B. Generate an application proxy Windows Installer file by using the Component Services tool. Generate an install script for each location that uses the Windows Installer executable (`msiexec.exe`) with the installation option of REMOTESERVERNAME set to the name of the server that is in their region.

C. Create a custom install script that uses the configuration classes in the `System .EnterpriseServices` namespace to set all the properties (including the server to connect to), create the necessary Registry entries, and register the components.

D. Upgrade the Windows 98 and Windows NT Workstation computers because they cannot run COM+ applications. Generate an application proxy Windows Installer file by using the Component Services tool. Generate an install script for each location that uses the Windows Installer executable (`msiexec.exe`) with the installation option of REMOTESERVERNAME set to the name of the server that is in their region.

4. You create a serviced component named MyApp that uses attributes contained in the source to dynamically register itself for COM+ services. MyApp uses transactions and role-based security. All the settings for MyApp, including the application identity, are currently configured properly on the development computer. MyApp is compiled into an assembly file named `MyAssembly.dll`.

You need to give MyApp to the administrator for installation into the production environment. You want all the COM+ configuration information for MyApp to be installed on the production computers.

What should you do? (Choose the best answer.)

A. Provide to the administrator the `MyAssembly.dll` file. Provide instructions to the administrator on how to use the Component Services tool to create the application with the correct settings.

B. Provide to the administrator the `MyAssembly.dll` file. Instruct the administrator to install it in the global assembly cache.

C. Use the Component Services tool to export MyApp to an MSI file. Provide the administrator the MSI file with instructions to run the installer.

D. Provide the administrator the `MyAssembly.dll` file. Instruct the administrator to use the .NET Services Installation tool (`regsvcs.exe`) to install MyApp.

5. You are working for a financial planning company. You create a serviced component named Portfolio that provides access to a client's portfolio. You declaratively secure Portfolio by using COM+ role-based security. You must ensure that security checks are enforced, and the component must not execute if an administrator turns off security for the COM+ application. Which of the following should you do?

A. To the project source code, add the following:

```
<Assembly: ApplicationAccessLevelControl _
(AccessChecksLevelOption.ApplicationComponent)>
```

B. Add the following attribute just before each method:

```
<ApplicationAccessLevelControl _
(AccessChecksLevelOption.ApplicationComponent)>
```

C. Add the following code in each method:

```
If Not ContextUtil.IsSecurityEnabled Then
    Throw New SecurityException ("The Portfolio" &_
 object requires that security is enabled.")
End If
```

D. Add the following code just before each method:

```
If Not ContextUtil.IsSecurityEnabled Then
   ContextUtil.SetAbort
End If
```

6. You created and tested a new serviced component named UsefulThing that will be distributed to your customers through a Windows Installer package. This package will register the component in the global assembly cache on each customer's computer.

You know that you will be providing future updates to UsefulThing. You will provide these updates to your customers. All updates to UsefulThing will be backward compatible. You will create Windows Installer packages for each update of UsefulThing that will register the updated assembly in the global assembly cache.

Which action should you take? (Choose all that apply.)

A. Sign UsefulThing by using a strong name.

B. Compile UsefulThing as a satellite assembly.

C. Add Registry entries to the setup project for the Windows Installer package to update the version of UsefulThing.

D. Increment the assembly version for each update of UsefulThing.

E. Include a version.config file. Increment the assembly version for each update of UsefulThing.

7. You need to deploy a serviced component named `ClientPortfolio`. This component will look up financial information for the company's financial planning application. You want to configure the COM+ application running the component to run under a user account called `PortfolioAcct`. This is a restricted account to maximize the security of the application. Which of the following should you do?

   A. Implement the `ISecurityIdentity` interface. Override the `UserName` and `Password` properties.

   B. Use the Component Services tool to set the `Identity` property of the COM+ application to `RemoteUser`.

   C. Add the following attributes to the `AssemblyInfo.vb` file:

   ```
   <assembly: ApplicationAccessControl(ImpersonationLevel = _
       ImpersonationLevelOption.Impersonate)>
   <assembly: SecurityAccount("PortfolioAcct")>
   ```

   D. Add the following attributes to the `AssemblyInfo.vb` file:

   ```
   <assembly: Impersonate("PortfolioAcct", Password="p@ssw0rd")>
   ```

8. You create version 1.0.0.0 of an assembly named `Bank`. This assembly contains two .NET Remoting objects called `Deposit` and `Withdrawal`. You register the assembly in the global assembly cache and configure the Remoting objects in the `Bank.config` file. You install it on the testing server of your company.

   You create a Windows application named `TestClient` on your workstation (which is a different computer than the testing server). `TestClient` references version 1.0.0.0 of `Bank`. `TestClient` is used to test all the functionality of the `Deposit` and `Withdrawal` objects. After successful testing, you release `Bank` to your customers.

   Later, you uncover some issues with the `Bank` assembly and must update it. You create version 2.0.0.0 of `Bank`, which is backward compatible, but you do not update any information in the `TestClient.config` file of `Assembly`. You register version 2.0.0.0 of `Bank` in the global assembly cache.

   Which version of `Deposit` and `Withdrawal` will `TestClient` use?

   A. Version 1.0.0.0 of `Deposit`; version 1.0.0.0 of `Withdrawal`.

   B. Version 1.0.0.0 of `Deposit`; version 2.0.0.0 of `Withdrawal`.

   C. Version 2.0.0.0 of `Deposit`; version 1.0.0.0 of `Withdrawal`.

   D. Version 2.0.0.0 of `Deposit`; version 2.0.0.0 of `Withdrawal`.

9. You create a serviced component. You need to ensure that the component can be accessed only by members in the AuthorizedUsers role. Which two attributes should you add to the component? (Choose two.)

   A. `<ComponentAccessControl>`

   B. `<Transaction(TransactionOption.Required)>`

   C. `<IsCallerInRole("AuthorizedUsers")>`

   D. `<SecurityRole("AuthorizedUsers", false)>`

10. You create one assembly that contains a number of serviced components. You are required to secure the assembly based on a number of COM+ roles. You need to ensure that role-based security is enforced in the assembly by using a directive in your source code. Which attribute should you use?

A. `<assembly: SecurityRoleLevel(SecurityAction.Assembly)>`

B. `<assembly: SecurityLevel("Assembly")>`

C. `<assembly: ApplicationAccessControl(AccessChecksLevel = AccessChecksLevelOption.ApplicationComponent)>`

D. `<assembly: ApplicationActivation(ActivationOption.Server)>`

11. You need to install a .NET serviced component in such a fashion that it can be shared by multiple applications deployed by different developers at different times. Where should you deploy the serviced component?

A. The `Windows` directory (for example `C:\Windows`)

B. The `System32` directory (for example `C:\Windows\System32`)

C. The global assembly cache

D. A shared directory on the network

12. Jennifer creates a .NET Remoting object named `Employee`. This object enables client applications (both Windows and Web forms) to access employee information contained in the company's HR application. As part of the requirements for the object, she needs to ensure that the client applications are securely authenticated before they can access the `Employee` object. She does not have much time left to deliver this component and would like to write the minimum amount of code. What should she do?

A. Write code to use the `Credential` cache object and other objects to authenticate the client with the remote object.

B. Host the `Employee` object in an Internet Information Services (IIS) virtual directory. Enable Basic authentication on the directory.

C. Host the `Employee` object in an Internet Information Services (IIS) virtual directory. Enable Windows authentication on the directory.

D. Use an `HttpChannel` and a `SoapFormatter` for the `Employee` object.

13. You are building a payroll application. You create an application called `PayrollServer.exe`. This server loads various .NET Remoting objects that are contained in the assembly file named `PayrollBL.dll`. The application is configured as a client-activated object and is configured to use the `HttpChannel` with the `SoapFormatter` in the configuration file `PayrollServer.exe.config`.

You deploy the application, but users complain that the application doesn't work some of the time. Upon further investigation, you determine that the application quits working when the server is rebooted. You need to fix the problem. What should you do?

A. Install `PayrollBL.dll` in the global assembly cache on the server.

B. Configure the server to run `PayrollServer.exe` whenever it is restarted.

C. Register the `PayrollBL.dll` assembly in the Registry with `regasm.exe`.

D. Register the `PayrollBL.dll` assembly in the Registry with `regsvr32.exe`.

14. How can you turn off an installer in a Windows service application?

   A. Set the `RunInstaller` attribute for the installer class to `False` as follows; then recompile the class:

```
<RunInstaller(False)> Public Class ProjectInstaller
```

   B. Set the `RunInstaller` attribute for the installer class to `True` as follows; then recompile the class:

```
<RunInstaller(True)> Public Class ProjectInstaller
```

   C. Set the `DoInstaller` attribute for the installer class to `False` as follows; then recompile the class:

```
<DoInstaller(False)> Public Class ProjectInstaller
```

   D. Set the `DoInstaller` attribute for the installer class to `True` as follows; then recompile the class:

```
<DoInstaller(True)> Public Class ProjectInstaller
```

15. You create a serviced component called `MyComponent`. You set the attributes correctly for dynamic registration and you try to use it logged in as Administrator, but it will not start. What other step or steps should be taken so the component can be registered? (Choose all that apply.)

   A. Register it in the Windows Registry by using `regsvcs.exe`.

   B. Give it a strong name.

   C. Add it to the global assembly cache.

   D. Create an application for the component by using the Component Services tool.

Answers to Review Questions

1. C. You want to implement the solution by using the least amount of code, so using IIS services for encryption reduces the amount of code that needs to be written. Using the `BinaryFormatter` will make the application perform better because the payload is more compact and the application takes less time serializing and deserializing the stream. The first answer could also be correct but it uses the `SoapFormatter`, which is significantly slower than the `BinaryFormatter`. This would be a better option if interoperability with other systems was important. The remaining answers are incorrect because they would require you to write the code for the Windows service host and the encrypting/decrypting streams from scratch (although you could potentially get better performance this way).

2. A. The .NET Installation utility (`Installutil.exe`) is transacted, and therefore if any part of the install fails, the whole install will fail. Because the install of `MyServiceC` failed, the installs of `MyServiceA` and `MyServiceB` had to be rolled back also. If you wanted to install the services without them all being in the same transaction, you would run `Installutil.exe` for each service.

3. B. You need to generate an application proxy that will connect to the server application. You need to make sure that the application proxy points to the correct regional server, so you need to install the application proxy and use the `REMOTESERVERNAME` installation option to specify the server name. Although it is true that Windows 98 and Windows NT clients cannot host COM+ applications, they can interact with the COM+ application through the use of the application proxy. You will not be prompted for a server name on install, and the default will be used (which is the name of the computer where the MSI file was generated via the export). The third answer could be done but would be more work than the correct answer.

4. C. An MSI file provides the most flexibility and is the standard way to install applications on Windows. It will also contain all of the properties that are configured on the COM+ application. The last answer D could work, but it is not the best answer because it might miss some of the settings on the COM+ application (it knows only about the attributes in the source code and is not the standard way to install applications on the Windows platform). The first answer could work but would be tedious and error prone. The second answer will most likely not work because the application might not be run by a user with Administrative privileges to have it dynamically register itself, and installing in the GAC has no effect on this.

5. C. The `IsSecurityEnabled` method of the `ContextUtil` object will return `False` if the security of the COM+ application is turned off by an administrator. You would check the return value of this method in an `If` statement, and the best course of action would be to throw an exception to indicate that this is the case. The last answer aborts the current transaction but does not prevent the component from running. The other answers try to set attributes to determine whether security is enabled on the application, which is not possible to do in .NET.

6. A, D. You will need to give the assembly `UsefulThing` a strong name to register it in the GAC and therefore enable versioning of the component. You will then need to increment the assembly version in the manifest by using the `AssemblyVersion` attribute (found in the `AssemblyInfo.vb` file in a VB .NET project in Visual Studio .NET). You do not need to make `UsefulThing` a satellite assembly. Satellite assemblies contain resources only (graphics, strings of text) and are usually used to add foreign language support to an application. Versioning information is contained in the manifest, not the Registry or a separate configuration file.

7. B.   You must use the Component Services tool to configure the Identity property of an application or use the COM interfaces to the COM+ catalog directly through COM interop. No attribute exists in the System.EnterpriseServices namespace that will allow you to configure the Identity property of a COM+ application. There is no interface that you can use to configure the Identity property in .NET.

8. A.   You never recompiled the application or updated the configuration file of the assembly, so you will not use another version of the assembly. When you compiled the TestClient application, the version of the Bank assembly it was binding to is stored in the TestClient's manifest.

9. A, D.   You need to enable access control at the component level and then use the SecurityRole attribute to specify which role the user needs to be a member of. The second answer is incorrect because the Transaction attribute is used to specify whether this component takes place in a transaction, which has nothing to do with security roles. The third answer is not an attribute that is available.

10. C.   This answer is correct because it shows the syntax for the attribute that enables assembly-level security checking. The last answer uses the attribute that sets the application to a server (out-of-process) application instead of a library (in-process) application, which is how the application is run, not secured. The remaining answers are not attributes in the .NET Framework.

11. C.   The GAC is where you would install any component that needs to be shared among multiple developers and multiple applications. The GAC supports multiple versions of the same component to be installed, which aids in avoiding versioning problems with applications. Applications will use the version they were compiled against. The first and second answers indicate locations where shared COM components are installed. The last answer could work in certain circumstances (all developers work for the same company and deploy their applications in the company), but the assembly would not be versioned and users of the component would likely have versioning issues in the future.

12. C.   Using IIS to host the Employee object would require writing the minimum code; the clients involve the use of Windows applications, which would be using Windows authentication. Basic authentication would require more coding to get all the clients to work with it. The last answer just describes the protocol and the format of the information sent, but does nothing to address the security concern. The first answer would work because you can programmatically control security, but would involve writing a lot more code than the IIS solution.

13. B.   Because the .NET Remoting object was created as an executable, whenever the server restarted it would need to be run again. You would configure the server to log on automatically and run the PayrollServer.exe. A better configuration would be to create a service out of PayrollServer.exe.

14. A.   Passing False to the installer will turn it off for the service after a recompile. The second answer would enable the installer, not disable it. The remaining answers refer to an attribute that is not in the .NET Framework.

15. A, B.   Serviced components require a strong name and registration in the Registry before they can be registered in the COM+ catalog on the machine. In addition, you need a type library generated for the serviced component. These steps do not change whether the method of installation is dynamic or manual (that is, using regsvcs.exe or the Component Services tool).

Deploying and Securing XML Web Services

MICROSOFT EXAM OBJECTIVES COVERED IN THIS CHAPTER:

✓ **Plan the deployment of and deploy an XML Web service.**

✓ **Create a setup program that installs an XML Web service.**

✓ **Publish an XML Web service.**

- ▪ Enable static discovery.
- ▪ Publish XML Web service definitions in the UDDI.

In this chapter, you will learn the basics involved in securing and deploying XML Web services. You will learn how to create a setup program for your Web service, as well as how to create the documents necessary for deploying it into the UDDI registry. Following that, you will see how you can implement authentication and authorization by using integrated security mechanisms as well as custom techniques. Finally, you will learn how to encrypt SOAP messages by creating custom SOAP extensions.

Deploying XML Web Services

There are two techniques for deploying an XML Web service: using XCOPY deployment or adding a Web Setup project to the solution containing the XML Web service that you would like to deploy. This section shows you the steps required in creating a setup program for your service. After you've learned how to create the setup program, you will learn how to publish your XML Web service to the UDDI registry.

Creating a Setup Program

One of the goals of the .NET Framework is the zero-impact install, which means you can install an application simply by copying the application folder and contents to the destination computer. This type of install is usually referred to as XCOPY deployment; on many occasions, you might not be able to use this type of deployment strategy. You might have an application that is dependent on a COM component, that needs to add an assembly to the global assembly cache (GAC), or you just desire a user interface for the installation process. For these reasons, you would create a setup program for your application. In Chapter 10, you built setup programs for different types of projects and application types.

In Exercise 11.1, you will see that creating a setup program for an XML Web service is not much different from any of the other setup projects that you have built.

EXERCISE 11.1

Creating a Setup Program

1. Create a new Visual Basic .NET ASP.NET Web service project named **WebServiceSetup**.

2. Switch to the Code view of Service1.asmx and remove the commenting from the sample `HelloWorld()` function.

3. In the Solution Configurations drop-down list, switch the build output to Release.

4. Build and test the project to make sure that it works.

5. From the Solution Explorer, right-click the WebServiceSetup project and choose Add ➢ New Project.

6. From the Add New Project dialog box, select the Web Setup project from the Setup And Deployment Project list. Name the Web Setup project **Setup11_1**. Your screen should be similar to the following one.

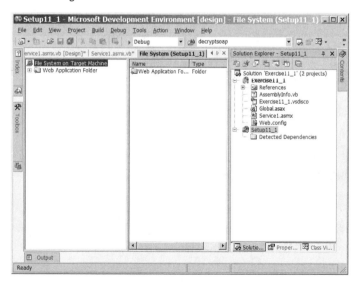

7. Right-click Web Application Folder and choose Add ➢ Project Output.

8. From the Add Project Output Group dialog box, hold down the Ctrl key and select Primary Output, Content Files, and Source Files to include the selected types in the setup package.

9. Build the Setup11_1 project, save all the files, and exit Visual Studio .NET.

10. Navigate to the Release folder for this project and double-click the Setup11_1.msi file to launch the Installation Wizard.

11. Click the Next button to view the Select Installation Address page.

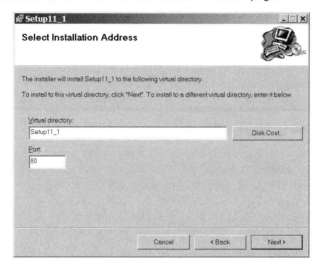

12. Verify that the address and port information are as desired and click Next to confirm the installation.

13. Click Next to install the XML Web service.

14. Click the Close button to close the Installation Wizard.

15. Test the newly installed XML Web service by browsing to `http://localhost/Setup11_1/Service1.asmx`.

16. Save and close.

Publishing XML Web Services

Now that you have built your XML Web services, you'll want a way for your customers to learn about and hopefully consume them. To make the information available to potential customers, you will typically publish information about your Web service either within your site or to a public directory. The process by which potential consumers locate available Web services is called XML Web service discovery.

XML Web service *discovery* is the process of finding and reading XML Web service descriptions (WSDL documents). This is an important first step in consuming a Web service. By taking advantage of the discovery process, a Web service consumer can learn how to interact with a particular service.

There are two kinds of discovery: static and dynamic. *Static discovery* is accomplished by creating an XML `.disco` file that contains links to other discovery documents, XML schemas, and WSDL documents. ASP.NET automatically exposes the contents of `.disco` documents that can be viewed by appending ?DISCO to the URI of the Web service file (`.asmx`). For example, if you wanted to view the discovery document for a Web service at `http://myServer/service1` `.asmx`, you would navigate to `http://myServer/service1.asmx?DISCO`. *Dynamic discovery* occurs when ASP.NET iterates through the folders of a web server to search for available XML Web services.

In addition to publishing information about your XML Web service within your site, you will probably want it published to a central directory of Web services. Next, you will learn how to enable both static and dynamic discovery, as well as how to create the necessary documents to send to the UDDI for publication.

Manually Enabling Static Discovery

The static discovery, or `.disco`, file is an XML document containing links to the documents that contain information about the service(s). The purpose of the `.disco` file is to have a single location to learn about the services exposed from a particular source.

The discovery file, typically named with the `.disco` extension, is an XML file that should contain a `<discovery>` element as its root, as in the following example:

```
<?xml version="1.0" ?>
<discovery xmlns:="http://schemas.xmlsoap.org/disco">
</discovery>
```

Add all of the references that you prefer to publicly expose to the `<discovery>` element. Service description references are specified by adding a `<contractRef>` with the `http://` `schemas.xmlsoap.org/disco/scl` namespace referenced. The `<contractRef>` element should have a `ref` attribute and a `docRef` attribute. The `ref` attribute should point to the WSDL of the service, and the `docRef` attribute should reference the service file (`.asmx`) itself. You can also include references to other discovery files by adding a `<discoveryRef>` element. The `ref` attribute of the `<discoveryRef>` element should point to another discovery file. The following example represents these settings:

```
<?xml version="1.0" ?>
<discovery xmlns:="http://schemas.xmlsoap.org/disco">

  <discoveryRef
    ref="http://www.myserver.com/myServices/Service2.disco"
  />

  <contractRef
    ref="http://www.myserver.com/myServices/Service1.asmx?WSDL"
    docRef="http://www.myserver.com/myServices/Service1.asmx"
    xmlns:="http://schemas.xmlsoap.org/disco/scl"
  />

</discovery>
```

Enabling Dynamic Discovery

Dynamic discovery is enabled by including a file named `default.vsdisco` from the root folder of the website. IIS will map the `.vsdisco` file to the `aspnet_isapi.dll` and the `System.Web` `.Services.Discovery.DiscoveryRequestHandler`. This handler will search the folder that the `.vsdisco` file is located in and all of its subfolders for XML Web service (`.asmx`) files, dynamic discovery (`.vsdisco`) files, and static discovery (`.disco`) files.

Similar to the static discovery file, the dynamic discovery file is also formatted as XML. The root element is named `<dynamicDiscovery>` and can contain one or more `<exclude>` elements with a path attribute that specifies the relative paths that are not to be searched. Visual Studio .NET will create a `.vsdisco` file automatically when you create an XML Web service project. The following code is an example of the contents of the `.vsdisco` file generated by Visual Studio:

```
<?xml version="1.0" encoding="utf-8" ?>
<dynamicDiscovery xmlns="urn:schemas-dynamicdiscovery:disco.2000-03-17">
    <exclude path="_vti_cnf" />
    <exclude path="_vti_pvt" />
    <exclude path="_vti_log" />
    <exclude path="_vti_script" />
    <exclude path="_vti_txt" />
    <exclude path="Web References" />
</dynamicDiscovery>
```

Publishing Web Service Descriptions to UDDI

Universal Description, Discovery, and Integration (UDDI) is a collection of specifications for distributed web-based registries of XML Web services. UDDI provides details about the XML Web services that a particular company exposes. In addition, it supplies Web service consumers with the location of endpoints for a given service as well as the binding information for a specific endpoint.

The UDDI Data Structure Specification defines the XML schema that must be used to describe types in the UDDI. Five data types are defined by the specification: `<businessEntity>`, `<businessService>`, `<bindingTemplate>`, `<tModelInstanceDetails>`, and `<tModel>`.

The *<businessEntity>* Element

The *businessEntity* element describes the business that is the responsible party for registering the XML Web service in the UDDI. This element contains details about the business, such as its name and contact information. The following XML shows a sample `<businessEntity>`:

```
<businessEntity businessKey="7F468458-1214-49BE-996E-F44622BAF924" operator="">
 <name>Weather Incorporated</name>
 <description xml:lang="en">
  Weather Forecast Service
 </description>
```

```
<contacts>
 <contact>
  <description xml:lang="en">
   Service Administrator
  </description>
  <personName>Thomas Anderson</personName>
  <phone>302-555-1212</phone>
  <email>neo@WeatherInc.com</email>
  <address>
   <addressLine>1313 Mockingbird Lane</addressLine>
   <addressLine>Wilmington, DE</addressLine>
  </address>
 </contact>
</contacts>
</businessEntity>
```

The *<businessService>* Element

The *businessService* element describes the XML Web service that the business entity is exposing. This element names the service, as well as associates it with a business entity and binding information. You can also assign categories to the Web service, such as industry, product, and so on. The following XML shows a sample `<businessService>`:

```
<businessService businessKey="7F468458-1214-49BE-996E-F44622BAF924"
                 serviceKey="3520889E-918E-4d78-AEF2-666334819141">
 <name>Business Service</name>
 <description xml:lang="en">Description goes here</description>
 <bindingTemplates>
  <!-- zero or more binding templates -->
   <bindingTemplate>
    Elements go here
   </bindingTemplate>
 </bindingTemplates>
</businessService>
```

The *<bindingTemplate>* Element

The *bindingTemplate* element describes the technical specifications that are required to bind to a particular XML Web service. The binding information is either an access point or a hosting redirector.

The `<accessPoint>` element describes the entry point. It contains an attribute named URLType, which is used to specify one of the seven types of entry points. These types are listed in Table 11.1.

TABLE 11.1   Valid *URLType* Values

Entry Point	Description
Mailto	The access point is an e-mail address.
Http	The access point is an HTTP-compatible URL.
Https	The access point is an HTTP Secure (HTTPS)–compatible URL.
Ftp	The access point is a File Transfer Protocol (FTP)–compatible URL.
Fax	The access point is a fax telephone number.
Phone	The access point is a voice telephone number.
Other	The access point is in some other format.

The following sample shows an `<accessPoint>` element:

```
<accessPoint URLType="http">
  http://www.abcinc.com/weather/weatherService.asmx
</accessPoint>
```

The following sample demonstrates a `<bindingTemplate>` element using an `<accessPoint>` element:

```
<bindingTemplate bindingKey="" serviceKey="">
  <description xml:lang="en">
    Weather Service binding template
  </description>
  <accessPoint URLType="http">
    http://www.abcinc.com/weather/weatherService.asmx
  </accessPoint>
  <tModelInstanceDetails>
    <!-- zero or more -->
    <tModelInstanceInfo/>
  </tModelInstanceDetails>
</bindingTemplate>
```

Instead of providing an `<accessPoint>` element, you can use the `<hostRedirectory>` element to point to another `<bindingTemplate>` for the specific binding information. The `<hostRedirectory>` element can also be used to allow for multiple binding templates to be associated with a single XML Web service.

The *<tModelInstanceDetails>* Element

The *tModelInstanceDetails* element contains zero or more `<tModelInstanceInfo>` elements. The `<tModelInstanceInfo>` element has an attribute named `tModelKey`, which identifies a specific `tModel` (explained in the next section). Also included in the `<tModelInstanceDetails>` element are a description of the Web method, a reference to the overview document, and instance parameters. The following sample shows a `<tModelInstanceInfo>` element:

```
<tModelInstanceInfo tModelKey="uuid:F3CD9457-9669-4E36-90E7-DEC7F512B8F3">
  <description xml:lang="en">
    Weather tModel
  </description>
  <instanceDetails>
    <description xml:lang="en">
      Weather instance details description
    </description>
    <overviewDoc>
      <description xml:lang="en">
        Weather service overview
      </description>
      <overviewURL>
        http://www.abcinc.com/weather/weatherService.asmx
      </overviewURL>
      <instanceParms>
        http://www.abcinc.com/weather/params.aspx
      </instanceParms>
    </overviewDoc>
  </instanceDetails>
</tModelInstanceInfo>
```

The *<tModel>* Element

One of the major goals of UDDI is that XML Web service descriptions are thorough enough to enable a developer to easily interact with a service that they don't know much about. To accomplish this goal, metadata must be attached to an XML Web service. The metadata could define how the service behaves, or what standards it complies to. The *tModel* element contains the information used to describe compliance with a specification, concept, or shared design. The `<tModel>` element contains a key, a name, an optional description, and a URL where you can find more information about the XML Web service. The following XML sample shows a document that can be used to register a `<tModel>`:

```
<tModel tModelKey="uuid:FD725AA4-A623-4372-A25E-4276FE7E7776">
  <name>Weather tModel</name>
  <description xml:lang="en">A TModel for the Weather Web service</description>
```

```
<overviewDoc>
  <description xml:lang="en">The Weather XML Web service tModel</description>
</overviewDoc>
<overviewURL>http://www.abcinc.com/Weather/overview.htm</overviewURL>
</tModel>
```

The <*publisherAssertion*> Element

It is not uncommon for a given business entity to represent a department or business unit from a large organization. To maintain a relationship between business entities, you would include the <publisherAssertion> element. In the following example, the businessKey value of E510D323-4DAB-4DD6-84C0-00F3D3CF2F34 represents the parent company of the <business-Entity> and the <toKey> value of 5F246BD1-1B4F-4182-B9C6-5D3CAF0ED3A6 represents the department or business unit:

```
<publisherAssertion>
  <fromKey>E510D323-4DAB-4DD6-84C0-00F3D3CF2F34</fromKey>
  <toKey>5F246BD1-1B4F-4182-B9C6-5D3CAF0ED3A6</toKey>
  <keyedReference tModelKey="uuid:FD725AA4-A623-4372-A25E-4276FE7E7776"
    keyName="Parent Company" keyValue="parent-child" />
</publisherAssertion>
```

In order to publish your business entity and XML Web services to a UDDI registry, such as http://www.uddi.org, you will provide the XML documents that you have created to a UDDI node. Microsoft and IBM have their own nodes: http://uddi.microsoft.com and http://uddi.ibm.com, respectively. You can also use the UDDI Programmer's Application Programming Interface (API) that is a part of the UDDI Software Developer's Kit (SDK).

> At the time of this writing, there is no private UDDI registry solution that can be used within a company's infrastructure. Windows 2003 Server is slated to include a UDDI registry service that companies can use as their own registry for both internal and external services.

Securing XML Web Services

XML Web services require as much, if not more, security than any other type of application. You've already learned, in the previous two chapters, the basic concepts of security within the .NET Framework. In addition to those methods, you can implement custom Simple Object Access Protocol (SOAP) headers to pass a username and a password with the SOAP request. If you're going to be sending security credentials, potentially over the Internet, you'll probably want to encrypt the data in transit.

In this section, we introduce you to authentication and authorization, as well as the techniques that you can utilize to implement them. Later in this section we show you how to implement security by using custom SOAP extensions as well as encrypting the data containing the security information.

Using Authentication Techniques

In the .NET Framework, *authentication* is the process of discovering and verifying the identity of a principal by examining credentials against some authority. Now, you will learn about Windows, Forms, and Passport authentication as well as how to create additional headers to your XML Web service in order to implement custom authentication.

Implementing Windows Authentication

Windows authentication enables you to utilize your existing Windows users and groups to provide access to your XML Web services. Internet Information Server (IIS) provides three ways to implement the authentication of the request:

Basic authentication   Transmits passwords in clear text (Base64 encoded), causing a security risk. Basic authentication is compatible with most web browsers.

Digest authentication   Hashes and then transmits passwords. Digest authentication is supported by Internet Explorer 5 and above.

Integrated Windows authentication   Transmits passwords that are hashed when using Windows NT LAN Manager (NTLM) challenge/response or a Kerberos ticket when Kerberos is used. Integrated Windows authentication cannot pass through proxy or firewall servers without using Virtual Private Network (VPN) technology.

In order to configure the application to use Windows authentication, you must set the authentication mode in the `web.config` file as follows:

```
<system.web>
  <authentication mode="Windows" />
</system.web>
```

Implementing ASP.NET Authentication

In addition to Windows authentication, ASP.NET has built-in support for Forms and Passport authentication. At the moment, Forms and Passport authentication are not recommended for XML Web services authentication. Instead you should use Windows authentication, or implement a custom authentication scheme. In the future, Passport authentication might become a more appropriate choice for XML Web service authentication.

Forms authentication occurs when an unauthenticated request is redirected to an HTML logon form. The requester supplies credentials to the form and submits it to the server, where it is verified. Having the Web request redirected to a user interface (UI), such as a Web form, where the requester enters their credentials is not conducive to the nature of an XML Web service.

Passport authentication is a centralized authentication service provided by Microsoft. Passport's best feature is that it allows for a single sign-on that can be used on multiple resources across the Web. One of the most popular sites that utilizes Passport authentication is eBay.

Implementing Custom Authentication by Using SOAP Headers

You could use the techniques you learned previously to authenticate an XML Web service request; however, many of them are not appropriate for authentication over the Internet. Windows authentication, for instance, would require that a Windows user account be created for each and every consumer of the XML Web service. A more conducive solution would be to store the credentials in a database, such as Microsoft SQL Server, and validate the credentials supplied in the request against those stored in the database.

One of the best approaches to passing additional data with a request to an XML Web service is a SOAP header. User and password information are added to the SOAP header by the Web service consumer and are passed to the XML Web service. After the header is retrieved, the Web service would carry out custom authentication.

To create a custom SOAP header, you define the class that inherits from the SoapHeader class. Located in the System.Web.Services.Protocols namespace, *SoapHeader* represents the content of a SOAP header. The following example demonstrates deriving a class from the SoapHeader class:

```
Imports System.Web.Services
Imports System.Web.Services.Protocols
Imports System.Xml
Imports System

Public Class AuthenticationHeader
    Inherits SoapHeader

    Public UserName As String
    Public Password As String
End Class
```

After you have created the custom SOAP header, you must create an instance of it to add to the Web method. The following example creates an instance of the AuthenticationHeader class defined previously and applies it to the Web method:

```
Dim AuthHead As AuthenticationHeader

<WebMethod(), SoapHeader("AuthHead", Required:=True)> _
  Public Function HelloWorld() As String

    'Code to validate incoming username and password
```

```
Return  "Hello World"

End Function
```

Of course, if your intention is to implement your own custom authentication, you must disable ASP.NET authentication in the web.config file for your XML Web service. The mode attribute of the <authentication> element should be set to None. This is demonstrated in the following example:

```
<configuration>
  <system.web>
    <authentication mode = "None" />
  <system.web>
</configuration>
```

In Exercise 11.2, you will derive a class from the SoapHeader class in order to pass the consumer's credentials in the SOAP header.

EXERCISE 11.2

Using Custom SOAP Headers for Authentication

1. Create a new ASP.NET Web Service project named **SOAPAuthExample** and switch to Code view.

2. Verify that the following Imports statements are at the top of the code file, and add any that are missing:

    ```
    Imports System.Web.Services.Protocols
    Imports System.Web.Services
    Imports System.Xml
    Imports System
    ```

3. Add the following class to the code file in order to create a custom SOAP header to pass the authentication information:

    ```
    Public Class AuthenticationHeader
        Inherits SoapHeader

        Public UserName As String
        Public Password As String
    End Class
    ```

4. The following code should be added to the Service1 class to create a Web method called myTime that returns a string and implements the custom header:

    ```
    Public AuthHead As New AuthenticationHeader()

    <WebMethod(), SoapHeader("AuthHead", Required:=True)> _
    Public Function myTime() As String

    End Function
    ```

5. Verify that the username passed in is `Customer` and that the password supplied is `p@$$W0rD` by adding the following code within the `myTime` Web method:

```
If AuthHead.UserName = "Customer" And AuthHead.Password = "p@$$W0rD" Then

    Return Now.ToLongTimeString

Else

    Throw New Exception("Access Denied")

End If
```

6. Build the **SOAPAuthExample** solution and add a new Windows Application project by right-clicking the SOAPAuthExample solution and choosing Add ➢ New Project. Name the project **SOAPAuthExample_Client**.

7. Drag two TextBox controls named **txtUsername** and **txtPassword** onto Form1 by using these details:

- Name: **txtUsername**, Text: **Username**
- Name: **txtPassword**, Text: **Password**

8. Drag a Button control onto the form named **btnCallService** with a Text property of **Call Service**. The following form represents how Form1 should appear.

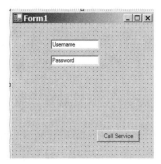

9. From the Solution Explorer, right-click the References item under the SOAPAuthExample_Client project and choose Add Web Reference.

10. In the Add Web Reference dialog box, type the following URL into the Address field: **http://*ServerName*/SoapAuthExample/Service1.asmx**. (*ServerName* should be replaced with **LocalHost** or the name of the server you are developing on.)

11. After the Available References window fills, click the Add Reference button to create the proxy class in the project.

12. Double-click the Call Service button to add an event handler for its Click event and switch to Code view.

13. Add the following code to instantiate the proxy class and invoke the Web service. You'll pass the values of the text boxes as the username and password arguments for the Web method:

```
Dim proxy As New localhost.Service1()
Dim Credentials As New localhost.AuthenticationHeader()

Credentials.UserName = txtUsername.Text
Credentials.Password = txtPassword.Text

Try
    proxy.AuthenticationHeaderValue = Credentials

    MessageBox.Show(proxy.myTime())

Catch exc As Exception

    MessageBox.Show(exc.Message)

End Try
```

14. From the Solution Explorer, right-click the SOAPAuthExample_Client project and choose the Set As StartUp Project option.

15. Launch the SOAPAuthExample_Client project and click the Call Service button, leaving the contents of the text boxes untouched—Username and Password—and obviously incorrect which causes the following message box to appear.

16. Click OK on the message box and type the following values in the respective text boxes.

- Username: **Customer**
- Password: **p@$$W0rD**

EXERCISE 11.2 *(continued)*

17. Click the Call Service button again, now with the correct values for the username and password.

18. Close the form and save and close the Visual Studio projects.

Now that you've learned some ways to authenticate the calls to your Web service, you need to learn how to determine who can and cannot execute the service.

Using Authorization Techniques

Authorization is the means of establishing whether a principal, or user, is allowed to complete a requested action. Authorization occurs after authentication, utilizing the requesting user's identity and role membership to determine which resources the user is allowed to access. There are two predominant techniques for authorizing the use of an XML Web service: file- and URL-based authorization.

File-Based Authorization

File-based authorization uses NTFS file security to determine whether the requesting client can access the resource. The only time that this can be used is when you are using Windows authentication. The actual authorization is performed by the file authorization module; it performs a check against the access control list (ACL) to establish the permissions that the user should have. This combines with *impersonation* to allow ASP.NET to make requests for resources by using the credentials of the client application that initiated the request.

Instead of implementing your own authentication and authorization scheme, you can use impersonation to let IIS authenticate the user, passing either an authenticated token to the ASP.NET application or an unauthenticated token (Anonymous). ASP.NET will then, relying on impersonation, use the token provided by IIS to access the resource.

To apply this technique to an XML Web service, you assign specific NTFS permissions to the .asmx file (or the directory that contains it).

In Exercise 11.3, you will secure your XML Web service by using file-based authorization.

WARNING File-based authorization can be implemented only on an NT-based operating system (such as Windows 2000, Windows XP, or Windows Server 2003), with the project files being saved in a directory on an NTFS-formatted volume.

URL-Based Authorization

URL-based authorization uses `<allow>` and `<deny>` elements in the application's `web.config` file to grant or deny access based on the ASP.NET URI that the client is requesting and the identity associated with the request. The authorization elements are located within the `<authorization>` element of the `web.config`.

You can allow or deny users access by using the `users`, `roles`, and `verb` attributes. The `users` and `roles` attributes have a value of a comma-delimited list of users and roles, respectively. In addition to listing the users and roles, you can use specific symbols that indicate a special meaning. The question mark (?) represents anonymous, or unauthenticated users, and the asterisk (*) represents all users. The first match to the identity of the request will apply. For this reason, you should put the `<deny>` elements at the top of the `<authorization>` element.

The following example prevents anonymous access and access by members of the Consultants and Temps roles to the resources of this application, while granting access to members of the Managers role and the Admin user:

```
<system.web>
  <authorization>
      <deny users="?" roles="Consultants, Temps" />
      <allow users="Admin" roles="Managers" />
  </authorization>
</system.web>
```

As you can see in the preceding example, you can specify the authorization settings for all the resources within the main application folder by placing your authorization details within the `<authorization>` element in the main `<system.web>` element of the `web.config` file. In addition, you can configure different authorization rules on each resource by adding a `<location>` element within the `<configuration>` element of the `web.config` file. The following example specifies authorization rules for `myService.asmx`:

```
<location path="myService.asmx" >
  <system.web>
    <authorization>
        <deny users="?" roles="Guests" />
        <allow users="Thatcher" roles="Employees" />
    </authorization>
  </system.web>
</location>
```

You can also specify a subfolder as the resource, as in the following sample:

```
<location path="ChildDirectory" >
  <system.web>
    <authorization>
        <deny users="?" roles="Guests" />
        <allow users="Thatcher" roles="Employees" />
    </authorization>
  </system.web>
</location>
```

In addition to permitting or denying certain users to access specific files or folders, you can also authorize which verbs are allowed to be used with each of the services. You can specify GET or POST by including the following type of elements within the <authorization> element:

```
<location path="myService.asmx" >
  <system.web>
    <authorization>
        <deny verb="GET" users="*" />
        <allow verb="POST" users="*" />
    </authorization>
  </system.web>
</location>
```

The preceding example prevents anyone from using HTTP GET to invoke the myService.asmx Web service and allows all users the ability to use HTTP POST.

The proxy class, when created with Visual Studio .NET or the WSDL.exe tool, exposes the Credentials property that you can set to a *NetworkCredential* object in order to pass credentials to be validated against password-based authentication schemes such as basic, digest, NTLM, and Kerberos authentication. The following example depicts assigning a new NetworkCredential object to the Credentials property of the proxy class:

```
Dim proxy As New localhost.Service1()
proxy.Credentials = _
    New Net.NetworkCredential("username", "password", "DomainName")
```

The domain name parameter is optional and refers to the Windows domain that is doing the authentication. In Exercise 11.3, you will create a Web service and restrict access by using URL-based authorization.

Exercise 11.3 requires Windows 2000, Windows XP, or Windows 2003 Server in order to support the creation of Windows accounts in the exercise.

EXERCISE 11.3

Implementing File-Based Authorization

1. Open a command prompt by clicking Start ➢ Run and typing **cmd.exe** in the Run text box.

2. At the prompt, type the following commands to create two user accounts on your local machine (press Enter after each command):

    ```
    net user /add user1 p@$$WOrD
    net user /add user2 pAsSwOrD
    ```

3. Type **exit** and press Enter at the command prompt to close the window.

4. Create a new XML Web service project named **FileBasedAuthExample** and switch to Code view.

5. Use the following code to create a Web method named secretMessage:

    ```
    <WebMethod()> Public Function secretMessage() As String

        Return "Secret Message to " & User.Identity.Name.ToString()

    End Function
    ```

6. Add a new XML Web service named Service2.asmx to the project and switch to its Code view.

7. Use the following code to create a Web method named publicMessage in the Service2.asmx code file:

    ```
    <WebMethod()> Public Function publicMessage() As String

        Return "Public Message to " & User.Identity.Name.ToString()

    End Function
    ```

8. Open the project's web.config file and notice that the authentication mode is set to Windows:

    ```
    <authentication mode="Windows" />
    ```

9. Remove the <authorization> element and its contents from the web.config file.

10. Add the following code on the line before the closing `</configuration>` element of the web.config file to permit User2 to execute the secretMessage service while preventing User1 from accessing the Service1.asmx service (replace *ComputerName* with the name of the computer you created the users on):

```
<location path="Service1.asmx">
    <system.web>
        <authorization>
            <deny users="?" />
            <deny users="ComputerName\User1" />
            <allow users="ComputerName\User2" />
            </authorization>
    </system.web>
</location>

<location path="Service2.asmx">
    <system.web>
        <authorization>
            <deny users="?" />
            </authorization>
    </system.web>
</location>
```

11. Build the solution and then right-click the FileBasedAuthExample solution from the Solution Explorer and click Add ➢ New Project. Select the Windows Application template and name the new project **FileBasedAuthExample_Client**.

12. Drag two Button controls onto Form1 with the following properties and values:

   - Name: **btnUser1**, Text: **User1**
   - Name: **btnUser2**, Text: **User2**

13. From the Solution Explorer, right-click the References item under the Exercise11_3_Client project and choose Add Web Reference.

14. In the Add Web Reference dialog box, type the following URL into the Address field: **http://** *ServerName***/filebasedAuthExample/Service1.asmx**. (*ServerName* should be replaced with **LocalHost** or the name of the server you are developing on.)

15. After the Available References window fills, click the Add Reference button to create the proxy class in the project.

16. From the Solution Explorer, right-click the References item under the Exercise11_3_Client project and choose Add Web Reference.

17. In the Add Web Reference dialog box, type the following URL into the Address field: **http://** *ServerName***/FileBasedAuthExample/Service2.asmx**. (*ServerName* should be replaced with **LocalHost** or the name of the server you are developing on.)

18. After the Available References window fills, click the Add Reference button to create the proxy class in the project.

19. From the Solution Explorer, right-click the localhost Web Reference and rename it to **svcSecret**.

20. From the Solution Explorer, right-click the `localhost1` Web Reference and rename it to **svcPublic**.

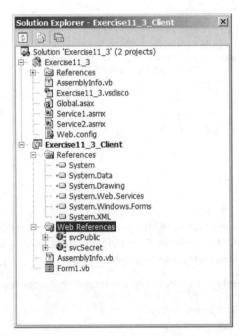

21. To create a subroutine in Form1.vb to call both services, use the following code with parameters for the credential information:

```
Public Sub CallServices(ByVal strUser As String, ByVal strPassword As String)

    Dim proxySecret As New svcSecret.Service1()
    Dim proxyPublic As New svcPublic.Service2()
    Dim myCredentials As New Net.NetworkCredential(strUser, strPassword)

    Try
        proxySecret.Credentials = myCredentials

        MessageBox.Show(proxySecret.secretMessage())

    Catch exc As Exception

        MessageBox.Show(exc.Message)

    End Try
```

```
Try
    proxyPublic.Credentials = myCredentials
    MessageBox.Show(proxyPublic.publicMessage())

Catch exc As Exception

    MessageBox.Show(exc.Message)

End Try

End Sub
```

22. Create an event handler for btnUser1 and type the following code in the procedure:

```
CallServices("User1", "p@$$WOrD")
```

23. Create an event handler for btnUser2 and type the following code in the procedure:

```
CallServices("User2", "pAsSwOrD")
```

24. From the Solution Explorer, right-click the Exercise11_3_Client project and choose Set As StartUp Project.

25. Launch the FileBasedAuthExample_Client project.

26. Click the User1 button to attempt both services as User1, who is denied access to the Secret Web service, but permitted to access the Public service.

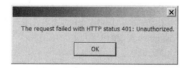

27. Click the User2 button to attempt both services as User2, who is permitted to access both services.

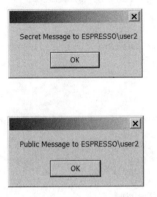

28. Close the application and save and close Visual Studio .NET

Encrypting SOAP Messages

Now that you have learned about authentication and authorization to prevent unauthorized access, you will need to secure the SOAP message itself. You must secure the contents of the XML Web service in transit between the server and the consumer. You can secure the SOAP messages by encrypting them before sending them.

Here you will be introduced to some of the techniques that you can use to secure all or some of the contents of the SOAP message.

Using SSL

One of the simplest ways to encrypt the SOAP message in transit is to use Secure Sockets Layer (SSL) connections. You need to obtain an X.509 certificate from a certificate authority (CA). You must enable SSL on your Web server after you have obtained a certificate. To enable SSL on IIS, you must open Internet Services Manager from the Administrative Tools on your Web server. Right-click the site on which you want to enable SSL and choose Properties. Navigate to the Directory Security tab, as seen in Figure 11.1, and click the Server Certificate button to launch the Web Server Certificate Wizard.

A major drawback to using SSL to encrypt the contents of a SOAP message is that it limits the protocols that you are able to use as a transport. You can use custom SOAP extensions to encrypt some or all of the SOAP message and still use it with any protocol you choose. Next, you will see the basic steps involved in using custom SOAP extensions for encryption.

FIGURE 11.1 IIS Directory Security tab

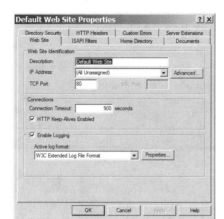

Selectively Encrypting Portions of the SOAP Message

You are the Web service developer of an Internet Web service provider. Some of the services that your company will provide require authentication. In some cases, credit card information might need to be transmitted across the Internet to be validated.

Your boss has volunteered you to be responsible for the security and privacy of the data that is being passed. The information must pass from the client to the Web service in a secure fashion. Many of the consumers will be using your Web service in their web applications, and therefore your service will need to perform as quickly as possible so as to not impact your customers' customers.

You know that using SSL causes all of the communication between the server and the consumer to be encrypted. Encrypting the whole message is not necessary in this case; the only data that must be secure are the authentication credentials and credit card data. Moreover, using SSL is often slow because the third party, or CA, needs to be contacted. One of the requirements posed to you is that the service must be as responsive and quick as possible.

You decide to alleviate this problem by creating a custom SOAP extension. By using a SOAP extension, you can encrypt only some of the requests or responses, or even specific parts of the requests or responses. You can also choose the type of encryption you would like to implement.

Implementing Custom SOAP Extensions

The .NET Framework makes it possible to interact with the serializing and deserializing processes for SOAP messages. To do this, you must create a class that is derived from the SoapExtension class, located in the System.Web.Services.Protocols namespace. You must also create a custom attribute that references the SOAP extension class.

To encrypt and decrypt messages by using this technique, you must apply the custom attribute to the appropriate XML Web service methods. A .NET consumer application of the XML Web service could also use the custom attribute. The attribute would need to be applied to the proxy class's methods that correspond to those services with the attribute applied.

The complete code for this topic is included on the CD that comes with this book, in the SOAPExtension.zip file. The code is a slightly customized version of sample code that originated from http://www.gotdotnet.com/team/rhoward. Rob Howard, a program manager on the .NET Framework team with Microsoft, makes this and several other .NET samples available for download from his page. This code is used with his permission.

After you inherit from the SoapExtension class, you can intercept the SOAP message in the ProcessMessage procedure, as seen in the following example:

```
Public Overrides Sub ProcessMessage(ByVal msg As SoapMessage)
        Select Case msg.Stage
            Case SoapMessageStage.BeforeSerialize
             'Nothing needs to happen here
            Case SoapMessageStage.AfterSerialize
                'Encrypt the data before serializing it to the client.
                Encrypt()
            Case SoapMessageStage.BeforeDeserialize
                'Decrypt the data before
                'deserializing it to .NET objects
                Decrypt()
            Case SoapMessageStage.AfterDeserialize
             'Nothing needs to happen here
            Case Else
                Throw New Exception("Invalid Stage.")
        End Select
End Sub
```

To implement selective encryption, you can create a custom attribute that you can apply to individual Web methods to require them to be encrypted. To accomplish this, you would inherit from the SoapExtensionAttribute class.

To enable this encryption on an XML Web service, you need to reference the Encryption assembly and add the attribute to the Web method, as in the following example:

```
<WebMethod(), EncryptionExtension(Encrypt:=EncryptMode.Response, _
    SOAPTarget:=Target.Body)> Public Function ReturnString() As String


        Return "This is an encrypted string"


    End Function
```

The client that uses this XML Web service would also need to use the extension in order to encrypt the request and decrypt the response.

> You can find more information about encryption schemes at `http://msdn`
> `.microsoft.com` and `http://www.gotdotnet.com`. There are also numerous
> books on the subject.

Summary

In this chapter, you learned about deployment strategies and ways to secure your XML Web services. We covered the following topics:

- How to create a setup program to install an XML Web service
- How to publish an XML Web service by using a static discovery document
- How to publish an XML Web service to a UDDI registry
- How to implement XML Web service authentication by using either Windows or ASP.NET authentication
- How to implement custom authentication by creating custom SOAP headers
- How to authorize access to resources by using file- and URL-based authorization
- How to encrypt SOAP messages by using SSL and HTTPS
- How to modify SOAP messages, like adding encryption, by creating custom SOAP extensions

Exam Essentials

Be familiar with the techniques of deploying XML Web services.   Make sure that you can create a setup program and a discovery document.

Know how to publish Web services.   You should know the schema and the meaning behind it in order to publish your Web service to a UDDI registry. You should also be able to configure static and dynamic discovery.

Know how to authenticate requests by using Windows and ASP.NET authentication.   Make sure that you can create custom SOAP headers to pass credentials to an XML Web service to be authenticated.

Be able to grant or deny access to XML Web services by using both file- and URL-based authorization.   Know how to restrict access to individual services and folders, as well as which verbs are allowed to be used by whom.

Key Terms

Before you take the exam, be certain you are familiar with the following terms:

authentication	impersonation
authorization	NetworkCredential
bindingTemplate	SoapHeader
businessEntity	static discovery
businessService	tModel
discovery	tModelInstanceDetails
dynamic discovery	URL-based authorization
file-based authorization	

Review Questions

1. You have developed an XML Web service that requires a shared assembly to be installed into the global assembly cache (GAC). You need to create a technique for the Web service to be installed on your customers' web servers. Which one of the following methods is most suited for this type of deployment?

   A. Use XCOPY to install the service.

   B. Create a setup program that installs the service as well as the assembly into the GAC.

   C. Create a discovery document to install the service.

   D. You must deploy your Web services to a UDDI registry for installation.

2. You are the developer of a simple XML Web service that returns weather information to its consumers. You have created the XML Web service by using Visual Studio .NET. The Visual Studio .NET solution is named myWeather, and the Web service project is named weatherService. What should you do to create a setup program for the weatherService Web service?

   A. Use the Package And Deployment Wizard to create a setup program for the myWeather solution.

   B. Add a Web Setup project to the weatherService project.

   C. Add a Web Setup project to the myWeather solution.

   D. Use the Package And Deployment Wizard to create a setup program for the weatherService solution.

3. You are the developer of several XML Web services that your company exposes for its customers. You would like your customers to be able to see all of the public XML Web services that you offer. Some of your customers will be using Visual Studio .NET, and others might be using Java and other tools to consume your services. Which of the following files should you create?

   A. .vsdisco file

   B. .disco file

   C. discovery.htm

   D. discovery.asmx

4. You are the lead developer of your company's XML Web services. You would like to publish the services into a UDDI registry, but first you must create the appropriate XML document to send to the registry. In which element will you specify information about your company?

   A. <businessEntity>

   B. <businessService>

   C. <bindingTemplate>

   D. <tModel>

5. You are developing an XML Web service that will require its consumers to authenticate over the Internet. You want to use your existing Windows infrastructure, so you have chosen to use Windows authentication. Many of your clients use their Internet browser to invoke the service. What type of authentication would you configure to allow for the highest amount of compatibility across browsers and through corporate firewalls, yet still verify who is and isn't allowed to access the service?

   A. Basic authentication

   B. Digest authentication

   C. Integrated Windows authentication

   D. Anonymous authentication

6. You have developed an internal XML Web service, named `enterTime`, that is used by employees of your company to enter their billable time. Your company uses Windows 2000 Active Directory to authenticate its users throughout the LAN. The `enterTime` Web service will be used only by employees who are locally attached to the corporate LAN. Which of the following elements would you put into the `web.config` file of your web application to achieve the highest level of security?

   A. `<authentication mode="None" />`

   B. `<authentication mode="Forms" />`

   C. `<authentication mode="Passport" />`

   D. `<authentication mode="Windows" />`

7. You are the lead developer of an XML Web service that calculates estimated shipping time between two locations. This service is designed to be used only by active customers. You want to implement your own custom authentication by using Microsoft SQL Server. You have decided to pass the credentials in custom SOAP headers and have set the authentication mode to `None` in the `web.config` file. What additional task must you perform to validate the credentials that are passed with the `WebMethod` call?

   A. Create the appropriate accounts in Active Directory.

   B. Within the Web method, validate the credentials against the database.

   C. Set the NTFS permissions on the `.asmx` file to grant access only to those who are authorized.

   D. None of the above.

8. You are the developer of an XML Web service that is restricted and allows only employees of your company to access it. The service is configured for Windows authentication. What is the fastest way to prevent a specific group from accessing the `service1.asmx` file?

   A. Configure file-based authorization and remove the groups' permissions from the ACL.

   B. Configure `service1.asmx` to use the `IsInRole` method of the `User.Identity` object to check the requester's membership in allowed groups.

   C. Add the `<allowed>` element to the `web.config` file and list the groups that are allowed in the `roles` attribute.

   D. Configure IIS to accept anonymous connections.

9. The following XML content is located in the `web.config` file:

```
<location path="weatherService.asmx" >
  <system.web>
    <authorization>
        <deny users="?" roles="Guests, Consultants" />
        <allow users="Thatcher, Tami, Rena" roles="Employees" />
    </authorization>
  </system.web>
</location>
```

Joe, Steve, and Jane are members of the Employees role. Thomas and Rena are members of the Consultants role. Which of the following users are allowed to invoke the Web service? (Choose all that apply.)

A. Joe

B. Jane

C. Thomas

D. Rena

E. Steve

10. You create an XML Web service named `getRecipe`. You need to make sure that the service meets the following URL authorization requirements:

- Anonymous access is not allowed.
- All members of the Cooks role should be allowed.
- An authenticated user named `tAnderson` is not allowed.

You have configured IIS to meet these requirements. Which of the following code segments should you put in the application's `web.config` file?

A. `<allow users="*" />`
   `<deny users="?" />`

B. `<deny users="?" />`
   `<deny users="tAnderson" />`
   `<allow roles="Cooks" />`

C. `<deny users="?, tAnderson" />`
   `<allow users="*" />`

D. `<allow users="Cooks" />`
   `<allow users="*" />`
   `<deny users="?" />`

11. You are creating an XML Web service that returns highly secure data to the Web service consumer. You create a class that derives from the `SoapExtension` class. Which method should you override in order to intercept the serialization process?

A. `ProcessSerialization`

B. `BeforeSerialize`

C. `AfterSerialize`

D. `ProcessMessage`

12. You are the developer of an XML Web service that processes credit card transactions for various e-commerce websites. You need to make sure that the credit card number that is transferred to your service is secure. The websites that use your service also want to make sure that they are transmitting the information only to your site. Which of the following technologies should you use to prevent the data from being intercepted on the Internet while requiring the least amount of developer effort?

A. Create a custom `SoapExtension` class.

B. Create a custom SOAP header.

C. Use SSL over HTTPS.

D. None of the above.

13. You have created a new XML Web service named `Prices` that exposes a Web method named `getBestPrice` that you would like to publish to a UDDI registry. You have already created `<businessEntity>` and `<tModel>` information, but you still need to provide an entry point for your service. Which of the following URLs would you use?

A. `http://www.abc.com/Svcs/Prices`

B. `http://www.abc.com/Svcs/Prices.asmx`

C. `http://www.abc.com/Svcs/Prices.asmx?getBestPrice`

D. `http://www.abc.com/Svcs/Prices.asmx?WSDL`

14. In order to allow an XML Web service consumer to specify the network credentials to pass into a Web service call, what property of the proxy object would you set to a `NetworkCredential` instance?

A. `Credentials`

B. `AuthInfo`

C. `Identity`

D. `Principal`

15. You are the developer of an XML Web service that accepts credit card information over the Internet. In certain circumstances a browser is used as the client, and you want to prevent a consumer from sending the credit information by appending it to the URL of the Web service. Which of the following XML segments should be assigned for this service?

A. `<deny verb="POST" users="*" />`

B. `<deny verb="GET" users="*" />`

C. `<deny verb="GET" users="?" />`

D. `<deny verb="POST" users="?" />`

Answers to Review Questions

1. **B.** Because of the requirement to install an assembly in the global assembly cache, you cannot use XCOPY, or zero-impact, deployment. A discovery document and UDDI are used for locating and consuming XML Web services, not for installing/hosting them. You must create a setup program that installs the service and the assembly.

2. **C.** The Package And Deployment Wizard was used to create installer packages for *previous* versions of Visual Studio. The Web Setup project cannot be added to another project, but only to a solution that contains the project to create the setup program for. Therefore, the third answer is the only possible correct answer.

3. **B.** The standard should be a `.disco` file conforming to the `xmlsoap.org` standard. A `.vsdisco` file is a proprietary Visual Studio .NET discovery file and doesn't follow the standards that non–Visual Studio .NET consumers would be looking for. An HTML file might be useful to provide more information about your services, but it isn't a standard or a part of discovery. The `.asmx` file is the actual service, not the discovery information regarding it.

4. **A.** The `<businessEntity>` element is used to describe the responsible party for the service in the UDDI registry. The `<businessService>` element describes the service, the `<bindingTemplate>` element describes the technical details of the service, and the `<tModel>` element specifies which standards the service meets.

5. **A.** Basic authentication is compatible with most Web browsers, even though it transmits the passwords in clear text. Digest authentication is supported only by Internet Explorer 5 and above, and Integrated Windows authentication cannot pass natively through corporate firewalls. Configuring anonymous authentication prevents the service from verifying who is who.

6. **D.** Windows authentication will provide the highest level of security for this scenario. Forms and Passport authentication are not currently designed for XML Web services, nor are they as secure as Windows authentication. Configuring the authentication mode to None would require that you implement a custom authentication mechanism, which is needed given this scenario.

7. **B.** If you are implementing custom authentication, you must write the code that verifies the credentials that the consumer supplies. There is no need, in this scenario, to create users in Active Directory. NTFS permissions aren't required because you are implementing custom authentication.

8. **A.** Given the scenario and the list of options, the best answer is using file-based authentication (NTFS file security). The second answer would work but it would require more time to configure than the first answer. In addition, the second answer would require the service to be recompiled each time that the roles that are allowed to access the service are changed. There is no `<allowed>` element that is recognized in the `web.config` file. Finally, anonymous access does nothing to restrict access to individual services.

9. **A, B, E.** Thomas and Rena are denied access through their membership in the Consultants role. Because Rena's `<deny>` element is encountered before her `<allow>` element, she will be denied.

10. B.   The elements are validated one by one. First, you must deny anonymous users: `<deny users="?" />`. Next, deny `tAnderson`: `<deny users="tAnderson" />`. Finally, allow the Cooks role: `<allow roles="Cooks" />`. The first answer is incorrect because it allows all users in first. The third answer is formatted incorrectly. The last answer allows all users before denying anonymous users and would allow `tAnderson` to invoke the service.

11. A.   You should override the extension's `ProcessMessage` method. The `SoapExtension` class does not have a `ProcessSerialization` method. The `BeforeSerialize` and `AfterSerialize` are `SoapMessageStage`s, not methods.

12. C.   Using Secure Sockets Layer (SSL) over HTTPS provides encryption of all the data, as well as a certificate authority (CA) verifying that the service is who it claims to be. A custom SOAP extension will not verify that the data is being sent to where it is intended; a third party must guarantee that. Custom SOAP headers don't provide any type of encryption alone.

13. B.   The extension `.asmx` must be specified in the entry point. The third answer is incorrect, because it is referencing the Web method and should specify the value that it is passing: `Prices.asmx?getBestPrice=1234`. The last answer is incorrect because the WSDL document is not necessary for an entry point.

14. A.   The `Credentials` property of the proxy object is what should be valued and passed to the service. There isn't an `AuthInfo`, `Identity`, or `Principal` property for all proxy instances.

15. B.   To prevent anyone from being able to send data to the service by appending it to the URL, you must prevent them from using an HTTP GET when requesting your service. The * is used to represent all users, and the ? represents only anonymous users. To prevent all users, you must deny everyone the ability to use the GET verb.

Glossary

AcceptChanges method   A method of the ADO.NET `DataSet`, `DataTable`, and `DataRow` classes. This method makes any user changes permanent in the `DataSet` and resets all values of the object to match the current values. After `AcceptChanges` is a called, the original database values are lost and rows are marked with a `RowState` property value of `Unchanged`.

ACID properties   A term used to describe important features of how transactions work. ACID stands for Atomicity, Consistency, Isolation, and Durability.

ADO.NET Toolbox components   Visual Studio .NET enables you to add commonly used objects, such as ADO.NET Connection, Command, DataAdapter, `DataSet`, and `DataView` objects to your project by selecting them from the Toolbox. The components can then be configured by using the Properties window or, in some cases, a wizard. The code that is needed to support these components is automatically generated and added to your project by Visual Studio .NET.

application domain   A Common Language Runtime feature that provides a new way of isolating managed code applications that are running on the same computer. Instead of requiring each application to run in a separate memory process on the computer, as in COM applications, you can run several application domains in a single process.

Application Proxy Remote Server Name   The name of the remote server that your components will be installed on; this is set when creating a Windows installer file (`.msi`).

assembly attributes   Attribute settings that are added to your application at the assembly level. Attributes can be set to control how your application works when running under Windows Component Services.

Assert method   This method of the `Debug` and `Trace` classes enables you to provide an expression that you expect to evaluate to `True` while your application is running as expected. When the test expression evaluates to `False`, the `Assert` method causes an error dialog box to be displayed and messages to be written to the Output window.

asymmetric cryptography   A type of cryptography that uses different keys to encrypt and decrypt data. Encryption algorithms add better protection by using asymmetric cryptography.

asynchronous callback function   A method that is specified to run when an asynchronous call to a remote object or web service has completed.

attribute   An XML element can contain one or more attributes, which carry additional data. Attributes are in the form of a name/value pair, and the attribute value must be enclosed in quotes. A given attribute name cannot be repeated for a given element.

authentication   The process of demonstrating who you are, to the system. This is most commonly accomplished by providing a username and password.

authorization   The process of verifying that a process has the required permissions to perform specified system actions. It is closely connected with authentication in that the identity of the user running the process often determines what the process is authorized to do. In .NET, authorization is provided by a combination of the Common Language Runtime's code access security and role-based security mechanisms.

AutoComplete attribute   When a method's `AutoComplete` attribute is set to `True`, the method's "vote" to commit or roll back the transaction will be set to `Commit` if the method completes successfully.

AutoLog property   A property of the .NET Framework `ServiceBase` class (the class that all Windows service applications inherit from). When this property is `True`, entries will be written to the Windows Application event log when the service is started, stopped, paused, or continued.

binary formatter   Creates a binary data stream containing the method calls and data that are passed between remote components. This binary data stream can be read only by .NET-compatible applications.

bindingTemplate element   One of the UDDI elements that are used to provide information about a Web service. The `bindingTemplate` element is used to describe the technical specifications that are required to bind to a particular XML Web service. The binding information is either an access point or a hosting redirector.

BooleanSwitch class   This class enables you to create an object in your application that indicates whether `Debug` and `Trace` messages should be output during application execution. This option can be set in source code or in the application configuration file.

BooleanSwitch.Enabled property   The `Enabled` property of the `BooleanSwitch` class determines whether `Debug` and `Trace` messages should be output during application execution. This option can be set in source code or in the application configuration file.

breakpoints   The Visual Studio .NET code editor enables you to set breakpoints that specify at which line of code the execution of your application should break (or be suspended) so that you can examine variable values and other application information. You can then continue executing code by stepping line by line. In Visual Studio .NET, a breakpoint can be defined to hit on only a specified expression value or hit count, and they can be saved with the solution.

businessEntity   One of the UDDI elements that are used to provide information about a Web service. The `businessEntity` element describes the business that is the responsible party for registering the XML Web service in the UDDI. This element contains details about the business, such as its name and contact information.

businessService   One of the UDDI elements that are used to provide information about a Web service. The `businessService` element describes the XML Web service that the business entity is exposing. This element names the service as well as associates it with a business entity and binding information. You can also assign categories to the Web service, such as industry or product.

channel   A defined mechanism for remote components to communicate with one another. The channel definition includes protocol (such as HTTP or TCP), port numbers, and (optionally) security features.

class   The source code that creates a template for an object.

ClassInterfaceAttribute   An attribute that can be applied to an assembly or class and that causes a COM interface to be generated automatically for your .NET component.

client-activated   A .NET Remoting object can be configured as either client-activated or server-activated. The lifetime of a client-activated remote object is controlled by the client; the object will remain activated on the server for multiple calls from the same caller.

Close method   This method of the `Debug` and `Trace` classes flushes the output buffers and closes the `TraceListeners`.

CLR Debugger (DbgCLR.exe)   A command-line utility that is provided with Visual Studio .NET. It provides debugging services with a graphical interface when the .NET Framework is installed but Visual Studio .NET is not present.

CLR role-based security   Grants permissions based on the identity of the user running the code and the roles to which they are assigned. It is often used to check whether a specific Windows user is authorized to access a particular system or network resource.

code access permissions   The capabilities that can be granted to applications, such as file and disk access, and access to other system resources.

code access security   Facilitates restricting the operation of code based on what the Common Language Runtime knows about the calling code. Code access security is implemented by combining .NET permissions with the concepts of evidence, security policies, and code groups.

code groups   Assemblies that are allowed similar permissions and are grouped together when defining security policy to simplify administration.

ColumnMapping property   This property of the `DataColumn` object controls whether a column is output as an XML element or as an attribute. The `ColumnMapping` property can be specified as either `Element`, `Attribute`, `Hidden` (that column will not be included in the XML output), or `SimpleContent` (the column data will be output as the text content of the row element).

COM+   A name that describes the Component Object Model (COM) and Windows Component Services as implemented on the Windows 2000 platform.

COM+ proxies   Wrappers that mimic the interface of the COM+ component locally, but contain only the code necessary to make a call to the COM+ application in another process or on another computer.

CommandBehavior   An optional parameter of the `Command.ExecuteReader` method. The most common use for this parameter is to take advantage of the `CloseConnection` option, but it can also be used for other optimizations, such as processing single row resultsets.

CommandText property   A property of the ADO.NET Command class. Use it to specify either a SQL statement, stored procedure name, or the name of a database table.

CommandType property   A property of the ADO.NET Command class. Use it to specify the type of query that will be run: an ad hoc SQL query (text), a stored procedure, or direct table access.

component   A compiled unit of executable code.

component interoperability   A set of standard interfaces that enable components to discover the capabilities of other components and call their methods.

Component Services tool   A Windows operating system utility enabling you to manage components that are hosted by COM+ Component services and .NET Enterprise Services.

ComVisibleAttribute   An attribute that can be applied to a class or member of a .NET assembly to determine whether the class or member is available to COM components that are interoperating with the assembly.

connection pooling   A mechanism that maintains a group of already initialized connections to the database. When a user requests a connection, an existing one in the pool can be made available quickly, assuming that there are available connections with the same userid. When the user releases the connection, it can be returned to the pool and recycled for the next request.

Connection.BeginTransaction method   Use the BeginTransaction method of the ADO.NET Connection class to create an ADO.NET Transaction object.

ConnectionString property   A property of the ADO.NET Connection class. It specifies the type of database server, location of the server, database name, user credentials, and other settings.

ContextUtil class   The System.EnterpriseServices.ContextUtil class has properties that give you information about the status of the current transaction and has methods that you can use to affect transaction outcome.

ContinueUpdateOnError property   This property of the ADO.NET DataAdapter determines whether the DataAdapter.Update method will stop processing when an error is encountered, or continue processing any remaining records and mark those rows in the DataSet where the update operation failed.

CreateAttribute method   This method of the XmlDocument class enables you to create new XML attributes programmatically.

CreateElement method   This method of the XmlDocument class enables you to create new XML elements programmatically.

cryptography   The process of encoding data to an unrecognizable form (known as ciphertext) for the sake of secrecy, and decoding it to obtain the original data (known as plaintext).

CryptoStream class   A member of the System.Security.Cryptography namespace, this class can read input data and write it as encrypted output to a stream object.

Data Adapter Configuration Wizard   A Visual Studio .NET wizard that helps you to configure an ADO.NET DataAdapter component. The wizard helps you select a connection and build SQL statements. Alternatively, you can use existing stored procedures or have the wizard generate the stored procedure code for you.

DataException class   This ADO.NET class is the .NET Framework class that enables you to catch specific types of data access exceptions.

DataRelation object   This ADO.NET object enables you to specify primary key/foreign key relationships between DataTables in the same DataSet.

DataRow object   This ADO.NET object enables you to work with the properties and field values of an individual row of data in a DataTable.

DataRow.RowState property   This ADO.NET property indicates whether the row has been Added, Deleted, Detached, Modified, or is Unchanged, since the data has been added to the DataSet or since the last time AcceptChanges or RejectChanges was called.

DataRowVersion enumeration   This set of enumerated values are used to indicate whether the data in a DataRow consists of Current values (changes that have been made to the data since the data has been added to the DataSet or since the last time AcceptChanges or RejectChanges was called), Original values (the same values as in the database), or Proposed values (while an edit operation is pending).

DataSet   This ADO.NET class is a disconnected local data store that can be used by client applications to work with data locally or to easily pass data from one component to another. Data stored in the DataSet is further organized into DataTable and DataRow objects.

DataTable class   This ADO.NET class provides a structure to hold the results of a single query inside the DataSet. A DataSet can hold multiple DataTables.

DataView class   This ADO.NET DataView class enables your application to create different ways to view the data in a DataSet, without changing the underlying data and without having to make additional queries to the database server. The DataView class has Sort, Filter, and RowFilter properties that can be used to create the alternative views of the data. The DataView class has a Find method to search the data.

DataViewManager class   This ADO.NET class provides a single object that can be used to make property settings, such as setting the Sort or Filter property, for any of the DataView objects associated with a DataSet.

DeactivateOnReturn property   A property of the System.EnterpriseServices.Context-Util class, this indicates whether the object has completed all of its work in the transaction.

Debug class   A member of the System.Diagnostics namespace, this class provides information to the developer during development and testing.

DEBUG compiler directive   In order for debug code to be included in your compiled executables, the DEBUG compiler directive must be set to True before compiling your application.

Debug configuration   Visual Studio .NET enables you to choose either a Debug or Release build for your application. The Debug configuration creates a .pdb (program database) file that contains what are called *debugging symbols* for your executable. This file is found in the project's \bin directory along with the executable file. A Debug build will also cause extra information to be added to the executable file so that the debugger can do things such as stopping at breakpoints and letting you step through your executing code. Use the Debug configuration when you are developing and testing your application.

declarative   A term describing permissions for code that can be specified declaratively, by applying attributes to assemblies, classes, or methods. Contrast this with imperative techniques, where security features are implemented in the application's source code.

DefaultTraceListener class   The .NET Framework class that is automatically added to the `Trace.Listeners` collection. This is the mechanism that is responsible for writing to the Visual Studio .NET Output window, by default.

DeleteCommand   This property of the ADO.NET DataAdapter class is one of the three related properties that hold the SQL statements (or stored procedure names) that will be used when the corresponding insert, update, or delete operations must be performed during an update to the database.

DiffGram   An XML representation of the contents of a `DataSet`. A `DiffGram` contains additional XML attributes that indicate which of the items in a `DataSet` have been modified, inserted, or deleted. Following the XML output of the data rows, the `DiffGram` contains a section of XML that retains the original values of the modified records. The new section of XML output begins with a `<diffgr:before>` element. If any of the data rows has an error, that information will be noted in another section of the output file starting with a `<diffgr:errors>` element.

discovery   The process that enables clients to obtain information about which XML Web services are available at a given endpoint (or on a web server).

distributed transactions   Transactional operations that involve more than one component, or perhaps even components running on different servers.

document encoding   Specifies the exact format of XML that will be created in the SOAP message by using a Web Services Description Language (WSDL) document.

Document Type Definition (DTD)   An older technology for validating the format of XML data. Although most tools can still validate by using the DTD syntax, XSD (Schema) is preferred for new development.

dynamic discovery   A process that enables clients to search all the directories on the web server until it locates an available XML Web service. Dynamic discovery is an alternative to static discovery, in which the client has prior knowledge of a specific URL for the web service.

element   The XML element is part of the markup that describes data.

Errors collection   The ADO.NET Exception class has an `Errors` collection containing one or more Error objects that contain messages sent from the database server.

event log   A log provided by the Windows operating system. All programs running on a Windows system can write status messages to an event log. These logs can be viewed by accessing the Event Viewer utility.

EventLogTraceListener class   A derived class of the `TraceListener` class, this will write trace messages to the Windows event log.

evidence   Information identifying the code and its origin. Common types of evidence considered when evaluating (or administering) code access security are the application directory, the publisher, website of origin (for code downloaded over the web), the strong name, and the security zone from which code originates.

ExecuteNonQuery method   This method of the ADO.NET Command class executes a query against the database and returns the number of rows affected. It is typically used with SQL insert, update, and delete queries.

ExecuteReader method   This method of the ADO.NET Command class executes a query against the database and returns the resultset to a DataReader object.

ExecuteScalar method   This method of the ADO.NET Command class executes a query against the database and returns a single value (the first column of the first row of the resultset).

ExecuteXmlReader method   This method of the ADO.NET SqlCommand class (supported only for the SqlClient provider) is used when executing a FOR XML query against the database which will return XML data to an XmlReader.

Extensible Markup Language (XML)   A markup language that enables you to add tags and attributes to a data file; these tags and attributes describe the meaning and structure of the data items. The XML standard defines a few simple rules that ensure consistency among all XML documents. These rules include case sensitivity, a uniquely named root element that encloses all the data, strict matching of start and end tags, proper nesting of elements within the hierarchy, and a few others. The XML standard was created and is maintained by the World Wide Web Consortium (http://www.w3c.org) and therefore is neither vendor nor platform specific.

Extensible Stylesheet Language (XSL) and XSL Transformations (XSLT)   A technology that can be applied to XML data files when you need to change an existing format of XML data into a new format of output. The two primary uses for this are to apply HTML formatting tags to XML data so that the data can be displayed on a web page, and to change the format of the XML markup (while retaining the data values) so that the XML file can be sent to another application or consumer that requires the new format.

file-based authorization   A type of authorization using NTFS file security to determine whether the requesting client can access the resource. The only time that this can be used is when you are using Windows authentication.

Fill method   This method of the ADO.NET DataAdapter class runs a single SQL query against the data source and creates (or adds to) a DataTable in the DataSet.

Find method   This method of the ADO.NET DataView class searches the data.

Flush method   This method of the TraceListener classes ensures that messages are promptly written to their destination text files or log files.

FOR XML clause   An optional modifier that can be added to a standard SQL query in Microsoft SQL Server 2000. Adding this clause causes SQL Server to return XML results for the query rather than a recordset.

ForeignKeyConstraint   This ADO.NET class enables you to specify a primary key/foreign key relationship between two DataTables (by specifying the appropriate DataColumns in the tables) for the purposes of enforcing referential integrity. The ADO.NET ForeignKeyConstraint can be set to either allow or disallow cascading updates and deletes on the related tables.

forward-only, read-only recordset   A type of resultset that enables you to access each row in the resultset only once. You cannot scroll backward, and the recordset cannot be updated by the user.

gacutil.exe   This command-line utility provided with Visual Studio .NET enables you to install an assembly in the global assembly cache (GAC), which is a central directory on the computer that holds all shared components.

Generate DataSet menu   After creating and configuring an ADO.NET DataAdapter Toolbox component in your project, you can use the Visual Studio .NET Data ➢ Generate DataSet menu choice to create an XSD schema and an Visual Basic .NET class, which define a strongly typed DataSet in your project.

GetElementsByTagName method   This method of the XmlDocument class enables you to identify all of the elements within an XmlDocument that match the specified element tag name.

GetXml method   This method of the DataSet class returns an XML representation of the data contained in a DataSet.

GetXmlSchema method   This method of the DataSet class returns the XSD schema for the DataSet.

global assembly cache (GAC)   A location to install assemblies that are shared by several applications. Assemblies must be assigned a strong name and installed into the GAC by using the gacutil.exe utility program.

Hosting a .NET Remoting object in IIS   Microsoft Internet Information Server (IIS) can be used to host .NET Remoting objects, simply by installing the remoting server's executables in an IIS virtual directory.

HTTP channel   The channel, for communication between remote components, that uses the familiar Hypertext Transport Protocol (HTTP) to pass data. By default, the HTTP channel uses the Simple Object Access Protocol (SOAP) formatter to send the message as an XML document.

Hypertext Transfer Protocol (HTTP)   An application-level protocol by which text and other types of data can be transferred over the Internet. HTTP is supported on all platforms. HTTP traffic is usually allowed to move through corporate firewalls with little interference on well-known port 80.

Identity object   An object that contains information about the identity of the user (such as their user ID) and the authentication provider used to determine and verify that identity.

Identity permissions   Permissions that are granted to code based on the user identity that it is running under and its origin.

ildasm.exe   A command-line utility program provided with Visual Studio .NET that enables you to view the Microsoft Intermediate Language (IL) code that is created when you compile your VB. NET source code.

imperative   A term used to describe techniques for specifying an application's security features that are implemented directly in the application's source code. Contrast this with the declarative technique of applying attributes to assemblies, classes, or methods.

impersonation   Enables a process to temporarily take on the identity of another user, whose authorization to perform certain tasks might be different from the user identity under which the process was created.

InsertCommand   This property of the ADO.NET DataAdapter class is one of the three related properties that hold the SQL statements (or stored procedure names) that will be used when the corresponding insert, update, or delete operations must be performed during an update to the database.

InstallUtil.exe   This .NET Framework Installation utility is used to install or uninstall a Windows service, and executes the installers that are contained in the Windows service's .NET assembly.

instance   A single runtime instance of an object, which has its own unique set of properties and data.

instrumentation   The process of adding features to your applications that provide the ability to measure performance and to track and troubleshoot errors.

integration testing   A type of testing used to ensure that calls are being made correctly to your component and that the return results are in the correct format. Integration testing tests the interface between two components.

IsolationLevel property   A property of the ADO.NET Transaction class that can be set to request that the database server place a high level of isolation, or protection, against other users changing (or even reading) the same data that your transaction is working with.

just-in-time-activation (JTA)   A feature that enables COM+ to activate an object instance very quickly at the time that a client application makes a method call on an object (not when the object is instantiated by a client). When that method call is complete, COM+ can also quickly deactivate the object instance and release any memory or other resources that the object is holding. By releasing these resources quickly, they can be made available to other users.

lease manager   A part of the .NET remoting architecture, this object is responsible for locating client-activated objects whose lifetime lease has expired and marking them as available for garbage collection.

lifetime lease   The predetermined lifetime of client-activated remoting objects or the amount of time they will remain active on the server if there are no incoming calls from the client. The lifetime lease can be extended at each client call, or to a specific amount of time by the client.

Load method   This method of the XmlDocument class enables you to load the XML contents of a disk file or a stream object into an XmlDocument object.

LoadXml method   This method of the XmlDocument class enables you to load the XML contents of a string into an XmlDocument object.

LocalSystem   One of the built-in Windows security accounts. It is the most commonly used setting for Windows services. It is a highly privileged account and is seen by other servers as an anonymous account.

managed code   All code written by using the .NET Framework tools and designed to run under the Common Language Runtime (CLR). Other applications that run on the Windows/ COM platform, such as COM components and Visual Basic 6 applications, are known as unmanaged code.

Marshal-by-Reference object   When this object is passed between components, a proxy object is created in the caller's process. This object shows the client the same interface as the remote object and enables the client code to make method calls as though it were calling a local object. When the caller makes method calls on the proxy object, the .NET Remoting infrastructure passes those calls to the remote server, and the call is carried out in the server's process.

Marshal-by-Value object   A Marshal-by-Value object is passed between components, by serializing a complete copy of the object and passing it through the remoting channel to the caller.

Merge Module project   A project that packages assemblies that might be shared by other setup projects. When this project is built, it will generate an .msm file that can be added to other setup projects. The .msm file contains all the files, Registry settings, and setup configuration for installing the assemblies. They must be used from within a setup project and cannot be run alone.

message queuing   A feature of Windows Component Services that enables applications to make asynchronous calls on components. The information about the call is placed into a message queue (persistent storage) on the server, and the component processes each message when it is available. This is useful for making calls on an application on a remote server that might not always be online or for balancing peak workloads. Messages wait in the queue until the server component is connected and is able to process them. Also called queued components.

Microsoft Installer file (.msi)   A set-up file that will install by using the Windows Installer (msiexec.exe). This is the customary way to package and install a Windows application on Windows; you can also use it to package and deploy an ASP.NET application to a web server or group of web servers. MSI files can also be published to Add or Remove Programs in the Control Panel console and deployed by using Active Directory Software Deployment Policies.

middle-tier components   In a three-tier application design, code is separated into a user interface tier, a business logic tier, and a data access tier. The middle-tier components provide the business logic of your application.

multicultural test data   Test data that is used to ensure that those items that vary from culture to culture, such as dates, currency, and separator characters in numbers, are interpreted correctly by your application.

MyTransactionVote property   A property of the System.EnterpriseServices.ContextUtil class that indicates the object's "vote" (commit or roll back) on the transaction status.

.NET Enterprise Services   A name that describes the .NET Framework capabilities to interoperate with COM components and to take advantage of the features of Windows Component Services.

.NET Enterprise Services role-based security   This security mechanism, based on COM+, is provided for compatibility with pre-.NET code, as well as to provide an easy way to implement role-based security when roles are not defined as Windows groups. This feature of Windows Component Services enables you to define which groups of users (roles) are allowed to make calls on a component, class, or method. You can apply role-based security in source code through properties and methods of the `System.EnterpriseServices.ServicedComponent` base class; you can apply a `SecurityRoleAttribute` to your class; or you can assign roles administratively through the Component Services management console.

.NET Framework Assembly Registration utility (`regasm.exe`)   See `regasm.exe`.

.NET Framework Installation utility (`InstallUtil.exe`)   See `InstallUtil.exe`.

.NET Framework Services Registration utility (`regsvcs.exe`)   See `regsvcs.exe`.

.NET Remoting objects   Objects that enable application developers to use a familiar object reference approach when making interprocess communication between two applications.

`NetworkCredentials` object   An object that is used to validate against password-based authentication schemes such as basic, digest, NTLM, and Kerberos authentication.

`NodeList` collection class   One of the base classes in the `System.Xml` namespace, this collection holds groups of related element nodes.

object   An in-memory construction of code and data that can be created from a class.

object pooling   A feature of COM+/.NET Enterprise Services that helps to improve performance and scalability by maintaining a defined number of objects in memory at all times, ready to be activated when a calling application makes a request. You can tune application performance by adjusting the minimum and maximum number of objects to be maintained by the pool.

`OleDbConnection` class   This ADO.NET class enables you to create a connection to databases such as Access, Oracle, or DB2 by using an OLEDB provider. Use this class for accessing older versions of Microsoft SQL Server (version 6.5 or earlier).

`OleDbDataAdapter` object   This ADO.NET class enables you to connect to a data source and execute a query to return records and fill a `DataSet`. If the user makes changes to the data in the `DataSet`, the DataAdapter is also responsible for sending the appropriate insert, update, and delete statements to the database.

`OleDbDataReader` class   This ADO.NET class enables you to process a forward-only, read-only resultset that is returned from a database query.

`OleDbError` object   This ADO.NET object contains one error message that has been returned from the database server. Error objects are accessed through the Exception object's `Errors` collection.

`OleDbException` object   This ADO.NET object represents a specific type of exception that is thrown when an error occurs during database access.

OleDbParameter object   This ADO.NET object holds information about a parameter sent to a stored procedure.

OleDbTransaction object   This ADO.NET object ensures that two or more database commands are executed successfully before the changes are committed permanently to the database. If any of the commands fail, all intermediate results are rolled back.

OnStart method   A method of the .NET Framework ServiceBase class (the class that all Windows service applications inherit from). You can add code to this event procedure to determine what happens when the service is started up.

OnStop method   A method of the .NET Framework ServiceBase class (the class that all Windows service applications inherit from). You can add code to this event procedure to determine what happens when the service is stopped.

OPENXML clause   OPENXML provides a rowset representation of the data in an XML Document, which can be used anywhere in a SQL Server 2000 query that tables or views would normally be used. This clause enables SQL Server to load XML data into database tables.

permission sets   Permissions that are grouped together for easier administration, if an application requires various types of permissions. The .NET Framework provides some built-in permission sets: Execute, Everything, FullTrust, Internet, LocalIntranet, and Nothing.

permissions   Capabilities that can be granted to applications, such as file and disk access, and access to other system resources.

Platform Invoke   A capability of the .NET Framework to make API calls directly to the Windows system DLLs (or other unmanaged code). Also known as PInvoke.

port number   Specifies an endpoint for communications coming into a server. Port numbers 0 through 1023 are reserved for common applications (for example, web browsers use port 80 by convention). You can specify any port number (up to 65,535) when you register a channel. Be careful that you are not trying to use a port that is already in use by another application running on the same computer.

Principal object   An object that contains an Identity object as well as information about the roles for which the user with that identity is authorized. Principal types are GenericPrincipal (not a Windows user), WindowsPrincipal (valid Windows user), and CustomPrincipal.

processing instruction   Part of XML markup that enables you to place application-specific processing instructions in-line with XML data. The syntax for a processing instruction uses the <? processing instruction ?> delimiters.

proxy class   When creating an application that consumes XML Web services in Visual Studio .NET, code for a proxy class is automatically generated when you reference an XML Web service. You can instantiate objects from the class and make calls on them in the same way as any other local class. By using the proxy class, you do not have to worry about the underlying details of creating the SOAP message and connecting to the Web service.

proxy object   A stand-in for the remote object, this shows the client the same interface as the remote object and enables the client code to make method calls as though it were calling a local object.

ReadXml method   This method of the `DataSet` class reads the data and schema (if a schema is available) into a `DataSet` from an XML data file.

ReadXmlSchema method   This method of the `DataSet` class reads the XSD schema, but no data, into a `DataSet` from an XML data file.

regasm.exe   A utility that enables you to register an assembly in the Windows Registry for use by COM objects.

RegistrationHelper class   This class in the `System.EnterpriseServices` namespace provides the same functionality as the `regsvcs.exe` utility through a programmatic interface. This means that you can create your own install application or extend the administration tool of your application to support installing components.

regression testing   A type of testing that is done when changes or additions are made to your application. In addition to testing the code that was actually changed or is new, regression testing tests all of the previously tested parts of the application to make sure the new code has not inadvertently caused an error to occur in another part of the system.

regsvcs.exe   A command-line utility program that is provided with Visual Studio .NET that enables you to register a .NET assembly so that it can be used with Windows Component Services or accessed by COM components. It will then generate a COM type library as if you ran `tlbexp.exe` on the assembly.

RejectChanges method   A method of the ADO.NET `DataSet`, `DataTable`, and `DataRow` classes. This method cancels any user changes and resets all values of the object to the original values, as they were when the data was retrieved from the database or the last time that `AcceptChanges` was called.

Release configuration   Visual Studio .NET enables you to choose either a Debug or Release build for your application. The Release configuration removes the debugging information from your executable and improves performance somewhat. Use the Release build to create a final version that will be distributed to your users.

role   A group of user identities that are granted permission to access code and system resources, usually based on the job role in the organization.

role-based security   See CLR role-based security and .NET Enterprise role-based security.

role-based security permissions   The set of permissions that are granted to a user because that user is a member of a specific group or role.

RowFilter property   A property of the ADO.NET `DataView` class that enables you to set matching criteria for individual field values in the view. Only those rows that contain data matching the criteria will be accessible through the `DataView`.

RowStateFilter property   A property of the ADO.NET DataView class that enables you to filter the DataView based on one of the DataRow.RowState values—either Added, Deleted, Detached, Modified, or Unchanged.

RPC encoding   A type of encoding that uses general rules from the SOAP specification and generates a format of XML with an element whose tag name matches the method name. Nested inside that element are additional elements matching the parameter names for the method. The SOAP specification does not require that these parameters appear in any particular order. An application that is receiving the SOAP request must be able to handle these variations in formatting.

runtime debugger (Cordbg.exe)   A command-line utility provided by the .NET Framework that enables you to debug .NET Framework applications when Visual Studio .NET is not available.

Save method   This method of the XmlDocument class enables you to save the XML data in the XmlDocument to a disk file or a stream object.

Secure Sockets Layer (SSL)   A technology that enables a web server to transmit encrypted data over an HTTP connection.

security account   A Windows user login or system account that provides the identity and permissions that the Windows service will run under.

security policies   Policies that are used to determine what permissions apply to particular code groups and users. They are typically set outside the application itself, and can be set by either a custom administration tool provided with the application or a standard tool on the platform, such as .NET's caspol.exe utility.

SelectCommand property   A property of the ADO.NET DataAdapter class that holds the SQL statement (or stored procedure name) that will be used when retrieving data from the database during a Fill operation. You must specify the query to be used for the SelectCommand manually. Visual Studio .NET can then automatically generate the queries that will be used for the corresponding InsertCommand, UpdateCommand, and DeleteCommand properties.

SelectNodes method   This method of the XmlNode base class enables you to identify a group of nodes in an XmlDocument by applying XPath pattern matching expressions.

SelectSingleNode method   This method of the XmlNode base class enables you to identify the first matching node in an XmlDocument by applying XPath pattern matching expressions.

serialization   The process of creating a representation of an object and its state that can be transferred across the network from one component to the other.

Server Explorer   A window in the Visual Studio .NET IDE that enables you to view information about the operating system and other programs that are running on your network servers. You can view information about Windows services, SQL Server, and operating system performance counters.

server-activated object   A remote object that is instantiated on the server only when a method call is received. If a server-activated object is created as a SingleCall object, then it is deactivated as soon as the method call is completed. A server-activated object that is created as a `Singleton` object will remain in server memory for an indefinite period of time, and a single instance of the object can service requests from many different callers.

Service Control Manager Shows you a list of all services installed on the computer. For each service, you can see the name, description, current status (Started, Paused, or Stopped), startup type (Automatic—starts automatically on boot, or Manual), and the identity that the service logs on as. By using the menus and toolbar buttons, you can issue commands to start, stop, pause, continue, or restart the selected service. You can also view a Properties dialog box that enables you to change configuration options for a service.

ServiceBase class The .NET Framework class that all Windows service applications must inherit from. It is a member of the `System.ServiceProcess` namespace.

ServiceController class This class provides properties and methods that enable you to create .NET applications that programmatically control and send custom commands to a Windows service. It is a member of the `System.ServiceProcess` namespace.

ServiceControllerStatus enumeration This property of the `ServiceController` class enables your application to test the state of a Windows service. Valid settings: `StartPending`, `Running`, `StopPending`, `Stopped`, `PausePending`, `Paused`, `ContinuePending`.

serviced component A component that is hosted by COM+ Component services or .NET Enterprise Services. Running the component in this environment provides infrastructure services that improve application performance and scalability, as well as provide security and transaction management features.

ServicedComponent base class All .NET components that will run under Windows Component Services must inherit from the `System.EnterpriseServices.ServicedComponent` base class.

ServiceInstaller class The `ServiceInstaller` class and the `ServiceProcessInstaller` class provide properties and methods that enable you to install a Windows service application. They are members of the `System.ServiceProcess` namespace.

ServiceProcessInstaller class The `ServiceInstaller` class and the `ServiceProcess-Installer` class provide properties and methods that enable you to install a Windows service application. They are members of the `System.ServiceProcess` namespace.

SetAbort method A method of the `System.EnterpriseServices.ContextUtil` class. When this method is called during a method call (usually in a error handler), it sets the object's transaction "vote" to roll back the transaction.

SetComplete method A method of the `System.EnterpriseServices.ContextUtil` class. When this method is called at the end of a successful method call, it sets the object's transaction "vote" to commit the transaction.

setup project A Visual Studio .NET project template that enables you to create setup files and Windows Installer files (`.msi`) to install your applications.

Simple Object Access Protocol (SOAP)   A standardized XML format that is used to exchange method calls and associated data between Web services. The SOAP standard is maintained by the World Wide Web Consortium (`http://www.w3c.org`) and therefore is neither vendor nor platform specific.

Simple Object Access Protocol (SOAP) formatter   The .NET Remoting infrastructure uses this formatter to write information in a standardized XML format that can be understood by many applications. This XML format contains the information about the method calls and data that are passed between remote components.

`SingleCall` object   A server-activated object that is deactivated as soon as a single method call is completed.

`Singleton` object   A server-activated object that will remain in server memory for an indefinite period of time. A single instance of the object can service requests from many different callers.

`sn.exe`   A command-line utility program provided with Visual Studio .NET. It enables you to create the public key/private key pair that is used when your assemblies are compiled and assigned a strong name.

SOAP extension   Classes that you create with your own application-specific processing. Your custom code will run each time a SOAP message is received or sent by a Web service. Your application-specific code can be used to alter the standard SOAP message, or to perform encryption, or message logging, or any other custom processing you require.

`SoapDocumentMethod` attribute   An attribute that can be applied to an XML Web service method or a method of a proxy class; this attribute indicates that the method expects document-based SOAP messages.

`SoapExtension` base class   A class in the `System.Web.Services.Protocols` namespace. SOAP extensions enable you to run custom code each time a SOAP message is processed. To create a SOAP extension, you must create a class that inherits from `SoapExtension` and override the methods of the base class.

`SoapExtensionAttribute` class   This class provides a means to mark a Web method, so that the specified SOAP extension will be run when the method is invoked.

`SoapHeader` class   The .NET Framework class that enables you to create custom header fields that can send application-specific information along with the SOAP message.

`SoapHeader` attribute   An attribute that can be applied to an XML Web service method or a method of a proxy class; this attribute indicates that the method can process a specific SOAP header.

`SoapRpcMethod` attribute   An attribute that can be applied to an XML Web service method or a method of a proxy class; this attribute indicates that the method expects RPC-based SOAP messages.

Sort property   A property of the ADO.NET `DataView` class that enables you to set the sort order for the rows included in the `DataView`.

SqlCommand.Parameters collection The ADO.NET collection containing Parameter objects, each of which holds information about a parameter that is sent to a stored procedure.

SqlConnection class The ADO.NET class enabling you to create a connection to databases such as Microsoft SQL Server 7 or SQL Server 2000 by using a native protocol.

SqlDataAdapter class The ADO.NET class enabling you to connect to a data source and execute a query to return records and fill a **DataSet**. If the user makes changes to the data in the **DataSet**, the DataAdapter is also responsible for sending the appropriate insert, update, and delete statements to the database.

SqlDataReader class The ADO.NET class enabling you to process a forward-only, read-only resultset that is returned from a database query.

SqlError object The ADO.NET object containing one error message that has been returned from the database server. Error objects are accessed through the Exception object's **Errors** collection.

SqlException object The ADO.NET object representing a specific type of exception that is thrown when an error occurs during database access.

SqlParameter object The ADO.NET object that holds information about a parameter that is passed to a stored procedure.

SqlTransaction object The ADO.NET object ensuring that two or more database commands are executed successfully before the changes are committed permanently to the database. If any of the commands fail, all intermediate results are rolled back.

stack walk A stack walk is a process that examines each of the procedures that are currently pending during application execution. When evaluating permissions for a given piece of code, the CLR examines the permissions granted to the current stack frame, and then starts traveling upward on the call stack, examining the permissions granted at successively higher levels of the call stack, for all method calls currently executing. In most cases, if a permission is not granted at all higher levels of the call stack, the permission is not considered to be in effect, even if it has been granted to the currently executing code.

static discovery A type of discovery in which the client has prior knowledge of a specific URL for the Web service. It is an alternative to dynamic discovery, in which the client must search all the directories on the web server until it locates an available XML Web service.

stored procedure Any Structured Query Language (SQL) statement or set of statements that are pre-compiled and saved on the database server along with the database definition. The Microsoft SQL Server database uses its own programming language, called Transact-SQL (or T-SQL for short), to write these queries.

STRIDE An acronym used by Microsoft to help you remember the common types of security threats: Spoofing identity, Tampering with data, Repudiation, Information disclosure, Denial of service, Elevation of privilege.

strong name   Uniquely identifies an assembly by using a combination of the name, version number, and culture information, along with a public key and a digital signature.

strongly typed DataSet   Also referred to simply as a typed `DataSet`, this is an object whose definition is provided at design time and expressed in the form of an XML Schema Definition (XSD) document. Visual Studio .NET will also generate a class in your project that expresses the definition in terms of object properties, methods, and events.

Structured Query Language (SQL)   A standard language for writing queries to access data in relational databases. It is a nonproprietary standard defined by the American National Standards Institute (ANSI) and the International Organization for Standardization (ISO).

symmetric cryptography   A type of cryptography that uses the same key to encrypt and decrypt data. This is used in traditional encryption algorithms.

System.Data namespace   The .NET Framework namespace containing all of the classes that provide database access.

System.Data.OleDb namespace   The .NET Framework namespace containing classes that perform database access by using OLEDB providers. Use these classes with databases such as Access, Oracle, DB2, or older versions of Microsoft SQL Server (version 6.5 or earlier).

System.Data.SqlClient namespace   The .NET Framework namespace containing classes that perform database access by using native SQL Server protocols. Use these classes with Microsoft SQL Server version 7 or SQL Server 2000.

System.Diagnostics namespace   The .NET Framework namespace containing classes that enable you to add tracing to your applications.

System.EnterpriseServices namespace   The .NET Framework namespace that includes classes enabling you to create .NET components that will run under Windows Component Services.

System.MarshalByRefObject   The .NET Framework class that .NET remoting objects must inherit from in order to use .NET Remoting's proxy/stub architecture.

System.Runtime.InteropServices namespace   The .NET Framework namespace that provides classes enabling you to create .NET components that can interoperate with COM components.

System.Runtime.Remoting   The .NET Framework namespace that contains classes enabling you to create components that can communicate with remote components.

System.Security namespace   The .NET Framework namespace that contains classes enabling you to add security features to your applications.

System.Security.Cryptography namespace   The .NET Framework namespace that contains classes enabling you to work with several types of encryption mechanisms in your applications.

System.Security.Permissions namespace   The .NET Framework namespace that contains classes enabling you to apply and verify permissions in your applications.

System.Security.Policy namespace   The .NET Framework namespace that contains classes enabling you to apply and verify security policies in your applications.

System.Security.Principal namespace   The .NET Framework namespace that contains classes enabling you to manage role-based security in your applications.

System.ServiceProcess namespace   The .NET Framework namespace that contains classes (including `ServiceBase`, `ServiceController`, `ServiceInstaller`, and `ServiceProcess-Installer`) enabling you to create and control Windows service applications.

System.Web.Services.dll   The .NET Framework assembly that must be referenced when you are creating an XML Web service.

System.Web.Services.Protocols.SoapHeader class   The .NET Framework class that enables you to create custom header fields that can send application-specific information along with the SOAP message.

System.Web.Services.WebService class   The .NET Framework class that all classes in an XML Web service must inherit from.

System.XML namespace   The .NET Framework namespace that contains classes enabling you to work with XML data files.

System.Xml.Xpath namespace   The .NET Framework namespace that contains classes enabling you to use XPath pattern matching expressions to locate nodes in XML data files.

System.Xml.Xsl namespace   The .NET Framework namespace that contains classes enabling you to perform XSL transformations on XML data files.

TCP channel   A channel for communication between remote components that uses Transmission Control Protocol (TCP), a lower-level network transmission protocol, and by default formats messages by using the binary formatter.

TextWriterTraceListener class   A class that can write tracing output to any .NET Framework stream object, such as a text file.

tModel   One of the UDDI elements that are used to provide information about a Web service. The tModel element contains the information used to describe compliance with a specification, concept, or a shared design. The element also contains a key, a name, an optional description, and a URL where you can find more information about the XML Web service.

tModelInstanceDetails   One of the UDDI elements that are used to provide information about a Web service. The tModelInstanceDetails element contains zero or more tModel-InstanceInfo elements. The tModelInstanceInfo element has an attribute named tModelKey, which identifies a specific tModel. Also included in the tModelInstanceDetails element are a description, a reference to the overview document, and instance parameters.

Trace class   This class from the System.Diagnostics namespace enables you to output messages from your application. These messages can be used to monitor your application's performance and troubleshoot any errors that might occur when the application is running.

TRACE compiler directive   In order for tracing code to be included in your compiled executables, the TRACE compiler directive must be set to True before compiling your application.

TraceSwitch class   This class enables you to create an object in your application that determines which Debug and Trace messages should be output during application execution, based on the setting for the Level property. This option can be set in source code or in the application configuration file.

TraceSwitch.Level property   A property that determines the priority level enabling you to determine which Debug and Trace messages should be output during application execution. This option can be set in source code or in the application configuration file.

transaction   A set of operations that must successfully complete together. If any one of the steps fails, then the results of all steps must be rolled back, or cancelled.

Transaction.Commit method   This causes the transaction to finish and all pending database changes to be written permanently to the database.

Transaction.Rollback method   This method causes the transaction to finish and all pending database changes to be rolled back.

Transact-SQL   The Microsoft SQL Server database uses its own programming language, called Transact-SQL (or T-SQL for short), to write SQL queries. Transact-SQL is based on the American National Standards Institute (ANSI) and the International Organization for Standardization (ISO) standard SQL language published in 1992, and also includes proprietary extensions.

Type Library Exporter utility (tlbexp.exe)   A command-line utility program provided with Visual Studio .NET that exports a COM-compatible type library from a .NET component.

Type Library Importer utility (tlbimp.exe)   A command-line utility program provided with Visual Studio .NET that translates COM type library information into a format that can be read by .NET components.

Uniform Resource Identifier (URI)   Any unique string that is used to identify the publisher of a particular Web service.

Uniform Resource Locator (URL)   A unique Internet address that is used to identify a specific website, web page, or Web service.

UniqueConstraint class   This ADO.NET class enables you to specify that a specific DataColumn in the DataTable must have unique data values.

uniquely named root element   A root element whose name is unique within that data file. Every well-formed XML data file must have a uniquely named root element.

unit tests   Tests that determine whether a single set of code, perhaps a single class or a component that contains a few related classes, is correctly performing its tasks.

Universal Description, Discovery, and Integration (UDDI)   A service for locating XML Web services by consulting online registries, such as uddi.microsoft.com, which contain information about available Web services. You can publish information about Web services that your organization wants to make available. You can manually search the UDDI registry sites or use the application programming interface (API) to access a UDDI registry server from your application.

unmanaged code   Applications that run on the Windows/COM platform, such as COM components and Visual Basic 6 applications. Unmanaged code is not executed by the CLR.

Update method   A method of the ADO.NET DataAdapter class. This method processes each row in the DataSet that has a RowState of Added, Deleted, or Modified and runs the appropriate SQL query against the data source for each row.

UpdateCommand   This property of the ADO.NET DataAdapter class is one of the three related properties that hold the SQL statements (or stored procedure names) that will be used when the corresponding insert, update, or delete operations must be performed during an update to the database.

URL-based authorization   Uses <allow> and <deny> elements in the application's Web.config file to grant and deny access based on the URI the client is requesting and the identity associated with the request.

Web Services Description Language (WSDL)   A defined format of XML tags that are used to describe the contract between the publisher of a Web service and their clients. A WSDL document shows all the methods of the Web service, the arguments that are passed when a method is called, the data types for the arguments, and the data type of the return value of the method call.

Web setup project   A template that installs your application in a virtual directory under the virtual root directory on a web server, as opposed to the file system. It is used to generate packages for installing web applications.

WebMethod attribute   Each method of an XML Web service that should be exposed as a part of the public interface of the service should be marked with a <WebMethod()> attribute.

WebService attribute   Each class in an XML Web service that should be exposed as a part of the public interface of the service should be marked with a <WebService()> attribute.

well formed   A term used to describe XML files that comply with standard rules, including the following: naming conventions for tag names, case sensitivity, the uniquely named root element, and proper nesting of element tags. Attribute names cannot repeat for an individual element, and all attribute values must be in quotes. An XML document that follows these rules can be read by any standard XML parser.

Windows Component Services   Part of the Windows operating system, these provide a hosting environment, or infrastructure, for middle-tier components. Windows Component

Services help you to manage distributed transactions, enforce role-based security, and increase performance by using object pooling and other features, such as message queuing and event notification.

Windows Installer 2.0 setup project   A Visual Studio .NET project template that enables you to create setup files and Windows Installer files (`.msi`) to install your applications.

Windows Integrated Security   An authentication mechanism that uses Windows operating system usernames and passwords, along with their associated groups and permissions, to verify users of your application when the application attempts to use network resources, such as connecting to a database server.

Windows service   An application that runs on a server or workstation computer and provides ongoing functionality without direct user interaction. Windows services are often used to perform system monitoring and other services that must run continuously.

World Wide Web Consortium (W3C)   An independent standards body that oversees application standards for the Internet such as HTML, XML, and all its related technologies. See `http://w3c.org` for more information.

`Write` method   This method of the `Debug` and `Trace` classes writes output as a text string.

`WriteIf` method   This method of the `Debug` and `Trace` classes writes output as a text string, if the specified expression evaluates to `True`.

`WriteLine` method   This method of the `Debug` and `Trace` classes writes output as a text string, ending with a line-termination character.

`WriteLineIf` method   This method of the `Debug` and `Trace` classes writes output as a text string, if the specified expression evaluates to `True`, and ends with a line-termination character.

`WriteXml` method   This method of the `DataSet` class outputs the data and schema (optional) from a `DataSet` to an XML data file.

`wsdl.exe`   A command-line utility program provided with Visual Studio .NET that enables you to generate a Web Services Description Language (WSDL) document describing the public interface of the Web service.

XML configuration files   Files used by the .NET Framework to hold application-specific settings. The advantage of holding these settings in configuration files rather than directly in your source code is that an administrator can make changes without having to change and recompile the original source code.

XML Data Reduced (XDR)   Before the W3C finalized XSD schema, some Microsoft XML tools used the XDR format for validation. XDR is similar to XSD.

XML Document Object Model (DOM)   This model offers complete programmatic access to XML data. The XML DOM is a W3C recommendation that provides a consistent object model for XML programming on any platform. When working with the DOM, you approach your

XML data as a tree of nodes. The classes in the .NET Framework `System.Xml` namespace implement the functionality of the XML DOM for .NET development.

XML namespaces   XML data files use namespaces for identifying the origin of the data, specifying standard versions for stylesheet and schema references, and qualifying the origin of tag names when consolidating data from different sources.

XML parser   Any computer program that can read and process an XML data file.

XML Schema Definition (XSD)   Also referred to as XSD schema, this is a standard way to define an exact format for a specific XML document. XSD enables you to specify valid element tag names, attribute names, relationships among elements and attributes, data types of element and attribute values, and more. Individual XML data files (instance documents) can be validated against the XSD schema. The XSD standard is maintained by the World Wide Web Consortium (`http://www.w3c.org`) and therefore is neither vendor nor platform specific.

XML Web services   Applications that accept remote procedure calls, and return results, over the Internet by using a standard SOAP message format.

XmlAttribute class   A member of the `System.Xml` namespace that enables you to work with XML data programmatically. The XmlAttribute class represents a single attribute in an XML data file.

XmlAttributeCollection class   This class in the `System.Xml` namespace extends the functionality of the `XmlNamedNodeMap` class and enables you to work with the set of attributes that belong to a given XML element.

XmlDataDocument class   A member of the `System.Xml` namespace that brings the best capabilities of a `DataSet` and an `XmlDocument` together. You can create a `DataSet` by retrieving data from a database and then create the `XmlDataDocument` by referencing the `DataSet`. This is called synchronizing the `DataSet` and the `XmlDataDocument`.

XmlDocument class   A member of the `System.Xml` namespace that enables you to work with XML data programmatically. The XmlDocument class represents a complete XML data file.

XmlElement class   A member of the `System.Xml` namespace that enables you to work with XML data programmatically. The XmlElement class represents a single element in an XML data file.

XmlNamedNodeMap collection class   One of the base classes in the `System.Xml` namespace, this collection holds groups of related attribute nodes.

XmlNode base class   This base class defines common properties and methods of all the types of nodes that can occur in an XML data file.

XmlNodeReader class   A derived class of `XmlReader`, this class provides fast, noncached, forward-only access to data in an `XmlDocument`.

XmlReader class   This base class provides fast, noncached, forward-only access to data in an `XmlDocument` and is implemented by the `XmlTextReader`, `XmlNodeReader`, and `XmlValidating-Reader` classes.

XmlReadMode parameter   This parameter of the DataSet class offers the following options: Auto, DiffGram, Fragment, IgnoreSchema, InferSchema, and ReadSchema. These options determine how the XML data is interpreted. If the DataSet already has a schema or the file has an in-line schema, the ReadSchema behavior will be used. If there is no DataSet schema and no in-line schema, the InferSchema behavior will be used and a schema will be created based on the contents of the XML data.

XmlSchemaCollection class   In order to perform schema validation on an XmlDocument by using a schema that exists in a separate disk file, you must first create an object based on the XmlSchemaCollection class and load that schema into the object.

XmlText class   A member of the System.Xml namespace, this class enables you to work with XML data programmatically.

XmlTextReader class   This class provides fast, noncached, forward-only access to data in an XmlDocument. XmlTextReader is a derived class of XmlReader.

XmlValidatingReader class   This class provides DTD, XDR, and XSD validation of data in an XmlDocument. XmlValidatingReader is a derived class of XmlReader.

XmlWriteMode parameter   This parameter of the DataSet.WriteXml method determines the format of the XML data file that is created. The valid values are DiffGram, IgnoreSchema, and WriteSchema.

XmlWriter class   This class provides a means to create a stream object or disk file that contains XML. The XmlWriter base class is implemented by using the XmlTextWriter class.

XPath expression   This expression can specify criteria for identifying a node by evaluating either the position of a node in the document hierarchy, data values of the node, or a combination of these criteria.

XPathDocument class   This class resides in the System.Xml.Xpath namespace. It is optimized for performance when you are performing searches using only XPath expressions or performing XSLT processing on your XML data.

XpathExpression class   This class in the System.Xml.Xpath namespace provides compiled XPath expressions.

XPathNavigator class   This class in the System.Xml.Xpath namespace provides optimized performance for XPath queries on your data.

XpathNodeIterator class   This class in the System.Xml.Xpath namespace enables you to process a selected set of nodes in an XmlDocument.

XslTransform class   This class from the System.Xml.Xsl namespace performs the stylesheet processing on your XmlDocuments.

Index

Note to the Reader: Throughout this index **boldfaced** page numbers indicate primary discussions of a topic. *Italicized* page numbers indicate illustrations.

D